THE MAJOR LATIN WORKS

OF

JOHN GOWER

THE VOICE OF ONE CRYING

AND

THE TRIPARTITE CHRONICLE

An Annotated Translation into English
With an Introductory Essay on the Author's
Non-English Works

By

ERIC W. STOCKTON

University of Washington Press · Seattle ·

1 9 6 2

Copyright © 1962 by the University of Washington Press
Library of Congress Catalog Card Number 62-20321
Printed in the United States of America

Qui legis hec eciam, te supplico, vir, quod honeste
Scripta feras, viciis nec memor esto meis:
Rem non personam, mentem non corpus in ista
Suscipe materia, sum miser ipse quia.
           (<u>Vox Clamantis</u>, Book II, Prol. 11-14)

Preface

These translations, long in the doing, need but a brief yet nonetheless sincere expression of gratitude to many people by way of preface. My greatest debt is to the Horace H. Rackham School of Graduate Studies, University of Michigan, for a most generous subsidy to help defray the cost of publishing this volume. I should like also to thank Professor Bartlett Jere Whiting of Harvard University for originally suggesting my work with Gower's Latin. Both he and Professor Francis P. Magoun, Jr., of Harvard University have gladly answered questions and borne patiently the lengthy time this book has required. Professor John R. Reinhard of the University of Michigan likewise responded to queries obligingly and permitted me to attend his fine seminar in Piers Plowman. Others who gave help and encouragement are the Reverend Paul E. Beichner of the University of Notre Dame, Professor Robert R. Raymo of Rutgers University, and the late Professor George R. Coffman of the University of North Carolina.

Professor Emeritus Bruno Meinecke of the University of Michigan lent wise assistance in solving difficulties in translating, and Mrs. Eileen Squires of Ann Arbor, Michigan, gave many hours of her time in helping to translate recalcitrant passages. These, the first published translations of Gower's Latin works, would have been far poorer but for her efforts. John T. Queenan's unpublished dissertation, A Translation from Latin to English of the Third Book of John Gower's Vox Clamantis (Rutgers, 1949), saved me from some mistakes. Special thanks are due to Professor John H. Fisher of Indiana University, who furnished much help, including a copy of his complete Gower bibliography; a version of this bibliography is forthcoming in the revised edition of John E. Wells's Manual of the Writings in Middle English, thus obviating the need for a bibliography in this volume. Professor David Fowler of the University of Washington read the entire manuscript and made valuable suggestions.

The staffs of the Widener and Houghton Libraries of Harvard University and of the General Library of the University of Michigan have been unfailingly helpful. The Horace H. Rackham School of

v

Graduate Studies of the University of Michigan, in addition to providing half the cost of publication, kindly gave me the grant of a summer fellowship in 1956 and also paid most of the cost of typing this manuscript. The University of Michigan College of Literature, Science, and the Arts, and its Department of English Language and Literature generously provided me with a semester of research in the fall of 1958, without which the translations would not have been finished. My typist, Mrs. Beatrice Conner, worked patiently, cheerfully, and successfully with a difficult manuscript. To all these people, my deepest thanks. I can lay claim only to those errors which remain, whether they be typographical, translational, factual, or stylistic.

Finally, I wish to thank one who not only bore with many delays and discouragements but at the same time gave help and enthusiastic reassurance. She opposes even identification, let alone dedication, but my gratitude to her is nevertheless profound.

Eric W. Stockton
Ann Arbor, Michigan
October 30, 1959

It is my further pleasure at this time to thank Mrs. Barbara Becker of Ann Arbor, Michigan, for compiling the Index, as well as to thank the Department of English of the University of Tennessee for defraying the cost of this Index. To repeat a quotation much loved by Gower, as St. Luke's Gospel truly says, "Omni habenti dabitur."

Knoxville, Tennessee
June 15, 1961

Table of Contents

THE MAJOR
LATIN WORKS
OF
JOHN GOWER

INTRODUCTION

Gower's Life; His Cinkante Balades

The fourteenth century in England would be fascinating even if it had not produced Chaucer. The medieval world was slowly breaking up; it had been an interesting world, and its passing away was no less interesting, though men in the time of John Gower (1330-1408) viewed its decline largely as a serious if reparable dislocation of society and Church. The turmoil was somewhat like that of our own age: The agency of internationalism was troubled by growing nationalism, the Christian Church was torn by ideological factions; knowledge of the sciences was increasing; wars were becoming deadlier; and the lower class was no longer content to remain the anonymous masses. As in our own century, England seemed to be at the top of Fortune's wheel; that height only made the subsequent fall the greater. The second half of the fourteenth century saw nearly everything go wrong for English politics, peace, and plenty, though not for literature.

The poems translated in this volume, however, are not the aesthetic glories of their time--which is not surprising in an age of Chaucer, Langland, and the poet or poets of MS. Cotton Nero A. x. Rather, these poems, John Gower's Vox Clamantis and Cronica Tripertita, are worthy of consideration after nearly six hundred years because they give copious, thoughtful comment upon an England in a time still somewhat dark, and because they also throw light upon other literature in an age rich in literature. The reign of Richard II, moreover, has never ceased to interest English readers and writers, whether dramatists and courtiers of the Elizabethan period, rebels of the seventeenth century, or Marxist theorists of the twentieth. Men of succeeding times have always found the precedents for action or inaction which they have looked for in the significance of the Great Revolt of 1381 and its aftermath; and John

Gower, wealthy squire of Kent born in 1330, is the poet of that Great Revolt, as well as the near perfect mirror of his times. He was an acquaintance in good standing with both Richard II and Henry IV, and he was keenly interested in all they did.

Indeed, he was interested in everything. His Vox Clamantis is a fairly systematic survey of the three estates (he had already done much the same thing in his French Mirour de l'Omme). No corner of English life eludes his eye, whether royal palace or villein hut, and no type of Englishman, whether king or serf, escapes his searching and exhaustive criticism. Then after completing his Latin magnum opus, he almost at once appended to the Vox Clamantis a prefatory account in dream-vision form of the Peasants' Revolt. Late in life he attached still another long section, called Cronica Tripertita, by way of conclusion. This second addition describes the deposition of Richard II and the ascension of Henry IV. Thus Gower covered not only the structure of society but something of its history as well. In all his major works --including his English Confessio Amantis--he tried to incorporate as much subject matter and as many literary genres as he could. An intense conservative in all his thinking, he tried to hold fast to everything, even while pessimistic about everything. As the Vox Clamantis puts it, "Si mala succedunt, deteriora time" (VII. 434). He was still voicing the same thought many years later in his short English poem, "In Praise of Peace: " "For evermor the werste is forto doute" (1. 138).

The known facts of John Gower's life are conveniently found in G. C. Macaulay's excellent edition of The Complete Works of John Gower, [1] with important additions and corrections in John H. Fisher, "A Calendar of Documents Relating to the Life of John Gower, the Poet. "[2] The exact year of his birth is unknown, but it is usually put at about 1330. Sir Robert Gower, a judge and landholder in Yorkshire,was perhaps his uncle. Traditionally, Gower was thought to be connected with the well-known Gower family of Stitenham, Yorkshire, which survives to this day. Macaulay opposed such a connection and instead placed the poet in what he took to be another Gower family, of Kent. Professor Fisher has recently shown, however, that the more traditional view is very likely correct, and that the poet's family was originally from Langbargh Wapentake, Yorkshire, and hence probably connected with the Stitenham Gowers. [3] The surname "Gower" probably derives from a thirteenth-century term for sporting dogs, animals which figured in the family coat of arms. [4]

The poet's uncle, and after him the poet himself, were large property owners, and many records survive which show that both men collected land and manors. "A good many of Gower's own real estate transactions appear to be joint ventures, and from this it might be deduced that whatever other profession he might have had, he was an 'investor' or 'entrepreneur' in real estate, the medium of exchange in those times. "[5] One of these transactions, Gower's acquisition of the Manor of Aldington in Kent, has created worries. Because the transaction smacks of having been "irregular, " Macaulay refused to identify the John Gower involved as the poet: "It is impossible without further proof to assume that the villainous misleader of youth who is described to us . . . as encouraging a young man to defraud the Crown by means of perjury, in order that he may purchase his lands from him at a nominal price, can be identical with the grave moralist of the Speculum Hominis [an alternate title of the Mirour de l'Omme] and the Vox Clamantis. Gower humbly confesses that he has been a great sinner, but he does not speak in the tone of a converted libertine: we cannot reconcile our idea of him with the proceedings of the disreputable character who for his own ends encouraged the young William Septvans in his dishonesty and extravagance. The two men apparently bore the same arms, and therefore belonged to the same family, but beyond this we cannot go" (IV, xv). It is now evident, however, that William Septvans (or Septvauns) was no mere boy, that one named "Gower" made a just recompense for the property in question, and that the 1366 inquiry into the matter "was undertaken to ascertain not whether the heir [i. e., Septvauns] had been defrauded but whether the king had suffered loss of income because the Septvauns holdings had been released prematurely" (Fisher, p. 17). Concerning the whole Septvauns affair Professor Fisher concedes that "Certainly at this distance it appears to be something of a mess, " while nonetheless maintaining that "Without more evidence it is idle to speculate on the legal and moral issues of the case" (p. 17).

It is nevertheless well to remember that the Middle Ages, being human, were shot through with contradictions, and that discrepancy between theory and practice was as much the rule as the exception. Was not Chaucer, a respectable gentleman and servant of the King, fined for beating a friar, and was he not also involved in a puzzling lawsuit charging him with abduction or perhaps even rape? As Gower himself expostulated all his life, the upper class was disgracefully corrupt, and modern historians agree with him. [6] The peasants did not revolt in 1381 against benevolent paternalism. As for Gower's apology for his sinfulness, that is undoubtedly the rhetorical device or topic of affected modesty or trepidation[7] --which of course does not prevent it from being sincere.

Of the poet's formal education we know nothing positive. He does not seem to have been a university man. He read widely, as will appear below, and except for scientific materials he assimilated his reading thoroughly. There is an old tradition that he was a lawyer; this is doubtful, in view of his chastising lawyers at every opportunity (as in Vox Clamantis, Book VI, Chaps. 1-6). Macaulay felt that at times Gower showed respect and special concern for merchants (Works, IV, xxvi-ii), but such concern is difficult to detect in the Vox Clamantis (see Book V, Chaps. 11-15). Undoubtedly, much of his time went to writing poetry, for his output was prodigious. As with regard to his education, there is similar uncertainty concerning whether he traveled abroad. Some lines in his major English work, the Confessio Amantis (1390) show close familiarity with nautical terms, [8] though any intelligent and inquiring Englishman could have picked these up, just as Shakespeare presumably did later. Gower says flatly in the Vox Clamantis (VII. 1295-96) that he always remained in his native land, though he lived for many years after so stating. In 1393 Henry of Lancaster presented his butler with a silver collar "'because my lord had given his collar to another esquire beyond the sea, '"[9] and there is indeed a record of Henry having given such a collar to "an esquire John Gower." There is no proof, however, of the esquire beyond the sea having been Gower. [10] He himself notes the English love of travel, attributing it to the influence of the moon (Confessio Amantis, VII. 749-54), yet he rarely if ever shows any first-hand knowledge of geography, and unlike Chaucer he is unable to localize foreign settings for his tales. Finally, the journey by ship in Book I of the Vox Clamantis is singularly unrealistic, and heavily dependent upon lines from Ovid and ideas from Virgil.

It is necessary to be equally tentative about whether Gower married when a young man. "From the Speculum Meditantis [a second alternate title of the Mirour de l'Omme] we learn that in early life he composed love poems, which he calls 'fols ditz d'amour' (27340), and from two other passages (ll. 8794 and 17649) we may perhaps assume that he was already married at the time when this work was composed. [It was finished about 1378.] In the former, speaking of those who tell tales to husbands about their wives' misconduct, he says in effect, 'I for my part declare ('Je di pour moi') that I wish to hear no such tales of my wife: ' in the second he speaks of those wives who dislike servants and other persons simply because their husbands like them, and he adds, 'I do not say that mine does so' ('Ne di pas q' ensi fait la moie'). If the inference be correct, his union with Agnes Groundolf in his old age was a second marriage. "[11] (This marriage is discussed below.)

Gower's "fols ditz d'amour" could well include his Cinkante Balades. This work, though dedicated to Henry IV probably soon after the latter's accession in 1399, is Gower's most youthful production, and it is hard to envision him as having written these graceful balades as an old man, thinking to please Henry. In the Confessio Amantis (I. 2708-33) he views love songs as the activity of a young and immature man, as "veine glorie" to be condemned by the priestly confessor. Very likely he collected his balades, some written earlier, and then added the dedication to Henry and the collection's final envoy at the time of presentation to the King. (Gower was given to keeping his own works by him and adding to them or changing them from time to time; such was the fate of both the Vox Clamantis and the Confessio Amantis.)[12] If the Cinkante Balades do incorporate any of a youthful Gower's "fols ditz d'amour, " he had little need, unlike Chaucer, to lament having written "many a song and many a leccherous lay, " for the sentiments of the balades are highly proper.

The form of the balades is no less conventional, though they remain Gower's freshest, least moralizing, and most lyrical pieces. They are nearly all very regular, each with three stanzas rhyming ababbcc (rime royal), or three stanzas rhyming ababcbc, and a four-line envoy, rhyming abab. The rhymes of each balade are alike throughout that balade. As in his other French poems Gower combines the English accentual with the French syllabic measure; there is a discernible iambic beat. The caesura is treated with the freedom of English poetry of that time rather than with the stricter regularity practised by contemporaneous French poets.

The speaker is more joyful in the first five balades than he usually is thenceforth, and the author seems to have recognized or attempted to make a distinction amongst the balades. Beside the envoy to Balade V is a French marginal note: "The balades from the beginning up to this point have been composed especially for those who expect their love through true marriage. " Then by the first stanza of Balade VI is a second marginal note: "The balades from here to the end of the book are for all the world, in accordance with the qualities and conditions of lovers who in diverse ways are troubled by the fortunes of love. " All the Cinkante Balades, however, (there are actually fifty-one, because two in succession are numbered as IIII in the sole surviving manuscript) read about the same, and there is nothing of marriage in any of them: Furthermore, there is little or nothing in them to indicate that such a division as the marginal notes furnish was the author's original intent. Rather, the old moralist was using his youthful songs as instruction for Henry IV as best he could; the marginal notes translated above were probably added shortly before presentation of the book to the King. Gower never lost an opportunity to instruct.

In the Balades there are several interesting references to figures in whom Gower showed a life-long interest. For example, Balade XIX, 19-22, mentions the story of Troilus, whom Gower mentions several times (e.g., Mirour, 5253-55; Vox, I. 993 and VI. 1325-28; Confessio, II. 2457, IV. 2795, V. 7597, and VIII. 2531). Therefore, Chaucer's dedication of his own Troilus and Criseyde to the "moral Gower" (and to the "philosophical Strode") is appropriate in that Gower had a knowledge of the story before Chaucer wrote his poem and maintained an interest in Troilus and Cressida for many years. There is another reference to Troilus in Balade XLIII, as well as others in the same balade to Lancelot and Tristan (ll. 17-18) and Gower's own Florent (l. 19), whose story Gower admirably tells in his Confessio (I. 1411 ff.). Other figures whose stories Gower tells much later in life are also alluded to: Paris and Helen in XIV, 7 (see Confessio, V. 7195 ff.), and Pygmalion in XXIV. 10 (see Confessio, IV. 371 ff.), for example. Likewise, some of the good details in the balades, such as that of the lover hearing the Mass but thinking of his lady (in No. XXIV) are later found in the Confessio. Gower's mind does evince some power for growth, though there is a regression in that there is much less lyricism in his later works than in the Balades. Even in them Gower's lyrical ability deserts him utterly in a few gauche spots, as in XXX, 5-6:

> Le Nief qe vostre bouche soufflera
> Me fait sigler sur le peril de vie. . . .

Yet this discussion of Gower's Cinkante Balades should not end on a negative note. Here is a translation of No. II by Henry Morley which will illustrate both Gower's lyric delicacy and his conventionality:

> "Winter departs, and comes the flowery May,
>   And round from cold to heat the seasons fly;
> The bird that to its nest had lost the way,
>   Rebuilds it, that he may rejoice thereby.
>   Like change in my love's world I now descry,
> With such a hope I comfort myself here,
>   And you, my lady, on this truth rely:
> When grief departs, the coming joys are near.
>
> "My lady sweet, by that which now I say
>   You may discover how my heart leaps high,
> That serves you and has served for many a day,
>   As it will serve you daily till I die.
>   Remember then, my lady, knowing why
> That my desire for you will never veer.
>   As God wills that it be, so be our tie:
> When grief departs, the coming joys are near.
>
> "The day that news of you came where I lay,
>   It seemed there was no grief could make me sigh;
> Wherefore of you, dear lady mine, I pray
>   By your own message—when you will, not I--
>   Send me what you think best as a reply

Wherewith my heart can keep itself from fear;
  And, lady, search the reason of my cry,
'When grief departs, the coming joys are near.

"O noble dame, to you this note shall hie,
And when God wills I follow to my dear.
  This writing speaks, and says, till I am by,
'When grief departs, the coming joys are near. '"13

This translation gives a very fair idea of both the strengths and limita-
tions of the Cinkante Balades, and its youthfulness, though sober-sided,
must place it among the products of a young Gower. The very last balade in the collection, unnumbered in MS. Trentham Hall, which indicates that it was added later, is highly un-amatory; the lady from whom
the lover implores help is now the Virgin. "This balade . . . does not
form one of the 'Cinkante Balades' of which the title speaks. It is a
kind of devotional conclusion to the series. The envoy which follows,
'O gentile Engleterre, ' does not belong to this balade, being divided
from it by a space in the MS. and having a different system of rhymes.
It is in fact the envoy of the whole book of balades. "14 The envoy begins
with the fine line, "O gentile Engleterre, a toi j'escrits" and ends with
a prayer for England and Henry IV. That king was little short of a god
to Gower, and England, too, could arouse his deep love (as in Vox, VII.
1289-1302).

Gower's Mirour de l'Omme

Thus far Gower's first major poem has been only mentioned. By
1378 or thereabouts he had completed a monumental work in French
known by the three titles of Speculum Meditantis, Speculum Hominis,
and Mirour de l'Omme. As does the Cinkante Balades, the poem survives in only one manuscript (Camb. Univ. Add. 3035), which was identified in 1895 by Professor Macaulay. It is a monument of perseverance
and good intentions, if nothing else: 29, 944 lines survive, with approximately two thousand more being lost (including the beginning and end of
the manuscript). Perhaps the missing lines had placed the whole poem
within the framework of a vision (cf. Books II-VII of the Vox Clamantis).
In any case, what is left is basically an allegory, within which is in-
corporated a critique of the three estates, a penitential manual, and
scriptural history, with the MS breaking off where a hymn of praise to
the Virgin begins. The entire poem is written in the same octosyllabic

lines as the Confessio Amantis, the meter being regular in the extreme. The lines are divided into twelve-line stanzas with the rhyme scheme aabaabbbabba, the then popular "Helinand strophe, " so called from a well known Old French poem. Such a stanzaic form assuredly demands dexterity, but far too much poetic effort obviously went into that rhyme pattern, at the expense of nearly everything else which might have made the poem readable. Instead, the tedium is seldom relieved by even a brief story (but see Works, I, xxxviii) or lyric passage, and the tone is one of unrelieved gloom. Here we have the moral Gower with a vengeance.

He himself implies that he wrote the poem before he wrote the Vox Clamantis[15] and there are a few allusions in it which help to date the poem thus early. First, Edward III is reproved in the Mirour (22801 ff.) as though he were still alive (he died in 1377). Shortly before this passage, however, Gower speaks of the Great Schism, which began in 1378 (see ll. 18829 ff.) Perhaps the Schism began while he was still writing the Mirour, though Macaulay thinks this passage was added later. Finally, Gower twice refers to Robin Hood (ll. 8659 ff. and 20887 ff.), and the earliest mention of him has long been thought to be that in Piers Plowman (B Passus V. 402), now dated between 1377 and 1379. [16]

The first 18, 000 lines of the Mirour de l'Omme describe the efforts of the Devil and Sin[17] to conquer Man. To gain help the Devil marries the seven daughters of Sin and begets five daughters upon each of them. Ll. 757-9720 exhaustively and exhaustingly describe these thirty-five daughters. God then gives the seven Virtues in marriage to Reason, and thirty-five more daughters are born (ll. 10033-18372). Thus far the work most closely resembles a manual of sins, and therefore corresponds fairly closely to the framework of the Confessio Amantis. [18]

After laboriously setting the stage for a psychomachia with thirty-five abstractions on each side, Gower does not reward the reader with a stirring allegorical battle, but instead abruptly declares that Sin is the victor, and then examines the whole of human society to prove it (ll. 18373-26604). This part of the poem corresponds closely in form and content to the critique of the three estates in the Vox Clamantis. The rest of the Mirour urges Man to reform, and recommends that he pray to the Virgin to intercede for him. Man is the source of all evils, and every class of society is equally guilty. The poem is a document to be read at most only once in one's lifetime. The sheer length and Gower's relentless moral earnestness are impressive but also oppressive. It is true that the Mirour does throw light upon its age: "In all the literature that has been published (in medieval England) it would be difficult to find a more perfect mirror of the social gospel as presented by the pulpit, in its artistry as well as its doctrine, within a single

10

frame, than his Mirour de l'Omme, or Speculum Meditantis."[19] Medieval preaching, then, must have been in no small measure a failure. It is not surprising that the French poem was largely forgotten for the superior Latin one which followed shortly after it, just as the Vox Clamantis in turn has been to a considerable extent forgotten for the Confessio Amantis, although less deservedly so.

The Voice of One Crying

If the Mirour is one of the longest poems in Anglo-Norman, the Vox Clamantis is one of the longest in Anglo-Latin.[20] Containing 10,265 lines, it is about the length of the Aeneid. Furthermore, a Dedicatory Epistle of 49 lines and a sequel, the Cronica Tripertita, were later added. Some critics have called the Vox Clamantis Gower's greatest work, though that honor must surely go to his English Confessio Amantis. The Latin poem survives in ten MSS, of which MS. All Souls College, Oxf. 98 (S), is the basis of Macaulay's critical text. "This MS. was certainly written and corrected under the direction of the author, and remained some time in his hands, receiving additions from time to time."[21] The existence of ten MSS shows that the poem was fairly widely read in the later Middle Ages in England, and it continued to be copied until about 1500. As for later readers, Macaulay notes (p. lxx) that MS. Hatfield Hall (H2) was owned and annotated by Lord Burleigh; and Bishop Thomas Fuller, who called Gower "Prince of poets in his time," translated I. 783-790 in his Church History of Britain. I can find no indication of other readers until Thomas Warton (History of English Poetry, Sec. XIX), and he seems to have read only Book I. Not even Milton, who read just about everything, gives indication of having read the Vox Clamantis. (This lack of readership is in contrast to the reputation of the Confessio Amantis, which has never ceased to have interest.)[22]

The title Vox Clamantis is messianic, going back to Isaiah 40: 3. It is fittingly translated as The Voice of One Crying[23]—in the wilderness which, in Gower's opinion, was England. The fourteenth-century John thereby intentionally connects himself with his predecessor John, both John the Baptist and the Apostle John. John the Baptist is the scriptural figure most closely associated with the phrase, "the voice of one crying in the wilderness,"[24] a phrase used to help prepare the way for the Lord, and which had political and homiletic currency in the fourteenth century.[25] The Apostle John, traditional author of the Apocalypse, paints a picture of what is happening and will happen to Gower's beloved England unless the voice is heeded. The poem's sequel, the Cronica Tripertita, describes the fulfillment of the dire prophecy and the eventual reestablishment of justice.

Books II-VII of the Vox Clamantis were begun shortly after the

completion of the author's Mirour about 1378, for Gower finished these
books before the Peasants' Revolt of 1381, and he must have needed
many months to write them. The revolt itself then moved him to write
Book I, which is an account of it. Books II-VII (originally numbered
I-VI, surely) comprise a critique of the three estates, with almost
unswerving attention to their wickedness. In the latter books all three
estates are guilty of causing the world's evils; [26] in Book I the peasants
alone are at fault. Such was Gower's wrath against the rebels, however,
that he surely would have taken the opportunity in Vox, V. 557 ff., for
example, to condemn the Revolt, had that event occurred by the time he
wrote the passage. In addition, Macaulay discusses manuscript evidence indicating that Book I was added later, together with a few difficulties in accepting such a theory. [27] He also cites internal evidence
for the separate composition of Book I with which it is hard to disagree:

> The first book, with its detailed account of the Peasants' revolt,
> though in itself the most interesting part of the work, has certainly
> something of the character of an insertion. The plan of the re-
> mainder seems to be independent of it, though the date, June, 1381,
> which is found also in the Laud MS. [which does not contain Book I],
>
> 'Contigit vt quarto Ricardi regis in anno,
> Dum clamat mensem Iunius esse suum, '
>
> was doubtless intended to suggest that portentous event as the oc-
> casion of the review of society which the work contains. The pro-
> logue of the second book, which introduces the teachings of the vision
> with an invocation of God's assistance, an apology for the deficiencies
> of the work, and an appeal to the goodwill of the readers, and con-
> cludes with a first announcement of the name of the succeeding poem,
> Vox Clamantis, would certainly be much more in place at the begin-
> ning of the whole work than here, after more than two thousand lines,
> and there is no difficulty in supposing that the author may have intro-
> duced the account of the Peasants' revolt as an afterthought. [28]

This quotation has been given at length because literary historians so
frequently continue to view Books I-VII of the poem as a continuous unit.
That Gower was quite ready to add an "afterthought" to the Vox Clamantis is also shown by his attaching to it the Cronica Tripertita. Such a
practice is medieval: Langland must keep adding to Piers Plowman
until the outlines of the final version become attenuated. Jean de Meun
must quintuple the length of the Roman de la Rose. Sheer length and
extensive form are impressive.

After he had completed Books II-VII Gower made a few changes in them, in an attempt to keep the poem up to date. The first twenty-nine lines of Book III, Chapter 1, underwent revision which makes new mention of the papal schism. Since the Great Schism began in 1378, it is reasonable to assume that the original opening of Book III was composed before that year. (There is another allusion to the Schism in V. 1009.) Then, perhaps when Gower returned to the poem to write Book I or perhaps later, he revised III. 1-29. (A second revision of the same lines embodies only inconsequential changes.) This attack on the Great Schism is of interest in that the event is not much discussed in the literature of the time. Even thus early, Gower adopts a nationalistic view of it. [29]

Also important is the revision of Book VI, ll. 545-580 and 1159-1200. In the original version of the first of these passages, Gower excuses the boy-king Richard II from blame for the realm's troubles, and lays it upon his advisers. In the revised passage he still takes the advisers to task, but boldly charges the King with the chief responsibility for the evil days upon which the country has fallen. [30] In the latter of the two passages Gower originally utters a hymn of praise to God for His blessings, and a prayer that the Lord guide and protect the glorious young king. The passage as revised calls upon Richard to reform his rule and to institute law and justice. For all his idolizing of royalty Gower is surely no sycophant. The poet is to be admired for speaking out fearlessly to his sovereign, a man who later ruthlessly exiled or executed several of the most important nobles of the realm. The year 1393 is a possible date for the revision of VI. 545-580 and 1159-1200, [31] for in that year Gower revised the Confessio Amantis with very similar intent, namely, omission of praise of Richard II, together with the different and additional purpose of sole dedication of the English poem to Henry of Lancaster. (The first version contains a dedication to Henry in the Latin lines at its end.) Gower showered Henry with every poem he could. Perhaps he did not rededicate the Vox Clamantis to Henry because such a change would have necessitated considerable revision of Book VI. That book contains praise for the Black Prince, Richard's father, and much advice to Richard which would not be applicable to Henry. What changes Gower does make in Book VI are sufficient to pave the way for his sequel to the Vox Clamantis, the Cronica Tripertita (c. 1400), in which Henry is further glorified and the "cruel" Richard brought to the depths of ruin, deposition, and death. The final version of the combined Latin poems is dedicated to Thomas Arundel, Archbishop of Canterbury and ally of Henry. Thomas plays a role in the Cronica Tripertita, being first banished by Richard and then recalled by Henry. Furthermore, his office figures in Book I of the Vox Clamantis; his predecessor Archbishop Sudbury is murdered during the Great Revolt.

The Vox Clamantis has usually called for mention of the Peasants' Revolt in the same breath on the part of literary historians. Many have implied or stated flatly that the uprising is the subject of the poem, although only one-fifth of it treats of that event. Gower himself is partly responsible for this unbalanced view. In a Latin headnote to the poem's table of contents, which is repeated at the beginning of Book I, he writes:

> In the beginning of this work, the author intends to describe how the lowly peasants violently revolted against the freemen and nobles of the realm. And since an event of this kind was as loathsome and horrible as a monster, he reports that in a dream he saw different throngs of the rabble transformed into different kinds of domestic animals. He says, moreover, that those domestic animals deviated from their true nature and took on the barbarousness of wild beasts. In accordance with the separate divisions of this book, which is divided into seven parts (as will appear more clearly below in its headings), he treats furthermore of the causes for such outrages taking place among men.

Anyone reading only that paragraph would understandably assume that the entire poem dealt with the Peasants' Revolt. [32]
Gower seems to have been aware that Book I would hold the most interest for his readers, and he accordingly plays it up once more at the expense of the rest of the poem in a concluding note (in Latin prose) to the Confessio Amantis. After stating that he wrote three books for the instruction of his fellow men, he devotes a brief paragraph to the description of each (i. e., Mirour, Vox, and Confessio). The paragraph on the Vox Clamantis, as does the whole note or "literary notice" of his works, exists in three versions, the two most complete of which are translated here:

> The second book, composed in the Latin language in hexameter and pentameter verses, treats of the astounding event which took place in England during the time of King Richard II in the fourth year of his reign, when the lowly peasants violently revolted against the freemen and nobles of the realm. Nevertheless, pronouncing upon the innocence of the said lord the King as excusable in this matter because of his minor age, the book declares that the blame, because of which--and not through Fortune--such enormities take place among men, clearly lies elsewhere.

14

The second book, metrically composed in the Latin language, treats of the various misfortunes occurring in England in the time of King Richard II. Whence, not only did the nobles and commons of the realm suffer torments, but even the most cruel King himself was finally laid low, falling because of his fault from on high into the pit which he had made. And the name of this volume is called The Voice of One Crying.

The first paragraph is readily seen to apply to the first complete version of the Vox Clamantis, Books I-VII, and to repeat the idea, as given in the poem's headnote quoted above, that the Peasants' Revolt is its burden. The second version of the prose paragraph refers to the poem in its final state, with the Cronica Tripertita added, and obviously furnishes another misconception, namely, that the deposition of the King is of paramount importance in the Vox Clamantis. Thus Gower himself fostered misleading ideas about the poem, and one of them became traditional. Undoubtedly, too, Fuller's spirited rendition of I. 783-790[33] served to magnify the importance of Book I. Finally, Gower's account of the revolt is the most interesting and original part of the Vox Clamantis, even if an "afterthought."

Though Book I with its allegory of the Peasants' Revolt was added later, it will be well to discuss it first, since it comes first in the poem as completed and has been first in importance for its reputation later. Gower's prose headnote to the Prologue to Book I, as has been seen, makes an attempt to link Book I to the whole poem. The Prologue itself is a somewhat labored apology for first, the validity of dreams, [34] and second, the author's limited ability--in short, a "modesty" prologue. In the first chapter the poet, speaking in the first person, gives a very flowery picture of a May morning, drawing heavily upon miscellaneous lines from Ovid. The scene is not of a poet falling asleep on such a morning; he is already asleep when the poem begins, and the May morning is part of the content of his dream. (Conventionally, a dream begun in the daytime, and a dream with a pleasant beginning, would have proceeded to a pleasant conclusion.) Then, at the end of the first chapter, he relates that he falls asleep and dreams what follows; he has, if only faintly, however, established that what has already preceded is likewise part of his dream. Thus, the dream-vision machinery creaks at the outset.

The dream proper of Book I is of the "premonitory" kind, and consists of three visions: that of Animals, that of Troy, and that of a Ship. The first one, that of Animals, is essentially a fusion of allegory and beast fable. It possesses considerable power. As the poet dreams he sees bands of rabble turned into asses, oxen, swine, foxes, flies, wasps, etc. Domestic animals and birds, too, become wild. These

15

are the peasants who revolted in June, 1381, forsaking their human nature and turning on their betters, both man and domestic animal. A Jay bird, who represents Wat Tyler, addresses the assembled throngs and incites them to battle (Chap. 9). At this juncture the beast fable is dropped, the assorted fauna being designated as men once more. The initial allegorized beast fable was a good idea, and it is thus a pity that Gower does not sustain it further. [35] As often, he has a hard time with inventio.

The peasants now assemble and arm themselves, and the second vision, that of Troy, begins when they attack (Chap. 13). (The name "Troy" for London is doubly appropriate: First, London was often given the literary appellation of Troy because of the legend that the Trojan Brutus had founded Britain [a legend used in Chap. 20]. Second, ancient Troy fell to invaders, just as London did to the mob.) The motif of the Trojan War prompts Gower to call his noble Londoners by the names of ancient Trojans. Simon Sudbury, the Archbishop of Canterbury, for example, becomes "Helenus," which was the name of Troy's chief priest. Many of the Trojan names, and all the Greek names which creep in (e.g., Ajax, Agamemnon, etc.) are, on the other hand, not meaningful at all. At best, such usages are questionable; Gower has to tell us, for example, that Helenus means Sudbury (I. 1001 f. and 1055-78); unfortunately for the author's moral purpose, the ancient Helenus was a traitor to Troy. Despite such onomastic defects, however, the murder of the Archbishop (Chap. 14) is effective narrative. The historical incident itself, of course, was sure fire.

In a bridge passage (Chap. 16) to the next vision, that of the Ship, the poet relates how he flew from the city of Troy to the woods and fields to escape death at the hands of the rebels. This chapter has had somewhat of a tradition as autobiography, though there are legitimate reasons for not accepting it as such. The entire account of the Great Revolt has hardly the character of eye-witness report; it is bookish, almost a gallimaufry of literary motifs. All of Book I is heavily reliant upon quotations from Ovid. It is Gower beating his breast and often feeling sorry for himself—understandably, for it was a painful time. Another reason for Gower's agrarian flight not being considered as autobiographical is that the dreamer finally escapes the mob by ship (Chap. 17), wherewith the third vision begins. The vessel in the Ship vision is surely allegorical: It is almost simultaneously a fictional means of escape, a tower (meaning the Tower of London), and the ship of state. At the same time it is the conventional symbol of the "ship of religion"[36] which offers escape from this world's problems. It is Gower's occasional practice to offer experience as literally his own which in reality could not have been. [37] He is not trying to deceive: The headnote to Chap. 20 says flatly that he saw his ship in a dream. All the while, Gower's escape by ship has a pagan model, that of Aeneas in

16

Aeneid, Book III. The English poet's ship encounters Scylla and Charybdis and then eventually makes port (Troy) safely, with all the nobility on board. The sequence of events on the voyage is not fully clear: In Chap. 19 we suddenly reach land, then just as suddenly we are back at sea.

The unreconciled elements in the three visions[38] which make up the dream of Book I have all the same a certain power. One might be tempted to argue that any confusion was deliberate on the part of the poet, in order to induce the atmosphere of a nightmare, save for the fact that similar hopping about and consequent impairment of structure is evident elsewhere in Gower, as in the _Cronica Tripertita_, sequel to the _Vox Clamantis_. There is nonetheless an attempt to unite the three visions. Chap. 18 links the Visions of Troy and the Ship, Chap. 19 does the same for that of the Animals and the Ship; in it, the Lord Mayor strikes down the Jay, Wat Tyler, whereupon Scylla gives up her prey. The total picture, however, is blurred, as is the precise role of the first-person narrator. Furthermore, some of the moral maxims with which Book I concludes (ll. 2071 ff.) are irrelevant.[39] The most important weakness of Book I is, as is in part true of the _Confessio Amantis_ later, failure of the attempt to encompass and fuse too many genres in one work: beast fable, dream vision, allegory, fictional autobiography, and history. Gower was no Dante. Such a failure is manifested by the tenuous device which Gower uses to link Book I with what follows: A voice orders the dreamer to set down in writing what he dreams of; but it is not clear whether the voice is indicating the dream in Book I or what follows in Books II-VII. Indeed, both must be meant. Gower is able to manage such a device because frequently in the original _Vox Clamantis_ he has made reference to the _vox populi_ as being his source.

Somewhat despite the incongruities of Book I, it remains a fairly effective prelude to Books II-VII, which are a critique of the three estates of the clergy, knighthood, and peasantry. It is an irony worth pointing out that Gower is so bound by the traditional view of society as consisting of these three strata that he to some extent slights his own group, that of the rising middle class. He does, to be sure, scrutinize merchants and tradesmen, but without awareness that his country was to become famous as a nation of shopkeepers and entrepreneurs. For him, the three traditional classes are immutably fixed.

Two thematic ideas run throughout the work, both of which were conventional in his time. First is the theme of the golden past: Times used to be good, but now they are bad, because men are bad. Second, when men now appear to be good, they are only concealing under a gleaming exterior the black evil which lies within them.[40] The purpose of his work is to urge men to reform themselves with divine help, since they are the sole cause of all evils. Just as our own age bathes the

American Revolution, the Gay Nineties, and Coolidge's Roaring Twenties in a golden glow, so did Gower and his age look back. In order to complain about the present, a standard is necessary, and the past uncomplainingly furnishes that standard. It is demonstrably true, however, that England had been better off militarily and politically earlier in the century. Gower realizes that the old Adam in human nature is wont to create troubles; he does not realize that he is unthinkingly following a convention as old as Genesis and Ovid's Metamorphoses which claims that the past was better. That convention was too much a part of his time. [41]

The poet states his conclusion that man is responsible for all worldly ills at the end of Book II, ll. 629-630: "I truly acknowledge that whatever happens in the world, whether it be good or evil, we ourselves are the cause of it."[42] After his review of society he then returns to this conclusion in Book VII, Chaps. 8 and 15. Gower places the responsibility squarely upon man and keeps it there. Always more nationalistic than Chaucer, he says that England was blessed by God above all other nations (VII. 17-36), yet has suffered a serious decline in weal. True enough, life is continually changing, and mutability is a hard burden to bear, but Gower will not allow his fellow men to put the blame upon Fortune.

He first describes Fortune at length (II. 51-198), being careful to point out that he is only reporting the common opinion of her. (He has obviously read his Boethius, but not taken Book II of The Consolation of Philosophy to heart.) He protests too much about the Lady. The reader begins to feel that Gower has the inclination to share the common opinion of her, Fortune being such an interesting and convenient explanation for man's ills. "Among the strange paradoxes of the Middle Ages none is more remarkable than the persistence, among the Christian conceptions of the Catholic Church, of the pagan goddess of Fortune."[43] Gower nonetheless overtly rejects such a scapegoat as Fortune. Indeed, it is blasphemy, he implies, to believe in Fortune, for God governs all things here below (Chap. 8). Idols of wood and stone are another scapegoat which man must eschew.

Nothing happens without cause, and most of the rest of the poem examines human society to show that man is the cause of the world's having fallen upon evil days. Since his criticism is so sweeping and severe, Gower protects himself: "I shall not find fault with individuals, but I do cry out against the faults which we see are reprehensible in individuals. I am not speaking of these things on my own part; rather, the voice of the people reported them to me . . ." (III. Prol. 9-12). Such indirection, a sort of shield of diplomatic immunity, is commonplace in the literature of complaint, though it does not do Gower's courage justice. He is not averse to speaking harshly both to and about the two highest individuals on earth, his king and his pope. And why the

18

pretense of mere reporting, to which he returns again and again in the
poem? It is not because Gower democratically holds the views of the
populace at large in high esteem; it is because all men are children of
God and are equal in God's sight, even though peasants do act like swine
and oxen. In addition, the formula vox populi, vox dei had some political currency in the fourteenth century. [44] A prince was to learn wisdom
from the voice of the people. Though he is not wholly consistent about
the maxim, [45] vox populi, vox dei is essentially valid to Gower, and it
is almost the last thought he leaves in the mind of the reader: "What I
have set down is the voice of the people, but you will also see that where
the people call out, God is often there" (VII. 1469-70). Gower sincerely
wants men to trust that his criticisms of them are not the grumblings of
a petulant old man, but are divinely inspired. Utilizing still another
convention or topic, he, like Milton, calls upon God for inspiration, not
the muses (II. Prol. 3-6).

Since men are the cause of the adversities which have befallen
them, Gower proposes to examine society in order to determine where
the blame lies. As in the Mirour, he finds that all three estates are
guilty—which is inconsistent with Book I, where only the serfs are reprehensible, with all others their innocent victims. The examination
begins with the clergy in Book III and continues into Book IV, altogether
for some 3,374 lines. On the basis of proportional treatment alone, the
clergy would seem to be most at fault, and this view is borne out in the
discussion. Their sins not only take longest to enumerate but are also
more grievous than those of other men, because they are the guardians
of men's souls, and because they have taken vows requiring duties much
stricter than those in their charge.

All ranks of the clergy are corrupt; where they appear otherwise
they are merely fostering a deceit to hide their wickedness. The bishops indulge in most of the seven deadly sins, with lust and avarice,
"the besetting sin of the Middle Ages, " predominating. The latter sin
has incited prelates to two villainies: First, they have erected a structure called "positive law, " which is not the word of Christ and hence
not morally binding, but law imposed by ecclesiastical fiat. What the
prelates give they can also take away--for a price. Hence, "positive
law" is solely a device to make money, for any infringements can be
rectified by cash payment. [46] Even worse, churchmen actually encourage immorality by deliberately putting men in the paths of temptation,
for, as Gower puts it more memorably in the Mirour (ll. 20149-50),
"The prostitute is more profitable . . . than the nun. " Second, clerical
avarice is the cause of wars--not wars for the souls of heathens, but
against the clerics' "evene Cristene, " in order to gobble up their earthly
possessions. Here Gower contrasts Christ and His disciples, who were
men of peace. [47] (Both of these charges were also Lollard complaints.)

Priests follow the evil ways of their bishops. Rectors of parishes are profligates, hunters, and merchants. Students at the universities and annuellers are indolent lechers. Yet all these men in holy orders claim they are no worse than other men, and they reserve the right to punish laymen, although they do not tolerate any lay interference in the judging of themselves. There is no need for either priest or layman to look for help from Rome, for the papal court is ruled by simony (cf. the Middle English poem, "The Simonie"). In Book III, Chap. 10, the pope (or his spokesman) actually boasts about Rome's indulging in luxuriousness, hatred, and vengeance. (Gower here uses the convention of "self-revelation.")

Book IV turns to the monastic and mendicant orders. Like the prelates, monks are primarily avaricious and lecherous, in contrast to the worthy monks of old. Monks used to be ascetics and now they are drunkards and gluttons. Similarly, the friars have ignored or forgotten the noble example of St. Francis, for their poverty and chastity are feigned, and their preaching is sanctimonious. They build palaces and overflow the earth with their numbers. Only in Chaps. 13-15 does Gower moderate his diatribe. He is gentler with the nuns, for they are but women, by nature the weaker creatures. If they sin even against chastity, they are to be more readily forgiven. The tone of Chap. 13 is somewhat like that of the Ancren Rewle, and becomes a welcome change from the precedent thunderings.

In Book V knight and peasant are more summarily but no less harshly dealt with. As is true of the clergy, the other two estates have suffered a falling off. Their golden age does not go back so far in time, however. In the previous two books, Gower is forced to return to Old Testament times to show the character of a good priest, to early Christianity to find pious monks, and (as was Langland) to St. Francis' days to find friars abiding by their vows. Knighthood, on the other hand, was honorable and peasants were loyal and industrious "only a short time ago," within the memory of the author. Once again, lechery and avarice are the two most widely practiced sins. The low point of the entire poem, I should say, is reached in Chaps. 2-8, in which Gower dwells almost obsessively upon the perils which female beauty presents to knights.

Conversely, Chaps. 9-14 are among the most interesting and valuable, aside from those of Book I, of the Vox Clamantis. We learn the typical view of a thoughtful, middle-class conservative toward the peasants: ". . . they are sluggish, they are scarce, and they are grasping." By implication Gower challenges the then current jingle,

When Adam delved and Eve span
Who was then the gentleman? 48

20

On the contrary, Adam is the prototype of the man divinely ordained to till the soil and earn his bread by the sweat of his brow. It is his necessary function to provide food and drink for the human race. Further, he himself is to be satisfied with rude fare and cease to demand wine and roasts. The description is a striking parallel to the well-known lines in Piers Plowman (B Passus VI. 304-321) on the peasant and his newly acquired tastes in matters of food. (Gower does not realize that all classes were then demanding more and more luxuries.)

In the whole of the 150 tales of the author's English Confessio Amantis there is not a single story of life in Gower's (and Chaucer's) England, or panorama of the city of London. Gower partly makes up for this omission in Chaps. 12-14 of Book V of the Vox Clamantis. Usury and Fraud, the daughters of Avarice, rule all activity in London. The rich are usurious, forgetting that the possession of wealth carries a responsibility. (Riches per se are of course legitimate. What else could the wealthy Gower say?) The smaller merchants and craftsmen of the city are all dishonest, for Fraud has them in charge. She governs vintner and baker, poulterer and butcher, chandler and cobbler, tailor and jeweler, both master and apprentice. For the most part, the picture comes alive. [49]

After concluding Book V with an attack on an unnamed mayor of low birth who is causing strife in the city and plaguing its citizens, Gower turns in Book VI to another violent tirade. Everyone in any way connected with the law, he says, is dishonest and will do anything to get money. Apprentices, lawyers, serjeants, judges, sheriffs, bailiffs, and jurymen are all open to bribes, so for the poor man there is no justice. Bad as lawyers are, however, there must still be law. Gower is always unwilling to abolish outright any institution. It is up to the King to set things right, but he is young and hence must be guided. From the older man to the younger then comes the giving of a lengthy piece of advice, a convention in English literature from Hrothgar to Polonius. In actuality, any king then did indeed have to work all things by counsel, so Gower is not supererogatory or pleonastic. If Richard II had taken these pious platitudes to heart, he would have done well. There is some justification for Gower later revising this passage from exhortation to condemnation.

Book VI ends with an interminable epic catalogue of biblical and classical saints and sinners. The saints are all deceased, but the sinners live anew: "Troilus, steadfastly faithful in love, is dead, and now Jason's love does not know how to keep faith. The faithful Medea is now dead and laid out in the earth, and the false Cressida takes pleasure in loving two men" (VI. 1325-28).

Book VII is a sermonizing summary of the previous five books, with Gower taking Daniel 2: 31 ff. as his text. (The Book of Daniel's account of the statue in Nebuchadnezzar's dream was then a widely popular theme.)[50] The materials out of which the members of the statue are fashioned allegorically represent the ages of the world: "The golden head of Nebuchadnezzar's statue has now been cut off, and the two feet of iron and clay still stand. The noble, golden race of men has departed from the world and a poor one of iron has sprung forth from it" (VI. 5-8). The iron of course symbolizes the hardness of men's hearts; all rich men are mercilessly avaricious. The clay symbolizes the frail flesh, which is doomed to death and corruption. Following still another formula, the poet then devotes seven macabre chapters (9-14) to an elaboration upon how this corruption attacks the dead body in the grave. There is a species of putrefaction in keeping with each of the seven deadly sins.

Two other ideas of importance to Gower appear in Book VII. In Chap. 8 he develops the conception of man as a microcosm (minor mundus) to whom the macrocosm is subject, a theme as old as the Timaeus.[51] The man of virtue will rule the greater world, which will furnish him with its blessings; the man of evil intent sets the universe awry and heaps misfortune upon it, so it is imperative that man live according to God's will. (Chaps. 5-6 of Book II also show that nature and the elements follow the bidding of the righteous man and wage war against sinners.) In addition, the idea of Courtly Love is briefly dealt with in Book VII. Courtly Love is of course of fundamental importance in the Confessio Amantis, Gower's best known work. In that English poem the Lover's confession to Genius the priest of Venus is a mixture of Christianity and Courtly Love. Only at the end of that poem is the latter kind of love rejected, and then because Venus tells Gower he is too old. The goddess of love, of all people, commands him thus:

> And tarie thou mi court nomore,
> Bot go ther vertu moral duelleth,
> Wher ben thi bokes, as men telleth,
> Whiche of long time thou hast write.(VIII. 2924-27)

The moral Venus should not be too severely blamed for rejecting the Lover after 30,000 lines, for in the Vox Clamantis, VII. 157 ff., Gower rejects Courtly Love as gallica peccata and those who practice it as meretrices. It is only right that Venus direct him back to what he had written.

The early chapters of Book VII comprise one last lament for the mutability of life, another reminder of the terrors of the damned, a call upon sinners to repent, and a final quick review of the three estates enmeshed in the seven deadly sins. Then comes the fine Chap. 24 telling of Gower's deep love for England and his sadness at his native

22

land's decay. The chapter ends with a cry for pity on God's part. The author then sets about the formal conclusion of his dream vision, a framework which he has only fragmentarily sustained throughout the poem. He cautions the reader once more that he is only reporting what the voice of the people put in his ear, but that men good and bad can profit from his book. In order not to seem self-righteous, Gower concludes the first version of the poem with a tactful formula: "I myself am the worst of sinners; but may the founder of the world grant me relief through a priest. Amen."[52]

These two lines are replaced by a transition to the Cronica Tripertita in the second or final version of the poem. Before examining the Cronica Tripertita, however, it will be well to discuss the Vox Clamantis further, not only because it was originally to stand alone, but also because its sequel is such a different kind of work, written much later (c. 1400), and less important for an understanding of Gower. It can readily be seen from the foregoing concise summary of The Voice of One Crying[53] that he is not a highly original thinker. His mind, although ever alert, is inexorably traditional in its outlook. Indeed, he is such a rock-ribbed conservative that, had he lived in this country in the present century, he would undoubtedly have "voted for McKinley all his life."[54] He is not superstitious, yet neither is he speculative. George G. Fox says in The Mediaeval Sciences in the Works of John Gower that the poet" is interested in facts rather than causes, and is satisfied with facts which do not appear to the modern mind particularly illuminating, nor do they seem to have shed in Gower's mind the clear bright light of knowledge which is power."[55] Fox's analysis was meant to apply only to Gower's knowledge and use of the sciences, but it is true generally. He is quite unable to escape the medieval passion for systematizing and pigeon-holing. He was of "an age when everything systematic was valuable just because it was a system; when every doctrine was profitable."[56] As in his other major works, in the Vox Clamantis Gower remains snugly within the tried and true strongholds of the three estates and the seven deadly sins. If he peeps out from behind a battlement, it is to view any slight fissure in the castle structure with alarm. On hardly a question raised in the poem does he show himself in any perceptible doubt about the true answer. Moreover, despite his many dire predictions, he rarely shows himself to be a prophet: ". . . with the passing of the cooling years, the wisdom of the simple peasants shines above the wisdom of the poet, as above the shrewdness of Richard and his counsellors."[57] On kingship, however, Gower does demonstrate a certain breadth of vision, and he is able, for once, to change his mind, as he does in regard to the degree of Richard II's responsibility. Gower would have been shocked at the suggestion, therefore, that his beloved monarchy "gave the coup de grace to the medieval order. . . ."[58]

Consistency, if not a jewel, is no hobgoblin to Gower. The Voice of One Crying manifests the contradictions of the age. The peasants are utterly to be condemned, yet Gower shares their hatred of foreigners and of lawyers. The Jews are enemies, yet the Old Testament patriarchs are models. War is bad and peace is good, yet there is no substitute for victory, especially if the enemy is heathen. He disbelieves in fatalism and chance fate, while at heart he is a fatalist, even as he argues for free will (II. 345-348). "Gentilesse" is a monopoly of the upper class, though all men are children of God. Money is an unmitigated evil; the poor should leave the rich alone with it. Lollardy is a dangerous schism; at the same time he agrees with Lollards on everything except dogma. Men have ceased to use their power of reason, thus endangering their salvation; faith is nonetheless the only road to salvation. Born in sin, man is innately imperfectible; the Vox Clamantis is to help correct his faults.

Few men, indeed, have ever desired reform so passionately. Here Gower is at one with Piers Plowman, which also urges for reform along established lines, never by violence and revolution. It has not been previously noted that Gower was very probably familiar with the B-text recension of Piers Plowman, now dated between 1377 and 1379. There is a possible allusion in the peroration of the Vox Clamantis: ". . . the bad man should know these writings so that he presently may become good, and the good man should seek them out so that he may do better" (VII. 1473-74). These lines are conceivably reminiscent of Piers Plowman's Visions of Dowel, Dobet, and Dobest. A clearer and more definite allusion to these same Visions occurs in the midst of Gower's account of the Peasants' Revolt: "One man helps in what another man does, and still another agrees that they would be bad, worse, and worst" (I. 1121-22). This scornful negation of Dowel, Dobet, and Dobest is quite in keeping with Gower's opinion of the peasantry, of course. Piers therefore could well draw Gower's fire. The hero of the alliterative poem is a peasant who is Christian, saintly and even Christlike. That is enough for Gower to think of it as "rum, ram, ruf." The whole English poem, often democratic in tone (as in B Passus XI. 192 ff.), is filled with sympathy for the poor, while not losing sight of their faults. Gower is humane enough to object to tyranny, to lawyers plundering the poor, to knights not defending the weak and helpless, and to the wealthy clergy and laymen not being generous to the needy; but he would never agree that a plowman could point the way to salvation, regardless of his awareness that the early Christians humbly held all things in common.

In spite of this difference, the Vox Clamantis and Piers Plowman are much alike in thought. The notes to these translations point out many parallels in their criticisms of the regular clergy, friars, bishops, and papal irregularities. Neither poet is a Lollard, though each echoes the Lollards' criticisms of the Church; and like them, each goes directly to the Bible and by-passes the clerical hierarchy in his search for truth. Most important is social, political and religious agreement. Each poet wishes the same fundamental structure of society, with due subordination of classes and performance of individual duty to sustain the social fabric. Compare, for example, the duties of knights as outlined in The Voice of One Crying, V. 4-8, and Piers, B Passus VI. 20-56. To both Gower and Langland every major institution is corrupt but any basic change is unthinkable. The remedy for all evil is one faith for all. Every person in the clerical hierarchy, the legal system, the government, and the merchant, artisan, and peasant classes is to follow the simple word of Christ.

There was another famous contemporary who proposed a somewhat different remedy. About the time the Vox Clamantis was written, John Wycliffe was achieving great popularity and notoriety. Until 1377 his work had been devoted toward reform of the Church in ways which Gower would have approved. In that year, however, he was indicted for nineteen heresies, and in 1379 he began to reinterpret or even question the doctrine of Transubstantiation. [59] Hence to Gower, Wycliffe is "a new Arius" and "a new Jovinian" (VI. 1267), and the poet attacks "those who are bringing on the great dangers of schism upon the people by getting out rash documents" (III. 1129-30). He does not mention Wycliffe by name, though he pointedly opposes him on the doctrines of Transubstantiation and Dominion: ". . . priests of today, whether the highest or the lesser, [i.e., whether good or bad,] effect the body of Christ and consecrate it. For when we consecrate the wine and bread on the altar, this becomes the true blood and flesh together" (III. 1819-20).

There is nevertheless much upon which Gower and Wycliffe could agree. Both are fearless speakers against episcopal and papal faults, and their criticisms of the friars are strikingly similar. [60] Both attack lawyers. Both oppose image worship, the Donation of Constantine, and the "Caesarian clergy." As does Langland, both rely heavily upon the Bible in deciding questions of good and evil. There are, indeed, echoes of the Wycliffite doctrine of Dominion in The Voice of One Crying, most notably in regard to Richard II (in Book VI, Chap. 8), though Gower does not extend it to priests, despite the fact that to have done so would proceed logically from the microcosm-macrocosm concept. The clergy are corrupt and so must reform, if the Church is to achieve its purpose of being men's means to salvation, thinks Gower. The Church is nonetheless doctrinally sound. He will have nothing to do with such radical ideas as substituting individual morality for the efficacy of the sacraments. Then too, Gower shares the Lollards' severe anti-clericalism, but would never dream of questioning the power of the pope to "bind and loose," or even considering disendowment. Wycliffe points toward the future, Gower looks back. [61]

Sources and Artistry of The Voice of One Crying

Gower not only adopts or echoes the ideas of other men, he also appropriates many of their verses. G. C. Macaulay, the editor of the critical text of Gower, comments on Gower's borrowings:

> One . . . matter affecting our estimate of the style of the composition generally has perhaps been sufficiently illustrated in the Notes of this edition, that is to say, the extent to which the author borrows in the Vox Clamantis from other writers. It is sufficiently obvious to a casual reader that he has appropriated a good many lines from Ovid, though the extent of this schoolboy plagiarism is hardly to be realized without careful examination; but his very extensive obligations to other writers have not hitherto been pointed out. He repeatedly takes not lines or couplets only, but passages of eight, ten, or even twenty lines from the Aurora of Peter Riga, from the poem of Alexander Neckham De Vita Monachorum, from the Speculum Stultorum, or from the Pantheon, so that in many places the composition is entirely made up of such borrowed matter variously arranged and combined. 62

The notes to this translation of The Voice of One Crying reproduce nearly all the editor's footnotes on Gower's sources, as well as adding quite a few more, and venturing to correct him in a number of instances. Not counting references and allusions to, and translations from, the Bible, the notes in this volume point out a total of over 1,300 borrowed or adapted lines. Hence, about thirteen per cent of the poem is borrowed or plagiarized. References to 142 of these lines make their first occurrence in this volume. With their kind permission, these notes also make mention of the 456 lines Father Paul E. Beichner, C.S.C., deals with in his "Gower's Use of Aurora in Vox Clamantis, " Speculum, XXX (1955), 582-595, and of the fifty-three lines dealt with in Professor Robert R. Raymo's "Gower's Vox Clamantis and the Speculum Stultorum, " MLN, LXX (1955), 315-320. Still more lines seem borrowed, e.g., V. 79-112, or VII. 591-604, but I am unable to cite a source. In an age when "schoolboy plagiarism" relies on The Reader's Digest rather than the Metamorphoses, however, it is not distressing-- save for source hunters more than half a millennium later--to find a fourteenth-century Englishman who sits down to write a Latin poem of 10,265 lines resorting to the use of other poets' verses.

Ovid is the most important source, furnishing the Vox Clamantis with some 537 lines. Gower does not borrow whole stories from him, as he does in the Confessio Amantis, where several tales from Ovid are pleasantly retold. [63] Instead, in the poem at hand, ". . . the perpetual borrowing of isolated lines or couplets from Ovid, often without regard to their appropriateness or their original meaning, often makes the style, of the first book especially, nearly as bad as it can be. "[64] Macaulay tends to exaggerate the number of lines borrowed inappropriately, and does not fully allow for Gower's incredible ability to make a smooth blend of lines from diverse sources. For example, Book III, Chap. 26, is largely a pastiche of borrowings from the Aurora, into which Gower has thrown isolated lines and couplets from three different poems of Ovid, but the result is a straightforward progression of clear thought. Book VII, Chap. 5, will serve as a further example: It is a lament on mutability and the wretched lot of man, with many lines taken from Alexander Neckham's De Vita Monachorum; but at VII. 483 Gower takes a line from Ovid's Ars Amatoria, III. 91, wherein a lover receives encouragement to seize the day, inasmuch as all things except the joys of love pass away! Again, as often, Gower is able to insure that there is no incongruity at all, despite radically different original contexts of the lines.

Macaulay is right in stressing the fact that the first book of the Vox Clamantis is heavily indebted to Ovid. A summary of Ovidian lines in tabular form shows that over half of those which Gower uses are in Book I--a likely indication that he composed this book somewhat hurriedly after the rest of the poem was complete.

Book	Number of Ovidian Lines	Number Not Previously Noted
I	270	33
II	22	1
III	47	10
IV	44	4
V	74	20
VI	29	15
VII	51	24
Totals	537	107

Another table will show that Macaulay is correct in claiming, "His knowledge of Ovid seems to have been pretty complete, for he borrows from almost every section of his works with the air of one who knows perfectly well where to turn for what he wants . . . . "[65]

	Number of Lines Borrowed
Metamorphoses	169
Tristia	79
Ars Amatoria	76
Fasti	61
Ex Ponto	58
Heroides	41
Remedia Amoris	38
Amores	15
Total	537

These tables include complete and nearly complete lines, or sometimes half-lines. They do not include many brief phrases taken from Ovid, [66] or some lines which fall halfway between paraphrase and plagiarism. [67]

Another feature of Gower's use of Ovid must be pointed out: Frequently, he is not content to leave well enough alone, but makes slight changes in lines or couplets. Some of these are harmless enough or necessary for adaptation, but others (as in VII. 327-328) are much for the worse, although some such seeming changes are very likely due to a corrupt copy of Ovid. (Many of these bad alterations are pointed out in the notes.) In a few instances (e.g., V. 399-402), it can be argued that Gower actually improves upon Ovid. At any rate, the Roman poet's influence upon him is sometimes admirable. For example, Vox Clamantis, VII. 471, is Ovid's, but it seems to have been the inspiration for Gower to then write the following line (472), which is a good one. In the Confessio Amantis Genius, the priest of Venus, is not at all reluctant to tell the Lover that the "clerk Ovide" furnished him with many stories. In the Vox Clamantis, Gower acknowledges his indebtedness only once (V. 384), and that is to escape accusation of having too full knowledge of immorality.

Close to Ovid in importance as one of Gower's sources is "the Aurora or Biblia versificata, one of the most popular and widely circulated books of the Middle Ages, . . . written by Petrus Riga, Canon of Reims, over a period of years sometime between 1170 and the end of the century."[68] With one exception (an exemplum in VI. 875-902) Gower again borrows only passages which fit into larger contexts of his own, as he does with Ovid; similarly, he mentions the Aurora and its author only once (III. 1853-54). This one lead enabled Professor Macaulay to trace about 235 lines borrowed from the Aurora. By using more and better manuscripts, the Reverend Paul E. Beichner, who is preparing the first printed edition of the Aurora, was able to add some 221 lines to those found by Macaulay. [69] Gower does not much use the Aurora for scriptural content, but for rhetorical excerpts. Or, if he does use it for content, he is apt to botch his material, as at III. 1840 ff. He is thoroughly familiar with the poem, but as the translation, notes, and Introduction below will show, he also knows the Vulgate well. At times, he might have been borrowing from either, or from the language of the Church liturgy.

From Alexander Neckham's poem De Vita Monachorum are borrowed 228 lines, of which twenty-three are pointed out for the first time in the notes to this translation. This fine satire is from the late twelfth century, as is another of which Gower makes use, [70] Nigel de Longchamps' Speculum Stultorum. [71] To mention the last of the medieval works from which Gower borrows freely, thirty-nine lines are taken from Godfrey of Viterbo's Pantheon, of which seven are here noted for the first time. The present writer has the uneasy feeling that he has missed still other lines in the Pantheon (and for that matter, in Ovid) which Gower has used. There are also a few miscellaneous borrowings mentioned in the notes.

As was Chaucer, [72] Gower was thoroughly acquainted with the Vulgate and made liberal use of it in his works. In the Confessio Amantis some fifteen tales, including a few of his best, are based upon the Bible. [73] In the Mirour and the Vox Clamantis, on the other hand, the references and allusions to the Scriptures are usually brief. One would expect Gower to show a preference for the sterner books of the Old Testament, but there are actually about as many references to the New Testament. His favorite part of the Bible is the Gospels, to which there are approximately ninety allusions in The Voice of One Crying. A great deal of the Sermon on the Mount finds its way into the Latin poem. Unlike the Mirour, the Latin poem does not contain many quotations from the Church Fathers, though the French poem shows that Gower knows much of them, if only in collections of quotations. Both of these non-English poems, to conclude, share in the practice of using only snippets of other works. The Confessio Amantis often borrows entire stories, while seldom following its sources slavishly. Thus Gower borrows lavishly throughout his poetical career (The Tripartite Chronicle will prove an exception). But he does not use his sources with maximum effectiveness until he finds his true talent, that of a teller of tales. It is unfortunate that he does not enliven his earlier works with rapid, clear narratives of Mozartian deftness such as those found in the Confessio Amantis. [74] Despite this stricture, the modern reader can express sincere agreement with Father Beichner's conclusion concerning Gower's use of sources in the Vox Clamantis: "When to his use of the Aurora is added that made of Ovid, of the De vita monachorum, of the Speculum stultorum, and the Pantheon, one is overwhelmed by Gower's industry. And yet I believe that he felt he was honestly presenting his views on his own day even though he often expressed himself in words and criticisms borrowed from his predecessors. "[75]

The Vox Clamantis does not emerge as a great work of art, despite much serious effort on Gower's part to make it one. Like the author of Piers, like Spenser, in a long poem he lacks architectonic ability. He erects an imposing but sprawling and shaky framework and then fills in the pieces as best he might, with some backtracking, rambling, and repetition. [76] There are nevertheless effective areas in the mosaic, such as some of the descriptions scattered here and there in the poem. Some examples are the banquet of the gluttonous prelates in III. 103 ff.; the sarcastic portrait of that stock figure the hunting parson in III, Chap. 16; and the picture of London commercial life in Book V, Chaps. 12-14, already referred to. The retelling of the creation of Adam in Book VII, Chap. 6, is well done. There is an occasional touch of wit, as in VI. 461-462. Unfortunately, Gower often pursues the rhetorical ornament of amplificatio to extremes, wearily dilating whatever he has to say. He takes to heart the medieval view that every author ought to beautify his verses in as many ways as he can.

Gower was surely well acquainted, as was Chaucer, [77] with at least one of the art of rhetorics current in his day, the most popular of which was Geoffrey de Vinsauf's Poetria Nova. [78] It would take a volume to catalogue all his uses of the various figures of rhetoric, [79] but these translations will furnish evidence of many of them. The following rhetorical devices will be easily recognized in the English translations: allegory, amplification, anaphora,. apostrophe, the catalogue or list, comparison, contrast, description, dialogue, etymologizing, example, exclamation, hyperbole, litotes, metaphor, oxymoron, parallelism (of several kinds: words, phrases, clauses, sentences), personification, repetition, representation, rhetorical question (as well as question and answer), and simile. Nearly all these are illustrated in the Poetria Nova. Even in translation, it will be apparent that metaphors are at times badly mixed (as in Cronica Tripertita, III. 17-26). Personifications and representations, so popular in the fourteenth century, are all too often mere labels, rather than effective instances such as that of Lady Mede in Piers Plowman.

Certain other figures, because of language differences, do not often carry over from the Latin into English, or are intentionally avoided in the English for the sake of clarity. Among these are alliteration (similiter cadens), internal rhyme (similiter desinens), chiasmus, hendiadys, and metonymy. The notes do call attention to many instances of plays upon words or paronomasia, and the translations attempt to reproduce as many of these as possible. The notes likewise indicate approximately one hundred proverbs or sententiae which occur in the two major Latin poems. [80] Gower was given to much use of proverbs and sententious remarks in his longer poems, though these are seldom as structurally or smoothly employed as they are in Chaucer. [81]

The Voice of One Crying tends to give the impression that Gower,

in order to write it, compiled a huge commonplace book with such headings as "air, " "bears, " "boars, " "dogs, " "fire, " "foxes, " "roses, "
"sheep, " "tears, " "water, " "wolves, " etc. The stock of images in this
poem (and in The Tripartite Chronicle) is small; accordingly he repeats
himself wearisomely. Bees are always stinging, dogs snarling and
biting, fire raging, roses bearing thorns, tears painfully flowing, and
wolves preying upon the poor sheep. [82] Gower has honorable classical
models for all this. Nevertheless, such lachrymose repetition serves
to thicken the atmosphere of the longer Latin poem, and to becloud an
occasional effective use of imagery. It is ironic that the poet believes
the cosmos obeys the will of the just man. The lugubriousness of the
worlds of nature and man always presenting obstacles to progress of
any kind makes the tone of The Voice of One Crying flat and heavy.
Even the sporadic irony groans with the weight of burdensome messages,
though occasionally its grimness does not lose its force, as at III. 1417
ff. The overcharge of gloom is a poetic fault which is in keeping with,
but which aggravates, the chief ideational one: "Gower was too obviously bent on fault-finding to be entirely convincing. . . ."[83] In re-
buttal of this condemnation it may be said, however, that greater men
than Gower agreed with his summation, "The world is al miswent"
(Confessio Amantis, Prol. 517): Compare for example, Dante, Purgatorio, 16: 58-60, which says the same thing.
        Although W. P. Ker's essay, "John Gower Poet, "[84] remains one
of the best general treatments of its subject, its author is unduly harsh
in complaining, "The Latin elegiacs of the 'Vox Clamantis' are generally detestable verse. . . ." A fairer estimate of Gower's metrics
is that of Macaulay:

    Gower's own style of versification in Latin is somewhat less ele-
    gant than that of Alexander Neckham or Peter Riga, but it stands
    upon much the same level of correctness. If we take into account
    the fact that the Latin is not classical but medieval, and that certain
    licenses of prosody were regularly admitted by medieval writers of
    Latin verse, we shall not find the performance very bad. . . . In
    any case it is certain that Gower expressed himself in Latin with
    tolerable correctness. He may have imitated the style of Ovid
    'studiosius quam felicius, ' as Leland observes, but the comparison
    with other Latin verse-writers of his time sets his performance in
    a fairly favorable light. [85]

The meter of the Vox Clamantis is nonetheless not as smooth as that of
the Mirour de l'Omme or the Confessio Amantis, for there is rarely an
irregular line in the French and English poems. Yet there is not a very

31

great number of irregular lines in the Vox Clamantis, though the use of
the elegiac couplet clogs the thought, for the sentences are cramped in
order to fit the couplets, with a continual "end-stopped" effect. (By
contrast, the sentences in the French and English works flow easily.)
Occasionally Gower varies the sentence structure to fit the sense, as
in Book I, Chap. 9, the famous passage translated by Thomas Fuller.
He also experiments with end rhyme from time to time, and writes the
Dedicatory Epistle and Cronica Tripertita in leonine hexameters, a
meter he came to grow fond of in his old age.

Ker remarks that "the Latin works altogether add nothing to
Gower's literary reputation, except that they show, like the English
and French poems, a talent for remembering words" (p. 455). The
latter half of this statement is certainly true, for the vocabulary of the
Vox Clamantis is large. Gower seems never at a loss for the term he
wishes, and he has assimilated Ovid's vocabulary almost in toto. His
stock of words comes in about equal portions from that Roman poet and
Medieval Latin, as do his constructions. There is also an appreciable
number of Anglicisms in both. For examples of Anglicized Latin constructions, see Vox Clamantis, VI. 288 and 1059-60, or VII. 18.
Struggling for quantitative meter, Gower badly overworks the words
sic, et, and que (often non-enclitic). These remarks, like Ker's
quoted above, may apply likewise to the Cronica Tripertita, with the
exception that its vocabulary is much less Ovidian, much more Anglo-
Latin.

Late Minor Works

Gower's life and works after finishing The Voice of One Crying
but before he came to write The Tripartite Chronicle may be briefly
considered here. In 1378 Chaucer gave Gower (and a certain Richard
Forester) his power of attorney to be used during his absence abroad.
There was therefore a close personal relationship between the two
poets at an early date, one which lasted for some years, for about 1386
Chaucer dedicated to the "moral Gower" (and to the "philosophical
Strode") his magnificent Troilus and Criseyde (V. 1856-57). About this
same time--the exact date is unknown--King Richard II asked him to
write "som newe thing, " as Gower tells us in the Prologue to the Confessio Amantis, 11. 22 ff. Gower returned Chaucer's compliment in
the first version of the Confessio, completed in 1390. The removal of
the compliment in a later (1393) version of the poem has caused some
speculation about a break between the two men. Of this, more later.
In a second version of the Confessio, Gower's chief change is the can-
cellation of some praise of Richard II, done a few months after the poem

had originally been completed. The third and final version of the poem was made not later than June of 1393. In it, Richard is all but dropped and the poem is dedicated to Henry of Lancaster, then Earl of Derby. Even the first version, it will be remembered, had contained a dedication to Henry in the Latin lines at the end. (In retrospect, it may be said that Gower was well in advance of the events of his time in singling out Henry so early, for it would have been hard to predict in 1393 [or 1390] that he would some day be King of England and--for Gower-- savior of the realm. He had every right to deluge Henry with poems and rededications later.) The gradual disfavor in which Gower came to hold Richard is apparent from the revision of the Vox Clamantis, and will become more apparent from the Cronica Tripertita. Similarly, it will become apparent that his admiration of Henry in that poem is of long standing. Gower must, however, have felt well disposed toward Richard to write the Confessio Amantis for the King's eye. A king's command is to be obeyed, but the length of the English poem is beyond the call of a subject's duty. In order to allow the poet time to compile its 34,000 lines by 1390, my conjecture is that he began to write it in the middle of the 1380's. [86]

Perhaps King Richard was responsible for Gower's using English for his frame story (see Prol. 22-25). Employment of his native tongue in poetry was a new departure for Gower. The fact that he wrote his first major work in French, his second in Latin, and his third in English has long attracted considerable attention, and Gower himself was understandably conscious of his feat. [87] His change from French to Latin to English has impressed critics in different ways. Some have thought that he was playing things safe linguistically, in order to insure a future reputation. During his lifetime, the English upper classes were shifting from using French to English. Given Gower's unsubtle and dogged temperament, however, it seems unlikely that he viewed his choice of English over French with such shrewdness or foresight. (Presumably, either language would have been acceptable to Richard II.) As for Latin, an educated man might well have wished, after having given his social views at length in French, to have his say in the most scholarly tongue, the one most likely to endure. (Bacon thought the same way over two centuries later.) Probably he was neither drifting with the times nor trying to predict them. Instead, conservative that he was, he retained all three languages to the end of his poetical career, employing all three for serious purposes. Even his major English work, the Confessio, incorporates a total of some three hundred Latin elegiacs, used in prefaces to books and sections of books. It is significant, too, that all his major works have Latin titles (with an alternate French one for the Mirour de l'Omme).

English was the least scholarly or learned language at his disposal; that may have been the reason for his adopting it to write of love.

Whatever the cause, the Confessio Amantis remains his most impressive work. It has affinities with the French and Latin works, yet in important ways is different from them. It is hoped that the present translations throw light upon it, but a full analysis of the Confessio Amantis is beyond the limits of this volume. [88] Suffice it to say here that when Gower turned to his native language, things went easier for him, both in versification and in utilization of sources. For his English poem he borrowed whole stories, not just lines; paradoxically, he thereby freed himself and found his true talent, that of a teller of tales, a teller who does not use his sources in scavenger fashion, and who does not hobble his poetic pace while rummaging through the books on his desk.

Gower continued to write shorter Latin works in the 1390's after he had finished revision of the Confessio Amantis in 1393. The longest of these, and one which can be dated, is alarmingly titled, "Carmen Super Multiplici Viciorum Pestilencia" (in Works, IV, 346-354). After he had finished his attempt in the Confessio to write a book "Somwhat of lust, somwhat of lore"(Prol. 19), Gower went right back to straight moralitas. The headnote to the "Carmen" says that it was written in "the twentieth year of King Richard," i.e., 1397. [89] The poem is composed of a mixture of sections in leonine hexameters and elegiac couplets (a mixture which is prelude to the linking of these verse forms in the combined Vox Clamantis and Cronica Tripertita.) The first section is an unconvincing argument "Against the Devil in the Cause of Lollardy" and a moving plea for the faith as of old. As usual, Gower is fearlessly outspoken and sincere, but to compare Wycliffe to Satan, however understandable, now seems unwarranted. It is equally far-fetched to accuse Wycliffites of luxuriousness, such as wearing fine linen under their outer garment of coarse wool: "Sub grossa lana linum subtile tenetur"(1. 35). The rest of the poem attacks the vices of Pride, Lust, and Avarice. The burden is exactly the same as in the Vox Clamantis, from which a scattering of lines are taken. Gower was presumably about to proceed through the seven deadlies again and then stopped short. Like Gower's other short Latin poems to be discussed below, it adds little or nothing to his thought, and hence neither it nor they are translated in this volume.

On Jan. 25, 1397/8 was issued a license for the marriage of John Gower and Agnes Groundolf, to take place within Gower's lodging of the Priory of St. Mary Overey (or Overes) in Southwark. His will of Aug. 15, 1408, is dated at the same place, so Gower must have lived in the Priory for his remaining years. His remarkable tomb still survives in the Chapel of St. John the Baptist, Southwark Cathedral, originally St. Mary Overes Priory and Church, though not in its original condition. [90] The marriage, possibly Gower's second, presumably took place in 1397/8, and Agnes Groundolf is one of the legatees of Gower's will. [91] Macaulay plausibly conjectures (in Works, I, lxxxiii-iv) that in 1397,

34

the year before the marriage, Gower wrote the Traitié pour Essampler les Amantz Marietz--a modern title for a work which had no medieval one (in Works, I, 379-393). The work itself consists of eighteen balades, each with three rime-royal stanzas, while the last balade has an envoy serving for the whole series and asking the reader's indulgence for the author's French. The apology is of course conventional modesty: The author of the Mirour and the Cinkante Balades had no real worries about his ability to use the French language. Gower had used this same balade form in some of the Cinkante Balades. Though technically as competent as those in that collection, the balades of the Traitié are weighted down with moralizing. Many of the essamples are the same as those which found place in the Confessio, e.g., Nectanabus, Hercules, Jason, and, not to forget the ladies, la fole pecheresse Heleine. The refrain of No. IX, "Horribles sont les mals d'avolterie," will give an idea of the whole series.

Seven of the ten surviving MSS of the Traitié connect it by means of a French headnote to copies of the Confessio: "Now that he has spoken above in English by way of example of the folly of one who loves passionately, he will at this time address to all the world in general a treatise in French, based upon learned authorities, in order to instruct married lovers, so that they may keep the faith of their holy matrimony through pure loyalty, and hold fast to the glory of God." The form and content of the sentence indicate it to be Gower's own. Furthermore, the headnote and Traitié are to be found in the Bodleian MS. Fairfax 3, an "exceptionally good" manuscript and "a copy which was probably made and corrected under the supervision of the author."[92] Thus the Traitié is made into a palinode for the Confessio Amantis, which had no need of one. Was Gower really stung by Chaucer's joke (in The Man of Law's Tale, ll. 77-89) that some tales in the Confessio Amantis were "cursed stories" and "unkynde abhomynacions"?

The poems in the Traitié pour Essampler les Amantz Marietz are obviously the work of an older and still more moral Gower than are those of the Cinkante Balades. In all the MSS of the Traitié the French balades are followed by thirty-six Latin lines (one MS omits a portion of these) which make doubly sure that love, though stormy, should be connubial. (Some of these lines are drawn from the Vox Clamantis; see V. 53 ff. and n.) The concluding couplet is autobiographical: "Hinc vetus annorum Gower sub spe meritorum / Ordine sponsorum tutus adhibo thorum." Let us hope that the good Agnes Groundolf received this prothalamium in the spirit of the Patient Griselda in Chaucer's Clerk's Tale, rather than that of Januarie's "fresshe May" in The Merchant's Tale.

Before proceeding to The Tripartite Chronicle, Gower's last major work, it will be well to speak a brief word about his remaining minor Latin poems (to be found in Works, IV, 343-345, and 355-368).

"De Lucis Scrutinio" (pp. 355-357) is a poem of 103 leonine hexameters lamenting the Great Schism. In it, Gower comes close to the Wycliffite position of advocating secular control of the Church, for he urges kings to take direct part in ending the Schism (ll. 27-30). Kings are to do this, as well as drive out the pagan, by the forceful example of their charity. The poem is still another run-down of the classes and groups of society. In each group he searches for "light" but finds only the darkness of sin. The short piece, "Ecce Patet Tensus" (pp. 358-359), consists of thirty-six elegiacs which lament the power of love to corrupt man. It echoes Vox Clamantis, Book V, Chap. 3, and contains some lines from that chapter.

"O Deus Immense" (pp. 362-364) is Gower's final statement to Richard II on the duties of a king. [93] As late as 1399 Gower, while greatly admiring Henry, has not yet given up hope for Richard. The poem is more democratic in tone than is usual with him: "Nomen regale populi vox dat tibi. . . ." (1. 61), but this is a standard medieval idea on kingship which need not be pressed too literally. There are also poems of praise and advice for Henry IV (pp. 343-345), one of which, "Rex Celi Deus" (p. 343), is largely an adaptation of lines in the original version of the Vox Clamantis, Book VI, Chap. 18, which Gower had previously used in praise of Richard II! The short poem, "Quicquid Homo Scribat" (pp. 365-366) exists in three widely different versions, which could well be given different titles. It constitutes Gower's farewell to writing. One version, which seems to be the first, says that he went blind in the first year of Henry IV's reign, i.e., 1400. A second version tells that he stopped writing in Henry's second year, and contains the moving lines. "Scribat qui veniet post me discrecior alter, / Ammodo namque manus et mea penna silent." Presumably, he dictated a very few short pieces after this date, however, for one of them, "Presul, Ouile Regis" (p. 368) refers to a great comet seen in March of 1402. The four-line poem, "Armigeri Scutum" (p. 367), which is carved on his tomb, is very likely Gower's last poem, one which he easily could have dictated. [94]

The Tripartite Chronicle

Although he went blind in 1400, Gower must have composed his last major work, The Tripartite Chronicle, in that year before losing his sight, for it is hard to conceive of his dictating it. Elegiac couplets would have presumably been easier to dictate than the difficult leonine hexameters in which the work is composed. Just as he affixed the Traitié to the Confessio Amantis, so he affixed the Cronica Tripertita to the Vox Clamantis late in life. The Cronica survives in six

36

manuscripts and has been thrice edited. [95] Macaulay's critical edition
(in Works, IV, 314-342) is again the basis for the present translation.
On Nov. 21, 1399, Henry made a grant "for life to the King's esquire
John Gower of two pipes of wine of Gascony yearly in the port of London. " Gower seems to be acknowledging the grant in his short Latin
poem, "O Recolende" or "Epistola breuis" (Works, IV, 345), and the
grant itself was no doubt made in recognition of Gower's long political
support of Henry, [96] which dates back at least as far as 1390 and the
first version of the Confessio Amantis. On April 5, 1400, the grant was
renewed. Perhaps by this date, perhaps later in 1400, the Cronica was
written. It incorporates Henry's coronation on October 13, 1399, the
brief insurrection against Henry in January, 1400, and Richard's death
a fortnight after the insurrection. That death is the last event in the
Cronica.

The whole poem is organized as a selection of historical episodes
from the years 1387-99, episodes which throw Richard II in an unfavorable light and Henry IV in a favorable one. It is thus far too unsystema-
tic to be technically called a "chronicle. " Gower probably chose the
title in order to give the illusion of completeness of coverage. He also
pretendedly "gives to his narrative [in about three places] the semblance
of having been composed as the events happened. "[97] This attempt to
achieve contemporaneousness, in addition to a half-hearted effort to establish a dream-vision framework at the outset, are two factors which
among others serve to make the poem sporadically obscure, or at least
awkward. The dream-vision framework, for example, is almost completely ignored at the end of the poem. The narrative is piecemeal.
Gower seems to have forgotten the skills as a teller of tales which he
shows in the Confessio Amantis. The historical line of thought is indeed
so disjointed that Part III (see especially ll. 3-6) may well have been
written after a delay since Part II.

Gower's choice of meter is unfortunate. Instead of carrying forth
with the elegiac couplets of the Vox Clamantis, he uses the difficult
leonine hexameter for the 1, 062 lines —a feat of virtuosity in itself. The
demands of rhyme for every hemistich, however, force him often to
contort his word order, sequence of tenses, and diction badly. There
is a corresponding loss in beauty of words and sentences. There are
far fewer figures of speech. There are, however, still many puns, much
use of litotes, some metaphors, and a few similes. The notes point out
the occasional proverbs; these are usually moralistic and less appropriately used than in the Vox Clamantis (e. g., Cronica, II. 345-348, and
III. 278-281). Because of the nature of the subject matter, as well as
the comparative rarity of the meter, less than a handfull of lines seem
borrowed. The notes to this translation of The Voice of One Crying endeavor to replace Macaulay's; those to this translation of The Tripartite
Chronicle supplement rather than replace his significant but lengthy

historical annotations, while at the same time presenting the English translation as a work capable of being read independently.

Just as the choice of meter is unfortunate, so is the attempt at allegory, especially in Part I, thus validating at least half of Henry James' stricture on allegory, to the effect that "it is apt to spoil two good things--a story and a moral, a meaning and a form. . . . "[98] Instead of calling his historical personages by name, Gower follows the literary convention of using heraldic terms, especially those based upon the names of birds and animals. As in that curious Middle English poem, Mum and the Sothsegger, [99] Warwick is "the Bear, " Gloucester is "the Swan, " and Richard Earl of Arundel is "the Horse. " These men are Richard II's opponents. The King himself is "the Sun" or "Phoebus. " (In Mum he is "the Hart. ") Such terms, which now strike us as pointless circumlocutions or subterfuges, constituted a literary motif or convention at that time, used in several other poems. [100] The labels derive largely from heraldic badges or cognizances and must have been as familiar to Englishmen at the end of the fourteenth century as such a name as "Old Hickory" is to our day. Whether familiar or not, Gower as much as apologizes (I. 43-47) for their cumbersome use. In addition, always anxious to insure clarity, he attaches a prose marginal note beside each paragraph of the Cronica Tripertita (these are herein translated as paragraph headings), often explaining directly the meanings of the symbols used. The notes to the translation sometimes perforce explain his explanations.

Part I of The Tripartite Chronicle deals with selected events of 1387-88. There is an attempt in ll. 9-10 to maintain that this part is a vision beheld in advance of the events related, as in Book I of The Voice of One Crying. Again, as in that poem, the happenings are reported to the writer by a "voice" which prompted his ear. Initially, it is clear that it is not the vox populi; at the end of the poem (III. 479) the voice is indeed that of the people.

In 1387, three nobles lead the opposition to Richard II's despotism. They are the Bear, the Swan, and the Horse, respectively the Earl of Warwick, the Duke of Gloucester, and the Earl of Arundel. "The shadowy one who bore the Sun" is Richard II (I. 57). On the King's side are the Boar (the Earl of Oxford), the Archbishop of York, and Michael de la Pole. Allied with the King's loyal opposition are the Earl Marshall, the Earl of Derby, and the Earl of Northumberland. The King's side quickly meets defeat. After this, five "Lords Appellant, " who are the Bear, Swan, and Horse together with the hardly mentioned Henry of Derby and the Earl Marshall, summon what is known to history--but not to Gower's poem--as the "Merciless Parliament" of 1388 (I. 129-130). Some of Richard's followers are executed, some flee the land, and some are exiled. The five impeccable nobles "thus molded a reformed, reinvigorated King" (I. 210).

38

Gower's own prose headnote to Part II is largely self-explanatory:

Here in the second part of the Chronicle he states how the King, pretending peace under the guise of feigned alliance, treacherously overthrew the three aforesaid nobles. He thus caused one of them to be strangled; another he had decapitated; while the third, alas! he destined to be imprisoned in exile, together with the Lord of Cobham, who had always been a true friend of the realm. And in addition, which was shameful, that same cruel King utterly expelled from his See the Reverend Father in Christ Thomas of Arundel, then Archbishop of Canterbury. And he most unmercifully decreed him to be held perpetually in exile.

Macaulay notes for Part II, "There is an interval of nearly ten years between the first and second part of the Chronicle. Our author proceeds to the events of 1397. He assumes that the king carried out a long-meditated plan of vengeance, cp. ll. 23 ff., but that was of course an afterthought by way of accounting for what happened" (p. 408). It is understandable that Gower skipped over the years 1388-97, for during this period his target Richard II ruled moderately well, if erratically; but the whole Cronica Tripertita is conceived to denigrate him and to elevate Henry IV. The poet should nonetheless have provided at least some sort of bridge between Parts I and II. Furthermore, he is too partisan: The King's victims are spotless, their opponents utterly wicked. Actually, there was of course good and evil on both sides. For example, Thomas Arundel, Archbishop of Canterbury, to whom Gower dedicates the final version of the Vox Clamantis and Cronica Tripertita combined, is remembered in history as the bigot who started the burning of heretics in England.

In Part II the Bear, the Swan, and the Horse again come on the scene, wholly loyal to Richard (an historical inaccuracy) and wholly virtuous. The crafty Richard II tricks them, and one by one their fates are related, with Gower never tiring of stressing Richard's shifty cunning. The Swan, the Duke of Gloucester, is treacherously murdered at Calais (II. 29 ff.)—though Gower neglects to mention that Gloucester's treachery preceded Richard's. The Horse (Arundel) and the Bear (Warwick) are seized and imprisoned. Parliament is summoned (II. 78) to pass sentence on the three. (Parliament was then a judicial high court.) As expected from a Parliament under the thumb of Richard, the trio are condemned to die. The unfortunate Swan, however, is already dead, having been mysteriously murdered; the account of his death (II. 85-118) is historically significant as a supplement to other documentation.

Arundel the Horse is deceived by a written guarantee of safety

39

from Richard II, and Gower portrays his death as a martyrdom (II. 118-158). (In actuality, Richard Earl of Arundel was a hardened man, by no means the pathetic saint Gower makes him out to be.) Next is the Bear's turn to be tricked by Richard (II. 159 ff.). He is persuaded to sign a confession of guilt, on the assumption that he is then to be released. But such a signature (as often in history) is the signer's undoing. Gower is not suspicious of Warwick's having thereby acknowledged any wrongdoing, but proceeds to make the most of Richard's perfidy, claming that the King jeered at his promise (II. 188). The Bear is then exiled to the Isle of Man and expropriated. There he dies of grief.

Lord Cobham, [101] the son of Richard Earl of Arundel, then flees to a Carthusian monastery for refuge (II. 220). Gower stresses Cobham's Christian virtue, glossing over a fact which he surely must have known, namely, that Cobham was a prominent Lollard. Sentence of death is passed upon him and then commuted to exile to the Isle of Jersey (II. 229-230). At II. 233 ff. Gower pulls out all the stops in lamenting the exile of Archbishop Thomas Arundel. He praises him lavishly as a "priest without peer" and prays for his safe return to England from his exile in France. There follows a lament on mutability; the nobles whose ruin he has depicted show that all life is uncertain. Gower then attacks Scrope, Bushy, and Green, partisans of the King who injured the Swan, Horse, and Bear (II. 320 ff.). (Surprisingly, Gower does not amuse himself with their names.) Part II ends with a series of proverbs and platitudes, not all of which are fully relevant to the situation at hand.

Part III of The Tripartite Chronicle, which is almost half the poem, is the most interesting. Gower now relates the stirring events of 1399, and approaches his material directly, with no allegory in his way. His sorrow turns to joy as Richard II meets with downfall and Henry IV with success. First there is a long diatribe (ll. 8 ff.) against Richard's cruelty and treachery, with special emphasis upon his "blank charters, " cartes blanches involving admission of debt and guilt which he forced members of his opposition to sign. Gower is right in judging these to be dangerous weapons in the hands of a man now almost out of his mind. Jealous of Henry's popularity, Richard banishes him to France (III. 85-86). Henry's father, John of Gaunt, "time-honoured Lancaster, " dies shortly thereafter, whereupon Richard seizes the Lancastrian estates. (This was a dangerous and foolish mistake; it alienated many from him, for property rights were sacrosanct.) The seizure helps to motivate Henry's return from France, in order to acquire property rightfully his by inheritance. In his returning fleet are Archbishop Arundel, brother of the Earl of Arundel (the Horse), and the latter's son Thomas. The Duke's return is described in highly pious terms (III. 150 ff.). The people flock to his side; Scrope, Bushy, and Green are soon dead, partly through Henry's agency, partly through the people's (III. 171 ff.). Gower taunts Richard II with the suggestion that he sailed for Ireland because of fear of Henry (III. 162-163). Richard is pictured as a fugitive, but still desperately plotting his tricks, and when he returns, the poet is delighted that the people turn against him. (For once, Gower expresses direct approval of the mob.) Gower then lectures him as if he were still alive (see l. 225), though of course he is writing after the event. Meanwhile, his hero Henry acts the gracious conqueror, recalls those exiled by Richard, and summons Parliament. Gower reports that Richard did not dare appear at Parliament, but that he abdicated (III. 287-291); he seems honestly unaware of the fact that Henry tricked Richard into doing so. [102] Just as Richard II's fall is as fatalistically depicted as though it were from the hand of Herodotus, so Henry's rise is destined by the hand of God (III. 317 ff.). His three-fold right to the Crown is explained (III. 332-337, and see n.). All is now sweetness and light in England. Gower exults in Henry IV's coronation, and rejoices to concur with the commoners once more, though he condemns them almost at once for desiring vengeance upon Richard's followers (ll. 394-396). Richard is then carried off to prison (III. 377), with no explanation for this action of Henry's. (There is likewise no account of the fact that Henry moved Richard from one castle to another; loyalty to him made Richard a dangerous prisoner.) At once there is a plot against Henry, which that invincible idol quickly and mercifully puts down (III. 400-419). Once again, every Englishman rejoices, with Gower ignoring the justifiable opposition to Henry IV.

There follows an interesting account of Richard's death by starvation in Pontefract Castle (III. 432 ff.) Gower repeats what was the general belief of his day, that Richard refuses to eat because he has lost hope and courage. This behavior is in implicit contrast with the bold Henry, who, "always a friend to piety," allows Richard a decent burial at Langley, a Dominican convent. (Such was not Richard's rightful burying place; but Gower makes nothing of this, though he has castigated Richard for similar offenses.) There follows an effective contrast between Richard II and Henry IV (III. 462 ff.), with Gower fairly accurate about Richard and much too partial to Henry. This discrepancy is understandable: Gower had long borne with Richard, yet at long last had come to pin his hopes for England on Henry. The dark Richard is, after all, still an enigma. The fiery Henry, the ambitious, unchivalric warrior who turned efficient politician, is, as Shakespeare well knew, almost as great an enigma. Gower cannot be blamed for not understanding that Henry's glowing deeds upon his accession were to stabilize his position, not to lay up treasures in heaven. To his credit, Gower is much interested in the problem of leadership in an age which needed it, and much interested in the question of succession to the Crown, a paramount problem in the latter half of the fourteenth century. Nearly everything Gower writes tends to turn into a Mirror for Princes, and

The Tripartite Chronicle indeed does so. Gower concludes that kings should live virtuously, for "he who is a sinner cannot be a ruler,"[103] as Richard's case proves. He praises Henry's mercy, yet he himself is human enough to relish a taste of vengeance toward the king he had tried so hard to instruct.[104] His Tripartite Chronicle, in any case, throws a little light upon a period needing all it can get.

Gower's will was drawn on Aug. 15, 1408, and proved on Oct. 24, so he died some time between these two dates.[105] His last years, spent in the Priory of St. Mary Overes with his wife, and where he was a canon, were not wholly as peaceful as his effigy on his tomb would suggest. There exist three records of mainprise during the years 1397-1405 which indicate that a certain John Gower was in trouble; one of these records definitely can be linked to the poet. Whether the trouble was personal, political, or financial is unknown.[106]

Gower's last datable poem has been seen to be the brief Latin piece, "Presul, Ovile Regis," with its mention of the comet of 1402. In honor of Henry IV's coronation on October 13, 1399, Gower wrote his second and last English work, "In Praise of Peace" (in Works, III, 481-492), dedicated to Henry IV. Gower was still mixing his languages: There is a seven-line Latin poem as headnote and another of fifty-six lines at the end of the English poem. The poem could well have been written to greet Henry upon the occasion of his coronation, or perhaps it is a bit later. "In Praise of Peace" is a powerful argument for peace, upon both Christian and secular grounds, and quite modern in its conviction that "The werre is modir of the wronges alle" (l. 106). (It seems to have had no effect upon Henry, who went right on making wars.) It will be remembered that Gower said he went blind in 1400 and that he ceased to write in 1401. The fifty-five smoothly handled rime-royal stanzas are such that he could have dictated them. Surely it was in some measure a tribute to Chaucer (who died in 1400) that he once again[107] used the seven-line stanza in English, just as Chaucer had in the Troilus and Criseyde dedicated to Gower?

The linking together of the names of Chaucer and Gower is traditional. The two men were compared in regard to art, story-telling, thinking, and learning in the fifteenth and sixteenth centuries, as late as Sir Philip Sidney's Defense of Poesie.[108] It is the Gower of the Confessio Amantis who figures in these comparisons, of course, not the author of the Vox Clamantis. This fact does not make any difference in any comparison of the two men's basic ideas, however, for the Prologue to the Confessio reads almost like an epitome of the thoughts in the major Latin works. Indeed, the Confessio as a whole ultimately emerges as moral. Gower was not the man to lose an opportunity to be didactic. As in most medieval writings, including the Confessio, the utile strives to outweigh the dulce.

Judged on the basis of his complete works, rather than just those stories of the Canterbury Tales "that sounen into synne, " Chaucer's writings are no exception. Since Elizabethan times he and Gower have been contrasted, rather than compared. This contrast is sound in regard to their disparate artistic abilities, but it has been wrongly extended to embrace all their thoughts and ideas. [109] They share the same fundamental beliefs on Church and state and on the existence of corruption in most spheres of life. Chaucer, like Gower, is a good Catholic. But because Gower's mind is the more medieval, he is more representative of the thinking of his class than is his greater fellow poet. Chaucer is able to play the bystander with amused, humane tolerance, and to watch his age pass in review. Gower becomes irritated and enraged when things go wrongly. Chaucer can readily characterize an actual yet perfect knight or parson, whereas Gower can only theorize on what the ideal knight or cleric should be. Chaucer's "povre Persoun of a Toun" is almost a line-by-line refutation (General Prologue, ll. 477-528) of Vox Clamantis, Book III. Aside from that same parson's brother the Plowman (General Prologue, ll. 529-541), however, Chaucer hardly shows more compassion for the third estate than does Gower. When Gower looks at the lowly peasant, it is with mistrust and aversion bordering upon hatred. Chaucer does not trouble to take the lengthy look at him which Gower does: It is significant that there is no real villein in the company of his pilgrims. Understandably, too, his few references to the mob or the "churles rebellion" are uncomplimentary or ironically negative. [110]

The two poets are in possession of comparable learning, both being well read. Chaucer has the inestimable advantage of wide acquaintance with Italian literature, whereas Gower has little if any. [111] Both are widely read in Old French and both make much use of the Roman de la Rose. Both are also learned in science, but Chaucer's knowledge of scientific works is much better understood and assimilated. Of neither can it be said that "His studie was but litel on the Bible, " for Gower and Chaucer are thoroughly versed in the Vulgate. [112] Both know and love Ovid, borrowing frequently from him, but Chaucer has much the better knowledge of Virgil. Both know the Aurora and the Speculum Stultorum. ". . . Chaucer is completely continental in his literary affiliations, "[113] and as for Gower, "It would be quite contrary to his practice to follow an English authority. "[114] (Both demonstrate at least some acquaintance, however, with the alliterative English poetry of their day.) Chaucer is averse to parading his learning in propria persona, and will usually get someone like his Physician or Chanticlere to do it instead; Gower is much readier to do so, and at an artistic sacrifice, as in Book VII of the Confessio. Chaucer always wears his greater learning more lightly and acquires it more casually, often reading only the beginning of a book. [115] Gower makes his way doggedly through the books which come to his hand. He is always Chaucer's superior in perseverance (or in

43

possession of leisure?), if in nothing else. (If the reverse had only been true, we should have read of Harry Bailey awarding a free supper at the Tabard.)

The important difference between the two poets is, of course, that Chaucer is of imaginative genius while Gower is not. Very often it is difficult to tell Chaucer's true feelings because he is so successful in putting himself in another's place. Gower never shows any sympathy for a viewpoint conflicting with his own. As an example of the difference in attitudes of the two men, observe the way in which each handles a hackneyed idea. [116] The Voice of One Crying, IV. 277-290, reads:

> The sea is the proper habitat of a live fish, and the monastery is the right home for a monk. Just as the sea will not retain dead fish, so the monastery casts out evildoing monks. A fish ought not to be out of the water, nor ought a monk to be away from his cloisters, unless you return to them, O monk in holy orders. If there were a fish that forsook the waters of the sea to seek its food on land, it would be highly inappropriate to give it the name of fish; I should rather give it the name of monster. Such shall I call the monk who yearns for worldly delights and deserts his cloister for them. He should not rightly be called a monk but a renegade, or what God's wrath brands as a monster of the Church.

Contrast Chaucer using the same proverbial idea of the fish out of water in his description of the Monk in the General Prologue, ll. 177-183:

> He yaf nat of that text a pulled hen,
> That seith that hunters ben nat hooly men,
> Ne that a monk, whan he is recchelees,
> Is likned til a fissh that is waterlees, --
> This is to seyn, a monk out of his cloystre.
> But thilke text heeld he nat worth an oystre;
> And I seyde his opinion was good.

In view of Gower's over-inflated, pedestrian preachment, Chaucer almost appears to be teasing him in the last line quoted.

Again, contrast an ironic handling by both men of the same scriptural passage. Gower is heavy-handed:

> For God commanded the human race to be fruitful; by His command man is to multiply. Thus, since his seed is copious the rector does

44

multiply, so that he will not be guilty in the light of God's mandate. Through such motives the rector approves the reasons that he may have lady friends, as long as he is in the scholarly profession. First he treats the subject of pregnancy, and in order to bear fruit he is highly repetitious about it. And he reads both the text and the gloss on it, so that the instruction will be clear to his students. [117]

Chaucer is rapid, and enjoys the Wife of Bath's mixture of heartiness, earthiness, and rationalization:

Men may devyne and glosen, up and doun,
But wel I woot, expres, withoute lye,
God bad us for to wexe and multiplye;
That gentil text kan I wel understonde. [118]

Once more one would like to feel that Chaucer was aware that Gower had ironically quoted the same text, too, and that his own tongue-in-cheek version would puzzle, if not worry, his friend. How could Gower appreciate Chaucer's seeming acquiescence to wrongdoing on the part of the Monk, and allowing the Wife of Bath to make such a statement unreprimanded? Gower's awareness of the difference of such parallel passages as these could well have helped lead to the supposed "break" between the two men. [119]

Yet in the end Gower's uncompromising seriousness wins out over the other's genial tolerance and profound devotion to art. Always more of a moral teacher than is usually supposed, Chaucer chooses his Parson's Tale and Retractation as his final and most medieval utterances. [120] Both poets are of an age, though only one is for all time. Not a second-rate Chaucer, Gower is a sort of Longfellow of the fourteenth century. Like the Bard of Brattle Street, he is well versed in several languages, he makes use of the frame story, he possesses almost "fatal facility" in versification, and he is "moral."

Remarks on the Present Translations

1. The aim throughout has been to render the original Latin, in accordance with Professor Magoun's keen, comprehensive, and demanding brief phrase, "as literally as possible within the limits of idiomatic Modern English," except as noted below.

2. Gower's considerable use of the historical present tense has often been changed to the past. Inconsistencies of tense have often been

45

eliminated. (". . . the mixture of past with present tenses is common in Gower. ")[121]

    3. There has been a minimum of emendation, and all emendations are enclosed within brackets.

    4. The paragraphing, "to which the author evidently attached some importance, "[122] is almost wholly Gower's own. Long sentences in the Latin, however, have frequently been repunctuated to make two or more shorter ones.

    5. There has been an attempt to regularize Gower's capitalization, especially with the word king. When capitalized herein, it means that Gower is thought to refer to a particular monarch. When lower case, it usually means any king.

    6. "Thee" and "thou" have been rendered as "you, " except when they apply to God, Christ, or the Virgin Mary, or when the translation attempts to recreate the flavor of biblical language in certain allusions to and translations from the Scriptures. (In this kind of passage the Douai Version, being a translation of the Vulgate, which Gower read, might well have been employed in place of the King James Version. The latter translation is here used, however, in order to keep Gower the more firmly in the tradition of the literature of England.)

    7. The notes attempt to place the poems within the concept of fourteenth-century English literature, by making numerous references to the other literature of the period, especially the works of Chaucer and Piers Plowman, primarily tne B-text.

* * *

    H. O. Coxe, Librarian of the Bodleian and first editor of the Vox Clamantis and Cronica Tripertita, wrote the proper words with which to conclude this Introduction:

> And with this, closes . . . our account of the 'Vox Clamantis, ' and if it be objected against the publication of such a poem, that there is much twaddle, still it must be allowed that there is much philosophy; or if little poetry, still there is much good hearty feeling that does honour to the writer; or if no new facts, still much that accounts for old ones which we did not so well know before; an insight into the moving principle that biased men's minds in those days, which we had not before; and this embracing every grade of society, the prelate, the priest, the friar, the King and his court, the soldier, the lawyer, the shopman, the apprentice, even the daily labourer, that after all we have much, for which our thanks are due to the 'moral John Gower, ' and it is but due to his morality--that after ages should be allowed the opportunity of benefitting by it. [123]

46

DEDICATORY EPISTLE[1]

John Gower, an old and blind man, has sent this epistle, written with a devout heart, to the Very Reverend in Christ the Father and His Eminent Lordship, Lord Thomas of Arundel, Archbishop of Canterbury, Primate of All England, and Legate of the Apostolic See. May our Lord Jesus Christ the Son of the glorious Virgin, Who lives and reigns as God forever and ever with God the Father and the Holy Ghost, favorably guide and sustain his office for the governing of His Church. Amen.

Thomas, successor to Thomas,[2] I render myself humble before you and I inscribe to you this present book which follows. Remember to heed the work which I am presenting to you, in order that your mind may be stimulated as it meditates upon it. As long as the Court of Rome destroys itself, which at present is seen to be divided, joy turns into sorrow.[3] And since Christ's law suffers because of this grievous age, I am sending you this book to read as a lament. But you who possess the radiant glory of divine healing power bestow that remedy upon the sorrowful so that it may cheer them [10]. Now that the light has failed and faith grows dim,[4] shed light on our affairs, you who are our Phoebus. And in order that you may become even more brilliant and glowing with perfection, I present you with this volume as a source of light. If you see something of judicious spirit clearly in such a mirror,[5] I think it shall not have been in vain. I am virtually blind, but granted that I cannot see what is going on, I shall still remember you in my heart through my mind's eye. However much halting old age racks me, the defect of my body has up to this time allowed my mind to remain active [20].[6] And so with Christ's help I am persevering actively in this work, in which I shall write down the manifest deeds of the world for you. Therefore, Father, I beg that while I am laboring

47

at my writings, you set the soul of a zealous spirit at rest. I have always loved you like a father and have hoped that in the end I would have your special favor. Now that my sight has been sundered from my body, [7] let your light shine forth and guide the footsteps of my soul. Do not let an old, sickly, and utterly wretched body be tormented, let it be helped along, with you for a protector [30]. And so as a guardian together in life and in death, take me, a blind man, unto yourself with your approval. Your worthy light, springing forth from a noble stock, ought not lie hidden under ashes in the world. [8]

Arundel shines with new light like the Sun, which produced you and which suckled you at its breast. [9] Since you are wholly manly, you are called Thomas, [10] after your ancestor, so that with God's help you are totally free from any taint. And so, now that you are a prelate consecrated to Christ's law, you should keep yourself spotless by it [40]. Your light is now serene and above reproach, and it shines brightly because nothing dishonorable has suppressed it. England, where those who would live rightly should be followers of your example, should rejoice that she is worthy of such a guiding light. All love shall prosper because of you and wrath shall decline, and under your care there shall be every good fortune. And since your light has thus spread and filled the earth, may God grant that such light be yours eternally. Gower asks these things, who is and shall be yours. [11]

THE VOICE OF ONE CRYING

BOOK I

Prologue

In the beginning of this work, the author intends to describe how
the lowly peasants violently revolted against the freemen and
nobles of the realm. And since an event of this kind was as
loathsome and horrible as a monster, he reports that in a dream
he saw different throngs of the rabble transformed into different
kinds of domestic animals. He says, moreover, that those
domestic animals deviated from their true nature and took on
the barbarousness of wild beasts. In accordance with the separate divisions of this book, which is divided into seven parts
(as will appear more clearly below in its headings), he treats
furthermore of the causes for such outrages taking place among
men.

Writings of the past contain fit examples for the future, for a
thing which has previously been experienced will produce greater faith. [1]
Granted that common opinion may hold that dreams contain no grounds
for belief, [2] nevertheless, writings from the time of the ancients inform us more reliably to the contrary. What dreams may mean is
clear from Daniel, and Joseph's vision in his sleep was not meaningless. [3] Indeed, the good angel who is the guardian of the inner man always protects him with vigilant love [10]. And granted that sleep may
envelope the outer body, the angel visits the interior of the mind and
sustains its strength. And often in a vision during sleep he furnishes

portents[4] so that the man may better understand the conditions of the time. Hence, I think that the dreams I witnessed at nighttime furnish memorable tokens of a certain occurrence. You can learn everything about it in this work—what sort of vision it was, and at what time in the year of which king it was.

If you should ask the name of the writer, look, the word lies hidden and entangled within three verses about it [20]. Take the first feet from "Godfrey" and add them to "John, " and let "Wales" join its initial to them. Leaving off its head, let "Ter" furnish the other parts; and after such a line is arranged, the right sequence of the name is clear. [5]

Do not propose anything in praise of the writer, however, but comprehend for yourself the subject matter which the writing will provide. For I shall write nothing in order that I may be praised, and my performance does not intend that I should have a care for my future reputation. I shall enter into the recent misfortunes that my country has exhibited, for it is a worthy labor to report the deeds of one's native land [30]. Although I may weep over it, I shall write of a tearful time, so that it may go down as an example for posterity. Just as our condition is mournful, so the poem is mournful, the writing being in accord with its subject matter. [6] The reader may judge everything of this book which is tearful to have been written with my own tears. [7] As I write these things my pen grows wet with profuse weeping, and while I am carried forward by my zeal, my heart and hand tremble. [8] And when I wish to write, my hand is burdened by the weight of the task, and anxiety takes away its strength [40]. One who looks further into this work and into the present time will find nothing consoling in the whole poem. If the voice in my frail breast were stronger, and if I had many mouths with many tongues, [9] it still would be impossible for me to tell all the evils which exist at this present time. My sensitivities are so tainted by the pollution of evils that my song flows in a poorer vein. [10] The road to Rome remains long when one's knee is crippled, and this book remains a long work for my limited ability [50]. Thus I ask for indulgence rather than praise, for my intention is good, even though my ability for the deed may be too small. Lend meaning to the Latin I have put together, my Muse, and lend fitting words for thy book, O Mistress. Filled with apprehension I shall sing of true dreams, the import of which disturbs the depths of my heart. May the one whom the Isle of Patmos received in the Apocalypse, and whose name I bear, guide this work. [11]

Chapter 1

Here he explains first under the reign of which king and also
in what month and year this event happened to him, the course
of which follows afterward. Moreover, in the light of what it
used to be, he commends the fertility of the land where he then
was. In it, as he says, delights of almost every kind join together. And he speaks furthermore of the pleasantness of the
weather and also of the serenity of the day, which nevertheless
preceded an extremely horrible dream.

It happened in the fourth year of King Richard, [1] when June
claims the month as its own, that the moon, leaving the heavens, hid
its rays under the earth, and Lucifer the betrothed arose at Dawn. [2]
A new light arose from its setting. Aurora shone from the setting part
of the world and brought forth the day. She furnished the day with light
and ushered in the marvelous stars, for her flight brings on the night
and her returning light the day. [3] Her fair rays shone from Phoebus'
reflection[4] and the joyful face of heaven glorified the earth [10]. After
the shadows of night had been driven away, [5] Aurora awoke in the morning, and everyone on earth adored her, seeing her so gay. With her
freshness she brightened the doorways rosy with splendor and the hall-
courts filled with roses. [6] In his chariot gleaming with bright emer-
alds, [7] Phoebus glowed warm with new fire in the sign of Cancer. He
fertilized, nourished, fostered, increased, and enriched all things, and
he animated everything that land and sea bring forth. [8] Fragrance,
glory, gleaming light, splendor and every embellishment adorned his
chariot as they were wont to do [20]. Its axle was golden and its pole
was made of none other than gold, and it flashed on its round wheels
with aureate splendor. Along the yoke a silvered row of gems glistened, and topaz made up its spokes. [9] And the fiery steeds of the
thunderer on high charged through the air, drawing his chariot behind
their backs.
        Clad in his purple robe he sat gleaming, [10] and all ages lay re-
vealed to his sight. Before his throne passed the four seasons of the
year, which were formed of their respective kinds of days [30]. But
at that time fair Summer stood near his right hand, bearing her garlands, and all created things loved her. [11]Then everything flourished,
then there was a new epoch of time, and the cattle sported wantonly in

the fields.[12] Then the land was fertile, then was the hour for the herds to mate, [13] and it was then that the reptile might renew its sports. The meadows were covered with the bloom of different flowers, and the chattering bird sang with its untutored throat.[14] Then too the teeming grass which had long lain concealed found a hidden path through which it lifted itself into the gentle breezes[15] [40]. Lucifer thawed out the frosty fields, and the mother bird sped to its work for its young.[16] Then icy, bristling Winter shed his hoary locks[17] and there was a return of a restful world. Whatever Winter had hidden it yielded from the icy cold, and the fallen snows passed away in the warming sun. The foliage shorn away by the cold returned to the trees, [18] and Summer's splendor held sway in every grove. She sprinkled the soil with dew, and bestowed grasses upon the earth, leaves to the woods, and welcome fruits to the trees [50]. The greening plain was renewed by a thousand different garlands of flowers and flourished under her sway. Flora sought out her realms and the field revelled, filled with the hues of flowers, and its face was joyful. Now the innocent rural maiden plucked violets to deck herself out; the earth bore them, although no one had sown them.[19] There were as many hues there as nature affords, and the ground was splendidly painted with different blooms.[20] O how I wished to enumerate the separate colors! But I could not; their abundance was too great in number[21] [60].

White lilies, mingled with red roses, perfumed the gardens just as in the private gardens of Paradise. Outside in the fields stood the primrose surrounded by hedge-rows, and each and every herb that medicine uses. The virtues of the herbs were such that they could bring aid to health with their seed, juice, or root. From the green turf the earth brought forth a rosy flower[22] which nature adorned in her fashion. Balm, spice, cassia with nard, and oil of myrrh made their abode there [70]. Purple violets, dewy roses, and lilies ever white chose to dwell in this spot. This sole region laid claim to all that land, air and sea fostered and held good. Here was the ornament of the globe, the flower of the world, the crowning glory of things, containing every delight that enjoyment seeks. It was planted with trees, sown with greenery, and surpassing in every gift which man asks for himself.

It was a second Paradise there, for whatever the human mind wished to have, the blessed earth brought forth[23] [80]. It was teeming with flowing fountains, filled with seeds, and marked with flowers and fruitful good things. Mingled with dew, the earth acquired sweet powers and nourished the various young grasses. By it the wood was decked with leafy branches, the garden with flowers, the field with blades of grass, and the soil with seedlings. The glade was renewed with foliage and every meadow grew green which Winter had subdued with muddy dirt. Zephyrs caressed the flowers brought forth unsown, [24] and the bright warmth from on high decked the earth [90]. And the season poured song into the birds, and every wooded meadow rang from the different voices above. [25] The cuckoo likewise called out, ever repeating from his full throat, and was witness of the new season. Aurora's messenger, the singing lark, fluttered above and sang in the ear of God on high. And the turtledove, rejoicing in the verdant season, promised her heart in faithful allegiance to her mate. [26] Philomena recovered her lost property of speech and by her notes proclaimed what had been done [100]. And Procne sang too of her sister's lost virginity--for so great are the tricks in love. The thousand thousands of birds sounded their melodies like organs, and a like number of flowers spread their perfume across the broad fields. They vied among themselves as to whether singing brought more pleasure to the ears or fragrance to the nose. The contention was mild, however, and the disharmony harmonious, for each group shone with like worth.

While nature filled the groves with the sweetness of her law and the birds re-echoed on every side [110]; and while the beauty of the flowers enveloped the spacious fields and green grass decked the blossoming meadows, gentle Eurus, rustling ever so sweetly, blew through the trees, and the gentle water sounded within its bank with a murmur. And so every animal rejoiced in the peaceful season and the fish sought out the depths of the stream against the sun. There was nothing alive which did not enjoy the delight of the season with its pleasant breeze. Whenever the eye saw such things it rejoiced and guided them through the cockles of the heart to the very depths of the man [120]. And the ear pulsated upon the sighs of the heart, through which Venus demanded the power of love in a youth. Lo, such was the day in which the pleasant season caused me to wander round in my joy.

An end awaits all things. Thus evening finally came, when the sunset claimed the day as its due. The quiet day had completed its customary hours and the tongues were silent, restrained from their sweet notes. Night had sunk in darkness the shining rays of the sun and sleep forced man to go to bed [130]. When there was no more daylight, then I turned my body to the couch, [27] where rest is wont to succor my weary limbs. Sadness often comes after joys, [28] clouds after Phoebus, and sickness after health. The day, once so bright, had hardly ended, when the dark aspect of night came on. Lo, black clouds covered the lurking stars, the golden moon fled, and night was without its light. Boötes had turned his wain with its downward-slanting pole, [29] nor was there then a set course provided for the heavens [140]. Instead the doomed constellation broke apart from the center and loosed ungovernable darkness upon the earth.

Sleep did not then soothe my eyes, and gone was my first heavy sleep, which the awakening of my frightened mind drove away. Indeed, my hair stood on end, and my flesh trembled, and the hollow of my heart grew weak, and my sense was carried away like water. While I was tossing about there in that way, I busily reflected in my mind as to what was the cause of the sudden fright on my part. Wakeful on my bed I pondered many things and poured out my thoughts, my heart wandering in different directions [150]. It was the time when all is silent, and when wandering dreams rush into some hearts[30] after the mind has been drugged. But neither sleep nor dreams had as yet imprisoned me, until my dread suddenly assured me that misfortune was at hand. It was the middle of the night, and my heavy eyelids were persuading the troubles from my eyes, but delay slowed up the process.[31] I spent the whole night in this way, awake with my worries and not knowing for what reason this fate was approaching. I reflected on times past and was afraid of the future [160]. Finally, darkness had closed my eyes. So, when the greater part of my wasted night was spent, sleepiness suddenly overtook my weary eyes. I took a little rest while Lucifer called forth its fire at dawn, and then I had a dream-vision.[32]

Chapter 2

Here his dream begins, in which he says that on a certain Tuesday he saw various bands of rabble, the first of which he beheld suddenly changed into the likeness of asses.

While a dull sleep bound my motionless limbs, my spirit itself was indeed stolen away. I thought that I was going to gather flowers in the fields, at the time when Mars himself claimed the day as his very own.[1] And I had not gone a long way when nearby I saw innumerable terrifying monsters [170], various rascally bands of the common mob, wandering through the fields in countless throngs. And while my eyes gazed upon the crowds and I was greatly amazed at so much rowdiness, behold, the curse of God suddenly flashed upon them, and changing their shapes, it had made them into wild beasts. They who had been men of reason before had the look of unreasoning brutes. A different shape marked the different mobs and so marked out each in its own form [180]. Dreams have significance; hence it is that I shall unfold these marvels. More on guard, therefore, by now I was thoroughly frightened.

I saw rebellious asses carried away by sudden revolt, and no one checked them by the bridle. For their vitals were filled with the raging of lions in search of their prey.[2] The halter had no effect on their unruly heads, as the wandering asses jumped through all the fields. Indeed, their braying terrified all the citizens, as they loudly redoubled their usual "hee haw" again and again [190]. The asses were violently wild and untamed, and each which had been useful lost its

54

usefulness. [3] They refused to carry sacks to the city any more and were unwilling to bend their backs under a heavy load. They did not care for the field grasses on the hillsides, but instead they now wanted greater delicacies. They drove others from their homes and wrongfully wanted to get the horses' rightful place for themselves.

The asses now took it upon themselves to enjoy jeweled saddles and always to have their manes combed [200]. Just as old Burnel[4] foolishly wanted his short tail newly made long, in order that the ass and the lion might have the same kind of tail, so these wretched creatures wanted new, straight backs. The ass fashioned himself as covered with a lion's skin, and his vainglory overstepped its bounds. By chance he sought an aid contrary to nature, since he could not attach a tail to his head. [5] Thus did the foolish asses try as they might to aggrandize themselves with what nature denied them [210]. They did not care for the tail which He who gave them their ears implanted in them, [6] but thought it too vile a thing.

The stupid meditation of the mind is wont to ponder many things which are more of a hindrance than its desires wish. Innate stupidity brings all griefs to the foolish and serves to reach a bad end. Great things are fitting for great people, and lowly things for lowly people, [7] but those who were the most lowly wanted to enjoy lofty things. An idea arose which had lasting effects and heedlessly started things which were an endless burden [220]. Thus did the fatuous asses, whom arrogance aroused, refuse their appointed duties by overthrowing all control. The madness in the air so ruined them that they seemed to be transformed into monsters. Those which I once could recognize by their long ears wore long horns in the middle of their foreheads. A two-edged sword does not cut more powerfully than those horns did, and they were drenched with the running gore of fresh wounds. Those which used to loiter because of a lazy disposition ran along with greater agility than hinds [230]. Does not the leopard outdo the ass in nimble jumping? But at that time the ass outdid it in jumping. Alas! The lowly ass then had a longer tail than the mighty lion itself.[8] Whatever the whim of the asses decreed had the force of law, and this innovation drove out all the justice of old. Their asinine behavior, however, labeled them as stupid and wild, for they had no power of reason. And since I had seen the senseless creatures, I was much afraid, and my trusty foot took me no farther [240].

Chapter 3[1]

Here he says that in his dream he saw a second band of rabble turned into oxen.

55

Behold, with them came oxen, which no one then dared prick
with a goad; indeed, everyone was afraid of them. Contrary to its
rightful duties, the ox refused to have a plowman and unexpectedly did
not now allow itself to be led. By pushing with its horn, the ox which
yesterday had gently been led by the horn to plow the fields was raging
today. Those which had recently been tamed now refused their bounden
duty, with forehead threatening and horns raised aloft. They declared
that they were no longer willing to be yoked to the plow, but they wanted
to bear their free necks upright [250]. Now they did not eat chaff or
coarse straw, but they sought out where the better grain was. Nature
forsook their transformed shapes and had caused the oxen to be like
monsters. They wore bear's feet and tails like those of dragons, so
that every trembling person shunned them. From their cavernous
mouths they emitted sulphurous flames which no water could put out,
when they had spread. But the devastating fiery flame consumed whatever was touched by its heat, whether it was stone or wood [260]. No
herdsman knew any defense against these droves; instead, they caused
great damage to city and countryside.

The mouths of the bulls of Colchis, which Jason's right hand subdued, did not so roar with sulphurous flames[2] but that these oxen set
even more fire to the crackling roofs, which they burned up with their
breath. The bull of Minos, [3] which Neptune gave him, did not so damage
the fields when it was raging mad but that these oxen laid waste the
farmlands even more, and in their madness they contrived truly horrible damages in the city [270]. Neither Nessus, changed into the likeness of a bull and defeated in arms by Aeacides[4] when waging war on
him, nor the Centaurs, nor even the fierce Minotaur itself offered such
fearful battle against men but that these oxen at this time, rashly abandoning their plows, committed an even greater slaughter of men.

They left their work implements scattered through the empty
fields and the plowshare did not get its rightful use. Behold, rakes lay
about on the ground, as did hoes and mattocks, [5] and they had no plow-
beam, moldboard, handle[6] or rope [280]. No yoke nor coupling-collar
nor tether was of any use; no tying-stake nor wagon tongue nor haft was
serviceable. There was no more use for the plow and the abandoned
share-beam lay idle. And they did not let the harrows perform their
tasks. Wagon and driver and cart came to a stop; they had no further
usefulness. One lawless course remained for the farmer, and they too
became ungovernable by reason. So, wherever you looked lay fields
without a tiller and empty lands which no one claimed [290]. [7] The granaries [would] await in vain the promised harvests, [8] if such an annual
practice were to tend the fields. The ox was a lion, the ox was a panther, the ox was a bear, but it was evident that the ox did not remember
its own nature. And so because I saw the oxen wandering destructively
and unbroken to the plow, my thoughts were disturbed. "Alas! O!" I

cried. "Tillage of the fields will come to an end, so my times should be afraid of famine. "

Chapter 4

Here he says that he saw a third band of rabble turned into swine.

My sleep grew even heavier and enveloped my weary limbs and increased my dreamings still more [300]. In them I again and again caught sight of mad, bristling swine standing about, filled with a devilish spirit. A great horde of them was brought together, tainting the air with their dung. A piglet madly pursued a hog, and a little boar a boar, and the pig-sty confined them no more. The boar-pig made a bargain with his toothless fellow: they joined together in order to tear up the soil the more. Breeding-sow and boar allied their fellow porker with themselves in order that they might do more damage and carry on more mischief [310]. I saw the soiled swine so damage the soil that the soil was scarcely safe in obstructing them. There was then no swineherd who drove them out of men's grain fields in the customary way. There was no one who could put rings in their noses so that the pigs would not dig most fearful ditches. And no one could then tie up their hairy necks; instead, every road was open to them. Nature wandered so far from her regular course that a pig did not keep to the behavior of a pig, but rather of a wolf [320].

Among them there was one wild boar which Kent had produced; [1] no country could produce one like it. It flashed from its eyes and it breathed flames from its chest. [2] Scarcely a single house was out of reach of its fire. [3]Lightning flew out of its mouth, and it set cities on fire with its breathings, and made war with its elephant-sized teeth. During its hoarse grunting, hot foam mixed with human blood flecked its shoulders. And it poured forth the hissing foam together with the fresh blood, [4] which the beast had spilled to the ground out of peoples' veins [330]. It hurled to the ground what it struck with its powerful head; no one had the strength to withstand its assaults. Its horrible neck stiffened as the standard-bearer for battle, and in its raging it had the look of a tiger. And its bristles, which wore the noxious badges of hell, stood on end like stiff spears. [5] Just as a loaded cart groans or rushing waters roar, so did its footstep rumble. The wild beast trampled on the crops growing in the stalk[6] and ground the grain into worthless chaff [340]. The boar grew so much that no grassy pasture could produce any savage beasts larger than that monster. No place that such a great beast menaced was safe, unless it be heaven, where evil cannot reach. When aroused, the beast's anger exceeded the furies of hell; the whole country trembled at its approach. Still another swine came from the North and met up with the boar, so that they could prepare pitfalls together. [7]

The Tegean wood did not produce such a savage boar, although the one in Arcadia was the biggest [350]. [8] It did not arouse Hercules' wrath in the mountains or oppose other people with such force as these pigs, which in my dreams I saw causing thousands more misfortunes in a thousand different ways. The fierce boar which Meleager[9] drove into the hidden shelter of the woods was not so violent but that wrath raged more in these pigs, and afflicted them more violently and brought on battles with their tusks. These so-called swine did not like dregs or swill and had no use for draff, which should have been their food [360]. They did not hunt for husks or acorns from the oaks of the forest for themselves, but seized upon what better things they saw. Thick lees and ordinary water were not a bit good enough for their drink; instead they gulped down fine wines. [10] When a countrified constitution indulges in unaccustomed wines, the body lies prostrate from drunkenness, as if it were dead. The gluttony of the pigs grew so that a rich man in the city could hardly procure his modest and proper foods. A sty was no longer tolerated as a lodging for pigs; they had to have a filthy bed or a [pillow][11] [370]. Indeed, they tramped into royal buildings with their filthiness and sought out the more noble ones in the middle of the city. They who had once been loathsome pigs now cultivated a haughty manner. Their grunting was like a lion that roared aloud, and Echo shook the woods at the sound of them. They were swine into which a cursed spirit had entered, just as Holy writ tells of. [12]

Chapter 5

Here he says that in his dream he saw a fourth band of rabble turned into dogs.

And afterwards I saw dogs standing about and barking as if there were tens of thousands, and the fields shook with their voices [380]. The winged herald of dawn had sung his song, [1] when the raging anger of the dogs struck the air. The morsel which fell from their masters' table was not food to these dogs, and they did not like any kind of bones. Instead they demanded better fare for their throats, they devoured any- and everything fat when they met up with it. But notice, well-bred dogs were not in company with them; they were worthless ones which had no

58

training. They neither went hunting nor rejoiced at the [sound of the] horn, and they persisted in nothing unless it was lowly [390]. They did not want to run through the woodland to catch the hare, nor to chase stags in their swiftness. Instead, they tried to bark at men's heels from behind, and caused them much loathsomeness.

Cut and Cur[2] ran swiftly together through the alleys, abandoning their wretched kennels for destruction. Even the shepherd's dog was on hand, and the one which guarded the church by barking at night; these two made trouble again and again. The broken chain loosed its dog to go free, the dog of every bakery and kitchen alike [400]. [3] And I saw the butcher's huge mastiffs coming, nor did the dog at the mill stay at home. The stable could not keep these old howlers from coming to join with their fellows. A one-eyed dog was there, and a three-legged one limped behind as if by stealth and barked as their companion. And then a snarler with a rough voice deserted the dung heap and panted to get new quarters. They were such that no one could stroke their backs, touch their tails, or hold their heads [410]. For they, always angry, bared their teeth at you, and their rough disposition contained no affection at all.

They all flocked together, both young and old, and they ran together and their jaws were ready with bites. They walked about proudly, with tails held high, and nothing was safe that they sought to tear to pieces. Teeth like a boar's marred the dogs' mouths, whose bite was deep and poisonous. The more food they ate the less they were satisfied; their insatiate hunger always clung to them [420]. Dogs to which a heap of dung had ordinarily been host at night kept their filthy limbs warm in soft beds. Their number was so great that none of them had any respect whatever for proper rank. O if anyone might have heard them then, [or felt] how the world trembled here and everywhere in terror at their voices, then he could say that no realm ever before heard howlings like these.

And when the noise of the dogs descended to Satan's ears, and hell rejoiced to hear the new sound [430], behold, then Cerberus the dog of the lower world and guardian of Hades lent an ear and went mad with joy. And in its madness it broke from its neck the fiery chains by which it was bound. Springing forth, it at once broke through the abysses of the center region and promptly hastened its journey to earth. Thus this comrade was joined with its fellows, like joined with like, [4] and an evil leader was in charge of evil dogs. So the savage leader of hell turned all the more savage, and himself made a dog of man [440].

When she assumed the shape of a mad dog, the grieving Hecuba[5] herself did not turn so fierce but that greater wrath raged within these dogs. And where they could fasten their bites they crushed every limb. The dogs which pursued Cadmus' grandson Actaeon[6] to tear him to pieces did not practise such wickedness. Geryon, [7] the huge giant with three dogheads which Spain bore long ago, did not so sharpen his bloody teeth by killing men, nor was he so murderous [450] but that even greater blood-drenched human slaughter was committed by these dogs of which I speak. Nor, when Diana was openly driven into exile from the city, did the dangerous beast which she sent to Athens to destroy the citizens offer such battles, [8] nor were so many men laid low by it. Nor was Cephalus' dog itself, which drove the beast right out of the city, of such strength as these were. Every citizen and freeman trembled together in fear of their biting [460].

Chapter 6

> Here he says that in his dream he saw a fifth band of rabble turned into cats and foxes. He says that the household servants were like cats. He says that since the criminals were free because the jails everywhere were broken open, the foxes then allied themselves with them.

While I had been thinking that I saw such things in my sleep, the onrushing vision produced even new monsters. I saw foxes and innumerable cats coming afterwards which behaved themselves like the dogs. Nothing that was above or beneath the earth lay hidden to them; instead, they saw everything. Whatever there was, they hunted it everywhere, they ran through fields and searched caves, grove, and meadow for it. Neither city nor stone fort nor wall duly forbade them entrance, when they wanted to go in [470]. They broke into strongvaults, and without a key they got into moneyboxes, in order that their booty might stand open to view. They gnawed through every iron trap with their fierce long teeth, so that nothing obstructed them. Moreover, no medical art could save the life of the living thing which their venom struck with a bite. Their bite was fatal, and the scorpion was not more fearsome than they. Wherever they went, death itself went as an ally.

Indeed, the gray foxes determined to leave the caves of the wood and go to the better-class homes of the city [480]. Broad daylight brought into the open the nightly thefts which used to be carried on in secret. From then on, neither the sheep nor the poor sheepfold meant anything to them, nor did the chicken nor the ewe satisfy them for prey. On the contrary, they seized things in the city which were of even greater value, and no law prevented them. The lowly fox, which used to live underground, climbed up into palaces and freely sought shelter anywhere. The foxes, which used to be hostile to dogs, made

mutually agreeable compacts of peace with them [490]. The [dog],
which once was gentler than a sacrificial animal, became a swift wolf
and fiercely guarded its tracks.

The cat also joined with them, and leaving its barns behind, the
bumpkin rushed into forbidden mischief. From then on the cat stopped
catching mice and did not care about following its natural ways. The
[cat] which duly used to drive pests out of the house then was noxious
and caused the houses to be noxiously infested. The mice of old which
gnawed their way into the city of Ekron, where the Ark of God was, did
not bite in such fashion [500]. [1] No such madness as this frightened the
Ekronites, and this time there was no such protection. On the contrary, the ghastly frenzy that I witnessed in these monsters was yet
more terrifying and oppressive to the citizenry everywhere.

Chapter 7

Here he says that in his dream he saw a sixth band of rabble
turned into domestic birds. He says that owls, that is, birds of
prey, mixed and banded together with them.

It was an amazing thing to me, as I watched such goings-on, and
the astonishment in my mind sank to the bottom of my heart. Among
brute beasts, there was no animal whatever which had been created for
a lowly status but that I saw every kind of them in the fields. And
mixed together this way they were the more to be feared [510]. Since
the stables were broken open, every beast was let free over the ridges,
over the hills, and over the paths. [1] The country-dweller of every kind
came and suddenly became taller than the corn crop risen from the
soil. As I turned my eyes in fear now here and now there, in watching
all the monsters in their places, behold, a flock of domestic birds appeared transformed. Their leaders were a cock and a gander. Those
which used to stay at home and tread on dung dared to assume the
eagle's prerogatives for themselves [520]. The cock seized the falcon's beak and talons for itself, and the gander wanted to touch the
heavens with its wings. And so the lofty [birds] sank down because of
the lowly ones, and the valuable fell because of the worthless ones,
since law and order were banished. And wherever the animals could
not direct their steps to seize their prey, the [birds] swooped over
everything.

Suddenly I saw the colors of the cock and the goose changed, and
a new shape enveloped them. New plumage with the blackness of a
raven transformed the cock, and the gander was instantly turned into a

kite [530]. It was not so much that they adopted the plumage of others
for themselves, but rather that they adopted like ways of behavior.
Going astray changed those which were once contented with very little,
and which used to feed naturally off of grain at the barns. For in order
to eat more, they demanded the fat carcasses of human bodies for
themselves, and these alone pleased them. Once so gentle, these creatures, which suffered anyone to call them and used to watch for the
hands which gave out their food, tried to snatch their plunder by force,
more savage and rapacious than falcons [540].

The cock, which used to sing at night so that everyone was wont
to enjoy hearing him, shouted hellishly. And the frightful sound of the
voice from its throat surpassed terrible thunder. And time and time
again the cruel Coppa, [2] following on foot, urged her cock on toward
various things which she had an idea were mischievous. The chatterer
made up in talk for what she could not do in deeds, and she alone incited a thousand to general wickedness. And when the gander coupled
with her, he deserted his own goose and aspired to new game everywhere [550]. The gander, which once in his simplicity had frightened
only children with his weak hissing, now terrified even adults with his
horrible noise, and wanted to tear the stronger ones to bits.

And the hostility ceased which once was wont to separate the owls
from other birds, and now there was love between them. They decided
that days were lawful for the things for which the dark form of night used
to lend furtive opportunities. [3] The owl flew out of its confinement as a
companion of the birds and freely joined with them in the fields [560].
This was a time when the owl might gather its wings so that it could
safely carry off its prey through the air. Indeed, that winged band
sharpened its feathers with iron, whereby men might die.

Chapter 8

Here he says that in his dream he saw a seventh band of rabble
turned into flies and frogs.

My continued sleep continued my dreams, and provided many
more new things to see. That the monsters' madness might grow
greater and their wicked violence be more abundantly increased with
evils, the entire species of flies came forth, which swore to pierce
every healthy creature with their bites and stings [570]. And the wasps
which once tortured "Waspasian"[1] returned and caused renewed misfortunes. Then the horrible raging swarm of flies grew so thick that
a man could scarcely hide from their stinging. Hence they caused pain

as if hell itself were raging; they stung everything, everything wounded suffered pain.

Banded together with the fly, the frog distressed many. One frog sped into mischief and another jumped to follow. See, the band of farmhands which Latona turned into frogs returned, and with renewed fury they created trouble [580]. [2] The vengeance of these strange frogs was overpoweringly frightful. They did great damage in all the houses: the frog ate up all the food and all the victuals, and spread its dire poisons in various places. These had been the frogs which barren Egypt once trembled at, and now they did harm of equal seriousness. Not a wise man in the land was unharmed by them; philosophers complained of the injuries done them. The frog was oppressive but the fly was more so: its violence was widespread and it tormented every place everywhere [590]. O heavy punishment, heavier than any that ever happened before! Worthy men suffered much from it.

The noxious fly of Egypt was not more horrible, and it did not frighten freemen more. On the contrary, these flying furies searched out all the inner rooms and dealt injury to honest men. They hurt nothing base, however, but tried to hurt those in the world whom a nobler rank distinguished. Thus one band helped another like it; thus the band from the country assisted the boorish behavior of the other, so that they mingled mischief with mischief [600]. The flies met together, the wasps conglomerated together, and they stirred up the air with their wickedness. The savage gad-fly was there, [3] the scorpion, the common fly, and the caterpillar. The locust was their ally in doing harm. They flew into cities and towns, wandering lawlessly, and no nets could withstand their force. No pot holding meat was then without a fly; no dish was so well shut but that if a new chink appeared, in came Beelzebub, the leader of this army of flies. And they followed him [610]. The torment then varied with the various kinds of flies, which dealt out harms in diverse ways. One struck and another plundered, one bit and another stung, and still another leaped forth and wounded with its bayonet.

The fly was a severe pest; never was there one any fiercer or more harmful to the world than it. [4] The day's madness and agitation were so great that no one could be safe any place. Flies which the white frost used to overwhelm became suddenly inflamed by only a very little warmth [620]. So with sudden vehemence, summer's heat scattered through the fields the flies which a mild winter used to hold in check. [5] O what an astonishing thing, when the vagrant locust claimed the fruits of the ant's labors for its own! O what an astonishing thing, when the fly, more rapacious than any hawk, swarmed forth everywhere after its spoils! O what an astonishing thing, when the filthy fly assumed the haughtiness of the proudly plumed peacock! O what an astonishing thing, when the fly, soaring on its tiny wings, was swifter than the lark [630]! O what an astonishing thing, when the puny fly tried to surpass the crane in its powers of flight! O what an astonishing thing, when the fly rose above the lofty eagle and longed to keep up with its pace!

This was the day which sent forth flies with the teeth of dogs, [6] and which abused the land with their offences. This was the day on which either fortune or places which no fly could reach were of scant help. [7] This was the day on which the warhorse yielded to the ass and was without honor in defeat [640]. This was the day on which the fierce hearts of lions trembled and were conquered, overwhelmed by the might of the oxen. This was the day on which the dirty swine polluted all the spruce fields with its filth. This was the day on which the dog became stronger than the bear, and the panther could not stand up to the cat. This was the day on which the fleet wolf wandered freely after prey everywhere in the midst of the fields.

This was the day when everywhere the weak man terrified the strong, the humblest the noble, and the little the great [650]. This was the day when the mighty oak suddenly fell, easily uprooted by an ordinary straw. [8] This was the day on which the fragile tile surpassed the durability of marble in its strength. Behold a day on which a straw held together other straws, straws which thought grain to be of no value. This was the day on which churlishness reveled in churlishness, while the state of the freeman suffered. This was the day which raised peasants to high place and put down the nobles, and did not allow them even to be their equals [660]. This was the day which was a dire stepmother to virtues and a mother to all the evil in the world. This was the day on which every man in the world who was wise longed for it to have passed on into the future.

This was the day on which everyone feared that the manifest wrath of God was approaching because of his sins. [9] This was the day which trembled forsaken throughout the world, as if it were full of the dread of judgment. This was the day which no record had previously told the like of, if we confess the truth [670]. [10] Alas, how terrible! Alas, how sad and bitter! How confounded with evils that day was then! May celestial vengeance, severe, swift, and direct, destroy those whom that day thus drove mad. Let that day be slow in coming back, let it not return in our lifetime, let there be no cause for it to return. If there is anything we ought first to ask this day, I implore that it return no more to these realms.

64

Chapter 9

Here he says that in his dream he saw that when all the aforementioned madmen stood herded together, a certain Jackdaw (In English a Jay, which is commonly called Wat)[1] assumed the rank of command over the others. And to tell the truth of the matter, this Wat was their leader.

When this great multitude of monsters like wild beasts stood united, a multitude like the sands of the sea [680], [2] there appeared a Jackdaw, well instructed in the art of speaking, which no cage could keep at home. While all were looking on, this bird spread his wings and claimed to have top rank, although he was unworthy. Just as the Devil was placed in command over the army of the lower world, so this scoundrel was in charge of the wicked mob. A harsh voice, a fierce expression, a very faithful likeness to a death's head--these things gave token of his appearance. He checked the murmuring and all kept silent so that the sound from his mouth might be better heard [690]. He ascended to the top of a tree, and with the voice from his open mouth he uttered such words as these to his compeers:

"O you low sort of wretches, which the world has subjugated for a long time by its law, look, now the day has come when the peasantry will triumph and will force the freemen to get off their lands. Let all honor come to an end, let justice perish, and let no virtue that once existed endure further in the world. Let the law give over which used to hold us in check with its justice, and from here on let our court rule [700]. "

The whole mob was silent and took note of the speaker's words, and they liked every command he delivered from his mouth. The rabble lent a deluded ear to his fickle talk, and it saw none of the future things that would result. For when he had been honored in this way by the people, he quickly grabbed all the land for himself. Indeed, when the people had unadvisedly given themselves into servitude, he called the populace together and gave orders. Just as a billow usually grows calm after a stiff breeze, and just as a wave swells by the blast of a whirlwind [710], [3] so the Jackdaw stirred up all the others with his outrageous shouting, and he drew the people's minds toward war. The stupid portion of the people did not know what its "court" might be, but he ordered them to adopt the laws of force. He said, "Strike, " and one man struck. He said, "Kill, " and another killed. He said, "Commit crime; " everyone committed it, and did not oppose his will. [4] Everyone he called to in his madness listened with ears pricked up, and once aroused to his voice, pursued the [prescribed] course. Thus many an unfortunate man, driven by his persuasive raving, stuck his hand into the fire again and again [720]. All proclaimed in a loud voice, "So be it, " so that the sound was like the din of the sea. Stunned by the great noise of their voice, I now could scarcely lift my trembling feet. Yet from a distance I observed how they made their mutual arrangements by clasping their hands. For they said this, that the mob from the country would destroy whatever was left of the noble class in the world.

With these words, they all marched together in the same fashion, and the wicked ruler of hell led the way [730]. A black cloud mingled with the furies of hell approached, and every wickedness poured into their hearts rained down. The earth was so thoroughly soaked with the dew of hell that no virtue could flourish from that time forth. But every vice that a worthy man abhors flourished and filled men's hearts from that time on. Then at mid-day the Devil attacked and his hard-shot arrow flew during that painful day. Satan himself was freed and on hand, together with all the sinful band of servile hell [740]. Behold, the untutored heart's sense of shame was lost, and it no longer feared the terrors of crime or punishment. And so when I saw the leaders of hell ruling the world, the rights of heaven were worth nothing. The more I saw them, the more I judged I ought to be afraid of them, not knowing what sort of end would be bound to come.

Chapter 10

Here he says that in his dream he saw joining up with the aforementioned madmen the cursed race of Cain, together with a multitude of King Ulysses' former followers, whom Circe had changed into beasts.

When hell raged together with the earth, the ferment was beyond measure, the frenzy was fierce, and the throng was immense. Approaching from all sides, the infamous assemblage of monsters was countless, just as the sands of the sea [750]. [1] This was the mad progeny of the Devil's breed, rendered horrible in the eyes of men and rash in the eyes of God, contemptuous of higher powers and ferociously eager for slaughter, [2] just as a wolf is when it goes mad with hunger for sheep. At once every wickedness of a worse vein broke out, and the atmosphere corrupted honest men.

The seven races which Cain himself fostered were reckoned as

66

comrades there among the madmen. Terrible, vile, quick for evil, and slow for good, each one contrived bad things in its own way [760]. The vicious spawn scorned the terrors to come, and all that they laid upon [others] they suffered equally themselves. [3] Each was ever fond of wrongdoing, and active in destruction, and was cruelly mad for slaughter like a butcher. [4]Isaiah, Isadore, and the Apocalypse tell (and the great Sibyl touches upon it in her books) that their name was called Gog and Magog, in whose deeds was utter wickedness. [5] These madmen did not know what a king or a law was; no rule or order restrained them [770]. They did not fear men and they did not worship the gods devoutly, but they did what the world considered most shameful. This vile tribe was wont to devour human flesh, and their beastly life gave a similar right to the people. There were many shameful things which their malign nature practised, and for this reason the malicious mob followed their bad example. Indeed, the raving frenzy of these malicious people joined with the madmen of whom I spoke before. Also, Ulysses' companions, whom Circe had transformed long before, met and allied themselves with them [780]. Now they wore the faces of men and now their transformed heads of wild beasts, and they had no power of reason.

Chapter 11

Here he tells how he heard their names and their horrible different voices in the vision of his dream. He also tells of John Ball, who then incited them to every crime and who was reckoned as a prophet among them.

[1]Wat calls, Tom comes to him, and Sim does not loiter behind. Bet[2] and Gib order Hick to come at once. Col rages, whom Geff helps to do damage. Will swears to join with them for mischief. Grigg grabs, while Daw roars and Hobb is their partner, and Lorkin intends no less to be in the thick of things. Hudd strikes while Tebb threatens those whom Judd tramples on. Jack tears down houses and kills men with his sword [790]. Hogg brandishes his pomp, for with his noble bearing he thinks he is greater than any king. The prophet Ball teaches them; a malicious spirit had previously taught him, and he then constituted their deepest learning. I recognized a great many of the madmen by these names, and there were a few others I remember. Time and time again they cried out with the deep voices of monsters and they kept making various noises in various ways.

Some of them bray in the beastly manner of asses, some bellow the lowings of oxen [800]. Some give out horrible swinish grunts, and the earth trembles from their rumbling. The frothing wild boar makes a great tumult, and the boar-pig cries out and adds to the din. And fierce barking weighed heavily upon the air of the city as the harsh, angry voice of the dogs flies about. The hungry fox wails and the cunning wolf howls into the air and calls together his runningmates. No less did the cackling gander strike the ear with its sound, and even the graves tremble with sudden anguish [810]. [3] Wasps buzz, and their sound is fearful, and no one can count the swarm of them. Together they make a roar like a bristling lion, and everything that was previously bad becomes worse. Behold the loud din, the wild clangor, the savage brawling--no sound was ever so terrible before. The rocks resound with its rumbling and the air reverberates the sound, and Echo takes up its reply. Its heavy roar terrifies the regions nearby with its din, so that everyone fears an evil outcome is approaching [820]. The infamous report of this period reached many people, [4] and just as many more were astounded at these monsters. The Jay, at whose name the earth trembled, terrorized great nations with his powerful storming. Rumor flies about and busies all the nobles with talk, but no wise man has a wise plan. [5] The unheard-of calamity weighs upon stupified ears, and via the ear a heavy anxiety comes upon the senses. People attempt to heal the malady, but it is incurable, and the physician's hand has no cure for it [830].

Chapter 12

Here he tells how, according to the vision of his dream, the aforesaid madmen appointed heralds and leaders for themselves, and in what fashion their young and old men were armed.

They set up heralds and leaders among themselves, and ordered their will to be sanctioned as law. Through the voice of a herald they issued their laws to the effect that every household which spoke ill of them would be burned down. The wretch who did not support their wickedness was to have his head cut off, and his house destroyed by fire. They chose comrades in crime and partners in madness, on whose hands that business would depend. And for this reason I envisioned as much harm as possible when the herald shouted in the ear of the unthinking marketplace [840]. The churl gave a thunderous shout, the quick-spreading fire was brought into a building, a great noise arose, and the house was filled with flames.

[1]The raging peasantry had made this decree for itself, namely, that all who could, both young and old, should bear arms. Those who were veteran soldiers[2] bore old stakes or poles rather than lack something to carry. Wearied with elderly years, and marked as they went along by a cough just like that of sheep, they supported their limbs with walking-sticks. Here came a lout carrying a quiver upside down; one carried broken bows, another a torch with no light [850]. [3] A man who shouldered a distaff did not think himself unarmed. In such fashion did even feeble old age rage in arms.

Meanwhile those whom youth had fired with rough behavior bore whatever cruder things lay at hand. [4] They carried an axe, a sickle which dark rust had badly corroded, and they cut people's necks with their pointed edge. A bumpkin carried a sword that barely half a sheath covered, and he struck at noblemen with it. The mattock took the place of the sword, the cane was brandished like a spear, and the hatchet was ready for use [860]. There was many a bow gnarled by smoke and age, and many an unfeathered arrow flew. Two- and three-pronged pitchforks were duly carried like a broadsword, and even the fierce hammer was wielded like a sword. A peasant said, "These arms belong on our shoulders, " and with such a cry he proceeded on his way. Thus the young men leaped across the fields like whelps and imagined that they outdid wild animals in their agility. There was a sling at hand and smooth stones, with which the peasant made various threats [870]. In their ferocity some carried clods and others carried branches torn from trees, when there was nothing else. Some held rocks, and they did not lack spears in their madness, [5] and they waged their cruel wars with deadly intent. This senseless band made the ground wet, [6] sprinkling it with the blood of worthy men. They gradually forced their way, step by step, not where reason but where whim directed them to go.

Chapter 13

Here he tells, according to the vision of his dream, how and when the said madmen, with the Devil instigating them, entered New Troy--that is, the City of London. For just as Troy was once pillaged, so this city remained almost destitute of all consolation for the time being, because of its shameful affliction.

On my right I then thought I saw New Troy, [1] which was powerless as a widow [880]. Ordinarily surrounded by walls, it lay exposed without any wall, and the city gate could not shut its bars. A thousand wolves and bears approaching with the wolves determined to go out of the woods to the homes of the city. There was no monstrous thing or species on earth whose fury could hurt the land but that it came forth and multiplied. Like a shower scattered by the east wind, some of their furor was at hand on every side. Then the monsters which previously had lurked in hiding went out into the open and were received by their companions [890]. The fierce and mighty beast, which used to rage not so much from fury as from hunger, came out of the woods and marshes. But it raged more from fury against the wasted city, which was stunned at the coming of such a strange calamity. They swore with savage rage in the woods that they would trample on justice in a mad frenzy by overthrowing all laws. So great was the number of these slaves of perdition that scarcely any wall could contain them.

Since madness prompted the goings-on, all restraint was gone, and the madness plunged into any- and everything forbidden [900]. Wanting not at all to be held in check, they hurried on of their own accord so that no one could block the course they had taken up. Everything was surrendered. We unlocked our doors to the enemy and faith was kept only in faithless treason. [2] Just as a spirited war horse snorts and leaps through the sounding air and remains unaware of the perils closer by, so the fierce peasantry started out heedless of their perils, and did not visualize their ultimate death from them. The slavish band, which utter lunacy possessed, tried to join the hand of victory with theirs [910]. [3] And so the savage throngs approached the city like the waves of the sea and entered it by violence. O what a tremendous affair and astonishing surprise sprang up unexpectedly with the approach of this calamity! The magnificent and palatial court in the city was changed and transformed completely into the likeness of a hut. And fate, which then became most faulty in its judgments, suddenly turned the meanest huts into palaces.

Behold, it was Thursday, the Festival of Corpus Christi [920], [4] when madness hemmed in every side of the city. Going ahead of the others, one peasant captain urged them all to follow him. Supported by his many men, he crushed the city, put the citizens to the sword, and burned down the houses. [5] He did not sing out[6] alone, but drew many thousands along with him, and involved them in his nefarious doings. His voice gathered the madmen together, and with a cruel eagerness for slaughter he shouted in the ears of the rabble, "Burn! Kill!" What had been the Savoy[7] burned fiercely in flames, so that Lancaster did not know which path to take [930]. The Baptist's house, [8] bereft of its master, fell to the sword and was soon ashes because of the flames. Holy buildings burned in wicked fires, and shameless flame was thus mixed with a sacred flame. The astonished priests wept with trembling heart, and fear took away their body's strength. [9]

He who hurls the dread thunderbolts with his awful hand[10] ordered that heaven vex the earth with fire. If any household stood firm and was able to resist such a huge misfortune without being overthrown, [11] it offered pious thanks to God [940]. I do not have to ask whether the domineering rabble yearned for the city's riches and committed thefts at that time. [12] Just as many ants are wont to carry off in a thin trail the grain they have found to underground storeplaces, [13] so the multitude of rash fools carried off stolen goods throughout the city; and no one could tell the number in the crowd. One clutched, another dragged, one stood still and another marched around, and the booty was quickly collected by many hands. Finally, Bacchus arrived and drowned their bellies in wine, and he brought that Thursday to a close [950]. It was night, and their eyes and thoughts were swimming with wine. [14] Their limbs were moving, but they had no control over where they put their feet.

After Aurora had put the starry fires to flight, [15] lo and behold, the growing misfortune caused fresh disasters. If Thursday's[16] violent wrath had been harmful before, the following Friday acted as if doubly agitated with rage. The swift furies darted here and there like lightning from the South. And woe and alas, wherever they went there were others like them. Then at the same time the wolf, the dog, and the bear pillaged together in the city and halted there [960]. Behold, even the old man Calchas, whose wisdom was greater than everyone's, then knew no course of action. Antenor did not know then by what means to arrange peace treaties; instead the great frenzy destroyed all his efforts. No difference marked the worthy man from the foolish: Thersites' heart became the same as Diomedes'. The orator Ulysses[17] was then of no help with his words of well chosen speech, and blessed discourse was not his. And since fate opposed all their great efforts, each man gave free rein to his own destiny [970]. Then neither war nor weapons nor horses were of assistance, and honesty did not possess its former worth. Just as the lioness rages when robbed of her nursing cub[18] and attacks the cattle near her, so the angry peasantry, bereft of the safeguard of justice, attacked the nobles with greater ferocity. Misfortune is common to all men, but nevertheless the same calamity does not confer the same status upon all.

O the degenerate nature of our former city, which allowed the madly raging rabble to take up arms [980]! O what a backward state of affairs it is that the unarmed knight shakes with fear and the barbarous mob has the leisure for fighting! The battles of Thebes, Carthage, and Rome were not more filled with madness than these. Neither Capaneus nor Tydeus prevailed; neither the former fierce warrior nor the latter made any attacks. Neither Palamedes nor Ajax survived, nor did Agamemnon's sword hold sway. The Trojan victory was lost in defeat, and Troy became a prey to the wild beast, just like a lamb to the wolf [990]. The peasant attacked and the knight in the city did not resist;

Troy was without a Hector, Argos without its Achilles. [19] No boldness of a Hector or Troilus defeated anything then, but instead those who were defeated suffered the whole affair without courage. Priam did not shine then with his usual honor; instead, the master put up with whatever the servant did to him. Even Hecuba's chambers could scarcely remain undisturbed, without suffering agitating the faint hearts within them. [20] Nor indeed could Ilion then defend from the madmen the man enclosed within its lofty towers [1000].

Chapter 14

Here he treats, as if through a symbol, of the death of the Archbishop of Canterbury, according to the vision of his dream.

The high priest Helenus, [1] who served Troy's Palladium[2] at the altar, perished when struck by the sword. He prayed beforehand that his life be spared him, but he did not move their cruel hearts for the better. What he said was quite sufficient, if grace might have touched their ears, but his words carried no weight. Whatever he said in warning examples went right out their ear, and the false-believing crowd was the deeper in villainy. Then the shouting resounded and a mighty tumult promptly arose and produced a great deal of sedition [1010]. Vicious people attacked the virtuous quarrelsomely, and the disgraceful crowd threw the sacred forum into confusion. Faith warred with Fraud, Virtue with Villainy, Wickedness with Piety, and Madness with Reason. [3] The Host, Impiety, entertained no pious affections in the heart, and Love, an exile, deserted the spirit. [4]

God knows those wild men were deserving of eternal fire and were unreasoning reprobates. [5] O the sorrow in these deeds, O the wicked deeds of sorrow! These foul exploits were more like those of hell than of man [1020]. This knavery was not human, for the Devil from the lower world was in charge of such rash doings. People were in such a frenzy that the rough mob did not know how to cherish God the Father, for they had lost Christ's love. [6] Here Virtue expired and a plethora of Vices arose; and as one deserted a place, another seized it. Hence Goodness fell, Piety perished, all Honesty was banished, and all things Good decided upon escape. Hence Love and Quiet, Peace and Calm of Mind, and Hope and Faith forsook their homes [1030]. The Temperateness fostering Sobriety, Moderation in action, and the Sense of Shame had delayed too long. Patience moved to a better abode, and its companion Humble-Mindedness followed it. When the band of Virtues was done away with, the unfriendly masses, the oppressive throng, and god-less violence broke out.

When a great assemblage had gathered together from all sides, the tremendous crowd rushed into mortal conflict. At the same time [there were] those who stood farther off, awaiting the end of the affair. One or two of them said [1040], "This prisoner is to die. He is to suffer capital punishment, and let his blood be on our heads forever." Words to the contrary of these were then spoken, but finally the chattering voices condemned the man unanimously. After the altars of the deity had been profaned, the enemy held every side and sprang[7] to the death of the presiding official. Feeling no pity, the murderers shouted, "This man shall be killed at our hands." Laying their hands on him, they cut through his neck with a scythe. No faith in Christ feared justice there [1050]. The official, however, bore all the villainy patiently, and after suffering such great wrongs, was at rest. Christ's righteous curse did not ignore those who cherished the head [of their Church] in this fashion, even though they were members.

Four men plotted an agreement for Thomas' death, and a hundred thousand brought about Simon's murder.[8] The King, moved in his heart, grieved for Thomas' life, and mourned Simon's last day. Thomas' death was caused by the wrath of a king, but Simon's death was caused by the utter madness of the masses [1060]. The cause is dissimilar, yet there was one death for the two. Each of the righteous men, however, suffered undeservedly. With its neck severed by the sword, the one head fell which God's altar considered more valuable; the neck of the other, whose torture was inflicted in the middle of the marketplace, suffered wounds, but the head remained intact.[9] A knight was the chief culprit in shedding Thomas' blood; a peasant furnished the weapons for Simon's murder. Nobles who did not fear Christ's Church were the cause of the martyr Thomas' murder [1070]; and the peasant class, opposed to justice in the realm, brought about Simon's last day in the city. Thomas sank down in the bosom of his Mother, and Simon fell by the sword because of the turmoil in the midst of his children. The King could have saved Thomas, but the royal power was without influence in regard to Simon's life. Thomas' death was avenged, and now vengeance for Simon's death threatens daily outside the door.

In the middle of the day, when the sun at its highest made the scantest shadows,[10] the Ephod was tinged with blood [1080]. Thus the pale, suffering victim, struck in the neck with an axe, spattered the ground with red blood.[11] He who was father to the soul was bereft of his body, and the shepherd shrank from the fields, cut to pieces by his flock. He who had been the protection of the soul had no protection, and the children whom the father cherished killed him. He who had been a cross-bearer and a Primate high in the esteem of their fathers was cast down and crucified all the more. He who had been a teacher of laws perished amidst lawlessness, and the shepherd was destroyed, cut down by the brazenness of his flock [1090]. He died before his day, without blame and without cause, so that both nature as well as God grieved. Although he was laid low by the treacherous regime of the serfs, he himself walks honorably along the eternal road. [12] Although he lost his outer self, his bravery as well as his virtue commended his inner self to God. And no matter what madness went on outside him, his temperate nature inwardly suffered in innocence. Howevermuch his wisdom was destroyed by the world, his goodness provided him a place in heaven with the wise [1100]. Howevermuch justice might seem laid low, he ascended to the stars and remained before God on high. They made him live whom they thought to kill; they could not take from God him whom they took from the world.

O who knows of such infamies in time past to be compared to the deeds which are mirrored in the Primate's murder? In the past he had willingly done many things for the good of all, yet of its own accord the rabble was averse to him because of his own worthiness. Even Nestor's years do not know of the commission of such a crime, and the deed becomes the more astonishing since it happens so rarely [1100]. To me, the things which were done in the past are not so grievous but that these things which are so well known to me at present are much more grievous. For the calamity which I now saw at hand in my own time brought about horrifying deeds of much greater suffering. O, the state of affairs now revealed to exist among the mob shows what vice long practised brings about. I believe they were worse than Cain, for he killed only his brother, [13] but this man was their father. I do not know who deserves the credit for such an outrage, but I do know that Troy in its ruin tolerated this crime [1120]. One man helped in what another man did, and another agreed that they would be bad, worse, and worst. [14] Justice demands that a man who commits a crime and another who agrees to it be equal partners in the legal action. O city which dares to stone prophets entrusted to you, you have reason enough to grieve for this. But the crazy peasantry, rather than the people as a whole, caused this crime, when they committed their first misdeeds. O cursed hand carrying the severed head! The guilt is horrible, the punishment will be eternal [1130]. O you who have treacherously done such a crime with God forbidding you, what penalty, what death will you be deserving of? O mad folly, boorish race, violent people, how the offense of your crime is above all wickedness! Tell me with what kind of boldness you can bring about such disasters. No one has ever equaled your treachery, your perfidies.

Hasten here, old men, gather together here, fair youths, see the wicked arms the peasant bore. Strike your breast, shed your tears,

lament for the body[15] whose unheard-of death is thus described [1140]:
as the tail of a wounded snake is wont to writhe, [16] he who used to be
our leader trembled and died. Alas! For there at the sacred altars
was an even more frenzied death, [17] and the high priest stood in less
esteem than a head of cattle. Be mindful of what is to come, and let
the unheard-of misfortune of this age be a lesson to the whole world.
Let those who serve the things of the spirit beware lest at the same
time the world place its concerns upon them. The things which Cassandra used to predict like a prophet came upon the city with most
severe oppressiveness [1150]. With His permission, God's gracious
hand allowed these evils, but God alone knows the reason for this. All
men, or at least those whom reason drew to the love of God, were
stunned by such an unwonted death. Priam could not save Helenus; [18]
rather, at that period of the King's command, justice was silent. Because the King knew that such was the course of things, however, he
lamented and mourned because of the love in his heart. The King
grieved for the deed, but he could not allay fate, nor carry out his rightful obligations toward Holy Church [1160]. I saw corpses cast out before the sacred portals, [19] and there was no place in which wrongdoing
did not go on.

Chapter 15

Here he treats further, according to the vision of his dream, of
the hostile persecution and murdering which the aforementioned
madmen carried on in the said city, alas! For the time being,
it was defenseless to a certain extent. And he treats of how this
kind of news terrified the neighboring cities.

All the citizens who had been prominent at this time lay like sheep
stretched out by the hand of death. The bodies dispatched in the slaughter were by no means carried off; instead they lay scattered everywhere
in the open roads. And because there were no tombs for these men, the
frenzied mob trod upon the dead bodies, torn limb from limb. They
placed the corpses of the slain to hang from the walls, and like crude
beasts they refused them even crude burials [1170]. There was horrible
butchery, while the earth grew red with blood. Wherever a fountain
swelled, it became red with bloodiness. Death was rampant in the
houses, death beat at the doors of the court of law, [1] and the peasant
himself gave orders for life or death. Whatever came by chance into
their hands succumbed, and the city which had been the greatest then

75

fell, overwhelmed by the slaughter. From the demolished castles they emptied the food they found, and they plundered everything they knew was of superior quality.

Then there was a new sorrow, and new lament, and grief overflowed. Wicked men turned aside from veneration of the King [1180]. [2] Old men whom a lifetime had guided through a hundred years wept over the misfortunes which one day brought. The madmen thirsted for blood more than a fish for water, and it was of no use to implore the blessing of peace. If a father spoke words of entreaty on behalf of his son, they both fell together, slain by a single word. If you had sought mercy and wept like the waves of the sea for it, nevertheless those tears would have had no influential voice. [3] Then the mob burned with more ungovernable fury, [4] so that mercy arrived at the point where its prayers were worth nothing [1190]. When prayers were used, the peasant raged even more violently, and he did whatever worse thing he could. The wild boar tumbling the swift dogs over and over in the midst of the forest with his murderous jaws [was] not so cruel in his anger as this. [5] But you might have felt your head cut off by their weapons quicker than you could speak one word to these madmen.

Confused by the great terror of such sudden destruction, the nobility scarcely knew whether its own class existed. The nobleman fled and wandered about, and there were no places quite safe either in the ramparts of the city or in woodland retreats [1200]. In seeking a measure of safety he approached a thousand houses, but nowhere could he find peace and quiet. The noble went now here, now there, like a raincloud in motion, [6] yet there was no sure safety. A man lay down in wellpits when he wanted to hide; he yearned for hiding places in hell rather than be on the point of death. But the woods were even frightened by the woods, the fields by the fields, [7] and city by city; one place did not know how to regard another. How suddenly did that madness, at whose deeds God shuddered, sprinkle the well-set dining tables with blood [1210]! [8] They drenched the scattered food with drops of gore, [9] and no spot or chamber furnished men a safe place. Then no safety could be found in the nature of a place unless it was under the earth or above the skies. The foreigner became a prey; [10] the native peasant drove him into the jaws of death, cutting him to pieces with swordbites. O the sorrow of the wife, when she saw the fatal sword by which her husband would fall, and he not guilty! He seizes her in his embrace and dries her tears with kisses, and says, "O let us seek the heights of heaven together [1220]"[11] The disheveled locks about his neck caught up his tears and his lips uttered piercing sobs. [12] With grieving heart I saw the woman bereaved of her husband often wet her delicate cheeks, [13] often wring her hands and tear her hair, and her nails lacerate her own skin. He who is the author of all cruelty, however, rejoiced at their afflictions and added to them. In such fashion did these monsters of men revel in cold blood, for impiety knows nothing of piety [1230].

Traveling through cities here and there, common talk spread the noise of this rumor and shook stout hearts. Because of its serious consequences the general disaster was talked about repeatedly, and a person did not know where he would fall in his fate. So the wicked slaughter terrified men even more, and no gifts of gold bought off its hand. While fear dried up the recesses of a man's heart, a sharp thirst drove him on and tortured his viscera. Then a heavy fear overcame the unconquered man whom no one had been able to defeat before [1240]. Then the shower of gore and[14] the land reddened with blood inwardly shook even a bold man. Nevertheless, no law and order helped relieve his affliction, and no one at hand lent him quick assistance. No one offered help in his bitter need; each was intent on keeping the slaughter in the balance. The hand of the nobles remained unmoved and did not oppose the wrathful time, but patiently bore every affliction. No strong man's strength was then secure; instead the Evil [One with a] tail weighed heavily upon his head [1250]. Each man's home then seemed forlorn to him, and no man was safe from the ulcer of death.

As long as the boorish peasant bore weapons he stained the knives he carried with much bloodshed. [15] The impious man wished to spare neither sons nor mother; he laid waste everyone's possessions, dwellings, courts, and the marketplace. No one could obtain mercy during this barbarism. Their assault struck terror into the whole countryside; for the entire multitude of rabble was then inclined to violent ragings, and there was not one nobleman to withstand them [1260]. [16] In all the realm there was not a sword or spear in the hands of a knight with which he might defend his duty, until the furor grew and the barbarous mob vaunted itself so that henceforward the wavering knight became quite meek. The suffering knighthood withdrew and handed its place over to the wrathful, while dishonesty crushed what had been honest. The spur took the place of the heart, and transgression that of justice, and there was no physician who knew a cure for the disorder. Thus neither the shield nor the lance of the nobles, with which their age-old honor should have been defended, offered any opposition then [1270]. And ineffectual justice came to an end and no longer had due control over the wild unconquered hearts.

The times allowed no remedies to cure the madness, but drunkenness ran riot in utter lawlessness. Those who wished to reproach these evils could not, and they shed tears in token of their feelings. Everyone wept tears fetched from the bottom of his heart, and expected that his end was at hand. Eyes which once had been dry and happy with laughter broke out in tears like flowing water [1280]. As a result, people who had been accustomed not to weep over any misfortune taught their eyes to cry. The grandfather wept, the sister wept, twin brothers wept, [17] and one's eyes suffered in sorrow only if they looked at nothing. The cry was, "O! Woe! Woe!" Everything was distressing, everything was full of anxious fear. Not knowing late at night what there might be in store for himself in the morning, everyone tearfully asked, "What way out is left for me?" Every man said, "O God, give us strength, I pray, and relieve our fear, [18] and let our wretched fortune now depart"[1290]. The peasant said to the nobles, "We have great power, and from this time on there will be an end of respect for you." O people stunned by the chilling fear of death, [19] how fickle a fate placed such evil things upon you! There is a reason hidden in the vaults above as to why such a great storm overwhelmed the nobles.

Peace and quiet perished, for the petty animals waged formidable war with undaunted spirit. I saw things which once had been prey seeking prey for themselves, and no prey withstood them [1300]. I saw the smallest whelps frighten the lion, and the leopard found no quarters safe for him then. The flock of sheep pointed its sharp horns at the shepherd, and they grew wet, stained by the blood which poured from his heart. With faith in Christ put aside, in their madness they reckoned a church and a brothel as one and the same. [20] The perfidious folly of the time then refused everything which God Himself or nature demanded. It did not fear God nor did it respect the laws of the world, but it declared that every criminal wrong was permissible [1310]. Thus all orderliness departed in disorder, and the state did not know what state it was in. [21]

The thistle destroyed the ears of grain, and the teasel grew up over them and spoiled the fields. Loot was taken, the shepherd seized, and the land pillaged. And He Who beholds all things suffered the times to be in darkness. Because of the sins of the people, punishment was then meted out even to the saintly, and the madmen thought that everything sacred was heinous. Since they feared neither God nor man, these men deserved to be enslaved to devils for their faults [1320]. In their usual fashion the commoners muttered shameless things deserving of resentment, and their grumbling started many brawls among the people. Usurping the rights of priests and taking away their functions, they incurred the wrath of God. Inwardly, the anger of this destruction flashed like a storm; outwardly, the noxious throng thundered noisily. [22] The madmen shouted together, the mournful earth re-echoed. Alas, that so many atrocities were committed in this age! A happy face was not to be seen in the city; its own countenance was in sympathy with the bitterness in its heart [1330]. There was no help and no peace for the troubled mind so that it could gain a period of sanity. [23]

So behold, the ancient charity of Troy was changed into anger, and song was silent everywhere, overcome with lamentation. All laughter was turned into tears, all honor into disgrace, and what had previously been enough into nothing. Tears wetted peoples' faces, and breasts trembled with fear, and grief consumed the joys which once had existed. You might have seen some lying on the ground weeping for others, and one's own sorrow was another's grief [1340]. And time and time again they stretched their arms to the sky [to learn] whether there might be a remedy for their ills from the powers above. A man who had been good was vexed all the more because of his goodness. There was frequent wailing everywhere, and fresh sorrow. "We have lost everything," they said, for no one in the city had any of the respect which his rank required. Wise men who once were rightfully eminent had their necks cut in two when the swords were put to them. As for those whom the madmen thought were men of wide experience, they cut up their bodies with the same kind of wounds and flung them to the ground [1350]. Mischievous gossip flew about and frightened timid ears, and a wise man did not know what justice could avail him. Every vice flourished, virtue perished, justice grew sickly, and the ruler did not have the wherewithal to rule. The savage lunacy brought about these and many other strange evils in the city, which no one had ever witnessed before. The same madness abounded in the land generally, not merely in the cities, but rather throughout the whole country.

Chapter 16

According to the vision of his dream, he here laments, as if in his own person, [1] for the sufferings of those who protected themselves by hiding in the woods and caves because of that fearful time.

As I saw things like these a ghastly fright seized me, [2] and my life seemed almost deadly to me [1360]. The image of death constantly troubled my heart within, and it struck at my vitals like a sword. Now midday had shrunk the shadows to brief size, and now evening and morning [were] of equal length. [3] Three and four times I witnessed bodies of my friends cast down to the ground, [4] and their death furnished indication that I would die. Looking at the faces of others dripping with blood, in my affliction I was fearful of my own death. Seeing the cruel hands, seeing the eye without the light of righteousness, [5] I said, "Now mankind is coming to an end [1370]," since beasts and warfare had seized control of men, and since there was no justice in their laws. This was a most definite reason for anxious fear on my part and the beginning of a worse fate for me. For since I had seen nobles yield to villeins in this way, there was no further hope of deliverance by fate. My home was

79

broken into by those whom hell sympathized with when it was broken out of, so that the order of things destroyed its own laws. Thus I fled from the impact of sudden destruction, not daring to approach the threshold of my ruined home [1380]. [6]

Then abandoning my own home, I ran away across alien fields and became a stranger in the wild woodlands. Lashed from behind by peoples' tongues, I often fell to the ground, and without any crime on my part I was often like a criminal. Thus wretched, I was arraigned in my absence, and although my cause was excellent, it perished since no one defended me. [7] Tracing my weary steps along the upward path alone, [8] I sought to find a safe road. Nevertheless, fear of this great madness added wings to my feet, and I was like a bird in my swift flight [1390]. [9] So, wandering here and there where chance led me as I went, I made a serious attempt for several places. My steps wandered, and my lips were silent; my eye was struck with amazement and my ear was in pain; my heart trembled and my hair stood stiffly on end. Panicky as a wild boar which a pack of dogs frightens by barking around it, [10] I thought about withdrawing to very remote places. Ah, how many times did I falsely say I had chosen a safe hour, which was suitable for my undertaking! [11] Even if it were more expedient for me to go somewhere, my foot often stood fixed in the middle of the road [1400]. All beauty was lost upon me in my sadness; I did not even look at the countryside, and a fruitful garden meant nothing. [12]

My mind was agitated, and for a long time I struggled with my thoughts [13] [as to] which spot was better for my life. Scarcely trusting myself and changing my wishes almost a thousand times in a single moment, I suffered in my wavering courage. If there had been any safe places, I would have willingly gone to them; but where I could not go in the flesh I was transported in spirit. On whatever day I wanted to go back home, the enemy seized the road to prevent me [1410]. And I was afraid lest I be captured at night, if I went ahead. Thus at no time did I have an opportunity. The enemy was close at hand on the right and pressed hard from the left, and each side terrified me with like fear. [14] Alas! How many times did I retreat into the shadows when I saw the maniacs, and my ear was always wide open. Alas! How many times did I hide in the woods, hardly daring to go into caves. Late at night I despaired over what the early morning might bring. Alas! How many times did fear, striking terror into my wits, say to me, "Why do you run away? You will remain alive only a short time here [1420]."[15] Alas! How many times did my mind forget what I was, as [in] its wonted way it clung to the past. Quite often when the sun was at its brightest during the day, darkness arose and came over my anxious eyes. [16]

Dreams mimicking my misfortunes frightened me, and my senses awoke to my own sufferings. [17] Thus my courage melted away because of my anxieties during sleep, just like fresh wax when fire is placed nearby. Or, even if I were refreshed by the semblance of a better dream, I gazed at the abandoned buildings of my native land [1430]. [18] Like the hare, I was often a traveler through the slanting shadows where the hollow valley was wooded. At no time did I then trust a plain clear of trees and open to view on all sides. [19] An ancient, thick wood, unviolated by any axe, [20] then became a safer dwelling-place for me than a church. My unaccustomed labor had so exhausted me that I could scarcely make my weary steps this way or that. So as I fled my own home, my mind was afraid of caves; it suffered that evil only to escape a worse [1440]. A little grass together with leaves modestly afforded me a bed under cover of a cloud. [21] I wished, had I been able, to conceal myself under the very bark [of a tree], for anything above the ground was not safe. Hiding for some days, and quaking at each and every noise, I took flight, all the while guarding against the perils which I had seen. Driving off my hunger by means of acorns, I covered over my body with grass which had been mixed with leaves, [22] and I did not stir a hand. Grief was my mind's principal concern, and my freely flowing tears were just like sustenance in the pit of my stomach [1450]. The grass was then my nourishment. At that time there was a powerful impulse to run through the spreading forests, since, at this juncture, castles were not of any use. I fed my hunger with my tears and with the dew; [23] in my faintness, I brought enough to my lips for food.

Even as I was grieving over these many things, I was very much afraid at this time; and above all, the wrath of God was a considerable cause of fear on my part. I was utterly dejected, since I was alone and was without any consolation. I was then forced, as though a wayfarer, to travel by quite unknown paths. These secret places increased my secret sorrows, [24] in view of the fact that every friend who might have been of comfort to my distress was gone [1460]. In my exile, however, my grief brought me no inconsiderable pleasure in the fact that I was able to wear my gloomy expressions while by myself. Thus, as I complained, there were tears upon tears, there were griefs upon griefs, yet there was no one who could furnish any remedy. The tears which sprang from my heart fell down my cheeks, [25] for I had an unpleasant anticipation of the fate which was to be mine. My tears were endless, except when a feeling of insensibility checked them, or a death-like numbness seized my spirit. [26] Then a fear quite like utter terror checked not only my rising tears but also the voice within me [1470]. [27] Pointing toward the sun's light, I stretched out my arms, and I made signs with them, because of the fact that my tongue could not utter a sound. And when the fierce, burning anger in my spirit had quite dried up my tears, [28] my sobbing clamored to have its turn next. [29] My mind, which was inwardly much agitated by these misfortunes and was burdened with frightening things, shivered like the surface of the sea. [30]

The strange-colored wanness of my face showed from without what lay hidden at the bottom of my teeming brain. Indeed, the trepidation and terror and the insane look upon my anxious face made me quite unrecognizable even to myself [1480].

While my mind was in an enfeebled state, the motion of my body, which in its leanness [scarcely] covered my bones, was painful; and my lips did not take any delight in food. [31] My human appearance now seemed taken away, and the pallor in my face betokened the grave. The blood left my mind and the color left my body, [32] and the earth's hue seemed more attractive than mine. I underwent long suffering because of the fact that my body scarcely possessed even a thin skin to cover my bones. [33] And suffering just as long a time in mind, too, I lost my color, and so I was like another self [1490]. It was with difficulty that I kept myself in sound mind, because no friendly fate provided me with any confidence. I was not at liberty to confide secrets to anyone; on the contrary, my silent lips withheld their words. If chance brought some friend thither to me, we both mingled our sorrowful tears together. [34] But I was rarely consoled with friendly words, [35] for there was hardly a single friend to be trusted then. That was a time of doubts, when a reliable man no longer considered the friend whom he used to have as reliable [1500].

One who before had always borne a true love for me--even his love had ceased in this time of adversity. [36] I then made search for faithful brothers, not those whom my father wished he had never begotten. [37] Whenever I was on the point of speaking, I considered myself to be in ambush; and looking upon the ground, I uttered only a few words. [38] When my lot forced me to say something to somebody, I passed the time idly with glib talk. Again and again a soft answer turned away wrath, [39] and my very safety depended upon agreeable words [1510]. And many a time when I wished my words to convey my inclinations, my halting tongue grew numb from a chilling fear. [40] In order that my talk might not consist of complaint about recent happenings and become burdensome to people, my tongue remained firmly tied because of the hostile circumstances, [41] I was often inclined to declare my mind, but I was fearful of handing myself over to the enemy, and then my tongue grew hesitant. Alas! A sad fate was persistently dogging me in my wretchedness, and an easier hour did not enter into my destinies. [42] If to live in misery is a kind of death, [43] I believe that at that time my life and death were just alike [1520].

So, wherever I looked there was nothing except the image of death, [44] which I believe no man can bear. I often wished to die lest I should see any such thing; or, I wished that I were safe from these monsters in the world. I decided I wanted to die, since it is written, "Death releases all things[45] and frees them from present woe." "Alas,

O Fortune, " I said, "Spare me completely in my suffering.   Let me
either wholly live or die. " But in the end I had only hope of death, and
I dared to approach no more the threshold of my home [1530].   Then
complaints unexpectedly sprang up in the recesses of my mind, and
because of my suffering they often spoke such words as these: "O my
garden, which this present wonder does not allow me to see, how much
better for you is your fate than mine![46]   Alas!   Since my death will not
occur in my own familiar bed, there will be no one to mourn for me
when I am buried. [47]   If my spirit departs now for heaven, no friendly
hand will anoint my limbs when they are laid out.   Still, if my lot has
rounded out the years which it was supposed to, and if the end of my
life is at hand this soon [1540], [48]   Thou knowest, O God, that I am not
making objections to Thy decrees.   As long as Thou punishest, I shall
suffer and confess that I deserved it. "

And when an even greater torrent of woe overwhelmed me and I
had been buffeted about by an even more barren fate, behold, Wisdom
sympathized with my sorrows and said, "Cease your tears, I pray, and
be patient.   Fate does not want your reproaches.   Instead, trust that
because God is displeased He is calling you to redemption.   You are not
suffering this torment as due punishment, you are suffering the wrath
of heaven. [49]   Do not be afraid, for every sorrow has an end [1550]. [50]
Through such precepts and through other means Wisdom warned me repeatedly that I should suffer without fear.   But granted that I was free
from personal blame, my mind was conscious of the fact that there
nevertheless was no hope of even doubtful safety.   There were no clever
means of removing the wrath of such a mighty God from myself and
bringing back happy times.   The discord in my weary mind was so
great I could hardly keep my senses.   What feelings then did I have,
or what feelings should I have had, when neither life nor death carried
the day for sure [1560]?   I turned over now this thing and now that in
my doubtful mind, so that I had no peace nor happy hour.   Since my
despair was greater during sleep, I said in a weak voice, [51]   "Cruel
sleep, why have you kept me so feeble?   Indeed, I should have been
overpowered by instant death before this. "[52]   Then as often as my mind
argued against any sorrows, it said, "Why do you weep?   You will be
here only a short time. "[53]

Thus did sleepless cares, which dreams brought to my sleepless
mind, waste away my wretched body [1570]. [54]   Fear overcame me, I
stood sorrowful in the darkness, [55] and the color in my face left my
cheeks.   Dazed by such a storm of ills, [56] I often was far out of my
mind [and] like a stone.   But when my senses returned, my sorrows
came back with them, [57] for life could not refuse death to my senses.
Longing for death in this way, I still feared the presentiments of death,

and my trusted mind did not inform me that there might be something better in store for me. I would have complained aloud, but my grief-filled heart prevented me, and did not permit any words at that time [1580]. By frightening away the approach of tears, my rage stood as a barrier to the sobs of my voice, and my tongue checked its course. [58] To die was life to me, to live was death; death was more welcome than life, and love of death smacked of living. Alone, poor, without hope, and almost forsaken by life, [59] I considered whether this lot was definitely mine. I was then suffering marvels much too long to be told in a whole year, and I scarcely recall them now. If anyone desires to know all my misfortunes, [60] a brief space of time does not possess limits within which I may tell them [1590]. And so in the midst of various sorrows, I still suffered weary times which constantly became more bitter to me.

Chapter 17

According to the vision of his dream, he likewise describes here, as if in his own person, the different troubles which befell those who went to the Tower of London to find safety. [1] And he describes the breaching of the same tower. Indeed, he pictures the said tower to be like a ship near the whirlpool of the perilous Scylla.

As I saw that law and order took no further cognizance of the world, and rumor of various calamities everywhere was on the increase, the astonishment in my dreams aroused more and more fear of them, and frequently presented dubious courses of action to me. Afraid of what I might do and not knowing what might be quite safe for me, I shed tears of anger. [2] I caught sight of a ship not far off, and I ran hurriedly [to see][3] whether my lot might be safer on it [1600]. Behold, a ladder stood plainly before me, and having climbed up by it, I went aboard, and a kind sailor gave me refuge. How many others of the noble class I saw board the ship, [4] men whom utter dread possessed. From the top to the bottom of their rank, there was scarcely any one of those who then were of noble stock but that he climbed trembling aboard the ship in the middle of the sea to seek peace, if there were any. But whatever others did, my one concern was always that I should be able to get away safely from the madmen [1610]. While boarding the ship I asked with frightened spirit that a favorable wind give me easy passage. [5] In my prayers I called out for Christ, Whom the winds and the sea revere, to give me a calm voyage across the sea: "Go Thou before me, O Star of the Sea, wherever I may be borne by the waves. Take charge of me; I shall be safe with Thee as my guide. "[6]

When the swell of the water had carried us far from shore and the ship's course enjoyed a fine running sea, then I asserted that I was quite safe from the madmen on land. But in this my hope was vain [1620]. For when my expectation of finding safety was a little greater, suddenly there was cause for grief. Shrouding its terrifying face in pitchy darkness, [7] heaven violently shook the ship's tackle from on high. The four voices of the winds howled so that no anchor could lend aid to the weak vessel. Beside himself with rage the South Wind flew forth on dripping wings, [8] and the raindrops caused great damage. The hanging Balance released waters from heaven[9] which the mightiness of the earth could not contain [1630]. They were hurled in unbridled course upon the surface of the waters, [10] so that a hugely swollen wave of the sea overwhelmed the land. The air roared through the ship with howling winds, and the ocean's driven billow rushed against the oars. A crashing sound arose, and the dense clouds poured themselves down from the sky, [11] and the ship was driven about by a series of calamities.

June's swelling messenger put on her varied colors and poured the waters back a different way. [12] But no drop which she poured was sweet; instead it was foul, bitter, sharp, vile, harsh, heavy [1640]. This flowing water, which penetrated to the hearts of those drinking it and at the same time shattered their viscera, was worthless to the taste. O happy was the man who escaped such cloudbursts, which were more grievous than Styx or Phlegethon! In a state of perpetual confusion, I still clung to the ship, which the furious wrath of the sea almost engulfed. In this flood of water the owl swam among the larks, the wolf among the sheep, the wicked among the upright. The furrowing keel suddenly sank from the force of this water, which advanced upon the bridge and forecastle [1650]. In the face of this unbounded fury even great whales shook with fear, as the sea's anger grew greater and greater. [13]Behold, the showers fell thick from the bursting clouds and the lightning's wrath thundered in mid-air. You would have believed that the whole sky fell into the deep, and from all sides Iris terrified the land with her threats. And the swelling sea mounted to the regions of the sky, as if it wished to leave its proper realm. All this time it spread itself far out and grew white with hissing foam. Everything that had previously been above came down [1660]. And now the surface of the water appeared tinted tawny, for it churned up the tawny sands from the bottom.

With their heavy surging and blowing the seas and winds furnished

what torments they could. The waters of the ocean were mingled with
the gusts of the skies, and the salt sea swelled up, mixed with rain.
The sails grew soaked by the black clouds, and no kind of shelter
helped one to cover his head with something dry. The contention of the
winds set the foaming waves in motion and the South Wind transformed
them into shifting floods [1670]. Gales sent from above gripped the
seas, so navigation was blind. Horrible night rushed down, and in the
darkness the flashing bolts of lightning brought light[14] with their bright
flames. During the night, when the sea began to grow white with surging billows and the East Wind rushed headlong to the fray, the captain
shouted, "Run to the sail and lower the yard at once." He gave this
command, [but] the blasts in his face drowned out his orders, and the
uproar of the sea did not let him be heard [1680]. Yet some hurried of
their own accord to draw in the oars, and everyone on his own effort
hurried to close the oar-holes. One bailed out the floods and poured
the sea back into the sea; another lashed the spars, which thrashed
about confusedly. [But] the winds warred and stirred up the angry
waves, and made further work on the part of the men useless. So great
a violent destructive force seized the ship that the captain lost his wavering courage. The captain himself trembled with fear, and confessed
that he did not [know] what the situation was, since the chilling fear in
his mind froze his heart [1690]. The men shouted clamorously, the
rigging rattled, and the captain himself did nothing further about the
oars. All was sea, a sea without a shore, [15] and the deep cast up its
monsters even to the King's throne.

Chapter 18

Here he tells, according to the vision of his dream, how the
storm grew so huge that everyone on the said ship was doubtful
of any sure refuge without divine aid. And each class, especially
the nobles, prayed to God very devoutly for this.

The two colors of red and grey painted the sky[1] and the wrath of
heaven was spread far and wide. The angry thunder roared above and
the seas below burst asunder, and the earth cast up the waters from
its very depths. The clouds poured out unheard-of cataracts of rain,
and the ship held out against innumerable waves on all sides [1700]. [2]
And thus did the wandering vessel, not knowing what fate it might undergo, swim amidst the waters of the ocean and the rain. And the sea
confounded our spirits with an alarming rumble, so that the fear of that
one sound alone was utterly terrifying. The sky was then gloomily

enveloped in dark shadows; one scarcely saw his hand before his eyes. Then portents threatening death came from the heavens, and each man awaited what fate had in store for him. The air above was filled with avenging flames, and on every side a violent frenzy stirred up the waters [1710]. Then the blazing fire roared fiercely, and scattered sparks flew about like bolts of lightning. The fire-belching stream so racked us that everyone remained silent with bowed head. Our skill failed, our spirits fell, and our strength grew weak; there was no hope of any kind.

And in addition to this a huge monster coming from the sea, and at whose breath the billows roared, loomed up[3] and plowed the waves, just like a ship tipped with a sharp prow. [4] And everything nearby dreaded it [1720]. The fierce creature was master of the wide sea under its breast, [5] and it demanded control of the seas, which it duly claimed as its own. It was brother to Scylla, raging more than Charybdis; and like the jaws of hell, it sought things to devour. When he saw this, even a bold man lost the inner strength of his heart, and trembling suddenly came over him. And the helmsman, forgetting his post, raised his hand towards the heavens and implored aid with his prayers. [6] His skill overwhelmed by the wind, the steersman no longer handled the helm; [7] instead, the ship plowed aimlessly across the sea, and his post was taken over by the wind [1730]. Then the feverish jaws terrified us as if we were all pieces of bait, and our minds lost their senses for lack of help. Stretching out his arms and hands to the sky and turning his eyes there in a spirit of dejection, each man asked for help. One man did not hold back his tears, another was struck dumb, still another called upon the saints; [8] and each invoked God for his deliverance. Entrusting all such things to God, the captain said, "May the Ruler of heaven grant me quick assistance. " A gap [in the ship] appeared which made an entrance-way for the deadly waves, [9] and there was no one who did not think of the coming of death [1740]. First it seemed like Scylla to me, and then Charybdis, as it was eager to devour the ship from both sides.

O, how like this ship was the Tower of London then, for a violent storm shook it--a Tower without walls, where stone became like paper, which even the loathsome fly crushed by piercing through it; a Tower where the gate would not close its bars, so that its hall suffered the shame of an attacker; a Tower where an approach for the madmen was wide open, and every entering peasant plundered the place and the property [1750]; a Tower where strength yielded to weakness; a Tower where no bravery came to men's assistance; a Tower wishing for help, with its protection gone and imprudently abandoned to itself; a Tower in disgrace because of bloodshed and infamous patricide, and whose reputation went forth ruined forever; a Tower where the leopard's[10] cage was broken open and it went away like a gentle lamb when it was driven

out; a Tower where a rotten tile weighed heavily upon the crown, so
that by chance the top fell under a weak foot [1760]; [11] a Tower not
scented with frankincense but fetid with ill health; and mourning, not
merrymaking, [12] and suffering loathsome things; a Tower divided like
Babel[13] with its tongues; a Tower like a ship of Tarshish[14] on the face
of the sea. Thus did the Tower suffer, overwhelmed in a whirlpool of
vice, and not knowing which way to find the path of righteousness.
Everyone suffered, but not as I did, for this shipwrecking Scylla was
on the lookout for my bitter destruction. With my eyes almost asleep,
I remained awake and witnessed these portents, for I was afraid of the
disasters to come from the whole affair [1770].

There was no doubt that I was terrified and alarmed in my
dreams, as I thought about suffering such things. I declared that I had
been led into uncertain dangers so often that the sea was safer for me
than my ship. [15] Violently agitated, I thus was afraid of Eurus and
Zephyrus and cold Boreas and rash Notus. [16] These four winds blew
over the four quarters of the globe, and nothing could stand in the way
of their blasts. Our fate was decided by hostile gales, and no fate
could have been sadder than mine [1780]. [17] Wretchedly I pictured the
fate contrived for myself, [18] and I judged that misfortune was at hand
because of my own unworthiness. Meditating to myself in this way, I
said in a low murmur, "My own guilt has brought the things I am now
suffering. " None of my faults lay hidden in the recesses of my heart,
but instead my deeds brought everything to mind. My heart remembered the crimes I had committed, so that the picture in my heart
stimulated my prayers. There was not a saint whom my tongue did not
pray to, for the portents of the sea boded destruction [1790]. Prepared
to appease the burning wrath of God with my supplications, I spoke in
tears as follows:

[19]"O creator of the human race, Christ the Redeemer, without
Whom there is nothing good on earth or nothing better, Thou spokest
and all things were established in Thy name. Thou gavest command,
and instantly all things were manifestly created. And at Thy word the
heavens were formed, and Thy spirit furnished every splendor for them.
And through Thee the waters exist, and also their fixed boundary, and
through Thee the fish exists and every species in the sea [1800]. Thou
hast created the air together with every kind of winged creature, and
Thou hast given breath to the wind in its four directions. And being
omnipotent, by Thy divine will Thou hast established the earth, which
Thy provident order rendered stable. And all earth-born animals live
because of Thee, and every reptile moves under Thy law. Finally,
man was made in Thine image and that of Reason, so that he might be
over all Thy handiwork. Urged on by the Old Serpent, he disregarded
Thy commands, and the bite of the apple was death for him [1810]. But
Thou wert made flesh from the flesh of the Virgin that Thou might

redeem him from death through Thy mercy. And thus because of our lust of the flesh Thou wert made the parent of our kind, whence Thou might be the more gracious unto us. As I believe Thou art God and my parent, I pray, O Father, rule Thou my fate more kindly! As Thou wert not ashamed to bleed on the Cross of death, [20] so spare me my misfortunes at this time! Thou Who snatchedst Paul from the sea, Peter from prison, and Jonah from the fish's belly, remember Thou me [1820]![21] God cannot fail those who trust in Him. He visiteth the sick, He raiseth those struck down, He furnisheth His help in abundance. I have sinned [but] I return [to Thee]; I implore Thee to have pity upon me who am to be pitied. The time is at hand; it behooves Thee to comfort the wretched again. Spare me, I pray, and hide away Thy thunderbolt, Thy weapons[22] which bring so much grief upon wretched me.

"O Thou to whom I pour forth my prayers, I entreat Thee, let my tearful voice enter into Thy divine ears! Now cold, sick, almost buried in the earth, I [shall be] saved by Thee, if I may now be saved [1830]. O heavenly powers, " I said, "lend help to our oars and provide safe shores for my wrecked ship![23] May she who cared for humankind by giving birth to Christ furnish help for my cares. I pray Thee, merciful God, that she who brought forth a flower while her own flower remained secure may be my mediator. Why dost Thou loose evils upon me which I never suffered before? Behold, we are dying together, be mindful of us, disaster threatens!" While I was prostrate in my prayers and fearfully awaiting the approaching destructions with no hope of safety [1840], suddenly a violent blast struck and drove to the bottom the ship which Scylla's wrath almost devoured. Nevertheless, the gentle power of prayer withstood the whirlpool's thirsty mouth, and instead it was not satiated. We are always in doubt as to what fate designs; there is neither a reasonable hope nor fear for us. The man who is overwhelmed by a sudden wave dies a more merciful death than the one who thrashes his arms about in the fearful seas.[24] Nevertheless, each man prayed unceasingly and offered his orisons in supplication and poured forth pious entreaties to the skies [1850].

Chapter 19

Here he depicts, according to the vision of his dream, a certain divine voice calling on high, and how God was finally placated by prayers and calmed the storms. And he depicts how the Jay, that is, Walter the captain of the madmen, was killed as if for a sacrificial offering because of his transgressions.

There was an outcry in the skies, there were tears and frequent groans, and the gods did not neglect to show mercy. But Neptune, who is god of the sea, demanded sacrificial offerings to calm the sea. Our gifts in conjunction with our prayers prevailed; because of the gifts the god listened more kindly, and he gave approval to the solemn promises of our prayers. When the mighty tempest of the swelling sea was raging furiously, and fatal dangers lay in sight, there was a certain Mayor William whom a righteous spirit deeply moved in the thoughts of his heart [1860]. This man held the sword by which that proud Jay fell, and he made peace with it. [1] A single bird perished so that a thousand thousand lived again, and the god stopped up the raging mouths of the sea. Even though it was late and after the mischief was done, the wretched, suffering ship was forced to take up arms. The Jay was dead! So those whom he previously killed, using his beak for a weapon, did not die in vain. The swordsman who struck with the sword perished by it, [2] and the wretched leader got a taste of his own work [1870].[3] Crime had to be piled upon crime, and corpse upon corpse, so that the tyrant might pay for the evil which he had committed before. The spirit of the dying man departed into the gentle breezes, and God knows whether it reached the pits below. Since he had taken to warfare in the shape of such a monster, the deluded peasant's prayers were ineffectual. Since everything the gods wished was carried out, his cursed lot came to an end because of his follies. But perhaps that day would have been the last of the confusion even if God had denied the necessity of this man's death [1880]. O how much comfort the mighty victor brought me, who lifted me to overwhelming heights of such a kind! O blessed hand, that so plentifully provided the sacrificial offering for which the sea's tempest grew quiet and subdued! For as God willed, even as the ocean wave was raging, the welcome hour of deliverance came. A voice from on high announced the fact that God had put aside His wrath for the time being. From the midst of the sky there was an utterance in a divine voice, and it spoke thus to our ears [1890], saying, "Now the time is fitting for Me, and behold, I proclaim My judgment with mercy." Suffering at this word, Scylla loosed its jaws. It at once spewed forth what it had previously swallowed up. And so by God's command the ship which the fierce whirlpool had sucked down was raised, and it clung to the surface of the water. Thus the harsh disturbance of before stood under control, so great was the force of the celestial voice. [4] And just on the point of failing, I revived at its words, as one's strength returns after drinking wine [1900]. [5]

The sailors shouted. They rushed forth together and each hastened to perform his duty. So in the midst of life and death they quickly re-established the course whither they thought they would travel more safely. They raised a small part of the sail which still remained undamaged, so that it might guide the vessel. The voraciousness and copious flow of the waters were so great that the earth could scarcely receive them again, once they were calm. [6] But He Who had compassion on the world and walked upon the sea with His feet[7] suppressed the horrors of the times and turned them into joys [1910]. He held the seas in check and shut the apertures of the sky and commanded the quiescent waters to die down. A mist sank down as the rain-clouds were swept away by the north wind, [8] and the uproar with the thundering voice raged no more. He calmed the waters of the deep and established a boundary for them, lest the sea's wrath damage the injured vessel further. Then He showed the earth [once more] to the sky and the heavens to the earth, [9] and restrained the angry furies of the ocean. Then, since the waves grew smaller, the shores grew larger; [10] peace returned, and safety was restored to the just [1920].

The powers of darkness fled from the clearing sky[11] and the long-awaited daylight shone more brightly. With its rays the risen sun revealed the broad earth, [12] and our earlier fate, dark with misfortunes, was no more. So the sea had a shore, and the riverbank held its full streams in check, [13] and the roads were again open to law and order. Just as God willed, when the sea grew calmer our joys, mingled with fears, grew stronger. All then praised Christ because He did not let them be destroyed by the storm's recklessness but rescued them [1930]. Then on bended knee and with hands stretched toward the heavens, I said, "Glory be unto Thee, O Christ!" Repeating this, I cast off the restraints of my cold fear, and the expectation of new happiness made the journey pleasant for me. When the sea had become pacified and the wind more friendly, [14] hope returned and raised the dejected spirits of the sailors. After regaining his powers, the timorous sailor sailed on, so that he might reach a peaceful port. The canvas flapped loudly, and with hope of a better fate the mariner gave the order to put on fresh sails and set sail [1940]. [15]

Chapter 20

Here he speaks of the ship he still saw in his sleep. That is, he speaks of his confusion of mind, as if he himself, while dreaming in his thoughts, had, as if by a ship driven rudderless by various winds, sought out all parts of the world in order to discover peace of mind. And he says that at last he reached the shores of Great Britain, where peace rarely exists. He also tells how a voice in his sleep ordered him to write down in full the things concerning the world which he had seen and heard during his search. And his dream ends in this way.

91

My eyes were still closed in sleep, in which my dreams dealt
constantly with the ship, which sought a safe haven. And fear could not
readily leave my wavering mind before it could reach port unharmed.
The oars were now gone, broken away by the winds on all sides, and
the ship held to the course where fate led it. Searching for calm shores
it tried everywhere, but it could not find a peaceful place. But alas!
With billowing waves the storm finally drove it into a harbor where
every evil raged [1950]. Since an island more oppressive than Scylla
received it, the ship was no less beset with dangers than when fleeing
Scylla. Indeed, this broad island was fortified all around, and was surrounded by the flowing waters of the ocean sea. Disembarking from
the ship and coming towards the harbor, I quickly reached the shore,
and a great crowd of people came to meet me. One man among them
happened to be worthier than the others. I inquired of him, "Tell me,
what island is this, and why are there so many people here, and what
kind are they [1960]?" The old man, who was standing at the harbor,
answered my questions with blunt words:

"This once used to be called the Island of Brut, an exile. Diana
gave it to him out of pity. [1] The people of this land are wild. Their
way of life involves far more quarreling than love. Because this people
sprang from different tribes, it has faults of a varied nature. They
are fair of form, but see, by nature they have more cruel fierceness
than wolves [1970]. They do not fear laws, they overthrow right by
force, and justice falls in defeat because of their violent warfare. This
rough, pernicious people devises more treachery, crime, fighting, uproar, and harm than laws. And in parts of this country the men have
spirits more turbulent than the sea itself. This land, which bloodshed
and slaughters and wars always control, was born of mixed stock. The
unsightly fields bring forth bitter wormwood, and by this fruit the land
shows how harsh it is [1980]. [2] [Yet] I do not think there is a worthier
people under the sun, if there were mutual love among them. "

I heard much more, and it all displeased me. Alas! Renewed
grief now disturbed my heart. Just when I was thinking that the divine
will was kinder to me, the harsh aspect of my fortune confronted me.
When I saw how relentless my fate was, I was crushed; and my feeble
hope ceased, succumbing to a strong fear. So, pierced by the hostile
shafts of fortune, I felt nothing but sadness in my breast [1990]. If I
had reached port I would have been frightened by it. That troublesome
land held more terror than the water. [3] Driven about amidst dangerous
lands and waters in this way, I did not know where I could safely find
refuge. I struggled with the treacheries of men and sea at the same
time, and the sword and billow caused twin fears. [4] Why did I escape
so many swords, and why did one of those gales which threatened so
many times not overwhelm my wretched head? [5] Because my fate led
me to stop in such a port where there was no peace, my hope now died

out [2000]. The color fled from my face and leanness shrank my limbs, and my lips took a bare minimum of food only when compelled. [6] As the gentle Zephyrus shakes the slender stalks of grain, and as the wintry breeze stirs the poplar leaves, [7] I myself lay trembling when I wished to proceed on my way. And a brooding grief dwelt in my heart. Whenever I bewailed my fate tears followed upon my words, and the ground took up the moisture from my eyes. God who vexed my spirits should have seen them now. There was no longer any country whatever my thought might turn to [2010]. So, again convulsed within my heart, I fell to the ground as if dead. Finally, when I opened my eyes and at last raised up my body, I looked behind and to every side. Behold, there was absolutely nothing there! Instead it was just as if the entire crowd and the ship were gone, and I was alone. When I reflected that I was by myself, I grew all the more melancholy over this, and my spirits became dejected. Suddenly, the celestial voice which I had heard before spoke to me in the following manner [2020]:

"Sadness will do nothing for you. If it is clear that you feared misfortune when the sea encircled you, nevertheless you should now guard yourself even more strongly. For a quarrelsome island where peace seldom lasts long has received you. Therefore it is less fitting for you to carry on worldly struggles, for the world holds out no peaceful rewards. If a war lies outside you, with God's help control yourself patiently by the peace within you. When its fury attacks, give way to its furious speed; every onset is difficult to face [2030]. [8] Cease to struggle; let the winds bear your canvas backwards, and as the waves beckon you, so let your oar proceed. [9] Whether the ground thaws by day or the stars coldly shine, you should watch toward which straits the wind blows. [10] As you look about you, seize upon your opportunities, such as they are, unless there are none seen at hand. Divine power sports with human affairs, and the present hour scarcely contains any firm assurance. [11] You should always act cautiously, and you should remember that things which seem auspicious to you can become trying even as you mention them [2040]. He who is silent is strong; he who says a great deal in haste is asking for reproaches to be made against him. Leisure nourishes the body, and the body takes sustenance from it, [12] but excessive toil on your part has an ill effect. Nature rejoices in moderation, but the abundance which is too great always makes a man poor. However that may be, I advise you to hasten to write down whatever you have seen and heard in this dream, when leisure affords you the opportunity. For dreams often furnish an indication of the future. "[13] And behold, the sound of the voice [2050] was heard no more after it spoke these words. And it happened at that moment that as the cock sang in its usual way at the dawn of day, then awaking from my deep sleep I was so benumbed that I could scarcely realize whether what I saw had been outside my body or within. But now that I woke up alive,

93

with my fear taken away, my trust in the Lord grew greater.

Chapter 21

On waking he here offers thanks to God, Who saved him from the sea during his sleep.

Viewing the world more clearly with my waking eyes, and observing that the daylight had grown stronger now that the clouds had been dispelled [2060], I perceived that the madmen had been subdued under the law of old and that a new mode of law had repaired the broken course of events. Patting my body's unharmed limbs, I rejoiced that my shoulders still supported my head. Friendship flourished as of old, and wrath's onslaught fled away, and at this time the rights of man were restored. Revived by fresh courage, I first offered canticles of praise to the Lord enthroned with glory on high. Nevertheless, I confess my strength did not fully return—I who had previously suffered such great harm so unexpectedly [2070]. The fish that has once been wounded by the treacherous hook often thinks that weapons lie hidden in the rest of its food. [1] One who sank to the ground yesterday is scarcely quite safe today. A shipwrecked man is afraid of even calm seas. [2] So as long as I recall that I had stood in danger, past injuries make me afraid of those to come. Thus when I am at sea, I am aware that I remember the storm, because it will not disappear from the channels of my thinking.

O woe is me, when I am compelled by my sorrow to remember that time, when all was sorrow [2080]! Now that I have escaped, however, and am away from the uproar but still alive, I joyfully render songs of praise to God. Now at peace, I praise Mary the Star of the Sea, [3] who calmed the rough waters lest I should perish. Above all, I rejoice that Scylla, into whose gullet I had been utterly thrust, did not devour me. [4] I dwelt in the midst of enemies and dangers, but through the mercy of God I am now free. Similarly, I passed by the dens and fearful jaws of wild beasts, yet was not regarded as a fatal morsel for them [2090]. Just as the rose does not know it is sharply prickled with thorns, [5] so I was snatched away from the sword of my attacker.

So when the peasantry had been bound in chains and lay patiently[6] under our foot, the ox returned to its yoke, and the seed flourished beneath the plowed fields, and the villein ceased his warring. Similarly, Satan's power lay prostrate, overwhelmed by divine might; but nevertheless it lurked in hiding among the ungovernable peasantry. For the peasant always lay in wait [to see] whether he by chance could bring the noble class to destruction [2100]. [7] For his rough, boorish nature was not tempered by any affection, but he always had bitterness in his hateful heart. In his subjection the lowly plowman did not love, but rather feared and reviled, the very man who provided for him. Their very peace and quiet stirred up these men, so that this goading fear became more sharply whetted in them and their burden weighed heavily upon them. The intelligent man who guards himself will not be deceived: because of past injuries he is wary of future misfortunes. [8] Yet God's right hand performed a miracle in order that that wrathful day might pass me by [2110]. The snare from which I escaped free was destroyed, and I was like a man refreshed by sleep. Just as I had fallen suddenly, God granted sudden relief from my misfortune, and He himself supported my faltering step. I see now that the dream sustains me; I now consider it my life, my heart is so greatly refreshed. [9] No matter how many thunderbolts heaven sent, it rescued me. The tempest frightened me, but it did not harm me. [10]

Thou Who kindly didst advise me to live when love of death was in my grief-stricken breast [2120], it is incumbent upon me, now that I am alive, to render praise unto Thee for Thy favor; for as my God Thou art more to me than life. I rejoice that Thou hast restored me, Lord, since the gateway to my happiness has long been shut. O if my country, which the sea did not swallow up, [11] might also know it should render devotion to God! The Lord punished it and then did not deliver it to the pangs of death, but stayed His hand from wrath. Whatever praise others may offer, I whom God plucked from the jaws of the sea in the midst of upheavals shall not remain silent [2130]. But since I was tossed this way and that on the billowing waves, my mind, now resolute, will utter what it drank in. Although the ocean's billow seized me, I praised God that my spirit did not succumb to the floods. Since my mind remembers them it will note down, writing as if in the form of a dream, the memorable things which I perceived with fear when I was awake. For because of them I am not yet at peace, but suffer them all secretly in my heart. In this dream I did not spend the hours which sleep requires, [12] although I do imagine seeing this calamity in my dreams [2140]. O wakeful sleep, in which I had a vision not of a sleep-inducing nature, but a watchful one! O wakeful sleep, you which brought on real dreams in which every man of the future will find a moral! O wakeful sleep, whose difficult meaning my writings must now tell! Because a voice ordered me to write the things I saw at other times, I wish with all my heart to be quite at leisure. Let the task of long standing which is wontedly mine now yield, and let my former care be banished by this new one [2150]. [13]

BOOK II

Prologue

Here he says that now that he is awake he intends to write, in
accordance with the voice which he understood in his dreams, of
the things which he saw and heard concerning the world. And he
calls this book The Voice of One Crying, since it was conceived,
as it were, by a voice crying over all things. For this reason
he invokes the Holy Ghost to the aid of this work.

I have seen and noted many different things, which my reminisc-
ing pen is eager to write down for you now. I do not invoke the muses
for my undertaking, however, nor do I make offering to the gods. But
I shall sacrifice to God alone. Merciful God of the spirit, fire the innermost depths of Thy servant's breast, kindling the feelings in his
heart. In Thy name, O Christ, I shall spread my net, so that my mind
may thankfully seize upon the things which it requires. [1] I pray that
this work, begun with Thy help for the praise of Thy name, may achieve
a fitting conclusion [10]. Likewise I beg of you, the man who reads
these writings, that you bear with them generously and not be too conscious of my faults. Embrace the matter, not the man, and the spirit,
not the bodily form in this material, for I myself am a poor fellow. On
the other hand, there is often precious material in a worthless min-
eral, [2] and after the commodity is extracted, it is highly valued. Take
what the honest intention in these writings offers you and do not
haughtily demand anything further. If this tenuous style of writing is
disturbing to your ear, [3] let it be as the means with which a physician
alleviates an ill [20]. And if I do not use well-chosen words in order
that these verses may be embellished by them, [at least] notice what

96

they mean. And if I who am unskillful treat of something unskillfully, you who read this take pity on my failure, and consider what is plainly revealed within the work. And if the inharmonious metres in my verses go astray, receive the harmonious offerings my soul intends for you. Whatever formalities of rhetoric these pages may lack, the fruit of the subject matter will not be the less for that. [4] Although outwardly these verses may be of only moderate worth, the inner worth in turn will be the greater [30].

No matter how much a dullness of perception may hinder me, I shall nevertheless render without any embarrassment the things for which my ingenuousness is adequate. Knowing very little used to be a great disgrace for an old man, [5] because of the magnitude of the time he had lost. But nowadays if old age is wise in any way or teaches what it has learned earlier, its voice hardly receives the welcome of a youth's. Even if they are fervent in their zeal, the words which old men write are, as a rule, acceptable to young men only quite rarely. Yet no matter how much the voices of the dogs may bark in objection, I shall not run away, but instead I shall sing out my words [40]. [6] Imbibe oil from the rocks and honey from the stones for yourself, [7] and single out the sweet notes from my harsh song. Whatever morality a piece of writing supplies for your inner being ought to have its place, for the sake of its teachings. He who brought forth words through the mouth of an ass[8] is my hope that my lips may speak resolutely in praise of him. Therefore, let my detractor yield to my ingenuousness, and do not let biting malice gnaw away at my writings. Let the reader's ears be spared any carping, and let unfriendly grumbling cease. Leave off your doings, you envious throng [50]. [9] Even if Simon is incensed and the Serpent swells with rage, [10] however, I intend none the less to finish the work I have begun. My eye is blind[11] and my ear is almost deaf; they furnish nothing for the depths of my heart in order that it may possess understanding. Yet if my heart knows something it does not teach, it is like a live coal: it lies hidden under ashes all the while. A shining light hidden under a bushel accomplishes nothing; and the feeling in the heart accomplishes nothing when the lips refuse to speak. [12] What if I do know but little? Surely it is fitting for me to write that little. It may indeed help another to learn [60]. In my poverty I shall therefore offer a little of what little I have, since I prefer to be worth a trifle rather than worth nothing. There is no one so poor that he cannot give something; if I cannot give gifts, I shall give words. [13] And yet to the man trusting in the Lord, no field of endeavor is impossible, when his work is of good intention. [14]

The man whom Christ's grace enriches will never be poor; the man whom God provides for will possess quite enough. [15] Sometimes lofty things are achieved by an ordinary intelligence, and a weak hand frequently manages great affairs [70]. Very often a small light dispels huge shadows, and a brooklet affords sweet waters. Certainly nothing which is right is hard for one who is willing; therefore, may God grant my discourse to be just as I wish it. I shall not, however, speak of my personal affairs in the words which follow, but I shall report them just like a well-informed messenger. As the honeycomb is gathered from the bud of various flowers and the sea shell is found and gathered from many a shore, [16] so many different mouths have furnished me with [the matter of] this work; and my several visions are the reason for the book [80]. I acknowledge that my verses have been written with many models and strengthened by learned men of old. And the name of this volume shall be The Voice of One Crying, [17] because the work contains a message of the sorrow of today.

Chapter 1

Here he tells, according to what he has heard from the general clamoring, how the course and condition of the world are being changed in many ways for the worse, especially in these parts. And he tells how each and every one blames Fortune[1] for this.

With fresh reed pen, I shall use tears in place of ink[2] for the things of which I shall write in serious vein. Solomon declared that it is vain to be a man, and that all is vanity: [3] and he declared that nothing is enduring unless one loves God. For as many as are born, the first voice is one of pain; every man begins to live by weeping. After baptism much temptation plagues them all: the craft of the Devil, the struggle of the flesh, burdensome lust. Now man exists and now he does not, he breathes and expires, he blooms and withers away, and no station remains permanently his in this world [10]. [4] Behold, a man begins to die when his mother gives birth to him from her womb; afterwards, a brief hour brings him to an end. Crying torments the baby, school the boy, lust the adult, ambition the man, and covetous desire the old man. Not one single day provides a man with so many joys but that during some part of it grief will afflict him.

Long ago, God granted that we[5] be happy, if it is possible that one may be happy on earth. Whatever the hand of the Most High could bestow upon His creatures, it bestowed this piece of good fortune upon us [20]: the glory, if such it is, of the highest kind of life was extended to us above all others. And then there was shouting everywhere that God had turned against us in particular, rather than against all people. So ran the common talk of the world, yet times were once happier for us than any people. And behold, our happy times of old have been

rudely wiped out, for a bitter day afflicts the present. As fast as
honors of a superior kind came, they underwent a loss of good fortune [30]. We flourished quickly, but that flourishing was short-lived,
and our brief fire was but of straw. 6 But trouble and cares and a fortune inferior to our accustomed ways7 are recklessly destroying what
was exalted. Our praises used to go forth among mighty nations, but
now that our lot has changed they present dangers.

Many people are consequently asking why the atmosphere of the
time is now worse than it once used to be. They ask why so many
strange and highly burdensome evils now attend us almost daily [40].
For nothing on earth happens without cause, as Job taught, 8 who suffered many ills. Nevertheless, all men commonly say that they have
nothing to do with cause, as if no one were responsible for things. In
fact they now blame fickle Fortune, saying that she is responsible for
them. Every man now reproves Fortune, since it unexpectedly alters
and changes what once existed in times past. And everyone can see by
this mirror of us that she who used to be gracious has now become all
too harsh [50].

Chapter 2

Here he reproaches Fortune and deplores the inconstancy of her
outcome.

O you who take the name of Fortune for yourself, why do you
violently overthrow those whom you once exalted? Betraying them into
much suffering, you are becoming a harsh stepmother to those for
whom you used to be a loving mother. Your destiny is wrathfully destroying those whom you have guided; you cast asunder into every harm
those whom you have joined together. 1 If there were any sense of
honor in your deceitful make-up, you would not be hostile to those with
whom you link yourself. A short while ago you were a rose in bloom;
but now, a nettle pricking troublesomely, 2 you hurt those whom you
used to favor [60]. Your wheel is much too inconstant, and the station
of rich and poor fluctuates with its sudden movement. But I prefer to
climb from the bottom to the very top of the wheel rather than to slip
and fall from the top to the bottom. A person above may disappear
down below, and one beneath me may appear above. And truly, prosperity that has fallen away is a burden, for I believe that the greatest
punishment a wretched man could have in his life is formerly to have
been happy. 3
O how true it is that much is given to him who has much, and he

who possesses little must lose that little [70]![4] This is clear to us, who used to be held in high esteem: almost all the people used to bow their necks to us. There used to be no country where we were not placed in high honor, but now our former praise is gone into exile. All the earth used to seek peace with us; now the enemy is waging war on every side. Behold, the enemy which appeared a short time ago with a smooth forehead now comes to meet us jutting forth his horns. And scarcely a place is safe for the one who used to be armed but now has a smooth forehead, because he has lost his horns [80].[5] They say that this land, which used to be quite fortunate, has lost its good fortune.[6] But say, Fortune, whether you are to blame, although I believe that you are not the cause of any of this. Whatever different reputation the voice of the people may give you, in my opinion I still reckon you as nothing. Whatever other people do, I cannot believe in fate,[7] at least as long as God is omnipotent. I shall not believe, Fortune, that you impose anything on me, as do people who grumble that fate is in your hands [90]. Nevertheless, in this document I have decided to describe what may be the figure they conceive of, but which is nothing at all to me.

Chapter 3

Here he describes Fortune according to others, who say that fate and chance belong to Fortune.

O Fortune, hear what is openly said to you: fickle in spirit, you are neither here nor there. You are two-faced: one of them looks about in an ugly way and your wrath fulminates from it; the other glows with a happy mien, and people who gaze at it conduct all their affairs prosperously. Accordingly, your hateful face often destroys happy hearts, and your lovable face lifts up troubled ones [100]. With one eye you cry and with the other you laugh, and in return a man does not recognize you. As long as you change and wear a double aspect throughout the world, it is plain you are not going about your way innocently. If I should remain happy on your wheel because of your favoring interest, even as I think I stand secure I suddenly fall. And in the darkness my heart is often apprehensive over the uncertainties of grief, even though new happiness comes to me upon the morrow. All things are hanging by your slender thread,[1] and the more one trusts in them the more he is deceived [110]. And if the glances of your eye are capricious, your pendulous destinies are, to a dangerous degree, even more capricious.

No bribes can help to hold you in check, and no household which relies on your wheel is secure. You are heavier than rocks, lighter than a gentle breeze, sharper than thorns, and softer than roses. You are fleeter than the sere leaves which lightly flutter along, dried out by the swift winds. And there is less weight to you than to the tip of a spear of grain which stands up stiffly, delicately parched by constant sunlight [120]. [2] Now you are at peace, tomorrow you will be calling for your weapons. Now your lot beams with joy, now it grows sallow with bitterness, in order that you may confer your uncertain goods and evils. You bestow all your rewards with both a niggardly and a generous hand, you carry out and take back your decrees for whom you please.

Iris does not have so many variegated colors in her clouds nor the month of March so many changeable moments but that you, wearing everything tinged with a different hue, divide your own seasons into a thousand more portions [130]. Your love is falser than any harlot, and you come and go like a wave of the sea. No one can know late at night what your will may be early in the morning, for your mind does not know how to concentrate. [3] You beam upon every nation, but you do not definitely settle down in any, and you make yourself like the blast of a whirlwind. Your kisses do not promise that you have made peace with me, for your beginnings refuse to have an end. Your plant is rootless, and does not possess the worth of a long-lasting flower, for it quickly wilts [140]. Your wisdom brings nothing that endures, but your gifts are all untrustworthy. Your prosperity is very near to disaster, and your glory, if it exists, is rightly short-lived.

Chapter 4

Here he treats further of the mutability of Fortune, according to what people say. He finally concludes, however, that the things which happen to men are due neither to fate nor to chance, but to their merits or faults.

All who desire the pleasures of the world are thwarted, for Fortune does not know how to give honey without gall. Fortune is a very good ally of envy, and she never remains quite sure to anyone, but instead is inconstant. What heedless wretch could be ignorant of Fortune's doings? She takes away the same thing she gives, she humbles the lofty [150]. Fortune moves her sphere like the wandering moon: she quickly waxes and quickly wanes. [1] She grows larger and smaller and does not remain fixed in her course. On her wheel she is now below and now above. "I shall reign, I reign, I have reigned, I am without reign"--just this quickly does her course beguile us all. Her decrees allow the moments of the day to change with innumerable alterations, and her decrees allow all that they ordain to pass away. Beware when Fortune favors, for her round wheel turns and hurls down what it bore aloft [160]. She drives away those whom she summons, she overthrows those whom she raises up. [2] She demands everything. She claims that deceit is her rightful property. Fortune wanders about, circling with aimless steps, and nowhere does she tarry for a day. [3] But she seizes upon whatever happiness chance has brought, and the man who was fat but a little while ago suddenly becomes thin. When Fortune is helpful and smiles with serene face, then riches attend upon all the favored kingdoms; when she flees, the riches flee with her, and the man who has been surrounded by a host of companions is now not even recognized by them [170]. [4]

The changing season of the year shows by its example how Fortune is necessarily varying in her ways. Fortune is not such a good friend but that she is false, as long as the law of her wheel governs her deceitful actions. Her wheel is forever turning lightly through a circle, and at no time does it remain fixed. This wheel does not except any people in the world; this wheel binds, punishes, and releases everything. You will not bend her with prayers, you will not appease her with gifts. No one will move her with any tears [180]. Nothing-- not sex, not condition, not rank or age—compels her to feel pity. If by chance she is judge, in her judgment townsman and farmer, king and peasant, white and black, learned and stupid, both rich and poor, the meek and the impatient, the devout, the wicked, the just, the unjust are all alike. Some she oppresses, others she comforts, and still others she raises up so that she may thrust them back down. [5] She calls to one as well as another, and mocks them each in turn. She sports and jests with things when her slippery wheel falls downward, and she makes everything slippery along with herself [190]. And this capricious wheel is whirled about in this way lest there be peace and quiet in our affairs.

Its violent motion overthrows whatever Fortune provides when propitious, and she herself has never rendered any station fixed. [6] Alas! Why was so much power granted to such a one? No rights in the world were rightly given to her. If she has any justice, it is said to be surreptitious, for by rights she has nothing over which she should rule. So say men who by chance believe that she has power to control everything which God created [200]. [7] But in spite of this, Fortune is nothing, and neither destiny nor fate nor chance has anything to do with human affairs. But each man fashions his own destiny[8] and opposes chance as he pleases and creates his own fate. And indeed, a free mind considers what it voluntarily does for its own benefit as done in the name of fate. For fate ought always to be the handmaiden of the mind, by which is chosen the very name that is to be its own. If your will is good, a good fate follows; if your will is bad, through the operation of your mind you cause fate to be bad [210]. If you should lift up your mind above the stars by the help of virtue, Fortune will conduct you to the top of her wheel; but if you should become corrupted by a heavy burden of sins, you will quickly bring your fortune to the bottom with you. It is to your advantage to shun the worse fate, for your soul is free to follow the one as well as the other.

Chapter 5

Here he speaks according to the Scriptures and relates how all creatures serve and obey the just man.

God has said that if a man were willing to observe the precepts He has enjoined, He in return would give him prosperity, fruitful fields, vineyards filled with clusters of grapes, and due moderation of sun and rain [220]. He would hold the heavens in check and render Saturn pleasing; Saturn, which had been a bane, would then become a blessing. [1] The sword would not pass through this man's boundaries, but instead all war would avoid them because of his goodness. So the just man has peace, plenty, and a sound body when he fears God. At the time when he stands out as just, prosperity stands with him; and if the just man falls, his prosperity will in justice fall away. For the prosperity of the just man who has been subverted is obverted, and because he has become evil, he will choose evil [230]. Thus God disposes the times according to our deserts, as is clear from examples, if you read what is worthy of remembrance. Favorably inclined toward men on earth, the Angel Raphael flew down from heaven to heal the blind Tobit. [2] The tormentors of the conquered lower world cannot oppose the command of a just man; instead they obey him. And subject to the law of the elements, the celestial bodies favor the just man and carry out his prayers.

[3]The man who is knowing in the virtue of God will dominate the stars, and all the power of heaven attends him [240]. Circle and cycle and every sphere on high are at the foot of the man whom God helps. The sun stood still upon Gibeon and could not continue in its paths, because the righteous Joshua requested it. At Joshua's command the sun's chariot did not dare run on but stood fixed, unmindful of its course. [4] Then too, a star revealed the announcement that Christ was born, through Whom the Lord conferred peace upon men of good will. [5] And we read that the holy Gregory allayed the plague in the air at Rome with the help of prayer [250]. [6] Striking with his rod, Moses divided the

sea so that the people on foot could enter it and remain dry. [7] When Peter's firm faith began to trust in Christ's words, the wave of the sea furnished a pathway for his feet. [8] Because of Elisha, iron, plunged beneath the whirling waters, sprang over them and returned to the surface. [9] The fiery furnace received the three Hebrew children, but the subdued flames spared them unharmed. [10] And the earth, which was level before, raised itself up for the blessed Hilary and the high seat received him [260]. [11] And when the streams leaped forth at Moses' command from the hard rocks of the desert, the people and cattle drank. [12] The king of the Macedonians united the divided mountains. [13] God so granted it to be because of just prayers.

Every wild animal in the word—the dragon as well as the lion--is subdued by the virtue of the just man; he subjugates them to himself. [14] And because of this fact, Babylon knew that Daniel was righteous and Rome felt that Sylvester was sacred. [15] And at Moses' command the birds of the air descended and gave themselves up as food for God's people [270]. [16] And a fish took care of Jonah for three days in the seas, until it cast him forth from its belly at the port of Nineveh. [17] Thus it is apparent that all God's creatures lend assistance to the just man and are subject to him. O how rich, how happy is man in his great reward! All the honor of the world is granted to him alone. He is happy above all others. Everything the fabric of the world contains arises for him and performs his bidding. [18] On the other hand, however, if a just man were to change his ways, he would at once feel their ill effects [280]. [19]

Chapter 6

Here he treats and relates according to the Scriptures how all creatures disobey and resist a sinful man.

[1] When David committed sin, the plague in the air grew thick and prostrated his people on every side. Sodom was utterly consumed by fire for its sins, [2] and Korah's household was burned because of his guilt. [3] Because of wickedness the torrent of waters descended in which the whole race of men suffered death. [4] And the solid ground was made liquid when the sundered clefts swallowed up Dathan and Abiram because of their vices. [5] And an angel of the Lord put the hosts of Syria to the sword, and made the leader Lysias take flight [290]. [6] And the demon Asmodeus slew the seven wicked husbands of Sarah by night, for God willed it so. [7]

Fortune can afford no salvation to the unjust man, for creator and

104

creation stand together in opposition. Fortune cannot confer anything of value upon a just man, for God is his help, and not fate at all. Who granted strength to Samson, wisdom to Solomon, or fairness to Absalom? Nature without doubt gave them their bodies, and she will accordingly insist that God's grace alone furnished the virtues of the soul [300]. It is therefore evident that Fortune can neither bestow anything upon us nor take anything away, since she has given us nothing. When Solomon ruled his kingdom so peacefully and his riches were so plentiful, and when David's sling overcame the giant Philistine in battle, [8] is it not plain that God brought these things to pass? And when the days of the dying Hezekiah were so prolonged and death departed from him, [9] or when Susanna was cleared from blame[10] and Esther was held in honor among her people [310], [11] tell me what favors Fortune conferred upon them then? None, I think, and I do not ask as one who now complains of her. Fortune is not to be worshipped in worshipping God; and fate cannot become good by doing evil.

How could Pharaoh blame Fortune when so many of his men perished violently?[12] Or why did Nebuchadnezzar dwell among cattle with his shape changed, unless his guilt caused this?[13] Or what of Saul, who destroyed his kingdom and himself? Was he not arraigned because of God's decree? [320][14] Did not white leprosy by chance attack Azariah, when he usurped the functions of the priests of the temple himself?[15] But what shall Ahab say? Because he made off with Naboth's field, his own avarice was the cause of his death.[16] Or Rehoboam? Because he scorned the good counsel of his elders, he suffered having his kingdom divided.[17] Or Phinehas and Hophni, whom the sword of battle slew [when] the ark was taken? Their former sin struck them down.[18] Or what of Eli, who fell backwards from his seat with his neck broken, because the news of it stunned him? [330][19] The lot of Fortune could not have brought such things upon them, but they happened to them because of their sins. Those who have done evil in the end reap evil rewards, [20] for evil rightly destroys the evil.

[21]When the Hebrew people had sinned in worshipping images, the wrath of the Lord handed them over to their enemies. When they moved heaven with their prayers and abandoned their idols, their enemies took flight—this with God's help. The kings of Judah then prevailed over all, as long as they did not transgress the laws of their God [340]. When they were righteous, the Jewish people always routed the enemy lines in battle. But when they had transgressed, then the enemy began to overwhelm them, defeated and captured on every side. So whatever happens to the human race, everything is wontedly due to merit or lack of merit. Thus the die of the world will be cast with varying luck, as long as the hand of the Most High is wont to sport with our affairs. [22]

Chapter 7

Here he speaks of God, the highest Creator, Who is both three-
fold and one. All created things are ruled by His wisdom and
direction.

God who alone governs all things is omnipotent. He forsees all
things while remaining all in all [350]. All that is to come is always
foreknown to Him, and He sees things as if done before they are done.
God [is] begetter before the creation, the first begotten creature, first
cause and mover. [1] All that is, had an appointed time for itself to
exist, but God truly existed before all time. God is all that is, that
was, that shall be, that He brings into being; yet temporal being is
not given to Him. No periods of time can make themselves coeval with
God, [2] so it is plain that He is the Lord God by prior right [360].
  God is the Father, Son, and Holy Ghost; thus the three-fold name
bespeaks three persons. And no matter what person, He is called the
Lord God, and God alone is the Lord, one and the same. [3] They are
three persons, but a single being; these three are one, not three, but
three in one. One essence dwells in these three, one God [is] three,
He can be nothing more nor less. [There is] one mind in the three, one
simple essence for the three, one goodness in the three, one wisdom
for the three [370].
  Fire, heat, and motion are three things, and they appear as such.
Just as a glowing fire always contains these three things, so the Father,
Son and Holy Ghost are all three in the Godhead, and they alike denote
one alone. [4] When the Lord proclaims, "Let us make man,"[5] He makes
known quite clearly what faith we should have in Him. He is known as
a three-fold person in one maker, although He remains one in His
divinity. [6]

Chapter 8

Here he speaks of the Son of God, our Lord Incarnate, Jesus
Christ, through Whom we are transformed from evil into good.

[1]Now it behooves us to trust in the Son Incarnate, Whom we worship in our faith as Jesus Christ [380]. The Son took up His task: as
God, He descended from the bosom of the Father, from the paternal
heart. Coming down to the world, He proceeded from the Father; but

He did not withdraw from the Father, He kept firm grasp on heaven. For He was always of the Father, always in the Father, always by the Father, always one with the Father. Having been made flesh, He assumed the flesh; having assumed it, He nevertheless did not cease to be what He was before. Thus the flesh was joined with the Word, so that the two might exist in the same person, the True God throughout [390]. He always remained what He was; that which He was not He acquired from the flesh of the Virgin, and He was that, [too]. A miracle equal to this is nowhere known. O Mary, no one could be equal to thy glory. Weak in the flesh but strong in divinity, less than the Father in the flesh but remaining His equal in divinity; through the one He takes nourishment, through the other He is nourished; through the one He feeds, through the other He is fed; through the one He rules, through the other He is ruled; through the one He is weak, through the other He is strong; through the one He lies in the cradle and seeks His mother's breast, through the other the heavenly band declares Him God [400]; through the one a narrow manger holds Him under a poor roof, through the other, guiding stars lead kings to Him; through the one [came] hunger, thirst, tears, toil, and sorrows, yet in the end He was able to overcome death. The priceless treasure was bought for a price, God Himself was betrayed and sold for a little money. And afterwards [there came] salvation, life, a breaking open of the cruel tomb. From it He rose again, seeking His Father's kingdom. And when the end of the world shall have come, He shall bestow upon all men what they have previously earned according to His judgment [410].

Thus perfect man and perfect God at the same time, He completely performs whatever is incumbent upon both. The fact that He suckled at the breast suggests that He is a true mortal; the fact that a new star bore Him suggests that he is God. [2] Because a manger held Him He is seen to be of mankind; because the three [wise men] honored Him alone with their three gifts, He is seen to be of God. So a poor one may be rich, a child may be God, a king may be without a bed, the Omnipotent may beg to feed upon the nourishment of milk. While He had a manger as His lodging, the fabric of the world was His home, and the lofty roof of heaven His chamber [420]. He came, inasmuch as bread may hunger, rest may toil, the fountain run dry, health suffer pains, light be blotted out by darkness, the sun lack light, joy be saddened, and life die. Moved by His love, He suffered of His own accord so that God would remain man in our flesh. Because Adam was the cause of our first sorrow, God with His strength made our burden lighter. The sin of the first Adam wounds all his descendants until the baptismal water of the later Adam heals them [430]. [3] The first Adam was lord over beast, bird and serpent, but our second Adam holds all things under His sway. [4] The Fall in time of old was to places of lamentation; the New Law has brought a way to places of rejoicing. [5] So it is

107

necessary that a man who wishes to be saved should have faith, and he should not know more than what is permitted him.

Chapter 9[1]

Here he says that everyone ought firmly to believe, and not investigate the grounds of faith more than is proper.

When God brought forth His creatures out of nothing into being, God was alone and without witness. Just as He wished to act alone, so He wished to know how alone, and He shared in this work with no one [440]. No substance, no delicate form, no lasting structure possesses any of our power of reason. Submit your mind to faith, for a mortal creature cannot understand the mysteries of eternal judgment. Sorrow does not know happiness, weeping does not know joys, death does not know life, and man does not know what pertains to God. Darkness does not embody sunlight, a blind man does not embody sight, nor does man's humble mind embody the loftiness of God. Indeed, you ought never search for the noble secret of the sacred soul, because you cannot penetrate it [450]. [2]

Since it is certainly not for us to understand the circumstances of the world, to what purpose does man labor to understand creation? For us to experience faith tested by reason—that task is not for human powers. It is not a human task to mount up to the stars; mortal man does not grasp that by his reason. The character of great virtue mounts to the heights, passes through the heavens, and dwells with God. The man who acts wisely should be only moderately wise in these matters, he should ask that he may possess the true faith [460]. Ills often agitate the wits; [3] it is not for men to know what God on high proposes. It is helpful for man to be in ignorance about a great deal; most facts offend the senses. Therefore, a man should acquire knowledge prudently. Let him entrust to faith what he would not have been able to trust to reason. Reason does not supply what a firm faith should provide.

Increase your faith, for true faith believes and hopes for what it does not see and hear, [4] and this is the way, the life, the salvation. [5] Faith furnishes evidence for things which cannot be understood by the mind or grasped by the reason [470]. Whatever true faith seeks to do it accomplishes; it succeeds in everything. Whatever is believed to be possible it can do. [6] The tongue is silent, the mouth does not speak, the mind fails, the ear does not hear, nothing exists here but faith alone. What does one spark avail the sun, or one drop the sea, or what

can our ashes be worth to heaven? Nevertheless, God wishes to be
worshipped by us with a loving spirit, the Infinite wishes to be worshipped by us insignificant ones, the Most High by the lowest. In loving Him let moderation vanish, let there be no bounds, for none has
loved Him according to His worth [480]. He teaches whatever is proper
and smoothes out the rough places, [7] cares for the weak, banishes
harm, and lifts up the fallen. The Cross and its nails sprinkled with
red blood were our salvation, for Satan was banished. [8]

    Everyone who meditates on Jesus ought to lay aside his former
ways and cultivate better things. Life is given to all though this name,
and no one can be blessed[9] except by the name of Jesus alone. There
is no saint like this Lord, Who alone was free from every taint, and
Who sanctified sinners [490]. And there is no other [God] but Thee,
since all those whom a golden shape falsely proclaims gods are surely
nothing. [10] Thus through Thee the Church blesses us generously with
its goods, and the synagogue is bereft of its goods. [11]

Chapter 10[1]

Here he treats of the fact that a graven or molten image should
not be trusted, and also that such things should not be worshipped. But he says that from seeing them in church, a mind in
trouble may be quickly moved to contemplating God alone.

    O cursed people, traitorous to God, surely pagans whom disbe-
lief does not allow to be holy! People to whom the true faith of Christ
is frightening, for apart from the true law of the Creator, they worship
creations of wood! Unmindful of His creator, man bows himself down,
prostrates himself, and worships wooden things [500]. He declares
that anything whatever is his god--wood, stones, things which he sees
carved like an image. Man, whom God raised up, lies prone before
ashes and prays to a statue carved from a tree trunk. He seeks help,
he begs for aid, and with his hands he implores the things which his
own hand created, but the mute things do not reply. How senseless and
lacking in reason it is for the master of things to make these things into
gods!

    O remember in your confusion of mind to Whom man's creation
belonged in the beginning [510]. Recall to mind the glory with which
God honored you when He gave you existence. [2] Was not all the world
first founded for you, and its treasures laid out for your enjoyment?
The world was not made for adoration but for use; it was made to be
your servant, not your god. Therefore, does reason urge you that what

the artisan melts in the fire or carves on smooth wood is a god? O wretched man, why do you say to yourself that false idols are gods, and why do you who are like a god yourself prostrate yourself before images [520]? Alas! This insanity of worshipping mute gods while they themselves know nothing is worse than all vices. Must salvation be imputed to images which possess neither motion, touch, taste, nor sight?[3] What is a brutish thing to a rational one? What is something that does not live at all to a living race? One part of a tree becomes a plow, one part an idol, and one part cooks food, yet the tree was one and the same. Look, I scorn two of the parts, but after it is carved the third part ought to be worshipped, for some reason or other [530]. "Let him who makes them and him who trusts in them be made like unto them."[4] So declares God Himself. The sculptor is worthier than his sculpture; it is therefore conclusive that the worker who worships his own work is all too foolish.

But I believe in our using graven images in a different way, and not for weakening our obligation to worship God. Instead we have them so that by means of them we can take better heed to offer our deepest devotions to the saints. We believe God exists, not gods, and no heathen rite binds us--away with it [540]![5] But when a man erects statues for the sake of money and decorates them so that he may expect to get hold of offerings from the people; when he contrives such a piece of work only because he is devoted to gold, this sort of art has no value whatever.[6] When God spoke to Moses from the mountain, the people saw no figure of God. For if the people had seen any likeness, perhaps they would have fashioned a work carved in the same shape. But God, who scorned the honor resulting from such a sculpture, did not wish to make known any likeness of Himself [550].[7] But I believe the image of God is a body united with reason. Through this He lays claim to worship for Himself.

Stamped on our minds, the sign of the Cross should everywhere be worshipped in honor of the crucified Jesus. The power of the Cross conquered hell, and after the Devil was overthrown, it repaired the work of our former ruin.[8] The Cross is the true salvation. The Cross is wood worthy of reverence, it is the death of death, the gateway to life, an everlasting glory. It purifies the feelings, cleanses the mind of its blight, brightens the heart, and chastens the body [560]. It furnishes understanding, increases strength, takes away the fear of death, and prepares the heart for battle. Liberty returns by the Cross, and the power perishes which once ushered in death when the Arch-enemy triumphed. Religion and the people's rites of worship pleasantly combine all sacred things together in the Cross. The gateway to Paradise lies open through the Cross; the flaming sword ceases to guard that far-off place. Behold in how many ways it shines forth, how beautifully each Testament proclaims it [570]. Wondrous indeed is the power of the Cross; one man alone from the high seat of the Father was stretched upon it, so that He might suffer. Christ harrowed hell with the power of the Cross, [9] and with it He brought back the sheep which had been lost. He ascended into heaven by the power of the Cross, and entering into its starry splendor, He returned to His Father's kingdom. The glorified body which suffered torments on the Cross is on watch in heaven, placed by the throne of God. [10] So by virtue of the Holy Cross and heavenly love and with the help of the New Testament, grace has arisen within the Church [580].

Chapter 11

Here he says that since God alone created all things, He alone should be worshipped by His creatures. And he also says that it is highly reasonable that He alone govern all things, and of His own free will pass judgment according to men's merits and demerits.

God is that which was and ever shall be, three in one. He has neither beginning nor end, yet He has brought about a beginning and end for all things. All things exist through Him, and without Him nothing exists. [1] Because He is sufficient unto Himself, He can do those things which He wills. He ordains, and what He has ordained to exist immediately does exist. I obey Him at whose command all creatures serve, I believe my God is from heaven. When the hand of God is extended, it supplies all things in abundance, and when He turns away, everything is turned away [590]. In His wisdom He allots all things with just judgment, for God cannot fail or be failed. It is quite rightly a fact that since God created all things, all things should be subject to His jurisdiction. Since all things were created solely through the agency of God, Fortune could not undo the work of God, could she? It is my opinion that she, who had no power in the beginning and will have none in the end, has no power over affairs in the meantime.

Who set in motion the massive bulk of the earth, the turning dome of heaven, or the stars? Was it not God [600]? Or who sweetened the waters flowing into the gentle rivers, or who made the ocean seas bitter? Was it not God? The founder of the world willed existence for what He founded in order that the whole fabric should serve God devotedly. He clothed the earth with greenery and the greenery with flowers; He caused the blossoms to swell into fruits. With the greatest devotion He took pains to enrich the earth and fructify it with abundance. And it was not enough that the world was teeming with rivers, springs,

111

gardens, flowers, and buds [610]; He prepared to bring new things to life, fashion their different shapes, and diversify them in their beauties. The earth acquired living things of diverse kind and groaned under the weight of its new burden. He caused what was proper for each to be near at hand, and He allotted [them] room according to their special properties, making some live in mountains, others in valleys, still others in woodlands, and many in plains. The bird took to the air, the fish chose the waters for itself, the cattle the plains, and all the wild beasts the out-of-the-way places [620]. 2 The Maker's skill lent form to the work and He fashioned it. The whole framework resulted from the Author's hand.

3Fortune contributed nothing, but because He alone created everything, He alone rules all creation. Nothing is fortunate or unfortunate because of fate; rather, God bestows His gifts according to man's deserts. The wise man who ponders the Scriptures will therefore say that, whatever happens, he does not hold Fortune responsible. I truly acknowledge that whatever happens in the world, whether it be good or evil, we ourselves are the cause of it [630].

BOOK III

Prologue[1]

Here he says that since the things which we in the world term
favorable or unfavorable happen to men not because of Fortune
but because of their merits and faults in God's worthy judgment,
he intends as a result to write of the state of men. He intends to
write of how they conduct themselves at present, according to
what he saw and heard in the dream spoken of above.

Since a good or bad fate is bound to be allotted to us more or less
according to our rightful deserts; and since the state of the world is
divided into three parts, so that it seems like the work of fate to all
men; and since our fate nowadays is quite adverse because of our vices,
everyone ought to consider happenings in the light of their causes. No
matter what rank a man is in, it would seem that fate turns out to be
responsible for the things which happen to him in this world. I shall
not find fault with individuals, but I do cry out against the faults which
we see are reprehensible in individuals [10]. I am not speaking of these
things on my own part; rather, the voice of the people has reported
them to me, and it complains of their adverse fate at every hand. I
speak as the masses speak, [2] and even as I write I lament over what I
say, namely, that no estate is pious as in days gone by. Let every man
probe his own feelings and thus see whether he is such a one as will remain undisturbed about this. No matter who he is, a man will say he
is innocent, for the whole population now cries out that every estate is
the injured party. [3] Indeed, an extensive guilt, not an insignificant one,
has with good reason tainted us, our country, and our times [20].
Nevertheless, I shall make no general conclusions from a particular

detail, and I do not propose to do harm to any estate.

We recognize that there are three estates. In his own way, everyone in the world lives under them and serves them. No estate is accused as being at fault, but when estates transgress against virtue, their fault declares against them. I shall write what others say, for I do not wish anyone to assume that this is a work of my own originality. He who arraigns vices is praising virtues, in order that the good man may thereby stand out all the more in his goodness [30]. Just as white is more plainly evident when placed next to black, so good things are made more readily apparent when they are placed by evil ones. Therefore, if a writer should touch upon evil men, this should not vex the good. Let the heart's balance weigh its burden patiently: truth does not refuse to be depicted, for it is the true account that ought to be written up, not the false talk of flattering guile. If I have any glimmer of sense, I pray that God increase it to the highest fruitfulness. If a piece of writing contains something good, may the fountain of goodness[4] distil it and may God grant that a man write good things [40]. May God make fruitful in his servant those writings which will be of use. Let man provide the proper seeds and God the grain. I confess I am overcome by the magnitude of the undertaking, but hope offers promise to me of bringing it to a good conclusion. Because hope offers promise, love embraces [the task], and faith[5] lends aid and counsel to them both. It suggests, incites, persuades, and vouches for the fruit of my labor. It cries out, "Begin, the task will be done."

Where my intelligence is too small lend thine, O God, and I beg Thou turn a kind face towards my prayers [50]. Grant favor to my undertaking, I pray Thee O God, so that this piece of writing may incorporate nothing inconsiderately. I do not aspire to reach the thrones of heaven, or seek to describe the mysteries of the lofty skies. Rather, I write of present-day evils which the common voice of mankind outwardly complains of in this country. Since a useful discussion contributes something even though the times are hostile, I intend for my words of good to bring evil to light. Let no tale-bearer try to impute any scandals, with which he may make light of the book's message in the ear of the hearer [60]. [6] Let no perverse interpreter arouse any wrath against me, [7] for I should not be speaking out except for the fact that things have gone so badly. Therefore I pray that [Thy] helping hand sustain aloft my feeble chariot, so that my wheel may run on a true axle. [8] May Thy favor assist and lessen the labor of writing, while the task remains steadfast in my trembling breast. Many things can corrupt perverted minds, yet those same things are quite harmless in their place. [9] My prayers for my labor shall be, God knows, that I may accomplish much and that others may profit from it [70]. Examine it, everyone, and choose your precepts from its words. Hatred does not prompt me to write this work. Even if this book is snapped at by its enemies, I still insist that they cannot hurt it. Go, my book, under the protection of Him Who makes the pathway of all His servants free, and let not evil tongues disrupt your journey. If you can pass by the hostile voices freely, my book, others will not heap any slanders on you.[10] My crying voice will not hesitate, for every man will be a great warrant for its utterance [80]. If it is clear that I often have made excuses for myself, forgive me. I am a shipwrecked man who is afraid of every sea.[11]

O Wise One, without Whom the wisdom of the world is as nothing, Thou into Whose service my devotions bring me, I pray Thee at this time, O merciful Christ, to grant that I can readily compose the verses I have striven for. Let my pen avoid what is turgid, let it refuse to write what is false; rather, let it now write what it sees to be true. Let it take care not to falter at the outset; instead, let what it puts in the very first line serve the whole work appropriately [90]. Let nothing that my writings are to offer offend the reader, unless it is the truth or very like the truth. Let my intent be true to Thee Who art true; let no man succeed in discerning any fabrication in it. Let the word fit the deed[12] and minister to the sense, and let whatever appropriateness it has be welcome. Let there be no flattery in my account, and let it not be hesitant. Let there be no praise for my accomplishment except Thine. Let me speak out so that henceforth vice will diminish and virtue flourish, in order that mankind may become purer in this world [100].[13] Guide Thou my footsteps, increase my understanding, reveal powers of perception to me, and shower words upon me. And since the state of the world is brought under a three-fold order, assist my writings in their three-fold course. Since they are dedicated to Thee, I pray as an untried mariner setting out upon the deep that Thy Holy Spirit direct my sails.[14]

Chapter 1

Here he treats of how the state or order of the world consists of three estates. They are, as he says, the clergy, knighthood, and peasantry. Through their going astray, the misfortunes of the world befall us. Hence we must first examine the waywardness of the clergy, especially among the rank of prelates, who are more powerful than the others. And he speaks first of those prelates who preach Christ's teaching, yet do the opposite of it.

[1]There are the cleric, the knight, and the peasant, the three carrying on three [different] things. [2] But I intend to write about the prelates first. The schism evident today shows that there are two popes, one a schismatic and the other the proper one. France favors the schismatic and declares that he ought to be revered, but England everywhere preserves the right faith. [3] I accordingly bequeath the good things said by my writings about this matter to good readers wherever they may be, and I bequeath the bad things to the bad.

As I seek for followers of Christ among the prelates [I find that] none of the rule[4] remains which used to be in force [10]. Christ was poor, [5] but they are overloaded with gold. He used to make peace, but they now wage war. Christ was generous, but they are as close as a money-box. Work occupied Him, but plentiful rest pampers them. Christ was gentle, but they are violent. He suffered humbly, but they

---

There are the cleric, the knight, and the peasant, the three carrying on three [different] things. The one teaches, the other fights, and the third tills the fields. First let us see what the cleric is. Behold, the whole world is now stunned by his example. The schism of today shows plainly that there are two popes, one a schismatic and the other the proper one. France favors the schismatic and declares that he ought to be revered, but England everywhere preserves the right faith. [3] I accordingly bequeath the good things said by my writings about this matter to good readers wherever they may be, and I bequeath the bad things to the bad [10*].

Every rule[4] of Christ rejects the delights of the world, but prelates now sin in this respect. Christ was poor, [5] but they are overloaded with gold. He suffered humbly, but they wish to be superior. Christ was meek, but their empty showiness makes them arrogant. He used

---

There are the cleric, the knight, and the peasant, the three carrying on three [different] things. The one teaches, the other fights, and the third tills the fields. First let us see what the clergy are. Behold, the whole world cleaves to them and shuns the rest of us. Evidently, prelates prefer to be waited upon first, for the pathway of learned men ought to be quite secure. I observe how much they teach with their moral words, but their deeds are not in harmony with what they say. Jesus undertook to do well and teach afterwards, [6] but that fashion does not continue now among prelates [10**]. He was poor, but they are overloaded with gold. He used to make peace, but they wage wars. Christ was generous, but they are as close as a money-box. Work occupied Him but plentiful rest pampers them. He was meek, but they rage more furiously than fire. He suffered humbly, but they wish to

desire to be superior. Christ was compassionate, but they seek after vengeance. He endured His torments, but fear of such torment puts them to flight. Christ was a virgin; they are rarely chaste. He is a good shepherd, but they devour the flock of sheep [20]. Christ was outspoken, but they make use of fawning words. Christ was righteous; they are more shifting than the wind. He took a stand against evils; they are quite tolerant of them. They sing out the praises of Christ's fast-days on a full stomach. Christ asked for water; they drink choice wines, and they replenish their bellies with as many sumptuous delicacies as the mind can conceive of. The food takes to their belly, and their belly similarly takes to the food, provided that Venus may stand at their side, once their gluttony has been pleasantly sated [30]. [7]

---

to make peace but they now wage war. Christ was compassionate, but they seek after vengeance. Piety rendered Him gentle, but wrath moves them frequently. Christ was outspoken, but they make use of fawning words. Christ was righteous, but they look to nothing except their own desires [20*]. Christ was trustworthy, but they are more shifting than the wind. He took a stand against evils; they are quite tolerant of them. Christ was a virgin; they are rarely chaste. He is a good shepherd, but they devour the flock of sheep. They sing out the praises of Christ's fast-days on a full stomach. They are clothed with soft garments, and He was barefoot. And what more sumptuous dishes could they provide themselves with, as if they were performing sacrifice at a festival of Bacchus. The food takes to their belly, and their belly similarly takes to the food, provided that Venus now stand at their side, once their gluttony has been pleasantly sated [30*]. [7]

---

be superior. He was compassionate, but they pursue vengeance. He bore his torments, but fear of such torments puts them to flight. He was a virgin; scarcely a one of them is chaste. He is a good shepherd, but they devour the fold [20**]. He was outspoken, but they make use of fawning words. He was righteous; they are more shifting than the wind. He took a stand against evils; they are quite tolerant of them. They sing out the praises of Christ's fast-days on a full stomach. He asked for water, they drink choice wines and they replenish their bellies with as many sumptuous delicacies as the mind can conceive of. The food takes to their belly, and their belly similarly takes to the food, provided that Venus may stand at their side, once their gluttony has been pleasantly sated [30**]. [7]

Christ refused whole kingdoms for Himself upon the mountain, yet
nothing is pleasing to these men except worldly glory. He used to be
completely simple in His way of life, and now the prelate thinks that
riches are his own way of life. Their wealth and their passionate greed
for it have grown large, and even though they possess a very great
deal, they seek after more. They once used to meditate upon the law
of God, and because of this, the Lord showed His face to them. Now a
greater respect for dignities has made its way into their minds; these
worthies obtain their due reward, yet everything is not enough for them
[40]. [8] One's worth is now in his wealth; property confers honors, [9]
and abject poverty is an object of utter reproach. When a rich man
speaks, [10] then every ear will pay attention, but the words of a poor
man are worth nothing. The intelligence of the wise man is as nothing,
if he is without property; worldly property now outweighs what one says
in significance. Even though he were to speak with the tongue of a Cato,
he will nevertheless be a fool; even though a rich man knows nothing,
he will nevertheless be wise. In their eyes, poverty in any man is con-
temptible, even though the man himself were worthy [50]; and in their
judgment, a rich man is not wicked, even though he is of an evil nature.
Without property there are no attainments, there is no true faith, no
gracefulness of speech, no originality of wit, no uprightness. Where
there is property there is an abundance of good sense. But no poor
man possesses wisdom; even if he were wise, he is still nothing but a
poor man. We reject the man whom the world rejects; and may perdition take him when he perishes. But we acclaim that man as worthy
whom the world's bounty has brought to worldly riches [60]. And so
the world is inwardly preferred by prelates, even while God Himself is
still outwardly represented by them.

We praise the years gone by, but we nevertheless waste away our
own. [11] The old way of life does not sustain our course. In those days
mortal sin had not driven Justice to flight. Now that she has been
violated, she has abandoned the earth to heaven. [12] Happy souls
used to shun this world, and their whole concern was to ascend into the
mansions on high. Neither Venus nor the vine used to weaken those
lofty spirits, which inwardly sought after God [70]. But now in these
modern times you can behold many spirits which conduct themselves
haughtily, quite apart from Christ's esteem. They now cater to their
fat, snug bodies; but such are not the delights born of true faith. These
pompous fellows declare openly that only the delights [found] under the
semblance of false piety, rather than the gentle rule of God, are satisfactory to them. [Nevertheless,] prelates suffer so many things for
the rewards of faith that we therefore are to reckon them as holy men.

Chapter 2

Here he speaks of those prelates who live luxuriously and yearn
immoderately for things of the flesh.

Behold, Thomas' post still exists, but his deeds no longer do,
and Martin's gentle rule has almost vanished [80]. [1] So the one who
used to be a shepherd is now a hireling; because he has fled, the wolf
is scattering the flock everywhere. The prelate does not strike off its
head with his sword, and he is not hardy enough to subdue his delicate
body with a close-fitting hair shirt. He now serves potted meats[2] for
his courses, and he prefers onions and leeks to manna. Alas! Such
are the people the bosom of the Church now nourishes--people who seek
after earthly vanities instead of things divine. The potted meats represent their carnal actions, which sensual desire enkindles in the flesh of
the clergy, so to speak [90]. [3] The blood-relations of the flesh are lust,
boastfulness, arrogance, ambition, envy, drunkenness, contentious-
ness, and deceit. Once the belly has been sated, the harlot flesh longs
to enjoy the lust of the flesh, and it seeks out the chambers of lust. So
as long as a wrongful affection for the belly is dominant in these men,
they are unable to reach the height of virtue.

Passion, idleness, abundance of food, and persistent impiety
overthrew Sodom. Beware of these things, prelate. But no matter
what the prelates say to my ears, the law still governs them according
to their own whim [100]. If they please the world and furnish things
pleasing to the flesh, then the virtue of the soul will rarely be pleasing
to them. When the feast has been spread and the wine has been poured
out in gold, [4] then the drinking goblet is in greater esteem than the
communion cup. Boasting of his table, the vain man does not hide his
golden flagons, from which he might enjoy a vain honor. His hall is
open to one and all, and viands load his table, and he indulges in entirely too much food and drink. [5] His long retinue of hangers-on is
beaming in the face, and their clothes glitter; the whole crowd is ready
for a slight nod from their host [110]. Yet the huge table is scarcely
enough for their "moderate" appetite, and the hall rings with calls for
the servants. These feasts are got up only for the rich and nobody else,
and a poor man cannot get a seat at one. And so their empty piety is
overcome by their greedy appetite. [6] "As long as the honor is ours,
the shame is not to be thought of. "[7]

And so the gluttonous prelate takes it upon himself to praise

Christ's fasting, yet he does nothing of the kind himself. But whatever land, sea, and air provide for his vice, his riotous hunger searches for it and gets it [120]. [8] His hungering soul wastes away, and his voluptuousness of the flesh stuffs the gullet in his throat to excess. So with his full belly, he is contented by big banquets all day, but at night he finds his pleasure among harlots. And when Bacchus has reddened both the sot's cheeks, Venus raises up his blind courage[9] with her goading. Such is this man's remarkable virtue, such is his blessed life, that when he has been feasted with delicacies, he lies with a prostitute. Anyone whom a bed warms with unchaste delights does not fear the chills of Acheron [130]. So he revels in the many pleasures of voluptuousness and caters constantly to his own desires. And so he wastes his life's empty hours, blissful in his play, lust, wine, and drowsiness. He does not realize that his body, which now feeds and pampers itself in so many ways, may feed an everlasting fire.

Chapter 3

Here he speaks of those prelates who yearn for worldly wealth, revel in the honor of authority, and want a bishopric not so that they may be helpful, but so that they may be autocratic. [1]

No honest man can serve two masters. [2] Nevertheless, the prelate in office does serve two: he says he is the servant of the Eternal King, yet he serves an earthly king and waits attendance upon him [140]. Peter was the bearer of the keys to heaven, but this fellow demands the keys to a king's treasure for himself. [3] Thus it is that the "devout" man is [now] grasping and the "meek" is haughty; and a man who is far too much attracted by this earth is "heavenly." In such a way will he keep a firm grasp on both Christ and the world—Christ will be his friend, but the world will be even more friendly. The question is often bandied among prelates as to which of them is more important, but there is no question aired as to which is better. Even if their outer appearance of goodness is conspicuous in the eyes of the world, they rarely possess it in the depths of their heart [150].

God has declared that whatever is helpful is our duty, but wrath is driving us into harmful controversies. I wish to be just, but I am being transformed into anger, and this ensuing anger is destroying my good principles. I castigate the flesh, I uphold the wretched, but in consequence of this my growing vainglory is robbing me of my goodness. [4] God's wrath denies any worthy reward to this passion for worldly praise and anger. And so my virtue is turned into a vice, with the result that the world rejoices while Christ passes out of esteem [160].

In former times holy orders demanded that a churchman do good, but now it is held proper to seek after a mitre that wields authority. When people were sinful, God's wrath used to abate, and He was unmindful of wickedness because of the priest's prayers. But now our Moses does not raise his hands in supplication, and in consequence Amalek harasses us with his sword. When Moses raised his hands, victory fell to Joshua; and when he lowered them, Joshua turned back, beaten by the enemy. [5] Similarly, the prelate, invoking heaven with his hands, tears, and prayers, instantly protects his people from their enemy [170]. But if the priest falls asleep, overcome with drowsiness, then the people fall subject to the vices of frivolity. Yet anyone can see, in Moses' prayers, what fruits the humble devotion of a just man may gain.

He who is a good shepherd is moved by pity for his flock and bears the responsibility for the sheep on his own shoulders. Even though he is free of any taint, he ascribes the shortcomings of his charges to himself. But Christ does not acknowledge that any offence has shifted over to him; rather, it is only among his charges that he is said to be at fault [180]. He does not cause his people to go astray, but on the contrary he takes their wrongdoings upon himself in order to do away with them. Yet people now say that there is a kind of priest in the world who teaches doing this but still does not do it. [6] Certainly a man who vitiates himself through his own transgressions rarely becomes another's salvation by his efforts. One who has given his all to the cherishing of this world cannot render any profitable service to his chosen God.

A priest is obligated to care for his needy flock in the world. When he sees its taints he should cleanse[7] them [190]. But if a priest knows that some important personages are tainted, he does not dare cleanse them, for he is afraid. [8] If others sin, what of it, as long as they can pay for it? And so the guilty man and woman are tortured by means of their purse. The priest drains the pockets of his flock and drags it among the thistles of lawsuits so that its fleece will be pulled out by them. The priest's new-fangled decisions declare that because the body has sinned, the sinner's purse should pay. [9] So in these days repeated lust means profits in the account book. One's sins are in arrears until his purse is opened [200]. When a man's treasure chest is full enough, his lust may have its fill; [10] the treasure chest's spawn renders the law subject to you. So it is fear and money that pay for sins. The whole business lies in their hands. In such fashion does the priest temper his vows for the sake of gain, and nod approval to our persevering in evil ways. He serves Mammon for tainted money, [11] but he does not help us to gain the kingdom of heaven.

[12]Nowadays a judge rages with anger if there is any downright wantonness and he does not know whom to hold guilty of unchastity[210]. If a reckless layman copulates with a reckless woman, the priest shouts out in church, and she trembles with fear. Yet if a cleric sinfully indulges in sexual intercourse, nothing is thought of it, for he himself may be both judge and party to his own case. In such fashion do these popular gods thwart the laws of the Almighty, yet if they render a decision in regard to me, I am guilty according to it. And in such fashion do they weigh other men down under a heavy burden, but how lightly the burden sits on their own shoulders! The woman taken in adultery was discharged; by this, Christ taught us to follow the example of forgiveness [220]. [13] But a purse of gold does not atone for such a crime; rather, a contrite spirit is the remedy. But nowadays there are no tears which can wash away a crime, if one's purse is ignorant of the law in respect to it. The purse can wipe out sin and can clear us from punishment. The purse is as strong as our court of law.

Chapter 4

Here he speaks of their positive laws. Although these are not necessary for the betterment of the soul, they nevertheless place countless stipulations heavily upon us almost daily, for their own profit. [1]

Christ does not grant me indulgence for wicked works, does He? I think not. Instead, He shows mercy after the deed is done. Or, does Christ declare something as forbidden which is not a sin? He does no such thing [230]. But now with their new decrees they declare a great many things as prohibited which the law neither of Christ nor of Moses prohibits. But if I were to pay out to them, they would pardon tomorrow what they pronounce sins today. Therefore I have a question on these matters. Either a thing is a sin in itself because, strictly speaking, it commits sin, or it is not wrong except for the fact that it is forbidden. If it is a sin, then why is it better to allow me, because of my money, to do that very thing before it is done? If it is something permissible, then why does their positive law conclude it is the more stringently to be condemned [240]? I do not think this arises from a sense of justice; instead their whim declares that there is money to be made by attacking in such fashion. The man who judges cases justly, with a zeal not for money but for God, performs a just deed. I believe it is fitting to bind by the laws of the Church anything in the world that is bound by them with just cause. [2] But God approves of nothing unjust, so another cannot assert what God Himself denies. Behold, Simon[3] is trying to fly higher and higher; he cannot be much afraid of falling down again [250].

The gentle Christ did not come to entangle the path of man; He pointed out the strait way. [4] We, on the other hand, contrive difficulties out of something simple and harshness out of something mild, and we deal in wickedness in place of piety. Christ's law, to be sure, was the kind which His grace rendered welcome, but our positive law is strict in its penalties. Christ's simple precepts are set down and contained in a few words; hence, His yoke provides only a gentle burden. [5] But the endless condemning on the part of our law is aggravating and scarcely has any end [260]. Christ's law is quite generous to men, but under our law no mercy is freely given without money. Everything happens through cause. [6] Thus it is that positive law, which the clergy has established, represents a big business. [7]The more birds the fowler tries to catch, the more nets he wants to spread; the more the clergy increases the number of positive laws, the more severe the people's pathway in this world becomes. For the more we walk through a tight place, the more quickly we are [apt to be] thrown to the ground when our foot slips, and trampled on there by the clergy [270]. When the clergy holds more of the world subject to itself, then the Church will make more profit here on earth. The richer the clergy is, the prouder it becomes because of it, and makes its laws according to its whim. The sun denotes the Church and the moon represents the congregation, but their guardians now do neither the one nor the other. [8] They are people who preserve neither the teachings of the Old Testament nor the new ones which Christ added to them. In former times a steadfast priest was spotlessly pure, helpful among the people, and very worthy in the sight of God [280]. But nowadays if he can grasp this vain world, praise from the lips of the people or of God is nothing to him.

123

Here he speaks of the churchmen who possess the world's temporal goods and neglect the spiritual.

[1] That angelic voice in the skies which once terrified Rome now is heard anew by our world. In the time of Sylvester, the same time when Constantine conferred earthly gifts upon him for his Church, the angel said, "Poison is now spreading within the Church. God's earthly dwelling-place is becoming worldly." And it was as the angel said: after possessions under the ownership of the clergy had heaped up, the poison stuck to it [290]. So now each of them is fond of his own gains, and because of his strong temptations he thinks that anything profitable belongs to him. As long as they care about adding lands to their monasteries[2] the laws of the Church are nothing to them. They are always hungering for this world and in turn the name alone of the Church is sufficient for them. It is known that the angelic order contains dominions and powers, and you see this likewise on earth. For since the clergy cannot join with them in rank, it makes a hierarchy for itself on earth [300]. So, since the prelate is in doubt as to how to get to heaven, he wants to enjoy the honors of this world for sure.

Christ said to Pilate that His kingdom was not of this world, [3] but the bishop does not follow Him now. Rather, they all wish to acquire the very opposite kingdoms and to wage war among men for them. They are not willing to battle with pagans in the cause of their faith, nor even spread the gospel according to the Holy Scripture. But if one were to oppose them in regard to their worldly kingdoms, they then put up a savage fight, Christian in least measure [310]. [4] And so, because the clergy is apart from Christ and takes up worldly quarrels, the Church is lacking in justice. Christ says, "By their fruits ye shall know them,"[5] and that precept is quite true. No matter how the clergy disguises its positive law, it will be chosen as witness for its deeds in public. Peter's shadow healed the sick; [6] neither our light nor our voice nor our prayer is worthy of rendering any assistance. Peter crossed over the calmed waters with dry feet; [7] the waves now drown our faith [320]. According to Christ's law we are ordered to reform a man who persecutes us through our prayers. Nevertheless, in accordance with our new-fangled positive law, we godlessly threaten him with the vengeance of the sword. Thus we destroy those whom we are obligated to raise up, and we lose whatever gifts Christ brought us. "Vengeance is mine,"[8] God says, but since the Pope is God on earth, let him vindicate himself first. [9]

Here he tells how Christ bestowed and bequeathed peace to His
disciples. But he says that because of their positive laws,
churchmen now institute and carry on wars even against Christians, for the sake of worldly goods.

Before the time of His death, Christ bestowed and bequeathed
peace to His disciples [330]. And since they loved nothing except
Christ alone, they dutifully suffered everything in the peace of Christ.
But since men now love worldly vanities to such an extent, the world
furnishes them wars which are for their own benefit. And since the
clergy now leads a warlike life, God the author of peace does not assist them. Christ said to Peter, "Whosoever of men taketh up the
sword shall finally perish with the sword."[2] I maintain that Christ's
meaning cannot be misinterpreted, no matter how destructive the
clergy's sword may be to it [340]. They strike with the sword; if anyone strikes back, the positive law of some new book damns him for it.
Peter preached, of course, but today's Pope fights. The one seeks
souls, the other greedily seeks riches. The first was killed for God's
law, the second kills, and yet God maintains no such law as that. The
one arouses faith through his innocence, not by force; the other rouses
armies on parade.
God wishes that our complaining be not rash, but may God avenge
the evils which we are now suffering [350]. We have conquered enemy
battle lines and hostile tongues, for the reason that vindictive anger is
foreign to our ways. Christ's behavior was not put to the test in times
of ease; His profound faith proved itself in times of stress. The gentle
patience which struggled within Christ in His sorrow surely contains
grounds for high esteem in our time. Christ was patient while suffering every abuse, but we of today become angry at the least little thing.
Its every labor prospered until the higher clergy forsook everything
under God's jurisdiction [360]. The piety in days of old used to implant faith, but our vindictive anger now uproots the proud deeds of
our forefathers. As David bore witness, "The sword does not save,
and he who shall put his trust in the bow is not saved thereby."[3] But
we are at variance with David's teaching as long as the hand of the
priest is armed with a sword. The ark was Moses' strength in days of
old, but our strength is the drawn bow, [4] which strikes down the people
of the world. God established the ark of the covenant in heaven so that
it might be there as a sign of peace to all mankind [370]. [5] On the other
hand, as long as we here on earth draw our long bow, it constitutes a
sign of bloodshed, with peace in exile. God saves those whom He

wishes to, but our clergy will be saved with weapons, persisting in the behavior of a knight.

[6]Behold, O Christ, Thou Who hast bound up Satan with Thy mighty power, we of the clergy have released him again. Now that he is released he has released all bondsmen, so that no one happens to render[7] his devotions to God. The monk does not know his abbot, and the monasteries in their present kind of order cannot even hold a prior in check [380]. Meanwhile the priest, ready for arms, holds on to a prostitute with his right hand and a sword with his left. Who in the world is better attested than such a fellow as being powerfully armed in order to fight well? At a time when nature urges copulation, every beast readily starts a fight because of its frenzied passion. But if this is the cause of the priest taking up arms, then war will last forever, far indeed from peace.

It is not the function of a knight to offer sacrifice at the altar, nor that of a priest to carry on wars of state [390]. If it is good for the clergy to win triumph for itself in battle, then what good are the deeds of a valiant[8] knight? We see the clergy fighting, which ought to be praying. They have a care for wars, not of souls. Why should the very man who dealt you one wound after another be called your physician? And a physician should not add ailment upon ailment, should he, so that your inner health flees farther away? Nature in her wisdom teaches this, that every medicine in the world by which I am made weaker is bad medicine [400]. If those who ought to restore peace practice war, I do not know how one can safely enter upon the path of peace. It is said that the fortune of any affair is known by its end, and that in doubtful affairs the test of one's actions is their outcome. [9] But God knows what sort of an end there will be for the wars of the clergy, or what fortune will follow.

Chapter 7

Here he speaks of how the clergy ought to be gentle and patient in the love of God and neighbor, and not warlike.

Virtue is always greater amidst adversity, [1] and behold, a light is wont to be brighter in the dark. Patience is a noble way of conquering; he who is patient conquers; if you wish to conquer, learn to be patient [410]. [2] Christ himself is your shield-bearer and standard-bearer if you are honest and act patiently. Others are ordered to fight with sword in hand, with weapons; it behooves us to fight with faith, hope, and compassion. The enemy of righteousness can do nothing

126

against a servant of the Lord. When he defends his position his cause will favor him. So when you have been imbued with righteous principles, then you can drive off your enemies by means of them. You may rout the enemies' missiles with the spears of Scripture, provided that you are well girded with heavenly virtues against the foe [420]. Isaiah together with Jeremiah shall battle in our behalf, and Joel together with Daniel, David with Samuel. The law of the Gospel, the voice of Paul, the word of the prophet are my three witnesses of whence is our salvation. [3]

David considered founding a temple to the Lord, but he heard from the Lord, "Thou shalt not be a builder, thou art a man of blood. Because thou art stained with blood, thou canst not build a temple worthy of me." He who sheds blood and embraces the sins of the world amidst warring is not fit to be a temple of God [430]. Such a man does not erect a sanctuary for Holy Church, nor does he establish a dwelling-place for holy faith. [4] For hatred is death, as the Scriptures say, and he who hates his brothers is his own murderer. [5] Then how can we, stained with the blood of the people, be servants of God's altar? Christ wishes life for the sinner, and that he not die, but be converted so that he may live for God. [6] Yet for the sake of the things of this world, we slaughter with the sword those whom Christ's blood made live [440]. Christ decreed what the laws of dutiful love were and asked nothing of the world for Himself except our hearts--not our heart's blood, but rather the spirit which loving affection preserves; and He claims that these are His laws. We, on the other hand, demand the surrender of the flesh-and-blood heart, because our wrath is so very fierce. I do not know whether we can conquer the world by such carnage; I do maintain this: it is repellent to God. For God abhors the church of an evildoer, and allows nothing to prosper under such a hand [450].

The faith of Christ and inner love of one's brother lend strength to those who know how to conquer the world. Brotherly love establishes peace, preserves agreement, binds friendships, and makes faith endure. Brotherly love does not know thirst for the possessions of others, nor does it ever demand things that are its own, nor how to keep its own. Brotherly love asks neither to vex nor to be vexed; it does not complain nor cause a man to complain. [7] The clergy wrongfully avenges its troubles by increasing suffering, and as long as it does battle, God Himself opposes it [460]. Profane love afflicts all men at every opportunity, but the hand of God preserves its own from their enemies. [8] Fear of God is prime wisdom, [9] the prime way of salvation, the prime light which brings prime rewards. Fear [of God] embraces love in a lasting alliance, and love unites this fear to itself in a similar alliance. The one virtue cannot be without the other, for fear and love are reckoned as the same. He is our Father, hence there is love for Him; He

127

is our judge, hence He is to be feared. And this fear and love bring many rewards [470]. It is not the fear of a slave but of a son, and it does not occasion begging, but instead provides[10] many recompenses for mankind.

Every man who loves Christ fears Him; he who fears [Him] does not commit an outrage by which he provokes God. This love inspires a man to catch a glimpse of heaven and it condemns the pleasures of the world as vain. It is therefore amazing how the discord among the clergy is not settled through the power of this love. Holy Writ teaches that all love of virtue is pleasing, and that worldly, ambitious honor is not [480]. Indeed, the world is a hindrance to those who love it, and in the end they get little profit from it. The Levites in the Old Testament had no lands, yet the world did not tempt them. [11] It is for God alone, and not another's concern, to attend to peace for the people. Therefore it is not good to engage in the earth's battles, since God is gentle and loves the blessings of peace.

Chapter 8[1]

Here he discusses further how it is in no way proper for churchmen to wage war impatiently against a Christian people. Instead, they should conquer all the world's evil only through their prayers and God's help, and without the impetus of anger.

As I ponder over my thoughts with meditation, dumbfoundment overwhelms me as to how merciful Christ's doctrine was [490]. Truly, Christ's example has taught us everything about peace, and our own cupidity brings on whatever war there is. Reason asks me how there should be a single warrior among the clergy, and rightly makes objection. [2] There are many reasons that it should not be like that, and Christ offers many instructions for guidance in this matter. And even if it should seem necessary [for the clergy to turn warrior], even if it is done on behalf of the world, the world's wisdom argues against it. For as long as they were men of peace and not greedy for fame, then this utter peace glorified them [500]. And even if it were proper for worldly men to fight over worldly things, such madness should nevertheless be far removed from the clergy. Things which are helpful to some people prove harmful to others; [3] what makes one man stand erect throws another to the ground. The offices of the clergy are not appropriate for the layman, nor is it seemly for the clergy to take up the layman's weapons.

Let others wage war and let patience rule the clergy. No matter

who may sound trumpets, we ought to be silent. The quicker one de-
sists from each and every victory in war, the greater his glory as a
victor will be [510]. [4] It is of no use for those who can bind all things
by word of mouth to employ force in any way. There is no need of
weapons where a hallowed voice is triumphant. [5] War is nothing to the
man who conquers through prayers. God enriched the clergy with such
a great gift that it is enough for it to offer solemn supplications with
its voice. Let him who wishes peace for himself remain quietly at
peace. The world does not oppress the man whom God helps. If by
chance you inquire of me, I am bound to answer that wars are designed
for the man who is a warrior [520]. O what a hard end impatience
comes to! A hasty retreat from it is apt to be troublesome. [6] As I see
it, rashness is disgracefully troublesome in those unrighteous ones
whom God's own righteousness rules over. Foolish vexation harms a
foolish man in many ways, and in the end he pays for his shame with
his own head. And when a man seeks to set his own powers over those
of Christ, and believes that war is stronger than His, then he will be
that much weaker; and just when he thinks he is winning he soon falls
in defeat [530].

Balaam wanted to complete his journey, but his ass, which saw
things of a divine nature, delayed on the way, even though beaten with
whips. [7] Similarly, if man is dominated by a headstrong will, the result negates the usefulness of his work. No matter in how many ways
human affairs may change, [8] experiencing a thing to the end everywhere
shows this: affairs clearly show by their outcome how great danger
can arise from the slightest cause. [9] In times of adversity there is
need for strong leadership, and it is wrong to rush our steps during
the midst of troubles [540]. [10] The wise Cato commands that we act
more calmly during hardships, [11] for haste makes waste. [12] How often
Fortune works in devious ways; [13] the patient man will accomplish
more than impetuous folly can. The clergy rightly teaches these
things, but behold, while it preaches to others, it acts just the opposite,
as if it were blind.

Shame now disgraces the learned man to whom sin is repugnant,
and he will have no praise for long. Nothing can free us of disgrace
except worldly prosperity, of which we have obviously had too much
for a long time now [550]. We have small talent for happiness, [14] and
our blind greed does not allow us to see things clearly. Riches de-
lude the foolish man time and again and cause him to be even more
greedy. In days gone by what sweet repose there was for the faultless
clergy! Now bitter anxiety is its teacher. The pleasure to be found in
chance happiness is greatly to be feared, [15] and often plunges the light-
hearted into vice. No one can see how easy the fall and how near the
ruin from chance happiness [560]. [16]

An inclination contented with little should not think of that little

129

as insignificant; only after the event does a thing show what it really was before. Nor should anyone esteem anything as great, lest by chance he lose it at some time. And rash people whom no cautiousness ever hinders should be wary, lest some violence hasten them toward their damnation. [17] More experience with reality will teach the clergy that worldly concerns are of no value. The vain man who shines with brilliant honor, and does not know what the heavy responsibility of honor is, resembles the beasts of burden [570]. It is an honor in the sight of God, I think, when pride does not vex the spirit, but instead keeps God's righteous laws. "He that is not with me is reckoned as against me; and he that gathereth not with me scattereth abroad."[18] These are the words of God, and positive law neither adds to nor takes away from the force of His law.

Chapter 9

Here he discusses the fact that just as it is not right for temporal lords to usurp control in spiritual matters, so it is not right for prelates of the clergy to undertake wars and temporal matters of that kind, which worldly pride and avarice bring about.

The signet ring and the pastoral staff are under the authority of the Pope. He possesses them as a spiritual symbol. And Caesar's[1] sceptre signifies the honor of the world as his, so that the affairs of the world are in part subject to him, as it were [580]. In caring for souls the Pope condemns them or gives [eternal] life; but Caesar rules their bodies, which are subject to his law. It is not allowable for Caesar to torture souls, nor does that concern belong under his power. Nor is it right that the Pope harass men's bodies with wars, for that business does not pertain to him. Let each do the work for which he came—at least he who bears the chief responsibility. The one who has souls under his care is higher, and his superior rank will glorify him [590]. Whatever the Pope does is permissible, as his office indicates. The person [may] make a mistake, but not the office. For his holy state transcends the world, and his right hand bears the keys of heaven. Hence he can open the heavens and shut the foul pit of hell. Things both above and below revere his laws. What he fetters is bound and what he releases shall be free, such power does he hold over our souls. [2]

The law requires that the things which are Caesar's be rendered unto Caesar and that the things which are God's be rendered unto God [600]. [3] It is Caesar's right that you should bow your head to him,

and you should bow your soul to the Pope; in this way you render each
his due. Caesar cannot have the rank of Pope, nor can the Pope assume Caesar's command for himself. It is not Caesar's place to tam-
per with spiritual matters, nor is it right that the Pope bear the arms
of a Caesar. Let the Pope keep what is his and Caesar what is his,
so that their duly established rights may endure equally for both. If
Caesar should usurp papal rights for himself, the Pope is not to allow
this, but is to resist it [610]. Therefore, what is a war which is
Caesar's to the Pope? For the God of the Church was a lover of peace.
But because the Pope seeks for the world through force of arms, he
will therefore find the same kind [of a world] he is looking for. If you
put a question to the world, it will answer, and it will give you back
the very thing which you propose to it.

The Church used to make the faithful secure, but in its impatience it now kills them through force of arms. The peasant loves the
farmer, the knight a man who carries on a hard fight, and the sailor
the pilot of the ship wandering uncertainly [620]. [4] Christ loves peace,
and peace claims the clergy as its own, and accordingly the clergy
ought to keep its members gentle. It is base to retreat and not stand
firm with steadfast foot; it is base to desert a ship in distress. [5] It is
even baser for them to declare that there is to be war in place of peace,
and to do away with Christ's laws just for the sake of this world. Almost all the realms which Christ's name fills carry on wars more
frightful than the treacherous Getans. [6] But it should be quite enough
that laymen have wars, were it not for the fact that the clergy strikes
with its own sword [630]. No matter what the laymen may do, I can
excuse the clergy even less, which Christ's rule of peace binds. But
because Christ has been put aside, the goods and chattels of the world,
which are as fleeting as shadows, are the cause of infamous battles.

The clergy claims to have under its jurisdiction whatever is done
among mankind in the realm of the spiritual. And it claims this by
right of the sword, yet its glory is higher than worldly concerns. Thus
the clergy now has two wings on which it flies, but it likes its worldly
wing better [640]. Thus the seeds of the stinging nettle are mingled
[with] pepper, [7] as long as the clergy of the world cleave to it like a
bridegroom. And as long as the haughty clergy mingle with the greedy
world, so that the people grieve, [hope of] salvation becomes feebler.
It is not enough for them to harass peaceful people, but they even distress Almighty God with their battles. It is written, "Thou shalt not
kill," but no one can find a safe place left in the world. Tell us, then,
where there is justice for us. Do you not know what to hold fast to in
the midst of such transitory concerns [650]?

[8]The lineal descent by right of His mother proclaims Christ as
the heir of the land in which He was born. If any of this world ought to
be our property, it should be Christ's part, which is made over to Him

by legal title. But a pagan interloper holds it now, and he pays no tribute into our treasury for it. But we do not carry on war against these men by attacking either their persons or their property. Our law is silent about this. No bull admonishes us about this, and no sweeping condemnation spurs us on, nor does our sword do battle [660]. "Let Christ Himself claim whatever things there are His, if He wants them; let Him fight for His own property. We are not interrupting our leisure for wars so far away, and not even an envoy is going there on behalf of Christ's portion. Instead we are fighting open battles over worldly possessions with our brothers, whom the water of baptism indicates as reborn."

Christ's mandate is that the clergy preach and thereby win their spiritual reward. [9] I do not read that the clergy should take up arms for worldly gain, but that it should refrain from that for love of God [670]. But the sermons of the clergy take no cognizance of the pagans in order to convert them, and it does not use its wealth for that purpose. Rather, it acquires castles and buildings and cities for itself, thus rejecting the things of the spirit which rightly belong to it, and slumbering unbecomingly where it ought to be vigilant. But it appropriates those worldly possessions which Christ nevertheless said were inappropriate for Him. And in appropriating these inappropriate things and rejecting the appropriate ones, the clergy disavows the actions which God has prescribed [680]. "Indeed, the prince of this world has come and he gets our services, since he pays big money. Our greedy spirit abhors Christ's poverty lest it disturb our bodily idleness, and His patient humility does not delight our hearts, for our haughty pride rejects this. Nothing restrains us except our own free will, and our feeble flesh controls its reins."

It is the author of the law which seems to spurn the law, and he does not keep to the paths which he preaches are his own [690]. He who is first taken in sin condemns sins, [10] and in corrupting others he commits even worse sins. One who wishes to know the faults of others should know his own, and make amends for what his sinfulness contrives. The one who bears Peter's keys in order to open the gates of heaven is the first to close them to men on earth. The more I think about this the more dumbfounded I am, for his shadow drives away anything that his light reveals. One man's greedy appetite has corrupted many thousands, and everything is tainted with a bad smell because of him [700]. O leader, sitting in high triumph with exalted pride, threatening much with look, eye, voice, and hand: malice pursues [you], and a bitter mob of hangers-on, and a sickly state of affairs, the black plague, and harsh pestilence. And that piety which used to remit our sins is now an avenger, avariciously seeking for transitory riches.

How grievous a pestilence, how wretched is the name of pride,

the root of sin, the fount and origin of evil! It has been the source of
wickedness, the cause of all suffering, the distress of virtue, a leap
dropping down to the pit of hell [710], the friend of avarice, extravagant
poverty, the beginning of fraud, false sentiment, wicked lust, restless-
ness of mind, impending strife, the mistress of death, a treacherous
spirit, devious reasoning, and empty honor. These are the properties
of a proud character, so to speak, and the master of hell is considered
first among such. He ushered in this capital evil, by which means he
rules every wretched head, and makes it the equivalent of his own
tail. [11] Man, the head of all things, was constrained to gratify his
vices, and freely learned to bear this yoke [720]--not that of the Lord,
which is said to be mild, [12] but rather the one which this invidious
enemy has placed upon him; not the yoke under which the freedom of
salvation is sought, but that which weighs heavily in a slavish fashion.
The first handiwork [of God], the first ornament, endowed with the
glory of pre-eminence, was the object of the first fall. Alas! Tell
me what the cause is of such a great catastrophe. The workings of a
proud mind were the source of it. O what haughty spirit, what dire
presumption, to occupy the place of the king of heaven, to be on a par
with one's judge [730], to set oneself up to be one's maker's equal, to
match God and not imitate Him, and not follow Him virtuously! In the
light of such examples it behooves us to rid ourselves of pride and to
do our duty with humble heart. Put aside uncertainty; hold it as certain that Christ's way was one of peace, and that He waged no wars.
If the head of the Church strays from its sacred course, see how the
sinfulness of the head makes the members sinful.

[In former times] the priesthood did not wage wars in the name of
Christ, but used to suffer dutifully [740]. Even though they were tortured with cudgels, they refused to torture anyone; and as long as they
acted patiently, they were victorious over everything. They conquered
evil with good, for Christ was their leader and granted the just petitions
of these righteous men. Peter sought spiritual gifts through his
prayers, and so he won his battles by his worthy supplication. This
was a victory for God's right hand; whatever he wished to be was
brought about through his powers. For he governed all things dutifully,
and weighed them with due consideration as he made his devotions [750].
So he who would look forward to Christ's mercy in his meditations
should not be arrogant or easily swayed.

Peter said that he had no silver and gold, but that God gave him
more precious gifts. He told the cripple to rise and he arose; he told
him to walk and go and he walked at once. [13] Now how does this concern us? Indeed, if any man asks us to cure him in this way, we are
no assistance. A haughty spirit does not have a gentle heart with which
it may pray suitably. Instead, God yields to humble prayers [760]. He
who used to be sweet is now spoiled by bitter saltiness, and he who used

133

to bear flowers now lacks genuine flowers. We are magnificent in our gold but destitute of virtue, for we have seen fit to pursue the things which belong to gold. If a person has gold, he evidently has enough, and thus is a man called blessed in this world. Almost all the world pours into the gaping mouth of the clergy, and its jaws devour everything made of gold. But that does not help the poor: not the least drop trickles back, but instead the clergy tenaciously keeps everything for itself [770]. Christ gave Himself as a gift of great value to the people, but we ingrates refuse it what we have.

O ruler of the Church, remember the times of Christ, if you would do things by the examples He furnished. He redeemed and brought back to life the sheep which you mercilessly slaughter with torture. He commanded Peter to forgive until seventy times seven times and to have mercy upon sinners.[14] But you strike with the sword of vengeance at the very first sin and have mercy on no man out of love [780]. Behold, Rachel wept and had no consolation for her grief, when the child of her womb forsook her.[15] O chosen race, O holy people, why is it that you utter harsh slanders in your judgments on the world? Alas! The one who is master of the Church's property, which rightfully belongs to the poor, wastes it in warfare. Alas! Because the justice of mercy is gone from the clergy, the one who should be head of the Church becomes its tail.[16] And health becomes sickness, life becomes death, a lifting up a fall, law a transgression, and the [Holy] Father himself an enemy [790].

Chapter 10

In view of the fact that churchmen write and talk about things pertaining to peace, he here asks how on the contrary they engage in and take charge of things pertaining to war. Afterwards, he himself finally answers this question.

In the books of the clergy of Rome I have seen this written: "Read these writings of ours in order that you may live better. Do you wish to serve God? Do you wish to learn what He demands? Read them, and then you shall know how this is possible. Love God with your mind. Seek, trust, and strive to serve Him." Thus is it ordered to be done, with this clerical book as my witness. "Since life is short, shun all the lusts of the body, and instead choose the gifts of heaven for your soul. Serve justice, let your ways be impartial to all. Do unto others as you would have them do unto you [800].[1] Love the Lord with all your heart, just as you should love your brother with all your soul.[2] Affection

for one's brother assuredly fosters love for God, and divine love flourishes in brotherly love. [3] Bring gifts to the afflicted and you will be
considered as bringing them to Christ; [4] bear no weapons with which
you might do injury, and fight no wars. Be gentle and patient, and let
your moderation be an example of peace to everyone, so that peace
may last the longer." Now that I have read that, I am at once struck
with amazement that I can see strife among the clergy [810]. So I
wanted to ask of the clergy who there might be that could give me a
reasonable explanation. The question was raised, and one churchman
stood up and answered my objections. Suggesting first that he possessed the highest honor of Supreme Pontiff, he said this about them:

[5]"The earthly powers have divided their command with me, and
I guard over the realms subject to the law of heaven. But since the
earth is near us and heaven is far away, [6] we like the earth more, which
is so close [820]. My palace is grand, and distinguished for beautiful
art. My chamber is noble and my couch is soft. I insist upon things
which are pleasant to the taste: I have sumptuous dishes of the best
fare; I drink wine; because it is so enjoyable, I am served food from
every wholesome kind of bird and fish. And for drink I procure every
kind of wine that the grape yields, so that by this means I may never
be thirsty. There are harmonious songs, timbrels, and gay poetry for
me; for me the minstrel renders ditties full of different jests [830].
The better things which earth and sea furnish and which the air provides are ready for me in the market-place, just as I would have them. [7]
I have a vineyard, I have enclosed gardens with a fountain, and I can
procure everything from the world I ask. In the fields which are endowed to me I have a fertile garden, [8] and I have splendid castles and
the highest honor in the city. The woods have brought forth game, and
the air the winged birds I must have, and the sea has filled its waters
with different fish. But such matters are not much to us, and these
creatures do not satisfy us, unless we have gifts of gold money [840].

"See the doors, which the doorkeeper watches with great care
so that no poor man will make his way in. The [papal] court drives
away those of whom it disapproves with this speech: 'Stand outside,
you worthless wretches, shed your tears outside the doors.'[9] The
doorkeeper is to shut out any hand that does not offer gifts and is ignorant of our ways. The man who wishes to be our friend should secretly
give us some gold. Without that, no kind of sacrifice is acceptable.
The hand which is full will be well received; the hand which is empty
should stay outside and be unhonored [850]. I reign with the highest dia-
dem, I free or fetter everything. I am master of the world. What
more could I wish for myself? Every living person worships me and
calls me master. I tread all the earth as if I were a second God. [10]
Our throne is exalted, so that we can give everyone both blessings and
curses with one and the same hand. And so with our power respected

everywhere, we are great within the Church and even greater in the world.

"We speak, and the thing is presently done; we give command, and behold, ready gifts of unexpected value mount up for us [860]. We take over all the kingdoms of this world which Christ refused, [11] and which our domineering vainglory has allowed. Thus we exalted ones have gathered[12] for ourselves everything from the earth that is full of enjoyment. The position we have assumed approves of what we are, because we who torment the earth are punishing idleness. Christ has given us a mild yoke, a light load, but we furnish heavier burdens for the earth. We determine justice for the people, but we are not bound by law. Whatever law I like shall have the force of justice [870]. The fact that I sin here on earth does not pertain to the judgment of men, so those deeds which please me are all permissible for me. And if by chance the world rebels against me in these matters, my hand is the stronger in a fight. For these reasons I as Pope promise that I will turn back in battle all the men on earth.

"A dispute once was created among the Disciples, but the example of a little child pacified their doings. [13] No one, however, could persuade us towards true peacefulness with any kind of moderating influence: our magnificence does not permit it [880]. Christ suffered His death while transfixed on the Cross, and His suffering was man's true salvation. Christ's patience was an example to all that we should be loyal friends to one another. But we consider that patience as a banner of vengeance, and we order vengeance carried on till the death of the people. And so we divert this pious banner away from piety, and what once was life itself is now destruction. Likewise, what once were the emblems of salvation are now the emblems of death, and the Cross which once brought peace now wages war [890]. Thus we carry the Cross of the Lord, but we do not follow the Lord with any of the spirit with which He bore the Cross. From now on our brute strength will make up for what our virtue cannot do. Not moral precept but mortal combat shall provide the way. Our left hand shall crush what our right hand once established; faith which is humble hatches no eggs. [14] We intend to scatter the harvest that others have reaped, and our fierceness shall devour the earth. So the untilled vineyard of the Lord receives none of our labors, and our violence becomes more warlike [900]. The more we are obligated out of piety to draw up the ox, the more fiercely we hurl it down into the pit. [15]

"Judea bears witness to what reward Peter received, and the people make known what treasures Paul received. But we with our gold shall not come empty-handed; the reward which is spiritual is nothing. Whatever the future life may bring, we fear no reproaches now, as long as the world is our friend. Fighting will help bring it about that our name be over every name, which is a rare honor [910]. According

136

to the laws of Mohammed, the man who scorns to hold his name sacred shall perish by the sword. Therefore, we now propose a decree that we shall insist upon by the sword, namely that our name henceforth be preeminent in all the earth. The man who contradicts the Emperor's command in this world is not thought of as his friend. Similarly, the man who does not place our high name in authority is the son of death, adjudged guilty by the edge of the sword.

"Thus we have come to send the world not peace but a sword, [16] and we do everything unheard-of, no matter what the harm [920]. Thus the head now rages against the body's members, and oppresses those whom according to its duty it should least offend. Thus the Father now becomes more like Saturn towards his children; he kills those whom by nature he ought to cherish. [17] Thus the shepherd devours the sheep which he is bound by right to feed, and he preys upon his own sheepfold. Thus we drive the world through fire like a harsh judge, [18] while we enjoy a wealth of fresh air. Let the priest sell his frock and buy a sword, and let every holy order cease its sacred works [930]. Let us magnify our name on earth so that others shall fear wars against themselves in the future. Let the pastoral staff be turned into a spear, and let the mitre become a helmet, and let peace rush[19] to the slaughter. Let the man who wishes to do good do it; we wish to be held in esteem above everyone, and to let others bear the burden.

"Thus we who bear the title of the highest cleric have blindly elected in our heart to pursue violence. Whatever their souls may do, we intend to subdue men's bodies, and positive law helps us [940]. For it is granted without any explanation that our hand take up any sword in order to make warlike assaults with it. So everyone is much afraid to dispute us, whose bold hand strikes hard in battle. But we by no means subject all the heathen nations to our peace, lest we should get hurt by them. We try to fight against Christians, who scarcely dare to assert their rights these days. Peter cut off an ear and Christ healed that wound as sound as it was before [950]. [20] But we lop off the whole head in our anger; we are sure that no one with such a wound returns afterwards to a sound state of health. Therefore our judgment is heavier than Peter's and our sword mightier than his." So the one now called Clement is far from being clement, and he is wrong in keeping this name, for his name lacks a prefix. [21]

Chapter 11

Here he speaks of the churchmen who adopt a holy name for themselves, but nevertheless lay hold of earthly possessions; and they do not help others out of charity by sharing these possessions.

137

[1]An angel, so one reads, spoke to Saint John, because the latter bowed down to worship it at some time or other: "See that thou shouldst not do this to me, the servant of God. Instead worship God with all the honor of thy heart [960]." [To which the Pope replies,] "Even though this celestial being refused such an honor while on earth, our court insists upon it for itself. Hence the knee is bent to us and kisses soothe our foot as if the foot of a second Christ were there."[2]

Christ commands that none of His Disciples seek to take the name of father for himself.[3] The saints in heaven proclaim a saint as one who is steadfastly worthy of their esteem in that kingdom. "We, however, bear both names among the people. 'Hail, O Father, hail, O Saint,' everybody greets us [970]. Great power was given us by Christ, and the world is eager to increase it everywhere. Let that be as it may; no matter who keeps a firm grasp on heaven, we know we can keep a firm enough grasp on the world. For the law, established as eager for war, now declares what the Church can claim by force. But whatever the clergy seizes and keeps from others, no man can take it back from the clergy." The clergy turns whatever it has to its own uses, but it [also] wishes to get its share from the laymen [980]. It declares that all its goods are sanctified and that no layman can lay hand upon them. It demands part of the layman's wealth in everything, but it is unwilling to share his misfortunes. If love were more common, then everything would be in common,[4] so that one man could clearly help another. But since the clergy nowadays has no common affection, it wants to keep whatever it has for itself alone.

According to ancient law a man could not consecrate to God anything plundered from an enemy [990]. But the clergy plunders districts ravaged by our Church, yet it says it holds such property sacred. In this way the clergy mulcts the laity but no one can mulct it, and so a singular kind of justice exists nowadays. The shepherd does not pasture his sheep, but devours their milk and flesh like the wolf itself. Similarly, one who is thirsty for pounds sterling has no appetite for books,[5] but instead construes "mark" in place of the Book of Mark. It is mindful of the man in high place, not God on high, and considers the best wines as more sacred than divine things [1000]. It does not seek the practise of virtue but the love of woman, and with this alone it tries to till the soil.[6] Thus its honor is not without onus, for the body [of the clergy] is resplendent with honor, but that body does not lift a finger concerning its onus.

Here he speaks about simony on the part of churchmen, and how
these voluptuaries claim they are the Church yet lay ever heavier
burdens upon others. In addition, he speaks of how they rashly
attack laymen with dreadful severity over a trifle.

Behold, as God is my witness the man who does not enter the
sheepfold through the door is known by this as a robber and a thief. [2]
And likewise the priest promoted in the Church through simony acts in
this respect like a thief. No one can offer gifts which please Christ by
stealing them; instead, God strikes his hand off for this [1010]. As a
result the [Church's] treasures grow large, but Christ refuses to receive them. Since they are of this world, the world shall keep them.
For as long as the clergy abuses its right, righteousness declares it
deserves to be deprived of it. The clergy calls itself the Church, as if
to say the layman shall not touch it, but on the contrary that is its own
privilege. Thus the arrogance of the clergy does not wish justice done
in the ordinary way, but in a furtive one. It rises up and subdues other
men and preys upon its subjects by means of its new-fangled law [1020].
So I see the pomp and pride of the world hiding under the pretext of
divinity, while God's justice does not endure.
    What is Holy Church except a faithful band of men? Hence it is
evident that the layman whom faith itself protects is a part of the
Church, and that a priest is not his better unless he lives better. [3] Who
would deny this to me? There is one God, one faith, one baptism; [4]
similarly, one Church unites us and holds us together. And just as a
single grain holds much within its hull, so one faith gathers many people together [1030]. Why then does the clergy want to keep the name
of Holy Church for itself, as if it were another God? It hangs the oppressive burden of its law around other people's necks, but is unwilling
to bear any load on its own shoulders. [5] It makes everything permissible for itself but forbidden for me. It takes its leisure, I sweat over
my toil. By its deeds it shows the way vices are committed, but its
words in your ear will sound just the opposite. Hence the bewildered
masses doubt whether they ought to believe first in the clergy's
speeches or its actions [1040]. But while prohibiting something to me
when they ought to be accused of the same thing, I scarcely trust their
words because their actions are guilty. [6] And in such fashion do I behold today's clergy acting proud, although the same faith rendered
those of old quite humble.
    These men order a man to submit by striking him on the jaw, so
that he will endure submission patiently. But if you offer any serious

resistance, they quickly curse your soul with a sentence of death. The man who kills a soul with the death penalty would have destroyed the body first, if he could have [1050]. Similarly, the shepherd does more harm than a cruel wolf by strangling the sheep which he ought to have taken care of. They bear the keys of heaven, but they do not enter themselves, nor do they allow the people whom they lawlessly rule to enter. Nor do they furrow the minds of the people with the plowshare of doctrine, [7] nor do they perform the work which necessity requires. They would like to puff themselves up as the blessed at Christ's right hand, but they would be unwilling to take up Thy chalice, O Christ. These fishermen stretch their nets for gain so that they may catch the world, not treasure for their souls [1060]. Living so wrongly they furnish an example for laymen, who follow them exactly in the way they have learned. In this way the sheep becomes tainted with the shepherd's stains, and each falls into the ditch like a blind man. [8]

Chapter 13[1]

Here he tells how the prelate ought to enlighten the people entrusted to him, not only by teaching but also by good works.

The man proceeding in darkness does not know where he walks, so that he does not see which road he must take. [2] And when the people go without instruction, they see that the one who is their prelate is not keeping the laws of God, since he neither teaches the Scriptures nor performs works of piety. Instead, he in his weakness is clearly given to vice [1070]. When the churchman's actions are not virtuous at all and when his lamp dies out with no light in the night, then he causes the people to go astray, and the blind follows the blind in the dark. [3] Utter ruin is the result of this. Therefore, let those who are leaders light up their torches more brightly, so that we may see the way. A lamp gleaming with fire does three things: it shines, it warms, and it burns. By reason of these three things the churchman has three [concerns]: his life is to show a brilliance, he is to show his warmth with love, and, since he censures sinners, he burns them [1080]. [4] When he binds his people to himself with heartfelt affection and protects and increases his flock with blessed prayers, then he serves God. He is seized with fear that someone may be led astray or that the wolf Satan may enter his sheepfold. He feeds his sheep and sets a holy example so that they may taste sweet honeycombs in their mouths.

The trumpeter often used to lend his help, and the good leader urge his fighting men forward by word of mouth. But it is more fitting for you, O priest, who are a spiritual leader, to utter words in harmony with God's law [1090]. Send out your deep voice like a guiding trumpet, and let the words from your lips direct the actions of your flock. Do not delay, cry out, tell the people their faults; but be righteous yourself, lead the way with your example. As long as the taste in the stream remains lastingly sweet, the waters from that fountain are drunk with great pleasure. 5 For the more blessed is the clergy's life in Christ, the more blessed will be the word which it teaches. God's word never returns without anything of value; rather, once it is sent forth, it brings back talents doubled in value [1100]. 6 The simple word of God, which His pure spirit sends forth, penetrates the bounds of heaven and bears back rich gifts for the earth. If it wishes, the sick soul which possesses such priests will find the path of salvation, once it is well. Those who relish nothing on earth, but seek after heavenly things, and hunger and thirst after God alone; 7 whom the splendor of books, not pounds sterling, 8 nourishes; they feed not upon the sight of gold, but the altar of God; 9 they, since they deserve a fitting reward for their labor, shall sow eternally and reap without end [1110]. When someone teaches what is right and in addition to this does what is right, it will profit you to do what his conduct prescribes for you. Once the starting gate is opened, the stout horse runs well, if he has others to follow and overtake. 10

The Scriptures of the Old Testament should be borne in mind. In this way the good shepherd can have a guide. When Jacob set out rods before his flock, this was a piece of wisdom worthy of remembrance. He laid them partly bare by pulling off the bark and left them partly covered with a peel of bark [1120]. After the bark was removed the whiteness in the rods glistened, as the splendid words of the Scriptures revealed. The bark is saved when the letter alone [of the Scriptures] is held to, and the pastor feeds his flock on the outward meaning. 11 But why will pastors speak out against such examples? In order to get the benefit of them for themselves but not to observe them. We think nothing of one on whose part neither a good life nor good teaching will help instruct the people. There are, however, those who are bringing the great dangers of schism upon the people by getting out rash documents [1130]. 12 Because of an unlearned teacher, students of ability often get little benefit from school. Similarly, if unfit churchmen fail to act, they lack effectiveness, no matter how much dogma they may have.

These reckless men ravage more violently than fire, and overwhelm fiercely, as a bear does sheep. When such a teacher utters anything harsh, he harms the man whose salvation he ought to be. 13 He inflicts injuries upon sinners, but he heals no injuries. What previously was bad he provokes into something worse [1140]. Thus the words of a haughty prelate cannot assist us, since a man of evil character is their

141

author. [14] And then there is the churchman who is good-natured, reproaching us with almost flattering talk. A guilty man is not afraid of that. Eli reproved his sons with a father's gentleness, not in the manner of a pastor and not with a serious tone. Eli was damned for their sins, since he was highly impious because of his pious words to his sons. So the pastor who does not reproach those in his charge will purchase the wrath of the Father on high and will belong in prison [1150]. [15]

These things are often written: "The saints held to the middle way. Do not aim too high, and do not act altogether basely." A prelate should not harass us too much with harsh justice, nor should he tolerate too much out of gentle innocence. If the rider's hand is not moderately light, the horse often rebels when the reins are pulled up. Sometimes a medicine will bring health and sometimes it snatches it away. There is nothing helpful which cannot also do harm. But the priest who holds the reins in check by paying attention to the proper time is that much more worthy to lead us a safe journey [1160]. Very often a sinner who would be quite impatient at harsh words mends his ways because of kind counsel. On the other hand, it sometimes helps for the priest's righteous indignation to attack unwilling rebels, without any good naturedness. [16] A severe disease is often allayed by bitter herbs, and a sharp thorn bears delicate roses. [17] Often you see that hard ground turned over by the furrowing plow[18] has a pleasantly soft surface.

A bishop should be anointed with oil, because it represents many things. And it is especially appropriate for him to follow them [1170]. The oil does four things which a good bishop ought to reserve for himself: it penetrates, it illuminates, it nourishes, and it anoints. [19] Nothing can penetrate except by virtue of strength, but that kind of virtue is a great help in penetrating. For when mildness has been combined with strength, the bishop's behavior will be both gentle and stern. He should do without beer, he should be sprinkled with oil, and holy love should anoint him, so that he may have no harmful guilt. [20] The more sublimely the voice of the teacher strikes within peoples' hearts, the more forcefully he will move them [1180]. Likewise, the virtue of the oil takes its virtues into due consideration: while it penetrates stout hearts, it regulates their actions quite gently. It is light for the blind, food for the hungry, balm for the sick; it sheds light upon them, it feeds them, it encourages them. The light is for guidance, while the food is to nourish the poor, and the balm spreads soothing words for people. [21] With David as witness, Christ was anointed with this oil, for His Father anointed Him with the ointment of joy. [22] Those who share Simon's sin—those who buy or sell or do not keep sacred trusts without pay—are not anointed with it [1190]. The man who sins in such matters is banished from God's people, for Christ drives such men from His temple. [23]

Here he tells how signs of the Antichrist have appeared in the Court of Rome, especially because of avarice on the part of certain people.

My mind, which is on the point of saying much more, grows weak with fear; it sinks feebly and trembles in silence. Christ and all Rome together shall be my witness, if I am allowed to touch upon anything pertaining to this vice. Rome slanders, scorns, and detests the hands that do not give freely, so everyone there receives one gift in exchange for another. God is no respecter of persons; [1] rather, He graciously watches over mankind's actions [1200]. But our own kind of grace welcomes those whom the world has enriched with gold and no others. The rich man who pays the price brings back prized gifts, for the whole court favors such a person. The man receiving unction does not enter there unless a drop of gold greases his palm. [2] A wealth of good morals accomplishes nothing when gold is lacking, for no worthy poor earn any assistance. If you knock on the door with gold, you will enter, and you will get what you ask for; and your gift brings you gifts in return [1210]. If you wish generous treatment, give generous gifts; for if you sow little, you will reap small rewards. [3]

The fool delights in bribery, but what shall the wise man do? [4] The clergy, which knows more about such matters, should answer for them. Believe me, bribes buy both gods and men. Even a great man in the world is appeased by the offering of presents. [5] But when Simon pays out his bribes for the sake of the world, there is no advancement for Christ through them. Christ urged that those who thirsted should come to the waters of their own free will, and behold, He slaked them at His fount [1220]. [6] But no thirsty person shall drink from our fountains without a cash payment, which he shall make in advance. Selling one thing for another is the practice our court follows, and with Simon's help it prospers. [7] Our court takes cognizance of no man without a bribe, and the empty hand goes away still empty. As long as a layman is willing to contribute, he takes precedence over theology. If you give me a gift, I will repay you with one. If Matthew, Mark, Luke, and John bring no gifts, they lose the favors which they seek [1230]. If a servant of the world should arrive, he is admitted and held in esteem; if a servant of Christ should arrive, no one takes care of him.

"If a pauper should come attended by the muses of Homer and brought nothing, he would return a pauper as before. [8] If a new Augustine made a request there and had nothing to give beforehand, he would wander on his way. The layman with gold can read and construe and sing well; if he has enough to offer, it is obvious he can do anything well. " See for yourselves what sort of piety this is, or whether justice will preserve her rights in such fashion [1240]. If by chance the Church crumbles to ruin because of these men, may the Most High raise it up again in His goodness, may He confound heresies and destroy schisms, [9] lest any [shepherd] lose his Christian sheep. In Thy mercy, O Redeemer, let those whom peace, reverence, and a single faith bind together return to Thee. [10] Antichrist will do things contrary to Christ by subverting morals and fostering vices. [11] I do not know whether he by chance has come in the world. I certainly see several signs of him now [1250]. Peter's ship is faltering; set it right before it perishes, O Christ, and do not let pride swallow it up.

Chapter 15

Here he tells how, according to common report, many strive for the honors but not the responsibilities of ecclesiastical office, so that the virtues of the Church are becoming fewer and its vices are in many ways on the increase.

O God, every heart is open to Thee and speaks its will to Thee, and no secrets lie hidden from Thy light. Thou knowest, O Lord, that Thy most excellent rule has fled as far as the distance from sunrise to sunset. That active faith which Thou wishedst to implant has almost gone astray now, because of the clergy. A world without justice has abolished the law that once was Christ's, and claims today's clergy as its own [1260]. Truly the name of saint does not make a saint; instead, one whom God approves is made a saint. "But if we glory in that name from the people and if the world praises us, such renown is enough for us. " Thus our Father's order is concealed by a masked face; by this means the post of honor has furiously plundered its charges.

The voice of the people agrees with the voice of God, [1] so that in critical times it ought to be held in greater awe. Common talk has taught me what I shall say, and my words contain nothing new [1270]. The Pharisees now ascend Moses' high seat, and the Scribes write down decrees, but they do not carry them out. [2] In earlier times a steadfast, humble, generous, pure, and moderate rule was revered in the churches. Now they have substituted idle, haughty, greedy, wanton plunderers in its place. Wrath has conquered the peacemakers, and pride the meek. Money controls the just men and Venus the holy ones. So justice does not govern affairs, but instead willfulness does, corrupted by evil and lacking in judgment [1280]. Likewise the earth now

144

worships false gods and is ruined by them, as long as the clergy's law knows nothing of God's. In plain words, false men determine what is right for you, and they do little or nothing for the sake of justice. They seldom follow Thee with examples of good works, O Christ, and they hold that Thy perfect law is null and void. They are careful to put off their own shoulders the things which Thy teachings put forth, and they order me to carry them out [1290]. But they wish to keep for themselves the empty glory which those teachings confer, and they take what is rightly mine away from me. They are not concerned about the firmament; instead they mask their faces like columns and call themselves temples.

Heaven was once corrupted, and the proud one fell headlong from its heights; and now that he is fallen, he occupies the depths. Similarly, Adam fell from Paradise because of his crime, just as Judas lost his high rank. Neither rank nor position makes a man blessed; rather, they are the downfall of those who wish to be superior. O God, Thou has made the Church holy unto Thyself; make also Thy churchmen holy for it [1300]. I pray, O God, that Thy mercy amend them, since Thou commandest us to trust our necks to these holy men. Make our leaders be what Thou hast decreed by Thy law, so that the right way of life may guide them. And even if their conduct is false and unsteadfast, grant that Thy people always retain their firm faith. And grant, O God, that the clergy can so restrain evil both by word and deed that it may be of help to us in this world. Let the long hoped-for and sweet remedy for our misfortunes come; even if it is late, it should be welcome [1310]. [3] If the clergy become good men, then we shall be better and God's glory so much the greater.

Chapter 16[1]

Now that there has been a discussion of those within the rank of prelacy who go astray, it is necessary to speak of wrongdoing on the part of curates. When stationed under prelates, these men negligently abandon the cure of their parishes' souls, thus bringing them into danger. And first he intends to speak of the curates who, in neglecting their cure of souls, stick close to the courts[2] in order to dance attendance upon important men.

I was writing of the faults of the negligent bishop exactly as I have heard them spoken of, and my pen stopped at that point. There are, however, other rectors not without the taint of wrongdoing who wield authority over the cure of souls. I intend to write of how this group contends with itself as to whether God or the world is more its concern. In considering the doings of rectors at the present time, I find what ought to belong to God belongs to the world [1320]. The curate, who is the bishop's right hand, is at fault because of the fault of the bishop, who is in charge of the cure of souls. He thinks a church is no good whatsoever, unless the prebend has been appointed through Simon's method. But a prebend of this kind succors the courtesan, not the poor; and similarly, he loves a goddess, not God. Just now there are many bad examples of such men, who neither tend to their cures chastely nor live providently. Their vesture has splendor, their food is customarily delicacies, and their bed loudly proclaims its unchastity [1330]. [3] You could learn from Christ's words that in times past His disciples did not have two coats. [4] But since these fellows are not disciples, they are not willing to follow the required practice in such matters. But they double not so much their clothes as their love affairs, and ecclesiastical rule regards nothing as more sinful. There is gold at hand to gird their unchaste loins, so that their foolish adornment brands them as worthless fellows. We see them degenerating in their splendors like the knight, except that only the spurs are missing [1340].

[5]The responsibility should belong to the one who has the honor. He who wants to share in the profits ought to share in the loss. A just faith demands this and the law has decreed it to all, but those who now have the cure of souls deny these edicts. They admit their curacies are fat, and they live off the fat, but they refuse to assume the responsibilities of the cure of souls. If a curate cannot live sinfully in one cure, then he wants to get a new and different one. After corrupting the first one, he then defiles a second; thus does he himself alter his own posts when they are not sinful [1350]. A letter bought from the bishop arranges things for the curate, and thus the curate's cure remains abandoned. He retains a lay priest to substitute for himself, while the courts of important men will retain him. When he aspires to honors he is drawn there like a bee, but he is backward and lazy in performing his duty.

He pretends whatever the world pretends, so that a court can believe him worthy. He speaks fawning words, and even a dog trained to bow does not bend down on its knee with such a humble expression [1360]. [6] He supplants his companions like a second Jacob, [7] and does everything to get the world's money. It doesn't suit him, however, to undertake anything without the help of the learned Simon, who is his advocate. Even though the front doors are shut, the greedy man picks his way and thus enters into the fold from another direction. [8] He is not concerned with the cure of souls at all, as long as the courts[9] of a magnate may be cultivated for his own profit. The soul's virtue is of no value to him, but the body's doings are. His post does not allow him to achieve his rightful reward [1370]. It is to the advantage of a man who is nothing in himself, and does not have what it takes to rise, that he be pulled up by somebody else's money. But this is absurd, for anyone who is puffed up because of another has puffed himself up more than he should have. [10]

[11]When a king's letter makes a plea to the Pope's ears and Simon is the go-between so that he can grease the right palms, [12] then our layman, having consulted with Simon, becomes a cleric fit to climb up to any and every rank on earth. The man who was a pauper yesterday, almost destitute and without any reputation, and who did not even possess the title of father [1380]; [13] the man whose coat was cheap, not full flowing but plainly too small and scarcely covering his knees--a closely woven garment now clothes him, and its fringe brushes against his feet and trails along the ground. His coat, which once was a stranger to his thighs, now warms his ankles and caresses his feet. [14] If you were to search for a mirror of the world in his coat, you could see the rector's many vanities.

If perhaps he cannot rise to the rank of bishop, he buys comparable clothes anyway [1390]. Almost all the world now trails after one who was recently only a young house dog. The riding crop now belongs to the one who recently was a groom; a lofty steed is now led by the reins up to his seat. He prospers in his affairs like a rich man, but he is poor in moral principles and governs his wealth foolishly. He is very eager that there be a great account made [of him] in worldly affairs, so that he may pay his obligations to his lord. But he should account to Christ about his cure of souls; his talents lie shamefully and unprofitably hidden in a pit [1400]. [15] Thus does a worldly court ruin Christ's servant, who is approaching a snare as long as he thirsts for riches.

Chapter 17

Here he speaks of the rectors who with the permission of the bishop pretend that they are going to school, so that they may practice vices of the flesh under the name of virtue.

There is another kind of rector, and he devises a pretext [for himself] by saying that he wishes to go to a school of religion. So, by reason of his petitioning with red [gold] and white [silver], [1] in order that the wanderer may be near those masters whom he loves all too much, the bishop nods approval that he may be so. Thus the roving rector wishes that under the guise of virtue he might duly busy himself in vices. Decretals and sacred theology are not a bit to his liking;

instead, his natural knowledge[2] is enough for him [1410]. That mistress teaches him a good many things, and he learns them; and he copies out at night what he studies during the day. For the sake of form he finally petitions the episcopal seat that he be placed in charge of things, and he pays out heavily in advance. In this way the curate is placed in the chair of the teacher, and makes his students read the sacred rites.

"Woe to him that is alone, " we read in Solomon's writings, [3] for no one looks after the man who is alone. For this reason it is the college's custom that everyone learned in his art ought to study with a female companion[1420]. God Himself made the first female companion in order that she might help man forever, and so He created her. Man was made first, and woman second, so that God might bring the human race into being through them. The discerning rector is very eager to carry out these precepts, and offers his devotions in a dutiful way. Who would not want the rib he feels missing from his side, the rib by which man is to be perfected? The first woman was created out of man's rib, and the rector accordingly wants to have his own rib [1430]. For God commanded the human race to be fruitful; by His command man is to multiply. [4] Thus, since his seed is copious the rector does multiply, so that he will not be guilty in the light of God's mandate. Through such motives the rector approves the reasons that he may have lady friends, as long as he is in the scholarly profession. First he treats the subject of pregnancy, and in order to bear fruit[5] he is highly repetitious about it. And he reads both the text and the gloss on it, so that the instruction will be clear to his students [1440]. For the sake of form the master often flogs the scholars so that the school is wary of his vigilant rod. The more formal[6] he is in the art of reading, the less need there is of subject matter. His toil does not excuse him, even though he were to teach night and day, to the point that his solicitude emptied his head. His topic, which he argues is profound, treats of and accomplishes many profound things on occasion. Ask a question, and being answerable for it, he has an answer for everything; and he does not allow anything to escape his logic [1450]. Yet often it is obscure to the teacher, and he himself so highly perplexed he ceases to remain in his chair. "The assigned reading is harmful, and when repeated it is ten times harmful; the more one reads of it the more one's senses are dulled. " And so learning renders our curate lazy, and through his long period of study he accomplishes nothing at home. He is stupid when he comes, but he will go away even stupider, as long as he is constantly going back to schools.

Such is the school in which the cleric studies, so that he may copy out the basic laws of nature in his own way [1460]. The practice that one form his own theory suits both pupil and master very well. This is the school to be bowed down to in worship above all others, a school in which every member revels in having a girl friend. Nevertheless, as long as the school is shared with girl friends it will ultimately make the guilty man bewail his deeds. So when the school confirms the pupil in ways of feminine companionship, he will become like a layman whenever he is a teacher. Alas! A mistress is dreadful, and a school in league with such intimacy is dreadful. The one ravages the body and the other makes away with one's wealth [1470]. It is a thing shameful to God and astounding to the people when the same man is both a teacher and a profligate.

While his bride the Church goes bare, his concubine is clothed; his forsaken bride perishes and his beloved prospers. After crying out that the faith pledged to it was broken, the Church now comes demanding its rights. But since its light has died out, its authority is dead; and hence the curate's bride departs, almost like an utter vagrant. The rector, applying himself to the study of vices, not morals, gives to Venus the tithe which ought to be God's [1480]. So the curate begets another just like himself, in order to fulfill his ordinary natural powers. So does the curate thrive on bodily passion like a layman, in order that he may be able to multiply his kind. And thus the school which used to be the mother of virtue is becoming a foolish stepmother because of its vices. 7

Chapter 18

Here he speaks of the rectors who live in curacies but neglect their cures. Inwardly their thoughts are especially concerned with hunting and lasciviousness.

There is a third kind of curate who fixes his attention on the world while he remains at home, living in his parish. The barren leaves of his parish come forth without fruit, since its foolish leader overshadows it in darkness (1490). He does no preaching to save souls, he does not visit the sick, nor is he moved by love to help the poor. 1He has a fat horse, while his learning remains meagre. An elegant saddle and a lowly mind are his ornaments. He blows upon a horn he carries at his side, and mountain and meadow re-echo from it; the hare flees the dangers evident from it. But his voice keeps quiet in church, lest it should drive the base hearts of his flock away from vice. His dog, which barks with faithful voice on the hunt, will certainly get whatever it wants to have [1500]. But as for the poor wretch who cries at the door and needs food--alas! Not a crumb nor a drop is given to him. 2 O God, how much praise does such a man, who gives a dog the food he refuses a man, deserve from Thee!

Holy days of feasting or fasting are hardly over but that he is
circling the meadow in the midst of his dogs. To him the noise of the
dogs as they bark together is a church bell on which hymns are played
to God. His mass is short but long are his devotions in the fields,
where he appoints his dogs as cantors [1510]. The hare and the fox are
what he wants most; as he speaks of God his mind is still on the hare.
Thus one fox chases another and hunts for something just like itself,
when all the while it is ravaging the young flock. For when wandering
about he investigates where the pretty women of tender age are, so that
he can glut his passion. Indeed, such a rector lies in ambush for women like a wolf circling about the sheep in the fold. When he sees an
old groom and a young bride, he pays a call upon people like this in
his charge [1520]. There the rector takes full control of the groom and
properly explains the bride's bounden duties. [3] Thus the rector takes
the good-looking bodies under his care and leaves the souls to wander
about corrupted.

Chapter 19

Here he speaks of the rectors who live in parishes, but nevertheless neglect the care of souls. Buying and selling all kinds of
temporal goods from day to day just like lay merchants, they
amass worldly wealth.

[1]In addition, there is a fourth kind of rector who does wrong
while dwelling in a parish: he goes around canvassing all the people
like a merchant. Once his mass is over, his mind is on the marketplace and then the tavern, as he tries to make a profit at a friend's expense. He squanders what belongs to the Church and pockets the gold.
He forsakes God to hold on to the world [1530]. He counts as wasted a
day on which he does not experience either a profit for himself or some
new sensual indulgence. And Avarice is his watchman, so that a pauper
can have no part of his riches. On no occasion does a poor man share
them, for his strongbox stands shut to him with a double lock. But his
sense of duty comprises something different in regard to a woman:
when Venus commands, then his hand is lavish. If a woman approaches
when his golden coffer is laid out on his spreading knees, the key will
give her access [1540]. He is harder than iron; nothing softens him;
but a woman's soft flesh overpowers him. As long as he has time for
unseemly money-making the rector will lay out his wares for a price, [2]

150

exchanging one thing for another. One hand scatters everything the other gathers in, just as a fool puts his balm in a sieve. [3] The foolish woman so preys upon the foolish man that by the end of the day he will have nothing left except a plucked beard.

O if sons could succeed curates and carry on their fathers' duties for the renown of the Church [1550], then I think those visitors to Rome who are hopeful at someone else's death could get little or nothing. [4] Such is the kind of devotion now promoted in the Church by our curates. May God be their judge.

Chapter 20

Now that the waywardness of those in the Church who have benefices has been told of, it is necessary to speak of stipendiary priests, at least of those who seek for and obtain the priestly office not because of the purity and integrity of the priesthood, but for the sake of worldly idleness.

[1]If I were to speak of the priests who are without curacies, we would see that they are equal to the others in their vices. Even if a priest does not occupy a church, annual services are just like a church. One priest now insists upon getting more than three formerly did; because he is consumed with avarice he is greedy for more [1560]. I see them going about the city on foot as if they were masters, led along by money just like a she ass is led to market. The laborer is still worthy of his hire, [2] in accordance with the worth that the labor fetches. Nevertheless, no one is authorized to traffic in divinity, so no mass can be sold to you. We believe that Christ, consecrated upon the holy altar, and having been sold once, does not wish to be sold any more. He who commanded holy gifts to be freely given gave Himself without any payment. [3] Then why do you, priest, insist upon money for yourself from them [1570]? Since you are clothed and your subsistence is satisfactory, why do you insist upon more, seeing that you should live for God? If you had any more money, it would be of no use to you, for illicit gain knows no bounds. Either you will go on buying and selling at Rome with Simon's gold, who would grant you preferment and for it take the money [you had] previously collected, and Simon would thus try to get what the mass gave you; or, a harlot would suck your full purse dry while you are revelling in lust, and give it back empty in a hurry [1580].

The harlot and the tavern take away what the Church has given. When these three get together they commit many infamies. Since I see

151

them like this, I would think they were some unheard-of kind of human monsters, if it were only rarely that I behold them. But since I can see every day the things I have spoken of, I am not at all surprised now at what I see. The cormorant often plunges its wings and legs in the stream and hides for long periods of time in bearing its young. It represents those whom dissolute lust of the flesh dominates completely and overwhelms with its grasp [1590]. [4] With the ancients it was possible to say, "This [is] a priest and this, a priestess, " yet in such regard we can only say, "These [are] men and these, women, " for they now fill the world with their offspring. [5] If there is piety in that, they are intensely pious. Night, love, and wine—three things which are well enough known to priests these days—do not counsel any self-restraint. [6] The course of [the priest's] prayers is brief, while on the other hand he insists on exchanging prolonged and tightly held kisses. Meanwhile the woman says, "O priest, how long a time until your arms may be around my neck [1600]? "

The man who seeks to keep his wife chaste nowadays and his chambers clean will wish that the pigeon and the priest stay away from his room; the one spreads dung and the other spreads lewdness. [7] A priest of God rarely rises sober from the table or chaste from a bed. When exhilarated by taverns his voice sings on high, but in churches it is all too mute. He is taught by his wine to worship a brothel, and he bends both knees in long prayer there [1610]. Thus he purges out the old leaven, since he spreads a new, but not as Paul has commanded. [8] The priest through whom the altar of the living God is defiled wishes to sacrifice on the altar of Baal. One woman is enough for me, but he needs a dozen; I see him going alone now like a young cock. Thus priests celebrate the sacred rites of Bacchus and sanctify drunkenness. The ancient pagan rite begins to be modern, and Christ's law almost perishes because of such men [1620]. And so they are now worshippers of temples and gods, and the goddess Venus stands in the highest esteem among them.

Chapter 21

Here he speaks of priests' habitual lust, and how by arrangement they get hold of peoples' money. By praying undevoutly for the dead, they do not properly discharge their burden of intercessions for the dead.

A voracious fire is consuming the earth and the things born of the earth; [1] wherever its onslaught rages it wipes out everything. In such fashion does a base sexual passion harm untutored laymen, because of the unchaste examples of priests. Their love of pleasure does not concern itself with anything ordinary or within reason; passion inflames their five bodily senses. Such punishment as this will attend those whom such infamy taints: fire and brimstone shall be their penalty [1630]. [2] But familiarity usually lessens one's sense of shame and emboldens a person whom it has influenced over a long period of time. [3] They do not think that they sin in that they often exchange kisses, for kisses usually mean tokens of peace. It is a most worthy cause to make a good peace; nor does love of goodness last long without peace. So love on the part of priests is a product of peace, for they indulge in frequent kisses as an habitual practice. This habitual custom is to be considered in another regard, too: a custom of long standing furnishes its own justification [1640]. [4] If, on the other hand, we were to speak of the law of nature, this has a glorious reputation among priests everywhere. And if their rights are established under such a guise, namely that long practice acquires the force of law, then I believe that priests are establishing laws by their practice, as long as they frequently give kisses in their lustfulness.

The priesthood signifies the bosom of the Church, so that by rights they should foster virtuous souls. But how will those who do not take care of their own souls care for the souls of others? [5] This is not reasonable [1650]. I do not know what service such people, who can do nothing serviceable for themselves, could render me. For it is known that God does not listen to sinners; homage to God from an evil tongue is shameful. The man who offers undevout prayers to God is asking for future damnation as his own judgment. One who causes [his own] damnation seems to have brought damnation [upon others]; he who tolerates what he can hold in check commits an offense. He inflicts death upon the helpless, if he has the power to prevent it and does not wish to, but instead allows an evil to exist [1660]. The bishop who ordains laymen to holy orders when they are not worthy of them is the cause of many an abomination. If anyone buys such things for money, he will deceive himself in doing so, or, God knows, he will ruin himself by such doings. I do know this, that a man who breaks bread with a hungry person (one whose weakness is clearly unfeigned), who helps the needy and visits the sick, deserves reward for his goodness. But the bishop makes a mistake to ordain men who are powerful and who conspire under the empty shadow of the priesthood for the leisure which the world at large posesses [1670]. And I believe that such bishops rightly lose their special gifts by hiring them out. [6]

Chapter 22

Here he discusses the reason for which it happens that laymen, as true friends of justice, abhor the habitual lasciviousness of priests. Quite often laymen attack this, reproving it severely.

The clergy says that however laden with crime it may be, it is not for the layman to accuse it. And out of partiality, one cleric pardons the sins of another because he himself stands lawlessly guilty of them. It does not wish to be accused by laymen; nevertheless, it accuses them, and seeks a free rein for itself. As a result, pleasure-giving acts of sin are unrestricted to the clergy, unless it be that the laymen's laws are forced upon it [1680]. A foolish priest results in a foolish people, and one who knows little good brings about much evil. A lawless clergy makes a lawless people, and in this way the clergy makes out a case for itself: for since the layman is without any law, he is unaware that the clergy which he sees abiding lawlessly is guilty. Yet if the clergy were wise, the people's wisdom would stand firm, with the result that both would stand together under the law. But since the fatuous clergy's lack of wisdom is now obvious, their life is accordingly held in disdain even by those of no understanding [1690].

Nature aids our power of reason with many examples; the more learned man governs his judgment by them. Hence it is that the lurking owl hates bright light, searches out its food at night, and is afraid of other birds. If by chance flocks of chattering birds fly against it, they pierce out its eyes, and cut and mangle it to pieces. This signifies the guilty priests who are corrupt in the flesh and stealthily commit their base acts of lust. Laymen, just like birds of the daytime, and afire with zeal for the law and love of God, try to hold them in check [1700]. [1] The false Judas was not thereby worthy of the esteem of Christ's servants. As long as a priest wears the yoke of lust, he should judge himself accordingly, if laymen nettle him about it.

In its just judgment the law wills that the abuser of justice leave off the vice concerning which a judicial decision was rendered for him. We are all brothers of the Church in Christ, and one always stands in need of another's help. But the law says this, that if thy brother trespass, rebuke him, and thereby make him return unto God [1710]. And if he heareth thee not, tell it unto the Church; but if he neglect to hear the Church and cleave to it not, let him be more unto thee as a heathen man, whereby no man can forbear to punish him for his faults. [2] Therefore, the priest who contributes to his daily transgressions ought by rights to enjoy no esteem. He shall not be exempt, for it is not right that anyone esteem a man who does not hold justice in awe. One who presumes to indulge in practices prohibited by law ought to go without the benefits conferred by law [1720]. In the end, everything that lies hidden will be revealed, [3] and rank and position will be no excuse. Tell me, what good was a contrived excuse when Adam wrongfully covered himself with fig leaves? [4] Or, what does it avail, if a priest conceal his sins of the flesh in darkness, bolstering himself with the honor of his rank?

Chapter 23

Here he writes in opposition to the fact that some priests say how they do not offend God more grievously than laymen by indulging in lust of the flesh.

A priest says[1] that he does not sin more than you when his flesh succumbs to the vices of the flesh. He says that just as others are made of frail flesh, so he has his bodily limbs [1730]. "I am just like another man," he asserts. "Why then shall I not keep women for myself, just as others do?" In such a way he fashions arguments for his misdeed, and says he is free to sin just like another man. In spite of this, I believe he is thinking contrary to the truth, for his state is holier than all others. Another course can quickly be adopted in which there is less blame, if one's course should turn out to be at fault. But the priest's holy orders cannot be entered into on the spur of the moment; instead, he expects to pass through its various stages [1740]. For first one rises through five positions[2] and is proven, for which reason he is to prepare for his post in every way. And every step is sanctified by a bishop and no other, so that it thereby may be the holier. The priest is anointed with an unction on his head and hands so that by this means he may be worthier than other men in this world. In receiving his yoke, he makes the vow of chastity from that time forth, so that as a purer man, he may keep his actions pure. And since he makes vows which are known in advance, I think that when he does just the opposite, his wrongdoing causes greater wickedness [1750]. In my opinion, the leader who should furnish an example of virtue, and yet is vicious, is more at fault than the one who is led. For these reasons, which I have carefully considered one by one, I conclude that priests are guiltier than you are.

Even though the priest may excuse himself by false words, he does not comfort the inner reaches of his conscience at all. On the contrary, since he is unmindful of the holy order he has taken, he is accordingly asking for further ill repute in his sphere of action. I do not

155

think that his rank makes the cobbler at one with the priest, nor does guilt weigh equally for them in the same balance [1760]. A priest and layman combined are not a shepherd, nor is their crime serious in the same degree. [3] The one vowed to be chaste when his tonsure was anointed, and every man of faith is bound by his vow. He would not be vested with a reward of such great honor, were it not for that fact that he was to undergo a greater responsibility for it. For the greatest king in the world cannot do what the least important priest in Christ can. Thus, since he is rightly placed before other men in esteem, the burden of righteousness oppresses him more severely because of his shortcomings [1770]. Alas! That a wicked hand, defiled by the pudenda of women should touch God's sacred objects on the altar! Christ abhors the deed [of] one who will handle the Lord's body, yet be basely attracted by a harlot. Alas! Those who should be servants of Christ are now agents of the Devil. Who will restore our source of strength?

Chapter 24[1]

Here he describes how each and every thing which concerns the office of priesthood signifies divine mysteries of great power. And he is to speak first, according to both [the Old and the New] Law, of sacerdotal vestments in their proper arrangement.

O how well it would be if the priest would consider what his privileges are--what his honor is, what his responsibility is, and what his glorious work. It would be a great surprise if a priest who made due reflection upon everything pertaining to himself and stood forth righteously were to bear his responsibility badly [1780]. Everything which that order claims as its own is seen to be sacred, so that these men should be all the holier as a result. It is not so much that he look to the performing of the mass, but that it is incumbent to be holy according to sacerdotal law. The various ornaments which the priest makes use of bear mystic signs of manifold virtue. His vestment is a surplice, which is otherwise called an alb, and which covers the priest's body down to his feet. Just as the alb is white on the outside, so the priest should be even whiter within himself, in order that he may have a good character in the world [1790]. Girded in an ephod, Samuel was eager to be a servant of the Lord, and his mother Hannah made a little coat for him. By this small coat is meant the doctrine of faith, through the grace of which his mother sustained his feeble spirits. By the ephod made of linen is meant bodily purity, which the priest preserves. [2]

156

There is also a girdle which chastely binds the coat, [3] lest the thigh become acquainted with shameful deeds[4] through lustfulness. The priest wears a humeral veil, so that in comforting our wretched souls he may bear them to better things [1800]. [5] And the wise priest fastens a headdress on top, in order not to allow his thoughts to go astray. [6] Clothing him is an encircling chasuble that glistens with gold, which is king over all metals because of its worth. And in similar fashion the priest shines with virtue, if he upholds the rank of his order well. The holy man wears gold on his clothes because God's glorious, shining wisdom is brighter in him than in others. [7] The border of the noble cloth[8] gleams in its course, lest a break in it be threatened easily [1810]. Likewise the good priest does not break himself off from the world, lest any rift of evil be seen in him. [9] Girded about with such purity, the priest adorns himself in order that all the world may hold sacred his virtuous offices. [10]

Vestments were woven for Aaron and his chosen ones so that each of them might enjoy the honor of priest. Similarly, priests of today, whether great or unimportant, produce the body of Christ and consecrate it. [11] For when we consecrate the wine and bread on the altar, this becomes the true blood and flesh together [1820]. He who made Christ's flesh in His Mother's womb makes His body consecrated upon the altar. [12] The shape of the altar is square, so that the Church's faith may be strengthened in the four quarters of the earth. [13] He who is fitted out with vestments and is worthy in his morals shall be ordained as priest; otherwise, he shall not be. Their calling demands that those whom such vestments and great glory adorn should be more like saints. The bishop who, contrary to what is right, confers such honors upon lay priests, brings disgrace upon the Church [1830]. Of those whom the bosom of the Church receives, it should recognize which are worthy of God and cast the rest outside. [14]

Chapter 25

Here he speaks of how sacrifices on the altar required according to the old law were symbolically by way of example for priests of the new law. [1] He says further that according to both laws those who sacrifice on the altar should be without blemish.

The old law prescribed animals, with which the people in former times sacrificed a burnt offering upon the altar to God. And a certain portion of an animal thus sacrificed always belonged to the priest. But through a hidden meaning this denotes for our priests their mystical

157

duties in regard to Christ's law. Our curates must keep well in mind that part of the burnt offering which pertains to the priest [1840]. By command of the sacred law, these are the parts which belong to the priest: the breast and the right arm, after it has been cut off. The breast is the seat of instruction, and every priest ought to teach those under his charge what is right. Even more powerful is the right arm, and it signifies that his deeds will be mighty, so long as he undertakes nothing improper. [2] The arm which is cut off shows that the priest may rise above the people by his [manner of] living, so long as he undertakes nothing ignoble. [3] It is not so much what he possesses [by being] in the order of priesthood, but that he possesses the heavy responsibility of a great office. For the old law, in conjunction with the new, everywhere makes clear that priests ought to be holy. Peter [of Riga] wrote what I have written in his _Aurora_, [4] and he will be a true witness and authority in this case.

The old law commands. and the new law confirms that everyone sacrificing at the altar shall be spotlessly pure. The deeds of his body should be free from any swinish taint by which he might displease God, and he should commit nothing dishonorable. He should have no taint and should not be guilty of carnal intercourse, lest his sinful action corrupt his pure goodness [1860]. [5] Still, I shall speak of those faults which are said to exist in the priesthood, so that the priest who reads this may be more mindful of them. [6]A man is said to be blind who is covered with the dust of the world and does not know how to take the road to the light of life. A man is half-blind whose inner mind is brilliant with intelligence but whose carnal doings cast a cloud over it. An aqueous film blinds the eyes of, and plainly marks out, the man who is puffed up with pride and ascribes only spotless deeds to himself. The man who is not able to understand small matters and who accomplishes what he does without any acute understanding has a small nose [1870]. [7] The man who does not understand what he reads yet makes out that he is learned has too big a nose. The man who acknowledges sweet as bitter and claims holy acts are evil has a crooked nose. The man is lame who knows his way, but cleaves to this world and is hesitant to run forward, with his fleshly body fettering his pace. The man who drags along slower than a lame man towards everything good is considered as having both a broken foot and a broken hand. The man is hunchbacked whom the burden of the world bends down, and does not allow his eyes to see the heights of the spirit [1880]. His fleshly desire, which commits many base acts in its wickedness, is recognized as being inflamed with lust.

If anyone feels that he is weak in respect to the vices mentioned above, the law commands that he should not consecrate bread to God. Stretching out his hands, Uzzah approached to lift up the ark, but death punished his overly bold hand. Hence people say that he deserved his violent end because he practised coitus with his wife the night before. This is to show that one who approaches the altar when he is defiled shall deserve the stroke of death [1890]. [8] Experience teaches that as long as an unclean hand grasps mud, it cannot thereby cleanse away filth. [9] A priest is said to show the way to others, and if he goes astray, all those whom he thinks he is leading go astray. Whether he is giving the sacraments or is teaching, this saying is plain: if the priest is wicked, others are worse as a result. Whoever proposes himself for the work of the priesthood is not free from responsibility, if he does his work well. Therefore you who wish to rise [to the priesthood] should be aware of this in advance, and if you rise to it, you should do what your priestly order enjoins [1900]. Bring to it not only your external appearance but also your principles and abilities, and you should make progress in the cure of souls.

Chapter 26

Here he says that sufficient maturity is required of a man before he assumes the rank of priesthood for himself. He also speaks about the shaving off of his hair, and says that such things are especially appropriate for priests as a sign of cleanness and purity. He says further that priests should not be indifferent to good works.

Before a priest takes office, he should be mature in age, so that he may be a seasoned leader. For the bloom of youth is more to the likes of the tempting adversary, and the ardor of both youth and the flesh is warm. Those whom dissolute, carnal lust has afflicted up to now ought not to be shepherds of the flock. [1] Their crown remains shaven so that they can rule for God and do noble works [1910]. Shaving does not pull out the roots of the hair; rather, shaved hairs grow more profusely. So even if you should banish all passions from your breast, you still could not escape them all. Therefore, you will not be shaved without the flesh always having a struggle; but you will have something within you with which you can always fight back. [2]

Even when you shun the world, you cannot become completely free of its dust. [3] For granted that you are shining with the highest virtues, you cannot eradicate all guiltiness from your spirit [1920]. There still remains a minimum of guilt which you retain, lest your spirit grow proud while you perform your many good works. [4] Accordingly, your payment for any such fault is absolved, provided that your spirit tremble with remorse for any sudden slip. The just person often falls, for every man remains frail, lest vainglory puff him up too much. The man who has suffered a slight setback will receive a favorable opportunity from God to rise up again even more strongly. You are the light of the world, [5] but you are hardly free from cloudiness, for no one has a life free of sin [1930]. [6] Good fruits often follow after temptations, and the struggles of the flesh have their reward. [7]

It would be helpful, to be sure, to extinguish those raging flames of passion and to keep your heart free from vice. [8] Do not let your eyes look upon anything by which they may be tempted; stop up your ears, lest a wicked sound enter there. It is safer and more fitting to withdraw in peace[9] than to wage the kind of war you cannot win. The unwounded gladiator, shining in his armor, is better off than when his weapons are drenched with his own blood [1940]. [10] And the priest, shining spotlessly in God's masses like a victor, in this way renders God peaceful toward himself as a reward. Consider quickly in your mind what kind of thing it is that you love, and withdraw your neck from a yoke that will chafe you. [11] A wise man ought to get rid of his flaws in their early stages, lest in his slackness he hit upon a cure too late. 1 Crush the harmful seeds of a sudden vice while they are still young, and let your steed check his pace at the outset. For time lends strength, time matures the tender grapes, and makes what was grass into a hardy crop [1950]. [13] If Venus makes an assault, life may be somewhat hard for you, but a newly kindled flame often dies down because of only a little water. [14] To redeem your body, you will suffer steel and fire, [15] and as much more as the healing of your soul occasions. If you banish idleness, Cupid's bow is broken and his torch lies extinguished in the dark. [16]

In order not to go astray, you must place a check on your sinfulness and shun wayward courses and idleness. Priests ought either to labor at something which is proper for them or exhort themselves through prayers [1960]. Paul made baskets in order to do away with idleness, for he did not wish to be wayward in any way. [17] Out of resting creeps the bitter plague of lust, hostile to one's reputation, and a costly glory for one's enemy. Out of resting proceeds an unfortunate lasciviousness, spiritual poverty, all criminal wickedness. Thoughts run to lust under the impulse of various suggestions, at least as long as the body remains ignorant of virtuous toil. God will certainly grant every advantage to industrious men. Work ought to bring considerable rewards [1970]. A prudent solicitude is good for the soul, for it undertakes the labor of being able to subdue the vices of the flesh. This solicitude is beneficial to the now subdued body in that it searchingly inquires how it may live on earth in a permissible way. As long as the flesh seeks after idleness and toil slumbers in exile, the pathway to wickedness is usually in readiness. Whenever a man's virtue will have no part of anything virile, the Devil highly favors his weak, womanly

160

behavior.[18] Idleness through lack of work is certainly harmful to such men; [19] for those of them who are Christians there can be no salvation [1980]. Indeed, this failing puts us far from God, while virtue puts us near Him; the former displeases God, the latter pleases Him.

Chapter 27

Here he speaks of the spiritual worthiness of priests, and of how they accomplish more than others, if they perform their duties well. Otherwise, they furnish more opportunity for transgression through their own bad examples.

A priest's honor is great, and his power is even greater, if he remains pious and good, and far removed from vices. With their hands they perform the rites of the highest sacrament, through which the flesh is made one with God by a word. And they can take away the sin for which our first parent fell by the sacred purification of baptism. They also celebrate our marriages according to the new law, and if they seek after righteousness, they will not engage in anything idle [1990]. They also offer pardon to those confessing they have fallen, and they provide an erring man a return to God. They also give us to partake of the heavenly host, and afterwards on our deathbed their unction awaits us. They also must assist the dead and buried, and offer up pious prayers in their masses.

They are the salt of the earth, by which we on earth are seasoned; without their savor man could scarcely be seasoned. [1] Elisha healed the waters with the salt he cast into them, and no bitter taste remained in them [2000]. [2] The salt signifies the knowing discretion of the just man, [3] whereby the man of discretion may season his people. [4] They are the light of the world. [5] For this reason, if they are in darkness, we in the world stand blind and uncertain. As God has declared, he shall be cursed who puts any stumbling block before a blind man that is hurt by it. He who has placed obstacles before a blind man shall, by his cursed deeds, show the pathway to sin. [6]

They are Jacob's ladder with its many steps, reaching to the heights of heaven; [7] by them the pathway will lie revealed [2010]. They are a holy mountain; through them every man of faith must mount the peak of virtues. They are our counsel, the right way to on high, the teachers of the law, and our new way of salvation. These good men close heaven and open it wide to people, and they can subject everything to themselves. It was said unto them, "Multiply, and yield much fruit." These words have reference to good morals. It was said unto them,

161

"Replenish the earth." Note what is said unto you: be full of good fruits in the Church [2020]. [8]

No worthless person should come before God, for no one lacking in virtue should be near God. [9] So the priest should reconcile both the righteous and the sinful to God, and pour forth the frankincense of prayers to heaven. Let him pray lest the just man fall away from justice, and let him pray that the dissolute man may rise up and weep over his extreme wickedness. [10] O what a shameful thing it is when a priest is like an ass, unversed in morals and lawlessly wild! Priests are like the stars of the sky in number, but scarcely two out of a thousand shine with light [2030]. They neither read the Scriptures nor understand them. Nevertheless, being tonsured, these men are apart from the common herd, and they think this is enough. There are some like this; and there are others whom an ardent virtue distinguishes in the Church, and who do many good works. Noah sent forth a raven and it did not return. He sent forth a dove and it did return. Similarly, in the Church there are ravens and doves. The good ones are without gall, while the bad ones are full of gall. "Tomorrow at prime," they sing, since they are slow to reform themselves; but the day of judgment often does away with such people [2040]. [11] Such are the black ones whom the bonds of this world shackle, and who are unwilling to thirst after the promised kingdom of God. [As for] the priest who upholds the laws of his order and who imparts holy teachings by both action and example, no esteem is too high for him, even when he is not held in honor by his order. Praise from the people is not enough for him, but God's praise is. I maintain that among the clergy, for those whom an ardent virtue shows to be good and true, their thanks shall be larger than they deserve.

Chapter 28

Now that he has spoken of the waywardness of those among the secular clergy who have usurped the office of the priesthood for themselves, he intends to speak a second time of the waywardness of scholars, who are called the little scions of the Church.

[1]We know that under the name of the clergy there are scholars, whom God calls the scions of the Church [2050]. The good scholar is a scion from the divine garden, and makes the fruits of the Church good. The cleric who is zealous for virtue and not for vice, and who reckons not the world but God for himself, is consequently thought of as belonging to God. And what he begins is brought to a good conclusion. The

just authority of a teacher outstanding in virtues rightly encourages the apt students. Those who stick to their studies and lift up their hearts and fix them on high are true offerings to God [2060]. [2]

But I think that nowadays although many among them are called, few are chosen as being upright in their ways. [3] For a long time in their behavior they have left off the virtue of study, and now they apply their studies vigilantly to vices. Scarcely a one studies for the sake of the necessary subject matter; instead the mere shadow of its outline is enough. A cleric used to go to school with a patient spirit, but now worldly glory is his master. He rambles here and there, a lazy, wandering drunkard, wayward and given to lust [2070]. A fruitful tree will not grow out of a barren plant, nor will a bad tree bring forth good fruit. [4] Old age often holds to what it held to as a youth. [5] If a youth is evil, he will scarcely be good when old. [6] It is the good root which brings forth seeds of goodness; utter badness sprouts forth from a bad root. Therefore everyone should punish his boys, seeing that the rod does not disturb the mind's proper activities. The youth who has a master of flowering virtue should learn what things are righteous [2080], and he will become well versed in them. But the man whom a dissolute teacher has instructed will rarely bear fruit.

Chapter 29

Here he inquires of the cause which persuades the minds of scholars to adopt the priesthood. He alleges that there are three causes in particular. He also discusses a fourth, which rarely obtains at present.

There are some nowadays who persist in zealous study, but I do not know what cause is responsible for this. Their intention judges all men, no matter what they do. God himself grasps what is in the heart. Now that I have made these remarks, explain the truth to me, scholar. Tell me what the underlying reason for your study is, when you first strengthen yourself for holy orders, when you first come to make yourself a priest [2090]. O what motive was then uppermost in your mind? Was this for love of the world or love of God? Either you tell me the particular source of your reason, or I want to tell you what I know to be true.

"As you may now observe, there are several reasons for which our order is widely esteemed throughout the world. In the first place, escape the everyday scourgings of the common law, which deals harshly with men. [1] Furthermore, I see that I do not have to sweat with toil, and so I can have the idleness I desire [2100]. The third reason [is that it] provides my food and clothing; and so I quietly persist in my pleasures. All my devotion is due to these things; for this reason the shaven tonsure can be seen as mine. This is the reason for going to school, which makes me study civil law and which skillfully teaches its logic. The school lets me progress upward to its highest levels, and in this way I try to rise into a good church. For I think that if his reputation prospers, a prebend will prosper, and so it is an easy task to devote some time to books [2110]. I like holy orders, and clerical learning is useful, as long as I get a fat profit from my study. Now I have told you the reasons that the position of a scholar is agreeable, so I confess I am guilty [of being one] for the sake of this world. For I don't think there is anything better for me than to enjoy the pleasures of the world while there is sufficient opportunity. "

But there is nevertheless a still better reason than all those, namely, that a school rejoices in having a good student. This reason, which virtuously embraces the work of a school, used to hold good in days of old but does not in our own [2120]. There used to be saints who disdained worldly pomp and longed for the highest good. And since becoming acquainted with schools incited their spirits to be holy, they gave themselves over to the pious study of Scripture. Ambition and love of possession did not move them, but they rightly went out of eagerness for virtue. In contemplating heaven they shunned the earth, and no lascivious purpose drew them aside. Nor did they wish to be in the service of a king, nor to have the name of rabbi among the people [2130]. [2] Nor did vain, sumptuous adornment, nor indulgence in wine, nor woman's love overcome them. Well versed in good morals, they furnished examples for those to come which the student ought to adopt for his own instruction. Today, however, virtue has been changed into vice, and what were once morals now bring on great disgrace. Their greed for worldly preferment now turns into worldly glory the writings which they say they are learning for the glory of God. What an astounding state of affairs! The scholar reads and studies about virtue, while his own actions become more and more vicious [2140]. So, because the clergy without the light of virtue is blind, we errant laymen wander about in darkness. [3]

BOOK IV[1]

Chapter 1

Since he has discussed the waywardness of the clergy, to whom
he looks especially for guidance for our souls, he now intends to
discuss the waywardness of men in monastic orders. And he will
speak first of monks and others who get possession of temporal
goods. While commending, to be sure, the sanctity of their
order, he rebukes in particular those whose actions are just the
contrary.

There are also cloistered men of diverse kind, concerning whom
I wish to write the little I know. As their actions show, some of them
are noted for property and some for poverty, but the poverty is feigned
to too great an extent. A monastic order is good in itself, but we say
that those who betray it are evil. I believe that those who live faithfully
in their cloister and who cannot be held guilty of worldly love are
blessed. A religious order will recognize as holy men those who put
their hand to the plow without looking back [10]. [1] God is present among
the monks who are willing to enter monasteries apart from mankind,
and the fellowship of heaven is theirs. When a man undertakes to love
two opposing things equally, the one love will detract from the effectiveness of the other. [2] I accordingly direct my words to those who presume to mask their faces under the shadow of a religious order, yet inwardly commit worldly sins. And no one else is going to be hurt by
what I have written; instead, every man shall bear his own burden. [3]
Nothing that I write is my own opinion; rather, I shall speak what the
voice of the people has reported to me [20]. [4]
There are certainly monks whom ownership of property has made

165

a claim on, men whom no religious order can hold in check through moral precepts. For some men of property seek the leisure of an order so that they cannot suffer any hardships. They avoid being hungry, and slake their thirst with wine. They get rid of all cold with their warm furred cloaks. [5] Faintness of the belly does not come upon them in the hours of night, and their raucous voice does not sing the heights of heaven in chorus with a drinking cup. A man of this kind will devour no less than several courses at table, and empties a good many beakers in his drinking [30]. Then he believes he has grown sick and demands to be made well again; and in such fashion does he devote himself to his sports. Indeed, it is only with difficulty that this man of professed vows is to be worn out from[6] drinking; thus, master monk[7] is willing to appear before God while in his cups. And while you are bringing him wine, he allures women to himself; wanton monasteries now furnish these two things together. If he can get to heaven after being inflamed with passion even while in his vestments; [8] and if his gluttony can gain a place among those above, then I think that the monk distinguished on these two counts will stand as Peter's fellow-citizen in the vault of the skies [40].

Chapter 2

Here he speaks of the monks who, contrary to the decrees of their order, are the first to abandon the virtue of self-restraint and partake again and again of the delights of the flesh.

Things which are dead by no means belong with the living; [1] and one who renounces the world does not return to worldly behavior. No matter how much he seems to be a sheep, neither tonsure nor the humblest garb is any help at all to him, if he is a wolf. For men can be deceived, but no one can deceive Christ, Who deceived no man. Indeed, He condemns the pretense of feigned religion and reckons its work as nothing. [2] Nevertheless, a monk withdraws from the world nowadays only in respect to his dress, and thinks that a religious order is sufficient for him in outer appearance alone [50]. The vestments will be the monk himself, and his thoughts will wander about in the world, heeding nothing beyond the material wealth of his order. Since he knows that bodies seldom thrive properly on slender rations for the belly, [3] such a monk demands plentiful sustenance for his gullet. And the more food he eats the more he craves, so that his belly may enjoy its pleasures, with the help of his gullet. Unmindful of his father, who used to bear burdens on his shoulders, the monk lugs the finest wines about in his belly. Such a man pours the fruit of the vine into his stomach as if it were a flagon, and he is not one to allow any place in his swelling paunch to be empty [60].

A monk ought to shun wine for many reasons, one of them being lest his flesh yearn for debauchery. A man should not spoil the good works of his brothers in religion, or sit around in a drunken state or have a fever from it. Nevertheless, the monk cares about nothing except stuffing his worthless body, yet his soul goes hungry every day. In these times snow-white bread, delicate wine, and meats provide monks with daily feasts. Just see how the cook bakes and roasts, freezes and melts, grinds and presses, strains and tests his performances [70]. [4] If a gluttonous monk can fatten his paunch, he thinks there is nothing in Holy Writ to the effect that one should work. Scorning manna, this kind of people demands that its cooking pots be black [with constant use], and prefers its vices to virtues. Lest hunger might weaken these fat fellows, their belly's harlot gluttony crams their faint stomachs full. A monk does not know what ought to be honored, but what ought to be esteemed for the belly. This, he says, is the way, the life, the salvation. [5] When the bell rings for the dinner pot, he runs at a fast clip, and not one crumb from the table escapes him [80]. But when the sluggard gets up at night and comes to prayers at a slow pace, he tries to be last. [6]

[7]When their order began, monks' homes were caves; now a grand marble palace sets them off. They used to have no steaming kitchen, and no cook served them delicacies roasted or baked by the fire. In former times no boiled food or dishes loaded with meat made monks fat. [8] Bodily gluttony did not afflict their souls, nor were they inflamed by lust of the flesh to seek out debauchery on the sly [90]. They who used to cover their bare bodies with the skins of animals[9] now cover them more comfortably with wool. Herbs used to furnish their food, a spring their drink, and a base hair shirt their clothing, yet there was no grumbling in those days. There was no envy or splendor in a monastery then; he who was the greater served as did the lesser. There was no great quantity of silver or chain of gold[10] that could corrupt their holy state then. Money did not touch their pockets, nor wine their palates, and no carnal flame burned in their loins [100]. They had a holy spirit which served their resolution well, and which persevered successfully in the work it undertook.

They were righteous men who shunned the world and who were burdened with no love of sins. The world did not draw them away from the right path, and the flesh did not beckon them toward heinous evils. [11] They put aside all the vanities which the world affords, and yearned only for the God of heaven. It was no disgrace then to take one's rest upon straw or to put hay under one's head [110]. [12] The forest was their home, herbs were their food, and leafy boughs were their bedding, [13] which the earth furnished without their even asking.[14] The hazel then flourished among them in high esteem, and the sturdy oak yielded splendid treasures.[15] They gathered the fruits of the arbutus and mountain [strawberries],[16] which were seasoned neither with salt nor with spices. And although they partook of acorns from Jove's spreading tree,[17] they grew strong from these foods. Contented with the modest things produced by Nature of her own accord,[18] they sent forth their humble prayers to God on high [120]. Admirable sowers of the seeds of justice then, now they reap their fruits eternally a hundredfold. But that ancient salvation of souls, which religious orders once possessed, has perished, undermined by the weakness of the flesh.

Chapter 3

Here he speaks of how the way of life and the rule which were originally instituted by the founders of monastic orders have in recent times been undone among a great many men, by their habitual practice of vices.

Men's thinking frequently turns toward new fashions, and the altered rule for monks will be a witness for me on this point. The original rule for monks has now become curtailed, for re has been subtracted from regula so that only gula is left.[1] And to drink wines freely by the tun is called moderation on the part of a monk, who gorges immoderately [130].[2] The monastic order commands silence during breakfast--so that no talkative tongue may disturb the ravenous jaws. When a monk drinks, he sits down first, so that his foot may not fail under the weight of his belly. And it is practical for a bloated monk's head to be shaved, lest long, flowing hair get in the way when he guzzles. Monks make mutual pledges that if one of them drinks to another, he will allow nothing to remain in the bottom [of the cup]. They drain their brimming beakers, and they fill up the emptied ones again, so that their ranks may make a celebration worthy of Bacchus [140]. Thus an oversized garment is useful to a corpulent monk, lest the outline of his fat paunch be plainly visible.

In a monk such as this the passion for eating is always seething; food and sleep furnish what he wants most. With his greedy jaws the greedy man devours what land and sea furnish and what the air provides.[3] Just as the ocean receives the rivers from all the earth,[4] yet the sea's swollen appetite remains ever keen [150]; and just as the billows swallow up like wells the streams coming from afar, yet are not filled up with water no matter how much pours in;[5] and just as the fire's heat burns up many huge logs, yet, the greater the supply, the more it requires for itself; 6 so does the gluttonous monk, out of fondness for his belly, dispatch a variety of banquets with his impious lips. He carries about a paunch heavy with a full load, yet his light-minded spirit turns away empty from Christ. After he has been consumed with drinking, the holy man does not stay active, but remains lumpishly and heavily in the spot he occupies. After wine has been drunk, the monk's feelings grow stupidly sluggish, and the heaviness of the cloister's burden is gone [160]. When the wine is poured out, his grateful inwards are delighted to be filled up; and after they are warmed, his spirits glow. Thus drugs make the holy man's slumbers long, 7 and drinking too much wine is the cause of his sleep. I do not know how a winebibber may remain properly chaste, for Venus rages as hotly with wine as a fire does with flame. 8 Venus is therefore quite happy to hide snugly beneath a garment of pain, 9 and carry on her wickedness under a religious facade.

Envy murmurs within the hollow of a monk's breast; his lips are outwardly silent, but his mind is busy within [170]. And when his tongue remains quiet, his hand, which is well versed in sign language, tells many a shameful thing on its fingers. 10 And so his talkative finger speaks out to make up for the verbal silence, 11 and runs riot in quarrels more than a harlot. His face swells with wrath, his veins grow black with blood, and his rolling eyes flash brighter than fire. 12 Often a blazing anger will color his eyes, 13 in which the idea of death for another is plainly visible. The pride in such a face is no less damnable 14 than if he were to cut down someone by the neck with his sword [180]. So no matter how much his order forbids contentious talking, he fights, and in his mind he cuts off a head with a sword. While he himself cannot speak, grumbling in the thoughts of his heart makes him hoarse with envy of his brother. His face is full of rage; he gives out growls instead of words, and he murders with his mind, since his hand cannot do so. Then the pallor of his face, the heavings of his chest, and the frightfulness of his aspect are harbingers of his disturbed thoughts. For whatever a man is afflicted with, his inner agitation affects his outer emotions in token of it [190].

The face expresses the state of one's mind and displays the wrath of a heart strongly aroused. For in the event that one express himself silently, no index of the mind can be more reliable than the face. 15 Whatever simplicity the blackness of one's garment may possess, experience teaches what lies beneath it. The monk prefers love to what is prescribed for him; he envies all those whom he cannot imitate. Each one rushes at once at the ringing of the bell, yet under the guise of their order they indulge in each and every vanity [200]. Outwardly, their voice sings in chorus, yet inwardly their spirit grumbles. Their lips implore a place in heaven, but their spirit a place on earth. Thus those in a religious order preserve only its outer form, not its essence. They stupidly cherish the body, now that they have enjoyed its fruits. So, outwardly their toil and wisdom are plainly visible, but what foolish concerns occupy them inwardly!

Chapter 4

Here he tells of the monks who secretly, and with the abbot not knowing about it, take it upon themselves to appropriate worldly wealth for wicked uses, contrary to the original commands of their order.

It is better to make no vows rather than break a vow, for no praise should be given to a liar. [1] Brotherly love ought to be mutual, at least among those whom a religious order binds together [210]. The present age, however, does not permit this; rather, envy provokes into anger whatever love there used to be. The half devil of a man in the cloister sneaks away, just like a bull in the fields which ruminates once again on the grasses. If you do not wish to be gnawed to pieces, you should partake of no banquets among them, where there is seldom any good faith. [2] As long as they are asking for your possessions, then they esteem you reverently, but they scarcely do so any more, if they merely wish to seem grateful. Nothing which their original founders bequeathed to them is of any use, unless it be the fact that they may plead for money every day [220]. Reason denies that a man can be both a property owner and a beggar, but a monastic order does not hold with that. Indeed, nowadays nothing on earth satiates these idle monks, who always have a constant hunger and thirst. One so reads of both Jerome and likewise of Benedict in order that we may follow them the more as models. They sold ornaments from their altar and distributed them among the poor for their rightful food. The Church's property belongs to the needy, and it is not allowable for members of religious orders to keep it, when they see need and want [230].

If you wish to give to a monk, he will take possession of everything that you offer; but he has nothing of his own, if you should ask for something from him. They are all in agreement on one and the same idea, which is that each one wants to keep his property for himself. So, the new type of religious order undoes whatever rules the old order formerly revered, because their ways have changed. We seldom see noblemen being made monks; rather, we usually see peasants, and therefore monks are more and more uncouth. Nevertheless, those whom a holy order makes into holy men of professed vows are quite

170

noble and worthy of honor [240]. But what shall I say for those whom neither order nor origin makes worthy? They certainly spend their time foolishly. Even if Benedict did found those who are maledict, God on His part will not give them His benediction. These writings of mine publicize those for whom the world has had more attraction than Christ, and who look back from the plow. [3]

Why, I ask, does one who forsakes everything covet anything? Why does one who vows good deeds return to evil ones? You who seek to gain heaven should little esteem the earth. If you desire what endures, shun that which passes away [250]. Those who have been made monks do not rightfully own property, do they? I do not rightfully know, but see what they do. If the guardian of a shrine seeks any personal property just because he is in a position to get hold of money, then he shall be witness for me. Or, whenever a monk in a position of authority puts by something as personal property, the result is proof of what he has done. For when he has his pile, then he enriches his "nephews" with it, and in such fashion does he provide for new cloisters. [4] He often calls "nephews" the children he begets to the glory of Venus, whom he worships devotedly [260]. Indeed, his children are often turned out under fictitious name, and so [only a] piety turned blind will help them.

In such fashion does imaginary almsgiving abound in corrupt monasteries, as long as a monk gives his donations to his own offspring. In such fashion does underhanded, monkish piety flourish, as long as it pretends that such things are given through love for God. When theft becomes lawful, then I can say that it is lawful to make such offerings to God. But the man who turns things held in common to his own private uses brings on God's curse by the character of his gift [270]. Monasteries are being bent toward ruin by such gifts; granaries are groaning with the weight of their grain. A hundred monks waste away just so two or three may have fat faces while they are in positions of authority. "Everything is ours, " they say; but the balance does not weigh equitably, as long as one man alone gets more than three.

Chapter 5

Here he speaks of how monks ought not to wander around outside the monastery.

The sea is the proper habitat of a live fish, and the monastery is the right home for a monk. Just as the sea will not keep dead fish, so the monastery casts out evildoing monks [280]. A fish ought not to be

171

out of the water, nor ought a monk to be away from his cloisters, unless you return to them, O monk in holy orders. [1] If there were a fish that forsook the waters of the sea to seek its food on land, it would be highly inappropriate to give it the name of fish; I should rather give it the name of monster. Such shall I call the monk who yearns for worldly delights and deserts his cloister for them. He should not rightly be called a monk but a renegade, or what God's wrath brands as a monster of the Church [290]. As for those who still remain within the monastery, yet with wandering minds look back on the world with new love in their hearts, their transgression disgraces such men in the eyes of God. Because of this they lose their cloister's rightful rewards. It is not a wise man who amasses goods for himself for several years and dissipates them in only one day. The monk who makes the rounds of town and country quite frequently commits a fault for which he perishes as a sinner. In spite of this, there are only a few at present who do not give over their errant hearts to sensual pleasures [300]. Solomon said that a man's foolish attire, which is outwardly visible, tells what is within. [2] But although a monk should array himself with humble garb, nevertheless you now see many sumptuous things on his back.

Chapter 6

Here he speaks of the monks who put on monastic garb not for divine service but rather for the enjoyment and honor of this world.

The raven is a black bird and a plunderer of corpses; a remarkable blind passion blackens it in a foul way. The lawgiver describes under [this] species of birds those whom worldly passion has cloaked with religion. He also touches upon the man whom the garb of a religious order masks in order that he may thereby enjoy a high reputation more readily [310]. [1] The bull is an unsightly monster; a field without grass is unsightly, and a plant without leaves, or a head without hair. [2] Even baser[3] is the monk who has put on the garb of a religious order yet lacks a monk's true nature.

Their ancient religious order commands that monks shun the world. They claim that they do shun it, but they seek it even by shunning it: the poor man whom villein stock has born to the plow wishes priority over the prior, although he is unworthy of it. Unmindful of his former status, he seeks within the monastery the honor which the world did not yield him [320]. Thus when they become monks, a religious order makes proud those whom by paternal rights nature created humble. They seek the title of lord, not monk, [4] and they make broad the path which was narrow. [5] Nothing burdensome concerns them, nor do they think it could. Therefore, they scarcely know of anything for which to petition God.

Chapter 7[1]

Here he speaks of how Patience together with other virtues have betaken themselves away from certain cloisters, with vices superseding them.

Abbot Patience is dead, and the monk Grumbler lives on, and there can be no peace in his cloisters. Abbott Chastity is also now dead, and Lust has succeeded him and is ruining the religious houses [330]. And Abbot Inconstancy has refused Constancy the monasteries that Hatred occupies and claims as his. Abbot Hypocrisy links up with Abbot Deceit, while Fraud aspires to achieve high rank. Monks of old used to plant the fruits of love; the modern monastic order now bears the fruits of Envy.

The rule of St. Bernard or St. Maure[2] is of no use to our modern fellow monks; on the contrary, it displeases them. A greedy fellow sets himself against St. Bernard and St. Maure, as does another, proud and envious; they now refuse to carry out the precepts of their order [340]. Thus Malediction has driven Benedict out of the monasteries, Gluttony has driven out Temperance, and Guile has driven out Faith. Gone is the Abbot Gentle whom gentle cloisters obey. The religious order's false shadow now conceals false men. What was once spirit is now a lifeless body, and Abbot World governs the whole undertaking.

Chapter 8

Here he says that wayward canons are to be censured for their transgressions, just as monks are.

By rights you should render a like decision in similar cases, just as the law says. No matter how many in the Church are confirmed as members of a religious order, if they are property holders, they are to be judged alike [350]. For a similar lapse, censure applies as much to canons whom sinfulness has led astray as it does to monks. In these

times, however, it so happens that many cut down on their rightful obligations, and once these have been trimmed off, they are silent about
them, as if [they were] under some new obligation. In their new fashion, they mollify with glosses the strict text their author had written.
It is sufficient, so they believe, to be recognized as being of a holy
order and to do little that the order requires.

[1]Even though the canon's name is taken from canon law, in
reality the facts rarely bear this out to you [360]. Granted that outwardly among the people they bear the appearance of saints, nevertheless their rule often fails in this respect. Underneath they wear white
vestments, but a black surface above these covers everything white. [2]
Too, their way of life will reveal itself in contrary fashion: outwardly
they pretend to be pure white, but inwardly they carry on black doings.
But I do not say this for the contemplation of those who innocently remain in their cloisters. Instead, I speak to those men who inwardly
search for the world, yet outwardly wear tokens of divinity [370].

Chapter 9

Here he speaks of how those in orders who live evilly are to all
other men whatsoever the most unfortunate.

[1]I think that unless they happen to be good, monks are born in
more inauspicious hours than other men. For a monk dies after having
professed to a pure life, because he cannot outwardly enjoy the good
things in the world like another man. And if he is inwardly covetous of
anything worldly, he loses the rewards of heaven. In such a case it is
evident that he is to enjoy neither the present life nor the one to come,
whereby he is doubly wretched. Having been dead to this life, he dies;
while at the same time he is to reckon both of his opportunities lost
through his second death [380]. And so, since he is dead in regard to
the world, because by his order's law he gets no pleasure from it; and
since no place in heaven remains for him unless he meditates upon
God alone in his heart and thereby is happy, I know not what fool is
stupider than the monk who deprives himself in such fashion of both his
blessings. Time passes away as useless for one whom the present life
has denied any pleasures, and for whom the second life does not include heaven.

Chapter 10

Here he speaks of how each person who considers entering into the vows of a religious order is under obligation to forsake all the vices of the world completely, and to acquire and preserve the virtues of the soul.

O companions of the cloister, who have taken vows in a religious order, I shall demonstrate in a few words[1] what and for what your task is [390]. Being an educated man, I have pondered the writings of the saints, which ought to be well heeded for your instruction. Holy words are more effective, when they are more clearly set forth. Therefore, you monks, see what is in them. You have taken your vows, brethren, you have taken your vows. Keep your vows and carry out the endeavors you have promised.[2] You have vowed to turn your ways toward the Lord.[3] God has chosen you; you should stand firm in love of Him. Monks' lives should keep to their strict purpose, and suffering hardships should not become irksome as time goes on [400]. The toil is slight, but the reward of the toil is great.[4] The former quickly passes by, the recompenses are without end. Hence holy monks should wash away their past sins by weeping and wailing with all their strength of spirit.[5]

He[6] who used to live proudly should now live humbly; each one who used to be wanton should now be chaste. Every empty honor should now become worthless [in the eyes of] one who used to seek after riches and strive for honors. A plain meal shall now furnish slender fare [for] one who used to delight in feasts and a rich table [410]. He shall beware of worldly vanities, no matter how delightful they are, for surely sweet things are often harmful to one's taste. The man who used to be happy in his excesses should now wash away his sins with tears. Let the garrulous man be silent; let the violent man grow mild in his wrath; let the envious man cast out the harsh poisons of envy. Each man whom the sword and rapine once pleased shall now become a pious and gentle lover of peace. Each man who used to swell up with the windy praise of flatterers should now value the praises of men as nothing [420]. And the man who used to hurt others with his cruelty should duly learn to suffer bitter things, after he too has been hurt. Let the man who was ready for quarrels and foremost in contentions now bear another's slanders bravely. The doves who used to quarrel shall now join bill to bill,[7] and their former angriness shall not last any longer. Similarly, even a brief fit of anger should be without sinfulness, for

175

a mind inwardly raging may be completely ignorant of one's actions. A true conversion like this, O brethren, is worthy of mercy; it can placate God when He has been offended [430].

Chapter 11

Here he speaks of how men in religious orders ought especially to avoid the companionship of women. [1]

[2]Shun a woman's conversation, O holy man; beware lest you entrust yourself to a passion raging beyond control. For the mind which is allured and bound over by a woman's love can never reach the pinnacle of virtue. Of what use is their prattling to you? If you have come in as a monk, you will go away a foul adulterer. Unless you turn aside from the venomous serpent, you will be poisoned by her when you least expect it. Every woman enkindles a flame of passion; if one touches her, he is burned instantly [440]. [3] If you ponder the books of the ancients and the writings of the Church Fathers, you may grieve that even holy men have met with ruin in this way. Did not woman expel man from the seat of Paradise? And was she not the source of our death? The man who is a good shepherd should therefore be vigilant, and he should everywhere drive these rapacious she-wolves away from the monastery.

Protect what is entrusted to you. Shepherd, what protestations will avail you who abandon the sheepfold to the swift she-wolf? The she-wolf stalking a lamb is often checked by a voice; [4] too, the lamb often perishes because the shepherd's tongue is silent [450]. The she-wolf draws near to many a sheep[5] and quite often lays waste the fold by her tricks when the shepherd is laggard. Just as the ravenous wolf, goaded with hunger and eager for blood, seizes upon the unguarded fold, [6] so the old serpent which profaned Paradise is eager to profane more holy cloisters. And for this reason the shepherd should drive away the she-wolves lest the flock fall into their maw, which it can never glut. Shepherds, watch out for wolves; guard your sheepfold, that they cannot stain your cloisters with the blood of the flock [460]. They kill souls, and send many of them to hell. Monks have no greater ruin to fear.

Woman, the death of the soul, should never approach monks. She should stay away from the holy band. Woman should keep at a distance from a gathering of holy men, for even if she cannot overpower them, she causes strife. [7] Therefore, O monks, take care lest lust of the flesh quickly dissipate the virtues of the soul. [8]Why does one who

176

blushes, because he does something shameful when I am looking, not blush all the more when God is looking [470]? If a judge of the nation knew of his deeds, he would be afraid; but the Lord knows the facts, so why is he not afraid? Similarly, when his enemy wickedly heaps misfortunes upon him and tries to trick him in a thousand ways, the monk should believe that God is always present everywhere, and should not think that he can conceal himself, were he to sin. He knows and sees all things, and nothing escapes Him. Everything is always open to His eyes. If He is silent and delays and has not yet punished crimes, He will punish them and will be a just judge of what they deserve [480]. Vain and fleeting pleasure, therefore, should not concern monks; instead they should cherish their bounden duties toward God. Let them do that for which they came, and fulfill their vows, and let no enemy gain a place in the monasteries. They should read, work, and pray in separate turns. [9] None of their time should be lacking in sacred pursuits. [10] They should always apply themselves diligently to useful and honorable employments; laziness is a highly pernicious quality. And the heat of lust, a thing provocative of evils, provides a vile dwelling place for their souls [490].

Chapter 12

Here he discusses, if only briefly, the things which, according to the stipulations of the founders, must in the end be strictly observed by those under the vows of a religious order.

The man who locks the age-old teachings of the saints within the chamber of his heart, and whose first intent is upon the ways of his order, knows well that within the cloister the world must be shunned. Nevertheless, at present it claims a place there. O good monk, you who forsake the world, do not return to it again, but rather shun what it teaches. Do not seek a soft bed where the flesh is pampered, do not seek a cloister where there is fancy dress and a book is a matter for jest. Let your heart be sorrowful and your hand generous. Let there be fast days. Let there be no unchaste love nor vain honor [500]. Let your drink be water, let your food be scanty, your clothing rough, [1] your sleep brief, your rest troubled, and let there be a rod for your back. Bend your knee, strike your breast, and pray bareheaded. Seek God, shun the world, forsake evil. Let your lips cleave to the earth and your mind to heaven. Let your tongue speak with humble heart and utter humble words. The man of undevout heart, who sows words without prayers, tills the barren sea coast, [2] for they are fruitless.

177

Not one's voice but one's vow, not a musical string but a heart string, [3] not one who cries but one who loves sings in the ear of God [510].

Let a humble spirit, clear eye, chaste body, pious heart, upright faith, and firm hope show you the way. If you wish to relish the sweet harmonies of heaven, you must drink from the cup of this world first. Properly calm and without a note of grumbling, you should subordinate yourself to your prior with humble heart. It is a monk's highest virtue to obey his prior and to refuse to bear the yoke of rule on his own behalf. Do not let your base garb or lowly place distress you; such things often disturb foolish men of your order [520]. He who reviles himself, thinks himself of little importance, and avoids the depths of this transitory world is wise and very close to heaven. He does not bear the empty title of monk without the substance.

Let the law of the Lord be your peace, the flesh your sacrifice, the world your place of exile, heaven your homeland, and God your life. Bear the irksome obligations given you; undertake them and make them welcome. In this way you will be a religious man in the Lord. No matter how lowly the things which the abbot recommends to you, if they are rightful, do them patiently [530]. Nor should you think it lowly, and even if it is lowly, it will give you pleasure, for your spirit will be pure in Christ. Just as young men submit to the commands of an elderly prior and do nothing contrary to the weight of authority, so the prior should treat young men kindly in matters of discipline, and conquer evil through a humble heart. Observe that the first yoke chafes the bullocks in harness, and the new saddle annoys the flying steed. [4] A harsh master oppresses a youth in the same way, and furnishes a cause for habitual grumbling to agitate his feelings [540]. Keep these writings in the cloisters of your spirit, O monk, and as a dead man apart from the world, live chastely for God. Purchase rest eternal through a little toil, and gain lasting joys through a brief sorrow. For if the burden of the flesh is nothing to you now, then rest and everlasting peace shall be yours without end.

Chapter 13

Here he goes on to speak about women who, in a nun's garb, enter upon the profession of vows under the veil of holy religion and do not observe the continence of their order.

I have now left off writing of the sins of the errant monk, and shall sing to you of woman veiled in religion. A monastic order is appropriate for men as long as they live virtuously, whereby they, apart

178

from the world, may reach the kingdoms of heaven [550]. It is also appropriate for virtuous women to fulfill their vows of chastity to God under the veil. Just as a holy order binds monks, it also binds nuns, so that both may shine in their merits for God. Nevertheless, if weak women in the cloisters go astray, their unchastity does not militate against them equally with men. For a woman's foot cannot stand as steady as a man's can, nor can it make its steps firm. Neither learning nor understanding, neither constancy nor virtue such as men have flourishes in woman [560]. But you often see women's morals change because of their frail nature, rather than by conscious choice. Quite frequently we perceive the very women whom their order thinks most sensible to be full of foolish behavior. And above all, those who know the Scriptures often fall because of an indiscreet secular crime. They think the Scriptures permit them to do as they do, because frequently they simply read the text and are not concerned about the gloss. The reading of Scripture teaches them to approve everything, and so, since they read about everything, they wish to make proof of everything [570]. [1] Nature's laws, which God in the beginning wrote down from her own lips, are to be fruitful and multiply. [2] And these are the Scriptures of God they wish to obey, and the regular laws of Nature which they wish to administer in dutiful spirit.

Woman strives for what is forbidden, [3] but she rarely does what is permissible without mentally grumbling. But nuns are made more perfect by the Scriptures [if] they patiently do what the Scriptures command them. It is written that the seeds which good earth will not receive do not bear any fruit at all, but lie dying [580]. [4] And yet a nun should be the kind of earth which lies in readiness, for there the seeds are multiplied tenfold. And since frail women sustain such a heavy burden, sometimes they rightly seek rest and quiet. Therefore it happens that on Venus' days[5] they eat meat because of their weak stomach. For to Genius, Venus entrusts for her worthy foster daughters[6] the pork dishes which he should prepare for his own nymphs. But when sated, their maw often grows too heavy and swells up because it is in pain, troubled by the weight of the food [590]. The swelling is too burdensome, and being tainted with poison, it is toxic to the stomach, and will bring on a fear of death. On the other hand, the food which is eaten secretly in the dark is injurious, and often causes heavy illnesses.

Chapter 14

Here he speaks of how ordinaries[1] on their official visitation, by
which they claim they reform women veiled in a religious order,
oftentimes make them worse.

Venus and Genius do not teach the cloister cells, which they now
govern in their fashion, to keep the laws concerning the flesh. Genius
is the convent's protector and confessor, and sometimes he holds the
rank of bishop. He visits the ladies in their cloister under the guise
of righteous authority, but when he comes to their bedchambers, he
casts righteousness aside and wields his power over them [600]. Although he may be in a fur-lined cape while he is giving instruction, he
nevertheless ministers his naked authority to them forcefully. By
Genius' decision they are stoned for their sins, but no mortal blow injures these women. [2] O the virtue of the cleric when he is the souls'
protector! How many blessed deeds of the priest are brought to light!
He should have a care for the women he thrusts himself upon as if he
were a second God, lest some rumor might fly outside the cell. "If the
father is a holy man, the mother is likewise a holy woman; but the child
is even holier, since it is begotten through the agency of the cloister
[610]." I should think this kind of unchastity highly damnable, unless it
were for the fact that woman fails because of light-mindedness. You
shall therefore not tempt them, for you know that a trivial cause could
ruin a thing so frail. [3] For unless a young woman is protected, she is
frequently weak to the extent that her nature teaches her to be. When
the young branch is growing in the green bark, any breeze shaking the
weak thing will hurl it to the ground. [4] In the cloisters where wise discretion is on guard, the growing crop is enclosed by high fences [620]. [5]
The frail flesh took its origin from the dust of the ground, but the soul
came from the mansions on high. [6] The spirit is willing, the flesh is
weak. [7] Therefore, do not stay in a place alone with a lone woman.
And a maiden ought not remain alone with one man; gossip considers it
wicked even though her body be not touched. And just as there is a
safeguard for the cloisters, so should there be one for the fields. Their
pastime should be proper and their work suitable. With no disgrace to
them, it should be permissible for nuns to participate in the diversions
which modesty and their precepts and duties allow [630]. But let not
waywardness ruin these weak, veiled women; let modest restraint assist them with a guiding hand.

What is it to me, if a wife dishonestly deceives her husband, who
knows nothing about her and does not see what she has done? But I
wonder at the dishonesty of the woman who deceives Him to Whose sight

all the ages lie revealed. If the brides of men should be pure, how much more ought the brides of Christ remain chaste in pure conduct for God. When a girl is to be a nun, first she is clothed in black garments and her hair cut off [640]. She disfigures her body on the outside in order that her spirit within may be beautiful and grow pure white, being filled with love of God. Since she is black on the outside, if she were to become even blacker within, she would not be like a handmaiden of God, she would be cast aside as infamous. But as long as she remains chaste, all the blackness on the outside shows that her mind is the more spotless.

Chapter 15

Here he speaks in praise of chastity, which is most highly in keeping for women who have made profession of vows in a religious order.

O how the virginity which follows the Lamb through all the vaults of heaven[1] shines above every glory! Wedded to the Godhead, it is radiant on earth, forsaking the actions to which the nature of the human body prompts it [650]. Just as the unchaste woman is fetid, the untainted chaste one is sweet-scented. The one possesses God, the other a corpse. Flowery garlands[2] heaped three-fold with a hundred fruits decorate the head of the virgin in God's presence. The rank of virgin transcends bands of angels and abides more in heaven than even the Triple Crown.[3] As John is my witness, the spirit of a virgin, imitating the prerogative of the eagle and yearning for the heights, flies up before God.[4] Just as a rose springing from thorns rises above them, so the status of a virgin surpasses others [660].[5] Just as a white pearl is pleasing, being highly valuable, so a virgin in a cloister is pleasing, having professed her vows to God. Such a nun is indeed highly worthy of the cloister and holy in merit, so long as she keeps her vows. But no matter what woman seeks the cloister under the veil, the rule which she obeys will sanctify her. If she has been a good woman, it will make her better, and at all times add more good morals to her good character. If she were defiled before she took the veil and live chastely from now on, her previous sin shall be as nothing [670]. Therefore it is not permitted for men to violate consecrated nuns, for the sacred veil carries the mark of chastity. How heavy a crime in our judgment does a man commit who takes it upon himself to violate another's bride! But be assured that the man who destroys nunneries and takes it upon himself to violate the bride of God sins even more heavily.

181

Now that he has discussed those in property-owning religious
houses who break their vows, it is necessary to speak of those
in the order of mendicant friars who go astray. And he will
speak first of those who conspire under the shadow of feigned
poverty for worldly riches, as if they would bring all the earth
under their dominion.

   While He was on earth, not all those whom Christ chose for Himself were faithful in keeping God's new law. Yet it is not fair that the
traitor's crime injure those who have cherished the true faith [680].
No spot is so barren that a useful plant may not be intermingled with
the unwanted, harmful ones in it. [2] Nor is there any spot so fertile
that a harmful, unwanted plant may not be intermingled with the useful,
good ones. Similarly, there is no large assemblage of just men in
which there is no mingling on the part of an unjust man. By like justice, their work shows which friars a religious order certifies as holy
are to be absolved [from any charges I may make here]. I do not wish
to scatter reproach against all because of a few; rather, each should
be judged on his own merits [690]. Nevertheless, coming as a messenger to those whom sin influences, I do report the necessary matters
of conversation which general talk has brought to me. [3] Just as a
shepherd separates the sheep from the goats, [4] so a religious order
separates those whom it feels to be upright from the wicked. I shall
write what the purport of this general talk contains, especially for those
whom their religious order brands as most guilty of transgression. I
do not wish to fix upon Peter the crimes that Judas committed; each
should bear his own burden. [5] I grant that the functions of the original
order were holy, and that in the beginning its founders were pious
[700]. A friar remains blessed who follows after them, who in renoun-
cing the world seeks to reach God, who adopts monastic poverty for
himself and bears it voluntarily, [6] and who patiently undertakes the work
of his order. Such a man is indeed to be praised for his high merits,
for the earth is restored through his prayers. But he who disguises
his outer appearance in the order and lacks its true essence, he who
preaches outwardly yet inwardly yearns for riches—to such men of the
present this book offers its message, since the voice of the people
furnished the things for it to say [710]. [7]
   The throng of friars overflows the mendicant order; the original
rule is dead, inundated by them. [8] These men, who used to bear hardships pleasing to God in accordance with the vow of their order, are be
coming soft. For the first time they are giving themselves a name

which must be described as "headless"; [9] those upon whom everyone confers opulence call themselves "inopulent." The friars maintain that they are disciples of Christ and that they are pursuing all their duties after His example. Their false faith claims this, but this is sufficient unto them, as those who know the Scriptures say [720]. [10] They are now acting like people who have no property, [11] yet under a pauper's guise they grab everything. I do not know whether it is a sign of favor or doom for these friars, but all the world abounds with them. They hold the Pope in their hands; he mitigates the hardships of their order and decrees that more and more things are now permissible. And if the papal authority rejects their suits, their perverse order will secretly make them lawful. There is no king nor prince nor great man in the world who should not confess his secrets to them [730]. [12]

And so the mendicants are mightier than lords, and from the world they secretly usurp what their order plainly forbids. I would say that these men are not disciples but rather gods: both life and death bring money to them. For a friar demands that he himself bury the dead bodies of those to whom he attached himself as confessor, if they were dignitaries. But if it should be a poor [man's] body, he makes no claim at all, since his piety takes no cognizance of anything unless there is money in it. They refuse to baptize mere faith, since a matter of business with no money in it will not be esteemed or performed at their hands [740]. [13] Just as a merchant buys every kind of goods in order that he can make a great deal for himself out of a great many people, so the greedy friar embraces every worldly cause in order that he may enjoy his various gains. They are men whom the grasping world has not frightened away; on the contrary, it shows a high regard for them, and has surrendered up its affairs to them. It is obvious that these converted men are subverted, so they should derive their true reputations from their deeds. [14] Thus the pharisaical branch has cut itself off from its source of life, and its fruit is pungently bitter to the taste [750].

Chapter 17

Here he speaks of the friars who hypocritically rebuke the people's sins when preaching in public, but nevertheless promote them zealously in private with blandishments and satisfaction. [1]

A friar's assiduous hypocrisy sows his words [2] in order that his harvest of profit in the world may thrive through them. He thunders out fearful sermons as he publicly damns the practice of sin, like a

very servant of God. But like a servant of Satan, he furnishes glosses
for them when he comes to sit down for a while in private chambers.
His gentle blandishment is soothing to the ear [of] those whom his deep,
resounding voice has goaded before. And thus does this sinner cater
to sins for others, for by encouraging vice he gets a profit from it
[760]. A friar knows well that when sin dies, then his revenue dies for
all time. Tell me where a friar will come three times, unless he may
take away money. He does not return by the road where his lot is un-
profitable. If you took away crime from the friars' foundations, [3] their
house which was lofty for so long would fall without a struggle.

O how the words of the prophet Hosea are now verified! Thus
did he speak the truth: "A certain tribe will arise on earth which will
eat up the sin of my people and know much evil [770]. "[4] We perceive
that this prophecy has come about in our day, and we give credit for
this to the friars. No matter what is necessary for their sustenance,
fate provides everything for them through sins. There are no such
sensuous pleasures as sometimes fail to yield a crumb to friars, if
they are confessors. Notice that doves come to spotless quarters, and
that an unclean tower does not harbor such birds. [5] Similarly, no house
except those of tycoons provides friars of today with guest accommoda-
tions where they wish to stay on [780]. [6] Ants never make their course
toward empty granaries, and a wandering friar will not come near when
one's wealth is lost. [7] With no thought of the blooms which it bore before, they disdain the thorn when the roses have fallen off. [8] In this way
do the friars scorn the favors of friendship from a man formerly rich,
when he can give no more. Many are friars in name but few by rights.
As some say, Falseness[9] is their prophet. Their cloak's appearance
is poor, but their money box is rich. They hide their shameful deeds
under sanctimonious words [790]. Poor without poverty and holy without Christ, thus does a man who is lacking in goodness stand out as
eminently good. They call upon God with their lips, yet they venerate
gold in their hearts, and on every side they seek to learn the way to it.
The Devil has placed everything under their foot, but their pretended
sanctity does not teach them how to hold on to anything. Thus does one
who "scorns" the world grasp in turn at the things of this world, while
his sheep's clothing conceals a hostile wolf. And thus the people, deluded by pretenses, will think of men whom deceitfulness inwardly rule
as outwardly holy [800]. There is scarcely a one who reproaches the
falseness of another; rather, each contributes to the trickery so that
they may be the more deceiving. Driven by the same vice, they are
thus tainted the more, and they taint all the earth with their dishon-
esties. In any event, may the Lord repress those whom He knows to
be sinning at this time against the age-old faith. I do not ask that they
be destroyed, but that the weak be strengthened, and that they submit
to the original way of life which their order imposed.

Here he speaks of those friars who, with an eagerness to instruct, aim at the highest teaching positions for the sake of worldly reputation and in order that they may become more privileged to hear confessions, as if they were exempt from the yoke of their order.

He who is a leader should become as a servant; Christ Himself acted as an example of this [810]. But when one who says he is a follower of Christ comes to high station, he does not keep to its proper ways. Behold, no matter what badges of a mendicant poor man he retains, a friar aspires to have his place of honor. He longs to bear the name of master in a school, but no rule binds him after he is exempt from episcopal jurisdiction. [1] He has a room to himself, he gets hold of some property, and then he thinks no monk is his equal. You would think that monks ought to pay homage to schoolmasters and bow down their necks at their feet [820]. Thus pomp and arrogance hide beneath theology, as long as the order [of friars] is inclined neither to lead nor to be led. Then the friar gains access to the highest chambers; there is no house whose door is closed in the man's face. When the chameleon looks at various things, it becomes changed itself and has just as many marks of color. [2] A friar is just like it; carefully weighing men's whims, he wants to be in exact conformity to them. And since the court feels that the friar is so like itself, in his presence it renders the decrees of the bishop null and void [830]. The friar wanders about outside and explores inside, and no place or affair is a mystery to him. Now he is a physician, now a father confessor, now a mediator, and he gives orders at every hand, both high and low. So the friar puffs about everywhere as if he were the spirit of the Lord, yet he comes to the bed when the husband is away. While the man is gone, the audacious, adulterous friar enters and takes over the role of another for himself. Thus does he approach the master bedroom with its smooth bed—a bedroom he has enjoyed again and again; yet quite often it will be for the very first pickings [840]. Solomon was begotten in this fashion by the woman who married Uriah, when a worthy intruder took his place. [3] The friar's devotion makes up for the husband's failures, and his growing progeny fill the paternal halls. The former beats the bushes while the latter catches the bird. [4] The one sows the piece of land, and the other harvests the field. They both run in the race, but long afterwards only one receives the prize, unjustly. [5] Thus the husband often has a share in the doings of others, but such matters are nevertheless in vain when he does not get the credit for them [850]. The married man believes and rejoices that he has fathered a child, yet not one fingernail

185

of the child belongs to him. Together with the husband, the hypocrite repeats sacred verses, as if God would stand by the word on his lips. With the wife he chants the praises of Venus, and fulfills his duty to the goddess with highest honor. Thus his lowly deed builds a lofty structure, yet his piece of work necessitates help when lacking the cover of night.

O the piety of the friar, who goes about helping everybody and bears another's burden so patiently [860]. O, he comes not so much to sanctify souls, but to sanctify our bodies with his sweat. He is a confessor not of the Lord, but of the ladies, and is blander than Titivillus[6] to them. He is a confessor just like a thief whom the gallows display, since he plunders[7] our prerogative over woman. He is a confessor who turns bad into worse, for in washing away uncleanness, he makes things even more unclean. A friar will give skin for skin, himself, his property, and all that he has for our wife [870]. [8] O who will give such a man his due reward, God or the Devil? —the last word is binding. [9] For a sinful end brings the wages of death, [10] while even an old sin is filled with new shamefulness. [11] The names of those who perform so many wondrous deeds while they live are written in the book of death.

I feel that Nature decreed something that is to be observed among bees so that a friar might take note: for if a bee stings, its mischief retaliates against it, so that it does not possess its sting any more [880]. And afterwards it keeps to the hidden recesses of its dwelling place and flies forth no more to make honey from the flowers of the field. O God, if the adulterous friar would only lose his swollen pricker in the same way when he has stung, so that he would not pluck women's flowers nor go wandering about in the world away from his home! Because the cause had ceased to exist, then any effect on his part would cease to exist. Because of that effect, many great dangers are now lurking.

Chapter 19

Here he speaks of how the friars who live in a disorderly fashion are not necessary in any way for the guidance of Christ's church.

One thing is astonishing to me. As I reflect upon it in my mind, I do not know what the ultimate reason for it might be [890]. It is said that before there was an order of friars, whatever ranks existed within the Church were well suited for it. The Pope was sovereign; he appointed others as deputies so that all the laws he made would exercise control over the people. The bishop has his own duty, and the curate under him directs the great masses of the people, in accepting the cure of souls. The bishop is the proprietary who confers a special property upon the curate, whereby he may perform his duties. The curate thereupon swears that in place of the bishop he will carry out in due time the duties which the bishop has set forth [900]. Does there seem, then, any reason or cause for a friar's appropriating the special role of another for himself? It is forbidden for the raven, which every flock recognizes as unwelcome, to take its place among white birds.[1] And all justice forbids that the friar who shirks his responsibility take his place among the members of the Church.

One should always act cautiously when things are uncertain, not so much for the world's sake as for God's. Still if one usurps worldly authority, the powers of the law hold him in check and do not allow him to transgress it [910]. If another man were to make away with worldly possessions which belonged to me, in such a case the law will repute him as dishonest. Just law does not give over to the prejudice of one party, so that one man may get another's place. One man cannot seize personal property which is another's unless he denies the fundamental justice of laws. But I do not know by what law a friar will justify his action when he steals what belongs to the soul. If he should say, "The Pope gives me dispensation," then let us see whether there were a suggestion made to him or he did it of his own accord [920]. We know that the Pope never granted such things on his own impulse, but the order frequently begs for them. The Pope can make a mistake, but He who sees his inner self knows whether it is for love of gain or love of God. [The friar's] tongue asks for the cure of souls, while his mind desires gold, and in this way he carries off both these possessions of ours by force. In cheating our souls such a man snatches away their well-being, and on top of this he tries to make away with our riches. Francis did not make such demands. Giving up everything, he suffered the poverty of mankind in his innocence [930]. The ground brings forth thorns when the plowman drowses in the fields, so that Ceres yields less of her riches for the harvest. The Church is troubled, wounded on every side by Envy's stings, which it feels have come untimely from the friars. Therefore, every good plowman will uproot these thorns lest this pharisaical plant defile a holy place.

Chapter 20

Here he speaks of how the friars who live in disorderly fashion
are not useful in any way for the common good.

Not for friars is the toil to bring back Adam's happy state, where
they would tend the vines or fields for themselves or for others. On
the contrary, the bodily repose which they strongly insist upon enfolds
them now, and no worldly cares oppress them [940]. Nor are they concerned with any outstanding feat of arms by which they zealously preserve the public's rights. Thus neither knighthood nor tilling the soil
distinguishes them; rather, each estate leaves them wandering about
in the world. And friars are not of the clergy, however much they
may try to usurp that rank, which their pretense of teaching permits.
Friars do not accept the clergy's burden but its honor, whereby they
insist upon occupying first place in the cathedral. They do not take
care of the people's souls and they do not succor their bodies, so of
what further use can they be for the common weal [950]? Just as you
cannot count the acorns on a spreading oak tree, [1] so you cannot reckon
the number of friars. Rather, just as a torrent swollen by waves of
rain or snow flows when melted by the warm west wind, [2] their order
has outgrown its religious garb and left off traveling its original paths,
while virtue has departed from their order. If right were done, the
poverty of the serfs requires that such men take to the plow.

David affirms that they are not in trouble as other men, neither
do they suffer any of the scourges of positive law [960]. [3] Neither royal
authority nor the bishop's decrees have the power to moderate the
friars' excesses. The world cherishes the things which are its own; it
has therefore conferred prosperity upon its beloved friars. They plow
not, neither do they spin; nor do they mow nor add store to the barns.
Yet the world does not feed them the less because of it. [4] Thus their
hearts rejoice and are not made weary with affliction, even while they
reckon earth as superior to heaven. Thus the friar exceeds his heart's
desire, [5] and he completes the course he wishes in the world [970].
Tell me what honor Hector's son would have, if he had renounced his
arms and foolishly boasted about his father's deeds? [6] And what good
is the apostate friar who calls upon Saint Francis and refuses to follow
him? But with their false words they darken the understanding of a
world without light, and their curses protect them in this. Thus even
where the order is not present, sinfulness lasts on in its shadow, and
the order now stands inviolate, as if behind a mask. Nevertheless,
honor is rightfully due those who obey Francis' rightful commands in
honest fashion [980].

Chapter 21

Here he speaks of the friars who oftentimes trap thoughtless boys, who do not possess mature judgment, into taking the vows of their order by enticing them with bland words. [1]

[2]I have a suspicion about friars, namely, that none of them is an adult when he first renounces himself. Boyish years did not attract Francis to the vow of an order when he took it. Similarly, impressionable boys were not the first to revere him, nor did a tale from a smooth tongue allure them. I am of the opinion that Francis had reached a mature age, when he took up his work with a knowing heart. And I think that his order brought men like himself to God, men following his teachings of their own free will and not because of a bribe or entreaty [990]. But the old practice is no more, for the friars' skillful deception now misleads young children, who know nothing of this matter. And accordingly the tender order asks only gentle things of a tender youth, and it remains only a shadow, almost like a stepmother.

Just as the fowler calls a bird to the snares when he plays his pipe, so does the sound from a friar's lips entice young children. Just as the bird is trapped, ignorant of the treacherousness of snares, so does a boy fall to the friar, for his treacherousness is hidden. And when he can trap a boy in this way, the older friar is bound as a result to acquire the name of father [1000]. Begotten of deceit, his offspring accordingly imitates the father and adds his own deeds of deceit to those of his father. And thus a single root by itself taints a hundred branches, which bear the fruits of deceit into the world. For when he has grown old, the boy deceived by an old friar acts deceitfully himself, because of such an example. Thus those who are first deceived afterwards deceive, and dishonesty spreads, aggravated by dishonesty. Thus the order becomes petty, yet the number of friars grows, since a wretched man is glad to have company in his miseries [1010]. [3] God Himself said, "Woe unto you who compass land and sea to make one proselyte for yourself."[4] That was said to the Pharisees, and I now can say those words to the friars with new justice.

Here he speaks of the apostasy of the order of mendicant friars, especially on the part of those who, through their feigned, hypocritical innocence, subvert the households of almost all important men and often cause incalculable transgressions by their falsehoods.

Just as many good things follow everywhere in the wake of a good friar, so it is obvious that many evils follow everywhere in the wake of a bad one. There are in truth three masters, of which each man serves the one by whom he wishes to be ruled. There is God, there is the world, and there is the Devil Apostate, in whose ranks the friar bears a burden of sin [1020]. For God's rule does not take cognizance of him, and no free company of knights grants him worldly rank. He does not possess God and he cannot possess the world, so he submits to the Devil's own yoke. Indeed, every corrupt apostate, either as an active agent of vice or as its well-wisher, lends aid to what he knows is evil. Solomon is witness that such a man is useless, and he commits the worst crimes of the spirit.[1] In every circle such a man frequents, by art or natural ability he accomplishes much that ought to be dreaded [1030]. No wall stands in his way, no enclosures withstand him, every impassable place stands as a thoroughfare for him. He travels through land, sea, and the whole world. He can choose anything that pleases him.

He relies upon deceit, he makes cunning speechs, he increases and heaps up and multiplies his trickeries. He promotes strife, he inflames quarrels into anger. He nourishes ill will and fosters envy. He breaks the bonds of peace, he disrupts the ties of nuptial love, and sets faith at variance [1040]. He suggests incest, he urges violation of chastity, dissolution of marriage, and defilement of the bridal bed. In falsely assuming faith, he counterfeits an honest face in order to conceal his deceit more carefully. He [is] at all times a faithful maker of promises while dealing out injuries; if he gives you opportunity, learn how his deceitfulness lies concealed. Beneath his coarse wool he wear fine linen; the innocence of his face hides a cunning heart.[2] As his tongue puts words in his venomous mouth, he makes poison into honey and honey into poison [1050]. As if deeds of vice were hiding under the cloak of virtue, and as if a lowly ape were to become a man, the proud friar--whom the spirit of God privately shuns--imitates a humble man of religion. This man in holy orders is eager to debase whatever virtue Francis piously prescribed. But he hides all this by an outward show and is deceptive with his air of decorum, while his inner feelings lie hidden, full of deceit.

You will find it written that the ostrich has wings equal to the wings of the stork and the hawk [1060]. But its wing does not succeed in so swift a flight, and brands as a sham the ostrich which flies by imitating them. In like manner, the hypocrite outwardly feigns deeds of gold, but inwardly his wicked mind entertains wishes of lead. [3] Indeed, there are many such, who color their words, stuff our ears, and utter aureate speeches. They are flowery in their talk, but there is no fruit in their action. They sway the minds of the naive by speaking sweetly. But the temple of the Lord shuts out such men, abhors the trappings of their speeches, and shuns their smooth talk [1070]. [4] Poets' writings, which painted language gilds over, are rendered with a golden tongue, but beware of them. [5] The simple word is good, and accordingly merits trust, [6] but the word of double meaning speaks apart from God to the mind. God despises all eloquence, when a polished exterior fosters poison under the honey of eloquence. [7] One who composes fine speeches and then acts evilly sins shamefully. For moral deeds ought to follow after moral words. [8] Those who are fond of higher learning sow stumbling blocks under a subtle and feigned disguise with their polished language [1080].

Quite often either money or the attainment of some empty honor makes friars' talk highly reprehensible. They frequently repay one with tares[9] under the guise of wheat, while their boastful teaching is eager with desire for praise. Often the zealous spirit of these experts ascribes accomplishments to their own merits and creates schisms. A soothsayer or a magician is a schismatic, since he confuses the truth which you believe and promotes what should be doubted. But you must prudently stop up your ears against the voices of enchanters, lest your heart cleave to them [1090]. [10] They are not true friars or faithful to the love of Christ's Church, such as is cherished in it. Rather, the tainted synagogue, which plainly does not teach the truth, will heed their instruction. Accordingly, that insolent multitude of children which the synagogue embraces[11] repeatedly works injury upon others. They are not true citizens of the Church; instead, their perfidious mother, the maidservant Hagar, bore them. So let Hagar be off, let the synagogue give place, and let Sarah bear the Church's faithful clergy [1100]. [12] Piety and love fashioned the origins of the friars, whom ambitious madness motivates at present. The friar is Hatred, which took its origin in hell and abhors the bonds of peace. This man of professed vows breaks his monastic laws and does not allow his fellow comrades to remain in harmony. But to the friar who realizes that he is sinful and does not stop it, I say these words: "Sin ought not extol the praises of evil to the righteous man. Light shines in darkness with greater glory [1110]. [13] Every man shall bear his own burden; [14] let the unjust one be blamed for his deeds and the just one be praised. "

191

Here he speaks of how the mendicant friars devote themselves to traveling about the world from place to place and idly seeking sumptuous pleasures. He also speaks of their unnecessary buildings, which are constructed in an excessively luxurious fashion, as if by the mightier potentates of this era. [1]

The dispersion of the friars, whom a devious wanderlust now drives throughout the world, resembles [that of] the dispersed Jews. [2] Neither the one nor the other remains fixed in one spot, but instead moves about by turns and exchanges different places everywhere. In such fashion does the irreverent [friar] stray about now in his compassing of the earth, and there is no home in which he does not seek lodging. Alms furnish plunder for him under the guise of a pauper, and he conceals the jaws of a wolf under his sheep's clothing [1120]. No man is worthy of good things without some effort on his part, [3] and accordingly they possess the means of expiation and purify[4] all the earth through their propitiatory offerings. I do not know whether heaven will shut the gates on high to them, but the sea, streams, and all the earth furnish a pathway for them. I have read that a plant which is often moved rarely flourishes, [5] but instead is usually poor because of its barren lot. Yet there is no rule but that it proves false in its turn, [6] for the friar's moving about causes him to flourish. For everywhere on dry land that he turn his steps, the world follows and waits upon him [1130]. Just as a snowball made of [smaller] snowballs usually grows in size when it is rolled along, and after a short distance becomes very large, so when a friar rolls himself along, the world redounds to him, and whatever he touches with his hand sticks to it. The renegade friar strengthens his ties with the world in such a way that they are almost always hidden.

But many seem to have certain virtues who possess not a whit of virtue or goodness. They will talk about such things, but there will be shameful things in their thoughts, and they delight in many of them to the point that they lack salvation [1140]. Their devotion aims at ornamentation of a church, just as if such things possess the marks of salvation. [7]A church built for them towers above all others; they set up stones and are highly fond of carved wood. [8] It has folding doors with elaborate porticoes, halls and bed chambers so numerous and various you would think it a labyrinth. Indeed, there are many entrance ways, a thousand different windows. Their house is to be an extensive structure, a house supported by a thousand marble columns, with decorations high on the walls. [9] It is resplendent with various pictures and every elegance [1150]. Every cell in which a worthless friar dwells is beautiful, decked with many kinds of rich carving. On the doorposts they carve figures which are to endure for a long age; by these they think to bind the hearts of the people. While fashioning[10] [a figure of] Christ, they long for the world and secretly follow it; yet together they sound His praise. Their holy devotion is feigned[10] under the guise of such a figure, and their house becomes quite a witness for this. Yet He who sees all and searches the depths of their heart knows that such a work is contrived on behalf of the world [1160]. But history teaches by the examples of Paris that a man should be content with a smaller house.[11]

No king in power has more magnificent chambers than theirs for himself. Thus the friars' attire does not become a mark of their simplicity; rather, the splendor of their houses marks them. Attentive toward the physical body of the Church and unfeeling toward its spirit, the whole assemblage of them is eagerly zealous for building. So the friars' pious devotion is outwardly plain to see, but the vainglorious spirit of their heart lies within them [1170]. Such men as these, who are without fruit, are like the [elm].[12] There is much impiety in them and little faith. Tell me, friar, what does it profit you, with your evil thoughts, to build so many noble houses? You yourself should be a dwelling place of the Lord, which you should ornament with holy conduct. As one who reverences religion you should love virtue.[13] In the end, all things are clearly revealed.[14] It will not avail you to pretend further; by it you will gain no inner satisfaction. Even if the world's fleeting praise is yours today, that praise will be your disgrace when you lose heaven [1180]. You are of a religious order; let it be your guide and do not depart from it. Otherwise, whatever you gain from it is fruitless.

Chapter 24

Here he speaks of how things which used to be virtuous are almost universally undone by vices, not only in the order of mendicant friars but also in every rank of the clergy. He says, however, that the way of life and rule according to certain regulations of Burnel are particularly observed, especially in these days.

Howevermuch their attire differentiates them, friars are just alike in their ways. No rule which was established long ago still endures; instead a new order makes over law anew. Indeed, according as the order of friars is let loose, the Church's monastic rule is made almost wholly new. Nevertheless, the holy order which Friar Burnel sanctioned[1] still remains, and it is growing larger [1190]. Now I shall not disclose all the stipulations that Burnel decreed, nor do I wish to disclose them. But I shall speak in turn of only two things he ordered, and which are like laws at the present time.

The first mandate he prescribed for you is that it is permissible to enjoy every pleasure—whatever in the world you like. If you wish to traffic in commodities, be a merchant. Moreover, if you wish to commit adultery, he allows you to be an adulterer. Any more things the flesh desires are now bounden duties for our blessed friar [1200]. This teacher further states through a second law that everything harmful to the flesh should keep its distance from you. Everything which pertains to the soul is reckoned as extremely loathsome, and the flesh is to partake of its delights. Give free rein to your heart, for no one will hold you in check. Go your way freely everywhere you wish. Well provided with delicate pleasures, Burnel's order stands highly esteemed, since it requires what men wish. From now on let Bernard and Benedict be nothing to me, and let Burnel be my prior [1210]. In this way there is plenty of rest for the flesh, and the worshipper's tongue, weary with prayer, may become almost totally silent. As long as his order wants to help us along with prayers like this, I leave the croakings to the frogs[2] and [want] no more of them. And if bad times come upon me, I believe that those of the clergy are far too much the serious cause of them. For who could bring us good times, as long as God's own order passes away because of the monastic order, and heavenly devotion flees from the rest of the clergy? Thus does our salvation flee from us on every side [1220]. For since our mediators themselves fail unbecomingly, we people wandering about in the world remain lazy.

What can the body do for itself unless there is a soul within it? What can it do unless a pious clergy amends us in this world? But one who wishes to examine the genus or species of the clergy from head to foot will scarcely make out a good man among them. Thus, where a way of life should instruct people to take the safe path, death instructs them; where light should do so, darkness does. I have discussed the clergy just as others discuss them. Because of them, sin has increased greatly among others on earth [1230]. For the flock is scattered without a shepherd, and behold, on every side it seeks the pastures of new sins.

---

[3]Now that the destiny of the clergy wavers from Christ's order, the world wrongly practices what God Himself forbids [1222*].

Burnel, as long as your teaching is widespread in the world, every man is deceived by it from top to toe. But when the blessed Gregory's teaching shone on earth, the true faith flourished and set everything at peace. But Arius is the new teacher now, as is Jovinian, [4] provoking schisms in the churches with their teachings. Thus where the rule of life should instruct people to take the right path, death instructs them; where light should do so, darkness does [1230*]. Therefore, let every good man, whether he be knight or peasant, offer his orisons to God, praying for the clergy.

BOOK V

Chapter 1

Inasmuch as there has been a discussion of those in the estate of
the clergy, who ought to govern matters of the spirit, it is now
necessary to speak of those in the estate of knighthood, who are
under obligation to assist and uphold temporal affairs.

I have said what may be said concerning the clergy, and I shall
speak secondly of how the knights' ancient order used to be appropriate
for them. In the beginning, knighthood was endowed with great honor.
It was first established for three reasons: first, it is to protect the
rights of the Church; second, it fosters the common good; third, it is
to uphold the right of the needy orphan and defend the widow's cause
with its power. [1] In such ways does the law will that the knight in arms
be ever ready to enter into battle [10]. Indeed, not long ago the knight
did conquer his enemies in such fashion, for which reason his fame in
the world lives on. A knight did not bear arms for fame, however, but
instead performed his deeds for the sake of justice. The worthy knight
who preserves the order's way of life ought to receive due praise for
it. But if a knight makes war for the sake of vain praise, his praise is
unwarranted, if it is granted under such a circumstance.
Now tell me another thing: what honor shall a conqueror have if
a woman's love can conquer him [20]? I don't know what the world will
reply to me about that. I do know he will have no praise from Christ. [2]
If a man wishes to enjoy honor, let him protect his honor, and let him
perform the work that his responsibility urges upon him. The end will
bring nothing but inevitable folly upon the man for whom Venus initially
leads the way to arms. It is not right that lead be mixed with shining

196

gold, nor that Venus prescribe the deeds of a doughty knight. A woman
does not often release a man whom she has ensnared so that he may
escape. Instead, she envelopes him with her silly love [30]. The man
who is once free and subjugates himself voluntarily ought to be reckoned
more idiotic than an idiot. It is practical for a knight to avoid battles
in which he might be made captive, when he cannot win. It is not for
the wise man to enter a ford in which he could be drowned, but rather
to check his course away from the destruction, once he has seen it.

Chapter 2

Here he speaks of how the knight who engages in the use of arms
when he is burning with lust for a woman's affection certainly
does not deserve the honor of praise for it at all. He also describes the inconstancies of such love, the passions of which are
highly at variance with each other, because of their mixed emotions.

O, if a knight were to think of the ways of love, which are changed
so suddenly, he would not suffer them. Love is not of one hue, but is
conflicting within itself; it tempers its vicissitudes intemperately [40].
Love conceals and reveals, disunites and reunites, and often drives
happy hearts mad with grief. Love is an unjust judge; marrying opposites, it makes the very natures of things deteriorate. In love, discord[1] is harmonious, learning is ignorant, anger makes jests, honor
is base, a poor man has plenty, joys grieve, praise reproves, despair
hopes, hope is afraid, harms are helpful, assets are harmful. In love,
anguish is tasteful, bitterness becomes sweet, winter is springlike,
chills perspire, sickness is strengthening [50]. So take greater heed,
knight, of the dangers you see. Read what forms love's sickness takes.
   [2]Love is sickly health, troubled rest, pious sin, warlike peace,
a pleasant wound, a delightful calamity, anxious happiness, a devious
path, dark light, gentle harshness, a light lump of lead, both a flowery
winter and a withered, flowerless spring, a thorny rose, a capricious
law without justice, weeping laughter, laughing lamentation, intemper-
ate temperance, a hostile ally and a gracious enemy [60], fickle constancy, a wish opposed to itself, hope despairing of itself, doubting
faith, black whiteness, bright blackness, bitter honey, delicious gall,
a prison offering pleasures, [3] irrational reason, foolish discretion, an
untrustworthy judge, an ignorant person reflecting upon everything,
food never digestible and drink ever thirsty, an insatiable mental hunger, a living death, a dying life, harmonious discord, a garrulous

197

mind, mute speech, a secret fever [70], poor prosperity, prosperous
poverty, a slavish prince, a subject queen and a destitute king, drunken
sobriety, demented clemency, the port of Scylla, a pestilential cure, a
way of health; love is a delightful serpent, a ferocious lamb, a gentle
lion, a timid hawk and a rapacious dove, a fatuous school turning out
an even more fatuous pupil, whose mind applies itself the more diligently as a result.

Chapter 3

Here he describes the beauty of a comely woman, for lust of
whom knights' hearts are ensnared and very often left destitute
of rational judgment.

[1] When the trembling lover admires a woman endowed with radiant beauty, the blush of the rose is in her face [80]. [He admires her]
golden hair, her well-shaped ears, [2] the smoothness of her brow which
is gleaming white, her youthful cheeks, her eyes which shine like the
sun and which a well-composed countenance graces, her straight nose
and delicately opened nostrils, her honeyed lips—and the breath of her
mouth is sweet—her even teeth, whiter than milk, and the beauty of
her mind, which is in keeping with her. The radiance from her face
brightens her ivory neck, [3] together with her throat of crystal [90]; and
the luster of her breast glistens whiter than snow, as if two dazzling
apples were affixed to it.

He beholds her long arms, just the least bit roundly plump, and
he thinks their embrace is a heavenly kingdom. And he sees her hands
and bejewelled fingers glitter—no soft wool is softer than they. He
perceives her youthful shoulders, unaccustomed to burdens; no boni-
ness shows in them, [4] so he marvels at them the more. From aside
he sees her extend her graceful figure, and no line is straighter than
she [100]. He observes her steps treading in the dance and notes the
measure of her paces. The singing sirens compare not at all with her
voice, and the voice of an angel sounds scarcely like hers.

And he sees her head encircled and glittering with jewels, and
the splendor of her clothes, which are highly becoming to her. She
approaches, decked out beyond measure, and wishes to appear beautiful, so that her lover may be more than half carried away with wonder.
All her limbs seem to be in such array that God [must] have fashioned
that handiwork in heaven [110]. Delightful are the part in her hair,
her serene brow, her milk-white neck, her mouth, her little lips, her
blush, and the bright light of her eyes. Beautiful are the crown of her

head, her brow, eyes, nose, teeth, mouth, cheeks, chin, neck, hands, breast, and perfect foot. The girl's beauty transcends humankind; she possesses a kind of divinity which surpasses the race of man. [5] Fortunate above all others whom grace of form adorns, she becomes a phoenix without peer [120]. [6] Splendid is her raiment, her head bound round with flowers, and a modest blush encompasses her pink cheeks. [7] Her figure pleases, and her snowy hue and flaxen hair; and her sparkling grace is artlessly achieved. [8] A man scarcely glances at her without being charmed by her to the point that, kneeling on the ground, he would offer his devotion. If she shows regard for the lover with her countenance, the man stands transfixed before her open eyes. [9]

When a man sees her womanly beauty--so sweet, elegant and fine, but more like an angel's [130]--he thinks her a goddess, and puts his fate of life and death in her hands. As he turns such marvellous beauty over in his mind, having been turned by it, he withdraws without turning around. [10] Outwardly, he does not show what the sight of her means to him; inwardly, the sting of love pierces his heart. He stands as motionless as a stone[11] and does not move from her sight, as if he were in a trance. His mind's eye grows dull, blind from the darkness of lust, and he sinks down to his own destruction [140]. He does not know what he sees, but he is consumed with what he sees. So he goes blindly mad because of his blind love. Colder than ice and hotter than burning fire, he both freezes with fire and burns with cold.[12] Just as a bird envelopes itself with birdlime by rolling about in it, [13] so does he grow the more ardent with love while defending himself against it.

Thus love conquers everything[14]--whatever nature has created-- yet love itself remains unconquered throughout everything. It imprisons and sets free, it fetters and unfetters, it subjugates everything to itself yet is unrestricted to all [150]. It constrains and appeases nature, it undermines and rebuilds it. And nature grieves because of love, yet is joyless without it. It militates against everyone; its rule excepts scarcely anyone, for it often causes even saintly people to be sinful. There is no one who can calmly go against its laws, but love itself bears everything calmly. Discretion fails the man whom virtue could not fail, and no man alive is safe in going against these things. Love with its pains[15] is not equal to the pain of retaliation. Love wounds the whole human race, but suffers no wound itself [160]. So when love is brandishing its piercing dart, fly a safe distance away from it. There are no arms which prevail in combat with love, nor does anyone have a treaty of lasting peace with it.

Love is a trusting thing, suddenly smitten with grief, [16] and the beginner does not know what end there will be for him. The knight does not lack for a battle who says within himself, "O how I keep silent, even while knowing that love burns me!"[17] The lover's mind is stirred in countless ways, as a rock is struck on every side by the waters of the sea [170]. [18] One of noble birth [may] lie prostrate under the effects of love and often recover, [19] yet more often he does not know what the noble course of action should be. Continually shifting into uncertainties in his imagination, love now lifts up the inner heart and now agitates it. Thus does blind love lead blind, foolish lovers, [20] so that no lover sees what is proper for himself. Tell me, what does not dare to rush into the madness of love? When one longs for embraces, he knows nothing of which he is afraid. He doesn't see the leaf for the trees, nor the grass for the open field, nor the waters for the brimming river [180]. [21] Instead he brings profits and losses upon himself as if he were blind, because impulse forces his mind to love. Neither heaven, earth, nor hell, neither sea, sky, nor air can hinder his undertakings by force. He will often lie freezing on the bare ground, suffering the heavy rain sent from a cloud in the sky. [22] Night and winter, long journeys and bitter sorrows[23] are the rewards love offers foolish lovers. There are as many sorrows in love as the groans you make; its madness and pity are equal on this earth [190]. The lover feels his injuries but nevertheless fervently assists in them, and pursues the source of his suffering.

Alas, that love is not curable by any herbs! [24] Neither brawn nor brain can escape its burden. No one can avoid this innate disease, unless it be that divine grace alone watch over him. O how grievous is the nature of man! Driven to his own destruction by it, it forces him to love. O the nature of man, which no one could bear! It does not even absolve him from the evil which it commits itself [200]. O the nature of man, which contains a mixture of two opposites, yet does not allow him to follow the promptings of both! Lust of the flesh wages battles with chastity; what the body wants, the spirit forbids. O the nature of man, which is fashioned in such a way, and cannot shun that which ought not be done! [25] O the nature of man, which frustrates the feeble power of reason, and possesses wickedness like a beast's! Arts are of no help; the wound rages incurable. [26] The wiser a man is, the madder he becomes as a result [210]. And if anyone should wish to curb his passion, [27] let him provide a means before he falls. In the meantime, until the seas grow calm and until love moderates its ways, [28] one should seize upon his salvation. You will conquer if you shun love, and you will be conquered if you resist it. Lest you be conquered like a lion, you must flee like a hare. [29] Nor does a woman escape the flames of love or its sharp arrows. [30] The weaker she is, the keener will be her passion. Just as a woman deceives men, so does a man deceive women, for love, foxlike, sings with the words of a wolf [220]. To beguile a trusting girl is not a praiseworthy honor, [31] but a deed of character. No art of man is more subtle than Venus'; by her art love long continues to demand its rights. [32]

Chapter 4

Here he says that when lustful love for women dominates a knight,
it veritably extinguishes all chivalrous virtue in him.

A knight does not rightly have to fear a bodily wound, since he
should receive the world's praises for it. But he should fear the wounds
of the spirit, which blind, incurable lust inflicts with fiery darts. Bodily
wounds are to be healed, but not even Galen will make a man well who
is sick with love [230]. [1] If the knight holds with womanish behavior,
his honor dies, bereft of his noble lineage. When a wise knight falls,
his fame forsakes him, as though he were fatuous and foolish. When
carnal love holds the mind ensnared, an intelligent man's reason becomes irrational. When the brightness of human intelligence is clouded
over by the shadow of the flesh, and the spirit of reason withdraws into
the flesh, man's reason stands utterly scorned. It is a slave to the
flesh, and scarcely retains the post of handmaiden [240].

Nevertheless, blind love does not weigh equally in the balance for
all men, nor deal out appropriate rewards to all. It often drives trustworthy people out of office for no reason and puts unreliable ones in
their place. It will refuse me a gift even when I deserve it, which it
will give to you without a trace of deservedness. Love blindly imposes
its obligations upon men, just as if you were to have to recognize different colors in the dark. [2] But almost every knight is a slave to love
now, and waits at its doors to receive his fate [250].

Chapter 5

Here he speaks of those knights of whom one will engage in feats
of arms for the sake of a woman's love and another for the sake
of wordly fame. In the end, however, both things pass away in
vain, without the reward of divine commendation.

One part of the knightly estate seeks after woman's love, and
another, what the world's lofty praise may extol to it. Everywhere the
knight aspires to and tries for new favor so that he may have fame.
But God knows by what right he desires honor, if the world or woman's
love will bestow it. If he wishes worldly praise, then he pours out the
wealth of Croesus in order that his lofty praises may be sounded,

because of his gifts. Then he sows gold, clothes, gems, and horses
like grain, in order that a crop of praises may grow in his ear [260].[1]
But if a knight chooses a woman's love for himself, then he will pay for
it more dearly than with his wealth. He will give up so many good
things for it—his body, his soul, his property, everything that Nature
or God has imparted to him. Nevertheless, when he shall have done
with his troublesome doings, yet at the same time every fickle compliment deceives him; and when neither the prattling talk of the world
reaches his ears nor virtuous love bestows its treasures upon him,
then the dupe will say, "Alas, how wicked Fortune is! For all my labor
turns out fruitless after such a long time [270]." The man who laments
for himself in this foolish way is too late, for he himself is the cause
of his suffering, and not another.

The world brings heavy burdens, but woman brings heavier ones.
It moves along, while she rushes; it buffets, while she kills. When a
knight thinks he has vanquished a woman's power, and with tender affection she grants everything he has asked, then he himself is thoroughly
defeated, just when he thinks he is thoroughly victorious, and the conquered woman reconquers him. And even if the knight chooses worldly
fame, surely it passes away vainly in a short time [280].

O why does a knight whose worldly honor remains without God's
esteem seek such honors for himself? Why does he believe that the
words of the prattling mob are an honor, and wish to possess them at
the price of death? Then, too, he fears nothing when he is overcome
by a woman, whereby he, guilty before God, loses a wealth of honor.
So why does a knight's undaunted courage wish in vain for things which
are senseless? His praises are sung in vain, unless God is the author
of them. And that honor which is noised about apart from God is a disgrace [290]. A knight is eager for any kind of praise or honor, when
God knows he is unworthy of it.

Chapter 6

Here he speaks for the moment in commendation of the good
woman: tried and true virtue of her sort transcends all earthly
delights. He also speaks of the bad woman, whose wiles a wise
man can hardly resist.

There was one woman through whom God on high came down, and
was made flesh of her flesh. Because of her honor, there are those
most praiseworthy women to whom the honor of praise ought deservedly
be paid. All good things come from a good woman, whose chaste love

202

provides love's riches. [1]A good woman is worth more than silver or gold; no fit value can be set upon her [300]. Tongue cannot recite nor pen describe the worth of her whom utter goodness properly distinguishes. Her noble husband dwells revered within his gates, and her household contains all that is good. Her servants are fitted out with garments which her hand, busy in its activities, fashions of double strength. No idleness attempts to run through her thoughts; womanly modesty effectively protects them at all times. For her merits, such a good woman should receive everlasting praise which no wicked, gossiping tongue can take away [310].

The woman who has acted just the opposite, however, does not thereby dishonor the others who are good. Although we may be speaking of a foolish man, his actions are nothing to the righteous one, nor do a thief's dishonest crimes involve honest men, but are as nothing to the good. Granted that the reputation of a harlot is inglorious, the woman whom a sense of decency watches over suffers nothing from it. Granted that a harlot is infamous, that shameful woman does not disgrace virtuous women by her own ill repute. One angel is good and another is bad, yet the sin of the bad cannot harm the good one [320]. The reputation of an infamous woman should not injure an honest one, nor have the power to take away her honor. While a foul, noxious weed may mingle with a rose, the rose is not otherwise than it was before. [2] When open guilt makes known its crimes, people cry out that this kind of conduct always has been and always will be just as they now observe it. But let what I may write here always be to the inviolate honor of those whose deeds a sense of honor watches over. Accordingly, what is of concern here [is that] the blame find out blameworthy women, whereby greater praise may be duly bestowed upon the praiseworthy [330]. It is helpful to know of evil, so that we can the more ably avoid it and beware of the slippery course before us.

All evils have usually proceeded from an evil woman; indeed, she is a second plague to men. [3] With her blandishments, a cunning woman gently touches upon a man's evil inclination and breaks down his manly honor. [4] Through her various wiles she destroys his feelings, his riches, his virtues, his strength, his reputation, and his peace. She deceives in a thousand ways and sets a thousand snares in order to catch one man [340]. Such a woman comes adorned with radiant jewels, gold and finery so that she can deceive. [5] Her clothes are well arranged, her rising breast is bound up, and the pattern of her bosom extends her neckline. She adorns her head with tinted hair and veils, and the golden splendor of gems decorates her handiwork. In order to sharpen the eyes of the frenzied man upon herself, there is one ring after another on her fingers. It is not her task to soften wool by spinning it, [6] but to be able to catch men when she is all decked out [350]. A showy woman lets herself be seen by people; perhaps there will be one out of many whom she can allure. [7]

Ah, how many times a lover is inflamed by false words, [8] when
the cunning tongue of some worthy beauty tempts him! If the woman
does not possess pleasing words to incite foolish men, there is charm
in her very defect: [9] with hands folded, she emits heavy sighs, and her
words do not lack their promised effect. Often a woman sounds somewhat raucous, but she laughs pleasantly, [10] and forces her hesitant
tongue to sound with a lisp [360]. [11] What can art not do? She learns
to weep becomingly, [12] so that by her look she deceives men whom her
talk does not attract. She deludes with her false expression and with
tears falling down her cheeks, and she pretends that she can hardly
speak. And as often as is necessary the sly mistress falls sick, and
outwardly her face suffers with pain. The Sirens were wondrous creatures of the sea, who with melodious voice detained whatever vessels
were sent to them. [13] Similarly, one who habitually listens to feminine
blandishments cannot safely retreat one foot from his downfall [370].
Just as one hand can paint many figures, and will vary its work in different ways, so one sole woman adds to the number of her various
lovers; and Venus forces them to believe in her foolish influence. She
alters what Nature has sensibly endowed her with, [14] and her cunning
tongue charms with its lispings. [15] Her fluency certainly torments a
good many foolish men, as she pleases now by laughing and now by crying. [16] She likewise adorns every part of her delicate body, and adds
to the beauty which God gave her [380]. I abhor relating the wickedness
of this discourse, which another and more experienced one has previously reported. Rest assured, I am going to repeat verses which the
poet Ovid set forth, and the words do not belong to me.

As a young woman tries to preserve her beauty and is anxious to
increase it in various ways, so an old woman aspires to renew the
beauty of her faded complexion, and will attempt the task with ointments. Just as the harsh winter causes lilies not to bloom, yet the
thorn which is left stands firm after the rose has dropped off [390], [17]
so does age despoil old women of their fairness, and there is a deep
wrinkle where there used to be a rosy hue. When her years take on
another color, then the old woman's hand covers her aged cheeks with
false coloring. For the fashion in such a case is that a woman beautify
her face, so that by means of ointments she may appear quite handsome
She skillfully marks her eyebrows and daubs her lips with rouge; with
blended tints, she helps them to be more becoming. She often dresses
her gray hair with medicinal herbs, and cleverly seeks for a hue better
than the original [400]. She often goes out with a thick set of tresses
she has bought, and makes another's locks her own. [18] And thus she
comes forth, covering her shoulders with golden hair, [19] and by her art
the old woman seeks to acquire the face of a young girl. She often puts
on yellow, she is veiled in a saffron robe, [20] whereby she appears less

impaired in her own complexion. The shameless woman has as many
flowers to attend to as the fresh earth brings forth in the warm spring-
time. [21] Do not believe that all women paint themselves in this way,
but each and every one uses her skill [410]. This one wants to be rosy-
hued and that one longs for snow-white beauty; one tints her cheeks and
another bathes hers. Still another fasts desperately and lets blood, and
she does this just so that she may become pale. For every woman who
is not pale thinks she looks countrified. "This is becoming, this is the
true color of a lover, " she says. [22] Woman assails our thoughts in a
thousand ways; if you don't look to yourself, you'll soon be captivated.
The poison of woman's love takes away your common sense, [23] and indeed, through grace alone does one escape its snares [420]. She grants
sweet embraces and plants tender kisses, but in her heart she silently
conceals venom. Many men have perished because of women's deceits.
Woman shrinks at nothing; she thinks anything is permissible. She
dares to do whatever her overpowering lust commands her, and her
fear and reason and very sense of shame vanish. Since it is usually
the case that beauty contends with a sense of shame, there can seldom
be a virtuous woman among comely ones. [24]

Woe unto the man whom a foolish mate has married in conjugal
union! His bed will not lack sorrow [430]. [25] The bride would have preserved the marriage contract, had she not been beautiful, and the facts
often show this clearly. [26] No watchfulness protects her whom Venus
excites, no boundary can be set for the foolish woman. When Venus
and the woman desire a time and place for themselves, what those two
want does not fail to come to pass. The woman's guard will be tricked
if he were Cato himself, while she, however, will not guard herself. [27]
Before a woman of Venus does not find a foolish lover and discover a
spot for her carrying on, then pigeons will begin to stay away from
towers, wild beasts will stay away from caves, cattle from grain, and
the cormorant from the sea [440]. [28] As many shells as the seashores
have; as many blooms as pleasant rosegardens have; as many sleep-
laden seeds as the poppy has; as many wild animals as the forest nur-
tures; as many as the fish that swim in the sea, or as the feathers with
which a bird softly beats the air[29]—these do not make up such a total
as can be called equal to the insidious evils a woman contrives.

The world is false but woman is falser, for Paradise perceived
her to be unfaithful [450]. [30] Behold, the world is a wolf in sheep's
clothing; where first it caresses, it finally bites. Yet it at least is
outside, but the serpent-like "turtledove" causes harms closer to home,
in the very bedchambers. For she is indeed a serpent who deceives
through a thousand meanderings and stings peaceful hearts. The man
who remains strong and wise after having been struck by her is of
heavenly nature, but earth itself cannot prevail against her. Neither
the strength of Samson nor the sword of David nor the wisdom of

Solomon is of any worth against her [460]. So why does the knight of today try to such an extent to overcome what so many men have not been able to conquer? There is not a man whom past perils make cautious, but instead he falls into the traps he sees. Who would forbid lesser men to adopt examples for their actions from the great? But our [kind of] love does not allow of this. The rash soldier takes up arms and enters the fray, unmindful of his former wound.

Chapter 7

Here he says that a properly constituted knighthood is responsible for the general establishment of security for all other classes of society.

O how knighthood stands out in the land as brave and noble, if it behaves well [470]! If he does not labor for worldly praise or gain, and if an untamable lust does not vanquish his heart of steel, then a knight will conquer with the glory of everlasting praise, and his eternal fame will make him renowned.

If knighthood were worthy, God would dwell within it, so that the knight might triumph with his unvanquished sword. If knighthood were worthy, its good repute, which now lies in bed overcome with sleep, would be wide awake. If knighthood were worthy, then the husband would prepare himself for his ventures together with his wife, with peace being restored [480]. If knighthood were worthy, then the Church's enemy would be overthrown by it, and the Church itself would grow in faith. If knighthood were worthy, then the harsh estimate [of it] which is noised about in the land would be of no importance. If knighthood were worthy, then peace, with which all prosperity would return, would not be slow in coming.

The knight who is worthy is ignorant of experiencing fear, nor does he suffer the inner vexations of a lukewarm spirit. [1] The knight who is worthy wipes out all worldly pride and fiercely conquers evil with a humble heart [490]. The knight who is worthy battles in behalf of Christ's name and defends the common cause with his valor. The knight who is worthy knows well and demonstrates that the beginning of peace in the world comes from the ending of war. Whatever esteem his code has in this world, such a knight is deserving of genuine praise.

Chapter 8

Here he tells how wickedness on the part of the knightly estate
harms and offends all other classes of society by its unseemli-
ness.

If, however, the knight were to bear his arms in just the opposite
way, many evil and fearful misfortunes would result. If knighthood is
bad, its shield is as nothing, its lance is as nothing, and its hand upon
the sword would not shine with honor [500]. If the knight is bad, who
in arms will defend us? If he is soft, he will cause hardships for us.
If knighthood is bad, what can the cleric and peasant do for themselves
when war looms at their doors? If knighthood is bad, then the fierce
enemy who ordinarily is law-abiding renews his activities. Thus the
good knight who carries our defenses in his hands brings good things,
and the bad knight brings on fearful evils. The clean hand strikes blows
of wondrous worth, while the one that is stained with its own filth flies
from the field [510]. Conscious of himself as he ponders his evil deeds,
[the bad knight] hesitates, and his performance is untrustworthy because of his wavering spirit. Feats of arms thrive upon good morals;
otherwise, good fortune vanishes. No virtue endures for long in company with vices.

Therefore, knight, be zealous for virtues. And resist vices, O
warrior, and strongly cherish your public duties. To conquer all the
hosts of the earth is not a bit to my advantage so long as I am conquered, defenseless, by a single vice. And what is not more severely
at fault than a knight slow to take up arms, yet eager for assize money
[520]?[1] When a knight stands before nearby enemies like a partridge
does [before] a hawk, his action is shameful. The man whom Mars'
glorious feats of arms do not delight cannot be worthy of Rachel's embraces.[2] The handsome woman who yields her love to such a man
makes a mistake, and does not know what honorable love is. Rather,
the infamous Leah[3] is more suitable for such a husband as has little
use for deeds of valor. Let such men go to Leah and attach her to
themselves; let the timid fellow who cannot be Rachel['s] be Leah['s]
[530].[4] Let no man be loved who is unworthy of love, and let the man
lack love who refuses its responsibility. When Jacob was smitten with
love, he did not possess Rachel's embraces without the anxious labor
of seven years' time.

But the knight whom the sake of gain moves to enter into battle
will have no righteous honor. It is the vulture's ghastly nature to want
[to eat] men, and to follow the camps of war in order to seize upon its
food. Those who want war and who follow the camps and are eager for

spoils and thirsting for loot are similar [540]. [5] This bird is terrifying, since it plunders like the swift hawk, and every flock of them is like a cruel wolf. O knight, you who prefer pleasures and abandon your arms and seek to have rest at home and plunder spoils from the poor like a lion: you seek the fat of the land for yourself, thereby causing others to waste away. Sluggishness motivates you and voluptuous lust urges you on, together with money and the driving force of avarice. Undertake the awesome duties of bloody warfare and I believe that your vices will flee you at once [550]. A knight should prefer honor to money, and in offering his prayers to God he will thereby conquer everything. But alas! I see that honor is now neglected for gold, and the world and the flesh are preferred to God. The number of knights increases but their activity decreases. Thus their honor is empty, since it is without responsibility. [6]

Chapter 9[1]

Now that he has spoken of those of knightly rank who ought to keep the state unharmed, it is necessary to speak of those who are under obligation to enter into the labors of agriculture, which are necessary for obtaining food and drink for the sustenance of the human race.

[2]Now you have heard what knighthood is, and I shall speak in addition of what the guiding principle for other men ought to be. For after knighthood there remains only the peasant rank; the rustics in it cultivate the grains and vineyards [560]. They are the men who seek food for us by the sweat of their heavy toil, as God Himself has decreed. The guiding principle of our first father Adam, which he received from the mouth of God on high, is rightly theirs. For God said to him, when he fell from the glories of Paradise, "O sinner, the sweat and toil of the world be thine; in them shalt thou eat thy bread."[3] So if God's peasant pays attention to the plowshare as it goes along, [4] and if he thus carries on the work of cultivation with his hand [570], then the fruit which in due course the fertile field will bear and the grape will stand abundant in their due seasons. Now, however, scarcely a farmer wishes to do such work; instead, he wickedly loafs everywhere.

An evil disposition is widespread among the common people, and I suspect that the servants of the plow are often responsible for it. For they are sluggish, they are scarce, and they are grasping. For the very little they do they demand the highest pay. Now that this practice has come about, see how one peasant insists upon more than two

208

demanded in days gone by [580]. Yet a short time ago one performed more service than three do now, as those maintain who are well acquainted with the facts. For just as the fox seeks his hole and enters it while the woods are echoing on every side of the hole, so does the servant of the plow, contrary to the law of the land, seek to make a fool of the land. They desire the leisures of great men, but they have nothing to feed themselves with, nor will they be servants. God and Nature have ordained that they shall serve, but neither knows how to keep them within bounds [590]. Everyone owning land complains in his turn about these people; each stands in need of them and none has control over them. The peasants of old did not scorn God with impunity[5] or usurp a noble worldly rank. Rather, God imposed servile work upon them, so that the peasantry might subdue its proud feelings; and liberty, which remained secure for freemen, ruled over the serfs and subjected them to its law.

The experience of yesterday makes us better informed as to what perfidy the unruly serf possesses [600]. [6] As the teasel harmfully thins out the standing crops if it is not thinned out itself, so does the unruly peasant weigh heavily upon the well-behaved ones. The peasant strikes at the subservient and soothes the troublesome, [7] yet the principle which the old order of things teaches is not wrong: let the law accordingly cut down the harmful teasels of rabble, lest they uproot the nobler grain with their stinging. Unless it is struck down first, the peasant race strikes against freemen, no matter what nobility or worth they possess. Its actions outwardly show that the peasantry is base, and it esteems the nobles the less because of their very virtues [610]. Just as lopsided ships begin to sink without the right load, so does the wild peasantry, unless it is held in check. [8]

God and our toil confer and bestow everything upon us. [9] Without toil, man's advantages are nothing. The peasant should therefore put his limbs to work, as is proper for him to do. Just as a barren field cultivated[10] by the plowshare fails the granaries and brings home no crop in autumn, so does the worthless churl, the more he is cherished[10] by your love, fail you and bring on your ruin [620]. The serfs perform none of their servile duties voluntarily and have no respect for the law. Whatever the serf's body suffers patiently under compulsion, inwardly his mind ever turns toward utter wickedness. Miracles happen only contrary to nature; only the divinity of nature can go against its own powers. It is not for man's estate that anyone from the class of serfs should try to set things right.

Chapter 10

Here he also speaks of the various workers from the rabble.
Employed under the supervision of others, they ought to be bound
over to their diverse tasks, for the common good.

[1]There is yet another group, associated with the peasants, which
is widespread, and which has no discipline [630]. They are those who
are unwilling to serve anyone by the year. A man will retain them for
scarcely a single month. On the contrary, I hire such men for even a
day's pay--now here, now somewhere else, now for myself and now for
you. There is scarcely one worker in a thousand of them who wants to
remain faithful to his bargain with you.

These are the people who behave basely within the house, as long
as your food and drink last. Because such a man is hired as a member
of your household, he scorns all ordinary food [640]. He grumbles
steadily that everything salted is harmful, and that he doesn't like
cooked foods much, unless you give him some roast. Neither weak
beer nor cider is of any use to him, and he will not return tomorrow
unless you provide something better. O why should a man whom water
drawn from a well has nourished ever since birth demand such delicious
drink? Born of poor man's stock and a poor man himself, he demands
things for his belly like a lord. The established law is of no help to
one, for there is no ruling such men, nor does anyone make provision
against their misdeeds [650]. This is a race without power of reason,
like beasts, for it does not esteem mankind nor does it think God exists.
I believe that in a short time the lords will submit to them, unless justice shall have been obtained by means of fear.

Chapter 11

Since no single region by itself produces all the various kinds of
things necessary for human use, merchants, among others, have
been appointed to assist the world's citizens. Through their
agency the goods of all regions are mutually shared. Consequently, he now intends to write of their actions.

If I turn in my writings to the noble city dwellers, what shall I
say but that they have an honor and they have an onus? It is an honor
that the citizen possess such great wealth; it is an onus that he then

seek after ill-gotten gains. It is an honor for a citizen to take the office of mayor; it is the onerous responsibility of his office to uphold the laws [660]. Honor is fleeting but the onus endures; for if he behaves badly, I know this, that the honor will not lighten his burden. The ordinary city depends upon two groups of people: there are merchants and there are likewise artisans. The one needs to have the assistance of the other, so that there is a general esteem between them. For bonds bind the two together quite strongly, so the two should be worthy comrades in esteem. As long as firm affection endures between the greater and the lesser, the city is happy and the state is prosperous [670]. Concord causes the smallest enterprise of the people to prosper; [1] discord causes the greatest affairs to sink into nothing. As long as unity of the people endures, justice will endure for both parties of the city, and everyone will approve conditions. And if it should be otherwise, then misfortunes for both parties plague cities, and the profits resulting from this are rare indeed.

[2]I can testify exactly as I have heard: just rule hardly sits upon the bench now. The man who clings entirely to worldly pomp in order to increase his reputation does not realize that he must hold [only] with God [680]. I do not judge or condemn any men in particular, but only those who have neglected God for the world; I believe that the man who wishes to render judgment from his heart upon an honest man will render himself accountable for it before God. For we are all so bent upon money at all hours that scarcely one festival day now remains for God. O how the Jew preserves the sacred Sabbath of the Lord, neither buying nor selling nor seeking for gain! [3] Divine law commands that man should keep his Sabbath holy and sanctify the day so that he may worship God [690]. Long ago, when God rained manna on the wilderness, what the people did then signifies a token for now: on the sixth day they did double labor, they lengthened their toil; for the seventh day is innocent of work. [4] But everything is permitted us under our present law. What are holy festivals to me when money is a consideration? [5] No one now cares how anyone makes money, as long as he can get his. Tell me what companion or dear friend you have whose friendship does not bring in any money to you [700]. Tell me what citizen in the city now remains without a share in the defrauding. Even if there were such a man, my city scarcely recognizes him.

Chapter 12

Here he speaks of the two daughters of Avarice, namely, Usury
and Fraud. They furnish secret indulgence for the citizens' business negotiations arising in the city. But first he will speak of
the nature of Usury, which confers its prerogatives especially
upon the more powerful men of the town. [1]

O how subtle are the sisters Fraud[2] and Usury! City dwellers
pay them their due, so to speak. They were begotten by various city
fathers, and their sole mother, Avarice, bore them. Usury's father
is important and rich in money, but Fraud was evilly begotten through
a vicious debauch. So the sister Usury, whom a rich man claims as
his offspring, is of nobler birth [710]. She exerts her effort toward
hiding huge sums of money under lock and key, and with them she carries out her crafty plotting. This sister prospers only by another's
misfortune, for someone else's losses bring a profit to her. It is this
powerful sister that has built the houses in the city, yet she destroys
the country homes. This sister enriches the city man, but robs the
knight of his gold and lays claim to his lands as her own.
The Lord has forbidden usury by eternal law; the Scriptures are
quite plain about this and should be read [720]. Wouldn't he be clever
who could put a gloss opposite this text which God Himself has handed
down? At the present time the merchant-citizen, who approves of his
being able to put a price on his usury, knows how to do this. Everything [about Usury] is openly exposed, for which reason he clothes her
with garments, in order that she may hide her secret doings under a
false pretense. Thus Usury's face lies hidden, painted with the hue of
Fraud in order that she may hence appear outwardly beautiful. But
even if the cunning fellow deceitfully alters her condition in this way,
Usury's reputation remains just as it was before [730]. Surely the merchant doesn't deceive God Himself with his precautions, when he conceals such evil deeds with his skill? Or is God blind, Who sees everything everywhere? He sees through the cloak of Usury and abominates
her.

Now that he has spoken of the power of Usury, he intends to speak of the subtlety of Fraud. According to common report, she subtly manages and arranges the things which almost each and every one must do in buying and selling.

The one sister provides heavy burdens, but the second one provides even heavier ones, for she is commonly found in all places. Fraud rushes wherever Usury goes; one finds the way and the other completes the job. Usury stays closely allied with those cities whose riches know no equal [740]. But Fraud usually stands close to all citizens and looks after them with all her might. She does her work stealthily, for the man she badly deceives feels the evil effect of it before he recognizes it.

Standing outside before the door the youthful Fraud shouts her different wares, whatever you might wish to have. She will say the names of this and that, of as many things as there are stars in the sky, as she calls and allures you. Those whom she cannot compel to come up by her words she compels by pulling. "Look, " she says, "Come here. Here is what you are looking for [750]. " In such fashion does the apprentice bring in people with his shouting, while the master is up to his secret trickery elsewhere. Indeed, when old Fraud utters her tricky words, no one can go away uncheated. If a smart man enters, she is smarter than he; and if a fool goes in, he goes away a bigger fool.

She puts everything at a double price, saying, "That's what Paris or Flanders has been paying. " Her words of promise make up for what in fact is deficient. She would wound Christ for a penny [760]. Certainly none of Christ's limbs will remain on Him when Fraud goes after her money with her oaths. [2] Nevertheless, we see that her households have often been plentifully filled in this way, yet those households contain nothing they rightfully should. And thus does the citizen hypocritically seek honor, so that people will greet him from afar on bended knee. For which reason it happens that he, a man who is more insignificant than everyone else, stealthily becomes quite important in the city. But when the time comes in which everything is openly revealed, what was once an honor will turn out to be a dishonor [770]. For when each man gets his due, then the crow covered with another's feathers will fly bare as it did before.

And Fraud comes out of the city to get wool from the country, with which she afterwards engages in dealings in the market. Does Fraud get the wines which Gascony produces? People rightly maintain that

this is harmful for them, but Fraud dwells within the cask and draws
the wine, wanting to sell it. And she often makes up new wine from the
old. Fraud also sells clothes, which she will make you look at in a
dark light, so beware of them [780]. Let your touch decide when the
light deceives your eyes, lest the clothmaker's trickery cleverly cheat
you. Therefore, away with that pretense which would sell, even while
denying Fraud, for she will give old, worn out goods mixed in with
new ones. Fraud takes a tithe for herself on the scales, or often takes
even a sixth part for herself through clever weighing.

Chapter 14

Here he tells in addition of how Fraud controls all the handicrafts
and food supplies of the city, through her clever managing. [1]

Craftsmen do not wish to put aside Fraud's ways; under her authority they now manufacture their products. She makes cups and purifies gold and silver, but from the pure metal belonging to you she takes
the purest for herself [790]. Out of glass she fashions jewels precious
to the eye, and she stakes her reputation upon them in order to deceive
you the more. If you have any cloth from which you wish a cloak to be
made and she cuts it for you, part of it will remain for her. No matter
whether the work is nothing at all or her measurement of the cloak is
dishonest, she takes more for the task than the whole thing is worth to
you. And what shall I say about black, white and gray fur garments?
Surely Fraud has previously been of "assistance" to them. On the face
of it, Fraud has been deceiving cleverly for quite a long time. What
she deceives today hasn't a leg [to stand on] tomorrow [800]. Fraud
also makes arms, selling inferior ones at a high price, and she lames
armor-bearing horses. Fraud starts the guttering of the candle made
of fat, with the result that the perpetual guttering is to her own benefit.
Fraud also manufactures saddles, boots, and shoes; she now makes
every art her own.
    Then too, Fraud sells meat and fish to people. She is in sympa-
thy with their tastes, for she takes a taste of the meat and fish herself
in advance. Fraud makes bakers mount the pillory because of their
bread, although the gallows of a thief would be more appropriate for
them [810]. As the jug bears witness, Fraud is mistress of beer, in
so far as Thetis[2] scarcely knows that Ceres in turn exists. Fraud the
cook both prepares baked goods and fixes roasts, and she calls the
crowd in for their food. Just as the shouting in hell constantly rages beyond measure, so does Fraud shout about her roasts in the ear of the

market. Fraud the hostess is delighted by pilgrims in her guest lodgings, but the pilgrim laments having had a bad hostess. Fraud is short in her measure; she cuts her hay short, but takes good care of the money [820].

Since she cares even about trifles, Fraud sells chickens and eggs —there is nothing on the market but that she controls it through her cunning. Fraud is known as general manager in the city. When she enters upon any business, it always pays. The deceits upon Fraud's lips are infinite, just as we must reckon the shores of the sea are. Fraud makes and sells her handiwork and also passes judgment on it. She is thoroughly guilty of an excessive desire to please. Even though Fraud is ruler, her activity does not further the common profit; but she keeps an eye out for her own gains [830]. So it is finally obvious, now that barren Honesty has departed from the city as an exile, Fraud is more and more fruitful. But I do not say that Fraud rules over all men, for Fraud brings in nothing to the honest citizen.

Chapter 15

Here he speaks of the rash and ill-willed citizen who, in choosing the office of mayor for himself, kindles malice among his fellow citizens. Hence, through his incompetence he disturbs and destroys the city's sound government. [1]

The bird blunders disgracefully which busies itself in fouling with its droppings the very nest of which it is guardian. [2] It is a disgrace for a citizen to deprive his fellows of high honor, whereby a peasant holds higher rank than the citizen. He rages fearfully among the people, at least while he holds a sword in his hand [840]. But when he rages in his office of judge, the man's power in the city is even more greatly to be feared. Just as a single spark can reduce a home to ashes, [3] so does one sole wicked man weigh heavily upon his native city. When a poor man is elevated in the city through an unexpected fate, and the unworthy creature is allowed to reach the height of honor, then Nature suddenly groans at the changed state of things and grieves at the unaccustomed rarity. When the new-found adulation of fools praises him, then the city's nobility can fear misfortune [850]. Fool smiles upon fool, the wicked man upon the wicked; the man of sense is delighted with a wise man. [4] Nothing is more troublesome than a lowly person when he has risen to the top--at least when he was born a serf. His thinking continues along the old way of a serf, let fate confer upon him whatever high rank it will. If [Burnell] the Ass is loaded with a race horse's saddle, [5] he nevertheless becomes no swifter in a race because of it. And the rude, untutored man is not transformed by an honor, but will be the cruder because of his rusticity [860]. All animals condemn the crow for dishonesty; so it is with the citizen who stands out badly in the city. No matter how a false destiny may place a man of no character in charge of a city, Fame[6] will ultimately establish who he is.

A wicked man whom God in due time allows to cause a great deal of agitation is often the scourge of many men. But in the end, all the villainy which he formerly committed at large among the people redounds upon his own head. One ounce of poison spoils a thousand jars of oil, and one single bad man spoils a thousand good ones [870]. One glowing coal sets many afire; similarly, one wicked man works much wickedness where he dwells. Yet when such a person has risen to the very top and intends to subject everything to his sway, behold, the wheel turns, and the one who formerly stood first in the city falls lower than everyone. [7] Fraud can flourish, but it cannot bear fruit, and its stunted plant does not strengthen its roots in the soil. The proof comes out in the end: [8] when someone who is swollen with avarice sets a price upon himself, he isn't worth much money [880]. Everyone can observe these things well enough in the mirror of today, yet there is scarcely a wise man who is on his guard, when he sees such doings.

Chapter 16

Here he likewise speaks of the citizen who is Talebearer, and a prattling sower of discord among his fellow citizens. He also tells of the various dangers that ensue by reason of an evil tongue.

As long as the talkative fellow, Talebearer, dwells in the city, he utters many slanders in abuse of people. For a talkative man harms other people like a second plague, and he often strikes as suddenly as a whirlwind. And since an evil tongue inflicts every sort of wickedness upon the world, I intend to speak of what its grievous powers are. A tongue sets quarrels in motion, a quarrel sets battles in motion, battles set people in motion, people set swords in motion, swords set schisms in motion, and schism brings ruin [890]. A tongue uproots rulers from their kingdoms, sends estates up in flames, and pillages homes. A tongue loosens marriage bonds, and makes into two what God has declared to be one. [1] Slandered wives shun their husbands, and husbands shun their wives, and they talk incessantly about the evils being done to them. This insignificant part of the body has learned to spare no one, and to speak falsely and facilely of both right and wrong. A moderate

216

anger on its part brings ruin to a whole multitude; by inflaming the mind it arouses the whole body [900]. It is not for nothing that a two-fold guard keeps watch over it, lest it impetuously pour out its words. Nature has wisely obstructed the palate with the teeth, so that by means of this barrier it can silence what is enclosed by remaining closed. By means of its sharp points, such a guard holds it in check, lest it suddenly do anything imprudently. [2] Farther outside, a second guardian, that of the lips, is furnished it, in order that this double door may shut off the course of the double-dealing one. The former bone-like arrangement corrects its excesses; the latter, fleshy and soft, makes its words mild [910]. Nevertheless, it sometimes secretly breaks through these approaches and rushes into words it cannot summon back. Its onset contains a thousand dangers, which swallow up all good fortune like a ravenous fire.

The man who can tell how many stars shine in the heavens and how many tiny bodies the dry dust contains[3] is scarcely wise enough to tell all the pestiferous seeds an evil tongue sows. No one can relate the evils that a prattler brings about in the city and the sufferings he causes with his deceitful tongue [920]. A prattling tongue is a bad thing, a worse thing, and the worst thing; however much it may lack bones itself, it can break bones. [4] Where the tongue of a chatterer rules is not a place of peace, and he who does not have peace does not have God. He who quarrels, lacking the peace of God, cannot achieve salvation; yet nothing lacking salvation is of any use. Discord takes away everything that peace acquires for itself, and demolishes whatever it erects. God is where love reigns; where there is no loving person, God cannot be present to guide our affairs [930]. Thus a garrulous tongue is heavier than a lump of lead; under its weight a city's honor falls. Let the citizen who intends evil for the city keep out of it, and let the gate not be opened to the false man. Although such a trickster may sing of the city's honor with his lips, he silently bears the seeds of secret treachery in his heart. Just as a fish is happy in water, so is the wicked man delighted when he sees misfortunes suffered by another. When one single person poisons the public fountain, a great plague suddenly comes and the people perish [940]. Let the citizen who stirs up and afflicts all the others be an exile, or else have the punishment of an early death. When one tooth is rotten it infects the whole head; if it is taken out, the pain from it stops. Similarly, let the malignant citizen be taken away, before civil honor loses its place in the city. For it is expedient that one man die, lest almost the whole population perish, overcome by his unwholesomeness.

[5]Ruler of the city, act so that there may be harmony, and give us peace, for peace engenders complete prosperity. Do not let your speech sound violent among the people; a city's love should be encouraged by gentle words. Compliance tames tigers and enraged lions;

little by little the bull submits to the rustic plow. [6] Thus prudence accomplishes what might cannot, and endowed with affable influence it fulfills its task. One anchor is not enough to hold ships which are tossed about, and one hook is not enough in running waters. [7] Nor can the person of a single man control all the vicissitudes of a city without the help of the people [960]. Stand up against the front lines, if you can, or discreetly carry out little by little what you cannot do all at once. When you rashly hark back to the circumstances of a long-standing injury, they often bring more trouble than relief. Some wounds we see are made bigger by treatment; it would have been better not to touch them. [8] You see mighty rivers arising from tiny springs; they are augmented by the waters gathered together. [9] Quite often a wound that at first was healable cannot receive help which has been long delayed [970]. [10] The wicked deed can be recalled to the point of nausea and the wound made fresh again, and the slightest harm may be grievous to those who are weak. [11] The scar not well healed will turn back into the old wound again, [12] the lack of earlier care having been the cause.

Just as a cinder which is almost out springs to life, should you touch it with sulphur, and from a very small fire will become a great one, [13] so does the man who rashly takes up an animosity of long standing arouse something he cannot easily endure. Any injury at all may rekindle extinct fires, [14] so that a previously forgotten wrath returns even stronger [980]. Anger, base wickedness, and a lust for gain spring up. [15] When there is no love, a city contains every evil. Reproaches are hurled, the air resounds with shouts, and each man invokes an irate God in his own behalf. [16] It is incumbent upon fellow citizens to hold their violent feelings in check. A glorious peace is appropriate for men, fierce anger for wild beasts. [17] There is no good faith where there is no love; but once love is gone, everyone in the city ignores his proper station. When the common people remain separated from men of wisdom, they enter into sly schemes [990]. [18] Fire and water are two things which show no mercy when they have mastery, and the ungovernable rabble is to be considered worse than them. [19]

Once peace, harmony, and justice used to set citizens right in their dealings and affairs. "Where are they now?" you may say. Not here. "Why, then, are they gone?" Malice and silver money are the reason. The profit that dishonesty acquires is not lasting, and love does not endure as the comrade of envy. Make pure your false oaths of time past, I beg of you; make pure today your past words of perfidy [1000]. In this way our fortunes will revive more than I would have believed they could, and what has now sunk basely will rise to high esteem. Sometimes the Deity is wont to be easily pleased; the day is usually brighter when the clouds have been driven away. [20] Peace is granted to the land in which there is an honest will for it; but a wicked man drives everything peaceful out of a city. Rome was head of the world for all time—at least when mutual love ruled the forum in the city. But once divided, it instantly declined, bereft of its honor, and utter disgrace destroyed its sway [1010]. [21] Glory did not depart from Athens as long as its citizens, in harmony together, did not hate each other. Afterwards, when a serious schism divided the city, from that time on it has not enjoyed any of its former greatness. But with God's help, may that fate withdraw from our city, which long shone with great honor.

BOOK VI

Chapter 1

Because of the fact that the sinfulness existing among all ranks
of laymen has been dealt with, he intends to deal in addition with
those who are termed ministers of the law. For it is right that
everyone be governed by the justice of the law, however much
these very men confound all justice by their chicaneries, and in
various ways debilitate it for the sake of worldly gain.

[1]How many there are nowadays who take their name from the law,
but who in part possess this name groundlessly. Apart from the law of
God and under the law of man they enjoy possession of their somewhat
false legal name. All love is far from them and all sin very close to
them, and every case is made for their own personal gain. Their work
and effort are primarily to be connected with their payment--without it
the utterance of their tongue is mute. But the one who devotes himself
to the true law and honestly furthers the justice of his neighbor's complaint [10] is, as the Psalmist sings, a man most blessed. [2] But our
time has few such as that. A struggle for gold so consumes the law
[like] a fresh ulcer that stricken justice is no longer safe.

I cry out what the voice of the people cries out, and I take note of
none except those whom wickedness stigmatizes. I therefore direct my
writings in particular to those whom the sin of avarice leads astray,
and not to the others. Under the cloak of law hides cleverness, whereby a law without justice daily devotes itself to carrying out its wishes
somehow [20]. When lawyers can twist this kind of law, they transmute
the justice begotten of their own words. Everything is tinted in the
guise of justice, whereby their sly administration of justice brings them

the more profit. They care not in what way a case is just or unjust, but that it be rich in returns for them. Nowadays when a lawyer knows that right is on the side of the opposite party, then he summons up his tricks. He disparages by his tricks what he cannot by law. When he cannot win a case, he harasses it [30]. But if he should win it, the custom of the law requires and vouches for his gaining the reputation of an intelligent man. Indeed, unless he knows how to mask the laws by his stratagems, then others will say that his work is a failure. Thus the action of a dishonest man succeeds in confounding the rights of an honest one, and [the former] thereby gets more for his money. So when a lawyer grows wise, he overwhelms the law with his numerous tricks. Thus the law is quite clear in form, yet in essence it is skillful chicanery, and it overthrows justice [40].

This is the garrulous, litigious tribe which much prefers to vociferate in false causes. The lawyer chooses to follow the way of the whore, who cannot love a man unless it be for a gift. And as you see, he is always for sale to everyone; if you give him gold, you can have his body. He never cares what sort or kind a man is, as long as he can get some money. [3] Just as the road stands open for the pilgrims to Rome who come to pay their devotions to holy places [50], so is there a common thoroughfare to lawyers' dwellings, and on it the people walk forth and pay them their tribute. Just as tyrants of old bound up righteous men who refused to make offerings to their gods, so does the greedy lawyer of today squeeze his neighbors who are unwilling to pay him his tribute. And so I see people now forced to make sacrifice to the advocate of the law, lest things go badly for them. Various people often make various presents to him, according as their means hold out [60]. Indeed, it is all right for you to offer reverently a gift of silver to him, if you have none of gold. If you haven't even silver, give him some presents, for there is nothing in the world that would satisfy him. For your gift he wants to get all the bounties that earth and the heavens above and the sea produce. He gathers from everywhere, both early and late, but while he takes all, he will give you nothing in return. [4]

The fowler does not seize birds with a single snare but with many, nor does one hook catch fish [70]. [5] Nor does the law, now transmuted into what are not laws, fashion only one net for its riches, but a thousand of them. Everywhere there is a case at law, whereby its dangling hook catches golden gifts for its spendthrift purse. [6] There is no path which it will not explore for the riches of gold, either by craft or cleverness, by force or desire. The delicate spider weaves its slender webs so that it can trap its prey in them. If a fly on the wing comes along, it is caught and falls, yet a hawk will pass through the middle without injury [80]. Whatever flies on strong wings will escape, but whatever is weak will stay there, wrapped around by the webs. In a similar way he greedy lawyer envelopes his trembling neighbors with the law and traps them. He oppresses timid people who have no defense, and binds them with the net of law. The innocent mob falls into his webs, and the lawyer's ruinous nets provide a way out for the man of prestige.

At night the bat swoops down to the ground; its custom is to use its wings for feet when walking [90]. Similarly, one whose mind is stocked with only worldly knowledge makes himself like this winged creature. For he flies about the world and seizes upon only worldly things, since he is ignorant of the true light. [7] The night owl is said to be sharp-sighted at night, and in the daytime tries to use less light. Those who are versed in the law imitate this bird, since they are engaged in the evils of darkness, and do not possess the benefits of the light. [8] Quite often, however, the prey which it seizes is its death, since its inevitable end lies in secret for it [100]. For the hawk is unexpectedly at hand, hungering to carry off the young fowls. Thus deceit often falls because of its own deceit, [9] the captor is captured, he who devours is himself devoured; the poor [fish] loves the hook by which he is caught.

Chapter 2

Here he speaks of the lawyers and advocates who amass huge pos-sessions by plundering the neighboring population and enriching themselves with the goods of others. It is said, however, that a third owner will scarcely enjoy these things.

[1]A lawyer swallows up his native land more than the ravenous Scylla swallows up the waves of the sea. A lawyer wants to get his money more than the hound wants to get its quarry in the spreading for-ests. [2] When it seizes its prey with its teeth in order to devour its flesh, the hound does not strangle its prey [110] more than the lawyer strangles his client with the law, in order that he may get himself a fee of money. Just as the hawk is wont to pursue frightened doves, [3] so does the lawyer pursue frightened people and throttle them. Just as the terrified, wounded lamb which has just escaped from a [grey] wolf trembles and does not remain quite safe; and just as the dove with its own blood smeared on its plumage still fears the claws with which it was clutched; [4] so trembles the wretch oppressed by the snares of law-yers, and hence cries in the ear of his God [120].

The physician wants suffering to be common so that another's mis-fortune may bring him welcome rewards; the lawyer wants people to be contentious, so that he can enjoy prosperity through their disputes. He profits from what you lose; and if you were to make a profit he wants to get his share along with you. When he has his right hand full, then he stretches out his left, which is still unsatisfied. So whichever way the wind blows, it always carries his tranquil sail to every sea [130]. Thus his purse is prosperous, bulging with other people's gold. [5] For the way of the law is that as soon as one can become rich in money, he then hungers for new lands.

Just as the she-wolf, constrained by hunger in the same fashion as her young, searches through the broad fields to get their food, so when the lawyer's progeny increases, he plots by means of every trick, to increase his wealth. Night and day without respite, he schemes to grab money, he tries his bargaining everywhere [140]. Then he joins house to house and field to fields, for he wishes to be alone with himself in the land. [6] The plunderer warms another's eggs like a partridge, but in the end it is clear what right he has to them. [7] The son quickly dissipates in vice what the father acquired for himself with great zeal and difficulty. And the giddy fool lets loose of the worldly accumulations which the clever man had gathered through his cunning. Thus a third owner will not enjoy that which is wrongly acquired, [8] but the world seizes back what it previously bestowed [150]. According to the sayings of Isaiah, there is clearly to be woe unto the lawyer, for he wickedly squanders the widow's house and home. [9]

Chapter 3

Here he speaks of those lawyers and advocates who, the more numerous they are, the more they swallow up their native land in their thirst for money. Weaving their subtleties under pretext of the law, they ensnare innocent, frightened people by their tricks.

When thorns have sprung up in great number, the crops are rendered smaller because of the overburdened soil. [1] And when the fat sow has suckled her young, her belly is made leaner by the piglets. And when the law swells the number of lawyers, then the plundered people in the land groan the more. Just as a torrent of waters inundates the engulfed crops and plucks and uproots whatever is sticking in the ground [160], so does the greedy man get men's accumulated riches which the surface of the earth holds, with the law being privy to this. Health cannot exist when the doctor injures the sick, and in his madness heaps harm upon harm. Likewise, when lawyers brood upon unjust cases, peace cannot remain secure for long. Such things are so constant in our days that a man will hardly escape safe and sound from this severe affliction. As long as a scale of gold weighs the laws, the balance will not be just; yet today's justice teaches this practice [170].

It is written that Chrysostom had a mouth of gold; [2] that quality was latent in his discourse. But powerful lawyers who are now swallowing everything made of gold actually do have golden mouths. Wares are sold by delicate weighing so that the buyer, tricked by this, may not know the market value of them. But behold, now there is an even more delicate weighing process, through which the words of the law are sold in their own way. Whatever laws may do, the law of the inner man bears the burden of the judge within him [180]. The Lord grants everything freely, but the miser of the law will not grant a single word unless he sells it. If they make fair promises, it would be right to promise only in just so many words, and to carry out their bargains according to their agreements. But they often insist on taking pay in advance for something they have not earned, no matter what follows in the end. Thus the crooked scale, which ought to be just, is ignorant of the weight of justice, so that it falls in the wrong way. Thus injustice is wont to be done under the name of justice, and what should be trustworthy becomes more and more without trust [190]. Lawyers declare that the law is sacred, but they demonstrate through their own deeds that it is wicked.

If a man assumes that something of wood is straight and puts it in sight under clear water, that which was straight appears in turn to him to be crooked. Behold, the law behaves like my idea. For if I now say to a lawyer that the law is clear, so that justice cannot fail me, he, in plotting for his own gain, will turn upside down whatever I may have said to him and suggest the many risks [200]. He makes bitter gall out of the sweetness of honey and pretends a rose is like a thorn. And just as the basilisk[3] poisons the air with the breath of its mouth, so that nearby life perishes because of the noxiousness, so does the man of law, well supplied with tricks on his tongue for our ears, poison with his words a law which is quite sound. And just as the fox terrifies the wandering sheep and seizes upon its prey, so does [the lawyer's] trickery make good faith vanish. It is more merciful to support the swimmer's sinking chin with even one finger than to drown his face in the flowing waters [210]. [4] I wonder at the fact that the counselor who ought to defend legally the causes of the poor instead aggravates their need.

How often do dreams—not an actual thing but the image of a thing seen in sleep--disturb men groundlessly. [5] Similarly, how often does a lawyer, pretending that there are dangers for you, change your course when it is quite right. He speaks to you with hesitant mind, for no man of deceitful mind can be assured in his speech. A question arises; he proceeds to deceive one's reason; by this he does not doubt to make you doubt [220]. He strikes fear into you by some trumped-up law in order to turn a man of reason into a brute. You will pay for one thing with your eyes in order that you may keep something inferior, until the law decides your case. Lawyers are clouds which darken the skies so that no one can see the light of the sun. For they obfuscate the clear justice of the law, yet their abominable darkness claims to be daylight. Splendor loses its radiance among these men; truth tells lies, fraud denies that honesty exists [230]. The law rampages, piety is dormant, wisdom fails, peace is a burden, and every lawsuit furnishes opportunities. And this lex, legis, [which is] from ledo, ledis, just as ius [is] from iurgo, administers justice at this present time. [6] But if the people would stand united in enduring love, then the status of the lawyer would be meaningless.

I grant that law is good in itself, but I now see its wicked masters distorting justice. It is not permissible to enter into conspiracy, so they say, but nevertheless they do not do what their own laws teach [240]. If the law makes it necessary that I act in opposition to a lawyer and I ask to have my own legal counsel, then they all say they are not willing to oppose a colleague. Thus they strike, but no one can strike them. The lawyer seeks worldly honors for himself, subverting justice with the vigor of his tongue. The law punishes others whom it wishes to, but not them; neither God nor mankind can keep them honest. [7]

Chapter 4

Here he speaks of how lawyers and advocates of the law, gradually rising in power and aspiring to the office of judge, finally reach the summit of a judicial bench. Sitting there in the seat of the scornful, [1] as it were, and struck with the blindness of greater avarice, they are of worse nature than before.

[2]A man is [first] an apprentice and afterwards a sergeant; finally, the office of judge will mark[3] him [250]. If he is greedy in the first rank, he is much more so in the second; and the third rank is guiltiest of all. And the law is so guided by heavy reins of gold that it cannot travel along honest courses. Law which used to be free is not free, but instead blind greed for money holds it fettered in a prison. Unless a golden key unlocks its closed doors, no one will have a way to enter it. Knocking with your hand or shouting with your voice will not help you at all to speak with the law, you who come without the key [260]. If money is not your guide and does not hire the guardians of the law, you can go away empty-handed. And thus a lawyer does not take up a case nor a judge decree a just judgment unless money is your guide.

225

[4]There are three things in particular by which the law is disturbed, so that it corrupts its office of justice: bribery, favor, and fear. Justice to the contrary, these three enter into agreements, with the result that nothing in the world stands in their way. Indeed, Solomon says that gold blinds the eyes of a judge, [5] and his decision is corrupted by money [270]. And we all know that one who is a friend of the judge can lose nothing by his verdict. We also know that if a case affects a powerful man, fear puts to flight the discernment of justice. Frequently the judge cannot endure his frightening threats and is swayed by his entreaties without any threats [being necessary]. When a great man's letter strikes the judge's ears, the might of his pen abrogates the justice which ought to ensue. But woe above all to the poor wretch who now seeks anything at law when he cannot give anything [280]! These things are common to us because under today's law justice refuses to act in a poor man's case. Thus with hesitation and with terrified ears, I seek sureties for the wrongs which are mine, but I do not find them.

Behold, the day in which law was a friend to justice! The law now acts quite contrary to its own pronouncements. A mask hides its face, and it confuses the text with the gloss; this changed law is turning into a school of logic. There are students of the law without numbers in the world; there are a great many leaves but very little fruit from them [290]. How often is wickedness contrived under an honest name and does trickery accomplish much under the guise of justice! Cautious men who see through such actions should in turn beware of such crimes. Great rivers are made smaller by many little streams, and a river bed is thus emptied of its waters. A hoard of treasure suffers an eclipse through many expenditures, and a rich man often becomes poor unless he takes precautions. Similarly, this wealthy land will be poor in a short time, unless the excess of laws is held in check [300]. Medicine does not know how to get rid of the troublesome gout, [6] and the law likewise has no cure for avarice. If my purse is effective, the law will be silent, overruled by it; when I am highly distinguished, I can banish all justice with gold. Or if my court is that of an especially great man, there is no need for the powers of the law; I have my say. Having lasted such a long time, this wound is becoming ulcerated; there is no room for a fresh injury.

Chapter 5

Here he speaks as if in a letter directed to the judges who put their trust in their transitory heaps of riches. In no way do they deem it fitting to establish God as their helper.

O you who hold in your hands the judgment, purchased for money, over life, death, and property [310], through what judgment do you think to save yourselves, since your law is wrongfully sold to others? O false and mighty lovers of this world, you who think earthly riches are gods; O you who strive so for mundane honors, you whose companion is never-ending anxiety: learn that lofty perches often await a violent fall and tumble down at high speed. Oftentimes an old tree falls before blasts of winds, yet a young shoot remains calmly fixed in place [320]. We know that lofty mountains, which cold and utter chill rack, grow white with snows. There the fury of the winds is harshest, while the nearby valley is pleasantly mild. Similarly, you men of power never lack adversities, nor is there any assured peace and quiet for you. [1]

Tell me whether rich men at any time lacked an enemy. On the contrary, serious misfortune often batters them. [2] Neither a purple vestment nor ivory makes for sound sleep, [yet] poverty lies safe on its lowly straw [330]. Sheer dread for what they could lose tortures misers, and the empty darkness strikes troubled men with fear. [3] The owner of gold is always afraid, and at every noise he thinks thieves are near. The rich man fears weapons, poisons, theft, and rapine; he cannot have unshaken confidence. Miserable greediness tortures him as long as he seeks after riches; fear tortures him when he begins to get what he has sought. Therefore, the rich man is wretched because a poor man seeks after his possessions, and he is wretched because he is afraid of losing them [340]. As he lies on his feather bed, his sleepless mind suffers torments, for it is seething, stirred up by various plots. He says, "I want to get the land of the wretch next door, for that field is next to mine." Thus he drives orphans from their paternal homes; he pursues widows and harasses them with lawsuits. He enjoys the satisfactions of the poor man's property, but he reckons the misfortunes of another as nothing. [4] If he could gain possession of the world, he would not care to know who God might be [or] anything further about God on earth [350].

Judge, the glitter of your gold is enough for your blind mind to be free of shadows, isn't it? You take the fertile gold for yourself, but never glance at your own barren existence. A judge is scarcely free of troubles in ascending the pinnacles of justice, so long as he is burdened with worldly affairs. 5 You try to extend the lengthy boundaries of your lands 6 and take no thought of your life's short span. Why do you seek silver for yourself? What trust do you place in gold? For the treasures of the earth are common to all [360]. Quite often you may perceive God's gifts given to His enemies, yet they have no praise in the sight of God. A pagan, a Jew, a bloody thief has such gifts; you should believe that God has given such things in anger. Whatever evil men happen to have I reckon as insignificant; the prosperity of the wicked is not a great good. O how often is the honest man poor and the scoundrel prosperous--here, but not in another place, since justice reigns there. The man beloved of God dies while the sinner lives on, but they are not equal in Christ's esteem [370]. The just man falls ill while the iniquitous flourishes in health, but in the end each shall bear his own burden. 7 But if a judge can find his salvation in the world, he does not care what his end will be.

O you who are greedy for everything, why do you abandon yourself? You own everything that is on earth, but you do not possess yourself. O you who know others but not yourself, you known to one and all, you do not know that your knowledge is worth nothing to you. Therefore, know yourself first and me second; make the right decision wisely [380]. You cherish all things which are of this world, you forsake all things which are Christ's, and believe that you have enough with nothing You win the world, you lose heaven; you sustain a worthless body, your spirit perishes. 8 So far as you are concerned, what is empty is filled, and what is fleeting is permanent; indeed, such a judge does not perceive his task well. You build castles and newly decorated chambers, and you cherish whatever is worldy more than divinity. You build huge buildings, you enclose them with a wide, deep ditch, 9 so that when closed, the front gates may shut out the public [390]. 10 Why should I mention a judge's clothing, his beds or his houses, the luxury of which can have no equal? One who saw what these dwelling places were would say at once they belonged to a second Jove. The pomp and splendor which you embody in your homes—will they not be everlasting for you, as long as you seize your plunder? But Babylon fell, and even mighty Troy, and world-ruling Rome scarcely retains her prestige. 11

Every earthly power has a sudden end and abandons what belongs to it in hasty flight [400]. Therefore be afraid, O judge, you who rise to great honors; remember that you are standing on a perilous spot. Everything of the world's which is dear to you will pass away from you, and God judges you on your own merits. And God's just law will then set aside the injustices which you now decree, and will render you your just burdens. When the terrible avenger sent by the just judge plunges you in the depths of the sulphurous lake, then, alas! you will wretchedly lament, although too late, that you placed your trust in such false things [410]. Neither jewels nor silver nor gold will descend there, no frail, wordly glory, which is so quickly lost. But it is in vain that I write of these matters to the people's judges; I have uttered wasted words. For that which is justice, or that which is the just kind of judge, is not to be seen at the present day. If there is a justice who acts falsely under such a title, he bears the empty title with no justice.

Chapter 6[1]

Here he speaks of the sinfulness of sheriffs, bailiffs, and also of jurors in assizes. Supporting unjust lawsuits because hired by the gold of the rich, they all unjustly slander and oppress the poor.

Now what, moreover, can I say to sheriffs? Do they not do harm to men in assizes [420]? The suit grows weak which affords no drop of grease by which their hand may be salved.[2] If your bribes in the law's assize are cut off, justice perishes and as a result your case is torn to shreds. But if your bribes are assessed beforehand, then you can make money at your assizes.

You can bring jurors into your service for a price, just as an ox is hired for the plow. And they will sell you false oaths for your money --thus does gold vanquish justice in my city [430]. So I see the rich man's unjust case allowed and the poor man's just case condemned. The [vis]count takes his beginning not from vicis but from vicium;[3] he assumes posts of justice out of greed. So I declare to sheriffs that, because they have been swayed by bribes, they do injury to the common people. Nor do jurors have a taste for anything, unless it is seasoned with the salt of the money you will furnish beforehand. Lawyers seize the wool and carry off the skin, so that nothing of a poor man's sheep will be left [440].[4] So, drawing my final conclusions from our foremost lawgivers, I say that the law of the purse is flourishing at present. Lawgivers take justice for their own now, as if a swine were to take pearls for its swill.[5]

[6]What is it to sell justice but to sell Christ, whom Judas' greed sold by treachery? But surely no one who is alive on earth today is like Judas? On the contrary, I believe many like him are alive. We know, to be sure, that Judas committed such a crime once, yet I gather he was penitent for it [450]. But nowadays, all men are so delighted to have got their profit that they sell [such] wares commonly. Judas returned the evil money which he received, yet it is doubtful that he thereby won forgiveness. Now, what will there be for those who sell justice to the wicked, for those who have a daily hour for such commerce? Just

229

as the very abyss of hell devours and holds tightly, with no man returning free from its mouth, so no one can take matters out of the hands
[of] those who sell the law and snatch at bribes [460]. And so, since
they are as grasping as hell, I believe that in the end hell will hold them
in its grasp.

Or what shall I say to bailiffs, who are like the swift furies of
Acheron? Beware of them even more. Where they enter the door, they
represent ominous troubles, for woes attend them in full force. Just
as the toad cursed the harrow, [7] so do I curse the many lawless masters of the law.

Chapter 7

Here he says that just as it is necessarily ordained for men to be
on earth, so it is right that laws be instituted for governing them,
provided, however, that the guardians of the law discern truth
from falsehood and render every man his due with impartial authority. Yet up to the present he absolves our king's innocence
of the sins and injustices now going on, because of his minor age.

Laws were established for the transgressor, so that each man
might receive his due rewards [470]. Nowadays, however, the good
man is punished and the other, the wicked man, is pardoned for gold,
as long as he is prosperous. To every thing there is a season, [1] and
the season itself has its own due seasons. Similarly, a lawsuit ought
to have its own justifications. What will the sea bring as it swells with
lofty waves, unless it have a ship which the rolling billow carries? But
what will the ship bring, unless there be a guiding sailor in it? Or
what good is the sailor, if he has no oar? What good is the sea, the
ship, or the sailor, even if he has an oar, unless they have a port and
there is a suitable wind for the water [480]? [2]

What is a people without law, or what is law without a judge, or
what is a judge, if without justice? If anyone looks at the doings in our
country, he will observe three things there which are frightening to me.
All misfortunes are burdensome, but none more so than when a just
man cannot get justice. Strife grows out of injustice, and as a result
one's customary affection leaves off, and the household grumbles. And
if grumbling comes, dividedness comes with it, and the land divided
does not stand firm [490]. And woe to that which cannot stand by itself,
whatever it may be; for it will suddenly fall to utter ruin.

For God is [my] witness, saying that kingdoms divided against
themselves shall not stand, [3] and I place trust in His pronouncements.

Therefore, all who govern kingdoms can see that the greatest part of our fate depends upon them. The people must atone for whatever errors the great commit, [4] since a weak head makes the members suffer. [5] If the leader loses the way, his followers among the people go astray, and the road by which they are to return is much in doubt [500]. Peoples have perished because of a king's sin, and writings rarely teach anything to the contrary. But royal goodness brings the joys of peace to the people, for God looks with favor upon the deeds of a pious king. To be sure, if a king is wicked, God, Who has power over everything, wills to punish him, since the law cannot. It would be advantageous for the people if every king would live honorably, since a two-fold destiny lies in his hands: the king who lives honorably is reckoned the sole salvation of the people, and the evil king commits actions toward their ruin [510]. For it is obvious that wicked deeds on the part of one whose established laws the people have to obey are highly injurious.

The greater a man is, the greater his crimes are. When he falls from his lofty position, he is harmed the more as a result. [6] I see many guilty men, but those who are lawgivers and yet remain lawless are guiltier than them all. When the corrupted power of a realm rages lawless, there can be nothing more grievous for the whole world. I think that cattle are more holy and susceptible of feeling[7] than one who makes the laws and does not obey them [520]. Wars alone with their triumphs are no ornament to a king's reign; rather, he should obey good laws at all times. A house cannot be built without timber, can it? But of what use is timber for it, if it has not been hewn? And once it has been hewn, what use is it, unless the hand of the toiling craftsman remains steady in joining things together? If these things have been combined, they will be thoroughly helpful, and if they are separated, no portion of them is of any use. [8]

Of what use is the earth by itself, unless people are on it? Or of what use are the people to it, unless a king governs [530]? Of what use is a king, unless he has sound counsel? And of what use is counsel, unless the king trusts it? [9] But in our land there is such disunion that each man now chooses to go his own way. Discord troubles the fellow-citizens in the city today, so that each one destroys the right of the other. Nor is the law heeded now by the rural leaders; rather, he who is most powerful is master. The clergy now blame the people and the people blame the clergy, but both persevere in their guiltiness [540]. Envious of one another, each man blames the other, and no group mends its own course. If you look at either rank, you will certainly say that we both have suffered in important ways.

[10]Now in particular does the voice of the people cry out, and I have fears within my trembling breast. [11] The high court which is obligated to uphold justice now travels its unjust ways. When the head is weak, the bodily members are deprived of health, [12] yet there is no physician who now takes care of our need [550]. The disease of vices has grown so great that no hand can check its excesses. Thus a pestilence is rising by which virtue lies overwhelmed, and it springs up into vice, which governs all affairs.

[13]The king, an undisciplined boy, neglects the moral behavior by which a man might grow up from a boy. Indeed, youthful company so sways the boy that he has a taste for nothing practical, unless it be his whim. The young men associated with him want what he wants; he enters upon a course of action and they follow him [560]. Vainglory makes these youthful comrades vain, for which reason they vainly cultivate the royal quarters more and more. They abet the boy king in his childish behavior, whereby he wields the authority of virtue the less.

There are also the older men of greed who in pursuing their gains tolerate many scandals for the boy's pleasure. Men of good character withdraw, those who are vicious come in, and the king's court contains whatever vice exists. Sin springs up on every side of the boy, and he, who is quite easily led, takes to every evil [570]. To boys, it is not

---

[10]Behold, a voice of doleful expression now speaks to the ears, and it says that there are many burdens in these days. The high court which should be our guide is lawless, and, as the voice says, it commits high crime. No tongue now speaks for the common good, but instead each man seizes upon the opportunities for his own profit [550*]. [14] A mob of flatterers proceeds to the forefront of the royal court, and the court cedes them what they order to be done. But the court banishes those who dare to speak the truth, and does not allow such people to be at the king's side. The boy is free of blame, but those who have instrumented this boyish reign shall not endure without a fall. So not the king but his council is the cause of our sorrow, for which the land grieves as if with a general murmur. If the king were of mature age, he would set right the scale which now is without justice [560*]. For a king's moderation moderates other men, and he is said to be the leader in the promotion of all justice. If he wishes to be a good king, those who are good are better instructed by his good character. If he wishes to be bad, a king singles out, extols, and cherishes hangers-on of a similar sort, in order that they may cater to him. But this latter thought pertains to one that maturity demonstrates as able to choose, not to a boy, since his blame is smaller then. It is not the law of nature or of reason that the evil which afflicts the world is that of a boy [570*]. To boys, evils are not wrongdoing but joking, not dishonor but glorious sport, and

wrongdoing but joking, not dishonor but glorious sport; but his destiny does arise out of this wrongdoing. There are, however, hidden causes which no one on earth can know, yet God knows them well. A mother, to be sure, does not know what fate is designed for her child, but in the end every secret is clearly revealed. [16] Everywhere the voice of the people of today, who are placed in doubt in the face of the enormity of evil, cries out about such things. I accordingly grieve even more than they over the disgusting things which I see, for which reason I offer the following writings for the boy king [580].

---

the origin of evil is not there. For Daniel has said that the impiety which the madness of the world embraces has arisen from older men. [15] Elders implant all the vice which the world has, and they sow poisons as if they had been scattered by a plague. For it is said that the wickedness of these men corrupts the thoughts of the whole world, for which reason God's anger rages. Deceit has now increased and integrity has disappeared, and what was once an honor is felt to be a disgrace [580*].

Chapter 8[1]

Here he says that because of the fact that all men whatsoever of earthly estate are governed under the justice of royal authority, he consequently intends to write this epistle, set forth for the sake of instruction, to our king now reigning at present. With the help of divine grace our king, who is now in his youthful time of life, may be more plainly instructed by this letter in his royal functions when he has afterwards reached more mature years. And first he says that however much the royal power may be exalted in any way above the laws, it is nevertheless only proper that his royal highness, by persevering in good behavior, zealously govern himself under the laws of justice as if he were a free man, and his people as if in the presence of the Almighty King.

Since every liege is subject to the law of his king and serves him with all his might, it is fitting that every liege should love him with faithful heart in a willing spirit. And it is proper for the king to guide the people entrusted to him and govern it with just law. Hence it is that for the honor of my king, I intend to set down a rule of conduct taken from many writings.

O pious king, hear what your kingdom's rule should be, in

harmony with the law and joined with God's justice [590]. When I grasp the reins[2] of the laws, I hold you in check more strongly than a fortress. While you fear no man, be fearful for yourself. For fear, a humble virtue, banishes all pride, and should be as a key to the [other]virtues. It is better for you, O king, to govern yourself according to the law than to subjugate all the kingdoms of the world to yourself. For the sake of the world, the fate of others is subject to you; for the sake of heaven, be subject yourself to God. Since the people subjected to you by law serve you devotedly, conduct yourself like a Christ toward your servants [600]. You who conquer others, strive to conquer yourself, and learn to subdue all excesses of passion. When punishing others you should wish to punish yourself, and when rendering justice to the people you should likewise render justice to yourself.

You who subdue others, work to subdue yourself. If you wish to be a king, rule yourself and you will be one. By what right could a man who does not even reign over the workings of his own mind say he was a king? The sovereign cannot confer well-being upon others as long as he is not ruler over himself, as he should be [610]. While all things are permissible to you, do not seek to permit yourself all things, for things permitted to you often bring harm. [3] You are above the laws, but live as a just man under them, and because of you there will be hope of welfare for us. Your wrath is death; you can do what is not allowed. Yet nevertheless, firm vows of justice must guide you. Although it may keep your peace of mind unimpaired, nevertheless the fact that everything is permissible does not prove it to be honorable. Granted that something is safe, you, strengthened in your honor, must nevertheless determine with strict judgment the things which you can do [620]. You should govern your actions quite moderately, unless the affair should require otherwise; severity causes hatred and bitter warfare. Do not let the general welfare of a mighty people escape your notice, but wisely beware of such a calamity. Pharaoh's life and Nero's wicked deeds teach what a just king must avoid.

O good young king, act so that through your goodness your youth may be properly dedicated to moral ways. What will your handsomeness or the noble name of your ancestors avail you, if you have become a slave to your own vices [630]?[4] Alexander the Great's teacher first taught him bad morals when he was a boy. [5] The boy king learned them, and afterwards when he tried to give them up, his early abuses stood in his way. Alexander conquered Darius together with Babylon, but he could not conquer the evil imprinted on his heart. The pot is wont to keep [the shape] which first moulded it, [6] as wise men have previously written in their precepts. Therefore, O king, drive wicked men quickly away from you, for a shame of long standing cannot depart from your door except with difficulty [640]. [7] Express approbation of good men,

flee the company of the immoral; the unfortunate hand which is drawn
out of pitch acquires a stain. [8]

Chapter 9

Here he tells how a king ought cautiously to shun those who counsel him evilly. He ought to annihilate them completely as traitors
to his kingdom. He ought also to investigate carefully the kinds
of ministers he has; those whom he finds straying from justice
he should correct with due punishment and penalize very severely.

You shall beware of false friends involved in base behavior, who
demand what is yours, yet have no wish to love you. You should avoid
being consoled by the bland words of the cunning, lest they cast your
personal reputation down to the depths. Listening to their words too
thoughtlessly, and believing what they say, often causes the beginning
of idle fears. A man who urges war, who advises plundering, and who
conspires to get your people's taxes [650]—O king, I implore you to
shut your ears to such men, lest your high renown crumble to pieces,
struck down by them. Let no greedy man dupe your royal council, but
consider such men as death. The evil is not on earth which is not
hidden in the recess of a covetous man's heart, when he is thirsting for
gain. He walks in darkness and performs the work of darkness, [1] and
he hates and impugns nothing except the need of peace. The man who
holds talk of peace while his thoughts dwell on evil, who brings honey
on his tongue but has poison in his heart [660][2]—this man is a wily, in-
imical friend for a king. He is always for sale since he devotes himself to gain. A viperous sort, both puffed up and filled with venom, he
contrives wars through his deceits, artifices, and cunning. He is always in the midst of plots and tries to injure the unwary, and he frames
his deceptions in secret. Prying into men's minds, he uncovers their
secrets, and he does his work like a Judas.
　　See who tempts you, O king, and who tries to subvert you and
persuade you to set aside God's commands [670]; see who he is or of
what kind or sort, or whether he wishes to tell you the truth. First
determine in your mind the feelings of the tempter, and pay attention to
whether he is acting calmly or hesitatingly, and whether he is proposing
something dubious for you as he fabricates his lies. Deceitful words
are always afraid of being found out. When there is ground for treachery, O gracious king, do not be credulous; if someone acts corruptly,
beware of his doings. Many a man does not believe [another man is not
to be trusted] until something harmful injures him; the wise ruler

provides for such actions beforehand [680]. Birds are often caught by pleasant sounds; [3] shun the honied words of a smooth tongue, O king. Give worthy, fitting rewards to worthy men, O king, and to the wicked give the rewards which their guilt has earned. Because Christ was merciful, the good thief won pardon; the bad thief deserved his penalty on the cross. [4] Base obsequiousness [may] wheedle a considerable gift from one's hands, but a man will mark what such actions are by their intention.

If a well established reason insists upon your punishing a crime, in that case do what a just man should do [690]. Do not let feigned piety mitigate the severity of your justice, but rather let the punishment carry out your decision. A judge's penalty which is put off will often bring on severe perils; one who suffers evil men to exist destroys good ones. Impose different punishments upon different crimes. There are a thousand forms of evil; there are a thousand remedies. [5] The sword is understood as indicating the badge of justice; even so, a king does not lay hold of his weapons in order that a traitor may perish: a king should order such men hauled up high by a noose, lest both his own position and that of the law be destroyed [700]. Act, O king, lest frenzied discord among the people should say, "The law governing our ancestral rights is without a king." And let it not be appropriate for the mob to say that a prince's shadow affords no refuge, because justice has been set aside. Let dishonesty perish through death, tormented with its own dishonesty, so that your royal justice may stand in honor. Let the people speak thus: "May there be glory forever to the king. Because of him, peace has flourished well; because of him, the guilty man pays for his deeds."

It is bidden that the sword always be brandished, in order that it may carry out judicial punishment the more promptly [710]. When the sword is at rest, it cannot hold the world in check. Let him who wishes to rule protect justice with blood. Arms bring peace; arms curb the rapacious. A worthy king should bear arms so that the guilty man may fear them. [6] [Yet] it is only right that you view your people with a tender heart, lest knights by chance do harm in your name. For if you are unwilling to punish your officials, the royal reputation bears the offense of their fault. A hawk flies forth after prey, and it serves its master's advantage by seizing food [720]. Similarly, there are those who in serving the king bring suffering upon the poor by taking too much for his benefit. [7] The poor man who cries aloud in destitution to the Lord has weight in his plea; He is mindful of His poor. [8] In the same fashion should the bishop who is a guardian of souls bear the responsibility of his office. His ultimate reward will be like his own meting out either glory or punishment will endure eternally for him. God will likewise confer just rewards upon you, O king, who rule our land with your laws [730]. Your power is great, O king, yet He Whose right hand weighs your every deed is even more powerful.

Chapter 10[1]

Here he says that a king ought to hold with sound counsel. He ought to support and encourage the rights of the Church and be a pious knight in his decisions. And he should value his own reputation above all worldly wealth.

Spurn the wicked, cherish the wise, curb the rebellious, give to the unfortunate, cast aside the criminal, have mercy upon the condemned. Whatever you do, your integrity should never be plunged into vice. Your reputation should be placed above money, and your duty above your affairs. You should contrive nothing for the sake of this world, O king, whereby you would be reputed as just among nobles but guilty before God. You should be eager to foster the Church with great piety; your crown, indeed, should be worn with its blessings [740]. When you resolve to attend to the complaints of the pauper and the widow, you should carry out judgment upon the wretched with compassion. Sometimes it is better to remit the decrees of the laws, lest mercy vanish because of your severity. So let your honor deem it fitting to be lenient with your subjects, for I believe that God often wishes the condemned man to live. Also, let noble and peasant bear an equal burden, and let nothing violate a secret at your hands. If your position seems arduous to you, you should certainly realize that faith is wont to be slow in matters of great moment [750]. [2] Do not place reliance in dubious things; a favorable hope is often deceived by its own presentiment, [3] and is a casting of mankind into affliction; [4] the beginning does not know what the end will bring. When necessity calls upon you to transact the business of the realm, let one old man together with another govern your counsel. [5] Whatever we may say will travel from the East to the West, [6] so do not let a talkative tongue learn your state of feeling. Evil counsel harms your royal honor and incites what once was peaceful good to wickedness [760].

Let an elderly man render justice to the people, and let respect be demanded, where there is maturity well versed in just laws. Even though the man himself be young, he whose wisdom confirms his mature intelligence is old enough. I do not approve of either old-fashioned, hide-bound intellects or of fatuous youth; [7] maturity does not confer her privileges thus. Very often a dotard has a juvenile character, while a young fellow exhibits the behavior of a elderly man. You should therefore examine both ages quite circumspectly, good king [770]. Put their actions to the test first; from this you may choose your men. The man who renders you service ought to be your servant, and not the worthless fellow who is eager for gold. The toil which looks forward to a king's acknowledgement is sweeter than the payment, and you can place your trust in it. The man who is peaceful, free from avarice, and generous toward everything good is the friend of justice. Make use of this type of counsel, good king, so that the chronicle of your everlasting glory may redound in the world. Fame, which flies freely and with no one prescribing fetters for her, [8] will proclaim either one thing or another, depending on your deserts [780]. Believe that a good name is better than treasures; it upholds honor, banishes scandal, and flourishes in esteem. Touch a wholesome flower; it will give off a pleasant scent. Similarly, the virtue of a good man is everywhere sweet to the scent. Consult with your doctors of law, withdraw from the associations of the wicked, and keep company with the good. You should gather wisdom from a learned mind just as you would gather grain from the harvest or drink from a refreshing fountain.

Chapter 11

Here he tells how a king's freedom by no means ought to fall into the servitude of vices. Rather, just as his power surpasses other men in the eyes of the people, so should the plenitude of his virtues shine brighter than others in the eyes of God.

Let no empty glory puff you up, I beg of you, O king, for a haughty life appears loathsome to people [790]. Even a small fly is harmful, so be circumspect in small matters. Royal sceptres do not make your people safe: little David conquered the great Goliath, for humble virtue vanquishes proud hearts. [1] The loving Christ raised the humble and cast the proud from His heart; therefore, rule your own kingdom devoutly, O king. Let your speech be trustworthy and your words well advised; act where, when, and with whom you should. Let your discourse in men's ears bring trust like the Scriptures: words conceived out of anxiety carry less certainty [800]. Do not let an angry impulse suddenly rush upon you, O king, but further the causes of justice with self-control. When wrath impels the spirit, it deprives it of the power of reason and negates the mind's allotted tasks. According to law, life and death are borne in your hands, so it is the more incumbent upon you to be farsighted in your dealings. No greediness ought to have the power to tarnish your reputation; instead, all the land should rejoice in your generosity. A noble king ought not to be the slave of

238

avarice, a king's character ought to be liberal in everything [810].

Through your merits, let your generous alms take care of the poor, by which means you can pacify God the King. Do whatever good things you can while you live this brief life; you will reap much if you sow a few seeds now. Do not give sparingly; rather, consider carefully to whom you give. Believe that it is quite enough to give intelligently. [2] The goodness which expends its gifts creditably does not come to nothing, for a gift brings worthy praise to the giver. It is often beneficial for a man to take a little water from a full stream, and the contents of the sea are none the less for this [820]. Similarly, when your alms are taken they will duly benefit the unfortunate, and the sum of your money will be none the less. If anyone gives to the unfortunate for love of God, his gifts endure for a time [but] his fame will be everlasting. Let your garments be divided up, let your gold and jewels be split into pieces, [3] offer to the poor what God has previously given to you. A sincere alms is the handmaiden of God, the antidote to death, the gateway to grace, the path of salvation. It contends against the sins of the giver, it pleads for its author, it redeems the worthy, it supplicates for the rich [830]. Sin is the death of the soul and death is the due punishment of sin, [4] but in this way the pious spirit does away with death.

Let the sin of gluttony be wanting in you, O king, for a king's worthiness ought to enjoy the honor of complete purity. Indeed, that vice damned our primeval parent with disgrace, so that the weak man fell guilty. [5] The Adversary tempted Christ with this vice, yet He Who is the true King scorned such an action. [6] Behold, when Saul wanted to fight, he imposed fasting upon all his men until he might subdue the enemy weapons [840]. [7] O king, banish your indolence, withstand your carnal passions, and stoutly take the path to righteousness. In order for your royal rank to rise above all your people, it should be so much the more noble in its deportment. O you of tender years and frank nobility, you in whom no deceitfulness is harbored, beware the weapons of treachery. [8] For your age does not allow of your being capable of deceitfulness, and your noble birth is opposed to your debasing yourself. Comeliness, breeding, honor, rank, grace, and power are yours. Your birth has conferred these generous gifts [850]. So let glory, virtue, and the blessing of good morals attend upon you, good king, and live with God like a mature man.

Chapter 12[1]

Here he speaks of how a king ought especially to abstain from the enticing voluptuousness of the flesh, because of divine displeasure. He ought to enjoy the lawful companionship of his wife, according to the stipulation of sacred law.

Above all, O king, avoid letting blind lust of the flesh arouse you toward its allurements. Instead, you as a husband should enjoy your own wife according to law, and not deprive your holy marriage of honorable praise. [2] No ancient writings about kings show that an appeased Venus and a kingdom stand together for long. The feat of a man directing his thoughts toward Venus and reason at the same time has never been believed possible [860]. Because of the many warning examples, you ought to avoid lust. Look at the doings of King David which the Bible has shown: as time passed, sin enveloped him until love of woman ravaged his heart. [3] What misery there was from that, and what punishment followed, to the point that it terrifies the mind of the man who reads of them. Let David's sin be a mirror for you: look into it, so that the fall of another may lift you up high. Fortunate is the man whom the trials of others make cautious, [4] so that he is wary beforehand of the paths which he sees [870].

Notice that while no treachery could defeat the Hebrew people, woman's guile conquered it through lust. You should be instructed by the example of Balaam as to how this was, by the way in which he instructed King Balak. [5]He gave Balak advice--by what cunning he might rout the Hebrews, by what tricks he might subdue the enemy onslaughts. "Hear what plan you can use, O king," he said. "These people do not conquer by their strength. Instead, they must always conquer by these two things: by worshipping God and by keeping their bodies chaste [880]. Choose out young girls whom charming speech and garments distinguish, so that you may defeat them not by Mars but by art. Let them clap with their hands, sport wantonly on foot, breathe the fire of passion at night, carry lutes, and surpass the stars with their beauty. Let the dalliance of love do the fighting, not the force of arms; let feminine bargaining do the fighting, not the iron spear. [6] In this way let beauty conquer the battle lines, let the fairness of the girls crush the men's defeated arms under foot. The wrath of the God of Heaven will accordingly rise up against them; thus you as victor will bear the people's joyful trophies [890]. "

The trusting king ordered this to be the plan. He prepared his outstanding young girls with their starry eyes. He made ready for the strange combat. He withstood the Hebrews, but not by means of the

240

long bow. He did not strike them with the sword or put them to flight
with blows. He did not fight with the corselets of his knights or the
reins of his horse, but with the lyres and choruses of women. One
woman sang, another dallied, and another furthered her charms with
art, in order that the two-faced beauty in her countenace might deceive.
She cast destruction through her face, showered sparks through her
eyes, and offered honey from her lips [900]. These beauties preyed
upon the feelings of the Hebrew people. They sinned, and the wrath of
God overwhelmed the sinners.

Take note how experience teaches you, [7] O king, and let this ancient example furnish you the way to be wise. See also, in the example
of King Saul, what surprising things a woman can do when she has power, O king. With the cunning of a demon the enchantress raised up the
prophet[8] and forced him to stand at the king's beck and call. She who
could subject the bodies of the dead to herself would have subjected
living men even more easily with her craft [910]. [9] But one who is forewarned is not deceived, [10] O king. Therefore you must take care that
you keep your body untainted. You are a king; one queen is sufficient
for you. [11] Join her to yourself, just as your cherished faith bids you.
If you shun the influence of vice in this way, O king, and keep your
good morals, you can accomplish anything you wish.

Chapter 13

Here he speaks of and points out to our present great, young king
the example of that most illustrious prince, his father. [1] He says
that when and where the virtue of necessity demands it, a king
ought boldly to exercise brave deeds of arms against his enemies.
And he says that in no adversity should he lose his steadiness of
bearing with others looking on.

It is also your concern, O king, to be your people's defender in
arms. And in order to defend justice with valor, remember your
father's deeds as a model for this. His undying fame is celebrated
everywhere even to this day [920]. His name shall never be effaced
from the earth. His feats of arms excelled Hector's. I direct my writings toward his praise and toward yours in order that you may be worth-
ily mindful of your father's honor. He was just, so he gathered just
men to himself; he was honorable, so he chose honorable men, and he
did not allow nettles to defile the rose. [2] He did not shower his gifts
sparingly upon one who was deserving of gifts. His hand was made
generous by a generous heart. He plundered foreign lands but he

protected his own, and he guided the good fortunes of the people entrusted to him [930]. Even if we all sing his praises, all our words are less than his deserts. No popular renown could express his worthiness; every voice is weaker than the praise it should utter. To speak briefly, he was as great a prince as could be celebrated by the words of his acclaimers.

France felt the effects of him; and Spain, in contemplating the powers with which he stoutly subjected her, was fearful of him. [3] Throwing his foes into disorder, he hurled his troops into the midst of his enemies and broke up their course of march like a lion [940]. [4] He pursued and destroyed them, he cut them down and killed them just as a wolf driven by hunger scatters a sheepfold. He was always sober in his actions but his sword was often drunk with the blood of the enemy. [5] Harshly assaulting his foes, he fought and overcame them. His sword point refused to go back into the sheath dry. [6] His hostile blade was sated with enemy gore; a torrent of blood slaked the thirst of his weapons. His broadsword was unwilling to drowse within the scabbard, it disgorged itself out of its mouth [950]. [7] Just as the wild boar tears the swift hounds to pieces with its deadly jaws when it is driven from the woods by their clamorous barking, so did he crush the bolder enemies near him, whom he struck with the murderous jaw of his sword. He won all his fierce battles like a lion. He attacked strongholds, annihilating the people. In order to seize booty, he boldly penetrated deep among his antagonists, and the enemies' necks were subjugated by his hand. Throughout the world his right hand bore down upon the necks of the haughty. So for that reason the leopard was said to be a lion [960]. [8]

The land was quiet under that great prince; no sword terrorized those whom his hand protected. Every man under his vine and under his fig tree, under its leaf and under its shadow, dwelt safely because of the sword of that noble leader. [9] The more his robust strength surged up, the more he thrived on his enemy, and the more prowess he had. [10] O king, remember your father's deeds, so that the praise which he earned may be bestowed upon you. Fortune favors the brave[11] and brings to fulfillment what courage wishes, and furnishes it strength [970]. [12]Peace excels over every good, but when our tried and tested rights call for war, it should be waged. There is a time for war and there are likewise times for peace, [13] but keep your self-control in all your actions. While Hector and Alexander were very noble, they could not stand firm upon uneven wheels. [14] Surpass your father's deeds and you will be called greater than he, and every voice will shout in honor of your glory. Do not slacken the reins in adverse times because of fear. If there is grief in your thoughts, grieve privately [980]. If grief assails your spirits, let a feigned appearance cheer your aspect, and let your face hide the fear in it. A happy countenance is a terror to

242

your enemies and a joy to your friends, for the face is the harbinger of the mind. [15]

Chapter 14

Here he says that a king should not make war without a demonstrably just cause. He says moreover that it is in keeping with royal authority and, for that matter, with wise, prudent rule, to treat its subjects more with love than with rigorous austerity.

Striving for the heights, the eagle flies higher than every winged creature; and it symbolizes the king pure in heart. Such men have fixed their heart upon heaven, just as the sacred writings of the harp-playing prophet attest. [1] The griffin, a winged animal, seizes men against their will with its four feet and terrifies horses [990]. [2] By this is designated the cruel villainy of potentates who ferociously waste men's lives. [3] Therefore, O king, in order to rule your realm peacefully with gracious love, it is better for you to adopt the nature of the eagle than to terrify the people dreadfully like the griffin. For love always transcends deeds of terror.

Not everyone who is afraid loves, but everyone who loves is afraid. [4] People in love suffer both love and fear at the same time. Love conquers all things; [5] love is a king's defense; his love for the people is an honor and glory to God on earth [1000]. The people are a king's soil; the king is a tiller who tills the soil. If he tills it badly, it brings forth thistles. If he tills it well, it bears grain. He who wields a king's command well is king, but he who rules unjustly amidst corruption is a tyrant. If a king lives off plunder, the people mutter curses and God's wrath is aroused. A just king wins both God and the people, and by this means the crown of his realm stands secure. Beat your breast, good king, in order that you can acquire the better things which prepare yourself for a king's rule [1010]. If nobility and noble names impress you, carry your own example of even greater nobility down to posterity. Even though you may be noble because of the illustrious name of your forefathers, you should match your ancestral deeds through your own good behavior. With one voice we pray in God's name for this, namely, that you unite your high birth with nobility of spirit.

Let the man whom God has made equal to you in character, worth, and rank be equal in your sight. And learn that there is a common origin for all men, and that there is one birth, one death, and one flesh [1020]. [6] Anyone who is illustrious because of goodness of spirit is noble, and anyone who likes an evil life is base. Indeed, the court of

243

heaven reveres good conduct, and the upright man, not the nobly born, reaches heaven. [7] Remember that brotherly love alone confers everything upon you. Brotherly love transcends the things of this earth, and with renewed strength ascends to things celestial and reaches the firmament and the stars. As long as it seeks for knowledge of God it is not afraid to soar to the stars, so that it may see Who is the God of Sion [1030], Who the Almighty King, what the vision of peace, what the region of heaven, or how great the glory of God. Such things are fitting for a king to meditate, in that he may be the better versed in them so as to render God His just due. You should strive to know yourself and to love God, for these are the two things, O king, which He decrees indispensable for you to know. This is the condition under which your Maker has conferred existence and your way of life upon you.

Chapter 15

Here he says that according to Solomon's experience, wisdom is superior to other virtues in the guidance of a kingdom, and it renders a king more acceptable to God and men.

O good young king, note what happened to the young Solomon, and then be mindful of yourself [1040]. As a boy of twice six years he was worthy of seeing God one night, since he had rendered holy offerings to Him. God addressed him: "Ask what gift thou wilt." And he said, "I seek wisdom, by which I may rule my kingdom." The kingly words pleased the Divine fancy, and God made this reply to him: "Thou hast not asked for long life nor riches nor triumph over thine enemies; therefore, what thou seekest shall be given unto thee. Thou shalt be not only wise but richer than all whom the earth has contained or can contain [1050]."[1]

O king, if you were to look at yourself well in this mirror, you could learn how very helpful it is to you. It is clear by this example that a king's wisdom must first be employed toward the governing of the people. Year upon year passes away but wisdom will always endure. No house standing upon this rock will fall.[2] It is a pleasing thing for an old man to be cheerful like a youth; it is even more pleasing for a youth to be an old man in his ways. God leads the man who with moral course follows where He wishes, and He safeguards his paths everywhere [1060]. Pray to God early in the morning that a happy day may cheer you. Pray in the evening that you may safely pass the time of night. For the king who is willing to submit himself to the highest King will obtain everything asked for during his rule.

Royal sceptres are held in the hands of kings in order to banish all evils, as if by a magic wand. Therefore, O king, perform your duties to your law. Do what is honorable for body and soul. Choose good men, banish the bad, be a lover of justice. Be dutiful and govern your people according to law [1070]. But in order that the law do good, let your approval lend assent to the law through Christ, without Whom no good law is bestowed. May you possess the honor of justice, a horror of destruction, propitious modesty, simplicity of spirit, and liking for familiarity. Thus, O king, if you as a wise man, wisely show wisdom toward all men, then you will savor the kingdoms in Christ with good relish. 3

Chapter 16

Here he tells how the kings of this earth must worship the God of heaven, who is King of Kings and Lord of Lords, with an especially pure spirit. And they must fear Him above all things.

O king, God has bestowed whatever you possess, and nothing that you have as your own or can have is from yourself. Know that you are a creature of God, and do not withdraw from His powers, if you wish to stand secure [1080]. You have a noble body and comely limbs, 1 so let the virtue of your spirit be all the greater. Just as your outer beauty is brilliant, let your spirit within be bright, so that your comeliness may be two-fold, O king. Good looks are a fleeting gift; handsomeness which is harmful to modesty often impedes the proper path of virtue. 2 Although beauty is a gift of God, the majority grow proud because of their beauty. Yet it is not tainted in holy men: not your beauty but a pure spirit is worthy of God. A blessed life is granted to righteousness alone [1090]. It is not fitting that the spirit within a king belie his handsomeness; rather, you should govern outward things from within.

O king, render your devotions to God, in honor of the God Who conferred your realms upon you, for which others revere you. No enemy assails the king who is dutiful to Christ; instead, destiny, which is subject to Fortune, favors him. 3 If you wish your enemies to fear your sceptre, you should fear the sceptre of God on high, and you will be feared. You should dread Him Who is enthroned on high in the vault of the heavens and at Whose command every knee is bent [1100]. He hurls down and raises up the world. He strengthens and enfeebles it, and He sustains every king's heart by His hand. He is the King in Whom kings reign forever; He is the King without Whom kingdoms fall enslaved; He is the King through Whom death finally seizes all kings, and

245

He rewards them according to their deeds.

Caesar was mighty, and more powerful than all the earth; an urn now contains the man whom the world did not contain. And likewise is the brave Alexander of Macedon now bones and dust, confined in a narrow plot [1110]. He was greater than the great world, yet paltry sands now cover the noble body of that vanquished exile. [4] Behold, nothing endures long for mortals. Behold, no honor, no glory staves off death: empty praises are of no use to the interred. Hell puts the guilty to frequent torture, even though they are famous. [5] O good king, be mindful of the future in the light of things past, and ponder the fact that nothing on earth is enduring. And since only the short span of this life is granted you, always live ready for every good work [1120]. Be subject to God, if you wish to conquer the world. He who serves Christ rules the choicest realms.

Chapter 17

Here he tells how a king, living in the affection of God and his neighbor, ought to make provision for himself with all diligence against that approaching death which spares no king.

Nature, under whose law the entire human race comes to an end, has decreed that all men be afraid of death. The learned man and the unlearned die, the poor man and the powerful. [1] Death makes all men alike through a like end. Here anointment and the royal badges of office can do nothing; they do not bring back health nor have they any healing power. No fame in worldly concerns can be retained, nor does the world then possess the wherewithal to defend itself [1130]. Learn that every honor is closely yoked to a burden, yet in the end the burden is greater than the honor. The more eminent you are, the more you should increase your anxiety, for exalted fame marches a precipitous path. [2] The life of man is reckoned as a battle, for on earth it is always waging three wars. [3] The king who would surpass the weak by means of war often recklessly comes to a foolish end. Therefore, O king, look well to yourself, for you are about to set out, seeking for the heights above or the depths below, but you do not know where [1140].

Remember that all the joyful things which people will say to you are a farewell, and that the leave-taking of pauper and king shall be one and the same. For no man can abide through his own efforts, no one can ward off his last day from certain death. Christ's sacred writings warn you that you are to withdraw yourself from the world, that you should begin to be a worthy traveler. In order to avoid a winter of vices deck yourself with the flowers of good behavior, go resplendent with the light of virtues. Pitch your tents as if you had been driven out of Egypt, and were eager to hasten toward your homeland [1150]. [4] Remember that you are made in the image of your Maker. Why? That you may follow Him, conforming to His law. Therefore, it is to your advantage that you love with all your might Him Who fashioned and redeemed you. O king, pray for the bounty of so great a King, that He may fulfill your life and protect your death. Do what you will, either good or bad, and such will you have for yourself, but I pray that God may direct you toward the better.

Chapter 18[1]

Here he briefly brings the king's letter to an end. He says that just as a king shall strive to elevate himself through the prerogative of his privileged status, and hence rule magnificently in the eyes of the people, so shall he present himself as humble and just in the eyes of God, in order to sustain the burden of his governing with full justice. Otherwise, the kingdom will not stand firm, because the king will be unstable.

His royal majesty is to be revered above all others, so long as he as king governs the affairs in his kingdom honorably [1160]. First he pleases God, and second he wins the hearts of his people; in this

---

Chapter 18*[1]

Here he speaks in conclusion of this letter, where he prays devoutly in behalf of the king's position that God may preserve his bloom of youth in all abundance, and that he may happily prolong his service toward the glory of God and of the people entrusted to him forever.

God, Who alone established the ages and Who alone rules all things established, is the King and Lord of heaven [1160*]. He produced the causes of things out of Himself, and decreed that within Himself there was to be a single beginning for things. He decreed that

247

way he enjoys a world that is good. He seeks for peace on earth and finds it, whereby he possesses the kingdom of heaven in the sight of God. Hence he is a great man while alive on earth, but he is even greater when dead and in heaven. He reigns in Christ in both places. These goods accrue to a good king through the goodness of the Celestial One; otherwise, his course will not stand thus.

If a king is vain, greedy, and haughty, so that he torments his kingdom, the land subject to him suffers [1170]. Everything that is pleasing to a king is not beneficial to him, [but] the things which justice grants him it allows without undue severity. The power of a king can accomplish wonders for a time, but in the end there is nevertheless sufficient proof of his idle deeds. [2] If a king's responsibility is weighed in the balance with his honor, his honor is not as great as his responsibility is considered to be. A king ought to weigh carefully the kingdom's laws, which are entrusted to him, and he ought to withhold justice from no man. Nevertheless, there is a cry nowadays among the people that because the law is failing, wrongdoing claims to be its own justification [1180]. In such a way does dishonesty, all decked out, enter by stealth into the good affairs of justice, and hence the law of today violates its secret trust. Where the law has withdrawn, sinfulness constrains kingdoms to its own purposes. For this reason, the king should by rights employ the treasures of justice.

---

through His own motion the world should forever remain fixed in a stable motion. With a mighty word He brought forth created things into existence, and He bound them by the law of His purpose. I pray that He keep my young king, and may his prosperous realms see him a healthy old man. May God Himself guide his youthfulness and prolong it forever, and always direct his actions for the better [1170*]. May no evil counsel have the power to influence you, O king, and may no betrayer of yours have the power to exist in this land. May every evil vanish lest it have the power to do harm, and may God grant that every good which is on earth be yours.

May it be granted to you, O king, always to hold the honored sceptre firmly in your hand during our lifetime. And may the day be near on which you, most handsome of kings, will go forth in aureate splendor behind four snow-white horses. [3] And may the shoutings of praise such as Augustus once had at Rome be yours anew [1180*]. Let the empire of our leader increase, let him increase his years, and let him protect our doors with his mighty crown. [4] O good king, may you stand sublime in a vanquished world, and may no lesser things be on your shoulders. [5] May the Supreme One from on high give to your right hand shining sceptres of gold which are of eternal glory. May He Who gave you your first realms give you assurance of your future realms, in order that you as a great man can enjoy great honor. So may your

Therefore, O king, you should wipe out crime in the kingdom and wisely govern what necessity urges upon you. Restore our common justice, now lost; bring law back to the realm, and banish all crime. If you wish to convert the kingdom subject to you, first make yourself return to God through Christ [1190]. And afterwards pacify your people toward yourself, not by means of terror but rather through love. As long as you hold the hearts of your people patiently in this way, you will stand out as noble everywhere in your kingdom. And as long as you administer laws tempered with righteousness, your every action will redound to your praise. On the other hand, however, if you turn yourself strictly to your own affairs, then the people which should be yours will turn itself away. O king, I now write these things to you both for the present and the future. Fate is ever changing on this fickle earth [1200].

Chapter 19

Since conditions everywhere through the whole world are changing because of the sins of today's people, just as you have heard from the common voice, let us as a result now look at the difference, pictured in examples, in the qualities of those who came before us —especially of those in the Church, which is divided at present.

---

fortune make constant progress, [6] in order that all the ages may call your praises to mind [1190]. I, a servant of the realm and eager for your honor, have written these verses to you for the glory of your rule, O king. Receive these writings, which I have composed with humble heart for you, good king, as gifts of God for your praise. For this instruction is not so much mine but His. He alone teaches and makes men well taught by His words. O youthful glory, royal honor, flower of youths, since there is goodness within you, I bid you goodbye. [7]

Chapter 19*

Here he recapitulates by means of symbols and examples from the Old Testament as well as the New. Through these he alleges that those who originally cherished the Church in all holiness, and spread the law of God and the faith of Christ, have long been dead. Others are now springing up in their place, especially from the clergy, who degrade the Church, strangling it with a whole multitude of vices.

The apples are falling from the branches, the acorns are shaken from the oak tree, [1] the flowers are withering away, the risen corn crop is drooping. The grain-bearing stock has stopped yielding grain, the temples now offer worthless frankincense to God. The hue which was once white is now the very opposite of white, [2] and the gem which used to sparkle now grows dim. Now it is that Babylon is venerated above all cities, and faith has no power to withstand this. The virtue of the modern Church lies buried in sleep, and the Synagogue becomes the bride of God, as it were [1210]. It is now evident that the righteous men of old have no followers; rather, all good men have passed away through death. Whereas those of that former time who were wicked — behold, they now live again, until now the way of the world is like them in all respects.

Noah the just has fallen in death, and Nimrod[3] arises in the Tower of Babel and scorns God. Japhet, who concealed the sins of his father, is dead, but the scoffing Ham now exposes them. [4] Abraham, who sought the wellsprings of faith, is dead, but Bel[5] is at hand and fabricates new gods [1220]. Isaac is dead, from whom the chosen race sprang, but the degenerate Cain[6] now stands in its way. Joseph, who was chaste, is dead, but Uzzah now pursues his carnal desires with love of lust. [7] Moses is dead, who was glorious according to the Old Law, but the trespassing Abiram still lives on earth. Death has laid Aaron low, whom God had chosen, yet the flame of envy offers incense to Korah. [9] Elijah is dead, who ascended to heaven in a chariot; [8] but Dathan, who deserves hell, lives on [1230]. [9] Micaiah is dead, and no second truth teller who dares oppose evils now lives in the world. For Zedekiah now claims to be above all the prophets, and everyone serves him at present. [10] Elisha is no more, nor is Naaman made well now, but Gehazi still wishes to acquire gifts for himself. [11] The dove flies forth from the ark and does not return. Indeed, the raven is now taking over its functions. Thus no one follows the examples of the Old Testament, so that the New Testament is becoming lost [1240].

Tell me where they are[12] who in Christ's ranks formerly made known their holy teachings through deeds and examples. Peter is dead, and the Liberius who now lives watches over his gates like Simon the Sorcerer. [13] I understand that Paul was once changed from Saul, and I now perceive that Saul has come back again from Paul. [14] We declare by our words that Gregory's writings must be obeyed, but by our deeds we cause them to be rejected. [15] We read of Martin's[16] gift, but we have a rich man's deaf ears, so that we give none of our goods [1250]. Tell where on earth there is another Tobit for the dead, [17] or tell where piety moves the hearts of today. [18] Job was patient in adversity and mild in time of change, and he remained so because of his steadfast spirit. But now, on the other hand, everyone is proud of his prosperity and grumbles in time of adversity.

250

Benedict, the founder of his order, is dead, [19] but Julian still lives and obstructs him. [20] If the salt of the earth is wanting, there is nothing with which it may be salted. [21] Because of this, the soul grows rank, reeking with the crime of fleshly lust [1260]. The corn does not die, but abides alone with itself; [22] and teasel covers the land and lays it waste. The vineyard does not remain alive, and thus it bears no fruit, but lies burning, parched, and barren. The light from Phoebus vanishes, with the gleaming of the stars destroyed, and the vanquished moon suffers eclipse. Now there is a new Arius, now there is a new Jovinian, so to speak; since they both sow heresy, they cause faith to doubt. [23] Behold, they say day is night, darkness is light, and injustice is right. Thus everything good perishes [1270].

Chapter 20

Here he treats of the fact that just as the wicked have succeeded the pious in the Church, so others have succeeded the leaders of all the world's knighthood, once renowned for their prowess. And these men have not become worthy of either divine or human praise.

If those who cherished divine law have passed away, so likewise have the world's valiant leaders. Trajan[1] the just is dead, yet behold, the tyrant Nero suppresses his just decrees. Justinian, the founder of the laws, has now passed away, but Dionysius condemns the keeping of those laws. [2] The chaste and upright Valentinian is dead; Tarquin rules the affairs of his domain. [3] The generous Alexander, once the best king, has died, and the greedy Croesus has succeeded him [1280]. The pious Constantine is dead and behold, Antonius now sits in his seat. [4] Theodosius, the fosterer of the Church, has gone, and Leo has succeeded him and wishes to destroy it. [5] The scoffer Constantius now profanes acts of faith, and Tiberius' gentle faith has perished. [6] Julius [Caesar] is dead, who conquered kingdoms in arms and made Rome the head over all. Hannibal is dead, because of whom Carthage once flourished, but now neither Carthage nor Rome flourishes [1290]. Hector, who once was to be feared because of his sword, now fears war more than the anxious Helen. Achilles has fallen and his sword is powerless; the weak Thersites has arisen in his place. [7]

Solomon the wise is dead and Rehoboam lives again, whereby young men are above the prudent counseling of their elders. [8] The love of Jonathan and David now stands sundered and the envious Saul burns with hatred. He also counsels the woman possessed by a demon now, [9]

251

for the grace of God has abandoned him as worthless [1300]. The obdurate heart of Pharaoh lives on; it feels the bitter wrath of God yet
does not fear Him. Thus the scar returns to the wound because there
is no cure, [10] and a worse fate grasps things which only a bad one held
before. Ahitophel's base advice is now heeded; Hushai counsels and no
one believes him. [11] Joab's envy kills the innocent Abner, and he allows
no one to be his equal with the king. [12] Cato, who was a just judge, has
retired from the city, and Pilate judges in his place [1310]. The honest
Abel now perishes, struck down by his brother's sword, yet the law approves this measure as permissible. Now I see Mordecai hung, but
Haman is snatched from the gallows; [13] the law allows such things at
present. The guiltless Christ is now crucified again, and, moreover,
Barabbas the thief goes free. Thus justice falls prostrate and is unable
to recognize a just man, and spiritual virtue does not govern man's acts
now.

Chapter 21

Here he speaks still further about the same thing, namely, how
others have arisen in place of those who in days gone by were
chaste and steadfast. Coveting the vanities of this age, they have
wholly lost a strong sense of shame.

Socrates, who curbed vices with virtue, is dead; Epicurus is now
at hand to tend to them [1320]. Diogenes, who forsook vanities, is now
dead, and the vain Aristippus possesses this world. [1] The pure Phirinus, [2] who castigated his body, is dead, and the adulterer Agladius[3]
lives anew in the city. Troilus, steadfastly faithful in love, is dead,
and now Jason's kind of love does not know how to keep faith. The faith
ful Medea is now dead and laid out in the earth, and the false Cressida
takes pleasure in loving two men. [4] The lewd Semiramis burns with desire in her loins, and even Cassandra can scarcely remain chaste now
[1330]. Penelope is dead, as is Lucretia of Rome, and Circe and Ca-
lypso rule their counterparts. Justine, who scorned wicked lusts, has
now passed away, and Thais is lying flat on her back. [5]
Now Paris' kind of love is commonly allowed in the world, so that
anyone may enjoy it at present without a war. Hymen does not preserv
people's troths, but Venus manages what is to be done in their bed-
chambers. Gold is engaged to be married, and the woman beautiful of
face prepares herself for Venus' bedchamber, ready for many men
[1340]. Formerly, mutual concern and companionable love used to hol
two people together, but now one woman allures five men to herself.

252

The law formerly held that two should be of one flesh together, [6] and now the new fashion holds for at least three. Now Venus gives the orders and Cupid has his armed camp, [7] and chaste love has disappeared at the present time. The bird cherishes what it should love; in the middle of the water the female fish finds the one with whom she may share her joys. The hind follows its mate; the serpent is embraced by a serpent; [8] even more are man and woman one flesh by marriage [1350].

Alas, where is plighted faith? Where is marital virtue? I have no answers, let another man supply them. An unfeeling expression which knows no sign of shame is a mark of esteem, and shame for a vice has ceased to be a shame. A blush used to deck a woman's cheeks; shamelessly, she now is more mad with passion than a sinful man. She is silent as a jackdaw, acts as chaste as a pigeon, and is as gentle toward you as a rose-bearing thorn. As I put up liquid in a sieve, so do I put up counsel in a woman[9]--but from this you can understand that I am in love [1360]. As long as the unctuous Jezebel reigns with her blandishing words, he who was once Joshua is turned into Ahab. [10] As long as the head inclines to vices, the members subject to it succumb to the same evils, whether by force or inclination. Thus lust stands decked in flowers and ornamented with vices, and the flower of virtue is trod under foot by men.

BOOK VII

Chapter 1

Inasmuch as there has hitherto been a discussion of all the classe
of society, throughout which sin has spread everywhere, in spiri
tual matters as well as temporal, he now intends to discuss, according to the opinion of certain others, the feet of the statue
which Nebuchadnezzar saw in a dream. Part of the feet was plair
ly of iron, and part of clay, in representation of this world's de-
teriorated state. We have quite clearly arrived at this state at
the present time, which in a way is the end of an era. And he wi
first explain the significance of the iron.

We can establish from our own evils what is wont to lie concealed
in ancient symbols. The ever-active misfortune of modern times reveals what the ancients were fearful of under the dark shadow of sleep.
The golden head of Nebuchadnezzar's statue has now been cut off, yet
the two feet of iron and clay still stand.[1] The noble, golden race of
men has departed from the world and a poor one of iron has sprung for
from it. No glorious fame of a magnanimous man, a man whose renown is acceptable to both God and man [10], now wings its way throug}
out the world. No generous man now scatters his gifts among the need
and the rich man scarcely feeds them at his table now. He scarcely
clothes the naked poor with piety, or receives the wanderers who he
knows lack shelter. No one remains who wants to take pity on those
thrust into prison, and no healthy hand aids the sick. Amidst the dis-
cords at present there is no ancient bond of love which comes to restor
us.

I think, indeed, that there are two causes in particular for which

254

this world has now ceased to be good [20]. Lust is found on the part of women of the very first rank; from it, laziness and dull repose take their origin. Accordingly, the knight whom a woman caresses in her bedroom with love is made sluggish in arms by her. And the cleric's lips are usually sealed by her, so that he cannot chant his prayers to God. Balaam's counsel[2] has conquered us through our women, with the result that God's people perish, struck down because He has been angered.

And the second cause is the avarice of the age, which is continually fostering fresh envy in the world [30]. It plunders, brawls, murders, and swears false oaths, so that peace cannot return because of its warring. Outwardly, greedy lords deal in the blessings of peace, but inwardly, wars still stand first with them. As long as it can store up more loot through war than through peace, avarice does not know how to love the good things of peace. And envy on your part does not permit you to conduct yourself peaceably toward me, for my tears are laughter in your ear. It is nothing to you if the downtrodden people bewail their sufferings, provided that the general misfortune brings in money to you [40].

And thus does avarice claim to subjugate the nobles' hearts; and they say that they wish to subjugate justice. Thus has noble honor given way, conquered by gold, and it is not eager to return to the seats of justice. The miser's taste for pieces of money is plainly hydropical: even as he drinks, his thirst yearns for more. Thus the rich man does not own property, but is owned by it, and thus the master himself serves his own servant. [3] Thus the rich man prospers outwardly, but inwardly he is destitute. Thus he has nothing so long as he thinks everything he has is nothing [50]. His stony hardness of spirit cannot melt, and he is not rescued from his cold aloofness by the treasure of piety. He scorns the poor man's tears, and wants to gain leisure and repose for himself through the oppressed poor man's toil. Thus his soul is indeed buried with coins of gold; he possesses them as gods, but does not know how to possess God.

Chapter 2

Here he speaks out in particular against those misers of the present time who are harder than any iron. Their riches can be of no value, as he points out, unless they are shared.

Alas! Why does one who seeks possessions pile up riches upon riches, when no one can make himself his own? He has no possessions, since whoever is possessed can possess nothing. He does not possess himself; therefore, he possesses nothing [60]. The owner serves what he owns; he does not possess but is possessed. Riches own the greedy man; wealth is master of the master. When you cannot be your own, nothing is yours. And no one can be his own; therefore, that which you own is as nothing. Indeed, if any [servant] subjects a master of property to himself, then the master's property is said to be his servant's. If the servant is duly acquired, [1] his possessions follow with him, and both the servant and his riches fall to the master. The servant [then] amasses wealth for his master, but amasses nothing for himself, it being plain that the master owns whatever the servant does [70]. The servant of avarice is not master of himself; when he misuses his proper authority, he deprives himself of his property. When you realize that nothing is your own, ample wealth is given you; and whatever things you keep are harmful to you, whatever things you share are helpful.

[2]For no one can be truly blessed who cannot share what is his with his fellow man. It is clear that one who can give nothing is quite destitute himself. When he fails to give to whom he should, the rich man is going to be poor. He is rich in what he possesses, but is poor in the fact that there is no one with whom he may share his wealth [80]. If your possessions are large, yet there is none to whom you give what is yours, then there is no abundance for you. If you have beauty, if you have fame, if you have a fine figure, if you have a cultivated mind, you are still poor, if another is untouched by all this. Dispense what you have for use, as utility advises; do not spend your wealth for the nourishment of avarice. Give to the needy, give to the poor, so that they may make use of your abundance. Love of liberality is an ornament to friendship. When you have every good thing at your command, it is either for consumption or for use; use things according to the inclination you have [90]. But there is so much avarice now that my writings mean nothing to a rich man's ears.

It is not much evident now that great and important men are miserly, but we do know that they are commonly guilty. Just as a hen fills her ample liver with kernels of grain and garners considerable food from the smallest things, the miser multiplies his monies and pockets them securely. To him there is nothing so scanty but that it enables him to get money. Such a man inflicts hunger on his own belly so that his coffer[3] may acquire more provisions [100]. Stingy and hard as iron, he protects his property with a niggardly heart in order that none will share it. And lest God might enter his heart, he loses the key to it, with which he wishes to lock out all pious action. Thus he does not know how to enjoy his acquisitions, and while he seizes everything, he does not have anything for himself. Thus almost all men have hearts of iron, since the head has fallen from the statue. [4] The times which once were golden are now plainly iron; thus does an ironlike nature dwell within

mankind [110]. The golden mean of worthiness which our forefathers
cherished is dead; behold, greed has destroyed it.

     The greedy man is the more wretched, not the one who possesses
less. [5] On the contrary, the man who is contented with what is his has
enough. [6] I do not condemn a rich man's riches [in themselves], however, but I approve of them, if they are given away when need requires.
The rich man is not to be blamed because he has money, but because he
does not help his brothers with it. [7] If his hand were generous, so that
he would provide a share for one in need, then his riches would be deserving of praise [120]. But scarcely a rich man lives in the world today who lays up wealth with which he may help either others or himself. [8]
The expression, "That which ye have hold fast, " which is written in the
Apocalypse, [9] now has the full force of a duty. The modern heart is girt
round with a vein of flint, and the unyielding breast contains seeds of
iron. [10] The rich man does not perceive the sounds of the poor man's
lament, but when within hearing he pretends to be a stone. There will
be a time when you who now shut out the needy will go to your last dwelling place as a pauper in need [130]. O you ages, you have now come
from gold to iron, [11] and whatever used to be noble is very base. The
greed of latter days is vanquishing our former good qualities, and Honor
does not know the land which should be hers. [12]

Chapter 3

     Here he speaks of the second portion of the statue's feet and of the
significance of this portion, which is of frail clay.

     The last age, that of clay, is at hand throughout the world. The
feet of the statue furnish me signs of it. [1] When a stone strikes it, the
potter's frail pot of clay is not broken into fragments more quickly than
man's frail nature lies broken, by the weight of its sin [140]. The layman is made of clay, but even more so is the cleric who causes evil
deeds to be done in imitation of himself. The world everywhere in-
scribes carnal lust as holy writ, so that not a letter of Christ's is to be
seen here. We can perceive that the one who commands us to subdue
the flesh is himself subdued, and that the learned man rejects his own
teachings. According to what he says, the cleric has a spiritual title,
yet his spirit is turned into carnal lust. Indeed, the sins of the flesh are
so commonly committed that continual practice of them is scarcely a
matter for shame [150]. It is as if the female has now become the lord
and master of the male, and the gentle, submissive, and compliant
handmaiden has become the man. Weak folly assails and conquers the

man of strength, and the man who should be wise falls, being made of clay. Because the cleric marches under the guiding banners of Venus, she now exacts tribute from all his people.

[2]The French sins now clamor to take possession of our households, which have recently fallen prey to them. Now it is permissible for every man to dance attendance upon another's wife, and this is called the noble rank's "love [160]."[3] This is not a vice for laymen, but a great mark of esteem; for a man becomes distinguished through adultery, while his adulterous wife courts dishonor for the sake of gifts. The husband who plays the same game is thereby absolved. Thus men and women now sell themselves as if they were whores, while Venus' generous hand is propitious. Thus do they puff themselves up under a false kind of love, and go in quest of shameful gains[4] through such wickedness. But the man who takes a bride because urged on by a cleric will contribute heavily to Venus, since the cleric may be adulterous in the matter [170]. For the poor friar takes back what he gives, and so, whether he gives or takes, he profits more. Thus does this age of clay complain in its feeble condition; [5] for every man is now easily broken to pieces.

But feigning hypocrisy commits its many base acts in secret, and tries to hide its lurking offenses. In outward appearance it thrives with the beauty of false pallor, so that its lean countenance may conceal its sordid deeds. But righteousness does not beautify the cheeks of its inner spirit; instead, that spirit offers curses to God while favoring the world [180]. The nettle steals the beauty of the rose, and lead hides its trickery under the guise of gold. Thus injustice hides within the just man, cursedness within the saint, and wickedness within one cherishing faith. Outwardly, [hypocrisy] wears the mantle of virtues, so that it may cover its inner guilt, lest someone shrink from it. Thus it outwardly appears as gleaming whiteness, but inwardly lurks the hidden blackness of utter pollution. Thus hatred flatters our ears like the voice of peace; its lips deal in amity and its fearful thoughts in threats [190]. [6] The raven is clothed with pigeon feathers, and the falcon[7] pretends to possess the mildness of the turtledove. Thus Satan's spirit wears the look of Gabriel; he has the head of a maiden[8] but the tail of a serpent. Thus in outward appearance [hypocrisy] displays honied goodness, but if you taste it, it is more like myrrh. Learn that hypocrisy is the devil's strongbox, in which every sinful wickedness lies shut up. A needle cannot be hidden in a sack without acting so that it outwardly feels hot, because of its point [200]; nor will hypocrisy lie hidden in such a fashion that it does not reveal itself, and that its virtue does not appear exposed or vitiated. Even while this vice wishes and burns impatiently to expound the gloss of its own viciousness, its wrath reveals it. It hides itself for a long time under the shadow of false piety, as soon as you wish to charge it seriously with anything. Thus does the wolf clad in sheep's clothing bare its teeth and openly show its tainted evil. Thus virtue toils on, overwhelmed by the fault of vice, and the freeman gets no justice from the serf [210]. The reins of a sense of shame are slackened for the gratification of vices, so that they may do away with the path which is pleasant for the virtues to travel. In short, I thus conclude that virtue everywhere lies prostrate, and vice occupies the better seats. And every precept is false, having been turned into its opposite, and everything in the modern world is filled with deceit.

Chapter 4

Here he speaks still further of the calamities happening in most recent times, which are represented in the variegation of the statue's feet. Indeed, he says that the virtuous aspects of human nature which formerly existed are all now changed into their opposites.

The bitter thing is now becoming sweet, the sweet is now becoming bitter, and the foul is becoming fair, since the fixed order of things is no more. Learning now becomes heresy, and sins become morals; craftiness becomes intelligence and plundered booty becomes lawful gain [220]. Holy orders become vagrant, the feigning hypocrite a saint, and the eloquent wise man a mute fool. The gentle confessor becomes an inveterate sinner: his words are saintly enough, but his actions themselves are evil. The fox now protects the chickens, and the wolf the sheep; the hawk protects the partridges, and the hearthfire the dry wood. Lying voices are teachers and prophets; trumped-up stories are in favor, and holy writ not at all. Useful doctrine is unwelcome, but the delight of Venus' prattlings is quite a joy to the ear [230]. Now love is lust and adultery is married, and incest prescribes my chaste duties to me. The clergy is turned into rabble, and now the rabble preaches God's works like the clergy. [1]

Servants are now masters and masters are servants, and one who has learned nothing thinks he knows everything. The peasant pretends to imitate the ways of the freeman, and gives the appearance of him in his clothes. And the gentleman changes himself into this base fellow and wants to enjoy his churlish vice [240]. Similarly, moderation is ostentation, modesty is boastfulness, laughter is buffoonery, and re-creation is vain and godless. The promoter of another's wickedness is now considered his special friend, and one standing in the way of his vices is his enemy. Now the flatterer blandishing in one's ear is held dear, and the ear considers the double tongue an orator. In the eyes of the king an immature boy is now wiser than Cicero and more welcome than Cato; [2] and his tongue's blandishments, which you observe extolling the world's princes, now have their reward [250].

All men now lack any distinction except that of the tongue, which sounds its harmonious words in the king's ears just like Echo. It blames what you blame, it praises what you praise, it says what you say, it honors what you honor. If you laugh, it laughs with you; if you weep, it weeps. And it will always equate your expressions with the force of laws. [3] Philemon's judgment is worth no reward, even when what he utters by word of mouth is the truth. [4] Fawning words now quickly clothe with linen the infant whom a shepherd's cloak once covered [260]. [5] No court preserves its ancient honor, no city preserves justice, and no land its faith. Arms are more of a business now than a mark of nobility; as a result, the tailor's boy now goes about in a helmet. The gilded spur[6] is all too common now, and for this reason there is not the honor in feats of arms that there used to be. And indeed, since the poor but proud man does not have the wherewithal to conduct himself with pride, he lives everywhere by plundering.

The weakness of the kingdom is growing, while its powers subside; thus you behold much chaff but little wheat [270]. The hearts of hares lie hidden [within men], yet their lion's jaws are open, now that leaden deeds have golden words. Now men are wont to spend long hours in talking until daylight is lacking for conversation; [7] and at discord in spirit, they postpone the more profitable matters which concern the realm. Today is converted into tomorrow by our actions; actions which are talked of remain to be carried out. Now pride, which scarcely stands half-safe on its own soil, wants foreign kingdoms subjugated to itself [280]. Boldness of tongue thunders strongly in its chambers about wars, but that ridiculous creature does not move a hand toward the battlefield. Taxes oppress us on all sides under the pretext of war, and I know that a thousand misfortunes are for the profit of one man. Our once customary liberty is now carried away with avarice, which burdens us in a highly unpleasant fashion. It readily promises every reward to the serfs, with the result that no one remembers when a man behaved well. The discipline of old does not serve as an example now; on the contrary, whim now governs our actions, instead of justice [290].

Gall is now honey, and malice is like love; [8] what lies exposed on the outside has nothing [to do with that which lies] within. Jacob's gentle voice and Esau's rough hand once acted falsely, but through this they furnished portents of the future: for no matter what good things that words now report to our ears, when action puts the deed to the test, it brings on wickedness. Justice is no more, and joint faith is no more; deceit and treachery have usurped their place. Now a friend's lamentations are as pleasing to his friend as organ music. [9] If one takes the lead, another will envy him [300]. A brother looks to his own advantage from a brother's misfortune, and a sister rarely expresses praise of a sister. A son feels that he now has a stepmother in his mother, and she feels that her sons are principally the results of her own wrongdoing. A daughter disparages her mother's actions, and the mother now spurns the daughter and hates her. A son now waits for his father's years [to be up] before their day, and [the father, because of] blind cupidity, does not see this with his own eyes. Even though he is the parent, he is no less undutiful than his sons, and he does not fill the depths of his heart with them [310]. No love spares anyone whom it can injure; any third person refuses to be what any two [others] have wished. The people remain lawless; there is no one who preserves justice, there is no one who says, "It is right to uphold justice." Men live by plunder. A guest is hardly safe from his host, and a father-in-law from his son-in-law, when the latter is without money. [10]

In these times many pay their respects with enduring hatred, and wrath speculates nauseously on its opportunity. [11] Actions cause hatred, the face implores love; [12] the mouth offers kisses, the hand strikes a blow [320]. There are as many caprices in men's hearts as there are notions in the world, and they do not possess any stable goodness for long. Just as Proteus resolved himself into gentle waves, and was now a lion, now a tree; now a goat, now a boar, [13] so is men's way of life inconstant at present, and I do not know whither I can safely go a step. When the fore part is visible and the hind part is hidden, it is not easy to know a cow from a bull. [14] Similarly, upon first consideration, [a man's] word is not fully understood; in the end, [however,] one who hides nothing will carry weight [330]. As long as you are fortunate, many are numbered as your friends; but if times should be hard, you will be alone. [15] Just as a hare protects itself by fleeing through different fields, love wanders and stays in no fixed abode. [16] In times of old, love flourished, but now that it is unbridled, it has scarcely any place where it may progress. The once venerable name of friendship is no more, and it loiters in search for a harlot. The ways of an earlier and honorable world are perishing, and now there is nothing that one ought not to believe [340]. [17]

Now love is forsaken, and it feels that it enjoys no favor. Abiding in hatred, it prefers your possessions to yourself. It is not a fact that a hare and a greyhound are one and the same. [18] I do not know what I see, yet I am not blind. Hatred is common now, but love hides alone throughout the world in desert places, like the phoenix. Now iron is hurtful and gold is more hurtful than iron; [19] every man is destroyed by the struggle for it. What now shall I say, when the right hand tells lies to the left? Will man ever believe this of himself [350]? On every occasion where there is profit or pleasure, the fashion is now that trust have no trust. And thus does the double and varied image of the statue's feet[20] signify how various are the deceits of men in the world. Misfortunes overflow everywhere, so that I, a freeman, cannot enjoy my peaceful ways in these times. Poverty alone remains free from envy; [21] no one on earth is eager to take its place. O fortunate and suffering poor man, you who remain free everywhere, without anxiety and with peace of mind [360]!

"O world, world, " people say. "O woe unto you, world, you who spawn baser and baser things!" I therefore wish to know everything-- what the world is in itself, or what its essential nature is, or what its condition. [22]

Chapter 5

Since everyone is complaining at present about the deceits of the world, he consequently intends to treat here of the state and condition of the world and also of the wretchedness of man's lot.

The world, to be sure, has given itself the name of being pure, but it rightly cannot be considered as free of impurities. [1] It is filled with uncleanness, filled with the seed of vices, filled with sins, filled everywhere with deceits. Times change, conditions change, and states change; no order of things endures for long [370]. [2] Learn how close and near destruction is, [3] such destruction, indeed, as has no remedy. Learn that whatever a fleeting pleasure embraces and falsely claims to be its own, it is as nothing. [4]

What is life at present? Temptation, a dangerous struggle. The line of battle is always here and the enemy is always at hand. [5] A thief envies our wealth, war envies peace, and disease health, and the flesh oppresses our old age. And so the beauty of a pleasing form perishes little by little, and none of the many things which have pleased us endure [380]. For things tasted are less relishing; one scarcely senses fragrances; one hardly perceives even clamorous noises by the ear. The eyes grow dim; of the whole [body], hardly the skin and bones alone remain, [6] bound together with their sinews. An aged man detests summers and finds faults with winters and chills, [7] and nothing can please the querulous oldster. He is troubled now with too much cold, now with too much heat, [8] and he never remains in a sound condition. His tooth aches, or his neck, or perhaps his tongue is tied, his spleen is swollen, his lungs grow weak, his liver suffers [390], his heart is faint, his kidneys are in pain, his bowels are loose, his arms have scarcely any strength, his feeble legs ache. [9] Faintness does not suffer his body, wasted by bitter cares, to sustain its powers for very long. Its every part is subject to not a few illnesses, and the wretched man lies utterly exposed to misfortunes. Yet the disagreeable fellow, consumed by his illnesses and his years, complains of the long span of his life.

For every power in which the worthless body takes pleasure has ceased to be, and it perishes, weighed down by sundry afflictions [400]. Are you wise? Wisdom withers away at death. Do you abound in riches? They flow away in a quick rush. Are you brave? Bravery dies. Are you honored? Honor slips away. Are you strong? Strength lies low at death. And when you perceive yourself succumbing, overwhelmed by your vices, I marvel that you say and think that you are strong. Lust wages its wars and you yield to its first blows; you must needs lower your neck to its base yoke. And you are likewise a slave to avarice and the impulses of wrath, and in the same way you carry out the shameful dictates of your ravenous gluttony [410].[10] So, everywhere you turn your face and your thoughts, you will realize that all things pertaining to the world and the body are vanities. If you should consider the body, in every respect you will see its frail nature, which cannot endure. If you should consider the world, in every respect you will see it wrongfully whirling about in its dubious affairs. One man complains of his vines having been shaken down by a hailstorm; another complains that his ships have sunk because of the high sea. Extravagance ruins one, pride another, and a raging tempest of grief agitates still another [420].[11] And thus the world changes in various ways, and whom it formerly raised up it casts down the more forcibly. This place is certainly transitory, and in its way is like a river, ebbing and flowing. If it entices one, it deceives him and is not to be trusted by him. Its delights always contain something for which you must suffer.

Something is always lacking in human affairs, and hence this life contains nothing wholly fruitful. No life can enjoy its sure reward before it has reached its worldly end [430]. If the blood of noble ancestors has exalted you, you should therefore lament the fact that you can degenerate. If fate has given you prosperity, prosperity yet vanishes because of fate. If misfortunes come upon you, fear even worse things. If fame persuades you that your wife is chaste, you should also lament accordingly that every woman is accustomed to deceive. One man bemoans the incestuousness of his debased wife, another is afraid of having been deluded by a false suspicion.[12] You should be afraid of losing the woman to whom many men sigh their devotions, or of not possessing her for yourself alone [440]. You should likewise be afraid lest some adulterer seduce her and she bring forth children of whom you will not be the father.[13] If, on the other hand, a host of worthy children grows up, you should accordingly grieve in turn that death will take them from you. If riches serve you for a brief hour, one day will snatch them away in order that you may grieve the more. If a robust youth promises long life, it deceives you, and Atropos cuts it short in order that you may grieve. If you possess the forceful wisdom of a keen mind, look upon Solomon so that you may grieve for your worth [450]. If your complexion, tinged with a rosy hue, gleams white as snow, you should accordingly grieve that crooked old age is approaching. [14]

Your mind has no rest here, but both within and without you wage restless battles with many things. [15] Make good your lost time while you can, for alas! Christ condemns what is done too little and too late. Let the man who has spent the last part of his life worse than the former part beware; if he loses his life, he has been a bad bargainer. [16] A young man should learn that life slips by at a swift pace, and what follows is not as good as what was before [460]. [17] The wave which has passed will not be called back again, and the hour which has passed will not return. [18] You think that because it moves slowly, time stands still, and the year completes its course with lagging steps. [19] When in fear of the hawk, the weary bird dares to come on trembling wings even to man's protection. [20] O corrupt old man, whom Satan awaits in the pit of hell, why do you run away, and for what reason do you not come to God? See how the frightful winter of old age comes with trembling steps, [21] and the handsome bloom of youth departs [470]. Life slips away secretly on the wing and deceives us, [22] and the swift course of the years flies like a shadow.

Those things which we call the elements also do not endure; [23] rather, the different elements suffer various changes. Bodies change, and we shall not be tomorrow what we are or have been; no age keeps itself the same. [24] Observe, what was once the sea is now most solid ground, and the wave of the sea now covers what once was land [480]. [25] The spring now flows but sometimes it is dry, with its streams dammed up, and behold, it does not remain in the same state. Iron wears away and flinty rocks diminish through use; [26] is not frail mankind broken to pieces even more? The palaces [which] now are resplendent under Phoebus and our leaders were once pastures for oxen destined to plow. [27] Where there are now castles there were formerly fields. They now deck temples with gems which they used to deck with leaves, and the high official used to feed his own sheep [490]. [28] And if I were to speak of the kingdoms of men, we know that no prince's empire endures for long in this world.

Things which time past brought the future will bring again; no state of things in the world is new. Who could say, "I remain undisturbed in the world"? And who does not have a thousand reasons for sorrow? [29] Wherever a man turns, grief or fear strikes him; no rank on earth is exempt. O how many tumults do even the hearts of kings suffer, and how those hearts rage with stormy passions [500]! Amidst royal banquets and feasts those vexed hearts are consumed with manifold terror. Surrounded by a thousand attendants and their weapons, [a king] cannot banish the fears from his trembling heart. [30] Thus the world corrupts everything through its wrongdoings, and at no time makes everything pure. Through a contradiction it claims for itself the name [of being pure], in which it by no means can share. [31]

Chapter 6[1]

Here he speaks of the beginning of man's creation. He also explains how the world was created for man's use and man for the worship of God. Therefore, if man does not dutifully worship his God, the world ought not be obliged to bestow any further those favors which are due man.

O, if I were to speak the truth, whatever wickedness the world contains, man alone is guilty of it [510]. [2] The writings of Genesis teach that when the maker had first fashioned the world, He created Adam and spoke as follows: "Let us make man, who can be like us. And in order that he may serve and worship us, let us breathe into him the sense of reason, love, the power to distinguish what he is and whence he is come. Let us breathe into him the knowledge of his maker, whence he may come to know and love his creator, and may come to know Who his author is, Who gave him essence, or for what reason the world serves and waits upon him [520]. Man alone shall comprehend the mysteries of the heavenly mind, and he alone shall inquire into all things. But he should investigate all things thoroughly—what necessity demands of him, or what he should believe is practical, or what he should think needful."

O what a sublime glory, a rare honor, a high distinction that man, sheltered by the earth, should be the image of God! That he should be a piece of work made in the pattern of his maker, and a creation likened to his creator! God created everything by His word. He applied His hand and fashioned the work [530]. A bit of earth is caught up, an insignificant lump is formed, and what was once soil becomes a solid body. He joined marrow-filled bones together with sinews. He sustained man's paces and connected his steps. In addition to these things, He laid out veins filled with blood, He clothed flesh with skin and hair. He poured the breath of life into the many internal organs, through whose functions all the bodily members become free [to act]: the mouth speaks, the hand works, the foot runs, the ears listen, and the eye alone beholds the heavens [540]. Man is made alive, the two-legged creature arises, the flesh exists, its companion the spirit exists, and man is complete. The flesh perceives the things which are of the flesh, the spirit longs for the lofty heavens and seeks its duties. [3]

265

Man stands created and marvels at himself and his movements, and does not know what he is and for what purpose he exists. He marvels at the role of his body, that his limbs have motion, at the skills of his hand, and at the joints of his feet. He stretches his limbs, relaxes his arms, and touches every limb of his body with his hands [550]. He marvels at whatever he beholds in himself, yet he does not see that the likeness which he bears is his very own. He marvels at the face of the earth and at the various shapes, and does not recognize them, since he does not know their names. He lifts his face, he raises his voice to the heights, he transports himself to the heavenly hosts, whence his spirit came. He marvels at the beauty and rounded shape of the sky, at the sidereal movements and the starry mansions. His new friend stands astonished, and ponders with him what the many [heavenly] bodies he observes may intend for them [560]. Nature, however, serves notice to him that he is man, that these are created things which he sees, that this earth is established for human use, that the world belongs to him and to God. His feelings flame into love for the author of it, and he now has recognized what it is to love God.

Chapter 7

Here he says that God the creator of all things has furnished all the pleasures of this world for human enjoyment. Therefore, it is proper that just as man enjoys those pleasures in keeping with the flesh, so ought he to return that wholehearted obedience welcome to God his creator, through the giving of thanks in keeping with the spirit.

Tell me, Adam, tell me, Mother Eve, tell me, both one and the other, tell me if you lack God's abounding grace. He has laid all things at your feet—both sheep and oxen, both the fowls of the air and the fishes of the sea [570]. Lo, the elements are propitious to you—the sun, the air, the skies, the earth, the wave of the teeming sea, and every other thing. For the author of things has so decreed it that every creature of the world should wait upon [man]; [1] that the creation should serve him and that he in turn should therefore wait upon only his creator. Raise your noble head and look about the world. Gather together all things, everything which His hands bestow upon you. All things are subject to you, all things serve you, all things answer and render obedience to you [580]. He who conferred so much upon you; He who accomplished so much for you; He who led forth His world into existence for you; He who caused disordered chaos and the seeds of so many things to stand forth at His command out of nothing: [2] He calmed the fierce motions [of chaos] with His skill, distributing its portions into four equal parts. [3] Having painted the sky with stars and called forth the seven planets to their appointed places even though they resisted, with the coming of the sun the heavenly leader, through the agency of twelve signs, He made time to pass through a like number of successive stages [590]. [4]

After He had decreed it, He Who adorned all the world with various and multiple kinds of good decreed that wild beasts were to be in the forests, lions in the mountains, cattle in the plains, and goats among the rocks. He covered the birds with plumage and adorned the sheep with wool, yet what they have is for your use. Look upon the delights of the world, at the gifts which the streams bestow upon you, and the riches which the wave of the teeming sea bestows upon you. Look upon the gardens with the trees set out, [5] the grasses, the shoots, the flowers, the leaves, and the fruitful good things [600]. In the presence of all these things, your mind should meditate upon Him Who made you, too, and upon how He brought forth good into existence out of nothing. For your spirit is His and your intelligence is His, and your reason is from His reason.

The author of things caused you to exist, and once things were set in order, He caused you to summon up names for everything. He gave you hope of progeny through a woman's love, an equal mate, and the trust of marriage. He made you almost equal to Himself; if I may say so, He took it upon Himself for you to be almost a second God [610]. He conveyed Himself into heaven, committed the earth to you, and divided the riches of the world with you. The sky accommodates you with the sun, the sun with light, the air with breezes, the sea with food, and the earth with a thousand good things. But what are you, then, in yourself? Who provides what you have? Of His own free will, God's gentle and ample goodness made both [what you are and what you have]. In bestowing you upon yourself He put forth Himself, and God had nothing better which He might give than that.

It is not fitting, is it, for any man whatever to grow insolent toward the mandates which God Himself has given [620]? Heaven cast down the proud one and earth despises him; the region of hell alone is fit for him. The whole race of men which our first father brought forth was tainted and corrupted by this vice. All mankind was corrupted in its origin, so that the world could not keep anything pure. [6] There was no one in the world who might make the world pure, nor anything in it which could attain the state of grace. But He Who single-handed founded all things through His goodness restored and amended His work [630]. He took the form of a servant and redeemed His servants, and caused what had been the devil's to be God's. [7] It remains for you to follow Him with devout spirit and to acknowledge Him as your Lord. If you follow His gentle precept wholeheartedly and do not undertake forbidden wrongdoing, you shall be blessed.

Chapter 8

Here he treats of how man is said to be a microcosm. It follows that according to that which man does well or ill, the world is good or ill in consequence.

O the goodness of the Lord, O what power, what grace, which made man to be so great! [1]Together with the angelic hosts, man possesses the wisdom whereby he knows that God is the supreme creator in the world [640]. Man feels, hears, tastes, sees, and walks; hence man possesses a kind of animal nature. Man also grows in height together with the trees; and by virtue of his special quality he possesses existence in the manner of stones. Thus man, who alone does everything, is a microcosm; [2] and man alone pays sacred devotion to God alone. [3]The man who is pure in his own right subjects the world to himself, and accordingly guides its circumstances for the better. If he is impure, however, he is injurious to everything which pertains to the world, and redirects its whole fabric for the worse [650]. He rules his world by his own command as he wishes: If he is good, it is good; if he is evil, it is evil. One who is a microcosm brings the greatest misfortunes upon the world, if he falls because guilty of impurities. If one who is a microcosm does not check his impurities, he weighs heavily upon everything in the world, which is impaired by his wickedness. [But] if one who is a microcosm worships the Omnipotent, he is the source of everything pure in human affairs. If one who is a microcosm meditates upon the laws of God, he will possess the great kingdom of heaven for himself [660].

Therefore, it is most fitting that man born of the creator return Him worthy gifts with humble heart. It remains for him to seek the love of his maker; it remains for him to know what he is and whence he came; it remains for him to realize above all that he alone is said to be a microcosm, because of the high degree of his fame. If he is a microcosm, if he inquires as to what order of things the framework of the world corresponds, he is to remember himself. If he is a microcosm, if he reflects upon what the origins of the world are, he is concerned with what and whence a man is [670]. If he does not know himself, he does not come to know Him by Whom or through Whom he was made, nor love Him.

Then too, a dual essence was made for him, because of the fact that God fashioned him, both spirit and flesh, in order that the spirit might serve its maker, the world might serve the flesh, and the flesh the spirit. [4] The flesh is a frail handmaiden whose mistress on high is the soul of God's reason. Nowadays, however, the flesh, conquered by the world, denies reason and leaves off submitting to the authority of its soul [680]. Thus the mistress is servant, thus her rule fails; and the soul, which should be the inner man, deviates from God to without. O stupider than a fool! Exchanging the things of heaven for the world and putting gold aside, you seek to possess clay.

Why, O lord of things, for what reason do you yearn to be a miniature copy of the Deity? You as a great man should yearn for what is greatest. The circle of the earth, and whatever is contained in it, is yours; everything is subject to your authority. Indeed, the parent of things, sent down from heaven above and descending to your [realms], was made man for your benefit [690]. Do not subjugate yourself to the kingdom of sin, do not follow after the transitory things which pass away so quickly. Rather, you should be content to transcend in spirit the lowly things of earth. Stoutly seize upon the pathway to the heavens above. [5] Even if you seek after great things, God is great above all things; even if you seek after good things, no one can express how good He is. Neither birth nor sex nor vain family ties are of any use to you at the approach of death. What help was it for Plato to have penetrated mysteries through his studies, and to have compiled his books of natural philosophy [700]? He knew the path of the sun, the regions of the sky, the courses of the moon, the stars both moving and fixed in the firmament on high, and many profound things in addition. And now the philosopher is ashes and his empty fame has perished. While Hippocrates investigated things and their causes, while he protected bodies by his medicinal powers, no such wisdom could save him. On the contrary, even the physician must suffer the law of death. [6] Thus it is clear that man's essential nature is mightier than any art, and it plunges into death those whom its course attacks [710]. Therefore, there is nothing better for you than to provide for that death which will be your end. You are always about to set out; you reach the close of life, and you do not know by what end or when it will be. The way to heaven is long and but few days remain for you. The man who takes the burden of the world upon himself delays his course.

Chapter 9

Here he tells how man, who is called a microcosm, will pass
away in body from the world into death. And just as man causes
the outbreak of this world's corruption through the sins of his
body while he lives, so he will afterwards be forced to suffer the
corruption of rotting away in his dead body. And first he tells of
the dead body's corruption following upon pride. [1]

O what will you say for yourself when the breeze does not rustle
your hair, and your jaws are withered up, and there is no passageway
for your voice, and the color of your face is bloodless, and your eyes
are motionless in their gloomy sockets, and your mouth cannot grow
moist [720], and inside it your tongue is frozen to the hard palate, and
your heartbeat cannot quicken your veins, and your neck cannot bend,
and your arms cannot embrace anything, and your foot is unable to take
a step? [2]
What does the proud dead man reply now? Let him tell what vainglory will bring him now. Gone indeed is all the honor of that lifeless
body, which belonged to the man who formerly scorned other men. And
because the body bore itself loftily a short time ago, its flesh is now
laid low as food for worms [730]. The eyebrow is not raised now as if
in disdain, nor at long last does his hand smoothe down both his sides. [3]
The power of death has overcome what powers he had, and a fly's back-
bone is stronger than his. If comeliness or beauty once flourished in
him, his vileness now causes even all cattle to hasten away. If he was
wise, he is now far different from a wise man: he is confined where he
knows nothing. Death quickly and briefly destroys the subtleties which
he pursued in long study [740]. Granted that he was skilled in the various arts, the man versed in the arts has fallen in his own way. [4] His
intelligent reason now perishes without reason, and death hurls into the
void what used to be reasoning. The learning which he taught is more
unlearned than an ass, and not one jot or tittle remains in his understanding. His mind does not presume to pass judgment on any men, nor
does his lifeless state allow him to vaunt himself. He who used to bear
the honor of feigned virtue hypocritically now openly shows what he was
[750]. The fact that he formerly knew the various kinds of tongues is
of no advantage to the man who is silent, with his mouth mute in death.
When one's hearing is gone, no organ nor harp notes delight him and no
music is pleasing. The one who has dissipated all his natural beauty
cannot now adorn his body through ingenious means. Splendor of dress
or mounting on horses cannot glorify at all a body now stiff. A beautiful home or the lackeying of servants is nothing to him. Now no one

greets him among the people in the market place [760]. Now a crawling thing shall be dubbed his servant and the grave his castle, and now a loathsome hole shall be given him in place of a bedchamber. Thus, since vainglory duped him, nothing now remains for him of which he will be proud.

Chapter 10

Here he tells of the corruption of the dead body following upon envy.

Behold the man who used to gnaw away with a doglike mouth because of envy. Now a dog or a worm is to gnaw him. Having scorned another's fame, which once used to vex him, now his deceitful, rotten tongue is silent. He laughed at the calamities of another and wept at his good fortune; now he cannot laugh because his mouth has no lips [770]. Once full of grumbling, his heart is now rotted away, and a broken pathway now lies open to the bottom of his heart. The pompousness which lies unpraised cannot now set aside a comrade's praise or place its own ahead of his. The gall formerly hiding under honey is now hidden itself, [1] so that the flesh, lacking a mind, cannot dissimulate at all. A mind burning full of envy can no longer sting each and everybody with the poisonous goad of malice.

Chapter 11

Here he speaks of the corruption of the dead body following upon wrath.

The man whom fiery wrath formerly inflamed when he was alive no longer shakes his head impatiently [780]. The silenced man, who a short time ago disturbed his neighbors with quarreling, makes no sound at the grave. Once loose-tongued, he can no longer be a talebearer. Death calls, he is silent, and says nothing back to it. The one who used to frighten a poor man with terrible threats now has no power against the grubworm. Rage does not incite a man to war, a man who does not have a peace treaty with the worm. Indeed, one will not have to fear the sword of the man who suffers a worm to pierce his heart [790]. The one who now lacks the active power of reason will not debase this power

271

of reason through scorn of the body.

Chapter 12

Here he speaks of the corruption of the dead body following upon avarice.

O what good is the avarice of former times to the miser now? Only a narrow wooden box remains his. He sought land with too much effort; he now owns seven feet of it, and no more.[1] The man who a short time ago was a plunderer, preying upon what belonged to others— now death seizes him for its prey like a plunderer. The man who formerly stretched his nets for stupid profits is now caught by a net from which he cannot escape [800]. He amassed many riches and guarded them very closely, but now another squanders his wealth. His property, which was huge almost without limit, is gone, and suddenly none of it remains his. In fact, his wife is delighted with the novelty of a second husband, and she does not keep her heart mindful of the former one.[2] The son and heir rejoices, forgetful of his father, and not one friend is left to him who has died. Thus the man who joined property with property and fields with fields[3] now gets nothing from his pursuits [810]. One day has taken away what a year brought him, and the toil of long duration turns out to be fruitless. The man who shut his purse to the poor is destitute himself, and all the abundance of his money is worth nothing to him. Neither cunning nor theft, neither defrauding nor false, perjured greed is now any help to his body.

Chapter 13

Here he speaks of the corruption of the body following upon sloth.

The man who used to be slothful no longer denies that he pampered his body's limbs for his pleasure. The man once given over to sleep now has abundant slumber in a long sleep from which he cannot wake up [820]. The man who a short time before sought out soft straw for his bed now is under the cold ground infested with worms. The man who once pursued leisure by shunning work—now there is nothing he may do to gain any strength. Although he might have been able to learn what is good, now no school teaches him to know what may proceed from

harmful things. Now he can lament all too much his long lost stretches
of days. Formerly he rarely prayed in church, but now he cannot be
carried from it, yet he does not pray at all [830]. [1]The man who sows
sparsely will reap sparsely; now when he cannot, he wishes he could do
what he formerly might have done.

Chapter 14

Here he speaks of the corruption of the dead body following upon
gluttony.

Gluttony, which he practised[1] daily a short time ago, is no pleasure at all any more to his belly or his throat. The entrails, which once
were loaded with the weight of foods, are now emptied and can hold
nothing. He used to relish spices and tipple sweet wines; and excre-
ments mixed with clay are now in their place. In his middle, where his
fatness used to lie snug, a worm now lurks which devours his fat [840].
His potbelly, which was big with drunken indulgence, is burst, and a
toad possesses his cavernous throat. The man who a short time ago
was redolent with food now serves himself nothing, and foul putrefaction
attacks his nostrils. Drunkenness, which once did not even yield to
fast days, now tastes nothing in its mouth, because its stomach is burst
into pieces.

Chapter 15

Here he speaks of the corruption of the body following upon
lechery.

O for the one who used to think the vice of lechery so pleasant!
Now a worm shall nibble his private parts. He does not sinfully make
the rounds of the brothels any more, nor can his hand enjoy base things
with its touch [850]. He cannot simulate with a wanton look from his
eyes, in order that he may entice a foolish woman to indulge him. No
beguiling songs composed in the language of Venus now help him with
their promises. Singing or going about in leather shoes is nothing to
him, [1] for his throat is no more, and his foot does not sustain him. Now
that he is dead, he does not commit incest, nor can he violate the honor
of virginity in his lust. Whatever his lasciviousness was previously, it

273

is now rottenness, and his heated passion during copulation is now frozen with cold [860]. Thus, whatever his body was a short time ago, it is now a corpse, and what was ashes before returns to ashes.

Chapter 16

Now that he has discussed how the human body is consumed in this world by the putrefaction of death, because of its various sinful pleasures, he makes further inquiry about man the sinner. He inquires why he, to his own detriment, is so intent upon and yearns so ardently for such fallible worldly pleasures.

Answer me, O proud man, what does pride avail you when putrefaction consumes your limbs in the earth? Ask yourself, you who are clad in silk, gems, and gold, what will ostentation offer you when death comes? Over what do you rejoice like a victor? This victory will forsake you, unless it be that you can withstand the onslaughts of vice. What will envy, the child of burning Aetna, do for you, when death shall have destroyed your heart and lips [870]? What do you think fury or wrath are worth to you, when death itself rages toward you with evil fury? Or what good are your times of sloth for you, when death endures to hurt you unceasingly? What will gluttonous delights bring you, when you will be devoured everlastingly in death? Or what do you think Venus will grant you at the end of your labors, when there ceases to be any passionate warmth in your limbs? What use to you are riches, the golden splendor of money? The final end swallows both into the earth [880]. Everything which a long, anxious year brought you a brief hour shall snatch quickly away altogether. Why do you conquer kings, why overmaster kingdoms, O tyrant? God, Who is preparing war for you, remains unconquered. What is fleeting fame to you, or honor, or empty ties? For all the useless glory of the world passes away.

Grief replaces the excessive joys of fools, and tears filled with sorrow dampen their laughter. Why are you proud of your body's beauty or of your family stock, you who pass on as food for worms, as ashes to ashes [890]? What if you can conquer lions in your strength--cannot a flea bother you? [1] What does worldly wisdom bring you except stupidity? Therefore, what a wise man knows apart from God is nothing. You have a worthless body fashioned out of dust, and a nature prone to every evil of the flesh. It begins in sorrow and ends in grief; why then do you wish that such handiwork as this be glorified? Since nothing belonging to the world is glorified by the body, it is nothing for you to glorify your body [900]. Nothing more of either your body or your property remains

274

for you except your rewards alone, be they good or bad. When that day comes which brings nothing if not justice for this body, then man will come face to face with his deeds. No man can rightly keep a permanent place here, but instead he will pass on to the uncertain paths of death.

Chapter 17

Here he speaks of how all the things of this world wax old like a garment, [1] and how in the twinkling of an eye they are locked up in sleep, so to speak. He also speaks in particular concerning the thought of death and the significance of its name.

All things are locked up more quickly than in the twinkling of an eye, and every man passes away as if asleep. Worldly joys beget ever-lasting sorrows and this short life brings life eternal [910]. [2] Everything which can be lost seems as nothing, and I do not believe whatever ceases to exist to have existed for very long. Tell me what salvation for our body is honor, wealth, fame, youth, beauty, ancestry, strength, wife, clothes, land, jewels or money, sceptre, kingdoms or gold, high station, an expansive estate and commodious home, great power, much learning, idle pleasure, or life. [3]

Experience teaches us such things as the fact that mortal flesh waxes old like a garment[4] and crooked old age comes at a swift pace [920]; that the span of our life is always growing shorter, and that man's day flees like shadow and smoke; that life is short; that death is un-fathomable; that no matter what grievous, harsh condition oppresses us all the time, [5] men can warn one another by example. Every saintly man who governs his actions well is king over himself; [6] the man who governs his actions badly shall be a foolish slave. You may have been called king, but why do you rejoice in an empty title, you who lie ruined, overwhelmed by your vices like a slave [930]? Why does one who rules kingdoms serve vices, and why is he not ashamed to be a lowly slave of the body? [7] As long as you wallow in vices, flashy clothes are of no use to you, and no purple will wash away your stains. Therefore, it is expedient that every wayfarer depart as lightly burdened as he can. The passing years rob us of everything, and approaching death seizes all our riches. Ashes return to ashes, the dissolution of the flesh shows the material clay of its origin [940]. God knows what will become of the soul in the future world, whether it will be unharmed or troubled, or how great or what sort of a thing it will be. Men know this, namely, that in this world the body can possess nothing permanently useful for the flesh. The living flesh is corrupted, and when dead it possesses

275

but a carcass, more vile than any living creature.

O the mirror of death! No matter how many look into it, if they see themselves clearly, no glory is visible. The course of hostile death is so backwards that it declares heads are equal to tails [950]. Death is named from a bite which was forbidden; in biting up everything it shows the meaning of its own name. [8] In our uncertain circumstances, nothing is more uncertain than the hour of death, [yet] nothing can be more certain than death. [9] As long as a man thinks it is insignificant, death deceives him, and even one who is quite healthy secretly conceals it [within himself]. [10] There is no astrologer nor physician who can prolong life through his healing power. Thus man and animal die in the same fashion, and both return to the earth in the same condition [960]. Nothing is excepted; it is evident that whatever has been created on earth has a death, just as it has a life.

Coming secretly to men's chambers, death flies on furtive wings, and unexpectedly overthrows what once existed in times past. It plunders riches, destroys men's strength, and separates friends. It cannot be bought off with gold in any way. It does away with men's actions, yet it surrenders those very men to their actions, so that a reckoning may be made at the feet of the judge—that same judge who judges all things justly, whom no worldly gifts can sway [970], and by whose judgment man shall receive fitting rewards for his labors, in keeping with his deserts, and without partiality.

Chapter 18

Here he says that although there is naturally only one burial for the just and the unjust, nevertheless, the death of the just man dispels all his sorrows and renders his spirit to eternal glory.

Both the just and the unjust pass away through death, and the earth devours both bodies in the same way. Nevertheless, their departure has different recompense, for death is joyful for good men and harsh for the bad. A man is therefore fortunate who has behaved well when alive, because when he is dying, he can receive God's blessings—the blessings, indeed, of heaven, where all joys are splendid and where life shall endure without sorrow forever [980]. Death, sickness, toil, enemies, crippled old age shall be no more; the happy mansion above does not contain them. The grace of the King shall be just to the souls on high, for whom He voluntarily suffered the bitterness of the Cross.

This is the place of peace and great honor, where there are no shadows, where there is day without night; where God washes away tears and lamentation, and where there shall be no more sorrow nor complaint. Neither death nor sickness, neither hunger, thirst, want, nor misfortune shall dwell in that place [990]. There light is continuous, peace everlasting, glory eternal, life blessed, salvation genuine, love unending. Hope, faith, goodness, renown, grace, virtue, feeling, love, piety, glory, beauty, and honor are there. Youthful flesh is without taint and age without senility, riches are without the disgrace of wrongdoing. Peace is without fear, all honor without pride, rest without toil, and salvation without grief. Joys remain consummate there; no suffering exists there, but every man has what he wishes [1000]. Life blooms perennial there, and the blessed vision of God, which is mighty above all things, stands forth in glory.

Do you wish that I describe to you in a few words what that place is? That is more than any man could express, more than could be explained by the mind's understanding, or more than the recesses of the heart could comprehend. How happy a place it is, how it should be cherished with fitting honor, the place in which all joys are met together! So, because glory is unending there, I cannot compose a suitable ending for my praise of it [1010]. There shall be full glory here for the angelic host in its entire number, glory which it once lost. Here shall be the highest honor of the human race, when the flesh is glorified at the resurrection of the body. Here shall be eternal rejoicing in the Lord by all men, when God shall have become all in all to everyone. And thus death takes away all harm from the just man's body, and destines the kingdom of heaven for his soul. When the just man dies, then he begins to live. This death, which benefits the dying man, is life-giving [1020]. This death leads not to an onus but rather to honor, for which reason the dead man possesses God in peace.

Chapter 19

Here he speaks of the sinner's two-fold death. Through one of them the body is destroyed here; through the other, the soul is tortured by everlasting torments, by God's fitting judgment.

Alas! How extremely unfortunate the man who conducted himself badly when alive! Because of this, a grave[1] punishment shall devour him in death. For a two-fold death is allotted to the wicked man; the first death is grave, [1] the second even more horrible. Killing the body, the first death removes it from the world, and it can do no further harm to itself. But the second and graver death fetches away the soul to the pit of hell, and renders to Satan what should be God's [1030]. [2] It places

277

in doubt what worldly pleasure is, and makes certain that every torture is in readiness—the torture of hell, where every suffering thrives, where one is always dying yet cannot die.

No voice can make known the wretched punishments, whose slow tortures are without end. Hence fear and trembling shall follow from them, and grief and distress. A death of unceasing pain rages without dying. You might say that to live or to die--to live in eternal death or to die in eternal death—makes no difference [1040]. Alas! I repeat so often about death, since that place inflicts nothing upon the wretched except the semblance of death—that place which dire hunger, cold, heat, darkness, gloom, and the shadow of night veil. Worms eat away the souls there, and fire consumes the bodies with its heat; the pain [is] too frightful. The tormentor there, who must always torture and will never cease, shall afflict the one tortured with burning pain.

Everything that once was pleasing to the flesh is overthrown, and bitter calamity perverts what used to be sweet [1050]. A base form disfigures what once was beautiful; pain destroys the creature that once was healthy; what once was strong is robbed of its powers; there the wise man is a fool and the rich man a pauper. What once was lust is worms and fire there, and what was gluttony becomes insatiable hunger. Vision is darkness and touch is a stinging scorpion, and one's steps hold the pathway into the fetters of death. The ears are tormented with noise and the nostrils with stench, and the taste gets a savor of what bitter things pains are [1060]. The eye weeps, the teeth gnash, and every limb is torn off in distress, so that it suffers endlessly. What was life is death, and what was the body burns forever in fire like a flaming torch. Alas, but the suffering soul, once created so pure as the image of God, is like the devil. Thetis[3] does not extinguish the bolts of lightning there nor does the physician's welcome remedy help against the viper stings. The continual grief there is like that of a woman in labor, yet the region does not expect to gain a period of grace [1070]. No one grasps in his mind the perpetual torment of the pain of hell, but the suffering there stands without equal. My heart trembles for my spirit, and my flesh for my heart, so that my feeble hand can write no more of this matter.

With what look or face, or in what company will the crown of the judge appear? His look is terrifying, his face like that of a madman, his horrible aspect threatens utter despair. The fury of the judge is brief, but his wrath[4] is without any remission of pain, and possesses no forgiveness or kindness [1080]. Our mother and the angelic host, indeed, the twelve-fold order [of angels] will attend him, carrying out his judgment. Here angel and man alike shall undergo torments; both shall pay the penalty according to their deserts. Like penalties shall affect those whom a wicked love of sinning formerly affected alike. There the good and the evil shall be separated, the one keeping to the right hand and the other to the left, [5] and they shall suffer judgment.

O how stern is the sentence which must be meted out to the unfortunate, to die in the perdition of everlasting death [1090]. This shall be
the day of the Lord, in the light of which the secrets which now lie hidden shall be clearly revealed. [6] This shall be the day of wrath, a fearful light in which not even an angel shall stand firm without fear. Since
the righteous man is to be saved only with difficulty at that juncture,
where will you flee, O sinner? What escape is there? Indeed, there
is none. It is therefore for the prudent spirit, the upright spirit, the
judicious spirit, to fear such an evil. O most fortunate the man who
can escape such a calamity, and live because of his worth's esteem
[1100]! O most fortunate, eternally fortunate, O safe and blessed the
man who can escape the heavy punishments of death, and experience the
joys of heaven with his God! Therefore, one should live wisely and reflect upon his deeds now, before that day of judgment comes.

Chapter 20

Now that he has discussed the joys which are destined for good
men and the punishments for the wicked, he further advises that
each and every man direct himself toward good morals. And he
further advises that the contrite man pray confidently and without
despair for indulgence concerning the good morals which he has
heedlessly neglected.

Since one brief hour threatens sudden disaster, and since a light
puff of air kindles the delicate breath of life, take thought of yourself,
dear one, as to who you are, and why, whence, for what, and of Whose
making you were created [1110]. Because the flesh is frail, untrustworthy, and easily swayed, it inclines to the worse, and is prompt to
pursue the worst. The spirit should shun this world and hope for future
things, always steadfast in love for its maker. In order that the flesh
may be subject to the spirit and obey it, the spirit itself should serve its
maker. In order that the impulse of the flesh may be kept within bounds,
death must be remembered, and the punishment of death must be kept
for the wicked. Man's living flesh cannot better be subdued than [by]
the fact that he bear in mind what it will be when dead [1120]. It is helpful and quite beneficial to have repented with continual weeping, as long
as opportunity for weeping is granted. God on high does not punish any
man for those crimes which he does not repeat, once he has confessed
them penitently.

Therefore, the man who is guilty must bear the pain of this life
until he has washed away all his sin. Having been thus purged, he may

escape that pain which endures without end, when the judge shall have come. [1] For one who does not serve God's commandments and meditate upon the end of life is forcibly dragged off to hell [1130]. Either the Scriptures deceive us or else you certainly ought to realize that only with difficulty does the human animal return to a state of grace. [2] For once overcome with vice, he becomes the slave of vice, and does not have the power to remove the yoke he has put on. Accordingly, never-ending punishment is necessarily due the one who expresses a lasting desire for sinning.

To be sure, it behooves God to forbear punishing and to be merciful; so strive to redeem yourself, even though it is late. God knows our deceitfulness, yet He considers a man contrite who seeks His help even at the very last [1140]. Do not despair; God is merciful, and he who denies that God is merciful denies that God exists. [3] He is accessible to all, just like a running wellspring; and just as there can be no wellspring without waters, so He cannot be without mercy. But since presumption often spoils too high a hope, assume a hope for yourself in a way that is fitting for you to do. In order that you may hope prudently, you must moderate your hope. Its reins have to be guided by pious fear. Your fear should not be excessive, because despair ruins the spirit; rather, fear God with a loving spirit [1150]. And your hope should not be presumptuous, but it should love in conjunction with fear. In this way, fear is a virtue, hope is a virtue, and both together are salvation. But to be sure, your spirit, remorseful in contemplating its end, should always fear adversities and hope to attain better things. In order that you may live more purely, always keep in mind the extreme penalty, for blows seen in advance are less hurtful. Have a care today, for the time of death is hastening near, and it will destroy all your riches at once.

Chapter 21

Here he says that there are few nowadays who, either through love of heaven or fear of hell, renounce the pleasures of this life. Instead, casting aside all reason, they ardently try to carry out whatever things the flesh yearns for.

The man who weighs everything justly when reflecting upon himself will, I think, perceive that, in the end, pleasures are vain [1160]. Nevertheless, nowadays everyone is infatuated with vices, because scarcely a man is heedful of his end. Every man adorns his body and delights in lust of the flesh, and his soul's cause is forsaken. Neither

the glory of heaven nor the pain of hell now has the power to recall
men's spirits from worldly ruin. Thus the world, the flesh, and the
devil everywhere lead men astray, so that scarcely a one knows the
path of Christ. In these times the flesh which is weak, the devil who
is clever, and the world which is wicked devote themselves to the kingdoms of men [1170]. And so the power of human reason perishes as if
it were that of a beast, so long as vice governs the actions of the body.

Now, I should say that man is an animal, but not a rational animal, as long as he lives in a condition like a brute beast's. A nature
ignorant of learning governs a beast, and it has no power of judgment
or reason. Man is therefore worse than a beast when his will alone
governs him contrary to nature. Alas! The body's strength in all its
limbs turns against nature and serves vices in its outward acts [1180].
And the soul's power of reason, corrupted by the vitality of the flesh,
knows nothing of inner virtue.

People of good character are now rapidly becoming the scorn of
the rabble, and learning vindicates the work of sin. A new wilfulness
now bridles the virtue which in its fashion of old used to make men
blessed. "I want this, I command this" are just like laws now among
those in the world to whom power has been bestowed. Righteous men
succumb, crying, "Alas! For a wicked band of men is ruining all the
kingdoms on earth [1190]." Force is obviating the laws, crimes are
upsetting good morals, and virtue is dying, battered in a whirlwind of
sin. The world is thrown into confusion, the order of things is confounded, and a great chaos is overwhelming everything at once.

Thus both parent and offspring in the land are base, because human nature scarcely remains in its rightful condition in the world.
Malice, ambition, gluttony, deceit, fearful passion, wrath, pompous
spirit, schism, love of praise, boastful honor, wicked love of gain,
evil indulgence in pleasure [1200], theft, rapine, wrongdoing, fear and
perjury are witnesses that the world now has no faith.

Chapter 22

Here he speaks of the various punishments now taking place almost daily in this age because of sin. These cannot in any way
be checked without the good works and prayers of righteous men.

Behold, the days which Christ foretold are come, and the fearful
words of God have long since become clear. Famine, pestilence, earth-
quakes, and signs from heaven have led the way, and now there is also
war. Nation struggles to rise against nation and people against people,

281

as every evil is manifest.[1] Thus the blood of man is now shed like that of cattle, piety lies low in defeat, and God allows these things [1210]. The avenger is here, his outstretched hand bringing deadly plagues uninterruptedly, yet no one fears them.

The judgment of the Lord often bides its time patiently; the good man shall be exempt from it, but no evil one shall. The man whom the Lord strikes can nowhere be safe, if his guilt does not leave him contrite. God does not wish death for sinners; rather, He wishes that the man upon whom He has shown compassion may be changed, so that his life may be spared him.[2] God is merciful. As we have it from the Scriptures, He said to the pious Abraham concerning Sodom [1220], "Find ten righteous men among so many thousands of wicked people and I will show them mercy. For it is fitting for me alone to show mercy upon the wretched; it is my concern to spare freely the many for the few."[3] O God, what then shall I say to Thee, why are our continual lamentations merely a trifle to Thee?

Are there even ten righteous men now, so that for the sake of their worth, the starry one may have a care about the evil days on earth? Unmindful of our suffering, God has either forgotten, or sleeps, or pretends [to sleep], or else His workings are obscure [1230]. To tell the truth, God is incensed. The fire is kindled against Jacob and the hidden anger is burning.[4] Thus does the creator terrify His creation and torment it because of the evil deeds which He sees.

O, one who with his mind's eye sees our wickedness prolonging its days in all ranks of society can then say that no man, from the beginning of time, has seen such crimes go so long unpunished. I do not know of any estate or rank but that it transgresses; I fail to know whom I should call righteous [1240]. Unless it freely atones for this, I fear that the general collapse of our well-being is near at hand. But since evils proceed from the highest stations in life, it is God on high Who should correct them.

Chapter 23

Here he speaks finally by way of recapitulating his treatise on all the worldly estates. One by one they are deviating from their rightful course. They are destroying their virtues by decreasing them, and they are furthering the things which pertain to vices by increasing them manifoldly.[1]

In former times the prelate carried on only the work of divinity; now, he cannot possess God because of the world. In former times the curate was devoted to his cure, and now he wanders about outside it, making the rounds of the whole population. In former times priests were chaste, and now they are lecherous. The leisure which they seek fosters the greatest harm [1250]. In former times scholars zealously taught good morals, but now, on the other hand, learning is corrupt. Indivisible Love bound monks together like a passion; now Envy strives to rule their cloisters. In former times Austerity used to subdue the friars in the flesh, but now their easy rule spares them. And in former times knighthood was prompt in service, but now their service is slow in coming, since their life is evil. In former times the merchant asked a fair profit for himself, and now he tries to get his profits dishonestly [1260]. Guileless Simplicity of Mind used to be associated with the peasant; now his untamed heart makes him savage. The law, which the power of money has everywhere subjected to itself, used to be just and propitious, sparing no one. Equal rank is now attained through inequitable doings, and every traveler goes beyond the bounds of his path.

Thus humble Piety is crushed and Pride reigns. Malice is wide awake and all Love grows drowsy. Fierce Wrath stays on and on, and meek Patience takes its leave. Sloth lives and Duty perishes [1270]. Immoderation, not Moderation, holds sway over our tables now, and Drunkenness crammed with food is rampant in vices. In former times modest Chastity helped to gird up the genitals, and now Lust wants to free them. Formerly, a generous hand scattered its gifts among the poor; now the grasping, miserly hand is greedy and shuts its purse.

Now tell me in how many vicious ways Pride alone has plunged the world toward doing various evil. Tell me how many armies following its banners that consuming Envy has subjected to its command, by force and fear [1280]. Tell me how many people have exerted themselves with greedy hands or rapacious spirit, while denying the laws of God. Tell me from how many delicacies does Gluttony lie in Stupor, how many foolish people in its turn this Stupor corrupts with fleshly adultery. Indeed, the flesh engulfs everything belonging to the soul, so that on every side the world subjects the impure soul to wickedness. The world's false charm has conquered everything, but it cannot purify impure men.

Chapter 24

Now at the end of his book he speaks in greater particular about the country in which he was born. Almost beating his breast, he laments how the honors and virtues of old are at present being undermined in many ways, because of the various transgressions overwhelming it, so to speak.

I love all the kingdoms which the Lord has established for Himself throughout the world and which bear standards in Christ's name [1290]. But above all I love my own land, in which my family took its origin. [1] Whatever other lands may do, I am not shaken by it, as long as I stand apart at a distance from them. But if the native land which bore me as a young child, and within whose realms I always remain fixed--if she suffers anything, my innermost feelings suffer with her, and she shall not be able to suffer her misfortunes apart from me. I am almost overwhelmed by the weight of her adversities. If she stands firm, I stand firm; if she falls, I fall [1300]. [2] Therefore, I bewail the schisms which, at least so others say, are so oppressive at this present time.

In my opinion, there is now one very bad fact which can be called the source and wellspring of evil. Alas! Because Justice, a fugitive, has withdrawn to afar, her associate Peace has also departed elsewhere. Peace, which in times gone by used to bestow kisses upon Justice, now has fled from the land, because Righteousness has vanished. [3] Many pernicious masters are now taking over the realm for themselves; Power and Whim give the orders, and are unaware of goodness [1310]. Now wherever an important man turns, the laws wrongly follow along, but the people suffer the burden of this. I myself am tormented not so much in body, but rather because of the fact that I own possessions of which I may make very little use.

It is not least of all that adultery is grievous now, for the flesh insists upon everything that is possible. Even if Venus does hold sway in other countries, they make up for this by their good qualities in other respects. For law is well established there, and judges for all men in common and decides cases without trickery [1320]. Neither rank, sex, bribes, entreaties, fear, nor anything else can withhold rights from the least of men. And so to a certain extent, Justice redeems their sin of the flesh, which falls because of its frail nature. But in this country not only are we mastered by the goad of the flesh, with which man is spurred on; but indeed, the law, ignorant of what is right, oversteps its boundaries. And so our native land goes astray with crooked steps, to such an extent that men say there is no longer any law and order in our realm. For this reason God [1330] is punishing these regions with a vengeance such as has been seen at no time from the beginning of the world. To be sure, there is not a single country which is utterly delighted with everything, but in ours the scourge is now becoming especially harsh. See, there is shouting everywhere, I do not complain alone. It is wrong to keep silent about such open sinfulness. So I weep tearfully. The law is false and I am played false; for my native land is filled with heavy evils.

Fate, which never used to use us harshly, now overwhelms us guilty people, hard pressed on every side [1340]. The earth, which used to be rich with every kind of metal, now does not contain its own weight in lead. [4] Once more valuable than silver or yellow gold, she who produced the noble[5] is scarcely worth a farthing. Once, whoever used to come here said, "Let us come to your ports, O land of plenty." Now you are thought of as barren, and indeed you are barren, for now neither morals nor riches are ever yours. Whither shall I be borne to seek solace for this unhappy state of affairs? No anchor now secures our ship [1350]. Thus my native land, which once was steadfast, is weakened by unjust legal decisions and by denying rights of man. Thus the Mistress of the people renders tribute to sin, and she stands apart from God, almost like a widowed woman. Thus she who used to be moral is now sinful; formerly law-abiding, now she is lawlessly fierce.[6] Thus she who once was generous now suffers poverty; she who once was holy is becoming the goddess Venus herself. She who used to be abundant with fruits is now sown with salt; and she who used to be a rose is now like a thorn [1360]. She who used to be beautiful is now thought of as a monster. Her head has turned into a tail, so that everyone treads her under foot. She who used to be the mother and friend of all honor is of late a wicked stepmother, spawning base scandals. She who used to be an angel is now a dark ingle, [7] and she lies listlessly in the shadows, confined by great squalor. The native land, which they say used to have Fame for a sister, is more infamous than all other regions. She who rightly used to be higher than all on earth is herself almost enslaved, now that God is elsewhere [1370]. Whatever honor she once had is gone because of her backsliding course, and she lies prostrate and weak everywhere. Discordant heresy now removes what is firm, tears down what is lofty, overthrows what is strong, and scatters countless evils everywhere. The nobles grow indolent, the clergy are dissolute, [8] the cities are quarreling, and the laws are unjustly severe. The untamed rabble are grumbling, the customary sinful abuses are on the increase. Thus the whole country is suffering. It is for this reason I think that the earthen foot rages against the head of gold, [9] and that the wolf is afraid of the lamb's useless horns [1380]. God views the world only in the light of men's merits, and man is actually the cause of his plight.

O land barren of virtues, bereft of sane counsel, wounded but possessing no cure, tell where your good fortune now hides, a fortune in which you once thought you had no equal on earth. If Lachesis directed that fate be treacherous toward you, she has now come to fulfill her treacherous agreements for you. Now Aurora, whose light shone brightly for others in the world, grows pale because of your black mischiefs [1390]. [10] And now the flower of youth, which once bloomed profusely for you, is withered and you are dying, superannuated by your vices. And now the prophetic owl, the loathsome bird, the presager of affliction to come, sings of your fate. [11] God knows that the cause for this land now standing without honor must be especially worthy of notice. I know this, that the country proverbially flourished for all men, and now everyone stigmatizes it as only a reflection [of its former self].

[12]Such things are reputedly brought about throughout the land by the law of fate, but I do not think it stands thus [1400]. It is not Fortune nor fate which causes us to endure such things, but our just deserts for evil deeds. Nevertheless, let the man who now believes that Fortune stands firm, yet who wishes to revoke her, wash away his sin, and he will accordingly revoke her. The ready grace of God will come to those seeking it, for God is turned toward those who are turned to Him. So long as the onward course of the land has spoken out in favor of benevolent peace; and so long as justice has made its works secure, faith has stood firm, and love remained flawless; then fate has bestowed every good thing, because peace has flourished [1410]. Our life should therefore be restored to God, lest our fortuitous fate become even more evil. [13] The age-old devotions of prayer should return to the Lord of Lords, so that the Lord may return with compassion for His people. Through this compassion, peace and honor will return, as well as the wholesome times which are now fled away because of our sinfulness.

Let the man who wishes the prosperity of old restored give up his former ways and repair them by his new ones. [14] God is gentle toward the meek and severe toward the wicked; thus every man can reach God by his own merit [1420]. Therefore, O Lord, let Thy grace, which once used to bring punishment upon the guilty, now help me through Thy compassion. Let Thy mercy receive us, lest the guilty people should say, "Where is your Lord, who is supposed to be so gracious?" Lend acceptance to our tears, merciful one, I pray, for Thou knowest we can possess no strength without Thee. Let Thy grace now contend in behalf of our faulty ways, and do not be mindful of our former sin. Thy grace was never unfeeling toward our causes; now where is it, which used to be our salvation [1430]? We are sinners and Thou art one of great mercy. Thy benevolence knows that we are Thy work; if man should sin much, Thou canst forgive even more. Our lot has furnished

Thee occasion for pardon. If men should sin again and again, send forth Thy thunderbolts, and the present age will be purified in short time. So, our maker, when Thou lookest about upon the world dependent upon Thee, make Thy creation peaceful. We, Thy servants, dear God, even though we are dilatory at present, believe that Thou, not Fortune, art God [1440]. We know that Thou alone art to be cherished above all, so Thou alone take pity on us, O God!

Chapter 25

Here he tells how he conceived of the things which he wrote in the present book concerning the transgressions of the world. He conceived of them as if in dreaming--not so much through his own part but through the general voice of the people. Nevertheless, he himself advises finally that if anyone feels that he is guilty of these things, he should penitently atone for his guilt with humble heart, before worse times befall us.

[1]I have compiled these verses, which a spirit uttered within me during my sleep. That was a hard night. But I, as an author, have not set down these lines in a book; rather, I am passing on what things I heard for you to read. It is not that a swelled head made me write them, but that the voice of the people put them in my ear. Let the man whose spirit is mordant be remorseful because of this voice, so that he may the better cure the vexations which he has previously suffered [1450]. But let the man who feels himself free from these go quietly on his way. Thus, let each man stand on his own merits. My opinion does not accuse one who is not burdened with guilt. No one is to be hurt by this, unless by chance he is guilty. Therefore, this should not offend you, for the galled[2] horse, not the sound one, refuses to bear the burden of a saddle.[3] I do not, however, charge anyone in particular with the burden of guilt, except to the extent that [every] man should examine himself within. I have not singled out anybody by a biting accusation, nor does my verse contain reproaches for anyone [1460]. While awake, I have set down these my writings which I received during sleep. What I have said should seem good to good people, and I leave what is bad to the bad. Everyone complains that the world has been laid waste by the vengeance of God, because of the gravity of our sin. Therefore, let the sinful man amend his faults with contrite heart, before we are all destroyed.

The man who keeps his heart pure sets the world right. Therefore, let him rule his heart, let him read these writings for himself.

What I have set down is the voice of the people, but you will also see that where the people call out, God is often there [1470]. [4] The man who is good listens to what is good, but the perverse man disregards it. Yet the man prone to what is good should listen to this. Likewise, the bad man should know these writings so that he may presently become good, and the good man should seek them out so that he may do better. [5] The world does not harm the righteous man as long as he is of good faith, but when he oversteps his bounds, the world takes up arms. The world will be such as a man shall have been during his life. Therefore, every man alive should withstand evil. Indeed, when the hidden guilt by which virtue is corrupted is not purged but is instead continued [1480], it deserves the bad fate which in the end is given it. [6]

[7]Here ends the book which is entitled The Voice of One Crying, issued especially concerning the period of the principal misfortune in England, which (as you have heard) befell the unfortunate Richard II in the beginnings of his reign—ostensibly as if from the rod of God. And furthermore, since he was not remorseful for this, but was instead hardened to a tyrant's ways, he did not desist from incessantly scourging his kingdom with constant oppressions, until he deservedly underwent the scourge of divine vengeance, even to the extreme of his own deposition. There were then three nobles of the realm who were especially disturbed about all this, namely, Thomas Duke of Gloucester, who is commonly called the Swan; Richard Earl of Arundel, who is called the Horse; and Thomas Earl of Warwick, whose name is the Bear. Together with certain other nobles allied with them, they violently revolted in order to destroy those who fostered the king's ill will. They revolted manfully and in righteous spirit for the glory of God and for the welfare of the kingdom, just as the writer intends to show clearly in the following chronicle, which is in three parts.

THE TRIPARTITE CHRONICLE

[Preface]

It is the work of man to pursue and seek out peace. The three nobles of whom mention is made below did this, as there was good faith among them.

It is the work of hell to disturb peace and to slay a kingdom's just men. The headstrong Richard was not afraid to do this, through devious trickery.

It is a work done in Christ to depose haughty men from the throne and to exalt the humble. God did this. He cast the hateful Richard from his throne and He decided upon the glorious elevation of the pious Henry, who was a man most pleasing in the estimation of all.[1]

May this tripartite chronicle which follows be heeded with experienced judgment; the part which appears first is the work of man, the second part is a profane work of hell, and the third part, through heavenly justice, is a work done in Christ. The man who is keenly discerning can learn wondrous things in it: what love is, and what wrath is; and finally there is this exclamation: "Love conquers all things."[2]

289

PART I

Here in the first part of the chronicle the compiler, after having characterized the times, then treats one by one the causes of the kingdom's being divided against itself.

Take the first letter of mundus and add to it C three times repeated, and take six periods of five years; and afterwards add ten times five, plus seven: Note the time when England was in upheaval. [1] When the turbulent Richard forsook loving-kindness, there arose a transgression of the law, originating with the King. For this reason Fortune sank down and the land went into a decline. The people which he did not rule well therefore revolted; [2] to this day the times bemoan what this chronicle touches upon. With this book as witness, the chronicle was written beforehand; it was spoken at another time, but it did not pass unheeded by the ear [10]. [3] You shall hear the amazing deeds which the wrath of the people committed. In every city the just man was terrified by them.

How the unfortunate King Richard persisted in his malice from bad to worse, not fearing the rod of God.

The King always had an obdurate heart, but such an affliction provided no remorse for one who was lacking in righteousness. He took the base, immature counsel of fools to himself, and caused the principles of older men to be rejected. [5] He absorbed the poisonous counsels of brash youths to the effect that he was to prey upon the goods of his nobles, whom he reduced to a state of weakness. In such fashion did the wicked King cling to wicked men and become their ally, since he had lost all piety [20]. Then he greedily presumed to make accusation against certain men, so that he might despoil them of their treasured possessions. There were three venerable nobles whom the wrath of the King took special note of, and he vowed to kill them. And he so wanted

290

the hide of the cat, once it had been skinned, that he feigned false charges locked within his treacherous breast.

Note the judges who wrongfully drew up documents under their seals, in order that they might specifically justify the King's wrongdoing against the three nobles he wished to kill.

In order that he might have the deed carried out quite circum-spectly, he had recourse to laws and drew them up to his own advantage. Corrupted by the persuasion of bribes and compelled by fear, men granted favorable judgment to the King, in a miscarriage of justice [30]. Then the lawyers compounded agreements, arranged whatever the King wanted, and duly affixed their seals. The King then rejoiced over this conferring of power, and spewed his poison to the utmost. Whereupon those young men who were his intimates were on hand to praise the King because he had thus subverted the law to himself. [6]

How the three aforesaid nobles, having been secretly forewarned about the King's maliciousness, were strengthened in their de-fense against him.

Observing this and fearing treacherous plots, others quickly de-termined what had to be done in defense. The King then hastened to give orders to this effect, that the three men should be sought out where they were and taken on the spot [40]. Then the three, who were just men and mighty in arms, arranged their affairs and put their strength to the task. It would be only fitting that I make reference to those nobles by their Christian name, and that I bless them. If I do not refer directly to the right names of the nobles, I shall nevertheless report them disguisedly, in hidden form. Even if I tend to write words which convey mysteries to your ears in the reading of them, those words none-theless report the truth.

Note the names of the three aforesaid nobles, in a figure of speech: the Earl Marshall; the most valiant Earl of Derby; [and] the Earl of Northumberland, whose Badge was a crescent moon.

There were the Swan, the Bear, and the Horse. Each of them was honorable; [7] they were not divided, but were seen to be as one [50].

The Wreathed Feather was allied with these three. [8] That noble who was youthful and upright as well, he who wore the S, also joined with the same group, [9] just as the trusted One from heaven was at hand. The Northern Moon[10] was not present for his share in the venture, but he accompanied the group in spirit.

How the King, whose Badge was the Sun, made request to the citizens of London for their help against the aforesaid nobles. But being apprehensive of the King's ill will, they did not consent to that at all.

The shadowy one who bore the sun[11] did not see the light, for during Troy's extremities he took vengeance upon the assembled peoples. It was first because of Troy that his sun sank to the depths: the people grew pale with fear at his eclipse, for he showed them no favor [60]. [12] The crowds resisted Phoebus, and he did not ascend the wall, for the Swan held sway with his wings.

How the King established the Earl of Oxford (who is designated as the "Boar") over Cheshire with the royal banner, in order that the latter might lead warlike bands against the three aforesaid nobles.

Phoebus' trickery moreover stirred the wicked crowds into disorder, as he exerted his efforts against the luminaries on the outside. Cheshire arose, where the Boar ruled over the leading lights. [13] The King's banner foolishly authorized him, but God thwarted the insidious plotter. For this reason their own treachery finally entangled the odious traitors. If power were sought on behalf of the wicked King, a contrary power was at work with the help of the Swan [70]. The Boar sought for ruses, tricks, and deadly lurking places, in order that the realm might perish and the King's arrogance be brought to bear. The Swan expressly provided for the things which he saw to be of assistance, and he himself protected the future welfare of the kingdom. The Boar led the people, whom he had incited to carrying arms, in order that by means of them he might freely pursue the nobles and utterly scatter them.

How on a certain Friday the Earl of Oxford, together with his followers, turned in flight near Oxford at the sight of the Duke of
Gloucester, who at that time was carrying a fox's tail on his
lance. And the castles, which the Earl had assigned to his own
family to be held under his banner, were in the end hurled to
the ground, unrelieved. [14] And indeed, the Earl himself crossed
the sea by ship as a fugitive, in order to protect his life in a more
secure way.

Since the Swan knew this, he went to oppose the oncomers, and
the warrior purged the realm, whereby its spirit revived. When Venus
ushered in her light, [15] fate brought back war. Thetis stood apart, [16]
as Cheshire fell victim to Mars [80]; the waters of the Thames received
the blood of affliction. The Swan was victorious on the wing, as though
its life were eternal. Then the Boar of Oxford retreated from the seat
of wisdom. While the impious man was near the city he cursed it. The
fleeing Boar did not remain there but crossed the shallows. There the
wretch was revived by the water. [17] The Boar fled from the fox's tail
like a lark. The tail hurled down castles numerous as the stars. Because the worthless man was found so wanting, he abandoned his castles
and sought for a ditch where he might live a pauper [90]. But neither
did the pomp of his castles avail the Boar nor was a pit given to him,
for he was driven from there as an exile. Thus, when he saw that Fortune had cut him off, he crossed over the sea to seek elsewhere to live.
Changed into a hare, [18] the Boar lost his place of honor, and no safe
place was open to him any more.

How, immediately upon the flight of the aforesaid Earl of Oxford,
Alexander Neville (the Archbishop of York), who had also been a
sharer in the wrongdoings with the King, guiltily escaped in a
similar flight overseas, because of fear of the Duke.

The odor of incense was then of no avail to York, but neither was
his mitre nor his wealth nor his lofty honor. Although he had been elevated on high at the royal side, the bishop fell from his seat and departed from his see [100]. The primate had been a trafficker in his
cure of souls and a spoilsman; and the man, whose previous guilt caught
up with him, withdrew as a pauper. Thus fled the Macedonian of New
Town, [19] this plunderer of the clergy, whom the Father of the Church
cursed, [20] since he had lived as he did.

293

How Michael de la Pole, Earl of Suffolk, who was then the King's Chancellor, also protected himself by sailing across the sea to safety elsewhere; for he sensed that he was guilty.

There was a haughty, treacherous, greedy, wicked Earl, who was Chancellor by means of a thousand trickeries. He hated the nobles and slandered their names[21] with backbiting; therefore, he finally became a fugitive. Thus God in heaven harshly purged the evils of Michael from the pool, [22] lest the Earl might rise again [110].

How the Bishop of Circencester, at that time the King's confessor, left his own region in flight and sought out foreign parts, conscious of his own guilt.

And there was another such, a fawning confessor and a professor of evil, who lay hidden under the wings of the King. This was a friar who was black within and without. In my opinion, his blackness besmirched the royal station. This biased man was a hidden enemy of the nobles, always stirring up anger rather than diminishing it. Nevertheless, he fled in the end, and the evils which he warranted for others he first paid for himself. [23] Thus did these aforesaid men fall victim to terror in their hearts, for they were living as fugitives from their own land [120].

How the three aforesaid nobles, meeting at London together because of the controversy, held a peaceful conference with the King, who was then living in the Tower. With due respect for the King's reverence, they came to obtain redress concerning matters which had been previously agreed upon. They therefore decided, with the King's consent, that Parliament was shortly to be held at London.

Then the three men who were full of good sense sought for justice, and they went to the King concerning it. The King was within the walls of the Tower and saw the nobles coming, and he acknowledged himself as unsmiling at the sight. After armed bands had entered the gates of the city, the bold nobles entered, following in peace. They reached the Tower, where they stopped, out of respect for the King. In order that they might remove the blame from his part, a course of action was found. To that end, Parliament was summoned, so that they might cleanse and repair the state of the realm [130]. [24]

How it was agreed, at the beginning of Parliament, that the absence of those who had fled the realm of their own accord (as has been shown) would be judicially made into perpetual exile, with no ransom.

The land was assembled, called together according to law. The King sat, and the voice of the Commons spoke in safety. It said, concerning those people who were collaborators of the King, that because of the fact that they were fugitives, such exile was to be the general sentence. Accordingly, they were banished from the land, not slain by the sword. The sentence of the nobles was made known far and wide.

How Parliament proceeded step by step with particulars against those who had been the infamous favorites of the infamous King. Of these, Sir Simon Burley, at that time the King's Chamberlain, was sentenced by judicial decision to the death penalty and was decapitated. [25]

When this had been done, they sought out the others who were in hiding, the chief of whom was the King's Chamberlain. The striped garment fell to the fate of the sword [140]. When it is not virtuous, old age is the more to be blamed: [26] even while the tears of the Queen implored medical aid [for him], the fallen man brought on his own destruction and lost his head.

How Sir John Beauchamp, at that time Seneschal of the King's household, and whom the King had given the title of Baron of Bridgenorth, likewise fell, losing his head because of the Court.

The Court condemned not so much the Seneschal's wealth of possessions, the ill-gotten gains which his destiny had pursued in its thirst for wrongdoing; rather, it condemned him to the fate of death. When he bowed his head, the sword was quick to provide justice for him. He certainly had despised the Swan and had always praised the ill-willed Boar, and infatuated the heart of the King. He was false, cunning, versed in trickery like a fox [150], envious, and with a tongue ever prating of peace. Thus fell the name of Baron Bridge of the North. [27] The King had wrongly given him this title of honor.

How Nicholas Brembel, who had been a citizen and Mayor of London, dishonorably lost his freedom of the city; for he was hauled to the gallows and hanged there.

There was a mayor of the city who was called Bramble. [28] He had vexed the nobles and given sanction to the plottings of the King. The King had cherished this man like a consort because he had accepted the decision of the Council. From it, he finally got his death: He whom the earth had previously upborne hung by the gallows, so the Londoner did not feel the stroke of the sword. [29]

How Sir Robert Tresilian, who was then Chief Justice of the King's Bench, ended the last day of his life through judicial decision, under that same penalty of the gallows. [30]

The one on the King's Bench who weighed the scales of justice [160], administered the law, and deprived others of justice, was a Cornishman. If one were to inquire into his crimes, there was no one worse or more dishonest than he. This scoundrel stirred up the nobles and often harassed them, for which reason the wicked man finally perished, harassed himself. Because of a crime outstripping what he had committed before, he was stretched on the gallows and overcome by hanging there. The sorry fate of hanging befell those dying men upon whose hands men's justice used to hang.

How the other judges, as exiles not under sentence of death, crossed over the sea from England to Ireland. As has been shown, under their seals they had confirmed the King's initial excesses against the nobles, at the importuning of the prelates.

The entire Court cried out against the other judges and recognizably false friends [170], as knowledge of past affairs became clear. City, country, and town condemned the false seals[31] which had given the King grounds, or rather a pretext, for his wickedness. There was no punishment which could have been sufficient for these wrongdoers, and the voice of the people said this openly and firmly. But out of feigned piety the King's priests quite presumptuously mitigated the punishment from due course of law. Accordingly, they did not fall by the sword, but crossed the sea into exile. Ireland received the ill-advised fools. Lawyers such as these were special favorites above all [180];

296

they showed great partiality toward the King's waywardness. In this instance fate decreed the men's destinies to be carried out in varying fashion; a guilty man received his deserts according as he had under-taken. One was banished from the state, another was decapitated; others were dragged to their funerals by a rope, once they had been killed. The reward was dissimilar, but the result was one and the same; no matter what a man had wished for, death finally resolved everything. [32]

How various friars, at that time the confessors of the various courts, were scattered everywhere like useless straw, [33] together with a great many other clergy.

In order that the King might be reformed and the kingdom made glorious, it remained to be sought how his guilt could make amends. At that time ungodly friars were his father confessors [190], and any fault confessed to them went unchecked. They who exculpated vice thirsted for vices; they who celebrated morals lacked a moral way of life. Thus the Church strayed from its path[34] into a pattern of wrongdoing, and that institution, guilty of its customary baseness, did not beware. Thus did friars vowed to holy things transgress, so that God became the avenger upon their persons. The group at the royal side was not spot-less, for which reason more than a hundred favorites were removed from there. The warblers grieved that they had lost the glories of their song [200], the scribblers lamented their writings hardened with deceit. Gone was the flatterer, the villain, the plotter, the false counselor, the schemer, the envious promoter.

How the aforesaid nobles, the principals in the quarrel, were flattered in order to see whether they might be swayed by en-treaties or bribes. But as the instruments of true justice, they stood firm together until the resolution of their grievance.

The struggle was extended, the Court did not cease contending, until all treachery was purged and got rid of. False men might tempt the just, but they might not get the better of them either by bribe or entreaty, with Christ the defender mediating. At that time those three stood firm, consolidated the realm, strengthened the law, and routed corrupt practices. They thus molded a reformed, reinvigorated King [210], [35] so that they had greater confidence, and they accordingly with-drew with praise. All the public commended and celebrated their good deeds in song, everywhere speaking and singing of these matters with praise.

In conclusion the compiler commends the deeds of the three afore-said nobles with praise. He prays devoutly to the Almighty in their behalf.

May there always be glory for the Swan in Christ's banner, [36] and may there be praise in this world for the Horse, whom the Swallow[37] marked with approval; and may the Bear enjoy honor from the lips of the people. These three were examples of good Englishmen: they up-held the realm and bore the burdens of others. May He Who is three and one render reward to these three. Amen.

PART II

Here in the second part of the Chronicle he states how the King, pretending peace under the guise of feigned alliance, treacherously overthrew the three aforesaid nobles. He thus caused one of them to be strangled; another he had decapitated; while the third, alas! he destined to be imprisoned in exile, together with the Lord of Cobham, who had always been a true friend of the realm. And in addition, which was shameful, that same cruel King utterly expelled from his See the Reverend Father in Christ Thomas of Arundel, then Archbishop of Canterbury. And he most unmercifully decreed him to be held perpetually in exile. [1]

In this second part of the chronicle the compiler first laments with grieving heart the grievous misfortunes which afterwards followed.

O alas for my spirit and alas for my speaking lips! And woe unto my pen, since I am to write of hellish deeds! With choking sobs and my face pale with tears, only with difficulty does my tongue[2] give utterance to those things which this Chronicle presents me. As you have heard before, the more that a disconsolate England delighted in the three men, the more Fortune threatened them. The false, two-faced King feigned all things and hid his plottings with deceit, although his ruin lay hiding in wait.

299

How these three nobles of whom you have heard obtained charters
of agreement from the King, in order to possess a more secure
peace with him; for they knew him to be treacherous.

At the royal side the Swan was placed as brother and associate,
and he performed those acts which he wished [10]. And the Horse was
likewise deluded by the caroling of the King, so that he did not see
through the deceits which he beheld. The Bear was also enchanted, as
though highly esteemed, and was unaware of the end toward which his
fate was working. But in order that they might remain safe according
to legal statute, they sought charters from the King, which they obtained. [3] Thus did they conduct themselves, and they reëstablished
themselves with the King, so that they lived after the fashion of a flock
with love for its shepherd. They plainly put their trust in him, but
time passed to no avail. Just when they thought they stood firm, suddenly their circumstances changed [20].

How the King, more cunning than a fox, plotted tricks with constant deceitfulness, in order to entrap the nobles through an
agreement of feigned peace.

Behold the wicked villain, hiding like a fox after a lamb. Thus
does betrayal await those toward whom the wrath of a tyrant inclines.
O the deceit, and O the treachery, which the King had so long represse
when the man unique in dissimulation poured forth his wickedness! But
then he spewed out his poison to the fullest extent. Having been long
puffed up with it, how often did the evil man inflict pain! [4] Thus, like a
whirlwind the violent young man made attack upon the rejected Swan,
even while it thought itself to be at peace.

How the King revealed, quicker than lightning, the hatred which
had long lain hidden in his heart, first for express vengeance
against the Duke of Gloucester (who is called the "Swan"). [6] Indeed, the King in his own person violently seized the said Duke
unawares at Pleshy, and ordered the man thus captured to be
brought to Calais without delay and strictly imprisoned there in
close custody.

O how Fortune does not remain fixed in one spot! [5] There is an
example of this in the course of this poem [30]. The King struck, and

the well-meaning Swan underwent heartfelt suffering, and the prostrated
one was not succored by the King. He was then captured at Pleshy, [7]
seized like a sacrificial animal; the King ordered battle waged, and
showed no willingness to take pity on him. His children together with
his wife grieved as though overcome by death. The King was fiercer
than a wolf, while the woman shed her tears. No sense of duty was of
any protection to him; the envious hand then took vengeance upon him.
The King remained hostile, and then there was not a single friend. O
kingly born! Like a needy pauper, the princely man lay basely dragged
down and lawlessly overwhelmed [40]. Those who seized the Swan when
they intended to take him captive were, of course, prime favorites of
the King. Thus with the imprisoning of the Duke in darkness, England
lost a shining light and grew wholly dark, with its luminary removed.
He who had always loved the King swam across the sea; a hundred
thousand wept because the Swan went away. He sought the haven of
Calais, where treachery--the wrongdoing of the King, which he spawned
through corruption of the law--hid its birth. He was suddenly shut up,
confined by a prison; he knew not for what purpose, whether for life or
destruction [50]. Then like a falcon taking to flight the King seized upon
the distinguished man, whereby he ruined his people, who were without
their defender.

> How the King, who disturbed the hearts of the nobles by torment-
> ing them through a thousand twists and windings, treacherously
> deceived Richard, Earl of Arundel (who is called the "Horse").
> The brother of the said Earl was Thomas, Archbishop of Canter-
> bury; to him the King offered assurances under oath that if the
> said Earl were voluntarily to come forth obedient to his King's
> presence, he might from then on be free to go wherever he wished,
> confident in the King's firm friendship and without any taint of dis-
> grace. And thus coming forth, the honest Earl was deceived by
> the dishonest King.

With the Swan out of the way, the King, seething in his evil heart,
sought to capture the Horse; and with hidden guile in his spirit he
plotted very cautiously to take thought with himself about this. So,
falsely swearing by Christ, he ensnared the Earl. He made his oath
while touching the book; and confirming the agreement, he definitely
made a promise and openly pledged his good faith, saying that he might
safely cross over[8] as a free man unentangled by any kind of trickery,
whenever he wished to come to him [60]. The Earl's brother, the Primate, eagerly received this oath of support from the King's lips. The

Archbishop was overjoyed, he was hopeful under such a compact; and thus the faithful man was captured through stratagems.

How Thomas, Earl of Warwick (by another name the "Bear"), innocent of guilt, patiently yielded when captured at London by the King's followers and was sent to prison. The tyrannical King declared that his Parliament at Westminster was to pronounce sentence next concerning this man.

When the Bear heard this, he did not withdraw afar off in consequence. Making the sign of the cross, he fixed his mind upon Christ; the patient and most devoted Bear did not raise alarms; rather, he awaited the evils which Fortune held in store. He remained at London and did not pass from the city gate, for which reason this man, guilty of no disgrace, was captured [70]. Thus the three men, abandoned as though a mere shadow, [9] remained confined in prison, through force and not by law of the crown. Then arrogance quickly waxed great upon the tyrannical throne; it spared no one so long as Fortune was favorably disposed toward it. Parliament decreed that their crime extended to the point that there should be a final judicial punishment. [10]

How, after Parliament had pronounced sentence, eight Appellants then appeared against the three said nobles, eager for their ruin. And since the King was unwilling to arraign the Duke of Gloucester in person before himself in Parliament, because of fear of the people, he pretended by a clever lie that the Duke, who hitherto had been held as a witness under lock and key in prison at Calais, had died in bed. And thus the pernicious King falsely condemned the absent Duke, without any response in his behalf.

At that time there were eight leading Appellants, [11] who made appeal against the three in order that they might harry them from this life. O who could take thought without bitterly weeping, as he examined the crime for which England lamented [80]? Behold, fatal days were at hand, in so far as the haughtiness of his retinue caused the haughty King to be more and more wicked. On the King's behalf it was cunningly arranged that the innocent Swan was to die without making answer. Although the King knew quite definitely that he was still alive, he pretended that the latter had passed away on his deathbed in due course. [12] Thus, when the Swan was not found, no one made answer to Parliament on behalf of one whom the King was hiding under lock and key. When he did not appear in order to aid himself according to law, they at once condemned the man, whom they afterwards expropriated [90].

How the King intended for the aforesaid Duke to be secretly condemned, just as you have heard. Therefore, a short time afterwards he sent certain assassins—men like confederates from hell—over to Calais, where the Duke was still imprisoned alive. Upon arriving there, under instruction from the King they contrived a violent murder: secretly and at night they pitilessly suffocated the unsuspecting Duke, who was suddenly pressed down to his death under the weight of a feather bed.

O hellish crime, for which men of today can weep, the fact that evildoers arranged for the murder of the Swan! They secretly obtained what they could not do openly; and since they feared the people, they carried on their activities in stealth. The assassins were ready, and one night the fanatics slew the prostrate Swan like a martyr. This wicked criminal act was carried out at Calais by order of the King, who was exultant when the murder was accomplished. From the sealed cabin of a ship England secretly received the body thus taken in murder and left by the enemy [100]. The body returned by sea and was not yet buried, for the King forbade a decent burial for it. Moreover, although the man had wished to occupy his proper place beside his father, only with difficulty did he enter into even a lowly tomb. O such wickedness, which neither the justice of the realm nor the law of Christ brought upon that nobleman! For his life perished, lawlessly put to sleep; and his death likewise affirmed that the place of burial he wished for was not to be his. [13] Alas! Who now lives that ever knew of such things as the son of a king having been put to death by a king [110]? Alas, that so outstanding a royal English family was undone by order of the King, with the criminal unapprehended. Alas, that certain ones, in the fashion of evil tormentors, silenced the enfeebled body of the beloved Duke with the weight of a feather bed, and committed murder upon the smothered man. All England was extremely grieved over this unwelcome report. May God grant this destiny, that the body now be buried and that the spirit reach a place eternally blessed!

How the Earl of Arundel, accused in Parliament by the infamous King, courageously made answer to the things which they brought against him. First, he pronounced in a clear voice that everything done by him had been done as a favorable declaration of his intent for the King's honor. Second, in the ears of all he very clearly set forth the King's charters, which attested to peace and agreement concerning this matter. But because of his own malice the infamous King, in whose presence no righteousness ever prospered, did not accept the Earl's answers. In a furious impulse he had the man, condemned by a death sentence, decapitated at the Hill of the Tower of London. There the Augustinian Friars carried away the head and the body with them to their church, amidst psalms, and devoutly buried him in a suitable place.

Now that the honest Swan has passed away, it is necessary to tell of the Horse. Fate did not wish to provide them with a similar death [120]. The King presided, and all his favorites then allied to him were there present, speaking many base things against the Horse. [14] He was alone and trusted solely in God; hence, he remained honorable and steadfast even to the extremities of death. The King first made accusation, and the Horse denied all wrongdoing. Displaying the King's seals, he showed his charter according to due course of law, by virtue of which he had thought himself to be quite safe. It did not go unnoticed that there was a previously recognized agreement. But by trickery the King warily rendered void the loyal Earl's answers, [15] and he dishonestly fashioned plots [130]. Then those conspiring with the King and those highly esteemed of the King confirmed everything he said. Alas! The sentence then carried out was all too repellent, terrible, deadly, for it was capital punishment. Led through the country, through the villages, he looked back upon his friends, who gave vent to many secret sighs. Prayerfully making many vows of devotion, everywhere those who beheld such calamities then wept. And there were other false men, knights who came forth as followers of the King, who were neither honorable nor merciful [140]. They then called out for capital punishment and ordered the evil fate to take place at a designated spot. Whereupon the Earl spoke this word to Christ: "Thou knowest all things: I am to die, since my enemy is thus determined. I perish tormented by foes, unrighteously oppressed. I proceed defenseless; therefore, have pity on me, I pray." With palms outstretched and psalms sounding on all sides, [16] thus did he undergo his final suffering and enter upon his punishment. But he did not lose his head without any thanks being rendered him, for thousands cursed the Hundred Parliament [150]. [17] At last[18] the body fell, while the spirit departed safely to the ethereal realms in the skies, where it dwells faithful in its love. Then the Augustinian

Friars of London lifted him up and took up the head together with the body. Nevertheless, they scarcely dared place it where they wished; rather, they arranged a hidden burial because of the King. May God grant that this become known so that he can still be buried, and may his heirs gain possession of their rightful estates for themselves.

How the Earl of Warwick, misled by the King's deception, acknowledged himself in Parliament as guilty, hoping by this means to earn the King's absolute pardon once and for all, as had been promised to him. But the King, whose intent was utterly false, hoped through such an acknowledgement to convict others who were in opposition. Returning evil for good to the said Earl, he expropriated him for the sake of a bribe; and he sent him into distant parts, in order that he might be kept there in prison as an exile forever.

Now that the Horse had been violently reined in and burdened down, they were hunting for the Bear, whom they wished to bait next [160]. The King's hungry, pernicious dogs were then ready at hand, and with their barking everywhere they did not keep the peace anywhere. They inflicted injury on every side, but the King gave no further heed to what more they could do; rather, he spread out his own nets. O! How clever his juvenile, violent piece of trickery then appeared! Because of it the Bear was then unable to enjoy his rightful renown. The King attested that if the Bear confessed he were guilty and did not oppose the things reported concerning him, he would offer him pardon, which the court would firmly uphold. And he would accordingly depart alive, and go away a free man [170]. And if he certified otherwise and insisted upon his rights, he would meet with his death; he was to endure the fate which he chose for himself. Those peers who were then advisers of the King probed the Bear and sounded out his wishes. One offered life and another rumored death; one consoled while another threatened. Each practiced deceits, with which he swayed the Bear's feelings; hence, he had the less understanding of what he could say to the King. And so, finally wearied by the stigma of guilt, he gave himself up to be convicted. This evil pronouncement was made [180]; by such a statement the crown's rights gained in power. The King put down three men, because one man spoke such things. [19] All the Bear's talk was concerning the King's pledges, and his every word was in response to what the King had promised him. But in truth, when he thought to have pleased the King in this way and hoped to have been safe, at the King's nod he then lost the bargain that the King had made him. For the King afterwards jeered at the agreement which he had promised;

and so the deluded Bear was imprisoned at the King's word, whose pious
talk became bitter to the taste [190]. Alas, what a sad affair! Alas,
what wrong there was in all this, when the King did not carry his own
agreement into practice! The King pretended he was ignorant of what
he dishonestly glossed over; the outcome has furnished extensive proof
of these matters. The Bear insisted upon what the King did not carry
out. Yet the King was not ashamed of his action, which was obviously
a piece of dishonesty. The King ordered that the condemned Bear, redeemed by none of his worthiness, be removed and taken away into exile. Then the Isle of Man, distant and full of dangers, confined the
Bear, whose sentence thrust him back into prison [200]. The fact that
he had inflicted such injuries was not enough for the King; he seized
his lands completely, once their owner was removed. He did not provide for the Countess, alone and abandoned to herself, but rather took
away the pittance which the court allowed. [20] Thus did the King ruin a
man whom the whole country mourned. May he soon pass away in
death, lest he suffer more. There yet remained an ominous Mount
Aetna[21] hidden beneath the wrath of the King, and he meanwhile felt its
consuming flames more and more. With burning eagerness the irate
King laid hold upon him; although the accused man was guiltless, he
soon died of grief [210]. However excellent in character the man may
have been, the pestilence which maddened the King was all the more
pernicious; from it the worst kinds of things arose.

How the King, seeking to injure everyone he could, finally brought
forth for the judgment of Parliament the innocent Lord of Cobham,
who had previously renounced the world for a home with the
Carthusians. Then the King protracted a delay. But Cobham,
yielding no quarter to the tyrant King through any persuasion of
blandishments or fear of threats, was found to be completely loyal
in all his responses. As though he had been confused by this, and
abhorring the man's firmness of purpose, the King dispatched
him into exile far from England, in disgrace but without the sentence of death. [22]

There was one worthy man, patient, honest and kind, prudent and
just, strong through the power of virtues; he was not envious, but a
genuine friend of the realm. As a thousand people have said, the King
hated the man in whom he recognized such good qualities--he was Lord
Cobham. The story has troubled those to whom he had been loyal, [23]
but since he in truth wished ultimately to please Christ, he transported
himself to a dwelling place at the sanctuary of the Carthusians [220].
Thus Christ received the man whom the royal authority wished to do

away with. This authority lawlessly took back the man whom Christ led. The King accused him of crime; Cobham denied all crime, justifying what he had done. Thus the matter proceeded to legal action. He was cognizant of the things which he said, and was not found to be insane in this regard; on the contrary, the King was certain that he displayed frankness. And so, since the truth-telling man was a friend to the three, the King condemned Cobham, but he did not shed his blood. Not having been sentenced to death, Cobham did not feel the stroke of the sword; nevertheless, he did undergo the alien scourges of exile [230]. [24] Hence I ask that this good man may come back honorably in the future, so that his friends may rejoice over his happy return. [25]

> How the King, who neither feared God nor esteemed mankind, was not ashamed, because of his hostility toward the Duke, to invent impossible reasons for hostility against the Right Reverend Father in Christ, Thomas of Arundel, Archbishop of Canterbury--even at a time when there was thought to be a bond of affection between them. Therefore, this same Thomas was suddenly changed from Archbishop into not being Archbishop. He completely lost all his worldly goods as well as his spiritual goods, because of the King's treacherous dishonesty. In addition, he was driven out without any worldly comforts; and crying out to God alone, he withdrew from England an exile and a pauper.

Alas! My pen is wet with tears, since a calamitous fate, the wickedness of which I shudder at, impels it to write. [26] It was not enough that the King distort temporal law, in order that the people dwelling under it might perish without that law; but he raged even more against Christ. For this reason I believe that I must not keep silence at this lamentable misfortune. The Primate of the English, who occupied the primal see with the support of the Most High while hoping for an even better sanctuary [240]--him the King harassed and drove from the see, while Simon abnegated Thomas' rights at Rome. [27] Born with the title of Earl, this Thomas was a worthy churchman, made a Doctor of Law, distinguished in the law, eloquent, virtuous, pleasing to Christ and celebrated among the people. [28] O that a prelate so pure and innocent was finally ensnared while at the very side of the King! Lurking in a fashion more cunning than an old fox, the King was eager to hurl Thomas down into ultimate destruction [250].

307

Here he declares how the aforesaid priest was the object, though almost unawares, of fictitious charges. Because of them, in absentia he unexpectedly incurred the sentence of exile by Parliament, as you have heard, which was contrary to all justice.

You have heard, with reference to the three, how the Bishop, as adjutant, was their protector, when the wicked King attacked them. In the role of pastor he strove at all times, not against the law, but to divert the King from his wrath. He was always such a man, so long as any hope remained, if he could save a follower in the face of death. The King bore this ill, namely, that the Chancellor showed steadfast love for those three at this juncture. The pious man was such a protector and mediator because they possessed the charters from the King, legally bestowed [260]. Like a priest, he thus made peace and put aside the sword of death, out of affection for the King. He would have accomplished these things had the King kept his agreement, but what he swore today his words denied tomorrow. Observe that because of this fault the King was especially angry toward the Archbishop, without material grounds; but other and more secret grounds were alleged, [29] just when money at Rome cunningly decided the Pope in Simon's favor. Behold, by means of these grounds, which were hidden within the King's heart [270], this misdeed overthrew Thomas, who had done nothing wrong. In addition, the King's previous hangers-on dissolved Parliament, which they had taken over by trickery. Accordingly, through judicial authority the King finally sent Thomas off into exile and did not release him for the sake of affection. Thus the priest without peer, whom the King greedily despoiled, then sought to reach distant, unknown parts. The pious Bishop then sustained his sad misfortunes for the time being, and hoped to regain his cure in the future. May Christ guide and save him and lead him back to safety [280], so that his every circumstance may be gloriously blessed.

Here he relates how scarcely a one of the three aforesaid nobles then heard any disheartening word spoken openly about death or exile.

O woe for that year in which haughtiness abounded in the tyrant! That wild beast, so to speak, crushed those whom he wished. Even as this wickedness continued it made the three men preëminent above all. Among the people there was a suddenly changed opinion concerning them. Certain confederates, certain men won over by bribery, were led to evil things, so that many people talked a great deal. At this time the Swan, the Bear, the Horse--not one is termed just. Yesterday they were praised, now they are cursed. Their early fame has fled, now that their good fortune has fallen low [290]; all their former praise has ceased, now that their good fortune has ceased. Love has now been forgotten, there is no friend for them. For this reason the aforementioned three are as dead as the shade of a corpse. [30] Blood relatives bloodily took their lives and denigrated the nobles' class in order to dissolve the relationship. Nothing stood in the way of that breed, and reason did not bring them back to their senses. Thus was that wicked day transformed. The stock has been extirpated, the bloom of the tree taken away, the scion perceives no indication that his name may endure. The father has withdrawn from the world alone, just as he entered it [300]. A fruitful unity has now been barrenly scattered. Yesterday rulers and today inferiors, thus have they been derided wherever seen. They closed doors where they had no keys, [31] yet abuse on the King's part was still not shut out. The one who turns from bad to worse does not turn back. So long as evils are sought for, to that extent worse evils follow. [32] Since he was doing his worst, he killed the three nobles. Because of this his pride undertook a too protracted flight. Then the deceivers, whom the court recognized as the more violent [310], laughed at the deeds they saw done to the three. They attributed ridiculous things to them, and placed three scandals upon them. This kind of thing was said, and is not yet renounced by word of mouth:

A song which malicious men composed in derision of the three nobles who had been tyrannically ruined.

"The Swan does not keep its wings forever, nor the Horse its hide; now the Swan is without wings, the Horse is flayed. The Bear, whom biting chains torment, does not bite. " Thus did the voice of the fatuous mob cry out in the city. Enemies were saying everything that could be said, imagining still more, and spawning lies. Scrope, Bushy, and Green, black men with no brightness in their hearts [320], meditated every crime so that they could do greater harm. By them the King was instructed and brought to all the evils which he later committed, at which all England trembled. The people, who witnessed their losses, wept to themselves. Since they did not hear a voice raised, they remained silent.

309

Here at the end he especially commends the virtues of the Duke of Gloucester and the Earl of Arundel, celebrating their deeds with praise. He moreover urges that they, with judicious spirit, not neglect to provide for themselves at present against the future, because of the things which happened in the past.

O mighty Duke, in knightly fashion you fought the French realms under the sword for the honor of the King. [33]

O Earl, you caused the fleet of the French, whom you vanquished to be conquered at sea on behalf of your King. [34] Alas, King, you who have betrayed such associates [330], may a ruinous destiny finally be your punishment. From a peaceful beginning of things, how often the end of the day is saddened. Let us therefore look into these matters: Trustworthiness, which a greedy spirit knows not of, is now rare. So long as lips are given to deceits, you should not believe everything that you hear. In days gone by the counsel for a wise man was to act with pretense toward one who pretended. Today's counsel is now such as yesterday's was: What is doubtful is deceptive, but when you shall see its purpose fully exposed, then at long last praise the times. In the twenty-first blood-filled year [340], [35] during the month of September, savagery held sway by the sword. As I listened in sadness, I entered into the writing of this poem. Lament, you who are alive, now that laments have subsided. These are a teacher's harsh words, which I wonder at the bitterness of: "While you may think you have acted for the best, there is a snake lying in the grass."[36] Whatever man says, whatever he does or contemplates, the destiny of the event always depends upon the word of God.

PART III

Here in the third part of the Chronicle he writes in conclusion of
how the aforesaid King put aside the law of both God and men.
He arbitrarily sent into exile for ten years the most vigorous
Prince, Lord Henry, then Earl of Derby (his father the Duke of
Lancaster being still alive). Afterwards, when the father was
dead and the son living in French parts, that same King, filled
with utter malice, through almost infinite subterfuges of deceit
ordered charges to be spitefully thundered against not only the
person of the absent man himself but also his heirs [10]. But the
Highest Judge, Who discerns truth from falsehood, did not bear
such great abominations of malevolence with impunity. He caused
the same Lord Henry (now Duke of Lancaster after the death of
his father) to return into England through His divine providence,
although the King was unwilling. Because of his arrival, the loyal
people of the entire realm, nobles as well as commons, praised
God as if with one voice. They renounced the pestilent Richard
because of his faults. They deposed him from his rank, elevated
the most gracious Duke (the previously mentioned Lord Henry) to
the throne of royal majesty, and joyfully crowned him on the thirteenth day of the month of October in the one-thousand-three-
hundred-and-ninety-ninth year of our Lord [20].

Here at the beginning of the third part of the chronicle the compiler reflects upon its end, rejoicing in the hope of future glory.

If we duly consider, we see these things plainly enough: If there
re sorrows after joys, [1] there are often peace and quiet after sorrows.
recently lamented for this broken kingdom overwhelmed by the King's

311

fierceness, but I have ceased my tears since then. I shall now smile upon an unsullied kingdom restored by the probity of its leader, and I shall not refrain from praise of him. O praiseworthy deed, O infinitely noteworthy deed for the glory of Christ, Who graciously led us forth out of the melancholy prison of R[ichard], then its jailer, as though he were a Herod reigning, and led us back to glorious realms [10]!

How King Richard, in order to ruin his kingdom like a tyrant, incessantly pursued all his stratagems for damaging the people -- like the mole, which ever spoils the land by digging it up.

When Richard II suppressed the honest noblemen, for whom all England wept, the world knew indeed that he thus aspired to swagger and strut all the higher, for he scorned and threatened his own kingdom. With more than his usual lurking fury, he gave vent to his rage and oppressed a people to whom he was unable to show mercy. Just as the undermining mole gnaws and digs up the soil without any respite from it, [2] so night and day this other mole, the more to undermine the kingdom which he was determined to ruin, added to his wrongdoing and applied his strength to this purpose [20]--even as the ranting Prince of Hell dominates the actions of the stage. [3] He occasioned heavy burdens with which he oppressed the people. Just as the furious Charybdis continually drinks from the raging whirlpool of the salt sea [and] vomits forth, so did the King spew out, upon a people existing—alas!--without law, the pent-up villainy hidden within his breast. [4]

Note how the King secured a committee for himself through subtle deceit so that he, together with certain persons designated by him, could continue the previously instituted Parliament wherever he wished to sit.

From the first he maintained in various places a commission always beholden to himself, through which he perpetuated every kind of evil. With the Crown remaining where the King's person was, the power of the commission depended upon his bodily presence [30]. [5] Thus, wherever the royal presence sat, it dealt out injury, with the result that no one knew what wicked deeds he stealthily entered into. This action of the King was an abomination of the law; the people certainly grumbled at it, but no one openly did so. Nevertheless, so that he might stand firm and continue this state of affairs, he produced special papal bulls on his own behalf. If anyone opposed the committee at all extensively in anything, either before or after the event, his opinion militated against him. The King had everyone browbeaten into implementing his wickedness, except for Christ, Who was no factor in this [40]. The people cursed whatever the clergy said, and invoked Christ's vindication for their grieving heart. But the pernicious King, having forgotten those religious observances which he once had adopted as his own, pressed forward to his cursed end. More and more ferocious in his plotting, feelings, looks, and action, he raged against the kingdom, which afterwards wept for his crimes. By conjecture, he happened upon harsh things which he had not even heard of with his own ears, evils of which his heart was unaware, with the result that he saw the people go to ruin.

Note the initial charters written under compulsion from the King, to which clergy as well as people affixed their seals in fright. Through this piece of cleverness the King ruined several parts of his native realm by plunder. [6]

Charters were written and were read everywhere, and he ordered these to be stamped with seals and honored by all [50]. The clergy carried this out—I do not know whether I ought to tell the truth, but the people were following their examples. As has been said, so long as it hoped for benefits from the King, the people, ignorant of the law, were ready for the royal commands. City, farm, and manor affixed seals to the charters, so that all the poison was scattered to the fullest extent. Everyone was deceived by him, everyone was reckoned as a traitor, for one's established guilt might be made a matter of record by means of a seal. Thus since every class was corrupted by these charters, it was fitting that each atone in some way, in order that it might obtain pardon for itself [60]. Then extortioners, more and more greedy for their maw, [7] set the people free, as though the latter were buying back their peace. But this trick was nothing but a pretended remedy, for their bite was daily more rabid. The King oppressed the people and knew not how to desist from it. He was always in upheaval, always menacing his realms.

Note the later charters, which were commonly called blank charters.

After the initial charters he further instituted other stratagems, but not a single word stood out clearly in writing. He even ordered the manors to sanction these with seals. Everyone asked complainingly what the end was to be [70]. And thus the common people, tricked by his veiled aspect, did not know what it was doing, so long as Fortune worked in this way.

How King Richard, being full of utter malice and because of sheer envy, cast into exile the most valiant Lord Henry, the then Earl of Derby and son and heir of the Duke of Lancaster, in order to destroy him.

Meanwhile it happened that while the country was divided, [8] a new strife was initiated which all England took note of. Then the noble Henry, a friend to all honor, came into full bloom and was mightier than all. Just as the rose is the crown of flowers, he was the best of good men, the protector of the English. Their light shone because of him, the model of virtues, the most excellent of the excellent. On the battlefields this lion crushed the weapons of the wolves [80]. His name acquired an honorable significance, so that Lancaster beamed upon this never-conquered man. While his father was yet alive, the King sent away this spotless man and banished him from his promising destiny. For the King knew that the country was devoted to him; hence, he was fearful of suffering the fate of having him for a follower. [9] The envious man nurtured this pretext locked within his heart, until he put down the man of honor and unjustly did away with him. He, on the contrary, had in his usual way been ever solicitious for the esteem of the King, from whom he had hoped for a different kind of reward [90]. Thus he had committed no offense, but because the King hated the actions of all honorable men, he repaid him with injuries. I have not written of all the benefits which the Duke conferred upon him; if the Duke had been given his just deserts, then he would have deserved no harm. For his final, especial reward he was given this painful exile, torn from the bosom of the King.

How the aforesaid noble Henry bravely transported himself with steadfast spirit to the realms of France, in order to remain there during his time of exile.

Pure in every way, this spotless man went into exile, and France received him whom the English King deceived. Being famous there, he was everywhere dear to that realm, where there was greater rest for him, yet he did not rest easy [100]. While he was seeking out his

314

relatives, from whom he sought justice for himself, death resolved everything[10] for his father, whom God absolved. Thus, with his father dead, he then had to inquire from the council joined to him what he had better do. And accordingly, when he had taken counsel, the knight demanded as the adult heir the properties which he recognized as his own from his father.[11] In the midst of rumors of this, emissaries came to make formal complaint before the King, and to seek action at law concerning it. But he, who gobbled up everything, did not listen to what the loyal man pleaded, but ordered the exile to be disinherited [110]. And so the noble Duke found neither a just king nor a just law when word of information came to him. Then after he had been dispossessed, he was illegally seized and carried off. The Duke had brought along no worldly goods in order to make himself comfortable.[12] Young crows whose mother devours them do not cry out more than the King's favorites cried out for the dukedom's castles, lands, and titles for themselves. The King, who did not proceed justly, broke up the properties, distributing portions in order that he might enrich his hangers-on with them. A widespread report confirmed what the King decreed [120]; this crime will now be recognized throughout the whole world.

Note how, after the death of his father the Duke of Lancaster, the latter's noble son, the aforesaid Earl (then legally Duke), came from the farther regions of France to Calais by a carefully planned route, in order to claim his inheritance.[13] Together with Lord Thomas, the Archbishop of Canterbury, as well as with Thomas, the son and heir of Richard Earl of Arundel (who, as has been shown, was already deceased), the Duke commended himself to Christ and boarded ship in order to sail across to England.

O how much God allows! Yet when the moment comes to an end, He then reveals how everything assuredly stands.[14] The Duke, at last aroused as though he were a new man, weighed and pondered everything in his noble heart, He perceived that the King had become a tormentor and the law distorted, and that in both ways the wrongdoing was highly oppressive. Crossing himself, he prayed for help in this matter to Christ, Who ordered him to strive for his property, so long as he was of good hope. Suddenly, and always with his honor intact [130], in knightly fashion the Duke crossed the pleasant regions of the French with a few men and did not remain in delay there. He came to Calais, where he demanded his own domains. It was right for the high-minded man thus to return with a small fleet, and the Duke was conducted from there in a peaceful ship. Thomas the Primate of the English, then an exile because of the trickery of evil men, was devotedly standing by there, in company with his nephew. [15] The royal Duke, as does a mother hen under its wings, guided them safely with him as his avowed followers.

How with Christ's help the noble Henry, the then Duke of Lancaster, sought port by sailing through the seas, finally reaching a peaceful shore near Grimsby.
How almost the entire country offered itself for the service of the noble Duke.

The Duke, the Earl, [and] the Bishop alike hopefully sought their melancholy comfort [140] when the winds were driving. Near sunrise the ships reached the port which fate decreed. As the Duke foresaw, he arrived at the Northern shore. Then with bolder countenance, he said exultantly to the people following [him] that he had been victorious in this as though in battle. With strong courage he gave stout hearts to his company, so that they might be of good hope, no matter what fate had prepared for them. So, hopefully rejoicing together and fearing nothing because they were of better cheer, they at once fastened the ships. Disembarking first, the Duke placed his foot upon his own soil [150], worshipped God on bended knee, and first prayed with devotions of sincere intent, with palms outstretched to heaven, that he might win the palm of victory. [16] In order that he might rise above the heinousness of war, he implanted a kiss upon the earth, and there the Duke made many devotions and pious prayers. He arose from prayer, and taking up his cross he found shelter for himself. And then what happy days he began to enter upon: When his native land knew that the Duke had returned safe, everybody ran to him, rejoicing everywhere.

How King Richard, at the time when the noble Duke Henry was landing, unfortunately spent some fruitless days in the realm of Ireland, to his own destruction.

Then Richard was a hare, and not a lion[160].[17] Fear constrained him; he appointed his forces elsewhere. He knew in advance by word of mouth of the Duke's purposeful approach here; for this reason he quickly departed and sought out his Irish dominions. [18] The man whom folly had afflicted then lamented, often in silence. Afterwards, the full-grown King broke out into much blubbering. Our Duke thus returned while the timorous King was gone; nor was he in any way presumptuous for he was resuming his own rights.

How three especial favorites of the King were seized and beheaded at Bristol. In the throes of death they reproached the
King's character again and again.

With bold countenance and with the people following him, the noble
Duke examined the kingdom to see whether any traitor might be found.
He accordingly came upon three men, former oppressors of the realm,
odious, more ambitious than all others [170]: Scrope, Green, and
Bushy perished, struck down by the sword. They had been like royal
cronies of the King. As for Scrope, the Earl and Knight, Bristol pronounced his actions base, so death was to be his fate. [19] The Duke decreed that Green was to be decapitated in like fashion, and the convicted
Bushy suffered similar blows, too. One kind of death suddenly laid low
these three men of one mind. The sword ultimately consumed them,
and just as they had harassed others, so they fell [180]. For this the
Duke was praised, and everywhere the kingdom was glad. Nevertheless, there were a great many then hostile to Henry; they tried to resist, but could not. They often spoke out and threatened him behind
his back, but they did not dare when they looked upon his face.

How King Richard, returning from the realm of Ireland, reached
the shores of Wales.

With the situation like this, the King remained where he remained
before, [20] until his whole following trembled uneasily. Such highly in-
experienced men rarely become prompt in action; similarly, all these
men hesitated to be helped from any source. Fortune then turned her
wheel away from them [190] and remained blind while the King crossed
over the seas. His own guilt cast [him] back into those snares which
he had fashioned; he was to be ensnared when he reached the shores of
his fatherland. With the wind not hindering him, but, indeed, driving
him forth, destiny provided an especially fatal port for him. Wild
Wales received his ships into her clasp. She quickly let them go when
she took thought of the King's deeds. Casting his lot, the King was con-
fident of gaining allies, but he found none when he returned with no
graciousness. And when they saw him thus, some laughed amid rebellious murmur [200], and some wept, grieving at heart. His good fortune, which he had been unaware of, then forsook the royal pomp; each
man suddenly changed course and did not take up arms. Then as the
King spoke he cursed his fate with grief; henceforth, he neither feared
Christ nor renounced the world. He was not contrite, he was unwilling
to give up his ways: just as he previously had gone astray, so he

continued on. Thus he was beside himself with wickedness, always lawlessly dangerous; such had he been in the beginning, and such was he
at the end. Just as the sly fox attacks the sheep which he rushes upon
to wound [210], so for a long time the young King, with the cunning
spirit of an old man's guile, surreptitiously sought out every evil by
which he might destroy the kingdom. Above all, however, he plotted at
that time to gain consolation by thwarting the Duke's destiny and putting
his associates to flight. To this end, deceitfulness was explored and
trickery carried on, to try whether anything might help, under compulsion of necessity. Nowhere was there any help; just as a bone without
marrow wastes away, the King, who lacked power, for that reason
withered away without strength. He fled through fields and through
castles, and if at that time he had known how to ascend beyond the stars
[220], then he would have wanted to transcend them. Thus his lofty
tumidity, once so vaunted, became timidity, hiding out like a contempt-
ible mole. The man whom Christ does not preserve does not preserve
himself, no matter how belatedly I say these things about you, Richard.[21]

How King Richard and his hangers-on gave themselves up to the
noble Duke Henry, who met them in Wales.

Vigilant against dozing, let everyone hear what is being said, and
let what is to be said serve as an example for kingdoms. The wheel of
Fortune is to a certain extent like the regular action of the moon, which
first shines at night and afterwards grows dark. Thus did it turn out
for Richard himself, of whom I have been writing [230]: When he was
in his plenitude, the times were propitious for him; but when he waned,
the dark clouds were heedless of his light. When he subverted himself,
he perverted his sunken hopes. There was no advantage for him from
wars, since the land stood in rebellion toward him; nor was the sea of
any help to him, since the fleeing sailor hastened away. There was no
hope furnished forth for him; instead, on all sides the fates buffeted
him and precipitously plunged him to the depths. There were accordingly no secret places or restful castles which then were secure against
his future destiny. The end was at hand, the King was taken and made
captive [240]; and such others as were associated with him, who followed his fortunes, were carefully taken prisoner. Thus the thwarted
King was held in check by virtue of the Duke.

How the noble Henry, together with King Richard and others, came to London, where this King was placed in the Tower and remained for some time under custody.

The month of August brought it about that the city of London was rejoicing and singing the Duke's praises. On hand was a gathering of people like the sands of the sea, [22] blessing the deeds of the great and powerful victor. R[ichard] went into the Tower, remaining under custody; thus did the leader of the English lie fallen, he himself the least of the little.

How the noble Duke Henry kindly recalled to their rights whatever nobles had been sent into exile by King Richard.

In order that his action might be plain and of no vain import [250], the Duke put his hand to clearing away the grain to the granaries. [23] He praised the just and censured the unjust. Some he strengthened, some he put down, others he raised up. Out of his goodness the Duke restored the Archbishop of the kingdom, whom the King had uprooted with merciless severity. The Duke rightfully brought back him whom the King had taken away—Humphrey the son, expropriated after his father's death. [24] Do not despair for yourself as a banished heir, Arundel, for you are to recover your good fortunes through the good fortunes of the Duke. The Earl of Warwick, whose arraignment the good Duke recognized as without foundation [260], he removed safe from prison. And in the same fashion the Duke caused Cobham to be recalled. Delivered from exile, that honorable man returned, rescued through his mediating advocate Christ, not through entreaty or bribery. The gracious Duke effected these many beginnings of good things. In order that such worthy and gracious deeds might be continued above and beyond this, Christ caused the Duke's spirit to remain steadfast in this purpose.

How Parliament was summoned at Westminster at the Feast of St. Michael, which was then at hand. Meanwhile Humphrey, the son and heir of the Duke of Gloucester, died because of bodily illness, as did his mother.

The Feast of St. Michael then being at hand [25] in London, Parliament was summoned in order that everything might be safe there. Everyone awaited the destiny that fate held in store for him [270], and

319

there was constant grumbling among the people at the reigning King. Meanwhile, the aforesaid Humphrey died while crossing back and did not remain in this world; the blessed man returned to God. Because her son had died, his mother soon afterwards passed away in a blessed death, once she knew of her son's burial. The Swan died first; hence, grief for her cygnet overcame the mother, and death did not spare her in the least. It was said among the ancients, "A dead man has scarcely any friends;"[26] let every man therefore beware for himself in advance. Let every righteous man alive beat his breast [280]; then he will not be joyful, for he will see that all is vanity. It now remains to write of things which the world still manifests, in order that this work may be a universal mirror for all.

How King Richard did not personally appear on the first day of Parliament; but by staying elsewhere, he completely renounced his title to the Crown, in a valid and binding way. Because of this, the noble Henry was elected to become king, with all the people shouting in his praise.

The previously instituted Parliament was then resummoned; because of it Richard's distracted activity came to an end. Behold, on Tuesday[27] there was no appearance on his part. He whom guilt drove from the House was not sitting in his seat. Fortune then denied a place on the bench to the tyrant, whose agitated thoughts made him shrink from the sight of the people. R[ichard] did not appear, but so long as he might still hold out elsewhere [290], he parceled out blame, yet he yielded his sceptre to[28] H[enry]. The latter seated some other nobles as friends of justice; to them the suppressed man confessed with his own lips. The entire court surrendered R[ichard], who was found wanting, to these respected men and others duly chosen. They deposed him, since they knew him to be fully disgraced, [29] and no one exculpate him, lest by chance he were to rise again. Then H[enry], the glory of the English and the best of good men, was chosen King, since it was fitting. Sunday saw this Parliament held [300], and on that account it did not express itself, but thereupon recessed. H[enry] nevertheless decreed the next day as the time for holding a new Parliament. [30] Because of this, the glory of the kingdom increased. When he had been finally crowned and elevated, then there were to be official proceedings concerning what the court demanded judicially. Meanwhile the people lived on, cherishing the hope that the new King would abolish the previous wrongs.

How Parliament was continued until after the coronation.

It was the sixth day of October when the new King arranged the new Parliament he wished. It was a court of formal allegations, and not judicial [310]; [31] nothing at that time was binding or had the weight of authority. [32] It was propounded that nothing peaceful could be accomplished until the King's person might be openly crowned. At this, all the people sprang up and rejoiced in their hearts that he whom Christ wished to be venerated was to be crowned in this fashion.

How the noble Henry, having been elevated to the throne of royal majesty, was crowned amid complete joy on a festival day.
Note how the right to the Crown accrued to Henry IV, now our most blessed King, in three ways: first, by succession; second, by election; and third by conquest without bloodshed.

He Who disposes human affairs and allots the times appointed for them, He fixed the day on which He blessed Henry. God predestined him to whom He gave the title to reign as King and to deal justly toward his realms. He whom God chose proceeded to the royal honor [320]; hence, he was crowned and glorified with fame. The solemn rites could be spoken on that happy occasion, and they were publicly held during those sacred, blessed hours. The famous festival of Edward the Confessor witnessed the noble celebration of King Henry. [33] The people sang in their hearts and broke out into ringing speech; everyone worshipped Christ, since He had raised up this King. A man could scarcely conceive or think there were such great and solemn rites as then shone gloriously. All the earth sang out in jubilation and praised God [330] and the just and pious Henry, strong and bold. Why he was crowned is approved by threefold right: he conquered the realm, and because of this, right is clearly on his side; he succeeded as heir to the kingdom and has not abdicated from it; in addition, he was chosen by the people and thus firmly established. In order that there might be agreement, no legal measure was omitted. Everything was in accord, and gave solemn promise of Henry's rights. [34]

How Parliament was now continued.

His spreading fame grew and filled all climes, so that the glory of his banner took precedence over all. He ruled like a mighty lion

321

over the reprobate, like a lamb over the innocent [340]; he filled his
long-standing enemies with terror and multiplied his friends. The
moon provided the day on which the country crowned the King, and the
following Mars permitted the country to resummon Parliament. The
King took his seat and all the nobles sat allied with him, and the more
judicious commoners were present. Such was the occasion and the
general judgment. Nothing was legally rescinded which had been correctly provided for. The just man accordingly rejoiced, since he was
protected; and the others, the wicked, dolefully feared their condemnation.

How Henry, the first-born of King Henry, then acquired the name
and rank of Prince, with the consent of all.

But since it is more fitting to tell of this benevolent man first
[350], I shall first relate in writing of things which are more pleasant.
Blessed with honor, Henry the son of Henry was confirmed as heir
and named Prince. [35] Thus the part of the tree which had been cut off
was anointed in the sight of the highest Judge and rejoined to its former
trunk. That was foretold and prophesied by the saints; God then ful-
filled it, and the land grew peaceful because of it. A joyful England,
happy for this deed, became filled with wonder and rejoiced in its heart
that this scion was raised from the family stock.

How the present Parliament confirmed the things which the Duke
of Gloucester and his associates had done in Parliament earlier,
during the time of Richard. And the present Parliament also
rendered wholly null and void the things which Richard had decreed in his last Parliament.

Then by the consent of the King as well as the approval of the
nobles [360], with the people shouting concurrence, Parliament stood
in session as before. Recalling the deeds of the barons, they proceede
in similar fashion concerning the deeds which they saw were for the
public good: they declared fully valid those things which the Bear, the
Horse, and the Swan (who was termed righteous) had recently done.
And the entire court rejected those things which Richard had done
through perverse, overbearing, and treacherous guile. And then they
dealt with that wicked act through which the gentle Swan had unjustly
met his death a little while before. As though one man, [36] all the peop
clamored to have [370] the vindication of true justice for this death.

322

The general love on the part of the people and the uproar on all sides were heeded by the King and admitted at law.

How the others who had been with the condemned Richard were indicted for their wrongs. Nevertheless, they remained unmolested, because of the King's utter kindness.

The unfortunate Richard, ever more wicked, was then everywhere in disgrace, offensive to one and all. He withdrew like one adjudged guilty and condemned of transgression, so that the overbearing man was carried off to prison. [37] His hangers-on, who had been duly indicted, were then called upon for their responses. These particular respondents submitted themselves [380] to the judgment of the King, on whose part the vengeance of the law was silent. For the royal mercy so tempered its bounds in every way that no death penalty was allotted them. Their honored name which was once so dear to them, however, was taken away by decree of the English. Their persons remained unharmed but their petty fame vanished. Duke reverted to Earl—thus did the court crush opposition--and the odious Bagot met with ruin. The merciful King kindly set him back on his feet and prolonged his span of life. Thus did the good Henry, no enemy to an enemy [390], quite graciously confer favors instead of condemnation, as was fitting. He loosened his gentle rein, since the happy occasion demanded it, and he thought to have pleased Christ by so doing. [38] This was not pleasing to the people, however; with loud voice, public opinion said that mammon had gotten the better of the law. The people wished for justice to be done, the King wished to show compassion; and so for the time being, Fortune was not of one mind. The King was excused, for they said that he had been swayed by counsel to this effect, for which reason this particular affair quieted down.

How a short time after Parliament was concluded, certain wicked conspirators traitorously revolted, at the instigation of the devil, in order that they might drive the good King Henry and his descendants from the land. The wrath of God came upon them in the City of Cirencester, miraculously destroying them at the hands of the mob.

Four authors of crime, more infamous than Judas [400], uttered praises with their lips [but] treacheries silently in their hearts. Like the bitterness of gall, Holland, Kent, Salisbury, and Spenser drew up agreements by which they sought to mislead Henry. [39] Those whom the good Henry let live and did no evil against, they hurled evils upon him, expecting him to meet with destruction. H[enry] indeed conferred peace upon them, while they were readying their arms, hoping for his imminent death. Thus did the highly ungrateful men return evil for good, although vengeance for the evil was upon their heads. For He Who knows the hearts of all men [410] laid bare their secrets. [40] Great punishment befell them. When they arose and intended sudden injury, they immediately lost their lives, once the danger had been seen. The assemblage was scattered into different places. God did away with them, yet He performed no miracles in this: The four arrogant men perished when beheaded by the country's people, with the Son of Mary concomitant. Behold the handiwork of God! Like one man, [41] the people arose on every side, in order that H[enry] might thus be protected.

How the King's sons were then saved a second time, in the Mayor of London's custody, for the sake of their own security.

The citizens of London [420] remained firm friends of the noble Henry, a fact which was very dear [to him]. The King gave orders and those at hand were quickly provided with arms, and they assembled a great company on his behalf. The city was then his helpmeet, and protected the King's sons like a nurse and cherished them like a mother. At this time the city was indeed a veritable chamber for the King; putting his trust in it, he was much pleased. So pious in Christ, he sensed the piety of its deed, so that he was saved and the kingdom made glorious. As though rousing from sleep, every Englishman sang out [430]; R[ichard] fell, H[enry] ruled, hence the realm was full of joy.

How Richard, when he heard of the recent death of those who had perished at Cirencester, put an end to himself by refusing all food in his anguish of grief.

At the time these things were being done Richard did not go forth into action, even when he recognized his dangers. Because the fate of his false companions was sealed, he wept for their deaths and scorned Fortune. He then saw full well that no false pretense was of any use to him; he grieved sorrowfully, as though overburdened with death. Behold, such was his grief that no hope of any kind could divert him from weeping while he yet lived. Nevertheless, the guards who were at his side often gave him aid [440], lest he were to fall into despair as he

prolonged his sorrows. But while he was shedding tears he neither
took comfort from their words nor looked kindly on their affections for
himself. He thus consumed himself, for he scarcely took food, nor did
he drink wine of his own accord whereby he might live. [42] Indeed, he
constantly wept, he constantly suffered from the fate to which he was
fallen, and he called to mind such of his comrades as had perished.
He sought only death, lest he might live longer, and thus his dying
pomp was laid to rest. England rejoiced that Christ had overthrown
him whom the people had greatly feared [450]; hence, the free land was
at peace. But in reverence to Christ, the worthy Henry, always a
friend to piety, caused his body to be buried with solemn ceremony, although without honor or praise. Langley is witness that Richard is
buried there. [43] It bestowed in a most special place the body which the
world at large refused to accept. Thus did the merciful and imperial
H[enry] kindly return good for evil to him who had concluded the last of
his life. The dead R[ichard] passed away, and the worthy H[enry] remained alive [460]; God extolled him, and took away R[ichard]'s good
fortunes.

Note here the goodness of the most blessed King Henry and the
wickedness with which, according to common report, the cruel
Richard tyrannically harassed his kingdom as long as he could.

If he be closely scrutinized through weighing and taking note of
various character traits, O how different R[ichard] seems from H[enry]!
Brilliant of speech yet inwardly dark with suffering, R[ichard] made a
pretense of peace even as he drew tight the bonds of death. R[ichard]
let loose destruction and the merciful H[enry] forsook bloodshed.
R[ichard] decreed servitude, and the merciful H[enry], well-being.
R[ichard] laid taxes upon the people and the merciful H[enry] alleviated
their taxes. R[ichard] hated the nobles and plundered their estates
[470]; H[enry] cherished them and restored their heirs to their homes.
The vindictive R[ichard] laid waste his kingdom and stood over everyone; H[enry] mitigated fear and brought back brotherly love. O God,
grant to Henry, whom I cherish and bless, a safe kingdom overturned
by no kind of violence. Grant him whatever happiness there is both for
this present life and likewise for the life to come. [44]

Here at the end he recapitulates, citing Richard's failings as an example for others.

This chronicle of Richard, who bore the sceptre of the lion, [45] was uttered by the people, as is clear; but his chronicle has not been a blessed one. Like the mirror of the world, to which no reflection can be restored [480], he passed away a blank, with nothing but blame remaining for his portion. Because he was haughty his honor has grown tarnished, his praise has become blame, his glory has died away, even if he now were to seek approval. Let those who are wise beware as they look upon this, for God abominates rulers on earth who live evilly. He who is a sinner cannot be a ruler; as Richard is my witness, his end proves this clearly. [46] Because of his faults, his senseless pomp met with ruin. Such was his life; this chronicle will stand accordingly.

Here ends the Chronicle, which is to be heeded with a watchful heart by kings both present and future.

TABLE OF ABBREVIATIONS

Am.	Ovid, Amores
Ars Amat.	Ovid, Ars Amatoria
AYLI	Shakespeare, As You Like It
Bal.	Gower, Cinkante Balades
BD	Chaucer, Book of the Duchess
Cant. Tales	Chaucer, Canterbury Tales
Carmen	Gower, "Carmen Super Multiplici Viciorum Pestilencia"
Chron.	Chronicles
Conf.	Gower, Confessio Amantis
Cons. Phil.	Boethius, De Consolatione Philosophiae
Cor.	Corinthians
Coxe	H. O. Coxe, ed. Poema Quod Dicitur Vox Clamantis, Necnon Chronica Tripertita, Auctore Johanne Gower
CT	Gower, Cronica Tripertita
CYT	Chaucer, Canon's Yeoman's Tale
Dan.	Daniel
Deut.	Deuteronomy
DNB	Dictionary of National Biography
Eccl.	Ecclesiastes
Ecclus.	Ecclesiasticus
Eph.	Ephesians
Etym.	Isidore, Etymologiae
Ex., Exod.	Exodus
Ezek.	Ezekiel
FrT	Chaucer, Friar's Tale
Gal.	Galatians
Gen.	Genesis
Gen Prol	Chaucer, General Prologue to The Canterbury Tales
Heb.	Hebrews
Her.	Ovid, Heroides
Hos.	Hosea
Inf.	Dante, Inferno
Is.	Isaiah
Isa.	Isaiah
Jer.	Jeremiah
Josh.	Joshua
Jud.	Judges
KT	Chaucer, Knight's Tale
Lear	Shakespeare, King Lear

Lev.	Leviticus
Macc., Mach.	Maccabees
Mars	Chaucer, The Complaint of Mars
Matt.	Matthew
MerchT	Chaucer, Merchant's Tale
Metam.	Ovid, Metamorphoses
MillT	Chaucer, Miller's Tale
Mir., Mirour	Gower, Mirour de l'Omme
MLT	Chaucer, Man of Law's Tale
MLN	Modern Language Notes
Mum	Mum and the Sothsegger
NPT	Chaucer, Nun's Priest's Tale
Num.	Numbers
Par.	Dante, Paradiso
PardT	Chaucer, Pardoner's Tale
ParsT	Chaucer, Parson's Tale
Piers	Piers Plowman
P. L.	Milton, Paradise Lost
Pont.	Ovid, Ex Ponto
PP	Gower, "In Praise of Peace"
Prov.	Proverbs
Ps., Psa.	Psalms
Purg.	Dante, Purgatorio
Rem. Am.	Ovid, Remedia Amoris
Rev.	Revelation
Rom	Chaucer, Romance of the Rose
Rom.	Romans
Romeo	Shakespeare, Romeo and Juliet
RvT	Chaucer, Reeve's Tale
Sam.	Samuel
Sat.	Juvenal, Satires
Smith-Heseltine	Oxford Dictionary of English Proverbs
TC	Gower, The Tripartite Chronicle
Tim.	Timothy
Traitie'	Gower, Traitie' Pour Essampler Les Amantz Marietz
Troilus	Chaucer, Troilus and Criseyde
Voice	Gower, The Voice of One Crying
Vox	Gower, Vox Clamantis
WBT	Chaucer, Wife of Bath's Prologue and Tale

Notes to the Introduction

[1] 4 vols.,(Oxford, 1899-1902), IV, viii-xxx. Vol. I contains the French works, Vols. II and III the Confessio Amantis and "In Praise of Peace, " and Vol. IV the Vox Clamantis, Cronica Tripertita, and minor Latin works. All references are to this edition, unless otherwise noted, and it is the basis of the present translations.

[2] JEGP, LVIII (Jan. 1959), 1-23. Professor Fisher is working on a complete biography of Gower.

[3] Fisher, "Calendar, " pp. 2-7.

[4] Fisher, p. 5.

[5] Fisher, p. 18.

[6] See, for example, Anthony Steel, Richard II (Cambridge, England, 1941), p. 57.

[7] See Ernst Robert Curtius, European Literature and the Latin Middle Ages, trans. Willard R. Trask, Bollingen Series 36 (New York: Pantheon, 1953), pp. 83-85.

[8] See Macaulay's n. to Confessio Amantis, IV. 1741; and to his references may be added I. 1164-66; III. 991 ff.; and VIII. 1890.

[9] Quoted in Macaulay, "Life of Gower, " Works, IV, xvii.

[10] Johan Vising, Anglo-Norman Language and Literature (London, 1923), says flatly that Gower "spent considerable time in Paris" (p. 82); but he may have been relying on the fact of the collar. (Gower's effigy on his tomb still wears such a collar.)

329

[11] Macaulay, "Life of Gower, " Works, IV, xxvi.

[12] This practice was common in the Middle Ages. Piers Plowman is another example.

[13] In English Writers (London, Paris, New York and Melbourne: Cassell, 1889), Vol. IV, Part I, pp. 166-167. The same volume contains a fuller description of the Cinkante Balades (pp. 161-168).

[14] Macaulay's n. to Balade LI, in Works, I, 470.

[15] In a passage of Latin prose at the end of the Confessio Amantis, Works, III, 479.

[16] Professor J. A. W. Bennett, "The Date of the B-Text of Piers Plowman, " Medium Aevum, XII (1943), 55-64; Bernard Huppe, "The Date of the B-Text of Piers Plowman, " Studies in Philology, XXXVIII (1941), 33-44. Gower's reference is thus about as early as Langland's. Both poets mention Robin Hood only to attack the interest in him.

[17] The genealogy of Sin and Death (ll. 205 ff.) is strikingly like that in Paradise Lost, II. 757 ff.

[18] The elaborate hierarchies of sins in the two poems are so similar that the resemblance was important in enabling Macaulay to identify the poem as Gower's long lost Mirour; see Works, I, xxxvi-ii.

[19] G. R. Owst, Literature and the Pulpit in Medieval England (Cambridge, England, 1933), pp. 230-231, quoted in George R. Coffman, "John Gower in His Most Significant Role, " Univ. of Colorado Studies, Series B (Studies in the Humanities), Vol. II, No. 4 (1945), p. 53

[20] I know of none longer in either language.

[21] Macaulay, in Works, IV, lxi. The MSS of the Vox Clamantis are fully described in IV, lx-lxxi, and are referred to by Macaulay and the notes to these translations as follows: S (All Souls College, Oxf. 98), G (Glasgow Hunterian Museum T. 2, 17), C (Cotton Tiberius A. iv), H (Harleian 6291), E (Ecton), D (Digby 138, Bodleian), L (Laud 719, Bodleian), L_2 (Lincoln Cathedral Library, A. 72), T (Trinity College, Dublin, D. 4, 6), H_2 (Hatfield Hall), and C_2 (Cotton, Titus, A, 13). MSS. for the Cronica Tripertita are SCHG, as for the Vox Clamantis, and also H_3 (Hatton 92, Bodleian).

[22] But see T. R. Lounsbury, Studies in Chaucer, 3 vols. (New York, 1892), III, 70: "The mere fact that no edition of the "Confessio Amantis" appeared from 1554 until 1857 [this ignores Chalmers' edition in British Poets, 1810] disposes of itself the fancy that Gower's popularity ever stood for a moment in rivalry with that of Chaucer. Caxton had, indeed, printed his poem. During the sixteenth century two other editions of it appeared. These were sufficient to supply the demand for that time and for the three hundred years that followed. " All the early allusions to Gower deal with him mainly as an English poet, and frequently place him on a par with Chaucer. Allusions from the fifteenth and sixteenth centuries are collected in Works, II, viii-ix. For a fuller list see Heinrich Spies, "Bisherige Ergebnisse und Weitere Aufgaben der Gower-Forschung, " Englische Studien, XXVIII (1900), 163-174, 207-208. See also Coffman, "John Gower in His Most Significant Role, " p. 52, n. 3. For later criticism see The Library of Literary Criticism, ed. Charles W. Moulton (Buffalo, 1901), I, 172-177.

Three recent and somewhat unexpected allusions may also be mentioned here: Ezra Pound, A B C of Reading (London, 1934), p. 88; Aldous Huxley, Eyeless in Gaza (New York, 1936), p. 105; Clifton Fadiman, Any Number Can Play (Cleveland, 1957), p. 386.

The most hostile reader, and therefore ignored by Gower scholars, is Coleridge: "I have never seen Lydgate's Troy Boke, published in 1513, but deeply regret that Mr. A. Chalmers [who edited the British Poets, 1810] had not substituted the whole of Lydgate's works from the MSS. extant, for the almost worthless Gower" (in Coleridge's Shakespearean Criticism, ed. Thomas Middleton Raysor [London: Constable, 1930], I, 108). It may be added in Coleridge's defense that only a man who had not read Lydgate's Troy Boke could make that statement.

[23] This English version of the title has some currency, as does that of The Tripartite Chronicle, in histories of literature. There is, indeed, no ready alternative to either, though Thomas Warton calls the Vox Clamantis the Voice of one crying in the Wilderness (History of English Poetry, Sec. XIX).

[24] Matt. 3: 3, Mark 1: 3, Luke 3: 4, and John 1: 23.

[25] Maria Wickert, Gower Studien (Kölner Universitäts Verlag, 1953), pp. 65 ff.

[26] See, for example, the heading of Chap. 23, Book VII.

[27] IV, xxxi-xxxii and lxvii.

[28] Page xxxii.

[29]He refers to the Great Schism much later once more in his "In Praise of Peace, " ll. 230 and 254 ff. (see Works, III, 488-489).

[30]On this accusation see Wickert, Gower Studien, Chap. 4, and George R. Coffman, "John Gower, Mentor for Royalty: Richard II" PMLA, LXIX (1954), 953-964.

[31]Wickert, in Gower Studien, says that these revisions were made after 1390 but that they portray the situation of about 1387 (p. 23).

[32]It was understood as such quite early: The heading of MS. Cotton, Titus, A, 13, is "De populari tumultu et rebellione. Anno quarto Ricardi secundi. "

[33]Quoted below in the note to these lines.

[34]George G. Fox, The Mediaeval Sciences in the Works of John Gower (Princeton, 1931), p. 111, says that Gower is in general uncritical about dreams, accepting them as supernatural revelations to man concerning what is to come.

[35]It was of course conventional to allegorize people as animals and birds. Gower does much the same thing later in The Tripartite Chronicle.

[36]There are analogous rescues or escapes by ship in Lydgate's Pilgrimage of the Life of Man, Thomas Usk's Testament of Love, and Dante, Purgatorio, 2.

[37]See Macaulay's n. on Confessio Amantis, I. 62.

[38]This discussion of the three visions is much indebted to Wickert Gower Studien, Chap. 2.

[39]Cf. The Tripartite Chronicle, III. 278-281.

[40]Still another theme is found in George R. Coffman, "John Gower in His Most Significant Role, " 52-56: "His most significant role is his explanation and illustration of the ethical basis of God's universe for this little world of man" (p. 60). Man's ethics are to be guided primarily by his reason, which will lead him to wisdom and virtue (pp. 53-55). Gower, however, usually places faith as superior to reason, as in The Voice of One Crying, Book II, Chap. 9.

[41] See for example Chaucer's "The Former Age" or his Clerk's Tale, 1139-40. All references to Chaucer are, unless otherwise noted, to The Works of Geoffrey Chaucer, ed. F. N. Robinson, 2nd ed. (Boston, 1957).

[42] See also II. 199-216.

[43] William Allan Neilson and Charles Jarvis Hill, eds. The Complete Plays and Poems of William Shakespeare (Boston: 1942), p. xvii. For the whole question of Fortune, see H. R. Patch, The Tradition of the Goddess Fortuna in Medieval Philosophy and Literature, Smith College Studies in Modern Languages, Vol. III, No. 4 (Northampton, Mass., 1922).

[44] Wickert, pp. 75 ff.

[45] The words of the people become vulgi vaniloqui sermones in V. 282, for example.

[46] As Chaucer's Summonour puts it, "Purs is the ercedekenes helle" (General Prologue, 658).

[47] The present translations and notes will indicate that Gower's love of peace has been exaggerated, though he has somewhat the reputation of a pacifist. He is too patriotic an Englishman not to look back nostalgically upon the days of Crécy and Poitiers; and in VI, Chap 13, he hopes that Richard II will emulate the military glory of his father, the Black Prince.

[48] In Confessio Amantis, IV. 2222-26, Gower echoes the old rhyme with approval.

[49] Gower had already done much the same thing in the Mirour, 6289 ff., though Avarice's "daughters" are not as effectively portrayed there. The daughters themselves are as old as Prudentius.

[50] Gower sustains the motif but feebly in Book VII; he tells the biblical story well in Confessio Amantis, I. 2786 ff. It is also briefly told in Piers Plowman, B Passus VII. 151-158. Cf. also Mirour, 1885-95 and Chaucer's Monk's Tale, 2143-82, and see n. on VII. 5-6.

[51] Gower probably took it from St. Gregory, Moralia, VI, 6. See Macaulay's n. on Confessio, Prol. 945 ff.

[52] VII. 1479*-80*.

[53] The poem is summarized at greater length by Macaulay in IV, xxxiv-lvii, and by Morley in English Writers, Vol. IV, Book I, pp. 177-192.

[54] As did a character in Theodore Morrison's novel, To Make a World (New York: Viking, 1957).

[55] Pages 48-49.

[56] W. P. Ker, Epic and Romance (New York: Dover, 1957), p. 346.

[57] Robert Dudley French, A Chaucer Handbook, 2nd ed. (New York: Crofts, 1947), p. 26. "Shrewdness" is too polite a word, unless one gives it its Middle English meaning, too: More than seven thousand victims were executed in the summer of 1381, as punishment for the Great Revolt.

[58] A. R. Myers, England in the Late Middle Ages (Harmondsworth, Middlesex: Penguin, 1952), p. xiv.

[59] G. M. Trevelyan, England in the Age of Wycliffe, 4th ed. (London, 1915), pp. 83-84; Encyclopaedia Britannica, 13th ed., s. v. "Wycliffe."

[60] Cf. Vox Clamantis, Book IV, and Wycliffe's Vae Octuplex, in Select English Works, ed. Thomas Arnold, 3 vols. (Oxford, 1869), II, 379-389.

[61] Gower condemns Lollardy further in his Confessio, V. 1803 ff., and in "Carmen Super Multiplici Viciorum Pestilencia, " 13 ff.

[62] Works, IV, xxxii-xxxiii.

[63] See Wickert, Gower Studien, pp. 174 ff., and Norman Callan, "Thyne Owne Book: A Note on Chaucer, Gower, and Ovid, " RES, XXII (1946), 269-281. It is worth mentioning here that the Latin and English poems of Gower usually borrow from different passages in Ovid, with surprisingly little overlapping.

[64] Page xxxiii.

[65] Ibid. The same can be said of his use of the Aurora.

[66] For example, illesos artus (I. 2063) occurs in Metamorphoses, XII. 489; formam rotundam (VII. 557) occurs in Fasti, VI. 280. Such examples could be multiplied.

[67] E. g., I. 2131 is a mixture of Metamorphoses, IV. 749, and Fasti, III. 595.

[68] Paul E. Beichner, C. S. C., "The Old French Verse Bible of Macé de la Charité, a translation of the Aurora, " Speculum, XXII (1947), 227. Karl Young, "Chaucer and Peter Riga, " Speculum, XII (1937), 299, also stresses the popularity of the Aurora. (Chaucer refers to it in BD, 1169.)

[69] "Gower's Use of Aurora in Vox Clamantis, " Speculum, XXX (1955), 582-595.

[70] Both poems are found in Thomas Wright, ed. The Anglo-Latin Satirical Poets and Epigrammatists of the Twelfth Century, 2 vols., Rolls Series No. 59 (London, 1872). The Speculum Stultorum was long attributed to Nigel Wireker.

[71] "Gower's Vox Clamantis and the Speculum Stultorum, " MLN, LXX (1955), 315-320. See also his "Mors Solvit Omnia, " MLN, LXXI (1956), 249.

[72] Grace W. Landrum, "Chaucer's Use of the Vulgate, " PMLA, XXXIX (1924), 75-100.

[73] Maria E. Neville, "The Vulgate and Gower's Confessio Amantis, " Ohio State Univ. Abstracts of Dissertations, No. 64 (for Summer Quarter, 1950-51) (Columbus, 1953), 387-398.

[74] On Gower's literary art in that poem see C. S. Lewis, The Allegory of Love (Oxford, 1936), pp. 198-222; Peter Frison, "The Poet in John Gower, " Essays in Criticism, VIII (1958), 16-26.

[75] "Gower's Use of Aurora in Vox Clamantis, " pp. 592-593.

[76] The Confessio Amantis embodies a similar flaw. The penitential structure is firmly outlined, but the examples confuse sins of Courtly Love with those of Christianity. Near the end of the poem, digressions become encyclopedic.

[77] J. M. Manly, "Chaucer and the Rhetoricians," Proceedings of the British Academy, XII (1926), 95-113.

[78] For the subject see Edmond Faral, Les Arts Poetiques du XIIe et du XIIIe Siecle (Paris, 1924). The text of the Poetria Nova is given on pp. 197-262. It was known to Chaucer.

[79] This has been done for the Confessio Amantis. See R. S. Daniels, Figures of Rhetoric in John Gower's English Works, unpubl. Yale diss., 1934. I have not seen the diss.

[80] Fifty-two of these are from Gotthard Walz, Das Sprichwort bei Gower, Munich diss., 1907. Walz's numberings of the proverbs are given.

[81] See B. J. Whiting, Chaucer's Use of Proverbs (Cambridge, Mass.: 1934). Gower's proverbs in his English and French works are treated on pp. 134-154 and 293-297.

[82] The image of the wolf devouring the fold, whether in sheep's clothing or in propria persona, was an extremely common one in medieval times, and often overworked (as in Gower). The Albigensian Crusade, for example, was to destroy the wolf and drive the wayward sheep back to the fold: See H. J. Chaytor, The Troubadours (Cambridge, Eng., 1917) p. 78; Dean Milman, Latin Christianity, Book IX, Chap. 8.

[83] Kenneth H. Vickers, England in the Later Middle Ages (London: Methuen, 1913), p. 234. The comment is made with regard to Gower's criticism of the friars, but is true in general as well.

[84] Quarterly Review, No. 394 (April, 1903), 437-458; reprinted in Essays on Medieval Literature (London, 1905).

[85] Pages xxxiii-xxxiv. Cf. Warton, History of English Poetry, Sec. XIX: "He . . . copied Ovid's elegiacs with some degree of purity, and with fewer false quantities and corrupt phrases, than any of our countrymen had yet exhibited since the twelfth century."

[86] The present writer hopes to demonstrate elsewhere that Gower's Confessio is much indebted to Chaucer's Troilus, which was finished c. 1386.

[87] See the concluding Latin prose paragraphs attached to the Confessio, in Works, III, 479-480.

[88] See n. 74 above.

[89] On this poem and its headnote see Coffman, "John Gower, Mentor for Royalty, " pp. 955-958.

[90] A picture of Gower's effigy may be seen in Richard Garnett, English Literature: An Illustrated Record, 4 vols. (London and New York, 1903), I, 177. See also Fisher, "Calendar, " pp. 3, 6.

[91] Macaulay, "Life of Gower, " pp. xvii-xix.

[92] Gower: Selections from the Confessio Amantis, ed. G. C. Macaulay (Oxford: Clarendon Press, 1903), p. 1.

[93] On this poem see Coffman, "Mentor, " pp. 958-964.

[94] The poem "Eneidos Bucolis" (p. 361) is not by Gower, and Macaulay conjectures that Ralph Strode wrote it, Strode having been known as a writer of elegiacs. Adding weight to this conjecture is the epithet morigeris in l. 6, as a possible echo of Chaucer's dedication of his Troilus and Criseyde to the "moral Gower" and the "philosophical Strode" (V. 1856-57).

[95] MSS. SCHG, as for the Vox Clamantis, and MS. Hatton 92, Bodleian Library (H_3); see Works, IV, lix-lxxi, for a description of these. The two earlier editions are described on pp. lxxv-lxxvi.

[96] These facts about the royal grants of wine and the interpretation of the "Epistola breuis" are due to Fisher, "Calendar, " p. 22.

[97] Macaulay's n. to Cronica Tripertita, II. 231 f.

[98] Hawthorne (New York and London, 1899), pp. 61-62.

[99] Ed. Mabel Day and Robert Steele, EETS, O. S. No. 199 (Oxford, 1936). The question of possible relationship between this poem and the Cronica Tripertita needs further study.

[100] See for example "On King Richard's Ministers" in Political Poems and Songs, ed. Thomas Wright, 2 vols. (London, 1859-61).

[101] Cobham, whose name was Sir John Oldcastle, was long confused with the prototype of Falstaff.

[102] See n. on III. 286.

[103] See n. on III. 486.

[104] Coffman, "Mentor, " takes a kinder attitude toward Gower's ministrations.

[105] Macaulay, "Life, " p. xvii.

[106] On these records see Fisher, "Calendar, " pp. 22-23.

[107] Gower had already used this stanzaic pattern in French and in "The Lover's Supplication to Venus, " Confessio Amantis, VIII. 2217-2300.

[108] See n. 22 above.

[109] Examples of important offenders are: James Russell Lowell, "Chaucer, " in My Study Windows (Boston, 1871), pp. 258-260; J. J. Jusserand, A Literary History of the English People (London, 1925), I, 264-72.

[110] These are KT, 2459; ClT, 995-1001; NPT, 3394-96; Troilus, IV. 183-84.

[111] On the question of Gower's knowledge of Italian, see nn. on Voice, II. 67-68, and V. 143-144. It may be added here that Gower's reference to Dante in the Confessio, VII. 2329* ff., does not seem based upon an Italian source. Rather, the marginal note, "Nota exemplum cuiusdam poete de Ytalia, qui Dante vocatur, " sounds suspiciously like Chaucer's WBT, 1125-26, though that work is approximately three years later than the first recension of the Confessio. It is worth noting that Gower drops the passage at the same time he omits the compliment to Chaucer.
See also Macaulay's n. on Confessio, II. 3095.

[112] See n. 72 above.

[113] A. C. Baugh, ed. A Literary History of England (New York: and London, 1948), p. 252.

[114] Macaulay, Works, III, 519, in n. to Confessio, VI. 1789 ff.

[115] John Edwin Wells, A Manual of the Writings in Middle English 1050-1400 (New Haven, 1926), p. 600; cf. J. L. Lowes, Geoffrey Chaucer and the Development of His Genius (Boston, 1934), p. 111.

[116] See n. on Voice, IV. 277-282.

[117] Voice, III. 1431 ff. The passage is from a longer one all in the same vein.

[118] WBT, 26-29. On the Wife and her Prologue cf. also Confessio, V. 455 ff.

[119] Cf. C. S. Lewis, "What Chaucer Really Did to Il Filostrato, " Essays and Studies, XVII (1932), 57-58.

[120] On Chaucer as a moral teacher see George R. Stewart, "The Moral Chaucer, " Univ. of California Publications in English (Berkeley, 1929), I, 91-109.

[121] Macaulay's n. on Confessio, I. 2176.

[122] Macaulay, in Works, IV, lxxvii.

[123] Poema Quod Dicitur Vox Clamantis, Necnon Chronica Tripertita, Auctore Johanne Gower (London: Roxburghe Club, 1850), p. xlii.

Notes to the DEDICATORY EPISTLE

[1]Dedicatory Epistle. "This Epistle, written apparently on the occasion of sending a copy of the book to the archbishop, is found only in the All Souls MS., and it is reasonable to suppose that this was the copy in question. . . . The piece is full of erasures . . . but the corrections are in the same hand as the rest. Having no other copy of it, we cannot tell what the original form of the erased passages [i.e.,ll. 8-11, 20, and 26-34] may have been, but it is noticeable that the most important of them (ll. 26-34) has reference almost entirely to the blindness of the author, and nearly every one contains something which may be regarded as alluding to this, either some mention of light and darkness, or some allusion to the fact that his only perceptions now are those of the mind. We may perhaps conclude that the Epistle was inscribed here before the author quite lost his eyesight, and that the book then remained by him for some time [i.e. underwent alterations] before it was presented. The illuminated capital S with which this composition begins is combined with a miniature painting of the archbishop" (Macaulay's note, p. 369). (Hereafter, any footnote or portion of a footnote enclosed within quotation marks but with no reference given will be understood to be quoted from Macaulay's footnote for the line or lines in question. This is done to avoid repetition of Macaulay's name several hundred times, for I quote nearly all his footnotes in whole or in part.) Macaulay's notes are to be found in IV, 369-416 of his edition of the Complete Works.

The All Souls MS (S) was used as the basis for Macaulay's edition of Vox Clamantis, and he says of it (Works, IV, lxi), "This MS. was certainly written and corrected under the direction of the author, and remained for some time in his hands, receiving additions from time to time."

Archbishop Thomas Arundel was impeached and exiled by Richard II in September, 1397, during the "Second Tyranny." He went to Paris and joined with Henry of Lancaster, who re-established him as Primate in 1399. See The Tripartite Chronicle, Parts II and III.

The Epistle could have been written before Arundel's exile, but more likely it was written after he returned. First, Gower would presumably have wanted him to have a copy of the Tripartite Chronicle, which the MS contains, and in which the Archbishop himself figures. Second, in l. 18 Gower speaks of himself as totally blind, and he is thought to have been blind "probably from the year 1400" (p. xxix).

The Epistle is written in leonine hexameters, the meter of The Tripartite Chronicle.

[2]Epistle. 1. The Thomas to whom Arundel was successor was surely St. Thomas à Becket, whose martyrdom is compared to that of Archbishop Sudbury in Voice, I. 1055-78.

[3]Epistle. 5-6. A reference to the Great Schism, which began in 1378. See Voice, III. 3-6.

There is a play in l. 6 upon peruertit ("destroys") and vertit ("turns").

[4]Epistle. 8-11. Ll. 8-11 are written over erasure.

[5]Epistle. 15. The word "mirror" is here understood in its frequent medieval sense of "picture of the world." Cf. TC, III. 480.

[6]Epistle. 20. L. 20 is written over erasure.

[7]Epistle. 28. There is a play in l. 28 upon diuisus ("sundered") and visus (sight").

[8]Epistle. 31-32. This sentence is probably an allusion to Matt. 5: 14-15. Cf. Mark 4: 21; Luke 8: 16, 11: 33.

In these notes references are given to the King James Version of the Bible (including the Apocrypha) whenever Gower quotes or alludes to the Scriptures. If the Vulgate numbering of chapter and verse differs from the King James Version, such difference is pointed out. If there is a significant difference between the meaning of the two versions, the Vulgate is paraphrased or quoted, from the "Vatican" or "Clementine" edition: Bibliorum Sacrorum Iuxta Vulgatam Clementinam Nova Editio, ed. Aloisius Gramatica (Milan, 1929).

[9]Epistle. 35. The word Arundella in l. 35 is here taken as a noun. But it could be taken either as an adjective, formed upon the basis of the Archbishop's name and modifying "light, " or as "swallow, " with a punning reference to the name. In the latter case, the translation would read, "The Swallow, which shines like the sun with new light . . . . " But this latter alternative is less likely, although Gower uses hirundo ("swallow") for the name Arundel in the Tripartite Chronicle, I. 215. The Latin form of the name itself is consistently Arundellia in that poem.

[10]Epistle. 37. L. 37 involves a pun upon Mas ("manly") and Thomas. This name meant "twin" in Latin; but Gower would not have to have known this fact to make his punning etymology of "a second Mas" or "doubly Mas. "

341

[11]Epistle. 49. After the Epistle in S and in five other MSS, namely CEHGD, a table of contents is given which for the most part duplicates the chapter headings as given in the text, and which is therefore not reproduced here. Macaulay points out some of the "slight" differences in his notes on p. 270 under CAPITULA.

After the table of contents, but preceding the Prologue to Book I, MSS. CEG have a drawing of a bearded man, probably resembling Gower, who is pointing a bow and arrow at a globe. The globe is divided vertically. Probably the lower half of the globe represents the masses or peasantry, while one upper quarter represents the clergy and the other the nobility. Above the archer and his globe appear four leonine hexameters in Latin which may be translated as follows:

> I hurl my darts at the world and I shoot my arrows;
> Yet where there is a just man, no arrow strikes.
> But I wound those transgressors who live evilly;
> Therefore, let him who is conscious of being in the wrong look to
> himself in that respect.

MS. L contains the picture and lines at the beginning of Book III. This page in MS. C is reproduced as the frontispiece of Macaulay's edition of the Latin Works. On these verses see Wickert, pp. 79 ff.

Notes to BOOK I

Prologue

[1]I. Prol. 1-2. Cf. Conf., Prol. 1-11, and Rom. 15: 4.

[2]I. Prol. 4. Proverbial (Walz no. 114b). "Cp. Conf. Amantis, iv. 2921 f. . . . " Cf. also Chaucer, Rom, 1-20. For the negative, cf. Troilus, V. 360-385 and 1276-77; NPT, 2940-41, 2969. All references to Chaucer are to The Works of Geoffrey Chaucer, ed. F. N. Robinson, 2nd ed. (Boston, 1957), unless otherwise noted. These notes make reference where possible to G. Walz, Das Sprichwort bei Gower, Munich diss., 1907. Walz's line references must be used with extreme caution.

[3]I. Prol. 7-8. These dreams are a commonly used motif. Cf. Villon, Ballade V. 4; Dante, Inf., XIV. 103-110, and Par., IV. 13-15.

For Daniel's interpretation of Nebuchadnezzar's dreams, see Dan. 2: 25 ff. Book VII of The Voice of One Crying is largely based upon a symbolic interpretation of his dream of the statue. Cf. VII. 5-6,

106-112, 136, 353-354, 1379.

    With I. Prol. 7-8 cf. Piers Plowman, B. Passus VII, 151-167, where Daniel and Joseph are likewise referred to as proof that dream interpretation is valid. Cf. also Chaucer, NPT, 3127-37 and BD, 280ff.

    For Joseph's two dreams, see Gen. 37: 5-10. I. Prol. 8 can also be translated, "Nor was Joseph's insight into dreams meaningless, " in which case Gower's line would refer to Gen. 40: 5-41: 57.

[4] I. Prol. 13. Cf. ll. 2049-50 below.

[5] I. Prol. 21-24. "We are here told to add to 'John' the first letters of 'Godfrey, ' the beginning of 'Wales, ' and the word 'Ter' without its head: that is, 'John Gower. '"

[6] I. Prol. 33-34. "Taken from Ovid, Tristia, v. I. 5-6. " See Arthur Leslie Wheeler, ed. and trans., Ovid: With an English Trans- lation: Tristia, Ex Ponto (Loeb Classical Library, London: William Heineman; New York: Putman, 1924), p. 209: "Mournful is my state, mournful therefore is my song, for the work is suited to its theme. " All subsequent translations from this, the Loeb edition of Ovid's Tristia and Ex Ponto, will be cited as "Wheeler. "

    The idea was proverbial. Cf. Chaucer, Gen Prol, 742: "The wordes moote be cosyn to the dede. " Professor Robinson notes fur- ther examples of the same idea. Cf. III. Prol. 95.

[7] I. Prol. 36. Adapted from Ovid, "Tristia, i. I. 14. " For paral- lels to the idea, see n. on II. 1.

[8] I. Prol. 37-38. "This couplet was originally Tristia, iv. I. 95 f.,

    'Saepe etiam lacrimae me sunt scribente profusae,
        Humidaque est fletu litera facta meo. '

The first line however was altered so as to lose its grammatical con- struction, and the couplet was subsequently emended. " See Macaulay's Textual Notes, p. 21.

[9] I. Prol. 43-44. Adapted from "Ovid, Tristia, i. 5. 53 f. "

[10] I. Prol. 47-48. Adapted from "Pont. iv. 2. 19[-20], where the comparison to a spring choked with mud is more clearly brought out. " Wheeler, p. 420: ". . . so my mind has been injured by the silt of mis- fortune, and my verse flows with a scantier vein. "

[11]I. Prol. 57-58. A reference to Rev. 1: 9.

"The author is about to denounce the evils of the world and proclaim the woes which are to follow, like the writer of the Apocalypse, whose name he bears. Perhaps he may also have some thought of the formula 'seint John to borwe, ' by which travellers committed themselves to the protection of the saint on their setting forth: cp. Conf. Amantis, v. 3416. " The formula occurs also, for example, in Chaucer's Mars, 9.

It will be noted that the dreams (sompnia) are premonitory, written as though in advance of the events related.

Chapter 1

[1]I. 1. "The fourth year of Richard II is from June 22, 1380 to the same date of 1381. The writer here speaks of the last month of that regnal year, during which the Peasants' rising occurred. " Violence first broke out on May 30 in Essex. It broke out on June 2 in Kent, where Gower lived and pretendedly was during the Revolt, and it was not fully put down there until the end of July.

"Easter day falling on the fourteenth of April in this year, would give the eleventh of June as the day to which Gower probably alludes. The meeting on Blackheath is commonly said to have taken place on the twelfth of that month" (Coxe, p. v. , note m).

[2]I. 4. Adapted from "Ovid, Her. xvii [Loeb ed. No. xviii]. 112. " See Grant Showerman, ed. and trans. , Ovid: With an English Translation: Heroides and Amores (Loeb Classical Library, London: William Heineman; New York: Putnam, 1921 and later printings), pp. 251, 253: "... Lucifer had risen, forerunner of the dawn.... " All subsequent translations from this, the Loeb edition of Ovid's Heroides and Amores, will be cited as "Showerman. " On Lucifer as Venus, see the n. on Troilus, III. 1417, in The Book of Troilus and Criseyde, ed. Robert Kilburn Root (Princeton, 1926), hereafter cited as "Root. "

[3]I. 7-8. "Godfrey of Viterbo, Pantheon, p. 24 (ed. 1584), has

'Luce diem reparat, mirandaque lumina praestat,
    sic fuga dat noctem, luxque reversa diem. '

He is speaking of the Sun generally, and the second line means 'Thus his departure produces the night and his returning light the day. ' As introduced here this line is meaningless. " But the line is not meaningless with reference to Aurora.

I have been unable to see the 1584 edition of the Pantheon, but

344

have used the edition contained in Germanicarvm Scriptorvm, Qvi
Rervm Gestarvm Historias Vel Annales Posteris Reliqvervnt..., ed.
Johann Pistorius and rev. by Burckhart Gotthelf Struve (Ratisbone,
1726), II, 1-392. For ll. 7-8 see p. 26 of this latter edition. (The
Pantheon is partly reprinted in MGM, Vol. XXII.) All contractions
and abbreviations in quotations from the Pantheon have been silently ex-
panded.

[4]I. 9. "Adapted from Ovid, Metam. ii. 110." See Frank Justus
Miller, ed. and trans., Ovid: Metamorphoses: With an English
Translation, 2nd. ed. (Loeb Classical Library, Cambridge, Mass.:
Harvard University Press; London: William Heineman, 1946 and
earlier printings), I, 69: "...jewels set in fair array gave back their
bright glow to the reflected rays of Phoebus." All subsequent translations from this, the Loeb edition of Ovid's Metamorphoses, are hereafter cited as "Miller."

[5]I. 11. Adapted from Ovid, "Metam. vii. 703 . . . ."

[6]I. 13. Adapted from Ovid, "Metam. ii. 113."

[7]I. 15. Adapted from "Metam. ii. 24."

[8]I. 17-18. "From Godfrey of Viterbo, Pantheon, p. 24 (ed.
1584)." See p. 26 of the 1726 ed.

[9]I. 21-24. Adapted from "Metam. ii. 107 ff. . . ." Miller, I,
67, 69: "Its axle was of gold, the pole of gold; its wheels had golden
tyres and a ring of silver spokes. Along the yoke chrysolites and
jewels set in fair array. . . ." On Phoebus' jewelled "car" cf. Antony
and Cleopatra, IV. viii. 28-29, and Cymbeline, V. v. 189-190.
  Macaulay suggests that "'alter ab auro' seems to mean 'different
from gold, '" but it is better rendered as "(none) other than gold."
  With ll. 21-24 cf. Conf., VII. 815-818.

[10]I. 27. Adapted from "Metam. ii. 23."

[11]I. 33-60. "This passage is largely from Ovid: see especially
Fasti, i. 151 ff. and iii. 235-242, iv. 429 f., v. 213 f., Metam. ii.
30, Tristia, iii. 12. 5-8." I have noted the borrowings below sepa-
rately for each line; Macaulay does so only for ll. 40 and 59.
  I. 33. From Ovid, "Fasti, i. 151." See Sir James G. Frazer,
ed. and trans., Ovid's Fasti: With an English Translation (Loeb Classical Library, London: William Heineman; New York: Putnam, 1931),
p. 13: "Then all things flower, then time renews his age. . . ." All

subsequent translations from this, the Loeb edition of Ovid's Fasti, are cited as "Frazer."

[12] I. 34. Adapted from Ovid, "Fasti, i. 156."

[13] I. 35. Adapted from Ovid, "Fasti, iii. 241."

[14] I. 37-38. Adapted from Ovid, "Tristia, iii. 12. 7-8."

[15] I. 39-40. Adapted from Ovid, "Fasti, iii. 239-240."

[16] *I 41-42. Adapted from Amores, I. vi. 65-66. As here, borrowings not noted by Macaulay are marked with an asterisk.

[17] *I. 43. Taken from Ovid, Metam., II. 30.

[18] I. 45-47. Adapted from Ovid, "Fasti, iii. 235-237."

[19] I. 55-56. Adapted from Ovid, "Tristia, iii. 12.5-6."

[20] I. 57-58. Adapted from Ovid, "Fasti, iv. 429-430."

[21] I. 59-60. Adapted from Ovid, "Fasti, v. 213-214."

[22] I. 67. Taken from Ovid, "Metam. xiii. 395."

[23] I. 79-80. Adapted from Nigel de Longchamps' "Speculum Stultorum, p. 47, ll. 9f. (ed. Wright, Rolls Series, 59, vol. i.)." The title of the volume is The Anglo-Latin Satirical Poets and Epigrammatists of the Twelfth Century (London, 1872). All references to the Speculum Stultorum are to this edition. This late twelfth-century beast epic, long attributed to Nigel Wireker, reached the height of its popularity in England from c. 1350 to c. 1450. See n. 25 below.

[24] *I. 89. Taken from Metam., I. 108.

[25] I. 92. Macaulay notes a total of some 13 lines borrowed from the Speculum Stultorum, and Professor R. R. Raymo adds 53 more references or quotes in the Vox Clamantis from the same poem. See his "Gower's Vox Clamantis and the Speculum Stultorum," MLN, LXX (1955): 315-320. All these additional borrowings are cited in the notes as "Raymo." I. 92 is from Speculum Stultorum, p. 28, l. 18 (Raymo).

[26] I. 99-102. For the story of Philomena and Procne see Ovid, Metam., VI. 440 ff. Gower tells the story in Conf., V. 5551 ff.

[27]I. 131. Macaulay notes, "ad ymum, 'to that low place, ' i. e. his bed. "

[28]I. 133. Proverbial (Walz no. 228b). Cf. TC, III. 1 (Walz no. 228a) and Mirour, 28597 (Walz no. 227). Cf. also Fasti, VI. 463, and Pont., IV. iii. 58.

[29]*I. 139. Taken from Ovid, Metam., X. 447. Boötes is the constellation known now as Charles' Wain (or the Great Bear). By midnight Boötes would have completed half his nightly journey. Thus it is now after midnight, since the tongue of his wain pointed downward.

[30]I. 152. "'Dreams cast the soul into wanderings': 'ruunt' is transitive, as very commonly. . . . " But it is perhaps better taken here as intransitive.

[31]I. 155-156.

. . . grauis et palpebra querelas
Ponderat ex oculis, set mora tardat opem.

Macaulay translates, "'and my heavy eyelid unclosed pondered over troubles, but no help came. ' This is the best translation I can give, but the explanation of 'ex oculis' as 'away from the eyes' must be regarded as doubtful. " The last clause may mean, "but relief was slow in coming. "

[32]*I. 163-164. Adapted from Ovid, Metam., IV. 629-630. Dreams had just before dawn were thought to be the most significant.

Chapter 2

[1]I. 168. "That is, on a Tuesday. It would be apparently Tuesday, June 11, 1381. The festival of Corpus Christi referred to afterwards (see 1. 919), when the insurgents entered London, fell on June 13. " The revolt actually began on May 30 in Essex. See n. on I. 1.

[2]I. 185-186. Possibly an echo of Ezek. 22: 25.

[3]I. 192. Literally, "and all that was usefulness lacked usefulness. "

[4]I. 201. "Burnellus: a reference to the Speculum Stultorum, p. 13 (Rolls Series, 59, vol. i). " The reference is to an episode in the

life of Burnell the ass. Cf. IV. 1190, V. 857, and NPT, 3312.

[5]I. 205 ff. "Cp. Speculum Stultorum, p. 13, whence several of these lines are taken." More specifically, ll. 205-206 are adapted from ll. 1-2 on this page, and l. 207 from l. 23.

I. 207. Literally, "since the tail could not attach itself to his head."

[6]I. 211. From "Speculum Stultorum, p. 15, l. 17." I. 213-214 are from ibid., "ll. 23 f."

[7]I. 217. Adapted from Speculum Stultorum, p. 16, l. 11 (Raymo).

[8]I. 234. Leopardus is the heraldic term for "lion passant gardant." The lion was (and is) a symbol of the royal house. The king's coat of arms contains three lions passant gardant. See A. C. Foxe-Davies, A Complete Guide to Heraldry, rev. ed. (London and Edinburgh, n. d), p. 173. Cf. Voice, I. 1757, and VI. 960; TC, III. 160.

Chapter 3

[1]Chapters 3-6 are largely in the historical present in the original.

[2]I. 263-264. For this episode in the story of Jason see Ovid, Metam., VII. 104 ff. The construction of this sentence is of a type common in Gower's works. Macaulay gives several parallels in his n. on Vox, I. 135. The story of "Jason and Medea" is told in Conf., V. 3247 ff.

[3]I. 267. "'The bull of Minos,' sent from the sea in answer to his prayer."

[4]I. 272. "Aeacides" is a mistake for "Alcides," a patronymic of Hercules, who was a grandson of Alcaeus. Gower's copy of Ovid was probably responsible for the error. For the story of Nessus see Metam., IX. 101-134; he was not changed into the form of a bull. Perhaps Gower or his copy of Ovid confused the words centaurus and taurus.

[5]I. 277-279. Adapted from "Ovid, Metam. xi. 34-36."

[6]I. 280. Reading capulus ("handle") with D rather than crapulus.

[7] I. 289-290. Adapted from Ovid, "Pont. i. 3. 55 f. "

[8] I. 291. Adapted from Ovid, "Metam. viii. 293. "

Chapter 4

[1] I. 321. The wild boar from Kent may represent Robert Cave, a baker of Dartford who led a mob of Kentish rebels. Wat Tyler may also have come from Kent, but Gower represents him as a jackdaw (in Chap. 9 below). See Charles Oman, The Great Revolt of 1381 (Oxford, 1906), pp. 34 ff.

[2] *I. 323. Taken from Metam., VIII. 356.

[3] I. 325 ff. Macaulay notes, "For this passage compare Metam. viii. 284 ff. " I. 325 is adapted from Metam., VIII. 289, and I. 327 is adapted from Metam., VIII. 287. See also notes 4 and 6 below.

[4] *I. 329. Taken from Ovid, Metam., VIII. 417.

[5] I. 335. Taken from Ovid, "Metam. viii. 285. "

[6] *I. 339. Adapted from Metam. VIII. 290.

[7] I. 347-348. It is difficult to explain this sentence fully. John Wraw led the rebels in Suffolk, and Geoffrey Litster in Norfolk, but neither met up with the "boar" from Kent, were it Wat Tyler or Robert Cave. Oman notes (p. 104) that "the Chronicon Angliae must be wrong when it says that he [i. e., Wraw] had met Tyler. . . . "

[8] I. 349-350. One of the twelve labors of Hercules was to destroy the Erymanthian boar which ravaged Arcadia or Tegea.

[9] I. 355. Meleager organized a hunt for the boar which Diana sent to ravage Calydonia. See Metam., VIII. 270 ff. The same story is alluded to below, ll. 453-455.

[10] I. 364. From Speculum Stultorum, p. 35, l. 20 (Raymo).

[11] I. 370. Reading [pulvinus] ("pillow") for puluis ("spice"). But the emendation may well be unnecessary, for a dandy might perfume himself and his room with the delicate odor of spices, as did "hende

Nicholas" in Chaucer's MillT, 3203-07.

There were many complaints in the second half of the fourteenth century about the lower class's newly acquired taste for luxuries, such as is described in ll. 359-372. Cf. Conf., I. 2976-86.

[12]I. 377-378. A reference to the Gadarene Swine. See Matt. 8: 31-32, Mark 5: 11-13, Luke 8: 32-33. Cf. l. 301 above.

Chapter 5

[1]I. 381. Taken from Ovid, "Fasti, ii. 767. "

[2]I. 395. "'Cut and Cur, ' names for mongrel dogs. "

[3]I. 399-400. Or, "Every broken chain loosed its dog to get away, the property of bakery and kitchen alike. "

[4]I. 437. Proverbial (Walz no. 248).

[5]I. 441-442. For the story see Metam., XIII. 405-406, 567-575.

[6]I. 445. For the story see Metam., III. 173-252.

[7]I. 447. The tenth labor of Hercules was to capture the oxen of the monster Geryon, or Geryones, which had three bodies. (Its dog Orthus had two heads.)

[8]I. 453-454. See n. on l. 355 above. In the next sentence the reference to Cephalus' dog is to Laelaps, a famous hunting dog. See Metam., VII. 771 ff.

Chapter 6

[1]I. 499-500. "See I Sam. v. The plague of mice is distinctly mentioned in the Vulgate version, while in our translation of the Hebrew it is implied in ch. vi. 5. " This implication is true, although the plague of mice refers directly to Ashdod, not Ekron (both were cities of the Philistines). The Vulgate, I Kings 5: 6, reads: "Adgravata est autem manum Domini super Azotios, et demolitus est eos et percussit in secretiori parte natium Azotum et fines eius. Et ebullierunt villae

et agri in medio regionis illius, et nati sunt mures, et facta est confusio mortis magnae in civitate. "

The King James version of I Sam. 6: 5-6 reads: "... for one plague was on you all, and on your lords. / Wherefore ye shall make images of your emerods, and images of your mice that mar the land. . . . "

Chapter 7

[1] I. 511-512. Taken from Speculum Stultorum, p. 29, ll. 7-8 (Raymo).

[2] I. 545. "Coppa: used as a familiar name for a hen in the Speculum Stultorum, pp. 55, 58, and evidently connected with 'Coppen' or 'Coppe, ' which is the name of one of Chanticleer's daughters in the Low-German and English Reynard. "

[3] I. 557-558. This sentence is thus translated in Macaulay's note.

Chapter 8

[1] I. 571. A bad pun on "Vespasian. "

[2] I. 579-580. Gower refers in ll. 579-580 to the story told by "Ovid, Metam. ii. 366 ff. " For the reference to Egypt (l. 586), see Exod. 8.

[3] I. 601-602. Taken from Speculum Stultorum, p. 30, ll. 3-4, as noted by Raymo. Both he and Macaulay point out that Torvus oester adest in I. 603 is from the same poem, p. 29, l. 4, and Raymo further notes that the phrase sine lege vagantes is from p. 24, l. 11.

[4] I. 615-616, "Cp. Speculum Stultorum, p. 24, l. 21 f. "

[5] I. 620. Taken from Speculum Stultorum, p. 24, l. 18; also, I. 621-622 are from p. 24, ll. 19-20, as noted by Raymo, who points out that the phrase sordida musca (I. 628) is from p. 29, l. 6.

[6] I. 635. "Cp. Speculum Stultorum, p. 25, l. 15. "

[7] I. 637-638. Cf. "Speculum Stultorum, p. 26. . . . "

[8]I. 652. "Stramine: probably an allusion to the name of Jack Straw, as 'tegula' in the next couplet to Wat Tyler." Chaucer uses the same pun on "straw" in Troilus, IV. 184.

[9]I. 667-668. Taken from Speculum Stultorum, p. 25, ll. 5-6 (Raymo).

[10]I. 669. Taken from Speculum Stultorum, p. 26, l. 3 (Raymo).

Chapter 9

[1]I. Chap. 9. Heading. "It seems to be implied that the jay, which must often have been kept as a cage-bird and taught to talk, was commonly called 'Wat, ' as the daw was called 'Jack, ' and this name together with the bird's faculty of speech has suggested the transformation adopted for Wat Tyler." Cf. Chaucer, Gen Prol, 641-643: "And eek ye knowen wel how that a jay/kan clepen 'Watte' as wel as kan the pope. "

There is a theory, moreover, that Wat Tyler and Jack Straw were one and the same, which many believed in the fifteenth century. For the whole question see Oman, p. 44, n. 3.

The meeting of the rebels and their choosing of Wat Tyler as leader took place at Maidstone on June 7, 1381. Gower does not exaggerate Tyler's oratorical powers in this chapter, although it is probable that the poet was no eyewitness of the meeting.

[2]I. 680. The expression is biblical. Cf. Rev. 20: 8: "The number of whom is as the sand of the sea. " Gower is fond of this simile; cf. l. 749 below, and TC, III. 246.

[3]*I. 709-710, Adapted from Fasti, II. 775-776.

[4]I. 716. 'Solue nephas, ' soluit, quis neque fata vetat. "There is no punctuation in S, but those MSS. which have stops, as CD, punctuate after 'nephas' and 'soluit. ' The line is suggested by Ovid, Fasti, ii. 44, 'Solve nefas, dixit; solvit et ille nefas. ' There it is quite intelligible, but here it is without any clear meaning. " But the meaning seems clear if a semicolon is placed after nephas, and fata interpreted as either "(his) determining will" or "calamities. "

Frazer, p. 59: "[He] said. . ., 'O rid me of my sin, ' and the other did rid him of his sin. "

Chapter 10

[1]I. 749. Cf. I. 680 and see n.

[2]*I. 751-753. Adapted from Ovid, Metam. I. 160-162.

[3]I. 762. "'All that they lay upon us, they bear equally themselves.' Apparently this is the meaning, referring to the universal ruin which is likely to ensue."

[4]I. 765-776. "These lines are taken with some alterations of wording and order from Godfrey of Viterbo, Pantheon, p. 228 (ed. 1584)." See the 1726 ed., p. 166, under the section entitled De Goth & Magoth, quos Alexander inter montes conclusit. See also Root's n. on Troilus, V. 1450; he quotes Isidore, Etymologiae, VIII. 8. Cf. Conf., V. 1133-54. Cf. also II. 263-264 and see n.

The Pantheon gives the usual medieval conception of the Sibyls; see pp. 157-161 (ed. 1726). Of the ten Sibyls, the tenth was called Tiburtina in Greek, Albunea in Latin, and to her were attributed verses predicting the coming of Christ (p. 157). Other verses predict the Last Judgment, in which the earth is destroyed, the wicked descend to hell and the righteous ascend to heaven (p. 161).

[5]I. 767. Gower (or rather, his source) is mistaken in this reference to Isaiah, who does not mention Gog and Magog. See A New Commentary on Holy Scripture: Including the Apocrypha, edd. Charles Gore, Henry L. Goudge, and Alfred Guillaume (New York: Macmillan, 1928), Part III, p. 703: "Gog and Magog came from Ezek 38 and 39, but through the medium of later apocalyptists who saw in them, not an invading prince and his land, but the world ranged against Israel under Satan's banner." See Rev. 20: 7-8 (Vulgate: Rev. 20: 7): "And when the thousand years are expired, Satan shall be loosed out of his prison, and shall go out to deceive the nations which are in the four quarters of the earth, Gog and Magog, to gather them together to do battle: the number of whom is as the sand of the sea." Gower thus views the Peasants' Revolt as the coming of the millenium.

Chapter 11

[1]I. 783-790. Thomas Fuller's translation of ll. 783-790 has for three hundred years been the best known part of the poem. It is here quoted from Macaulay, p. xxxvii:

Tom comes thereat, when called by Wat, and Simm
as forward we find,

Bet calls as quick to Gibb and to Hykk, that neither would
tarry behind.

Gibb, a good whelp of that litter, doth help mad Coll more
mischief to do,

And Will he does vow, the time is come now, he'll join
in their company too.

Davie complains, whiles Grigg gets the gains, and Hobb
with them does partake,

Lorkin aloud in the midst of the crowd conceiveth as deep
is his stake.

Hudde doth spoil whom Judde doth foil, and Tebb lends his
helping hand,

But Jack the mad patch men and houses does snatch, and
kills all at his command.
Church History, Book iv (p. 139).

[2]I. 784. Bette is a male name. Skeat notes (Piers, B. Passus
V. 32), "It is the same as Bat, i. e. Bartholomew." The names Tom
and Wat also occur in the same passage (ll. 28 and 30), thus showing
clearly that Gower was using lower-class nicknames. Watte surely
stands for Wat Tyler, just as Balle does for John Ball.
    The names Watte, Hikke, and Dawe (i. e., Davie) are found in ll.
316-320 of the same Passus. But it is possible that Gower had some
of the actual leaders of the revolt in mind: "The life of Richard by the
monk of Evesham. . . says, – 'capitaneos eis praefecerunt, hujusmodi
nomina imponentes, Jak Sherp, John Wraw, Thomas Meller, Watte
Tayler, Hobbe Carter et Jak Straw; ' p. 24." (Quoted from Coxe,
p. viii, note q.)

[3]I. 810. . . . que subito fossa dolore pauent. "It is difficult to
see how this line is to be translated, unless we suppose that 'fossa' is
a grammatical oversight." "Graves" seems applicable to fossa here;
the word can also be the neuter plural form of the past participle of
fodio, meaning "the things which have been pierced" by the cackling of
the gander.

[4]I. 821. Adapted from "Ovid, Metam. i. 211. "

[5]I. 825-826. This statement was no exaggeration. The inability
of the upper classes to plan any sort of immediate defense against the

rebels was striking. See Oman, p. 48.

Gower here uses Rumor, rather than the commoner name Fama for "Lady Fame" or "Dame Rumor. "

Chapter 12

[1] I. 843-864. These lines are fairly accurately translated, with the Latin text parallel, in G. G. Coulton, Europe's Apprenticeship (London: Nelson, 1940), pp. 259-260.

[2] I. 845. Gower is right in stating that there were old soldiers (veterani) in the mob. See Oman, pp. 36-37.

[3] I. 849-50. "Adapted from Amores, iii. 9. 7 f., but not very happily. " Showerman, p. 481: "See, the child of Venus comes, with quiver reversed, with bows broken, and lightless torch. . . . " This borrowing would seem to be about as "happy" as many of Gower's uses of Ovid.

[4] I. 855 ff. "With this passage we may compare the description in Walsingham [Chronicon Angliae, 1322-88, ed. E. Maunde Thompson (Rolls Series, London, 1874)], vol. i. p. 454. . . . " Cf. also G. M. Trevelyan, England in the Age of Wycliffe, 4th. ed. (London: Longmans, Green, 1915), p. 213.

[5] I. 871-873. Adapted from Ovid, "Metam. xi. 29 f. "

[6] I. 876. Macaulay translates, "'These fools boast [ferunt] that the earth has been wetted, ' &c. "

Chapter 13

[1] I. 880. "New Troy" is of course London, the legendary founder of which was the Trojan Brut, from whose name "Britain" was supposedly derived. "One of the charges against Sir Nicholas Brembre in 1388 was that he had designed to change the name of London to 'New Troy. '" See n. on TC, III. 174-175.

London is called "the toun of newe Troye" in Conf., Prol. 37, and "Troy" in TC, I. 58.

[2]I. 903-904. Adapted from "Ovid, Ars Amat. iii. 577 f. " (Here Macaulay's note reads 904 instead of 903 f.) See J. H. Mozley, ed. and trans. , Ovid: The Art of Love and Other Poems: With an English Translation (Loeb Classical Library, London: William Heineman; New York: Putnam, 1929), p. 159: "Let all be revealed: we have flung our gates open to the foe, and in faithless treason let us keep faith. " All subsequent translations from this, the Loeb edition of Ovid's Ars Amatoria and Remedia Amoris, are cited as "Mozley. "

[3]I. 909. Adapted from Ovid, "Metam. viii. 421. "

[4]I. 919. "Corpus Christi day, that is Thursday, June 13. " Gower's date is correct for the burning of the Savoy, as described below, ll. 929 ff.

[5]I. 923-924. Taken from Aurora, Mach. 37-38. The borrowings from Peter of Riga's versified Bible, Aurora, are listed by Father Paul E. Beichner, C. S. C. , in his "Gower's Use of Aurora in Vox Clamantis, " Speculum, XXX (1955): 582-595. I am most grateful to Father Beichner for permission to make use of his findings in the Introduction and Notes to the present translation. The numberings of the lines of the Aurora, including passages noted by Macaulay, are those of Father Beichner's forthcoming edition. Borrowings not noted by Macaulay are designated "Beichner" in these notes.

[6]I. 925. Perhaps an ironical reference to celebrating the sacred ceremony of Corpus Christi.

[7]I. 929. "via salua: apparently meaning 'Savoye, ' the palace of [John of Gaunt,] the duke of Lancaster in the Strand. In the next line 'longum castrum' looks like 'Lancaster, ' but it is difficult to say exactly what the meaning is. " "Lancaster" is surely right. Gaunt, the patron and friend of Chaucer, was one of the men most hated by the rioters. Being on an expedition in Scotland, Gaunt himself escaped death at their hands.
     The destruction of the Savoy was utterly complete. See Oman, pp. 57-58, and his translation of the relevant part of the Anonimalle Chronicle, pp. 194-195.
     Gower's method of translating parts of proper names by phonetically or semantically similar words was a fairly common practice. See his own Cronica Tripartita, I. 55, 103, 109, 154, etc. , and BD, 1318, where "long castel" means Lancaster. Similarly, in Romeo, I. i. 102, Villafranca is "Freetown. "

[8]I. 931. "Baptisteque domus. This is the Prior of St. John of Jerusalem at Clerkenwell, which was burnt by the insurgents because of their hostility to Robert Hales, the Master of the Hospital, then Treasurer of the kingdom. Walsingham says that the fire continued here for seven days. " Hales, widely known as "Hobbe the Robber, " attempted to collect the unpopular poll tax of 1381, which was the immediate cause of the revolt. He was dragged from the Tower of London by Tyler and his men on Friday, June 14, and beheaded along with Archbishop Sudbury (see below, Chap. 14).

[9]I. 933-936. Adapted from "Ovid, Fasti, vi. 439 ff. , where the reference is to the burning of the temple of Vesta. Hence the mention of sacred fires, which is not appropriate here. " Perhaps Gower was thinking of candles or lights burning in the church, though the building itself, aflame or not, would be "sacred" to him. Frazer, p. 353: "Holy fires blazed, fed by wicked fires, and a profane flame was blent with a pious flame. Amazed the priestesses wept with streaming hair; fear had bereft them of bodily strength. "

[10]I. 937. Taken from Ovid, "Metam. ii. 61. "

[11]I. 939-940. Adapted from Ovid, "Metam. i. 287 f. "

[12]I. 941 ff. "This accusation, which Gower brings apparently without thinking it necessary to examine into its truth. . ., is in direct contradiction to the statements of the chroniclers, . . . but it is certain that dishonest persons must have taken advantage of the disorder to some extent for their own private ends, however strict the commands of the leaders may have been [against plundering], and it is probable that the control which was exercised at first did not long continue. The chroniclers agree with Gower as to the drunkenness. "

[13]I. 943-944. Taken from "Ovid, Trist. v. 6. 39 f. "

[14]I. 951. Adapted from "Ovid, Fasti, vi. 673. "

[15]I. 953. Taken from Ovid, "Metam. xv. 665. "

[16]I. 955. "Thursday" is literally "Jove, " and in the next line "Friday" is "Venus. "

[17]I. 962-967. "It is probable that the names here given, Calchas, Antenor, Thersites, Diomede, Ulysses, as well as those which follow in ll. 985 ff. [i. e., Capaneus, Tydeus, Palamedes, Ajax, Hector, Achilles, Troilus, and Priam], are meant to stand for general types,

357

rather than for particular persons connected with the government. In any case we could hardly identify them. " See also Introduction, p. 16.

Gower was thoroughly familiar with the story of Troy, as we know from the Confessio Amantis, through his reading of Guido delle Colonne and Benoit de Sainte-More.

[18] *I. 973. Adapted from Metam., XIII. 547.

[19] I. 983-992. Taken from Aurora, I Kings, 559-566 (Beichner). Quoting this passage from the Aurora, Father Beichner points out (Speculum, XXX, 592-593 and n. 17) that Gower ". . . even borrowed some of the few Classical allusions with which Peter Riga had ornamented his writing. "

[20] I. 997. "This looks like an allusion to the princess of Wales, the king's mother, whose apartments in the Tower were in fact invaded by the mob. Similarly in the lines that follow 'Helenus' stands for the archbishop of Canterbury. " There is an interesting episode in the invasion of Joan of Kent's apartments: "The rebels also searched the Princess of Wales's room; one ruffian, it is said, wanted to kiss the terrified lady, who fainted and was carried off by her pages, put into a boat, and taken round to the 'Queen's Wardrobe' near St. Paul's" (Oman, p. 66).

"The man" referred to in l. 1000 is undoubtedly Richard II; "the lofty towers" are the Tower of London. Wat Tyler and others actually broke into the Tower even as Richard was conferring with other rebels at Mile End on June 14.

Chapter 14

[1] I. 1002. The name "Helenus" (also used in l. 1155) is singularly ill-chosen. First, the ancient Helenus was a son of Priam and Hecuba, who represent King Richard and his mother in this poem, I. 995-997 and 1155. Second, the ancient Helenus was a traitor to Troy.

[2] I. 1001. The Palladium of Troy was a statue of Pallas which fell to Troy from heaven, and on which the safety of the city was thought to depend.

[3] I. 1013-14. Taken from Aurora, Gen. 1275-76 (Beichner).

[4] I. 1015-16. Taken from Aurora, Gen. 1279-80 (Beichner).

[5]I. 1017-18. Taken from <u>Aurora</u>, Jud. 225-226 (Beichner).

[6]I. 1019-23. Written over erasure in MSS. SCHG. "The text of
these five lines, as we find it in DTH$_2$, that is in its earlier form, was
taken for the most part from the <u>Aurora</u> of Petrus (de) Riga, (MS.
Bodley 822) f. 88 v° [Jud. 227-230 in Beichner's ed.], ... "

> Not the piercing bramble, but the glistening olive, the choice
> fig, the pleasing vine were repulsive to them [1020]. Almighty
> God did not rule over them, nor did a loving spirit [<u>spiritus al-
> mus</u>, the Holy Ghost?]; neither law nor Christ had mastery over
> them; and indeed they did not worship the Creator with any
> honor.

"He is speaking of the parable of Jotham in the Book of Judges [9: 5-
21]. "

[7]I. 1046. Taken from Ovid, "<u>Fasti</u>, ii. 228. "

[8]I. 1055. Four knights of Henry II murdered Thomas à Becket,
Archbishop of Canterbury, in 1170 in his cathedral. This martyrdom
was very much in the minds of Englishmen for the next three hundred
years, so Gower's comparison and contrast between Becket's murder
and Simon Sudbury's on June 14, 1381, is quite appropriate.

[9]I. 1066. An accurate account of the execution, which took place
on Tower Hill before a delighted mob of thousands. "The headsman's
work was so badly done that eight strokes were spent in hacking through
the unhappy prelate's neck" (Oman, p. 67).

[10]*I. 1079. Taken from <u>Metam.</u>, III. 50.

[11]I. 1081-2. Adapted from Ovid, "<u>Tristia</u>, iv. 2. 5 f. "(Macaulay's
note is to l. 1081 only.)

[12]I. 1094. Adapted from Ovid, "<u>Fasti,</u> i. 122. "

[13]I. 1117-18. A reference to Gen. 4.

[14]I. 1122. This is possibly a satirical reference to the Visions of
Do-Wel, Do-Bet, and Do-Best in <u>Piers Plowman</u>. The name of Piers
became a watchword among the peasants, as is shown by the curious
rhyming letters of John Ball, which were "full of dark sayings" and
revolutionary in intent. Thus it is understandable for Gower to attack
some ideas in <u>Piers Plowman,</u> although the poem itself is conservative
politically. See Introduction, p. 24. Cf. V. 921-922, VII. 1473-74,

and TC, II. 306-307.

For Ball's letter to the leaders of the commons in Essex, see Illustrations of Chaucer's England, ed. Dorothy Hughes (London, 1918), pp. 233-234.

[15] I. 1137 and 1139. Taken from Aurora, Gen. 1351 and 1353 (Beichner).

[16] I. 1141. Adapted from Ovid, "Metam. vi. 559. "

[17] I. 1143. Adapted from Ovid, "Metam. vii. 603. "

[18] I. 1155. See n. on l. 1002 above.

[19] I. 1161. Taken from Ovid, "Metam. vi. 602, " Miller, I, 385: "Before the temple doors I saw the corpses cast away. . . . " Macaulay adds, "Considering that the line is borrowed from Ovid, we cannot attach much importance to it as indicating what was done with the body of the archbishop. " The disposal of his body is unknown, but his head was put upon a pole, with his mitre nailed to his skull, and paraded around the city. Then it was set over the gate of London Bridge, where Tyler's later replaced it.

Chapter 15

[1] I. 1173. "ostia iuris; cp. Walsingham, i. 457, 'locum qui vocatur "Temple Barre, " in quo apprenticii iuris morabantur nobiliores, diruerunt. '"

[2] I. 1179-80. Taken from Aurora, Mach. 49-50 (Beichner).

[3] I. 1188. Adapted from "Ovid, Her. iii. 4. "

[4] I. 1189. Adapted from Ovid, "Metam. v. 41. "

[5] I. 1193-94. Adapted from Ovid, "Ars Amat. ii. 373 f. . . . "

[6] *I. 1203. Adapted from Metam., IV. 622.

[7] *I. 1207. Adapted from Metam., VIII. 585.

[8] I. 1209. Adapted from Ovid, "Metam. v. 40. "

[9] I. 1211. Taken from Ovid, "Metam. xiv. 408."

[10] I. 1215-16. "A reference probably to the massacre of the Flemings." This occurred on June 13 and 14. Some Lombards were also attacked. Gower was usually hostile to Lombards (see Conf., II. 2077-2144, and Mirour, 23257-68 and 25429-49), but it would suit his purpose here to adopt a different opinion.

[11] I. 1219-20. Taken from Ovid, "Fasti, iii. 509 f."

[12] I. 1221-22. Taken from "Ovid, Amores, iii. 9. 11 f."

[13] I. 1224. Adapted from Ovid, "Her. v. 68."

[14] I. 1241. Reading et with S rather than vt.

[15] I. 1253. Adapted from Ovid, "Metam. vii. 599."

[16] I. 1260. During the first few days of the revolt, the only exception to this statement was Henry Despenser, Bishop of Norwich. See Oman, pp. 129-134.

[17] I. 1283. Adapted from Ovid, "Her. viii. 77."

[18] I. 1289. Taken from Ovid, "Metam. ix. 775."

[19] *I. 1293. Taken from Metam., XV. 153.

[20] I. 1306. An unpardonable untruth. "In East Anglia, as in Herts or Kent or Essex, we find no sign whatever of a tendency to church-breaking or other sacrilege. It is one of the most notable features of the rebellion throughout the whole of England" (Oman, pp. 101-102).

[21] I. 1312. Literally, "and the state does not know what it is to have a state."

[22] I. 1325-26. This awkward couplet involves a play upon turbine ("storm") and turba ("throng").

[23] I. 1331-32. Taken from Speculum Stultorum, p. 56, ll. 11-12 (Raymo).

Chapter 16

[1] I. Chap. 16. Heading. "quasi in propria persona: cf. Conf.
Amantis, i. 60, margin, 'Hic quasi in persona aliorum quos amor alli-
gat, fingens se auctor esse Amantem, ' &c. The author takes care to
guard readers against a too personal application of his descriptions. "
This statement of Macaulay's is important, for the description of the
flight to the woods has long been cited as an accurate narrative of Gower's own actions. Many members of the nobility and upper classes did
have to flee in much the same manner as Gower describes, however.
See Oman, p. 41, and Introduction, p. 16.

[2] I. 1359. Adapted from Ovid, "Metam. xiv. 198. "

[3] I. 1363-64. Adapted from Ovid, "Ars Amat. iii. 723 f. "Mozley,
p. 169: "and now midday had drawn short the unsubstantial shadows,
and evening and morning were of equal length. . . . "

[4] I. 1365. Taken from Ovid, "Metam. xiv. 206. "

[5] I. 1369. Adapted from Ovid, "Metam. xiv. 200. "

[6] I. 1379-80. Adapted from Ovid, "Tristia, v. 4. 33 f. "

[7] I. 1385-86. Adapted from Ovid, "Her. xx. 91. f. " Showerman,
p. 281: "Now, unhappy, and my cause, though excellent, is lost because no one appears for me. "

[8] I. 1387. Taken from Ovid, "Metam. xiv. 120. "

[9] I. 1389-90. Taken from Aurora, Jud. 211-212 (Beichner).

[10] I. 1395. Adapted from Ovid, "Metam. iv. 723. "

[11] I. 1397-98. Adapted from Ovid, "Tristia, i. 3. 53 f. " Wheeler,
p. 23: "Alas! how many times did I falsely say that I had a definite
hour suited to my intended journey. "

[12] I. 1401-1402. Adapted from Ovid, "Fasti, v. 315 f. "

[13] I. 1403. Adapted from Ovid, "Metam. xv. 27. "

[14] I. 1413-14. Adapted from Ovid, "Pont. i. 3. 57 f. "

[15] I. 1420. Adapted from Ovid, "Her. iii. 24, used here with a change of meaning." Showerman, p. 35: "'Why do you weep? But a short time, ' he said, 'will you be here. '" The same line is borrowed in toto below, 1. 1568.

[16] I. 1424. Adapted from Ovid, "Ars Amat. ii. 88. "

[17] I. 1425-26. Taken from Ovid, "Pont. i. 2. 45 f. " (Loeb ed.: I. ii. 43 f.)

[18] I. 1429-30. Adapted from Ovid, "Pont. i. 2. 49 f. " (Loeb ed.: I. ii. 47 f.)

[19] I. 1433. Taken from Ovid, "Metam. iii. 709. "

[20] *I. 1435. Adapted from Metam., III. 28.

[21] I. 1442. Adapted from Ovid, "Her. v. 14, where we have 'Mixtaque' instead of 'Copula. '" Showerman, p. 59: ". . . where mingled grass and leaves afforded us a couch . . . . "

[22] I. 1445-47. Adapted from Ovid, "Metam. xiv. 214-216. "

[23] I. 1453. "Adapted from Metam. iv. 263. . . The change of 'mero' to 'meo' involves a tasteless alteration of the sense, while the sound is preserved. " Miller, I, 197: ". . . her hunger fed by naught save pure dew and tears. . . . "

[24] I. 1459. In part adapted from Ovid, "Rem. Amoris, 581. "

[25] I. 1465. Taken from Ovid, "Metam. ii. 656. Our author has borrowed the line without supplying an appropriate context, and the result is nonsense. Ovid has

'Suspirat ab imis
Pectoribus, lacrimaeque genis labuntur obortae. '"

Miller, I, 107: ". . . she sighed deeply, and with flowing tears. . . . "
But Gower's line is hardly nonsense. Pectoribus can be taken as an ablative of origin after aborte, and genis as an ablative (or locative) of place, although the construction is weak.

[26] I. 1467-68. Taken from Ovid, "Pont. i. 2. 29 f. " (Loeb ed.: I. ii. 27 f.)

[27] I. 1469. Adapted from Ovid, "Metam. xiii. 539. "

[28] I. 1473. Taken from "Ovid, Metam. viii. 469. "

[29] I. 1474. Literally, "to have the remaining turns. "

[30] I. 1475. Taken from "Metam. iv. 135, borrowed without much regard to the context. " It seems necessary to take pallidiora in the active sense of "frightful, " "frightening, " rather than the passive sense of "pale with fright, " "affrighted. " (Ovid uses the word in this latter way in Her., XII. 97.)

[31] *I. 1482. Taken from Tristia, III. 8. 28.

[32] I. 1485. Taken from "Ovid, Her. xiv. 37, where however we have 'calor, ' not 'color, ' a material difference. " Showerman, p. 173: "My blood retreated, warmth left my body and soul. . . . "

[33] *I. 1488. Taken from Tristia, IV. vi. 42.

[34] I. 1496. Taken from Ovid, "Her. v. 46. "

[35] I. 1497. "The expression 'verbis solabar amicis' is from Ovid (Fasti, v. 237), but here 'solabar' seems to be made passive in sense. ' Frazer, p. 279: "I consoled her with friendly words. "

[36] I. 1501-1502. Adapted from "Ovid, Pont. iv. 6. 23 f. "

[37] I. 1503-1504. Adapted from "Tristia, iii. 1. 65 f. "

[38] I. 1506. Taken from "Fasti, i. 148, not very appropriate here. " But this borrowing seems as appropriate as many others. Frazer, p. 13: ". . . and with eyes turned to the ground I spoke in few: . . . "

[39] I. 1509. Cf. Prov. 15: 1.

[40] I. 1512. Taken from Ovid, "Her. xi. 82. "

[41] I. 1514. Adapted from "Her. xiii. 86. "

[42] I. 1517-18. Adapted from Ovid, "Her. iii. 43 f. "

[43] I. 1519. Adapted from Ovid, "Tristia, iii. 4. 75. "

[44] I. 1521. Adapted from Ovid, "Tristia, i. 11. 23. "

[45] I. 1525-26. Omnia solvit mors is proverbial. See n. on TC, I. 187.

[46] I. 1534. Adapted from Ovid, "Tristia, v. 4. 4. "

[47] I. 1535-36. "1535 ff. Cp. Tristia, iii. 3. 39 ff. " I. 1538 is much adapted from Tristia, III. iii. 44, and I. 1537 from Tristia, I. v. 11.

[48] I. 1539-40. Taken from Ovid, "Tristia, iii. 3. 29 f. "

[49] I. 1549. Taken from Ovid, "Fasti, i. 483. "

[50] I. 1550. Proverbial. See William George Smith, comp. , The Oxford Dictionary of English Proverbs, with an Introduction by Janet E. Heseltine. 2nd ed. , rev. Sir Paul Harvey (Oxford, 1948), s. v. "Everything hath an end"; hereafter cited as Smith-Heseltine. Cf. Troilus, III. 615.

[51] I. 1564. Taken from Ovid, "Her. xiv. 52. "

[52] I. 1564-66. Taken from Ovid, "Her. x. 113 f. " (Loeb ed. Her. X. 111f.)

[53] I. 1568. "See note on l. 1420. "

[54] I. 1569. Taken from Ovid, "Metam. iii. 396. "

[55] I. 1571. Adapted from Ovid, "Metam. xiv. 210. "

[56] I. 1573. Taken from Ovid, "Metam. vii. 614. "

[57] I. 1575. Adapted from Ovid, "Metam. ix. 583. "

[58] I. 1581-82. Taken from Aurora, Gen. 1317-18 (Beichner).

[59] I. 1585. Adapted from Ovid, "Metam. xiv. 217. "

[60] I. 1589. Taken from Ovid, "Tristia, i. 5. 45. "

[1] I. Chap. 17, Heading. It is unlikely that Gower actually took refuge in the Tower. As does that of Chapter 16 the heading of this
chapter says that he relates the story quasi in propria persona. As
for the ship, an escape via "The Ship of Religion" is a fairly commonplace motif, and cannot be trusted to represent autobiography. It
occurs, for example, in Deguilleville's The Pilgrimage of the Soul, a
widely read book in that century. See Introduction, pp. 16-17.

[2] I. 1598. Literally, "anger sprinkled my eyes. "

[3] I. 1600. Such omission of the purposive infinitive is a fairly
common kind of ellipsis in the poem.

[4] I. 1603-04. Gower probably does not intend here to include himself in the noble class. His only title was that of esquire.

[5] I. 1612. Adapted from Ovid, "Her. xix. 52. "

[6] I. 1615-16. On these lines Macaulay comments:

"It seems probably that this is a prayer to the Virgin Mary,
whose name 'Star of the Sea' was used long before the fourteenth
century. . . . For Gower's use of the expression cp. Mirour de
l'Omme, 29925, 'O de la mer estoille pure, ' and later in this
book, 1. [2083, not Macaulay's 2033], 'Stella, Maria, maris,
'Here, however, we might translate, 'Be thou a star of the sea
going before me, ' taking it as a prayer to Christ. "

The Virgin Mary is probably referred to as noua stella in II. 414,
and she is praised in II. 392 ff., but it is surprising how little she is
mentioned in this poem, in view of Gower's reverence for her in the
Mirour, 27361-29945 (where that poem breaks off, because of a defective MS).

[7] I. 1623. Taken from Ovid, "Metam. i. 265. "

[8] *I. 1627. Taken in part from Metam., I. 264.

[9] I. 1630. Adapted from Ovid, "Fasti, iv. 386. " Gower substitutes celestes for caelestis. Frazer, p. 217: ". . . the Balance hung
in heaven released the heavenly waters. " The Balance is either the
constellation Libra or the sign of the Zodiac of the same name. See
Conf., VII. 1101-20.

[10]I. 1631. Taken from Ovid, "Metam. i. 282."

[11]I. 1635. Taken from Ovid, "Metam. i. 269."

[12]I. 1637. Adapted from Ovid, "Metam. i. 21." Miller, I, 21: "Iris, the messenger of Juno, clad in robes of many hues. . . ." Gower's meaning in ll. 1637-1644 is apparently that the rainbow Iris brought back sea water to the clouds instead of pure rain water, such was the degree of confusion. Then it rained salt water.

[13]I. 1653 ff. "From this point to the end of the chapter the description is mostly taken from Ovid, Metam. xi. 480-523, many hexameters being appropriated without material change. . . ." The passage from Ovid describes a storm at sea, and is from the story of Ceyx and Alcyone, Metam., XI. 266-748. (Gower tells the same story in Conf., IV. 2927 ff., as does Chaucer in BD, 62-269.) The list of Gower's borrowings follows:

Line Numbers		Miller's Translation
Vox, I	Metam., XI	(Loeb ed., II, 155, 157)
1653	516	Behold, the rain falls in sheets from the bursting clouds. . . .
1655	517	. . . and you would think that the whole heavens were falling down into the sea. . . .
*1657 (adapted)	518	. . . and that the swollen sea was leaping up into the regions of the sky.
1659	501	At other times the waves spread out, white with hissing foam.
1661	499	Now the water is tawny with the sands swept up from the bottom of the sea. . . .
1665 (adapted)	519-520	. . . with the waters from the sky the ocean's floods are mingled.
1667 (in part)	519	The sails are soaked with rain. . . .

Line Numbers		Miller's Translation
<u>Vox</u>, I	<u>Metam.</u>, XI	(Loeb ed., II, 155, 157)
*1673 (adapted)	521	. . . and the black night is murky with its own and the tempest's gloom.
1675	480	. . . when as night came on, the water began to whiten with the roughening waves. . . .
1677 (adapted)	482	"Lower the yard at once, " the captain cries. . . .
1679-1684	484-489	So he orders, but the blast blowing in his face drowns out his orders, nor does the uproar of the sea let his voice be heard. Still, of their own will, some hastily draw in the oars, some close the oar-holes, and some reef the sails. Here one is bailing out the water and pouring the sea into the sea, while another hastily secures the spars.
1685	491	. . . the raging winds make their attacks and stir up the angry waves.
1689 (adapted	492	The captain himself is in terror and admits that he does not know how the vessel stands. . . . (Macauley notes, "The line is taken away from its context, and consequently gives no sense. . . ." The line seems to fit Gower's context acceptably only if emended).
1691	495	All is a confused uproar-- shouts of men, rattling of cordage. . . .

[14]I. 1673. Tetraque nox premitur, tenebrisque micancia lumen in the text, but the comma could follow tenebrisque instead of premitur.

[15]I. 1693. Taken from Ovid, "Metam. i. 292. "

Chapter 18

[1]I. 1695. "From Peter Riga, Aurora, (MS. Bodley 822) f. 16 v⁰ [Gen. 745 in Beichner's ed.]. "

[2]I. 1697-1700. "Cp. Aurora, f. 15v⁰ [Gen. 695-698 in Beichner's ed.]. . . . "

[3]I. 1717-18. Adapted from Ovid, "Metam. iv. 689 f. " Miller, I, 227: ". . . there came a loud sound from the sea, and there, advancing over the broad expanse, a monstrous creature loomed up, breasting the wide waves. " The second half of l. 690 is borrowed by Gower in I. 1721.

[4]I. 1719-20. Adapted from Ovid, "Metam. iv. 706 f. "

[5]I. 1721. Adapted from Ovid, "Metam. iv. 690. " See note on ll. 1717-18.

[6]I. 1727-28. Taken from Ovid, "Tristia, i. ii. 21 f. "

[7]I. 1729. Taken from Ovid, "Fasti, iii. 593. "

[8]I. 1735. Taken from Ovid, "Metam. xi. 539. "

[9]I. 1739. Adapted from Ovid, "Metam. xi. 515. "

[10]I. 1757. On leopardi see n. on I. 234. Gower could well mean "leopard" and not "lion" here, for wild beasts were caged in the Tower in his day.

[11]I. 1759-60. The "tile" stands for Wat Tyler, as in l. 653 above, and "crown" is both a symbol of the king and the cornice of the Tower. "Top" (caput) means both "leader" and "top of the building. "

[12]I. 1761-62. There is a play in these lines upon Turris ("tower") and thuris ("frankincense"), and another upon lugens ("mourning") and ludens ("merrymaking").

[13]I. 1763. "Like Babel": Babilonis ad instar. Gower should have written Babelis. For the reference to the Tower of Babel, see Gen. 11: 1-9.

[14]I. 1764. Ships of Tarshish are proverbial for large, powerful vessels bound on a long voyage and suffering destruction, as in Isa. 23: 14: "Howl, ye ships of Tarshish: for your strength is laid waste. " Cf. Isa. 2: 16; 23: 1; Psa. 48: 7 (Vulgate, Psa. 47: 8). (In the Vulgate version of Isaiah 23: 1 and 23: 14, the Ships of Tarshish are simply "ships of the sea. ")

[15]I. 1774. Adapted from Ovid, "Fasti, ii. 98. "

[16]I. 1775-76. Adapted from Ovid, "Amores, ii. 9 f. "

[17]I. 1779-80. Taken from Ovid, "Tristia, v. 12. 5 f. "

[18]I. 1781. Taken from Ovid, "Metam. xiv. 213. "

[19]I. 1793-1810. Based upon Gen. 1-3 (or Psa. 8). Cf. VII. 511 ff., and also Aeneid, VI. 574 ff.

[20]I. 1817. Literally, "to be bleeding from the death of the cross. "

[21]I. 1819-20. For the reference to Paul's deliverance at sea, see Acts 27: 14-44. For Peter's escape from prison, see Acts 4: 1-21 and 5: 17-19. For Jonah, see Jonah 1: 17-2: 10, and cf. II. 271-272.

[22]I. 1825. Adapted from Ovid, "Tristia, ii. 179. "

[23]I. 1832. Taken from Ovid, "Tristia, i. 5. 36. "

[24]I. 1847-48. Adapted from "Ovid, Pont. iii. 7. 27 f. . . . "

Chapter 19

[1]I. 1861-62. Mayor William Walworth struck down Wat Tyler at Smithfield on June 15.

[2] I. 1869. Based upon Matt. 26: 52.

[3] *I. 1870. Adapted from Ovid, Ars Amat., I. 654.

[4] I. 1898. Taken from Ovid, "Fasti, iv. 542."

[5] I. 1899-1900. Adapted from Ovid, "Pont. i. 2. 9 f."

[6] I. 1907-1908. "From Godfrey of Viterbo, Pantheon, p. 82 (ed. 1584)." See the 1726 ed., p. 61:

Tanta fit ingluvies et aquarum fluxus abundans,
Quod decimo mense vix tota revertitur unda,
Vix quoque sedatus terra resumpsit aquas.

(This is from a description of the biblical flood.)

[7] I. 1909. "'But he who walked upon the sea, ' &c., that is, Christ."

[8] I. 1913. Adapted from Ovid, "Metam. i. 328."

[9] I. 1917. Taken from Ovid, "Metam. i. 329."

[10] I. 1919. Adapted from Ovid, "Metam. i. 345."

[11] I. 1921. Adapted from Ovid, "Metam. v. 286, where we have 'nubila, ' as the sense requires." Gower substitutes numina. Miller, I, 259: ". . . and the dusky clouds were in full flight from the brightening sky.

[12] I. 1923. Adapted from Ovid, "Metam. ix. 795."

[13] I. 1925. Taken from "Metam. i. 344." (Loeb ed., I. 343.) Miller, I, 27: "Now the sea has shores, the rivers, banks full, keep within their channels. . . ." Gower substitutes sic, his favorite Latin word, for iam as the first word in the line.

[14] I. 1935. Taken from Ovid, "Metam. xiii. 440."

[15] I. 1939. Taken from Ovid, "Metam. xiii. 419."

[1]I. 1963-64. "This alludes to the supposed reply made by Brutus (son of Silvius), when he consulted the oracle of Diana in the island of Leogecia, 'Brute, sub occasum solis, ' &c. , as told by Geoffrey of Monmouth. " See The Historia Regum Britanniae of Geoffrey of Monmouth, ed. Acton Griscom (London and New York, 1929), p. 239. Cf. Mirour, 25253-54.

[2]I. 1970-80. These lines are largely a pastiche made from Ovid's complaints about the Getae. *I. 1970-72 are taken from Pont. , V. v. 46-48, *1976 from Tristia. , I. xi. 34, *1978 from Tristia, I. xi. 32, and 1979-80 from "Pont. iii. 8. 15 f. " See n. on III. 628.

[3]I. 1991-92. Adapted from Ovid, "Tristia, i. 11. 25 ff. "

[4]I. 1995-96. Adapted from Tristia, I. xi. 27-28, as indicated by Macaulay's n. on "1991 ff. "

[5]I. 1997-98. Taken from "Tristia, iii. 2. 25 f. "

[6]I. 2001-2002. Adapted from Ovid, "Her. xi. 27 f. "

[7]I. 2003-2004. Adapted from Ovid, "Her. xiv. 29 f. "

[8]I. 2029-30. Adapted from Ovid, "Rem. Amoris, 119 f. "

[9]I. 2031-32. Adapted from Ovid, "Rem. Amoris, 531 f. "

[10]I. 2033-34. Adapted from Ovid, "Her. ii. 123 f. " Showerman, p. 29: "Whether by day the soil is loosed with warmth, or whether constellations coldly shine, I look ever forth to see what wind doth sweep the straits. . . . "
The expression is the proverbial "see which way the wind blows. " Ll. 2034-46 are a series of proverbs and sententiae.

[11]I. 2037-38. Taken from Ovid, "Pont. iv. 3. 49 f. "

[12]I. 2043. Adapted from Ovid, "Pont. i. 4. 21. In Ovid we read 'animus quoque pascitur illis, ' and this probably was what Gower intended to write [instead of using corpus twice in the line]. " Wheeler, p. 289: "Leisure nourishes the body, the mind too feeds upon it. . . . "

[13]I. 2049-50. Cf. I. Prol. 13 above.

[1] I. 2071-72. Adapted, somewhat for the worse, from Ovid, "Pont. ii. 7. 9 f. " Wheeler, p. 351: "The fish once wounded by the treacherous hook fancies the barbed bronze concealed in every bit of food. "

[2] I. 2074. Taken from Ovid, "Pont. ii. 7. 8. "Wheeler, p. 349: ". . . . the shipwrecked man shrinks even from calm waters. " The expression became proverbial: See Jakob Werner, ed. Lateinische Sprichwörter und Sinnsprüche des Mittelalters (Heidelberg, 1912), T-35 (hereafter cited as "Werner").

[3] I. 2083. See n. on ll. 1615-16 above.

[4] I. 2085-86. Taken from Aurora, Gospel, 697-698 (Beichner).

[5] I. 2091. "Cp. Hist. Apollonii Tyrii, xli, 'Sicut rosa in spinis nescit compungi mucrone. ' The couplet (ll. 2091-92) means, "As unwittingly as the rose escapes the prick of its own thorns, so did I escape the blows of my attacker's sword. " Gower uses a very similar line in Conf., V. Latin verses, x. 1.

[6] I. 2094. There is a play upon the two meanings of paciens: "patient" and "suffering. " The idea was proverbial; cf. Troilus, IV. 1584 and n. Cf. also III. 742. The next line, *2095, is adapted from Fasti, I. 703.

[7] I. 2099-2100. Gower's complaint is in a sense justified. There were outbreaks of violence almost annually after 1381 for many years, although none of them was on the scale of that year. Over 7000 rebels were executed after the Great Revolt of 1381, which died down sooner than might have been expected.

[8] I. 2108. Proverbial. See Smith-Heseltine, s. v. "Forewarned, forearmed. "

[9] I. 2115-16. Taken from Aurora, Gospel, 699-700 (Beichner).

[10] I. 2117-18. Taken from Aurora, Gospel, 857-858 (Beichner).

[11] I. 2125. Taken from Aurora, Gospel, 859 (Beichner).

[12] I. 2139. Adapted from Ovid, "Pont. i. 5. 47. " Wheeler, p. 293:

"When I have devoted to sleep what hours my frame demands. . . . "
Gower is here apologizing for representing his dream vision as being
of such length that an ordinary night's sleep would be too short to encompass it. (Conrad's Lord Jim makes a similar demand upon veri-
similitude.)

[13]I. 2150. Adapted from Ovid, "Rem. Amoris, 484. "

Notes to BOOK II

[1]II. Prol. 7-8. Taken from Aurora, Exod. 247-248 (Beichner).
Invoking the aid of the Holy Ghost remained a literary convention as
late as Paradise Lost.

[2]II. Prol. 15. "Cp. Speculum Stultorum, p. 11, 1. [14]. . . . "
(Macaulay refers to 1. 41.)

[3]II. Prol. 19. There is a play here upon stylus ("style") and stilla
tus, which may mean "stale" or possibly "overly copious" or "drooping; " literally, "distilled. " The word may also mean "metrical. "
   This line is one of several indications in the poem that literature
was often orally delivered in the Middle Ages. On this matter see Ruth
Crosby, "Oral Delivery in the Middle Ages, " Speculum, XI (1936), 88-
110, and H. J. Chaytor, From Script to Print: An Introduction to Medieval Literature (Cambridge, Eng., 1945), passim. Cf. below, 11. 49
and III. Prol. 60. The Vox Clamantis, however, was of course intended
to be seen and not heard.

[4]II. Prol. 18-28, Cf. Conf. Amantis, VIII. 3110 ff. and 3062* ff.,
for a similar conventional apology.

[5]II. Prol. 33. Taken from Speculum Stultorum, p. 50, 1. 25 (Raymo). Gower always represents himself in his writings as being old.
True, he was approximately fifty when he wrote the poem, which is old
by the standards of his time, but he continued to write copiously for
another twenty years.

[6]II. Prol. 39-40. This couplet contains a play upon canina and
canam.

[7]II. Prol. 41. Adapted from "Deut. xxxii. 13. . . . " ". . . and
he made him to suck honey out of the rock, and oil out of the flinty rock
The expression was proverbial (Walz no. 1016).

[8] II. Prol. 45. An allusion to Balaam's ass. See Num. 22: 21 ff. The motif was conventional. Cf. III. 531-532.

[9] II. Prol. 49-50. Adapted from "Fasti, i. 73 f."

[10] II. Prol. 51: Si tamen incendat Sinon Excetraque sufflet, is a troublesome line. "The supposed mischief-maker is compared to Sinon, who gave a signal by fire which led to the destruction of Troy; cp. Conf. Amantis, i. 1172 [or Aeneid, II. 79 ff.]. I cannot satisfactorily explain 'Excetra.'" MS. L reads Symon excetraque, and D reads si non excecraque. I adopt Symon from L in view of Gower's many references in the poem to Simon, the archetypal briber (see n. on III. 249), and of the inappropriateness of a reference to Sinon here. Excetra is a Classical Latin word meaning "serpent." Its capitalization indicates that Gower may have meant "the old Serpent," Satan himself. Hence the couplet may mean that Gower will not desist from his task because of bribery or the ragings of the Devil.

[11] II. Prol. 53. The statement about the poet's blindness is not to be taken literally here. He was not blind until approximately twenty years later. See Introduction, p.36 and Dedicatory Epistle, n. 1.

[12] II. Prol. 57-58. Macaulay's note points out that ll. 57-58 are "From [Alexander] Neckam, De Vita Monachorum, p. 175 ed. [Thomas] Wright, [The Anglo-Latin Satirical Poets and Epigrammatists of the Twelfth Century] (Rolls Series, 59, vol. ii)." Neckam here alludes to Matt. 5: 15, Mark 4: 21, Luke 8: 16 or 11: 33. Cf. Dedicatory Epistle, l. 34 and n.

All future references to and quotations from Neckam's De Vita Monachorum are to this edition.

[13] II. Prol. 64. Adapted from "Ars Amat. ii. 166."

[14] II. Prol. 66-67. Probably an allusion to Mark 9: 23.

[15] II. Prol. 68. Proverbial (Walz no. 193b). Cf. Conf., V. 2400-2401 (Walz no. 193a).

[16] *II. Prol. 77. Taken from Ars Amat., III. 124.

[17] II. Prol. 83. See Introduction, p. 11. The phrase "the voice of one crying in the wilderness" describes John the Baptist in Matt. 3: 3, Mark 1: 3, Luke 3: 4, and John 1: 23. Its import is Messianic in Isa. 40: 3. On the poem's title see Wickert, pp. 65-67.

Chapter 1

[1]Chap. 1. Heading. Gower does not capitalize fortuna, but it is clear that he means the goddess Fortune or Fortuna. "With the general drift of what follows cp. Conf. Amantis, Prol. 529 ff. "

[2]II. 1. Cf. "Conf. Amantis, viii. 2212. " Cf. also Voice, I. Prol. 36; TC, II. 4 and 233-234; Troilus, I. 7, and IV. Proem, 12-14.

[3]II. 3. A reference to Eccl. 1: 2 or 12: 8.

[4]II. 10. Or, "and no station (status) on the wheel of Fortune (in orbe) remains fixed for him. "

[5]II. 18. "nos: meaning [we,] the people of England, as compared with those of other countries. " Gower is often nationalistic: cf. VII. 1289 ff. and see Macaulay's Introduction, p. xxix.

[6]II. 31-32. Adapted from "Tristia, v. 8. 19 f. "

[7]II. 33. Taken from "Tristia, v. 5. 47. "

[8]II. 41. "Job v. 6, 'Nihil in terra sine causa fit': cp. Mirour de l'Omme, 26857. " The sentence is not given in the King James Version.
Cf. also III. 263.

Chapter 2

[1]II. 55. Perhaps an allusion to Matt. 19: 6 or Mark 10: 9: "What therefore God hath joined together, let not man put asunder. " Cf. V. 893-894.

[2]II. 59. "This is the usual opposition of rose and nettle, based perhaps originally on Ovid, Rem. Amoris, 46: cp. Conf. Amantis, ii. 401 ff. "

[3]II. 67-68. "Cp. Boethius, Consol. Phil. 2 Pr. 4, 'in omni adversitate fortunae infelicissimum genus est infortunii fuisse felicem. ' So Dante, Inf. v. 121 ff.,

> 'Nessun maggior dolore,
> Che ricordarsi del tempo felice
> Nella miseria. '"

Here the thought is only coincidentally similar, for Gower probably did not read Dante. See Paget Toynbee, Dante in English Literature from Chaucer to Cary (c. 1380-1844) (2 vols., London, 1909), I, 17: "On the whole. . . it seems probable that Gower had no direct knowledge of Dante. " But see ibid., n. 2: "[There is possibly a reminiscence of Inferno v. 121-3 in the second book of the Vox Clamantis (ll. 67-8). . . . Gower may, however, have borrowed the sentiment from a passage in Chaucer's Troilus and Cressida, iii., 1625-8; or he may have taken it direct from Boethius, who was Dante's, as well as Chaucer's, authority.]" Albert S. Cook, in "Dante and Gower, " Archiv für das Studium der Neueren Sprachen und Literaturen, CXXXII (1914), 395, unconvincingly maintains that Gower read Dante. But the English poet's mention of him in Conf., VII. 2329* sounds very much as if Gower had Chaucer's WBT, 1125-26, in mind.

[4] II. 69-70. A reference to Luke 8:18: ". . . for whosoever hath, to him shall be given; and whosoever hath not, from him shall be taken even that which he seemeth to have. " (Approximately the same is repeated in Luke 19:26 and Matt. 13:12 and 25:29.)

The marginal reference Lucas: Omni habenti dabitur is given in Conf., V. 7719-20. But these lines are amusingly different:

> What man hath hors men yive him hors,
> And who non hath of him no fors. . . .

[5] II. 77-80. The reference is probably to enemies in general. The tropological meaning of cornua ("horns") is "strength, " "might, " "courage, " etc.

[6] II. 71-82. A frequent lament in Gower's day. Cf. VI. 937 ff.

[7] II. 86-87. Cf. ll. 345-46 and 629-30 below, where Gower similarly concludes against fatalism. At heart, however, he is a fatalist: cf. Conf., I. 1714, "Bot nede he mot that nede schal, " and III, 352 ff., as well as ll. 347-48 below. More important, the account of the downfall of Richard II in the TC is fatalistically conceived throughout.

Chapter 3

[1] *II. 109. Adapted from Ovid, Pont., IV. iii. 35. Wheeler, p. 433: "All human affairs hang by a slender thread. . . . "

The expression is proverbial (Walz no. 214c). Cf. Conf., VI. 1513-14 (Walz no. 214a), Mirour, 10948-50 (Walz no. 2146), Troilus, III. 1636, and Piers, B Passus VI. 246-247.

[2]II.117-120. Adapted from "Her. v. 109 ff. In l. 117 'siccis' is substituted, not very happily, for 'suci.'" Showerman, pp. 65, 67: ". . .but you--are lighter than leaves what time their juice has failed, and dry they flutter in the shifting breeze; you have less weight than the tip of the spear of grain, burned light and crisp by ever-shining suns."

[3]II.134. Literally, "does not know how to keep a central place," or "place of focus."

Chapter 4

[1]II.152. Proverbial (Walz no. 213).

[2]*II.159-161. Adapted from the Pantheon, p. 165 (ed. 1726). The idea was proverbial (Walz no. 208). Cf. Conf., VI. 1509-11 (Walz no. 210).

[3]II.163-164. Adapted from "Tristia, v. 8. 15 f."

[4]II.167-170. Adapted from "Tristia, i. 5. 27 ff."

[5]*II.187. Suggested by a line in the Pantheon, 1726 ed., p. 165.

[6]II.193-194. Taken from Speculum Stultorum, p. 31, ll. 3-4 (Raymo).

[7]II.199-200. Macaulay objects, "There seems to be no grammatical construction here." But the couplet is clear in its meaning, if somewhat awkward.

[8]II.203. Proverbial (Walz no. 202).

Chapter 5

[1]II.221. Saturn was traditionally a planet of evil influence. Cf. III. 923, and see Conf., VII. 935 ff.

[2] II. 233-234. A reference to Tobit 11.

[3] II. 239ff. "With this passage cp. Mirour de l'Omme, 27013 ff., where nearly the same examples are given. The classification is according to the nature of the things affected, first the heavenly bodies, then the elements of air, water, fire, and earth, and finally living creatures. This arrangement is more clearly brought out in the Mirour." Cf. also Conf., VII. 511-520. II. 239 is proverbial: cf. Conf., VII. 651-654, and Mirour, 27001 ff.

[4] II. 245-246. Taken from Aurora, Josue 169-170 (Beichner). Cf. Mirour, 27014-18; and see Josh. 10: 12-14.

[5] II. 247-248. A reference to Matt. 2: 9-10. Cf. Mirour, 27019-21.

[6] II. 249-250. Cf. Mirour, 27022-24.

[7] II. 251-252. A reference to Ex. 14: 15-22. Cf. Mirour, 27079-80.

[8] II. 253-254: A reference to Matt. 14: 25-31. Cf. III. 319-320 and Mirour, 27037-39.

[9] II. 255-256. A reference to II Kings (Vulgate, IV Kings) 6: 4-7. Cf. Mirour, 27040-42.

[10] II. 257-258. The "three Hebrew children" (pueros) are, of course, Shadrach, Meshach, and Abednego. For this story, see Dan. 3: 15-27.

[11] II. 259-260, "Cp. Mirour, 27031, and n." "The story is in the Legenda Aurea: it is to the effect that in an assembly of prelates Hilarius found himself elbowed out of all the honourable seats and compelled to sit on the ground. Upon this the floor rose under him and brought him up to a level with the rest." (Macaulay's n. on Mirour, 27031).

[12] II. 261-262. A reference to Num. 20: 7-11.

[13] II. 263-264. This story of Alexander the Great is told in Godfrey of Viterbo's Pantheon (1726 ed., p. 166) (See n. on Voice, I. 765-776.) George Cary, in The Medieval Alexander (Cambridge, Eng., 1956), points out that Gower usually used Alexander as an example to be

avoided (pp. 253-255). For the story alluded to here, see also Historia de Preliis, Par. 77.

[14] II. 265-266. Cf. Mirour, 27046-48.

[15] II. 267-268. "Cp. Mirour, 27049 ff." The reference is to Dan. 6: 16-23.

[16] II. 269-270. A reference to Ex. 16: 8, 11-13.

[17] II. 271-272. A reference to Jonah 1: 17-3: 3, where we find that the city of Nineveh was actually "three days' journey" from the "dry land" upon which the whale "vomited out Jonah." Cf. I. 1819-20, and Mirour, 27056-60; cf. also Chaucer, MLT, 486 ff.

[18] II. 273-278. These lines are in such direct contradiction to Book that when Gower added the latter to the poem he surely overlooked them.

[19] II. 277-280. Cf. Mirour, 27065-27072.

Chapter 6

[1] II. 281 ff. "See Mirour de l'Omme, 27073 ff." The reference to David is to II Sam. (Vulgate, II Kings) 24: 10-17.

[2] II. 283. A reference to Gen. 19: 24-25.

[3] II. 284. For the reference to Korah, see Num. 16: 30-35. Cf. VI. 1228, and Mirour, 2344-47.

[4] II. 285-286. A reference to the biblical flood, Gen. 7.

[5] II. 287-288. For the reference to the fate of Dathan and Abiram, see Num. 16: 25-33. Cf. VI. 1227-28, 1230, and Mirour, 2341-43.

[6] II. 289-290. A reference to II. Macc. 11: 1-12.

[7] II. 291-292. A reference to Tobit 3: 8.

[8] II. 305-306. For the story of David and Goliath, see I Sam. (Vulgate, I Kings) 17: 32 ff. Cf. Mirour, 2173-84.

[9] II. 307-308. A reference to II Kings (Vulgate, IV Kings) 20: 1-6.

The same story is told in Isa. 38: 1-8.

[10] II. 309. For the story of Susanna and the elders, see the Vulgate, Dan. 13, which is the Apocryphal History of Susanna.

[11] II. 310. See the Book of Esther (the Vulgate includes six and a half additional Apocryphal chapters).

[12] II. 315-316. A reference to Exod. 14: 27-28.

[13] II. 317-318. A reference to Dan. 4: 33 (Vulgate, 4: 30).

[14] II. 319-320. See especially I Sam. (Vulgate, I Kings) 13: 9-14, 15: 10-35, 26: 21, and 31: 1-13.

[15] II. 321-322. A reference to II Chron. 26: 16-21. In the King James Version Azariah is known as Uzziah, while Azariah is the name of the chief priest, who rebukes him. Uzziah is "Ozias" in the Vulgate.

[16] II. 323-324. The reference is to I Kings (Vulgate, III Kings) 21: 1-22; see also 21: 28-29. Cf. Mirour, 4957-61, and Conf., VII. 2527 ff.

[17] II. 325-326. The reference is to I Kings (Vulgate, III Kings) 12: 6-24, or to II Chron. 10: 1-15. Cf. VI. 1295-96. Gower tells the story of Rehoboam in the Conf., VIII. 4027 ff. Dante sees him as an example of pride laid low in Purg., 12: 46-48.

[18] II. 327-328. The reference is to I Sam. (Vulgate, I Kings) 2: 12-17, and the couplet is adapted in part from 4: 11: "And the ark of God was taken, and the two sons of Eli, Hophni and Phinehas, were slain." Cf. Piers, B Passus X. 280-283.

[19] II. 329-330. The reference is to I Sam. (Vulgate, I Kings) 4: 17-18: "And the messenger answered and said, Israel is fled before the Philistines, and there hath been also a great slaughter among the people, and the two sons also, Hophni and Phinehas, are dead, and the ark of God is taken. /And it came to pass, when he made mention of the ark of God, that he fell from off the seat backward by the side of the gate, and his neck brake, and he died. . . ." Eli's sin was his failure properly to check his sons' misdeeds. See III. 1145-48.
Cf. Piers, B Passus X. 280-283, and C Passus I. 103-124, in both of which the application is different.

[20] II. 333. Based ultimately upon Gal. 6: 7, or Job 4: 8.

[21]II. 335-344. Cf. VI. 871-902. Lines 335-338 are taken from Aurora, Jud. 5-8 (Beichner).

[22]II. 345-348. See n. on II. 86-87 above. In l. 348 the verb ludere ("sport") does not do justice to Gower's general seriousness, but merely carries out the figure of playing at dice.

Chapter 7

[1]II. 353-354. "Cp. Godfrey of Viterbo, Pantheon, p. 9 (ed. 1584). . . ." (Page 17 in 1726 ed.)

[2]II. 357-359. "These three lines are from the Pantheon, p. 9." The 1726 ed. (p. 16) runs somewhat differently:

Omne quod est, esse cum tempore, protulit ex se,
Nulla coaeva Deo tempore, nosse queo.

[3]*II. 361-363. Taken from Godfrey of Viterbo, Pantheon (ed. 1726), p. 17.

[4]II. 371-374. "Taken with slight change from the Pantheon, p. 10. (1726 ed., p. 18.)

[5]II. 375. A reference to Gen. 1: 26: "And God said, Let us make man in our image. . . ." Cf. I. 1807-8 and see n. Cf. also VII. 511 ff

[6]II. 377-378. "From Aurora, (MS. Bodley 822) f. 7 v° [Beichner edition: Gen. 187-188]." Gower expresses himself similarly on the Trinity in Conf., VII. 73 ff.

Chapter 8

[1]II. 379-390. Cf. John 1: 1-14.

[2]II. 414. Macaulay translates, "That which the new star brings argues that he is God." Gower has already called the Virgin Mary a "star" in I. 2083 and perhaps in I. 1615. See n. on I. 1615.
II. 414 may have been suggested by the Pantheon (ed. 1726), p. 231:

Nata maris stella, regina Maria novella . . . .

[3] II. 429-430. Taken from Aurora, Exod. 1291-2 (Beichner).
"Baptismal water" is literally "wave" (vnda).

[4] II. 431-432. Taken from Aurora, Gen. 187-188 (Beichner). For
the original reference to Christ as a "second Adam, " see I Cor. 15: 45:
"And so it is written, The first man Adam was made a living soul; the
last Adam was made a quickening spirit. " The concept of Christ as a
second Adam was very common in the Middle Ages and later. Cf., for
example, P. L.: XI. 383. The concept is symbolically treated in Purg.,
32: 37 ff.

[5] II. 433-434. Taken from Aurora, Num. 425-426 (Beichner).
"The New Law" is, of course, "the New Testament. " ("The Old Law"
is a frequent term for "the Old Testament. ")
On this terminology of "Old Law" and "New Law" see R. H.
Bowers, "A Middle English Treatise on Hermeneutics: Harley MS.
2276, 32v—35v, " PMLA, LXV (1950), 597, n. 33.

Chapter 9

[1] With this chapter cf. ll. 54-77 of Gower's Carmen Super Multiplici Viciorum Pestilencia (Works, III, 346-354), where many of the
same lines are used. Chapter 9 is an elaboration on Adam's sin as contained in Gen. 3: 22: "And the Lord God said, Behold, the man is become as one of us, to know good and evil . . . . "

[2] II. 449-450. Taken from Aurora, Exod. 85-86 (Beichner). This
is a common medieval idea. Cf., for example, Piers, B. Passus X.
116, and Skeat's n.; Conf., Prol. 352-4.

[3] *II. 461. Taken from Ovid, Ars Amat., II. 43. Mozley, p. 69:
"Ills often stir the wits . . . . " The expression is proverbial (Walz no.
130).

[4] II. 467-468. An allusion to Heb. 11: 1.

[5] II. 468. An allusion to John 14: 6. Cf. IV. 78.

[6] II. 472. Perhaps based upon Mark 9: 23.

[7] II. 481. Based upon Luke 3: 5 or Isa. 40: 44. Cf. III. 251-252.

[8]II. 483-484. Taken from Aurora, Jud. 91-92 (Beichner).

[9]II. 487-488. benedicti . . . nemo potest: "The MSS. give 'bene-dicti, ' but it seems probable that 'benedici' was meant. " I have trans-lated as benedici.

[10]II. 489-492. Taken from Aurora, I Kings 61-64 (Beichner). There is possibly an echo here of I Tim. 1:15.

[11]II. 493-494. Taken from Aurora, I Kings 85-86 (Beichner).

Chapter 10

[1]II. Chapter 10. "Cp. Isaiah, xliv. 9-20. " Cf. also Exod. 20: 4-5. Gower is at pains to avoid both Wycliffite iconoclasm and the im-age worship then alleged by reformers. His position is strictly ortho-dox. Cf. Conf., V. 1497 ff., where Gower discusses the origins of idol worship.

[2]II. 509-512. These lines expand Eccl. 12:1: "Remember now thy Creator in the days of thy youth. . . . "

[3]II. 521-524. Perhaps an allusion to Psa. 115: 4-7 (Vulgate, 113: 4-7).

[4]II. 531-532. A slightly altered quotation from "Psalms, cxiii. 8. " King James Version, Psa. 115. 8: "They that make them are like unto them; so is every one that trusteth in them. "

[5]II. 540. Literally, "let it be far from the world. "

[6]II. 541-544. For a similar charge that priests fostered idolatry for the sake of gain, cf. Piers Plowman, C Passus I. 95-124.

[7]II. 545-550. See Exod. 33: 18-20.

[8]II. 555-556. A reference to the Harrowing of Hell, in the Apo-cryphal Gospel of Nicodemus. See Arthur Westcott, The Gospel of Nicodemus and Kindred Documents: Translated with an Introduction (London: Heath, Cranton and Ouseley, n. d.), pp. 96 ff.

[9]II. 573. See n. on ll. 555-556.

[10]II. 573-578. Based on part of the Apostles' Creed: ". . . He descended into hell; The third day he rose again from the dead: He ascended into heaven, And sitteth on the right hand of God the Father Almighty: From thence he shall come to judge the quick and the dead. "

Chapter 11

[1]II. 584. Based upon John 1: 3.

[2]II. 619 ff. Macaulay notes, "Cp. Ovid, Metam. i. 74 ff. " The parallels in diction are few, although the general idea is the same. Miller, I, 7: ". . . the stars and divine forms occupied the floor of heaven, the sea fell to the shining fishes for their home, earth received the beasts, and the mobile air the birds. "

[3]II. 623-630. Cf. VII. 1399 ff. and see n. on VII. 1400. On the idea of man, and not Fortune, being the cause of all ills, cf. Dante, Purg., 16: 66 ff., esp. ll. 82-83. Cf. also Conf., Prol. 520-528, 544-549, and 905-909

Notes to BOOK III

Prologue

[1]III. Prologue. Much of this prologue sounds as though it originally began the entire poem: see especially ll. 89 ff. Perhaps the critique of the three estates which begins in Book III was written even before Book II, which is more or less an independent essay. Macaulay suggests, "There seems . . . to have been an alternative numbering, which proceeded on the principle of making five books, beginning with the third, the second being treated as a general prologue to the whole poem. In connection with this we may take the special invocation of divine assistance in the prologue of the third book, which ends with the couplet,

'His tibi libatis nouus intro nauta profundum,
Sacrum pneuma rogans vt mea vela regas. '" (P. xxxi, n. 2)

It should be noted that Gower likewise invokes divine assistance in II. Prol. 3-10.

[2]III. Prol. 11-13. "The author characteristically takes care to point out that in his criticism of the Church he is expressing not his own private opinion, but the 'commune dictum, ' the report which went abroad among the people, and the 'vox populi' had for him always a high authority. Cp. Mirour de l'Omme, 18445 ff., 19057 ff., and see below, l. 1267 ff., iv. 19 f., [691 f.,] 709 f. [and vii. 1447-48, 1470]." It is well to add, however, that the idea of vox populi, vox dei had been proverbial from Hesiod onward; it appeared in St. Thomas Aquinas, Dante, et al. Actually, Gower did not at heart subscribe to it; the vox populi, after all, manifested itself most noticeably to Gower in the form of the Peasants' Revolt. See also n. on TC, I. 9-10, and Wickert, pp. 73-79.

"With what is said in this Book of the condition of the Church and the clergy we may compare the author's Mirour de l'Omme, 18421-20832. "

[3]III. Prol. 18.   lesum is the legal term for "injured party. " Gower often makes use of legal terminology in the poem; however, his knowledge of it is such as any intelligent layman could acquire.

[4]III. Prol. 39.   The fountain of goodness probably refers to Christ. Cf. ll. 83 ff.

[5]III. Prol. 45-46.   An allusion to I Cor. 13:13.

[6]III. Prol. 59-60.   See n. on II. Prol. 18-28.

[7]III. Prol. 61.   Adapted from "Pont. iv. 14. 41.

[8]III. Prol. 64.   Adapted from "Pont. iv. 9. 10.

[9]III. Prol. 67-68.   Adapted from "Tristia, ii. 301 f. " Wheeler, p. 77: "All things can corrupt perverted minds, yet all those things stand harmless in their proper places. " Cf. Bal., XLIX. 1.

[10]III. Prol. 75-78.   These lines involve plays upon liber ("book"), liberat ("makes free"), and liber ("free").   There are also overtones of the following idea: "Go, my book, under Him Who liberates all serfs . . . . If you can pass by as a freeman . . . . "

Such an address to one's book is an old literary convention.   Cf. Chaucer, Troilus, V. 1786 ff. and see Robinson's n.

[11]III. Prol. 82.   Adapted from "Pont. ii. 2. 126. " Cf. I. 2074 and see n.

[12]III. Prol. 95. Proverbial. Cf. I. Prol. 33-34 and see n.

[13]III. Prol. 100. The first of many puns in the poem upon the two words mundus, "pure, " and mundus, "world. " I have indicated these puns in the notes only where the translation does not make it clear that they occur. Sometimes the verb mundare, "purify, " is substituted for the adjective. In any case, when the words "pure" and "world" occur within the same sentence, a pun is always intended.

[14]III. Prol. 106. Sacrum pneuma continues the nautical metaphor in its meaning of "sacred wind, " as well as the religious metaphor in its meaning of "Holy Spirit, " or "Holy Ghost. " The concluding couplet (ll. 105-106) of the Prologue to Book III is taken from Aurora, Lev. 25-26 (Beichner), and in that poem it concludes Peter of Riga's prologue to "Leviticus" (Beichner, p. 588).

Chapter 1

[1]III. 1-28. The text of ll. 1-28 is as given in S, the final form. The intermediate text (of which line numbers are marked with one asterisk) is as given in CHGEDL, and the original text (of which the line numbers are marked with two asterisks) is as given in TH$_2$. "It will be noticed that the lines as given by TH$_2$ make no mention of the schism of the Papacy. " Since the Great Schism began in 1378, we may conclude that the first version of these lines was written before that year.

On the subject of the Great Schism, see Walter Ullmann, The Origin of the Great Schism (London: Burns, Oates, 1949).

[2]III. 1. John T. Queenan, A Translation from Latin to English of the Third Book of John Gower's Vox Clamantis, Rutgers Diss. (New Brunswick, 1949), translates tres trina gerentes as "each complementing the other. " This translation is hereafter cited as "Queenan. "

[3]III. 6(8*). This is typical of English sentiment at the time of the schism in 1378. The popes at Avignon were under the influence of France, England's traditional enemy. But cf. Piers, C Passus XXII. 411-431 or B Passus XIX. 407-427 for the sentiment of a "lewed vycory" against all popes (and cardinals). Nor does Gower exclude even the "true" pope from blame in Book III.

[4]III. 10(11*). "Rule" (regula) refers to a monastic rule, or complete set of instructions.

[5]III. 11(13*). The words Christus erat pauper are from Speculum Stultorum, p. 110, l. 107 (Raymo).

[6]III. 9**. Cf. ll. 183-184 below and see n. on ll. 177-182.

[7]III. 27-30. Cf. Piers, B Passus XIII. 60-67.
Gluttony and lust were thought to be closely associated. Cf. Piers, B Passus I. 30 and VI. 267-269.
Cf. also III. 125-128, IV. 35-36, 61-62, 165-168, Conf., VI. 502 ff., Eph. 5:18, and Pard T, 481-484. The Middle-English word "likerous" meant both "lecherous" and "gluttonous."

[8]*III. 39-40. Adapted from Fasti, v. 31-32.

[9]III. 41. Adapted in part from "Amores, iii. 8. 55."

[10]III. 43. The proverbial "money talks." The succeeding lines suggest a similar proverb, "When money speaks the truth is silent." They also involve plays upon census ("wealth," "property") and sensus ("intelligence," "understanding").

[11]III. 63. Adapted from "Fasti, i. 225."

[12]III. 65-66. Adapted from "Fasti, i. 249 f."

Chapter 2

[1]III. 79-80. "Thomas' post" refers to the Archbishopric of Canterbury, once possessed by Thomas à Becket; the criticism is at variance with I. Chapter 14. "Martin" refers to St. Martin, the founder of French monasticism. He established a monastery near Tours in A.D. 365.

[2]III. 85. "Potted meats" is ollarum carnes, the Vulgate phrase for "fleshpots." The play upon words is repeated in l. 89.

[3]III. 85-90. "Chiefly from the Aurora of Petrus (de) Riga, (MS. Bodley 822) f. 71."
"It would seem that Gower read 'Gebas' (which has no meaning) for 'Cepas' . . . ." Cepas and Gebas, however, are variant forms of the same word, meaning "onions."

[4]III. 103. Taken from Speculum Stultorum, p. 57, l. 7 (Raymo).

[5]III. 107-108. Adapted from Speculum Stultorum, p. 57, ll. 3-4 (Raymo).

[6]III. 115. Adapted from "Metam. xv. 173. "

[7]III. 116. This line contains the first of many puns in the poem upon honor, meaning "honor, " and onus, meaning "onus, " "burden, " "responsibility. " These puns are not pointed out in the notes unless the translation does not make them obvious.

[8]III. 119-120. Cf. Chaucer, Pard T, 517-520.

[9]III. 126. Cornua ceca ("blind courage") involves an obvious indecent allusion. There is also another possible allusion in the fact that cornua could mean the points of a bishop's mitre.

Chapter 3

[1]III. Chap. 3. Heading. "Cp. Conf. Amantis, Prol. [298] (margin), where this is given as a quotation from Gregory. " See Macaulay's note on Conf. , Prol. 289.

[2]III. 137. Based upon Matt. 6: 24. The expression became proverbial.(See Werner, n-29 and n-262.) Cf. IV. 13-14. Father Beichner cites l. 137 as an example of the difficulty in sometimes distinguishing Gower's short scriptural paraphrases from Peter of Riga's (Speculum, XXX [1955], 587).

[3]III. 141-142. "Cp. Mirour de l'Omme, 18553 [ff]. "

[4]III. 153-157. Taken from Aurora, Lev. 365-369 (Beichner).

[5]III. 167-168 are "From Aurora, f. 37. " Ll. 165-168 refer to Exod. 17: 8-16; these four lines are all from Aurora, Exod. 333-336 (Beichner).

[6]III. 177-182. Taken from Aurora, Lev. 441-446 (Beichner). With ll. 174-184 cf. Chaucer's Parson, Gen Prol, 496 f., 515-528, and see Robinson's n. on l. 497, which refers to Matt. 5: 19 and Conf. , V. 1850. Cf. also l. 9** above, and ll. 191-192 below.

[7]III. 190. "Cleanse" is literally "anoint" (vngere).

[8]III. 193 ff. "With this passage compare Conf. Amantis, Prol. 407-413, and Mirour de l'Omme, 20161 ff. In all these places a distinct charge is brought against the clergy, to the effect that they encourage vice, in order to profit by it themselves in money and in influence: 'the prostitute is more profitable to them than the nun, ' as our author significantly says in the Mirour (20149). "

Conf., Prol. 407-413:

> And upon this also men sein,
> That fro the leese which is plein
> Into the breres thei forcacche
> Her Orf, for that thei wolden lacche
> With such duresce, and so bereve
> That schal upon the thornes leve
> Of wulle, which the brere hath tore . . . .

Macaulay paraphrases this in a note: "The sentence here is a little disorderly and therefore obscure: 'Men say that they drive forth their flock from the smooth meadow into the briars, because they wish to seize and by such ill-treatment take away the wool which shall remain upon the thorns, torn out by the briars, ' &c. " The same idea is more clearly stated in Mirour, 20161-69,

[9]III. 197. Cf. Chaucer's Summoner, Gen Prol, 656-658.

[10]III. 201. Dum loculus pregnat satis, impregnare licebit. Queenan: "When the purse is sufficiently pregnant, it will be permissible to cause pregnancy. "

[11]III. 207. Literally, "He spends the Mammon of tainted money. " Another allusion to Matt. 6: 24, as in l. 137.

[12]III. 209 ff. "Cp. Mirour de l'Omme, 20113 ff. "

[13]III. 219-220. A reference to John 8: 3-11. Cf. l. 691 below, and IV. 603-604.

Chapter 4

[1]III. Chap. 4. Heading. MSS. LTH₂ substitute the following for this chapter heading: "Here he speaks of how new things are decreed

as sins for us almost daily, by means of positive laws. Before they are committed, however, the prelates offer dispensation for them for the sake of money, and they freely allow them to be committed for the sake of gold. " MS. L terms the positive laws as diligentibus, which can mean both "unremitting" and "profitable. " In the Table of Contents, MS. L reads as L does here.

"For this attack on the 'positive law' of the Church, cp. Conf. Amantis, Prol. 247, Mirour, 18469 ff. The 'lex positiva' is that which is enjoined not as of inherent moral obligation, but as imposed by Church discipline. " (Chaucer mentions "positif lawe" in KT, 1167.)

For Gower's strictures in this chapter against pardons and indulgences, cf. Piers, B Passus VII, 168-194.

[2]III. 243-244. Taken from Aurora, Deut. 61-62 (Beichner).

[3]III. 249. This is one of many references to Simon the Sorcerer. See Acts 8: 9-24, "Cp. Mirour, 18997 ff. " Cf. also ll. 1189-90 below, for example, and Conf., Prol. 204, 241-242, and 438-443.

[4]III. 252. Probably a reference to Luke 3: 5 (or to Matt. 7: 13-14 or Luke 13: 24). Cf. II. 481, and IV. 324.

[5]III. 258. An allusion to Matt. 11: 30: "For my yoke is easy, and my burden is light. " Cf. l. 721 below.

[6]III. 263. Omne fit ex causa is biblical and proverbial. Cf. II. 41 and see n.

[7]III. 265 ff. "Cp. Mirour 18505 ff. "

[8]III. 275-276. Perhaps Gower was thinking of I Cor. 15: 40-41. III. 275 is from Peter of Riga's interpretation of creation in Aurora, Gen. 109 (Beichner). See Gen. 1: 14-18.

Chapter 5

[1]III. 283 ff. "Cp. Mirour, 18637 [ff.], Conf. Amantis, ii. 3486 [ff]. " This is an allusion to the celebrated fabrication of the Donation of Constantine, according to the terms of which the Emperor gave the Lateran to the Church as its initial temporal possession.

For the voice of the angel in the sky, cf. Piers, B Passus XV. 519-529 or C Passus XVIII. 220-232, and see Skeat's note on the latter. Cf. also Conf., Prol. 858-859.

[2]III. 293-294. A just criticism. The Church owned one third of the land in England in the fourteenth and fifteenth centuries.

[3]III. 303-304. A reference to John 18: 36.

[4]III. 307-310. Cf. ll. 651 ff. below.

[5]III. 313. A quotation from Matt. 7: 20. Cf. Matt. 7: 16.

[6]III. 317. A reference to Acts 5: 15.

[7]III. 319-320. A reference to Matt. 14: 29. Cf. II. 253-254.

[8]III. 327. Quoted from Romans 12: 19. Cf. Piers, B Passus VI. 228.

[9]III. 327-328. There is a play here upon vindicta ("vengeance") and vindicat ("vindicate").

Chapter 6

[1]III. Chap. 6. "With this chapter compare Mirour, 18649-18732."

[2]III. 337-338. This is not an exact quotation, but is based on Matt. 26: 52: "Then said Jesus unto him, Put up again thy sword into his place: for all they that take the sword shall perish with the sword." (Cf. Rev. 13: 10.) In the verse quoted, Jesus speaks to an unnamed follower who struck off the ear of one of His persecutors. But in John 18: 10, Peter is named as the one who struck the blow with the sword. Gower refers to Peter often in order to draw a contrast between him, the first pope, and the popes of his own time.

[3]III. 363-364. David makes a statement somewhat like this to Goliath in I Sam. (Vulgate, I Kings) 17: 47.

[4]III. 367-368. Ll. 367-368, as do ll. 369 and 371, involve a play upon archa ("ark") and arcus ("bow").

[5]III. 369-370. Taken from Aurora, Gen. 743-744 (Beichner).

[6]III. 375. The following appears in the margin at l. 375:

Note here concerning the war on the part of the clergy in the time of King Richard in Flanders; for at that time not only the secular but also the regular priests took to plundering in mortal battles there, like laymen.

"The note which we find here in the margin of SCHGD refers to the crusade of the bishop of Norwich in Flanders in the year 1383, which probably took place soon after the completion of our author's book. It is added in SCHG in what appears to be one and the same hand, possibly that of the author himself. If we may judge by the manner in which the campaign in question is referred to by contemporary chroniclers, it seems to have been considered a public scandal by many others besides Gower. "

[7] III. 376-378. There is a play upon soluimus, solutus, and soluit ("released") and soluere ("render").

[8] III. 391-393. This sentence contains a play upon valet and valent ("be good, "be worthy") and validi ("valiant").

[9] III. 403-404. Proverbial (Walz no. 4c). Cf. III. 537, VI. 1174, and Conf., V. 7817-20, and VI. 2383: "An ende proveth every thinge. " Gower's exitus acta probat is from Ovid, Her., II. 85 (not noted by Macaulay). Cf. Matt. 10: 26 and I Cor. 4: 5.

Chapter 7

[1] III. 407. Proverbial (Walz no. 224). Cf. Bacon, "Of Adversity, " and AYLI, II. i. 12.

[2] III. 409-410. Proverbial (Walz no. 89). Cf. Troilus, IV. 1584.

[3] III. 421-424. III. 421-422 are taken from Aurora, Josue 29-30, and III. 423-424 from Aurora, Deut. 197-198 (Beichner).

[4] III. 425-432. "Cp. Aurora, (MS. Bodley 822) f. 103 [Beichner ed., II Kings 129-136]. " The reference is to I Chron. 22: 7-8; see also II. Sam. 7: 2 ff. and 12: 1 ff.

[5] III. 434. A reference to I John 3: 15. The sentence (III. 433-434) is taken from Aurora, Deut. 73-74 (Beichner).

[6] III. 437-438. Perhaps a reference to Luke 9: 56. Cf. John 3: 17, Matt. 9: 13, Mark 2: 17, etc.

[7]III. 456-458. These lines contain a play upon the words querit ("demand, " "ask") and queritur and queratur ("complain").

[8]III. 461-462. Taken from Aurora, Gen. 1103-1104 (Beichner). Each line contains a proverbial idea. For l. 461, cf. Troilus, I. 976-979 and Purg., XVII. 91-93. For l. 462, see Walz, no. 195.

[9]III. 463. Based upon Psa. 111 (Vulgate 110): 10.

[10]III. 472. The line involves a play upon the verbs parit ("occasion") and parat ("provide").

[11]III. 483-484. This is probably a reference to Josh. 14: 3-4. See also Deut. 14: 27-29 and Josh. 21: 41-45 (Vulgate: 21: 39-43).

Chapter 8

[1]III. Chap. 8. With this chapter cf. Piers, C Passus XVIII. 233-261.

[2]III. 493. The line involves a play upon ponit ("asks") and opponit ("makes objection").

[3]III. 503. Taken from Speculum Stultorum, p. 14, l. 25 (Raymo). The idea is, of course, the proverbial "One man's meat is another man's poison. " See Smith-Heseltine, s. v. "Meat, One Man's. "

[4]III. 508-510. Taken from Speculum Stultorum, p. 62, ll. 9-12 (Raymo).

[5]III. 513. Taken from Speculum Stultorum, p. 62, l. 13 (Raymo).

[6]III. 521-522. Taken from Speculum Stultorum, p. 21, ll. 1-2 (Raymo).

[7]III. 531-532. Taken from "Aurora, f. 75 v⁰ [Num. 499-500 in Beichner's ed.]. " The reference is to Num. 22: 21 ff. Cf. II. Prol. 45 and see n.

[8]III. 535. Taken from Speculum Stultorum, p. 54, l. 25 (Raymo).

[9]III. 537-538. Taken from Speculum Stultorum, p. 54, ll. 27-28 (Raymo); with this idea, cf. ll. 403-404 and see n.

[10]III. 539-540. Taken from Speculum Stultorum, p. 20, ll. 27-28 (Raymo).

[11]III. 540. Taken from Speculum Stultorum, p. 21, l. 7 (Raymo).

[12]III. 541-542. Literally, "Hurrying too much does the deed more slowly." Proverbial (Walz no. 7c). "Cato" refers to The Distichs of Cato. Cf. Conf., Prol. 650, and III. 1680.

[13]III. 543. Taken from Speculum Stultorum, p. 21, l. 1 (Raymo); the idea is proverbial. Cf. Troilus, III. 1212-16, and IV. 3.

[14]III. 551. Taken from Speculum Stultorum, p. 21, l. 23 (Raymo).

[15]III. 557. Taken from Speculum Stultorum, p. 21, l. 25 (Raymo).

[16]III. 559-560. Taken from Speculum Stultorum, p. 40, ll. 15-16 (Raymo).

[17]III. 561-566. Taken from Speculum Stultorum, p. 27, ll. 23-28 (Raymo).

[18]III. 574-575. From Matt. 12: 30 or Luke 11: 23.

Chapter 9

[1]III. 579. The word Cesar in this chapter means not only "Caesar" but also "emperor," and frequently designated simply temporal power, as in Matt. 22: 21, Mark 12: 17, and Luke 20: 25. Hence it is that Wycliffe attacked what he called the "Caesarian clergy."

[2]III. 593-598. A reference to Matt. 16: 19. This is a text which Wycliffe attacked. Cf. Piers, B Passus VII. 173-180.

[3]III. 599-600. Based upon Matt. 22: 21, Mark 12: 17, or Luke 20: 25. Cf. VII. 1030. The same verse is quoted in Piers, B Passus I. 52-53.

[4]III. 619-620. Taken from "Pont. ii. 5. 61 f."

[5]III. 623-624. Taken from "Pont. ii. 6. 21 f."

[6]III. 628. The Getans or Getae were a barbarous tribe which lived along the Danube near its estuary on the Black Sea. The poet Ovid

lived among them in his exile and refers to them fairly often in his Tristia and Ex Ponto. The tribe was a mere name to Gower, of course, although he may have connected them with the Goths, as do some today.

[7]III. 641. "See Ars Amat. ii. 417, where we find 'semine, ' a reading which is required by the sense, but not given in the Gower MSS. " Mozley, p. 95: ". . . or they mingle pepper with the seed of biting nettle. . . ."

[8]III. 651 ff. Cf. Conf., IV. 1659 ff. Cf. also ll. 307-310 above. The hypothetical quotation beginning at l. 661 is reminiscent of Chaucer's Monk: "Lat Austyn have his swynk to him reserved!" (Gen Prol, 188).
See Matt. 1:1-17 for Jesus' genealogy. A different genealogy is given in Luke 3:23-38.

[9]III. 667-668. A reference to Matt. 10:5-10.

[10]III. 691. An allusion to the Scribes and Pharisees who took the woman in adultery, the story of which is referred to above, ll. 219-220 See John 8:3-11; cf. IV. 603-604.

[11]III. 717-718. A harsh couplet. It contains a play upon capitale ("capital, " "deadly") and caput ("head").

[12]III. 721. A reference to Matt. 11:30. Cf. l. 258 above and see n.

[13]III. 753-756. A reference to Acts 3:1-8.

[14]III. 777-778. A reference to Matt. 18:21-22.

[15]III. 781-782. A reference to Matt. 2:18. Cf. Jer. 31:15.

[16]III. 788. Cf. l. 718 above.

Chapter 10

[1]III. 800. Based upon Luke 6:31, or Matt. 7:12.

[2]III. 801-802. Based upon Matt. 22:37-39, Mark 12:30-31, or Luke 10:27.

[3]III. 801-804. Taken from Aurora, Deut. 37-40 (Beichner).

[4]III. 805-806. Based upon a verse such as Matt. 25: 40.

[5]III. 815 ff. "What follows is spoken as in the person of the supreme pontiff: cp. Mirour, 18505-18792, where somewhat similar avowals are put into the mouth of a member of the Roman Court." Gower is here using the literary convention of "Self-Revelation." Other examples are that of Faux-Semblant in the Roman de la Rose and Chaucer's Pardoner in the Prologue to his Tale.

[6]III. 819. "Cp. Conf. Amantis, Prol. 261,

'The hevene is ferr, the world is nyh.'"

[7]III. 831-832. Cp. Chaucer, Pard T, 517-520.

[8]III. 835. Taken from "Fasti, v. 209."

[9]III. 843-844. Taken from Aurora, I Kings 419-420 (Beichner).

[10]III. 854. sic deus alter ego. Queenan: "as if I were God's alter ego."

[11]III. 861-862. A reference to Matt. 4: 8-10, or Luke 4: 5-8.

[12]III. 863. traximus can mean "squandered" as well as "obtained," "gathered."

[13]III. 877-878. A reference to Mark 9: 33-37. Cf. Matt. 18: 1-4, and Luke 9: 46-48. The dispute is so called only in Mark.

[14]III. 896. The expression was proverbial.

[15]III. 902. An allusion to Luke 14: 5.

[16]III. 919. Based upon Matt. 10: 34.

[17]III. 923-924. Cf. II. 221 and n. The mythological Saturn dealt harshly with his sons, Jupiter, Neptune, and Pluto, who later overthrew him.

[18]III. 927. Probably an allusion to the judicial sentence of ordeal by fire. "Ordeals of God" had been abolished in England as early as 1219, but they continued in Germany and Italy, in spite of their complete

prohibition by Pope Innocent III and the Fourth Lateran Council in 1216.

[19]III. 934. Reading _ruet_ with MSS. CH, rather than _ruit_.

[20]III. 949-950. A reference to John 18: 10-11, where Peter is named. Jesus heals the wound in Luke 22: 50-51. Cf. Matt. 26: 51-52 and Mark 14: 47, and see n. on ll. 337-338 above.

[21]III. 955-956. "I take this concluding couplet as a remark made by the author on the sentiments which he has just heard expressed by the representative of the Pope. It practically means that 'Clemens' is not a proper name for the Pope: it is in fact a 'headless name' and should rather be 'Inclemens.' Compare the address to Innocent III at the beginning of Geoffrey de Vinsauf's Poetria Nova:

'Papa, stupor mundi, si dixero Papa _nocenti_,
Acephalum nomen tribuam tibi: si caput addam,
Hostis erit metri, ' &c. "

See Edmond Faral, Les Arts Poetiques du XIIe et du XIIIe Siècles (Paris, 1924), p. 197, where the text is somewhat different. (Gower makes the same play upon a word with and without a prefix in IV. 715.)

It should be added that while Gower places his papal spokesman at Rome, he is also undoubtedly attacking Clement VII of Avignon. (England generally held with Urban VI at Rome. Cf. III. 5-6 above.)

Chapter 11

[1]III. 957 ff. "It seems best to take what follows as, in part at least, a dialogue between the author and the representative of the pope, who has just spoken. Soon however the speech passes again entirely to the author. The Biblical reference here is to Revelation, xxii. 8 f. The same use is made of it in the Mirour, 18736 ff. "

[2]III. 963-964. An allusion to Luke 7: 45.

[3]III. 965-966. A reference to Matt. 23: 9.

[4]III. 985. An allusion either to Acts 2: 44 or to 4: 32; the thought that the early Christians "had all things in common" was much in the minds of reformers in the fourteenth century. Cf. Conf., V. 1-5, and VII. 1991 ff.

[5]III. 997. This involves a pun upon _libras_ ("pounds sterling") and

libros ("books"). In the next line, a mark was a unit of money worth 13s. 4d., i.e., two thirds of a pound. Cf. 1. 1106 below, and Speculum Stultorum, p. 106:

Praesul amat marcam plus quam distingere Marcum,
Plus et amat lucrum quam fecit ipse Lucam.

[6]III. 1001-1002. The couplet contains a play upon morem ("practice") and amorem ("love"), as well as another upon solo, which here means both "alone" and "soil."

Chapter 12

[1]Most of this chapter is written in rhyming hemistichs.

[2]III. 1005-06. A reference to John 10: 1 Cf. 11. 1365-66 below.

[3]III. 1025-26. Gower seems almost to voice the Wycliffite doctrine of Dominion here and below, 11. 1141-42 and 1672-73. See also TC, III. 486 and note, as well as Introduction, p. 25.

[4]III. 1027. Based upon Eph. 4: 5.

[5]III. 1034. There is no punctuation in the printed Latin text at the end of this sentence.

[6]III. 1042. Cf. Piers, B Passus V. 42-45.

[7]III. 1055. The image of doctrine as a plow was then a common one. Cf. Piers, B Passus XIX. 257-261 (Queenan).

[8]III. 1063-64. An allusion to Matt. 15: 14, or Luke 6: 39. Cf. III. 1073-74 below, and Piers, B Passus X. 276 and XII. 185.

Chapter 13

[1]III. Chap. 13. With Gower's criticism of bishops in this chapter, cf. Piers, B Prologus, 78-82.

[2]III. 1065-66. An allusion to John 12: 35. Cf. I John 2: 11, and 1. 2142 below.

[3]III. 1073-74.   Another allusion to Matt. 15: 14 or Luke 6: 39.
Cf. l. 1064 above.

[4]III. 1077-80.   "These four lines are from the Aurora [MS.
Bodley 822], f. 21 v⁰ [Exod. 809-812 in Beichner's ed.]" See Exod.
19: 16-19.   The "good leader" thus probably refers to Moses, who long
had a military reputation; cf. Machiavelli, The Prince, Chapter 6.
   "He burns them" means that he consigns them to hell-fire.   Burning of heretics did not really get under way in England until 1401.   See
n. on TC, II. 246.

[5]III. 1095-96.   Adapted from Pont., III. v. 17-18.

[6]III. 1099-1100.   An allusion to the parable of the talents, Matt.
25: 14-30.   Cf. l. 1400 below.   Cf. also Piers, B Passus VI. 240-248.

[7]III. 1106.   An allusion to the fourth beatitude, Matt. 5: 6.

[8]III. 1107.   See n. on l. 997 above.

[9]III. 1108.   Perhaps an allusion to Matt. 23: 17.

[10]III. 1113-14.   Adapted from "Ars Amat. iii. 595 f. . . . The
original application is to the effects of rivalry in stimulating the passion
of lovers. "

[11]III. 1118-24.   "These lines are almost entirely borrowed from
the Aurora, (MS. Bodley 822) f. 21 v⁰ [Gen. 1080-83 and 1091-94 in
Beichner's ed.]. "   The biblical source is Gen. 30: 37 ff.   The illustration and interpretation here are poorly chosen.   What is worse, Jacob
is used as a bad example below, l. 1361.

[12]III. 1129-30.   An allusion to Wycliffe and his followers.   Cf. IV.
1227*-28*, VI. 1267-68, and the feeble argument against Lollardy in
the first section of the Carmen Super Multiplici Viciorum Pestilencia,
in Works, IV, 346-348.

[13]III. 1137-38.   Taken from Aurora, Lev. 335-336 (Beichner).

[14]III. 1141-42.   Now Gower echoes the Wycliffite doctrine of
Dominion.   See n. on ll. 1025-26 above.

[15]III. 1145-50.   "Almost verbatim from Aurora, f. 93 v⁰ [I Kings
129-134 in Beichner's ed.]. "   The reference is to I Sam. (Vulgate: I

Kings) 2: 22-25 and 4: 17-18. Cf. II. 329-330 and see n. Cf. also Mirour, 19117-22.

[16]III. 1143-64. Cf. the portrait of Chaucer's Parson, Gen Prol, 515-526.

[17]III. 1165-66. Proverbial (Walz no. 232).

[18]III. 1167. The words Sulcis obruta are from Ovid, Metam., I. 123-124. See n. on l. 1055 above.

[19]III. 1171-72. "Cp. Aurora, f. 44 v⁰ [Beichner: Exod. 803-804],

'Est olei natura triplex, lucet, cybat, unguit;
Hec tria mitratum debet habere capud. '"

[20]III. 1177-78. Taken from Aurora, Lev. 319-320 (Beichner).

[21]III. 1185-86. "Cp. Aurora, f. 44 v⁰,

Lux est exemplo, cibus est dum pascit egenos,
Vnctio dum populis dulcia uerba ferit. '

Gower is right in reading 'serit, ' which is given in MS. Univ. Coll. 143. f. 13. " Macaulay's line reference is to 1183 f.; he then quotes the line used in 1185-86. The slip is probably due to the fact that all four lines (1183-86) are from the same passage in the Aurora (Exod. 805-808 in Beichner's ed.).

[22]III. 1187-88. Taken from Aurora, Exod. 1133-34 (Beichner).

[23]III. 1189-92. Taken from Aurora, Exod. 1139-42 (Beichner).

Chapter 14

[1]III. 1199. Based upon Acts 10: 34.

[2]III. 1206. "Cp. l. 1375. " Cf. also VI. 421-422.

[3]III. 1211-12. Proverbial (Walz no. 257b). Based upon II Cor. 9: 6. Cf. Mirour, 7567-68:

Escharcement qui semers
Escharcement puis siera . . . .
(Walz no. 257a).
401

[4]III. 1213. Adapted from "Ars Amat. iii. 655. "

[5]III. 1215-16. Adapted from "Ars Amat. iii. 653-654. "

[6]III. 1219-20. Probably a reference to John 4: 14. Cf. John 6: 35 and 7: 37-38.

[7]III. 1223-24. Cf. Piers, C Passus III. 243-244.

[8]III. 1233-34. Based upon "Ars Amat. ii. 279 [f]. " To Gower, Homer was, of course, a mere name.

[9]III. 1241-43. Taken from Aurora, Gen. 843-845 (Beichner).

[10]III. 1246. Taken from Aurora, Gen. 876 (Beichner).

[11]III. 1247-50. "Cp. Mirour, 18793 ff. "

Chapter 15

[1]III. 1267. "Vox populi, &c. : cp. Speculum Stultorum, p. 100, 1. 4, and see also the note on iii. Prol. 11. "
The expression was proverbial (Walz 201b). Cf. Mirour, 12725-26 (Walz 201a).

[2]III. 1271-72. "Cp. Conf. Amantis, Prol. 304 ff. and Mirour, 18805 [ff]. "

[3]III. 1309-10. Taken from Speculum Stultorum, p. 62, ll. 1-2 (Raymo).

Chapter 16

[1]"With the remainder of this Book, treating of the secular clergy, we may compare Mirour de l'Omme, 20209-20832. " Cf. also Conf., III. 2491 ff., and V. 1860-99. Chaucer's Parson, as he is described in Gen Prol, 477-528, is the exact opposite of the clergy of whom Gower complains in Chapters 16-20.

[2]There is a play here upon curas ("cure of souls") and curiis ("courts"). Cf. ll. 1367-68 below.

[3]III. 1325-30. Cf. Piers, B Passus III. 148-153.

[4]III. 1331-32. A reference to Matt. 10: 10, Mark 6: 9, or Luke 9: 3. Cf. Luke 3: 11.

[5]III. 1341 ff. "Cp. Mirour, 18889 ff."

[6]III. 1359-60. "Cp. Conf. Amantis, i. 1258 ff." Cf. also Merch T, 2013-14 (Queenan).

[7]III. 1361. For the story of Jacob supplanting his brother Esau, see Gen. 25: 29-34 and 27: 1-36. See also n. on ll. 1118-24 above.

[8]III. 1365-66. An allusion to John 10: 1. Cf. ll. 1005-1006 above and see n.

[9]III. 1367. Cf. Chapter 16, Heading, and see n.

[10]III. 1371-74. Taken from Speculum Stultorum, p. 12, ll. 21-24 (Raymo).

[11]III. 1375 ff. "Cp. Mirour, 20287 ff." Cf. also Conf., Prol. 207 ff.

[12]III. 1376. Cf. l. 1206 above, and VI. 421-422.

[13]III. 1380. Literally, "and the title (honor) of father did not possess him."

[14]III. 1384-86. III. 1384 is taken from Aurora, Gen. 1226, and III. 1386 from Aurora, Gen. 1390 (Beichner). Cf. Pars T, 416-420.

[15]III. 1400. Another allusion to the parable of the talents, Matt. 25: 14-30. Cf. ll. 1099-1100 above.

Chapter 17

[1]III. 1405. "prece ruffi . . . et albi, 'by reason of the petition of the red and the white, ' that is, presumably, by the influence of gold and silver, 'dominis' in the next line being in a loose kind of apposition to a dative case suggested by 'Annuit. '" I take dominis as a dative of compounds after astet, however. In either case the construction is

403

awkward. The terms "red" and "white" for gold and silver were common in alchemy; see George G. Fox, The Mediaeval Sciences in the Works of John Gower (Princeton, 1931), p. 131. Cf. Mirour, 6210-11.

[2] III. 1410. "natural knowledge: " ars . . . nature.

[3] III. 1417. Quoted from Eccl. 4: 10.

[4] III. 1431-32. A reference to Gen. 1: 28, likewise used ironically, as here, in IV. 571, and Chaucer, WBT, 26-29. Cf. also ll. 2017 and 2019 below, and Conf., V. 6421-23, and VIII. 1 ff. See Introduction, pp. 44-45.

[5] III. 1438. "In order to bear fruit" is literally "in order that birth may result" (Vt veniat partus).

[6] III. 1443. "formalis, that is, 'eminent, ' from 'forma' meaning 'rank' or 'dignity, ' but here also opposed to 'materialis. '"

[7] III. 1485-86. It was a common Lollard complaint that the Mother Church at Rome had become a very stepmother to the Church in England.

Chapter 18

[1] III. 1493 ff. "Cp. Mirour, 20314" [ff]. The sporting parson was quite a recognized figure in the fourteenth century . . . . " Cf. Chaucer's Monk, Gen Prol, 166-178, and Piers, B Passus III. 309-312. Cf. also B Passus V. 413-426, in which there is a vivid description of Sloth, a priest who prefers hunting and harlotry to visiting the poor, fasting, and religious observances.

[2] III. 1501-2. Cf. Piers, B Passus X. 58-70.

[3] III. 1521-22. This sounds like a reference to the jus primae noctis. The prerogative was largely monetary rather than sexual in feudal England, however. See Karl Schmidt, Jus Primae Noctis: Eine geschichtliche Untersuchung (Freiburg im Breisgau, 1881), passim.

Chapter 19

[1] III. 1525 ff. Cf. Piers, C Passus XIII. 224-228.

[2] III. 1543. This line involves a play upon merces ("wares") and mercede ("price").

[3] III. 1546. "Apparently a proverbial expression used of wasting valuable things. " See Smith-Heseltine, s. v. "Water In a Sieve. " Cf. Mirour, 17656-58; and Conf., III. 433. Cf. also VI. 1359 below.

[4] III. 1549-52. "If benefices went from father to son, little or nothing would be gained by those who go to Rome to seek preferment, for an heir would seldom fail. " For a related idea, see Chaucer, RvT, 3977-86. Cf. also IV. 247-248 and 263-264.

Chapter 20

[1] III. 1555 ff. "Cp. Mirour de l'Omme, 20498 ff. The priests here spoken of are the 'annuelers, ' who get their living by singing masses for the dead, the 'Annua seruicia' spoken of below . . . . " Cf. Mirour, 20497-502; Gen Prol, 507-510, and Piers, B Prologus, 83-86. This was an important criticism, in Gower's eyes, for he left provision for "annuelers" to sing masses for his own soul.

[2] III. 1563. Taken from Luke 10: 7 or Matt. 10: 10.

[3] III. 1569. An allusion to Matt. 10: 8.

[4] III. 1587-90. "Taken with slight change from Aurora, (MS. Bodley 822) f. 65 v⁰ [Lev. 711-714 in Beichner's ed.]. "

[5] III. 1591-93. At first glance a puzzling statement. Macaulay translates, "'With the ancients it is possible to say, 'hic et hec sacerdos, ' that is, 'sacerdos' is both masculine and feminine. " I take the lines to be an overly condensed statement of the following: "With the ancients it was possible to single out a priest or a priestess because of his or her holiness. But the priests of today are so unchaste that they have, as it were, populated the entire world with offsprings exactly like themselves, so that for two reasons there now is no way of distinguishing priests from any other people. "

[6] *III. 1595. Adapted from Amores, I. vi. 59.

[7] III. 1601-4. Based on an old proverb. See Smith-Heseltine, s. v. "Pigeons and priests." Cf. IV. 777-778, and see n.

[8] III. 1611-12. A reference to I Cor. 5: 7: "Purge out therefore the old leaven, that ye may be a new lump, as ye are unleavened . . . . Probably a pun is intended on expurgat fermentum, which can mean both "purge out the leaven" and "vomit up beer."

Chapter 21

[1] III. 1623. Taken from Aurora, Deut. 161 (Beichner).

[2] III. 1628-30. Taken from Aurora, Gen. 924, 929-930 (Beichner).

[3] III. 1631-32. Taken from Speculum Stultorum, p. 12. ll. 27-28 (Raymo). The idea is proverbial. See Smith Heseltine s. v. "Familiarity breeds contempt."

[4] III. 1640. Proverbial. See Smith-Heseltine s. v. "Custom."

[5] III. 1649-50. Possibly an ironic echo of Matt. 27: 42, Mark 15: 31, or Luke 23: 35; Matt. 27: 42: "He saves others; himself he cannot save."

[6] III. 1671-72. This last sentence is another hint of the doctrine of Dominion. See n. on ll. 1025-26 above.

Chapter 22

[1] III. 1693-1700. "Adapted from Aurora, f. 65 . . . [Lev. 703-710 in Beichner's ed.]." On the owl, cf. Conf., I. 1727-28.

[2] III. 1709-14. Based upon Matt. 18: 15-17 and Luke 17: 3, but not a direct quotation.

[3] III. 1721-22. Based upon Luke 12: 2, Matt. 10: 26, or Mark 4: 22. The expression was proverbial (Walz, no. 30c). Cf. IV. 1177 and VI. 576.

[4]III. 1724.   Taken from Aurora, Num. 468 (Beichner).

Chapter 23

[1]III. 1727.   Literally, "priests say, " but Gower changes to the singular in l. 1730.   With ll. 1727 ff. , "Cp. Mirour, 20713 ff. "

[2]III. 1741.   A reference to the five minor orders of ostiary, cantor, lector, exorcist, and acolyte, which lead up to the major orders of subdeacon, deacon, priest, and bishop.   (By another reckoning, priest was the lowest rank of the major orders.)

[3]III. 1759 ff.   "Cp Mirour, 20725 ff . . . . "

Chapter 24

[1]"Thirty-one of the fifty-six lines of the chapter are compiled from various places in the Aurora" (Beichner, Speculum, XXX [1955], 591).   Father Beichner cites (loc. cit.) this chapter and the next as illustrations of Gower's use of Peter of Riga's figurative and moral interpretations of Mosaic law.

[2]III. 1791-94.   Adapted "from Aurora, f. 93 v°, and the succeeding couplet is adapted from the same source [I Kings 121-126 in Beichner's ed.] . . . . "   In ll. 1791-92 the reference is to I Sam. 2 (Vulgate, I Kings): 18-19.

[3]III. 1797.   "Cp. Aurora, f. 46 v° [Exod. 919 in Beichner] . . . . "

[4]III. 1798.   "Shameful deeds" is facta pudenda, which contains an obvious allusion.   Cf. VII. 168.

[5]III. 1799-1800, "Cp. Aurora, f. 45 v° [Exod. 847-848 in Beichner]. "

[6]III. 1801-1802.   Adapted from "Aurora, f. 46 [Exod. 897-898 in Beichner]. "

[7]III. 1807-1808.   Adapted from "Aurora, f. 45 [Exod. 827-828 in Beichner]. "

[8]III. 1810. "Cloth" is _texilis_, which must mean the same as _textilis_.

[9]III. 1809-12. Adapted from "_Aurora_, f. 46 [Exod. 899-901 in Beichner]. "

[10]III. 1813-14. "Cp. _Aurora_, f. 46 v° [Exod. 925-926 in Beichner]. " The latter line contains three plays upon words:

Vt totus mundus munera munda sacret.

[11]III. 1815-18. Taken with few changes, and those not for the better, from "_Aurora_, f. 45 [Exod. 821-824 in Beichner] . . . . "
In ll. 1815-16 the reference is to Exod. 28: 1-4. In Exod. 28: 5-8, and in Peter of Riga's version thereof, Gower finds many of the details of the sacerdotal vestments which he employs in ll. 1787-1814.

[12]III. 1819-22. Taken from _Aurora_, Exod. 1043-44 and 1047-48 (Beichner). Gower's remarks are directed against Wycliffe, who by 1379 or 1380 was "arguing against transubstantiation. His propositions as to the nature of the sacrament were indeed very moderate, but for those days bold in the extreme . . . " (Trevelyan, _History of England_, p. 248). Cf. VI. 1267-68. See Introduction, p. 25, and Robinson's n. on _Pard T_, 537 ff.

[13]III. 1823-24. Taken from "_Aurora_, f. 43 v° [Exod. 735-736 in Beichner]. "

[14]III. 1831-32. Taken from _Aurora_, Lev. 107-108 (Beichner).

Chapter 25

[1]III. Chap. 25. Heading. The terms "old law" and "new law" in this chapter are of course synonymous with "Old Testament" and "New Testament" respectively. See n. on II. 434.

[2]III. 1846. "Nothing improper" is _nulla sinistra_, the word _sinistra_ having the additional connotation of "left" (as opposed to the "right" arm).

[3]III. 1841-48. "These eight lines are taken with insignificant changes from the _Aurora_, f. 63 v° [Lev. 579-586 in Beichner]. " The details come originally from Lev. 7: 32-35.

408

[4]III. 1853-54. "The reference here given by Gower to the _Aurora_ of Petrus (de) Riga has led to the tracing of a good many passages of the _Vox Clamantis_, besides the present one, to that source."

[5]III. 1859-60. Taken from _Aurora_, Lev. 173-174 (Beichner).

[6]III. 1863-84. "These lines are almost entirely from _Aurora_, ff. 66 v°, 67. The arrangement of the couplets is somewhat different, and there are a few slight variations . . . . " The arrangement of the couplets is as follows in Beichner's forthcoming edition: Lev. 793-794, 799-804, 805-808, 819-820, 797-798, 809-812, 795-796, 813-814. Omitted from Lev. 793-820 are verses 797-798 and 815-818.

[7]III. 1869-70. The references to noses in ll. 1869, 1871, and 1873, as well as the references to lame men in ll. 1875-78 and the maimed and hunchbacked in ll. 1877-79, are part of the borrowing from Peter of Riga, Lev. 793-820 (Beichner). See Lev. 21: 17-21, where it is commanded that no man with a blemish be a priest of God. Peter of Riga interprets the blemishes symbolically here, of course, although that fact hardly justifies Gower's inept borrowing of the ideas.

[8]III. 1885-90. Based originally upon II Sam. 6: 6-7 (Vulgate, II Kings), or I Chron. 13: 9-10. "Our author still borrows from the same source, though from a different part of it. We find these lines nearly in the same form in the _Aurora_, f. 103 [II Kings 119-124 in Beichner] . . . . " Cf. VI. 1223 and see n.

[9]III. 1891-92. Biblical (Ecclus. 13: 1) and proverbial: see Smith-Heseltine s. v. "Toucheth pitch." Cf. _Mirour_, 1232-36, and _Conf._, II. 574-575.

Chapter 26

[1]III. 1905-8. "These two couplets are from _Aurora_, f. 69 v°, where however they are separated by four lines not here given [Num. 143-144, 149-150 in Beichner]."

[2]III. 1911-16. "Cp. _Aurora_, f. 69 v° [Num. 127-132 in Beichner] . . . . "

[3]III. 1917-18. Taken from _Aurora_, Deut. 189-190 (Beichner).

[4]III. 1919-23. Taken from _Aurora_, Josue 257-261 (Beichner).

[5] III. 1929. Quoted from Matt. 5: 14.

[6] III. 1930. Proverbial (Walz no. 190). Cf. I Kings (Vulgate: III Kings) 8: 46.

[7] III. 1931-32. Taken from Aurora, Num. 403-404 (Beichner).

[8] *III. 1933-34. Adapted from Rem. Amoris, 53-54.

[9] III. 1937. Taken from "Rem. Amoris, 669. "

[10] III. 1939-40. Adapted from "Tristia, iv. 6. 33 f. "

[11] III. 1943-44. Taken from "Rem. Amoris, 89 f. "

[12] III. 1945-46. Adapted from "Rem. Amoris, 115 f. "

[13] III. 1947-50. Adapted from "Rem. Amoris, 81-84. " III. 1949 is proverbial (Walz no. 6).

[14] III. 1952. Adapted from "Her. xvii. 190. "

[15] III. 1953. Adapted from "Rem. Amoris, 239. "

[16] III. 1955-56. Adapted from "Rem. Amoris, 139 f. "

[17] III. 1961. Cf. Piers, C Passus XVIII. 17-18:

Paul after his prechynge · panyeres he made,
And wan with hus hondes · all that hym neodyde.

Skeat's note (II, 224) is as follows:

"Panyeres, baskets. The word is curiously chosen,
as St. Paul was a tent-maker; Acts xviii. 3.
Yet Chaucer seems to have the same idea--

'I wol not do no labour with my hondes,
Ne make baskettes, and lyve thereby . . .
I wol non of the apostles counterfete.

Prol. to Pardoneres Tale [444-447]. " See Robinson's n. on Pard T, 443 ff.

[18] III. 1977. Taken from Aurora, Exod. 21 (Beichner).

[19] III. 1979. Taken from Aurora, Gen. 343 (Beichner). The idea

in this and the previous sentence is proverbial: see Smith-Heseltine, s. v. "Devil find a man idle. "

Chapter 27

[1] III. 1997-98. Based upon Matt. 5: 13. Cf. Luke 14: 34 and VI. 1259.

[2] III. 1999-2000. Adapted from "Aurora, f. 140 [IV Kings 95-96 in Beichner]. " The biblical reference is to II Kings (Vulgate: IV Kings) 2: 21-22.

[3] III. 2001. Taken from "Aurora, f. 60 v° [Lev. 395 in Beichner]. "

[4] III. 2002. Taken from Aurora, Lev. 398 (Beichner).

[5] III. 2003. Cf. 1. 1929 and see n.

[6] III. 2007-8. Taken from Aurora, Lev. 777-778 (Beichner). See Lev. 19: 13.

[7] III. 2009 is taken from Aurora, Gen. 1043 (Beichner). See Gen. 28: 12.

[8] III. 2017-20. "From Aurora, f. 8 [Gen. 209-212 in Beichner]. " The quotations in ll. 2017-2019 are based upon Gen. 1: 28. Cf. ll. 1431-32 above and see n.

[9] III. 2021-22. Taken from Aurora, Exod. 1305-1306 (Beichner).

[10] III. 2023-26. Taken from Aurora, Num. 253-256 (Beichner).

[11] III. 2035-40. Borrowed "From Aurora, f. 15 v° [Gen. 723-726 and 729-730 in Beichner], but one couplet is omitted, and so the sense is obscured. After 'sunt sine felle boni' (l. 2038), the original has,

'Cras canit hinc coruus, hodie canit inde columba;
Hec vox peruersis, congruit illa bonis.
Cras prauum cantant, dum se conuertere tardant,
Set tales tollit sepe suprema dies. '

The meaning is that the bad priests cry 'Cras, ' like crows, and encourage men to put off repentance, while the others sing 'Hodie, ' like doves, the words 'cras' and 'hodie' being imitations of the notes of the two birds. The expression 'Cras primam cantant, in l. 2039, is not intelligible, and probably Gower missed the full sense of the passage. " Father Beichner points out (Speculum, XXX [1955], 592, that "'Cras primam cantant' is a misreading on the part of someone for 'Cras praui cantant; but the chief difficulty is that Gower has not carried through the figure to say something about the dove, for the sound of the crow, cras 'tomorrow, ' in paralleled by the sound of the dove, hodie 'today. '" Cras primam can, moreover, be taken to mean either "tomorrow at prime" (i. e., the canonical hour of nine o'clock a. m.), or "the first day after tomorrow. " In l. 2040 there is a play upon two possible meanings of tollit: "uplifts" (the good priests) and "does away with" (the bad). The expression, 'Cras! cras!' became proverbial; see Werner, C-116 (also 117), as well as G-60.

Chapter 28

[1]III. 2049 ff. "Cp. Mirour de l'Omme, 20785 ff. "

[2]III. 2050-60. Taken from Aurora, Lev. 65-66 (Beichner).

[3]III. 2061-62. An allusion to Matt. 22:14. Cf. Matt. 21:16.

[4]III. 2071-72. An allusion to Matt. 7:17-18, or to Luke 6:43.

[5]III. 2073. Proverbial (Walz no. 137).

[6]III. 2074. Proverbial (Walz no. 255b). Cf. Mirour, 20827-28 (Walz no. 255 a).

Chapter 29

[1]III. 2097-98. "Cp. iv. 959 and note. " Macaulay there notes, "A reference to Ps. lxxii. 5 . . . . " The King James version is Psa. 73: 5.

[2]III. 2130. An allusion to Matt. 23:8.

[3]III. 2142. An allusion to John 8:12, or 12:35. Cf. I John 2:11, and ll. 1065-66 above.

[1]Book IV. "The matter of this book corresponds to that of the Mirour de l'Omme, ll. 20833-21780."

Chapter 1

[1]IV. 10. An allusion to Luke 9: 62. Cf. ll. 245-246 and V. 569 below.

[2]IV. 13-14. An allusion to Matt. 6: 24, Cf. III. 137.

[3]IV. 18. An allusion to Gal. 6: 5: "For every man shall bear his own burden." Cf. ll. 698 and 1111 below.

[4]IV. 19-20. "Cp. Lib. iii. Prol. 11." Also see n.

[5]IV. 26. Cf. Mirour, 20866-67.

[6]IV. 33. There is a play in this line on fessus ("wearied") and professus ("man of professed or religious vows").

[7]IV. 34. "Master monk": "'dompnus' or 'domnus' was the form of 'dominus' which was properly applied as a title to ecclesiastical dignitaries, and it seems to have been especially used in monasteries . . . . Cp. l. 323 of this book and also 327 ff. "

[8]IV. 37. Literally, "with his vestments inflamed."

Chapter 2

[1]IV. 41. Probably an allusion to Luke 24: 5.

[2]*IV. 43-48. Taken, with minor changes, from De Vita Monachorum, p. 175.

[3]IV. 53. The phrase in ordine ventris means both "in respect to the belly" and "in the monastic order of the belly."

[4]IV. 69-70. Cf. Pard T, 538.

[5]IV. 78. An allusion to John 14: 6. Cf. II. 468.

[6]IV. 79-82. Based upon Speculum Stultorum, p. 42, ll. 13-16, Gower's indebtedness falling between "plagiarism and paraphrase" (Raymo, p. 319).

[7]IV. 83 ff. With this paragraph, cf. Piers, B Passus XV. 263-303 or C Passus XVIII. 6-36.

[8]IV. 87. "Cp. Godfrey of Viterbo, Pantheon, p. 74 (ed. 1584). " (1726 ed., p. 56).

[9]IV. 91. Adapted from the "Pantheon, p. 74. " (1726 ed., p. 56).

[10]*IV. 97. Taken from the Pantheon, p. 56 (ed. 1726).

[11]IV. 105-106. Taken from Aurora, I Kings 225-226 (Beichner).

[12]IV. 109-110. Adapted from "Fasti, i. 109 f. "

[13]IV. 111. Adapted from "Ars Amat. ii. 475. "

[14]IV. 112. Adapted from "Fasti, iv. 396. " Frazer, p. 219: "which the earth yielded without sollicitation . . . . " Macaulay objects that "Gower has not improved the line by his changes. " But the change from nullo sollicitante to nulla sollicitate does not interfere with the meaning, although Gower's meter becomes questionable. Macaulay glosses sollicitas as "labour"; it surely must mean "solicitation, asking. "

[15]IV. 114. Taken from "Fasti, iv. 400. "

[16]IV. 115. Taken from "Metam. i. 104, but Ovid has of course 'fraga. '" Gower has fragra, which is meaningless. I have translated as [fraga], "strawberries. " Miller, I, 9: "Men . . . gathered the arbute fruit, strawberries from the mountain-sides. . . ."

[17]IV. 117. Adapted from "Metam. i. 106. " As Macaulay points out, Gower's "'patule glandes' is nonsense. " I have translated patula with Ovid. Miller, I, 9: ". . . and acorns fallen from the spreading tree of Jove. " (The oak was sacred to Jove.)
Ll. 115-117 provide two examples of Gower's unwillingness to

borrow in toto, his inability to let well enough alone, or, more unlikely, his occasional lack of comprehension of his sources. At times, however, he probably had a defective copy of Ovid before him.

[18]IV. 119. Adapted from "Metam. i. 103. "

Chapter 3

[1]IV. 127-128. Regula means "monastic rule" and gula "Gluttony. " Cf. ll. 715-716 below. For the rhetorical figure, see n. on III. 995-996.

[2]IV. 129-130. The couplet contains plays upon modio ("a liquid measure, " "a tun"), modus ("moderation"), and absque modo ("immoderately").

[3]IV. 145. Adapted from "Metam. viii. 830. " Cf. Pard T, 518-520.

[4]IV. 147. Taken from "Metam. viii. 835. "

[5]*IV. 149-150. Adapted from Metam., VIII. 836.

[6]IV. 151-153. Adapted from "Metam. viii. 837 ff. "

[7]IV. 163. Adapted from "Ars Amat. iii. 647. "

[8]IV. 165-166. "Cp. Conf. Amantis, Prol. 473 ff. "

[9]IV. 167. A garment of pain means a hair shirt.

[10]IV. 169-172. It is well established that monks enjoined to silence in the cloister made use of sign language, but not that they used it for the purposes Gower indicates.

[11]IV. 173. Taken from Speculum Stultorum, p. 52. l. 1 (Raymo).

[12]IV. 175-176. Adapted from "Ars Amat. iii. 503 f. . . . "

[13]IV. 177. Adapted from "Metam. viii. [466]. " (Macaulay notes l. 465.)

[14]IV. 179. Adapted from "Ars Amat. iii. 509. "

[15]IV. 193-194. Proverbial. See Smith-Heseltine, s.v. "Face is the index of the heart (mind), The."

Chapter 4

[1]IV. 207-208. An allusion to Eccl. 5:5.

[2]IV. 215. Si non corrodi vis, tu corrodia nulla
Inter eos sumas, est vbi raro fides . . . .
"'corrodium' (or 'corredium') is the allowance made from the funds of a religious house for the sustentation of a member of it or of someone else outside the house: see Ducange under 'conredium' and New Engl. Dict. 'corrody.' Gower himself perhaps had in his later life a corrody in the Priory of Saint Mary Overey, of which he was a benefactor." Corrodium has the meaning which Macaulay adopts for it, but another widespread meaning was "feast" or "banquet," which is much better adapted to the context here, in view of the pun upon corrodi ("to be gnawed to pieces").

[3]IV. 243-246. With IV. 243-244, cf. Mirour, 16127; with IV. 245-246, cf. ll. 9-10 above and see n.

[4]IV. 247-248. Cf. ll. 263-264 below and III. 1549.

Chapter 5

[1]IV. 277-282. A common idea. See Introduction, p. 44 ; cf. Mirour 20845-46, and cf. Piers, B Passus X. 291-313 or C Passus VI. 147-150 and see Skeat's note (II, 67) on the latter. Cf. also Chaucer, Gen Prol, 179-183 and see Robinson's note; Troilus, IV. 765; and Smith-Heseltine, s.v. "Fish out of water."

[2]IV. 301-302. "The reference is to Ecclus. xix. 27 . . . ." The Latin text is quoted in part in the margin of Conf., I. 2705.

Chapter 6

[1]IV. 305-310. Adapted from "Aurora, (MS. Bodley 822) f. 65
[Lev. 675-676, 679-682 in Beichner]. " Moses is the lawgiver meant in
l. 308 (see Lev. 11: 15), but the interpretation is, of course, Peter of
Riga's.

[2]IV. 311-312. Adapted from "Ars Amat. iii. 249 f. . . . . " There
is substitution of pecus monstrum for pecus multilum. Mozley, p. 135:
"Ugly is a bull without horns; ugly is a field without grass, a plant without leaves, or a head without hair. " Macaulay suggests, "The word
'monstrum' in Gower came probably from a corruption in his copy of
Ovid. "

[3]IV. 311-313. These lines contain a play upon the two basic meanings of turpis: "ugly, " and "shameful" or "base. "

[4]IV. 323. A play upon dompni and domini. See n. on l. 34 above.

[5]IV. 324. Probably an allusion to Matt. 7: 14. Cf. III. 252.

Chapter 7

[1]IV. Chap. 7. "With this chapter compare Mirour de l'Omme,
21133 ff. The capital letters of 'Paciens, ' 'Castus, ' 'Luxus, ' &c. are
supplied by the editor, being clearly required by the sense. "

[2]IV. 337. St. Maure was a disciple of St. Benedict (A: D. 480? -
543?), the Italian monk who founded the Benedictine order.

Chapter 8

[1]IV. 359-370. Cf. Mirour, 21157-68. With l. 359, cf. Speculum
Stultorum, p. 92:

Lex sine lege Dei, canon sine canone Christi.

[2]IV. 363-364. "The habit described is that of the Canons of the
order of St. Augustine. "

Chapter 9

[1]IV. 371-388. Cf. Mirour, 21061-72.

Chapter 10

[1]IV. 390. Unlike Chaucer, Gower rarely makes reference to brevity, and rightly so.

[2]IV. 395-396. "Cp. Neckam, De Vita Monachorum, p. 175 . . . ,

'Vovistis, fratres, vovistis; vestra, rogamus,
Vivite solliciti reddere vota deo. '"

[3]IV. 397. Taken from "De Vita Monachorum, p. 176. "

[4]IV. 401-402. Taken from "De Vita Monachorum, p. 178. " (Macaulay notes only l. 401.)

[5]IV. 403-404. Adapted from "De Vita Monachorum, p. 177. "

[6]IV. 405-430. "Most of this is taken from Neckam, De Vita Monachorum, p. 176. " Gower modified slightly ll. 407, 408, 413, 417, 421, 422, 424 and 430, and inserted his own ll. 410-412 and 426-428, as well as taking l. 425 from Ovid, as noted below.

[7]IV. 425. Taken from "Ars Amat. ii. 465. "

Chapter 11

[1]IV. Chap. 11, Heading. Unlike Chaucer, Gower seldom has a good word to say for women. But cf. V. 293 ff.

[2]IV. 431-446. "Taken with slight alterations from De Vita Monachorum, pp. 187, 188. " Gower adds ll. 432, 438, and 440, but Macaulay's note is otherwise correct, although ll. 445-446 are considerably changed.

[3]IV. 431-440. Such strictures against woman are a medieval commonplace. Cf. Chaucer, NPT, 3164 and see Robinson's n.

[4]IV. 449. Adapted from "Fasti, ii. 85 . . . Our author has inter-changed the sexes [of the wolf and the lamb] for the purpose of his argu-ment, the man being represented as a helpless victim. " Frazer, p. 63: "Often at his voice the wolf in pursuit of the lamb stood still . . . . "

[5]IV. 451. Adapted from "Ars Amat. iii. 419. "

[6]IV. 453-454. Taken from "Tristia, i. 6. 9 f. "

[7]IV. 461-466. Taken with slight alterations from "De Vita Mon-achorum, p. 188. "

[8]IV. 469-490. "Nearly the whole of this is taken from Neckam, p. 178. " "490" is evidently a mistake for "480, " since ll. 481-490 are not from this source. In the lines borrowed, Gower has altered the sequence of lines at times and has made trivial changes in ll. 469-470 and 478-479.

[9]IV. 485. This injunction is based upon the Benedictine Rule.

[10]*IV. 486. Taken from De Vita Monachorum, p. 177.

Chapter 12

[1]IV. 501. Adapted from Speculum Stultorum, p. 35, l. 1 (Raymo).

[2]IV. 507. Proverbial for toiling in vain. Cf. Ovid, Tristia, V. iv. 48.

[3]IV. 509. Non vox set votum, non musica cordula set cor. . . .

[4]IV. 537-538. Adapted from "Rem. Amoris, 235 f. "

Chapter 13

[1]IV. 569-570. The couplet contains a play upon the two meanings of probare: "to approve, " and "to put to the test" or "to make proof of. " They also contain an allusion to I Thess. 5: 21: "Prove all things; hold fast that which is good. "

The same ironic use is made of the verse in Piers, B Passus III. 333-339, where Conscience corrects Lady Meed.

[2]IV. 571. A reference to Gen. 1: 28, made ironically both here and in III. 1431-32, as in WBT, 28-29.

[3]IV. 575. Adapted in part from "Amores, iii. 4. 17. "

[4]IV. 579-580. A reference to the parable of the sower. See Matt. 13: 3-8, Mark 4: 3-8, or Luke 8: 5-8.

[5]IV. 585. "Venus' days" are, of course, Fridays--but with an amatory overtone, as the next two sentences show.

[6]IV. 587. There is a marginal note in S at l. 587: "Note that according to the poets the Priest of the Goddess Venus is called Genius. " "'Genius' is here introduced as the priest of Venus and in l. 597 in the character of a confessor, as afterwards in the Confessio Amantis. The reference to the 'poets' in the marginal note can hardly be merely to the Roman de la Rose, where Genius is the priest and confessor of Nature, but the variation 'secundum Ovidium' of the Glasgow MS. does not seem to be justified by any passage of Ovid. The connexion with Venus obviously has to do with the classical idea of Genius as a god who presides over the begetting of children: cp. Isid. Etym. viii. 88. The marginal note in S is written in a hand probably different from that of the text, but contemporary. "

Chapter 14

[1]IV. Chap. 14, Heading. Here "ordinaries" are priests deputized by a bishop to visit nunneries, principally to hear confession. Cf. the Ancren Rewle, Pt. v, with its warnings on the strict protocol necessary for nuns in making confession.

[2]IV. 603-604. Perhaps the translation should read, "By the (judicial?) decision of Genius, (some) women are stoned for their sins, but no fatal blow (i. e., from a stone) injures these women (i. e., those in the convent, in contradistinction to those on the outside). " The allusion is once more to the woman taken in adultery (John 8: 3-7). Cf. III. 219-220, 691. aggravat ("injures") can also mean "make heavier, " i. e., "impregnate"; lapidate ("stoned") may well carry the overtone of "testicles" (see NED, s. v. Stone, sb., 11.).

[3]IV. 614. Taken from Speculum Stultorum, p. 41, l. 14 (Raymo).

[4]IV. 617-618. Adapted from "Ars Amat. ii. 649 f. "

[5] *IV. 620. Taken from Ars Amat., III. 562.

[6] IV. 621-622. An allusion to Gen. 2: 7: "And the Lord God formed man of the dust of the ground, and breathed into his nostrils the breath of life; and man became a living soul."

[7] IV. 623. Adapted from Matt. 26: 41 or Mark 14: 38. "Gower apparently took this text to mean, 'the spirit is ready to do evil, and the flesh is weak': cp. Mirour, 14165 [-67]."

Chapter 15

[1] IV. 647-648. An allusion to "Rev. xiv. 4 . . . ."

[2] IV. 654. The phrase florida serta is taken from Fasti, VI. 312.

[3] IV. 656. The Triple Crown refers to the pope.

[4] IV. 657-658. "Apparently referring to Rev. xii. 14."

[5] IV. 659-660. "Cp. the Latin verses after Confessio Amantis, v. 6358." In his note (Works, III, 507) to the latter passage, Macaulay points out, "The idea expressed is that though examples of virginity can only be produced through marriage, yet virginity is nobler than marriage, as the flower of the rose is nobler than the stock from which it springs . . . ." Cf. WBT, 71-75. The idea of the rose and thorns here is proverbial; cf. Troilus, I. 948-949.

Chapter 16

[1] IV. Chap. 16. With this chapter on the mendicant friars, cf. Mirour, 21181 ff. Cf. also Piers Plowman, A Prologus, 54-64 or B Prologus, 58-67.

[2] IV. 681-682. Adapted from "Pont. iv. 4. 3 f."

[3] IV. 691-692. Cf. ll. 709-710 below and see n. on III. Prol. 11.

[4] IV. 693. An allusion to Matt. 25: 32-33. Cf. VII. 1087-88.

[5]IV. 698. Another allusion to Gal. 6: 5. Cf. 1. 18 above and see n. Cf. also 1. 1111 below.

[6]IV. 703-704. The distinction between voluntary poverty (a virtue) and involuntary poverty (a source of sinful discontent) was a commonplace. Cf. Pard T, 439-441 and WBT, 1178-1206.

[7]IV. 710. Cf. 11. 691-692 above and see n. on III. Prol. 11.

[8]IV. 711-712. For another complaint on the numbers in religious orders, especially those of the friars, cf. Piers, B Passus XX. 262-270 (C Passus XXII. 264-272). Cf. also WBT, 866-868.

[9]IV. 715-716. "Acephalum. This name was applied in early times to ecclesiastics who were exempt from the authority of the bishop: see Ducange. The word is differently used in iii. 956, and by comparison with that passage we might be led to suppose that there was some reference here to the 'inopes' and 'opem' of the next line." The reference is certain. Cf. 1. 128 above, and see n. on III. 955-956.

[10]IV. 719-720. Probably an allusion to Matt. 6: 2, 5, 16: "Verily I say unto you, they have their reward."

[11]IV. 721. Partly from Speculum Stultorum, p. 87, 1. 29 (Raymo).

[12]IV. 723-730. "Compare with this the contemporary accounts of the controversy between FitzRalph, archibishop of Armagh, and the Mendicant Friars, who are said to have bribed the Pope to confirm their privileges (Walsingham, i. 285), and the somewhat prejudiced account of their faults in Walsingham, ii. 13. The influence of the Dominican Rushook, as the king's confessor was the subject of much jealousy in the reign of Richard II." Cf. 11. 829-830 below, and TC, I. 111. On Rushook see Anthony Steel, Richard II (Cambridge, Eng., 1941), pp. 157-158 and 164.

[13]IV. 735-740. "Cp. Mirour de l'Omme, 21469 ff." Cf. also Piers, B Passus XI. 73-80.

[14]IV. 747-748. Taken from Speculum Stultorum, p. 45, 11. 11-12 (Raymo).

[1]For a related criticism of the friars' preaching, namely that they undermined faith, see Piers, B Passus X. 71-77.

[2]IV. 751. Sermones means both "words" and "sermons."

[3]IV. 765. De fundamentis can also mean "utterly."

[4]IV. 769. A reference to "Hos. iv. 8: cp. Mirour, 21397, where the saying is attributed to Zephaniah."

[5]IV. 777-778. Adapted from "Pont. i. 9. 7 f." Wheeler, p. 45: "You see how the doves come to a white dwelling, how an unclean tower harbors no birds." Cf. III. 1601-4; Gower now echoes the other form of the same proverb seen in those lines: "Pigeons and priests (Doves and dominies) make foul houses." "Dominies" were Dominican friars.

[6]IV. 779-780. Cf. Piers, B Passus X. 92-100.

[7]IV. 781-782 are adapted from Tristia, I. ix. 9-10 (Macaulay notes only that l. 781 is taken from "Tristia, i. 9. 9").

[8]IV. 784. Adapted from "Fasti, v. 354."

[9]IV. 788. "Falseness": Pseudo. "See Mirour, 21625 ff." Macaulay's note on the Mirour lines is as follows: "It seems that the word 'pseudopropheta' used in Rev. xix. 20 and elsewhere was read 'pseudo propheta,' and 'pseudo' taken as a proper name . . . ." Cf. Conf., V. 1879.

Chapter 18

[1]IV. 816. That is, he forsakes all his vows, whereas he has been released only from those which would interfere with his teaching, such as that of mendicancy.

[2]IV. 826. Cf. Conf. Amantis, I. 2698 ff., and Bal., XVI. 1-2.

[3]IV. 841-842. A reference to II Sam. (Vulgate, II Kings) 11: 25-5 and 12: 24. The "woman" was Bathsheba and the "intruder" was David. Solomon, however, was born not of their first and adulterous

union but later, in wedlock. Cf. Conf., VI. 95-97.

[4]IV. 845. Proverbial (Walz no. 85b). Cf. Conf., II. 2355-56 (Walz no. 85a).

Cf. also Mirour, 8899-8901, where the application of the proverb is perhaps the same as in the Latin:

> Quique ses buissons vait batant,
> L'oisel au mari nepourquant
> Demorra . . . .

[5]IV. 847-848. "The wording is suggested by I Cor. ix. 24. . . . " Cf. Mirour, 14365.

[6]IV. 864. On Titiuillis Macaulay refers the reader to Dyce, Skelton, II. pp. 284 f. The full reference is The Poetical Works of John Skelton, ed. Alexander Dyce, 2 vols. (London, 1843), II, 284-285, where a number of appearances of the name are cited or referred to. See also The Oxford Companion to English Literature, ed. Sir Paul Harvey, 3rd ed. (Oxford, 1946), s. v. "Titivil."

[7]IV. 866. "Plunders" is rapit, which carries the connotation of "rapes."

[8]IV. 869. "Cp. Job. ii. 4 . . . . "

[9]IV. 872. "vltima verba ligant. As in a bargain the last words are those that are binding, so here the last word mentioned, namely 'demon, ' is the true answer to the question." The expression is proverbial. Cf. Troilus, II. 260 and see Robinson's n.

[10]IV. 873. Based upon Rom. 6: 23. Cf. VI. 831-832 below.

[11]IV. 874. Proverbial (Walz no. 31c). Cf. VI. 640. Macaulay notes, "'Men sein, Old Senne newe shame, ' Conf. Amantis, iii. 2033 [Walz 31a]." In addition, Walz (no. 31b) notes the further parallel in Conf., VII. 5115.

Chapter 19

[1]IV. 903. Adapted from "Metam. ii. 632 . . . . Gower's line seems to have neither accidence nor syntax." But the only change necessary is Macaulay's own equating of vetitur with vetatur in his glossary.

424

Chapter 20

[1] *IV. 951. Adapted from Ars Amat., III. 149.

[2] IV. 953-954. Taken from "Fasti, ii. 219 f. "

[3] IV. 959-960. "A reference to Ps. lxxii. 5 [King James Version: 73: 5: "They are not in trouble as other men; neither are they plagued like other men. "]. . . . The first half of this psalm seems to have been accepted in some quarters as a prophetic description of the Mendicants. " Cf. III. 2097-98 and see n.

[4] IV. 965-966. Based upon Matt. 6: 26-28.

[5] IV. 969. "Cp. Ps. lxxii. 7 . . . . " (The King James Version is Psa. 73: 7.)

[6] IV. 971-972. "Cp. Mirour, 21517 ff. . . . " Hector's son was Astyanax.

Chapter 21

[1] IV. Chap. 21, Heading. Gower's charge was true. A law was passed in the fourth year of Henry IV to the effect that no youth should be received until after he had passed his fourteenth year, without the consent of his parents or guardians. See Coxe, p. xxviii. Wycliffe made the same charge against the friars: See Thomas Arnold, ed. Select English Works of John Wyclif, 3 vols. (Oxford, 1871), II, 380-381.

[2] IV. 981 ff. "Cp. Mirour, 21553 ff. " St. Francis was 20 or 21 at the time of his conversion.

[3] IV. 1010. Proverbial (Walz no. 222). Cf. Conf., II. 261-263 (Walz no. 221), and CYT, 746-747.

[4] IV. 1011-12. Based upon Matt. 23: 15.

[1]IV. 1027-28. Perhaps Gower had in mind such a verse as Prov. 2: 4, but I am unable to supply a more exact reference.

[2]IV. 1047-48. Taken from Aurora, Deut. 89-90 (Beichner).

[3]IV. 1059-64. "These six lines are taken without change from Aurora, (MS. Bodley 822) f. 65 [Lev. 683-688 in Beichner's ed.]. " Beichner (p. 585) cites ll. 1059-80 as an example of Gower's borrowing assorted lines from the Aurora and making them fit smoothly into his own context.

[4]IV. 1065-70. Taken from Aurora, Deut. 29-34 (Beichner).

[5]IV. 1071-72. Taken from Aurora, Josue 99-100 (Beichner).

[6]IV. 1073. Taken from Aurora, Deut. 35 (Beichner).

[7]IV. 1076. Taken from Aurora, Deut. 36 (Beichner).

[8]IV. 1078. Taken from Aurora, Gen. 962 (Beichner). Cf. Chaucer, Gen Prol, 742 and see Robinson's n.

[9]IV. 1083. Perhaps a suspicion of Lollardy, or heretical teaching; Gower uses zizannia rather than lollia for "tares. " Cf. Chaucer, Epilogue to MLT, 1173-83, and Robinson's n. on l. 1173.

[10]IV. 1087-90. Taken from Aurora, Num. 451-454 (Beichner).

[11]IV. 1096. Taken from Aurora, Gen. 1160 (Beichner).

[12]IV. 1099-1100. "Cp. Aurora, f. 19 v° [Gen. 941-942 in Beichner's ed.]. . . . " Ll. 1097-1100 refer to Gen. 16.

[13]IV. 1110. Perhaps an allusion to John 1: 5.

[14]IV. 1111. Another use of Gal. 6: 5. Cf. ll. 18 and 698 above.

[1]IV. Chap. 23, Heading. For other attacks on the extravagance of friars' churches, see Piers, B Passus III. 59-72 (C Passus IV. 63-74) and B Passus XIV. 197-199, or C Passus XVII. 40-42.

[2]IV. 1113-1114. Adapted from Aurora, Gen. 1573-74 (Beichner). Father Beichner comments (p. 583) on IV. 1113-18 as an example of Gower's using a borrowed passage to fit another context. In the Aurora, fratres meant the brothers (Solomon and Levi), not the friars.

[3]IV. 1121. Proverbial (Walz no. 78).

[4]IV. 1122. There is a pun on lustrant "purify by means of propitiatory offerings" and "wander over" or "traverse."

[5]IV. 1125. Proverbial. Cf. Troilus, I. 963-966, and see Robinson's n. on 964.

[6]IV. 1127. Proverbial. See Smith-Heseltine s.v. "Rule without some exceptions."

[7]IV. 1143 ff. "Cp. Mirour de l'Omme, 21403 ff. and note." Macaulay's note on Mirour, 21403 ff: "The passage of the Plowmans Crede relating to this subject is well known." See Pierce the Ploughmans Crede, ed. W. W. Skeat (Oxford, 1906), Preface, pp. xxvii-xxix and ll. 156 ff.

[8]IV. 1144. There is a suggestion of image worship here, a practice Gower attacked in Book II, Chapter 10.

[9]IV. 1145-48. "These lines are partly from Neckam's Vita Monachorum, p. 192 . . . . Gower alters the first sentence by substituting 'valuas' for the verb 'vallas.' 'It has folding-doors, halls, and bed-chambers as various and as many as the labyrinth.'"

[10]IV. 1155. Fingentes in l. 1155 and fingitur in l. 1158 can mean both "fashion" and "feign."

[11]IV. 1161. "'historia parisiensis' in the MSS. I cannot supply a reference." Gower may have been thinking of Alexander Neckham's account of his quarters on the Petit Pont in Paris when he was a student there. See Urban T. Holmes, Jr., Daily Living in the Twelfth Century (Madison: University of Wisconsin Press, 1952), p. 73.

[12]IV. 1171. Reading [vlmo] rather than vlno. An alternative is [alno] ("alder"). (Vlnus is an "ell" or a "measure of land" [Classical Latin ulna].) See Smith-Heseltine, s.v. "Ask pears of an elm, To, " and Metam., XIV. 661 ff.

[13]IV. 1175-76. "From De Vita Monachorum, p. 193."

[14]IV. 1177. Biblical and proverbial. See n. on III. 1721 and cf. VI. 576.

Chapter 24

[1]IV. 1189 ff. "The reference is to the Speculum Stultorum, where Burnel the Ass, after examining the rules of all the existing orders and finding them in various ways unsatisfactory to him, comes to the conclusion that he must found an order of his own, the rules of which shall combine the advantages of all the other orders. Members of it shall be allowed to ride easily like the Templars, to tell lies like the Hospitallers, to eat meat on Saturday like the Benedictines of Cluny, to talk freely like the brothers of Grandmont, to go to one mass a month, or at most two, like the Carthusians, to dress comfortably like the Praemonstratensians, and so on. What is said here by our author expresses the spirit of these rules rather than the letter." Cf. I. 201, V. 857.

[2]IV. 1214. "The expression 'Linquo coax ranis' is said to have been used by Serlo on his renunciation of the schools: see Leyser, Hist. Poet. p. 443." The full reference is to Polycarp Leyser, Historia Poetarvm et Poematvm Medii Aevi, 2 vols. (Frankfort Am Main and Leipsic, 1741) I, 443.

[3]IV. 1222* ff. The text is from STH2; the original version, ll. 1221*-1232*, is from CEHGDL.

[4]IV. 1227*. Another allusion to Wycliffe. Cf. III. 1129-30 and VI. 1267-68 and n.

Notes to BOOK V

Chapter 1

[1] V. 4-8. Cf. ll. 4-8 and Chapter 9 below with Piers, B Passus VI. 20-56, on the proper relationship between knights and the peasantry, and the duties of both classes. On knights, cf. also Miour, 23592-24180.

[2] V. 13-22. Cf. Conf., I. 1610-44 and 2651-57.

Chapter 2

[1] V. 45. "Architesis. It must be assumed that this word means 'discord, ' the passage being a series of oppositions. "

[2] V. 53 ff. "Est amor egra salus, &c. Compare the lines which follow our author's Traitié, 'Est amor in glosa pax bellica, lis pietosa, ' &c., [given in French Works, p. 392, and Latin Works, p. 359, ll. 1-15,] and Alanus de Insulis, De Planctu Naturae [in The Anglo-Latin Satirical Poets and Epigrammatists of the Twelfth Century, ed. Thomas Wright, 2 vols., (London, 1872)], p. 472 (Rolls Series, 59, vol. ii). " Cf. also Bal., XLVII. 1 ff., and Romeo, I. i. 182-187.

[3] V. 65. Gower begins a new paragraph after "pleasures. "

Chapter 3

[1] V. 79 ff. "There is not much construction here; but we must suppose that after this loose and rambling description the general sense is resumed at l. 129. "

[2] V. 81. Aures patulas mediocres.

[3] *V. 83 and 89. These lines contain details from Metam., III. 422. (This is from Ovid's telling of the story of Narcissus.)

[4] V. 98. "Nee Patet os in eis: cp. Chaucer, Book of the Duchess, 942. " Cf. also Conf., VI. 778.

[5]V. 117-118. Taken from Aurora, Gospel 117-118 (Beichner).

[6]V. 113-116, 119-120. Taken from Aurora, II Kings 47-48, 45-46, and 43-44 (Beichner). There is a play in l. 120 on Felix and fenix.

[7]V. 121-122. Adapted from "Her. iv. 71 f."

[8]V. 123-124. Adapted from "Fasti, ii. 763 [f]."

[9]V. 79-128. Father Beichner comments (pp. 588-589) that Gower's effictio of a beautiful woman is in part taken from the Aurora's description of Absalom and the Virgin Mary!

[10]V. 134. An awkward line: Ipse volutus ea non revolutus abit.

[11]V. 137. "As stille as any stone" is a frequent simile in Chaucer.

[12]V. 143-144. Gower was fond of these and similar oxymora. Cf. Conf., VI. 249: "In cold I brenne and frese in hete"; Conf.,I. 1708-10; VII. 4300-2; Vox, I. 1583-84 and 2141-45; and Bal., III. 1-2; IX. 24-29; and XLVIII. 1 ff. The similarity between Vox, V. 143-144 and Troilus, I. 420, is remarkable but probably coincidental. Chaucer had already used a similar series of paradoxes in BD, 607-612. (He translated those in Troilus, I. 420 from Petrarch, Sonnet 88 or Rima, 182: 5, as Root's note on the passage points out.) Such figures of speech became conventional in the Elizabethan sonnet, probably because of Petrarch, and long remained so. Cf. P. L., II. 595. They were already conventional for Gower, who would not have needed to read Petrarch to learn them. (On Gower and Dante, see n. on II. 67.)

[13]*V. 145. Cf. Ovid, Ars Amat., I. 391.

[14]V. 147. Proverbial. Gower writes amor omne domat instead of the more usual amor omnia vincit, which appeared on Chaucer's Prioress' plaque, Gen Prol, 162, as well as in TC, Preface 9.

[15]V. 159. There is an obvious and obscene pun in Non amor in penis est . . . .

[16]V. 165. Taken from "Metam. vii. 826." The same line is adapted in l. 199 of Gower's Carmen Super Multiplici Viciorum Pestilencia (Works, IV, 350).

[17]*V. 168. Adapted from Her., IV. 52.

[18]V. 169-170. Adapted from "Rem. Amoris, 691 f."

[19]V. 171. Adapted in part from "Her. iv. 161."

[20]V. 175. Proverbial (Walz 173a), and based in part upon Matt. 15: 14 or Luke 6: 39. Cf. Conf., VIII. 2130-31 (Walz no. 172b). Cf. also Ecce Patet Tensus, ll. 5-6, in Works, IV, 358.

[21]*V. 179-180. Adapted from Ovid, Tristia, V. iv. 9-10.

[22]*V. 185-186. From Ovid, Ars Amat., II. 237-238.

[23]*V. 187. From Ars Amat., II. 235.

[24]V. 193. Adapted from "Her. v. 149."

[25]V. 199-206. Cf. Ecce Patet Tensus, ll. 23-28.

[26]V. 209. Adapted from "Metam. x. 189."

[27]*V. 211. Adapted from Her., XVI. 231.

[28]V. 213. Adapted from "Her. vii. 179."

[29]V. 215-216. Proverbial. See Walz no. 180, which gives a reference only to the Carmen Super Multiplici Viciorum Pestilencia, 207-208, where the same lines are used.

[30]*V. 217. "Arrows" is literally "bows" (arcus). V. 217 is adapted from Ars Amat., III. 29.

[31]V. 221. Adapted from "Her. ii. 63."

[32]*V. 224. Adapted in part from Ars Amat., III. 42.

Chapter 4

[1]*V. 229-230. Cf. Ovid, Pont., I. iii. 21-22.
[2]V. 247. Proverbial. Cf. Troilus, II. 21.

Chapter 5

[1]V. 259-260. "Cp. Mirour de l'Omme, 23920, Conf. Amantis, iv. 1634. "

Chapter 6

[1]V. 299-308. "The description is taken of course from Prov. xxxi. "

[2]*V. 323-324. Adapted from Ovid, Pont., II. iv. 14-15.

[3]*V. 333-334. Cf. Ovid, Tristia, III. vi. 17 and Metam., II. 170. The description of the bad woman which follows also owes something to Prov. 7:10 ff.

[4]*V. 335-336. Adapted from De Vita Monachorum, p. 186.

[5]V. 341-342. Macaulay's note: "341 ff. Cp. Neckam, De Vita Monachorum, p. 186. " The reference should apply only to ll. 341 f.

[6]*V. 349. Taken from Metam., II. 411.

[7]V. 352. There is a play upon trahendo ("by spinning") in l. 349 and trahit ("allures") in l. 352.

[8]*V. 353. Adapted from Ars Amat., III. 481.

[9]*V. 355. Adapted in part from Ars Amat., III. 295. Cf. Lucretius, III. 1153-69, for a similar idea.

[10]V. 359. Adapted from "Ars Amat. iii. 289. "

[11]V. 360. Adapted from "Ars Amat. iii . . . 294. Presumably 'bleso' in l. 360 is a mistake for 'iusso. '" But such an assumption is not necessary, for Gower's meaning is clear. Mozley, p. 139: ". . . and the tongue is compelled to lisp at their command. "

[12]V. 361. Adapted from "Ars Amat. iii. 391. "

[13]V. 367-368. Adapted from "Ars Amat. iii. 311 f. "

[14] *V. 375. Taken from De Vita Monachorum, p. 186.

[15] V. 376. "Cp. Ars Amat. i. 598. " (The line also occurs, with one change, in De Vita Monachorum, p. 187). Mozley, p. 55: ". . . make your crafty tongue stumble in stammering talk . . . . " The expression subdola lingua is also used above, l. 354.

[16] *V. 377-378. Adapted from De Vita Monachorum, p. 187.

[17] *V. 390. Adapted from Ars Amat., II. 116.

[18] V. 399-402. "Taken with slight changes from Ars Amat. iii. 163-166. "

[19] V. 403. Adapted from "Metam. ii. 635. "

[20] V. 405. Adapted from "Ars Amat. iii. 179. "

[21] V. 407. Adapted from "Ars Amat. iii. 185. "

[22] V. 413-416. Taken from "De Vita Monachorum, p. 186. " Putatur is substituted for videtur in l. 415. See Wright's textual notes on these lines.

[23] *V. 417-419. Adapted from De Vita Monachorum, p. 187. Ten lines intervene after l. 417, and minor changes are made in the lines borrowed.

[24] V. 421-428. Adapted from "De Vita Monachorum, p. 189. " Only l. 427 undergoes any significant change at Gower's hands, although he rearranges the sequence of the lines of his source.

[25] V. 429-430. Taken from Speculum Stultorum, p. 58, ll. 1-2 (Raymo).

[26] V. 431-432. Cf. Chaucer, WBT, 257-261, 1213-16.

[27] V. 433-438. Cf. Chaucer, WBT, 357-361, and Ovid, Am., III. iv. 5-7.

[28] *V. 439-440. Adapted from Pont., I. vi. 51-52.

[29] *V. 443-446. Taken with but minor changes from Tristia, V. ii. 23-26.

[30]V. 449-450. MSS. CEHGTDL read, "The world is false but woman is falser, and indeed she fetters foolish men by her arts. "

Chapter 7

[1]V. 487-488. From Aurora, Deut. 199-200 (Beichner).

Chapter 8

[1]V. 520. "Cp. Mirour de l'Omme, 23701 ff. "

[2]V. 523. From Aurora, Deut. 201 (Beichner). On Joseph, Rachel and Leah, see Gen. 29: 16 ff.

[3]V. 527. See n. on l. 523 above.

[4]V. 529-530. From Aurora, Deut. 203-204 (Beichner).

[5]V. 537-540. From Aurora, Lev. 671-674 (Beichner).

[6]V. 556. "The neglect of the burden of a charge, while the honour of it is retained, is a constant theme of denunciation by our author: cp. iii. 116, and below, ll. 655 ff. " This statement could be made more generalized, in order to say that Gower frequently attacks the contrast of virtuous appearance with evil reality.

Gower makes complaints similar to those in this chapter concerning the numbers and wrongdoings of knights in Conf., VIII. 3011 ff.

Chapter 9

[1]V. Chap. 9. See n. on ll. 4-8 above.

[2]V. 557 ff. "With this account of the labourers cp. Mirour de l'Omme, 26425 ff. It is noticeable that there is nothing here about the insurrection. " Thus it is all the more likely that Gower added Book I after he had written the rest of the poem.

Cf. also Conf., V. 6961-65.

[3]V. 561-568. An expansion of Gen. 3: 19: "In the sweat of thy face shalt thou eat bread, till thou return to the ground. . . ." Cf. Piers, B Passus VI. 235-236. In this chapter Gower tries to refute the widely current jingle of that day:

> When Adam delved and Eve span,
> Who was then the gentleman?

In Conf., IV. 2222-26, however, he echoes it with approval.

[4]V. 569. Another reference to "not looking back from the plow" (Luke 9: 62). Cf. IV. 10, 245-246. Cultor has the meaning of "worshipper" as well as "peasant" or "tiller." Cf. ll. 617 and 620 below.

[5]V. 593. Adapted from "Metam. vi. 318."

[6]V. 599-600. At first glance this sentence would seem to refer to the great uprising in 1381, but surely such an occurrence would have called for fuller treatment at Gower's hand, especially in view of his general opinion of the peasants and their proper place. "The experience of yesterday" really means "recent experience" as opposed to that of the good old days, to which Gower is always harking back.

[7]V. 603. Vngentem pungit pungentem rusticus vngit.

[8]*V. 611. Taken from Ovid, Metam., II. 163.

[9]V. 613. "A quotation from Pamphilus: cp. Mirour, 14449." Mirour, 14449-52 and Macaulay's note:

> Pour ce nous disoit en ses vers
> Pamphilius ly sages clercs,
> Qe joyntement dieus et labour
> Nous apportont les biens divers . . . .

"The reference is to a dramatic love-poem in Latin elegiac verse with the title Pamphilus, or Pamphilus de Amore, which was very popular in the thirteenth and fourteenth centuries. Pamphilus (or Panphylus) is the name of the lover who sustains the chief part, but others besides Gower have supposed it to be also the name of the author. The line referred to here is,

> 'Prouidet et tribuit deus et labor omnia nobis, '
> (f. 6 v⁰).

[Gower substitutes Contulit for Prouidet in V. 613.] I quote from a copy of a rare fifteenth-century edition (without date or place, but supposed to have been printed about 1490 at Rome), in the Douce collection, Bodleian Library. It has the title 'Panphylus de amore, ' and ends, 'Explicit amorem per tractus (i. e. pertractans) Panphyli codex. ' The book is not without some merit of its own, through to a great extent it is an imitation of Ovid. It is quoted several times by Albertano of Brescia in his Liber Consolationis, and was evidently regarded as a serious authority: see Chaucer's Tale of Melibee, which is ultimately derived from the Liber Consolationis. It is referred to also in the Frankeleins Tale, 381 f. [Robinson ed., ll. 1109 f.],

> 'Under his brest he bar it more secree
> Than ever did Pamphilus for Galathee.'"

The reference to Melibee is l. 1556. In a note on that line Professor Robinson mentions the edition by A. Baudouin (Paris, 1874); I have not seen the poem.

[10] V. 617. There is a play in ll. 617 and 620 upon the two basic meanings of cultus, namely, "cultivated" and "cherished." Cf. l. 569 above.

Chapter 10

[1] V. 629 ff. Piers, B Passus VI. 304-321, is a very close parallel to ll. 629-648.

Chapter 11

[1] V. 671. Proverbial (Walz no. 240).

[2] V. 677 ff. The trend of thought in this paragraph is uneven.

[3] V. 687-688. Gower seldom praises the Jews (but cf II. 341-342, and Conf., V. 1608-1736). Usually, he is hostile to them, as were nearly all his contemporaries. But cf. Piers, B Passus IX. 83-87.

[4] V. 693-694. "Cp. Aurora, f. 36 . . . [Exod. 277-278 in Beichner's ed.]."

[5] V. 694-695. Cf. Piers, B Passus VII. 18-22.

Chapter 12

[1] V. Chap. 12. Heading. Cf. Coxe, pp. xxxiii-xxxiv: "Usury too was now at its height. In the Parliament Rolls of the 14th year of this

[i. e. , Richard II's] reign is a complaint of the Commons against the horrible and abominable vice of Usury, called 'Chevance, ' and praying that the laws against it of the 25 Edw. III may be confirmed. "

[2]V. 703. "The capitals which mark the personification of 'Fraus' and 'Vsura' are due to the editor. 'Fraus' corresponds to 'Triche' in the Mirour de l'Omme: see ll. 25237 ff. "
      For a similar picture of Avarice and Usury as merchants, cf. Conf. , V. 4383-4430.

Chapter 13

[1]V. Chap. 13. With Chapters 13-14 cf. Mirour, 25705 ff.

[2]V. 760-762. "Cp. Chaucer, Cant. Tales, C 472 ff. " The passage is Pard T, 472-475. It was thought that each time someone swore by a limb of Christ, that limb suffered another wound. (The Pardoner also talks of fraudulent vintners, ll. 562-566; cf. ll. 775-778 below.)

Chapter 14

[1]V. Chap. 14. Heading. Cf. Piers, B Passus V. 200-227 and C Passus IV. 77-120 for other descriptions of the dishonesty of merchants and craftsmen.

[2]V. 812. "'Thethis, ' ('Thetis, ' or 'Tethis') stands several times for 'water' (properly 'Tethys'): cp. vii. 1067. The line means that the water is so abundant in the jar that it hardly admits the presence of any malt ('Cerem' for 'Cererem'). " (The confusing of "Thetis" with "Tethys" also occurs in Shakespeare, Troilus and Cressida, I. iii. 39.)

Chapter 15

[1]V. Chap. 15, Heading. "It is difficult to say who is the bad mayor of London to whom allusion is here made. The rival leaders in City politics were Nicholas Brembre and John of Northampton. The former was lord mayor in the years 1377, 1378, and again in 1383 and 1384, when he was elected against his rival (who had held the office in 1381, 1382) in a forcible and unconstitutional manner which evoked many

protests. Brembre, who belonged to the Grocers' company, represented the interests of the greater companies and was of the Court party a special favourite with the king, while John of Northampton, a draper, engaged himself in bitter controversy with the Fishmongers, who were supported by the Grocers, and was popular with the poorer classes. In the Cronica Tripertita [I. 154-159] Gower bitterly attacks Brembre (who was executed by sentence of the so-called 'Merciless Parliament' in 1388), and we might naturally suppose that he was the person referred to here; but that passage [i. e., this passage in The Voice of One Crying] was written before the political events which led to that invective and in all probability not later than 1382, and the references to the low origin of the mayor in question, ll. 845-860, do not agree with the circumstances of Nicholas Brembre. Political passion in the City ran high from the year 1376 onwards, and the person referred to may have been either John of Northampton or one of the other mayors, who had in some way incurred Gower's dislike; cp. Mirour, 26365 ff. " Very likely, no particular person is meant; the chapter is generalized.

[2]V. 835-836. Proverbial (Walz no. 260b). Cf. Mirour, 23413-14 (Walz no. 260a) and 2893-95, and Werner, m-51. The crow was thus thought to befoul its own nest.

[3]V. 843. Proverbial (Walz no. 246, where the reference is to l. 843, but ll. 975-976 are quoted). Cf. Mirour, 10959-60 (Walz no. 245). Cf. also Ecclus. 11: 34.

[4]V. 851-852. Proverbial. See Smith-Heseltine, s. v. "Fool praises another, One. "

[5]V. 857. There is a play in this line upon sella ("saddle") and Asellus. Because the latter word is capitalized, Gower undoubtedly again means Burnell (cf. IV. 1190 etc.)

[6]V. 864. "Fame" (fama) in the sense of Lady Fame in Chaucer's House of Fame.

[7]V. 876. Proverbial (Walz no. 205f). Cf. II. 175 and 159-160. There are several parallels in Gower's other works, e. g., Mirour, 10942 and 22101 (Walz nos. 207b and 207c); Conf., VII. 2393 (Walz no. 2096).

[8]V. 879. Proverbial. Cf. Conf., V. 2817-20 and VI. 2823; Troilus, II. 260; TC, III. 123. See Smith-Heseltine, s. v. "End tries all, The. "

[1] V. 893-894. An allusion to Matt. 19: 6 or Mark 10: 9. Cf. II. 55, and see note.

[2] V. 901-906. For parallels to Gower's terming the teeth as a barrier for the tongue, see the n. on Lear, II. ii. 9, in Sixteen Plays of Shakespeare, ed. George Lyman Kittredge (Boston: Ginn, 1946), pp. 1172-73. Cf. also Chaucer, Manciple's Tale, 322-324.

[3] V. 915-916. Adapted from "Tristia, i. 5. 47 f. "

[4] V. 921-922. "Cp. Prov. xxv. 15 . . . . " Cf. also Conf., III. 463-465, and Skeat, Early English Proverbs, no. 79. Perhaps 1. 921 is another satiric allusion to the Vision of Do-wel, Do-bet, and Do-best, in Piers. See n. on I. 1122.

[5] V. 949 ff. This paragraph and the next consist of a list of proverbs and maxims which Gower compiled from Ovid. They are given here without much thought as to organization or the Vrbis rector, at whom they are directed.

[6] V. 953-954. Taken from "Ars Amat. ii. 183 f., but Ovid has 'Numidasque leones [instead of tumidosque leones]. "

[7] V. 957-958. Adapted from "Rem. Amoris, 447 f. "

[8] V. 965-966. Taken from "Pont. iii. 7. 25 f. "

[9] V. 967-968. Adapted from "Rem. Amoris, 97 f. "

[10] V. 969-970. Adapted from "Rem. Amoris, 101 f. "

[11] V. 971-972. In part adapted from "Rem. Amoris, 729 f. "

[12] V. 973. Adapted from "Rem. Amoris, 623. " Cf. VI. 1303.

[13] V. 975-976. Adapted from "Rem. Amoris, 731 f., 'Ut pene extinctum cinerem si sulfure tangas, Vivet, ' &c. The reading 'sub' must be a mistake on the part of our author for 'si. '" But the subjunctive tangas is sufficient, without si, to establish a conditional clause, although sub sulfure is an awkward phrase.

[14] V. 979. Adapted from "Ars Amat. iii, 597. "

[15]V. 981. Taken from "Ars Amat. iii, 373. "

[16]V. 983-984. Adapted from "Ars Amat. iii, 375 f. "

[17]V. 985-986. Adapted from "Ars Amat. iii. 501 f. "

[18]V. 990. Taken from "Fasti, iii, 380, absurdly introduced here. " But the borrowing seems acceptable enough. Frazer, p. 147: ". . . he formed a very shrewd design. "

[19]V. 991-992. "Cp. Conf. Amantis, Latin Verses before Prol. 499. "

[20]V. 1003-1004. Adapted from "Tristia, ii. 141 f. "

[21]V. 1009-10. A reference to the Babylonian Captivity, or Great Schism. Cf. III. 4-6.

Notes to BOOK VI

Chapter 1

[1]VI. 1 ff. The first four chapters of Book VI should effectively dispose of the conjecture that Gower was a lawyer. He condemns them uncompromisingly. With VI. 1-468, "compare Mirour, 24181 ff. " With Chap. 1 cf. Piers, B. Passus VII. 39 ff.

[2]VI. 11. A reference to "Ps. xiv. 3. " The King James Version is Psa. 15: 3.

[3]VI. 44-45. Cf. Piers, B Prologus, 210-215.

[4]VI. 59-68. On lawyers' receiving gifts, cf. Chaucer's Man of Law, Gen Prol, 316-317.

[5]VI. 69-70. Cf. Her. XIX. 13.

[6]VI. 74. de burse gurgite: "for its spendthrift purse. " The phrase can also mean "for the bottomless abyss of its purse, " or "by the weir of its purse. "

[7]VI. 89-94. "From Aurora, (MS. Bodley 822) f. 6 [Lev. 751-756 in Beichner]. . . ."

[8]VI. 95-98. Taken, with minor changes, from "Aurora, f. 65 [Lev. 689-692 in Beichner]. . . ."

[9]VI. 101-102. "Cp. Aurora [f. 64 (Lev. 663-664 in Beichner)],

'Inprouisus adest cum pullos tollere miluus
Esurit, in predam non sine fraude ruit.'

This is adapted by our author to his own purpose, but as his meaning is altogether different, some obscurity results, and he does not make it clear to us how the biter is bit." But the biter is bit in the next chapter, where it is shown that the avaricious lawyer builds up a large estate only to have it wasted by his son and heir. (Macaulay's note reads, "Cp. Aurora, 64 f.")

VI. 102 is proverbial (Walz no. 109b). Cf. Conf., VI. 1379-81 (Walz no. 109a), and RvT, 4321.

Chapter 2

[1]VI. 105 ff. Chapter 2, which is written with real feeling, ironically places Gower on the same side as the peasants, who hated lawyers and attacked them in the Great Revolt.

[2]*VI. 107-108. Cf. Metam., VII. 65, and Her. XII. 123.

[3]VI. 113. Taken from "Metam. v. 606."

[4]VI. 115-118. Adapted from "Metam. vi. 527 ff." Miller, I, 325: "She trembled like a frightened lamb, which, torn and cast aside by a grey wolf, cannot yet believe that it is safe; and like a dove which, with its own blood all smeared over its plumage, still palpitates with fright, still fears those greedy claws that have pierced it." I have read "grey" (cani) with Ovid rather than Gower's canis.

[5]VI. 129-131. There is a play upon aura ("air," "wind") in l. 129 and auro ("gold") in l. 131. Ll. 129-130 are based on a proverb: see Smith-Heseltine, "Wind blows, As the."

[6]VI. 141-142. Adapted from "Is. v. 8 . . . ." Gower himself was land hungry, however. See Intro., pp. 4-5 and cf. ll. 341-348 below.

[7]VI. 144. "By comparison with Mirour, 24580 ff. we may see that the dissipation of the property by the son is here alleged as a proof that it has been ill acquired . . . ."

[8]VI. 149. Proverbial (Walz no. 25). From Juvenal, Sat. XIV, 303.

[9]VI. 151-152. A reference either to Isaiah 1: 23 or, more probably, to 10: 1-2.

Chapter 3

[1]*VI. 153-154. Cf. Metam., V. 485-486.

[2]VI. 171. Gower may have learned the Greek meaning of "Chrysostom" from Godfrey of Viterbo's Pantheon (ed. 1726), p. 276: "Eo tempore Joannes Chrysostomos, qui interpretatur os aureum . . . ."

[3]VI. 203. "Basiliscus: cp. Mirour, 3748 ff. "

[4]VI. 209-210. Adapted from "Pont. ii. 3. 39 f. "

[5]VI. 213-214. This idea contradicts I. Prol. 4 ff.

[6]VI. 233-234. "'And this lex, legis, from ledo, ledis, as ius from iurgo, administers justice at this present time. ' It is meant that the administration of law, as we see it, suggests the above etymologies. "

[7]VI. 241-248. "Cp. Mirour, 24253 ff. "

Chapter 4

[1]VI. Chapter 4, Heading. "Sitting there in the seat of the scornful" is an allusion to Psa. 1: 1.

[2]VI. 249 ff. "Cp. Mirour, 24349 ff. . . ." (Ll. 24349-96 of the Mirour are translated in Edith Rickert, Chaucer's World, edd. Clair

C. Olson and Martin M. Crow [New York: Columbia, 1948], pp. 159-160.)

VI. 249: Est Apprenticius, Sergantus, post et Adultus . . . . I do not find that Adultus was the name of a separate legal rank, in spite of the capitalization.

[3]VI. 250. In addition to "mark, " notabit can also mean "brand with infamy. "

[4]VI. 265 ff. With this paragraph cf. VII. 39-61 below; cf. also Piers, B Passus III. 12-19.

[5]VI. 269. The reference is to Ecclus. xx. 31 . . . . "

[6]*VI. 301. Taken from Pont., I. iii. 23.

Chapter 5

[1]VI. 313-326. "These fourteen lines are taken with some alterations (not much for the better) from Neckam, De Vita Monachorum, pp. 180 f. " L. 318 seems to be Gower's own.

[2]VI. 327-328. "Cp. De Vita Monachorum, p. 182, ... "

[3]VI. 327-332. Cf. Piers, B Passus XI. 258-260, and WBT, 1187 ff.

[4]VI. 329-348. Macaulay notes, "De Vita Monachorum, p. 181 [pp. 181-182]. Most of the lines 329-348 are borrowed. " Those original with Gower would seem to be ll. 331-332, 336, 342, 344, and 349.

[5]VI. 355-356. "Cp. De Vita Monachorum, p. 182 . . . . "

[6]VI. 357. Taken from "De Vita Monachorum, p. 190. "

[7]VI. 359-372. "Most of these lines are borrowed with slight alterations from De Vita Monachorum, p. 191. " Ll. 361, 362, 368, 370, and 372 (which is another allusion to Gal. 6: 5) are Gower's own. With VI. 360, cf. Troilus, IV. 391-392.

[8]VI. 383-384. An allusion to Mark 8: 36. "For what shall it profit a man, if he shall gain the whole world, and lose his own soul? "

[9] VI. 389. "Cp. De Vita Monachorum, p. 192, 'Cur ampla aedificas busto claudendus in arcto?'"

[10] VI. 387-390. "Cp. Mirour, 24733 ff. "

[11] VI. 397-398. Cp. "De Vita Monachorum, p. 193 . . . . "

Chapter 6

[1] VI. Chapter 6. "Cp. Mirour, 24817-25176. "

[2] VI. 421-422. "For the idea contained in 'vnccio' and 'vncta' cp. iii. 1376. " Cf. also III. 1206.

[3] VI. 433. "'The word comes receives its beginning not from vice but from vicium. ' That is, apparently the prefix which makes 'comes' into 'vicecomes' is to be derived from 'vicium. '" Vicecomes is a common term for sheriff.

[4] VI. 439-440. "Cp. Mirour, 25166 ff. "

[5] VI. 443. An allusion, of course, to Matt. 7: 6.

[6] VI. 445 ff. "With this compare the corresponding lines in the Carmen super multiplici viciorum Pestilencia, under the head of 'Avarice' (246 ff.),
'Vendere iusticiam nichil est nisi vendere Cristum, ' &c. "

[7] VI. 467. Proverbial (Walz no. 49b). "Cp. Mirour, 24962 f. "

Chapter 7

[1] VI. 473. A quotation from Eccl. 3: 1: "To every thing there is a season, and a time to every purpose under heaven. " Cf. Conf., VII. 3594-95. This biblical verse is very frequently quoted in Chaucer; see for example, Troilus, II. 989; III. 855.

[2] VI. 475-480. These lines seem borrowed, but I am unable to cite a source.

[3] VI. 493-494. A reference to Mark 3: 24, Matt. 12: 25, or Luke 11: 17.

[4] VI. 497. Taken from Horace, Epistles, I. ii. 14. Harper's Latin Dictionary, s. v. Achivus: ". . . whatever wrongs the (Grecian) kings are guilty of (before Troy) their subjects must suffer for; but it soon became a general proverb: whatever errors the great commit, the people must atone for . . . . " (Walz no. 242b). Cf. Conf., VII. 3928-31 (Walz no. 242a).

[5] VI. 498. Proverbial (Walz no. 241c). Cf. 1. 549 below and PP, 260 (Walz no. 291a), and "Cp. Mirour, 22835 f. " (Walz no. 291b).

[6] VI. 513-514. The idea is proverbial. Cf. Troilus, II. 1380-83 and see Robinson's note.

[7] *VI. 519. Adapted from Metam., I. 76.

[8] VI. 523-528. "The idea of the passage seems to be that good laws are as the material, and the ruler as the builder of the house. "

[9] VI. 529-532. "Cp. Conf. Amantis, vii. 2695 ff. "

[10] VI. 545 ff. Ll. 545-580 are the revised text as given in MSS. SCEHGDL, while ll. 545*-580* are the original version as given in TH$_2$. "The chief difference introduced is in the direction of throwing more responsibility on the king, who however is still spoken of as a boy. Thus instead of 'Stat puer immunis culpe, ' we have 'Rex puer indoctus morales negligit actus' (or more strongly still 'respuit'). "
    Cf. Piers, B Passus XIX. 462-476 and C Passus XXII. 467-481. Skeat's note on C Passus XXII reads: " '"Then(I grant) that thou mayest have what thou askest for, as the law requires, ' (c); 'Thou mayest take in reason, ' etc. (b). The change is very significant; the king is no longer to take, but to ask for what he wants. Richard II. was rapidly falling into disgrace. "

[11] VI. 545-546. This is seemingly an accurate premonition of the Great Revolt which followed, rather than hindsight.

[12] VI. 549. Proverbial (Walz no. 241d). Cf. 1. 498 above.

[13] VI. 555 ff. The author of Piers was also very bold in criticising Richard II: see C Passus IV. 201-215. Gower much exaggerated the youthfulness of Richard's advisers. Cf. also TC, I. 15-16, and see n.

[14]VI. 550*. Proverbial (Walz no. 128b). Cf. Mirour, 6357 (Walz no. 128a).

[15]VI. 573*-574*. The reference is to Daniel 13: 5 (Vulgate).

[16]VI. 576. Biblical and proverbial. See n. on III. 1721 and cf. IV. 1177.

Chapter 8

[1]VI. Chapter 8. With this chapter cf. Conf., VII. 1825-48, 2709-64, and 3067-94; VIII. 2109-25.
"The ensuing Epistle to the young king, which extends as far as l. 1200, assumes a more severely moral form owing to the alteration of the preceding passage, the exclusion of all compliment ('regnaturo' in this heading for 'excellentissimo') and the substitution of 'doctrine causa' for 'in eius honore. '"

[2]VI. 591. The line contains a play upon frena ("reins") and freno ("grasp").

[3]VI. 611-612. An allusion to I. Cor. 6: 12 (or 10: 23).

[4]VI. 629-630. Cf. "Neckam, De Vita Monachorum, p. 185, . . .'"

[5]VI. 631-632. The teacher of Alexander was, of course, Aristotle, who had acquired a reputation as a Don Juan in the Middle Ages. Cf. Conf., VII. 4255-61.

[6]VI. 638. Proverbial. The line can also mean, "the pot is wont to retain the tinge which first stained it. "

[7]VI. 640. Proverbial. Cf. IV. 874 and see n.

[8]VI. 642. An allusion to Ecclus. 13: 1. Cf. Mirour, 13684-87.

Chapter 9

[1]VI. 657. An allusion to John 12: 35. Cf. I John 2: 11.

[2]VI. 659-660. From Aurora, Mach. 35-36 (Beichner). Cf. Ovid,

Am. I. viii. 103-104. There is a pun on venenum ("poison") in l. 659 and venalis ("for sale, " "venal") in l. 662.

[3]VI. 681. Proverbial (Walz no. 1111).

[4]VI. 685-686. From Aurora, Gen. 1053-54 (Beichner). See Luke 23: 32-33, 39-43.

[5]VI. 696. Taken from "Rem. Amoris, 526. "

[6]VI. 709-714. These lines are part of the evidence that Gower was no pacifist, despite Book III, Chapters 6-10, as well as In Praise of Peace. Cf. Chapter 13 below. Gower is not for peace at any price: see Conι., VII. 3524 ff. The words Arma ferunt pacem in l. 713 are from Speculum Stultorum, p. 30, l. 1 (Raymo).

[7]VI. 719-722. "Cp. Aurora, (MS. Bodley 822) f. 65 [Lev. 699-702 in Beichner] . . . . "

[8]VI. 723-724. From Aurora, Lev. 305-306 (Beichner).

Chapter 10

[1]VI. Chapter 10. With this chapter cf. Conf. , VII. 3873-90.

[2]*VI. 750. Taken from Her. , XVII. 130.

[3]*VI. 752. Taken from Ovid, Her. , XVII. 234. The expression became proverbial (Walz no. 144).

[4]*VI. 753. Adapted from Metam. , I. 246.

[5]VI. 755-756. Cf. Conf. , VII. 4135-39.

[6]*VI. 757. Adapted from Tristia, IV. ix. 21.

[7]*VI. 765. Adapted from Ars Amat. , III. 557.

[8]*VI. 779. Adapted from Metam. , III. 700, with considerable change in meaning. Texts CEH retain Ovid's solvente, which Macaulay adopts. I have read iubente ("prescribing") with SGDL.

Chapter 11

[1]VI. 793-794. "Cp. Aurora, f. 96 v⁰ [I Kings 313-314 in Beich-
ner] . . . ."

[2]VI. 816. Adapted from "Amores, i. 8. 62 . . . . "

[3]*VI. 825. Adapted from Amores, I. x. 61.

[4]VI. 831-832 An allusion to Rom. 6: 23. Cf. IV. 873 above.

[5]VI. 835-836. It was an old idea that Adam (and Eve) ate the
apple in Eden because of gluttony: cf. Mirour, 7769 ff. and 8750
ff.; Conf., VI. 1-14; Dante, Purg., 103 ff., and Par., 13: 38-39;
PardT, 504-512. The idea lasted as late as P. L., IX. 739-743. But
Gower of course knew that Adam's fateful and fatal sin was pride: see
Voice, III. 729-730, and VII. 619-624; Carmen, 96.

[6]VI. 837-838. For the account of Satan's tempting Jesus to turn
a stone into bread, see Matt. 4: 1-4 or Luke 4: 1-4.

[7]VI. 839-840. "Cp. Aurora, f. 95 v⁰ [I Kings 265-266 in Beich-
ner]. " The original source is probably I Sam. (Vulgate: I Kings) 7: 5-
11.

[8]VI. 846. From "Fasti, ii. 226. "

Chapter 12

[1]VI. Chapter 12. With this chapter cf. Conf., VII. 4215-56, and
IV. 1476-77.

[2]VI. 853-856. Richard II and Anne of Bohemia were married in
January, 1382 (they both were only fifteen at the time). But Gower is
perhaps speaking in general terms, for only Book I and the revised passages of Books III and VI were written as late as 1382.

[3]VI. 863-864. From Aurora, III Kings 269-270 (Beichner). Peter
of Riga is probably referring to the account of David and Bathsheba in
II Sam. (Vulgate: II Kings) 11: 2-17, although the thought is generalized.
Perhaps he refers to 24: 10-17.
For ll. 862-864 cf. Traitié, XIV.

[4]VI. 869. From Speculum Stultorum, p. 145, ll. 13-14 (Raymo).
Cf. Troilus, I. 203.

[5]VI. 875-902. "Taken with few alterations from the Aurora, f. 76
[Beichner: Num. 509-540, omitting 523-524 and 537-538]. The passage refers not to the well known account of Balaam and King Balak of
Moab in Numbers 22-24, but to another account. According to it, ". . .
Balaam was a Midianitish prophet who counseled his people to tempt the
Israelites into various immoralities" (Gerald Se Boyar, A Handbook of
the Bible [New York, 1940], p. 28). This second tradition is referred
to in II Peter 2:15, Jude 11, and Rev. 2:14. Cf. VII. 27-28.
    Cf. also Conf., VII. 4406-68, where the same story and moral
are given.

[6]VI. 886. "acuum ferrum: in the original 'Minitans ferrum.' Apparently our author took 'acus' to mean a spear or javelin. The choice
of the word in this passage is unfortunate." (Acus commonly means
"needle"; perhaps Gower intended to write acutum.)

[7]VI. 903. Gower has te docet experimentum for the proverbial
experientia docet. Cf. Conf., I. Latin verses ii. 3.

[8]VI. 907. From "Aurora, f. 100 [I Kings 539 in Beichner]."

[9]VI. 905-910. A reference to I Sam. (Vulgate: I Kings) 28:7 ff.
The enchantress here is the Witch of Endor. Cf. I Chron. 10:13 and
ll. 1299-1300 below, and see n. Cf. also Conf., VI. 2384-90.

[10]VI. 911. Proverbial. See Smith-Heseltine, s.v. "Forewarned,
forearmed."

[11]VI. 913. Cf. Traitié, XVII, refrain: "A un est une assetz en
marriage."

Chapter 13

[1]VI. Chapter 13, Heading. Richard II was the son of Edward,
Prince of Wales, the Black Prince. For a view opposed to Gower's on
the much-admired Black Prince, see Steel, Richard II, pp. 39-40.

[2]VI. 926. Possibly an allusion to the badge of the House of Lancaster, which was a white rose. Properly speaking, however, Richard

449

II was not of this house, but was the last of the Plantaganet line.

[3]VI. 937-938. Gower and Langland seem to agree in approval of British invasions of France: cf. Piers, B Passus III. 187-204 and C Passus IV. 233-263. Lines 937-938 are Gower's own, but they are in a long passage (ll. 929-967) which is largely a pastiche of quotations from some of the most heroic passages in the Aurora. See Beichner, pp. 584-585.

[4]VI. 939-940. From Aurora, Mach. 83-84 (Beichner).

[5]VI. 942-944. From Aurora, Mach. 96-98 (Beichner).

[6]VI. 945-946. From Aurora, Mach. 179, 134 (Beichner).

[7]VI. 947-950. "Taken from the description of Saul at the battle of Gilboa, Aurora, f. 100 v° [I Kings 549-550, 547-548 in Beichner]. "

[8]VI. 955-960. From Aurora, Gen. 1583, 1586, 1585, 1578, 1601, 1606 (Beichner). For the meaning of "leopard" here see n. on I. 1757.

[9]VI. 961-964. The ultimate source is I Kings (Vulgate: III Kings) 4:25. The lines, however, are from Aurora, Mach. 277-280 (Beichner).

[10]VI. 965-966. From Aurora, II Kings 33-34 (Beichner).

[11]VI. 969. Proverbial (Walz no. 204b). Cf. Troilus, IV. 600-602 and see Root's n. Cf. also Conf., VII. 4902-4903 (Walz no. 204a).

[12]VI. 971 ff. Macaulay notes, "Cp. Praise of Peace, 78 ff., " but the parallel is not very close except in l. 78:
Pes is the chief of al the worldes welthe . . . .

[13]VI. 973. Based upon Eccl. 3:8.

[14]*VI. 976. Adapted, though not very happily, from Pont., III. iv. 86. The line and its context in Ovid are as follows: "Moreover frail couplets could not support the weight of so vast a triumph upon their uneven wheels. " (Wheeler, p. 405.) The "uneven wheels" refer to the uneven line lengths of the elegiac couplet.

[15]VI. 984. Proverbial (Walz no. 119).

Chapter 14

[1] VI. 987-988. David and one of his Psalms, such as 139: 8 (Vulgate: 138: 8) or 112: 7-8 (Vulgate: 111: 7-8) are meant. The lines are Peter of Riga's; see n. 3 below.

[2] VI. 990. "'horret equos' seems to represent the 'equis vehementer infesti' of Isidore, Etym. xii. 2. "

[3] VI. 985-992. Adapted "From Aurora, f. 64 v° [Lev. 651-658 in Beichner]. " On the passage, see Beichner, pp. 589-590 and n. 11, where it is pointed out that Aurora, Lev. 654 (Gower's line 988) is actually based upon Psa. 73: 9 (Vulgate: 72: 9).

[4] VI. 997. Proverbial (Walz no. 178).

[5] VI. 999. Proverbial (Walz no. 105b), going back to Virgil, Eclogue x. 69. Cf. Chaucer, Gen Prol, 162.

[6] VI. 1020. A reference to Eph. 4: 5.

[7] VI. 1019-1024. "From Neckam, De Vita Monachorum, p. 185, with slight alterations. "

Chapter 15

[1] VI. 1041-50. "Taken with slight changes from Aurora, f. 108 [III Kings 37-46 in Beichner]. " The lines are based upon I Kings (Vulgate: III Kings) 3: 5-13. Cf. Conf., VII. 3891-3912.

[2] VI. 1056. An allusion to Matt. 7: 24-25. Cf. Luke 6: 47-48.

[3] VI. 1075-76. These lines contain plays upon the two basic meanings of sapio, "to savor" and "to be wise, " or "to know. "

Chapter 16

[1] VI. 1081. From Speculum Stultorum, p. 17, line 15 (Raymo).

[2] VI. 1085-86. "From De Vita Monachorum, p. 184. "

[3]VI. 1096. <u>Subdita fortune sors magis immo favet</u>. The line may also mean, "Instead, a more fortunate destiny subservientlyfavors him, " or, " Instead, destiny, in place of (or substituted for) Fortune, favors him. "

[4]VI. 1107-12. Taken, with slight alterations in ll. 1108 and 1111, from "<u>De Vita Monachorum</u>, p. 193. " See Wright's textual note on l. 1107.

[5]VI. 1115-16 are taken from "<u>De Vita Monachorum</u>, p. 183. " The two lines are separated by four others in the original.

Chapter 17

[1]VI. 1125. Proverbial (Walz no. 152). Cf. <u>Conf</u>., II. 3246-47 (Walz no. 15a).

[2]*VI. 1134. Adapted from Ovid, <u>Tristia</u>, IV. iii. 74 (Walz no. 82).

[3]VI. 1135-36. Proverbial (Walz no. 147b) and biblical. Job 7: 1: "<u>Militia est vita hominis super terram</u>. " (The King James Version is, "Is there not an appointed time to man upon earth? ")
The "three wars" are with the world, the flesh, and the devil.

[4]VI. 1145-50. From <u>Aurora</u>, Num. 23-26, 29-30 (Beichner).

Chapter 18

[1]VI. Chapter 18. The revised text is as given in SCHEGH (over erasure in all except E). The original form, which is marked by an asterisk after the chapter and line numberings, is as given by DTH$_2$. Both forms are given by LL$_2$, with the original first. "A considerable part of the erased chapter reappears in the poem 'Rex celi deus, ' &c., addressed to Henry IV: see p. 343 [of the <u>Latin Works</u>]. " Thus Gower uses the same lines to praise and pray for Henry IV which he had originally used in respect to Richard II and then retracted.
The same lines stand at the end of Gower's <u>In Praise of Peace</u>. See <u>Works</u>, III, 492-494 and notes.

[2]VI. 1174.   Proverbial.   Cf. III. 404 and n.

[3]*VI. 1178*.   From Ars Amat., I. 214.

[4]VI. 1182*.   Literally, "his increased crown" (aucta corona).

[5]VI. 1184*.   Or: "may all things here below (cunctaque . . . in-feriora) be on your shoulders, " i. e., "belong to you. "

[6]*VI. 1189*.   Taken from Tristia, IV. v. 25.

[7]VI. 1198*.   The pun is better in the Latin: Vt valor est in te, sic tibi dico vale.

Chapter 19

[1]VI. 1201.   Adapted from "Metam. vii. 586. "

[2]VI. 1205.   Taken from "Metam. ii. 541. "

[3]VI. 1216.   For the reference to Nimrod see Gen. 10: 8-10 and 11: 1-9.

[4]VI. 1217.   For the reference to Japhet, who covered the drunken and naked Noah, see Gen. 9: 18-27.

[5]VI. 1220.   Bel is a Babylonian god, referred to, for example, in Isa. 46: 1, and in the apocryphal book Bel and the Dragon.

[6]VI. 1222.   Five MSS have Ishmael, meaning the son of Nephaniah (Jer. 40, 41).

[7]VI. 1223.   ". . . Uzzah (2 Sam. vi.) . . . is selected as a type of carnal lust, apparently on the strength of the quite gratuitous assumption adopted [from the Aurora] in Lib. III. 1885 ff. " (See n. on those lines.) In III. 1885 ff., as in Dante, Purg., 10: 55-57, Uzzah has his more usual reputation of a presumptuous office seeker.

[8]VI. 1229.   A reference to II Kings (Vulgate: IV Kings) 2: 11.

[9]VI. 1227-30.   For the references to Abiram, Dathan, and Korah, see Num. 16: 1 ff.   Cf. II. 284, 287-288.

[10]VI. 1231-34. For the references to Micaiah and Zedekiah see II Chron. 18: 6-24 or I Kings (Vulgate: III Kings) 22: 7 ff. Gower tells the story of Micaiah in the Conf., VII. 2527 ff.

[11]VI. 1235-36. For the references to Elisha, Namaan, and Gehazi see II Kings (Vulgate: IV Kings) 5: 1-27.

[12]VI. 1241 and 1251-52. A direct expression of the medieval ubi sunt motif, of which the whole of Chapter 19 is an echo.

[13]VI. 1243-44 "Liberius: pope from 352-366. A. D. He is mentioned here as a type of unfaithfulness to his charge, because he was induced to condemn Anasthasius. " For the reference to Simon the Sorcerer see Acts 8: 9-24.

[14]VI. 1245-46. The Apostle Paul had the name of Saul before his conversion. See Acts 13: 9.

[15]VI. 1247-48. Pope Gregory the Great (c. 540-604) is meant.

[16]VI. 1249. Saint Martin (c. 316-397) is meant.

[17]VI. 1251. ". . . 'for the dead, ' that is, to bury them charitably, as Tobit did. " See Tobit 1: 20-21. See also note on l. 1241 above.

[18]VI. 1251-52. See n. 12 above.

[19]VI. 1257. Saint Benedict (c. 480-c. 543), founder of the Benedictine Order, is meant.

[20]VI. 1258. Julian, Roman Emperor from 361 to 363, opposed Christianity.

[21]VI. 1259. Based upon Matt. 5: 13. Cf. Luke 14: 34 and III. 1997-98 and see n.

[22]VI. 1261-62. "Cp. John xii. 24. "

[23]VI. 1267-68. "Perhaps an allusion to Wycliffe, who seems to be referred to as a new Jovinian in a later poem, p. 347. " See the Carmen, l. 32, and cf. III. 1129-30 above and see n. See also n. on III. 1819-22.

[1]VI. 1273. "Troianus: i. e. Trajan, whose name is so spelt regularly by our author." Cf. Conf., VII. 3144, and Mirour, 22168, in both of which lines the name is "Troian." In a note to the latter line Macaulay remarks, "The justice and humanity of Trajan were proverbial in the Middle Ages, owing chiefly to the legend about him connected with Gregory the Great." The legend was that Gregory successfully interceded with the Lord for the delivery of the pagan Trajan's soul from hell. See Skeat's note on Piers, C Passus XIII. 75 (where the name is again spelled "Troianus"). Cf. Dante, Purg., 10: 73-76, and Par., 20: 43-48.

[2]VI. 1275-76. Justinian the Great, Emperor under whom Roman law was codified, lived A. D. 483-565. By Dionysius, perhaps Gower means the third-century bishop of Alexandria, who was (falsely) accused of Arianism.

[3]VI. 1277-78. "Valentinianus: cp. Conf. Amantis, v. 6398 ff. " There he is cited as a worthy example of virginity. Valentinian III was Emperor from A. D. 419? to 455, and supported the ecclesiastical supremacy of Pope Leo I. Tarquin the Proud, who raped Lucretia (mentioned in l. 1331 below), died c. 510 B. C. Gower tells the story of "Tarquin and His Son Aruns" in Conf., VII. 4593 ff., and of "The Rape of Lucrece" in Conf., VII. 4755 ff.

[4]VI. 1281-82. Gower refers to Constantine the Great, the first Christian Roman Emperor (A. D. 324-337). Antonius, a fourth-century Bishop of Fussola, was a profligate and the center of a scandal. Gower tells the story of "Constantine and Sylvester" in Conf., II. 3187 ff.

[5]VI. 1283-84. Emperor Theodosius II called the Council of Ephesus in A. D. 431. "Leo" is probably Leo the Isaurian, who became Eastern Emperor in A. D. 717, and who engaged in controversy with Pope Gregory II.

[6]VI. 1285-86. Constantine, a fourth-century Emperor of the East, defended the Arian side of the Trinitarian controversy. Tiberius is probably the Tiberius Constantine of Gower's "Tale of Constance" (Conf., II. 587 ff.) and of Chaucer's MLT.

[7]VI. 1293-94. Eacides: "Aeacides" was a patronymic of Achilles, who killed the scurrilous Thersites.

[8]VI. 1295-96. Cf. II. 325-326 and see n.

[9]VI. 1299. Another reference to Saul and the Witch of Endor (cf.
VI. 910), here called Phitonem mulierem. The name commonly applied to her in Gower's day was "Phitonissa." Cf. Chaucer's FrT,
1509-10. Cf. also ll. 905-910 above, and Conf., IV. 1935-37; VI.
2384-90.

[10]VI. 1303. Cf. V. 973.

[11]VI. 1305-6. A reference to II Sam. (Vulgate: II Kings) 16: 20-
17: 23.

[12]VI. 1307-8. A reference to II Sam. (Vulgate: II Kings) 2: 13-
3: 30.

[13]VI. 1313-14. A reference to Esther 3: 1 ff.

Chapter 21

[1]VI. 1321-22. For Gower's "Tale of Diogenes and Aristippus, "
"Cp. Conf. Amantis, vii. 2217 ff. "

[2]VI. 1323. Phirinus is Gower's spelling for "Spurina" in all three
of his major poems: cf. Mirour, 18301-312 and see Conf., V. 6372-
94 for his story. In a note on the latter passage, Macaulay points out,
"The anecdote is taken from Valerius Maximus, Mem. iv. 5 . . . ."
Spurina was a handsome Roman who destroyed his own beauty in order
to preserve his virginity.

[3]VI. 1324. I am unable to identify Agladius. Does Gower mean
Aglauros (Agraulos), whose story is told in Metam., II. 559-561?

[4]VI. 1325-28. On this reference to Troilus and Cressida, see
Introduction, p. 7.

[5]VI. 1333-34. Thais was the Athenian mistress of Alexander the
Great and, after his death, of Ptolemy I. Justine was St. Justina, who
converted the pagan magician Cyprian, when he tried to seduce her.

[6]VI. 1343. An allusion to Gen. 2: 25.

[7]VI. 1345. Adapted in part from "Amores, i. 9. 1. "

[8]*VI. 1347-49. Taken from Ars Amat., II. 481-483.

[9]VI. 1359. Cf. III. 1546, and see n.

[10]VI. 1361-62. "Perhaps an allusion to the case of Edward III and Alice Perrers. "
For the reference to Jezebel and Ahab, see I Kings (Vulgate: III Kings) 19: 1-21: 26.

Notes to BOOK VII

Chapter 1

[1]VII. 5-6. "Cp. Conf. Amantis, Prol. 595 ff. " For Nebuchadnez-zar's dream and Daniel's interpretation of it, see Dan. 2: 31-45. Cf. I. Prol. 7 and n., and see below, ll. 106-112, 136, 353-354, 1379. Cf. also Dante, Inf., 14: 103-110.

[2]VII. 27. Reading Consilium with CEHDL rather than Concilium. Cf. VI. 871-902 and see n.

[3]VII. 47-48. "Cp. Conf. Amantis, v. 49 ff. " Cf. also Chapter 2 below.

Chapter 2

[1]VII. 67. Macaulay rightly glosses euinco as "acquire, " although he queries this meaning. See Harper's Latin Dictionary, s. v. evinco, II. A. 2, "to recover one's property by judicial decision. "

[2]VII. 75-92. With this paragraph cf. Piers, C Passus XIII. 235-248.

[3]VII. 100. Loculus has the two meanings of "coffer" and "coffin. " The ambiguity is probably intentional.

[4]VII.108.   A reference to the statue, or image, in Nebuchadnez-zar's dream.   See above, ll. 5-6 and n.

[5]VII.109.   Proverbial (Walz no. 99).

[6]VII.110.   Proverbial (Walz no. 95b).

[7]VII.115-118.   Even the author of Piers Plowman is reluctant to condemn riches per se, although he feels that poverty is better.   See C Passus XIV. 26-32.

[8]VII.121-122.   The author of Piers similarly complains of the avarice of the rich.   See B Passus X. 23-31.

[9]VII.123.   Based upon "Rev. ii. 25. "

[10]VII.125-126.   Adapted from "Tristia, i. 8. 41 f. "

[11]*VII.131.   Adapted from Metam., XV. 260-261.

[12]VII.134.   Nec scit honor solium, quod solet esse suum.

Chapter 3

[1]VII.136.   See n. on ll. 5-6 above.

[2]VII.157-168.   The only reference to courtly love in the entire poem.   The concept originated in France, so Gower is right in terming it Gallica peccata.   Courtly love of course is an important aspect of the Conf. Amantis.   See W. G. Dodd, Courtly Love in Chaucer and Gower (Boston, 1913), and on the whole problem see Alexander J. Den-omy, The Heresy of Courtly Love (New York: McMullen, 1947).
With ll. 157-168 cf. Mirour, 8917 ff., and Traitié, XVII; XVIII. 1-21.   Cf. also VI. 1343-44.

[3]VII.159-160.   Nunc licet alterius sponsam quod quisque fre-quentet Est status ingenui, dicitur illus amor. "It is difficult to construe this couplet satisfactorily, and the reading 'Est' [given in S] seems quite as good as 'Et' [given in CEHDL]. " But et is much the better reading, and with the placing of the comma after frequentet instead of after in-genui, together with the adoption of et, there is no difficulty with the couplet.

[4]VII. 168. There is an obscene allusion in lucra pudenda. Cf. III. 1798.

[5]VII. 173. In causa fragili sic causat fictilis etas.

[6]VII. 189-190. Written over erasure in the text. MSS. EHT read as follows:

> Thus it gleams outwardly like a heap of gold,
> yet inwardly its putrefaction is rank, and its flesh
> is food for worms.

MSS. DL have both this latter reading and the one in the text.

[7]VII. 192. nisus ("sparrow hawk") is the reading in EHT instead of falco.

[8]VII. 194. "caput ancille: an allusion to the form in which Satan is supposed to have appeared in the garden of Eden."

Chapter 4

[1]VII. 233-234. Perhaps an allusion to John Ball.

[2]VII. 247-248. From Speculum Stultorum, p. 12, ll. 9-10 (Raymo).

[3]VII. 255-256. Adapted from "Ars Amat. ii. 201 f." Mozley, p. 79: "If she laughs, laugh with her; if she weeps, remember to weep; let her impose her laws upon your countenance." Macaulay here notes, "In adapting the couplet to his purpose our author has contrived to make it unintelligible." But Gower's construction, although somewhat awkward, is not unintelligible. Literally, it reads, "And it will always establish the laws as equal to your expressions."

[4]VII. 257-258. Philemon is the pious old man who, with his wife Baucis, hospitably received Jupiter and Mercury. See Ovid, Metam., VIII. 618 ff. Here he is a rather inappropriate prototype of judicious forthrightness.

[5]*VII. 259. Adapted from Metam., II. 680-681.

[6]VII. 265. "Fuluus . . . talus: referring to the gilded spur of knighthood; gold is 'metallum fuluum.'"

459

[7]VII. 273-274. Adapted from "Tristia, v. 8. 27 f. "

[8]VII. 291. Proverbial (Walz no. 36a). Cf. l. 775 below.

[9]VII. 299. Cf. La Rochefoucauld: "Nothing is so pleasing to us as the misfortunes of our dearest friends. "

[10]VII. 315-316. Adapted from "Metam. i. 144 f. "

[11]VII. 318. Tempus et ad vomitum ruminat ira suum.

[12]*VII. 319. Adapted from Am., III. xi. 43.

[13]VII. 323-324. Adapted from "Ars Amat. i. 761 f. "

[14]VII. 327-328. Taken from "Fasti, iv. 717 f. The application belongs to our author. " It is obviously inappropriate: Ovid is talking about the sun passing through the sign of Taurus in the zodiac. Frazer, p. 243: "Whether that victim is a cow or a bull, it is not easy to know; the fore part is visible, the hinder part is hid. "

[15]VII. 331-332. Adapted from "Tristia, i. 9. 5 f. "

[16]VII. 334. Taken from "Ars Amat. iii. 436. "

[17]VII. 340. Taken from "Tristia, i. 8. 8. "

[18]VII. 343. There is a play upon lepus ("hare") and leporarius ("greyhound"). I take the line to mean that love cannot be both love and hate at the same time; therefore, it is now turned to hate.

[19]VII. 347. Adapted from "Metam. i. 141. "

[20]VII. 353. See n. on ll. 5-6 above.

[21]VII. 357. Proverbial (Walz no. 106 b). Cf. Mirour, 3337-8 (Walz no. 106a) and WBT, 1183-90.

[22]VII. 361-364. "Cp. Mirour, 26590 ff. "

[1] VII. 365-366. Another play upon mundus ("world") and mundus ("pure"). Cf. ll. 505-508 below.

[2] VII. 369-370. Proverbial. Cf. Troilus, III. 813-815 and see Robinson's note.

[3] VII. 371. From Speculum Stultorum, p. 31, l. 1 (Raymo).

[4] VII. 373-374. From Speculum Stultorum, p. 31, ll. 5-6 (Raymo).

[5] VII. 375-376. "From Neckam, De Vita Monachorum, p. 177." With this paragraph cf. Piers, B Passus XX. 166-197 or C Passus XXIII. 167-198.

[6] VII. 379-383. "Taken with slight change from De Vita Monachorum, pp. 183 f."

[7] *VII. 385. Taken from De Vita Monachorum, p. 184.

[8] VII. 387. Taken from "De Vita Monachorum, p. 195."

[9] VII. 389-392. "Taken with slight change from De Vita Monachorum, p. 197, and so also 395 f."

[10] *VII. 405-410. Taken from De Vita Monachorum, p. 186. Ll. 407-408 are used in Carmen, 173-174. (With ll. 427-430 below, cf. Carmen, 288-293.)

[11] VII. 417-420. Taken, with slight alterations, from "De Vita Monachorum, p. 196." Sixteen lines intervene after l. 418 in the original.

[12] VII. 437-438. Taken from "De Vita Monachorum, p. 196."

[13] VII. 441-442. Adapted from "De Vita Monachorum, p. 189."

[14] *VII. 452. Adapted from Ars Amat., II. 670. Cf. Carmen, 186.

[15] *VII. 454. Adapted from Tristia, II. 236.

[16] VII. 458. This line contains the proverbial words caveat . . . emptor.

[17] VII. 459-460. Adapted from "Ars Amat. iii. 65 f. "

[18] *VII. 461-462. Taken from Ovid, Ars Amat., III. 63-64. The expression is proverbial (Walz no. 237).

[19] VII. 463-464. Taken from "Tristia, v. 10. 5 f . . . . " et eo is substituted for adeo in l. 463. Wheeler, p. 247: "One would think that time stood still, so slowly does it move, and the year completes its journey with lagging pace. " Macaulay objects, "The couplet has neither sense nor appropriateness as given here. " But Gower's meaning is clear: the sinner thinks he has ample time to repent because time seems to move slowly, but he is deceived.

[20] VII. 465-466. Taken from "Pont. ii. 35 f. "

[21] *VII. 469. Taken from Metam., XV. 212. Cf. Carmen, 187.

[22] *VII. 471. Taken from Metam., X. 519. (The line in Ovid's Amores, I. viii. 49 is almost exactly the same.)

[23] *VII. 473. Adapted from Metam., XV. 237.

[24] *VII. 475-476. Adapted from Metam., XV. 215-216.

[25] *VII. 479-480. Adapted from Metam., XV. 263-264.

[26] *VII. 483. Taken from Ars Amat., III. 91.

[27] VII. 485-486. Adapted, somewhat awkwardly, from "Ars Amat. iii. 119 f. " Mozley, p. 127: "The Palatine whereon now Phoebus and our chieftains are set in splendour, what was it save the pasture of oxen destined to the plough? " In my translation, I have followed Macaulay's suggestion that "'qui' is evidently a mistake for 'que. '" In Ovid, Palatia meant the Palatine, one of the seven hills of Rome, together with the Temple of Apollo and the palace of Augustus; in Gower, palatia means "palaces. "

[28] VII. 489-490. Taken from "Fasti, i. 203 f. " Frazer, p. 17: "They decked with leaves the Capitol, which they now deck with gems, and the senator himself fed his own sheep. " In Ovid, Capitolia meant the temple of Jupiter at Rome; in Gower, capitolia must mean "temples. " The reference to the "senator" is out of place in Gower, but his attack upon extravagance in ecclesiastical architecture and the negligence on the part of the clergy toward their "sheep" may be valid.

[29] *VII. 496. Taken from Rem. Am., 572.

[30] VII. 499-504. Taken, with minor changes, from "De Vita Monachorum, p. 181." Two lines intervene in the original after l. 502.

[31] VII. 505-508. Cf. ll. 365-366 above and see n.

Chapter 6

[1] VII. Chapter 6. Chapters 6 and 7 are largely an expansion of Gen. 1: 26-2: 25. Cf. Conf., VIII. 26 ff., and Mirour, 97-180.

[2] VII. 509-510. "Cp. Mirour, 26605 ff. and Conf. Amantis, Prol. 910 ff." Cf. also ll. 1399 ff. below and see n.

[3] VII. 543-544. Cf. Rom. 8: 5.

Chapter 7

[1] VII. 574. "[man]" is "him" in the text.

[2] VII. 583. Cf. II. 437.

[3] VII. 585. I. e., the four elements.

[4] VII. 587-590. These lines are difficult to render literally, but the general meaning is clear. With them cf. Conf., VII. 685-698 and 955-978, and Psa. 8: 4-10. The "twelve signs" are, of course, the Zodiac, and the "like number of successive stages" are the twelve months.

[5] VII. 599. "Arboribusque sitis. There must be something wrong here, but the variant [satis] given by D does not help us." But sitis as the past participle of sino, here in the ablative plural agreeing with arboribusque, makes perfectly good sense.

[6] VII. 631-632. Perhaps an allusion to the Pope's title, "Servant of the servants of God."

[1]VII. 639 ff. Macaulay notes that the quotation is from Gregory the Great. I quote his note on the Conf., Prol. 945 ff.: "This is one of Gower's favourite citations: it occurs also Mir. 26869 [ff.], Vox Clam. vii, 639. It is quoted here from Moralia, vi. 16 (Migne, Patr. vol. 75, p. 740): 'Homo itaque, quia habet commune esse cum lapidibus, vivere cum arboribus, sentire cum animalibus, discernere cum angelis, recte nomine universitatis exprimitur.' In the Mirour it is given as from the Homilies; see Hom. in Ev. xxix. 2 . . . ."

[2]VII. 645. "minor est mundus homo, 'man is a microcosm': cp. Mirour, 26929 ff." Cf. also Conf., Prol. 947, and see Fox, Medieval Sciences, Chapters 2-3.

[3]VII. 647 ff. "Cp. Mirour, 26953 ff." Ll. 647 ff. contain a plethora of plays upon the two meanings of mundus.

[4]VII. 673-676. Cf. Traitié, I. 1-21.

[5]VII. 685-694. "From Neckam, De Vita Monachorum, pp. 197 f." L. 694 is changed somewhat, and in the original, six lines intervene after l. 686 and four after l. 690.

[6]VII. 699-708. Taken "With slight changes from De Vita Monachorum, pp. 193 f." On the idea that all men must die, cf. Conf., IV. 2245-47.

Chapter 9

[1]VII. Chapter 9. Heading. The idea in Chapters 9-15 of corpses decaying in different fashions, according to the different sins their owners committed while alive, is not original with Gower. Cf. the pictures of death rotting corpses in MS. Brit. Mus. Addit. 37049. A similar idea persisted long after: cf. the old Spanish ballad, "Despues que el rey don Rodrigo," esp. the line quoted in Cervantes, Don Quixote, Part II, Chapter 33:

> "They [i. e., worms] are eating me, they are eating me now,
> There where I most have sinned."

See the Samuel Putnam translation (New York: Viking, 1949), p. 730, and n. 12, p. 1008.

[2]*VII. 717-724. For the most part adapted from <u>Metam.</u>, VI. 303-309, where Ovid is speaking of Niobe.

[3]VII. 732. <u>Nec manus in longum planat vtrumque latus</u> . . . . Perhaps Gower means that the proud man can no longer slap his thighs in self-congratulation, or preen himself. Mrs. Eileen Squires suggests, "Nor does the hand make level for long either of its sides": "This refers to the custom of approval with palms up, and of disapproval with palms down. " (Personal letter to the translator.) Cf. 1. 850 below.

[4]VII. 742. <u>in sua arte</u>: "in his own way, " and "through his own artfulness. "

Chapter 10

[1]VII. 775. Proverbial (Walz no. 36b). Cf. 1. 291 above.

Chapter 12

[1]VII. 796-797. The traditional answer to the question of Tolstoi's short story, "How Much Land Does a Man Need? "

[2]VII. 805-806. Gower is right in pointing out that widows in medieval England usually did not long remain unmarried. (The same was true in Elizabethan times.) Chaucer's Wife of Bath at once comes to mind.

[3]VII. 809. An allusion to Isaiah 5: 8.

Chapter 13

[1]VII. 831. An allusion to II Cor. 9: 6 or Gal. 6: 7.

Chapter 14

[1]VII. 833. "He practised" is literally, "was his. "

Chapter 15

[1]VII. 853-855. Probably the leather shoes (coreis) were fancy. Cf. Chaucer's Nicholas and Absolom in Mill T, 3213-18, 3318, 3331-33, with this passage.

Chapter 16

[1]VII. 892. "For the idea cp. Mirour, 1784 ff. It is originally from Augustine." Macaulay's note to the passage in the Mirour: "Aug. in Joann. Ev. i. 15, 'Quid est quod te inflas, humana superbia? . . . Publicibus resiste, ut dormias: cognosce qui sis.'"

Chapter 17

[1]VII. Chapter 17, Heading. The expression "waxes old like a garment," in the Heading of Chapter 17 and in l. 919 below, is biblical. See Psa. 102: 26 (Vulgate: 101: 27) and Isaiah 50: 9 and 51: 6.

[2]VII. 909-910. Taken "From De Vita Monachorum, p. 178."

[3]VII. 911-918. Taken "From De Vita Monachorum, p. 179, with slight variations."

[4]VII. 919. See n. on Chapter 17, Heading.

[5]VII. 919-924. Taken without change from "De Vita Monachorum, p. 180." L. 922 is probably an allusion to Job 8: 9: ". . . because our days upon earth are a shadow." The expression was proverbial (Walz no. 149).

[6]VII. 927. Walz (no. 126) lists this as a proverbial expression, equivalent to others such as Ein jeder ist Herr in seinem Hause, "Every man's house is his castle," etc., but the parallel is not at all close.

[7]VII. 929-932. Taken, with minor changes, from "De Vita Monachorum, p. 180." Two lines intervene after l. 930 in the original.

[8]VII. 951-952. Gower (wrongly) establishes an etymological relationship between mors ("death") and morsus ("a bite") together with mordens ("biting").

[9]VII. 953-954. Proverbial (Walz no. 156, where there is a quotation in n. 1 from Bernard, Epist. 105: Nil mortalibus vel morte certius vel incertius hora mortis.

[10]VII. 955-956. "Cp. Mirour, 11404 ff. , where the often quoted lines of Helinand's Vers de Morte are given. "

Chapter 19

[1]VII. 1024. For the pun in ll. 1024 and 1026 cf. Mercutio in Romeo, III. i. 101: "Ask for me tomorrow and you shall find me a grave man. "

[2]VII. 1030. Perhaps an allusion to Matt. 22: 21, Mark 12: 17, or Luke 20: 25.

[3]VII. 1067. "Thetis, used for 'water' or 'sea': cp. v. 812. "

[4]VII. 1079. "furor breuis, ira set: the words are suggested by the common expression 'ira furor breuis, ' but the sense is different. This is frequently the case with our author's borrowings, e. g. v. 213, vi. 101. "

[5]VII. 1087-88. An allusion to Matt. 25: 32-33. Cf. IV. 693.

[6]VII. 1091-92. An allusion to Luke 12: 2 or to Matt. 10: 26.

Chapter 20

[1]VII. 1125-28. From Aurora, Deut. 243-246 (Beichner).

[2]VII. 1132. From Aurora, Exod. 202 (Beichner).

[3]VII. 1141-42. The idea in ll. 1141-42 is a common medieval one. Despair was a great fault, for it usually predicated a disbelief in God's benevolence or omnipotent power to save, although not in God's existence, as here. Cf. Conf. , IV. 3389-3514, Piers, B Passus V. 449-455, and Chaucer, Pars T, 692 ff.

467

Chapter 22

[1]VII. 1203-1208. A reference to the four horsemen of the Apocalypse. See Rev. 8 ff. VII. 1208 also contains an allusion to Isaiah 2: 4: ". . . nation shall not lift up sword against nation . . . . "

[2]VII. 1217-18. For the idea, see Mark 2: 17 and Luke 15: 7, 10, and esp. I Tim. 1: 15. (The ultimate source of the concept was perhaps Ezek. 33: 11-19.) Gower is very likely echoing the words of the Absolution or Remission of Sins from the Mass; cf. the American Book of Common Prayer (New York, [1945]), p. 7.

[3]VII. 1221-24. A reference to Gen. 18: 23-33.

[4]VII. 1231-32. Based upon Psa. 78: 21(Vulgate, 77: 21): "Therefore the Lord heard this, and was wroth: so a fire was kindled against Jacob, and anger also came up against Israel. " There "Jacob" means the descendants of Jacob, i. e., the Israelites, who in this line represent the English.

Chapter 23

[1]VII. Chap. 23, Heading. The wording of this heading lends weight to the idea that Books II-VII were written first. See Introduction, pp. 14-15.

Chapter 24

[1]VII. 1292. In qua principium duxit origo meum.

[2]VII. 1289-1300. These lines are ably paraphrased in George R. Coffman's "John Gower in His Most Significant Role, " in Elizabethan Studies and Other Essays in Honor of George F. Reynolds, University of Colorado Studies, Series B. Studies in the Humanities (Boulder, Col., 1945), Vol. II, No. 4, p. 58, n. 12.

[3]VII. 1305-1306. "The reference here and in the next lines is to Ps. lxxxiv. 11. " The same verse is quoted in Piers, B Passus XVIII. 421. King James Version: Psa. 85: 10.

[4]VII. 1342. "An allusion apparently to the debasement of the

coinage. " The line could also be interpreted literally, for some English mines had been exhausted before Gower's day.

[5] VII. 1344.   "Nobile que genuit, 'she who produced the noble, ' i. e. the gold coin of that name, called so originally because of its purity. "

[6] VII. 1356.   There is a pun here upon legifera ("law-abiding") and sine lege fera ("lawlessly fierce").

[7] VII. 1365.   There is a play here upon angelica ("angelic") and angulus ("dark corner" or "lurking place, " "ingle").

[8] VII. 1375.   clerus dissoluitur can mean both "the clergy are dissolute" and "the clergy are disunited, " the latter interpretation referring to the Babylonian Captivity.

[9] VII. 1379.   Alluding to Nebuchadnezzar's statue, and meaning that the peasants are insubordinate to the nobility. See n. on ll. 5-6 above.

[10] *VII. 1389.   Adapted, inappropriately, from Metam., VII. 209.

[11] VII. 1393-94.   The owl was, as here, a traditional bird of ill omen. Cf. Metam., V. 550, for example.

[12] VII. 1399 ff.   Once again Gower throws the burden squarely upon man. Cf. VII. 509-510, 1381-82, 1469-70, and II. 623-630. Cf. also Conf., Prol. 499-528, and Dante, Purg., XVI. 66 ff., esp. 82-83.

[13] VII. 1409-11.   MSS. EDLTH$_2$ read, "and as long as faith has stood firm and ruled over all, then glory and salvation have remained ours. It follows that our deeds should be made virtuous anew through God . . . . "

[14] *VII. 1418.   Taken from Fasti, IV. 596.

Chapter 25

[1] VII. 1443-81.   Chap. 25 is written largely in rhyming hemistichs.

[2] VII. 1455.   "galled" is literally "humpbacked" (gibbosus).

[3]*VII. 1455-56. Cf. _Tristia_, V. xiv. 16.

[4]VII. 1470. "'Vox populi, vox dei': a sentiment repeated by our author in various forms; cp. note on iii. Prol. 11. " Cf. also III. 1267 and n.

Ll. 1469-70 are written over erasure in SCEHG. The original version, given in DLTH$_2$, is as follows:

> You should take warning from these writings as to what evils exist, and accordingly render yourself up to God.

[5]VII. 1473-74. Perhaps an echo of _Piers_ and its vision of Dowel and Dobet. Cf. I. 1122 and n. , and see Introduction, p. 24.

[6]VII. 1479-81. These concluding three lines, leonine hexameters written over erasure, are as given in SCEHG. "They seem to have been substituted for the original couplet in order to point more clearly the moral of the _Cronica Tripertita_, which is intended for a practical illustration of the divine punishment of sin. " The original couplet, as given in DLTH$_2$, is as follows:

> I myself am worse than all men; but may the founder of the world grant me relief through a priest. Amen.

[7]VII. Prose Link. "It will be seen that in these later years Gower has almost brought himself to believe that the events of the earlier part of the reign were intended for a special warning to the youthful king, whom he conceives as having then already begun a course of tyrannical government. At the time, however, our author acquitted him of all responsibility, on account of his youth. " On this matter, see Maria Wickert, Studien zu John Gower (Kölner Universitäts-Verlag, 1953), Chapter 4.

The concluding Prose Link is as given in SCHG. In EDTH$_2$L, there is only, "Here ends the book which is entitled The Voice of One Crying. "

[8]VII. Prose Link. "The swan was used as a badge by the duke of Gloucester and also (perhaps not till after his death) by Henry of Lancaster. For the horse and the bear as cognizances of Arundel and Warwick see Annales Ricardi II (Rolls Series, 28. 3), p. 206. " See also Introduction, p. 38.

Notes to THE TRIPARTITE CHRONICLE

[Preface]

[1]These three prose paragraphs are marginal in the MSS, as indeed are all the paragraph notes in the three parts of the Tripartite Chronicle. These marginal notes from the MSS are inserted throughout, however, like chapter headings, though they are left unnumbered. The paragraphing is almost wholly that of the MSS.

[2]"These seven lines must be regarded as a metrical preface to the Chronicle which follows." The expression Omnia vincit Amor in l. 7 is of course proverbial. Cf. Voice, V. 147 and see n.

Part I

[1]I. 1-3. "The date thus indicated is MCCC + 30 + 57, i. e. 1387."

[2]I. 7 refers to the Peasants' Revolt of 1381 and Book I of the poet's Vox Clamantis; thus does Gower link his sequel the Cronica Tripertita to the earlier poem—as well as by the connecting prose link.

[3]I. 9-10. Gower fuses several ideas here, in a not completely clear way. First, he says that he did not compose the poem as the events it describes occurred. Second, he maintains, feebly, that he wrote the Chronicle (or at least Part I) in advance of those events, which is pretentious and absurd. Third, they were reported to him, as was the Vox Clamantis, by a "voice" which prompted the ear. But the next two lines make clear that it is now not the vox populi he heard. Yet at the end of the poem (III. 479) he returns to that voice. Indeed, throughout the Tripartite Chronicle he is inconsistent concerning the role of the common people. Here (ll. 11-12) he blames them for helping Richard II; at other times he portrays them as standing helplessly by, and then at the end as rallying to Henry IV.

[4]I. 4-12. "These lines are written over erasure in SCHG. The original version of them is not extant . . . ."

[5]I. 15-16. A frequent charge against Richard in that day, but largely groundless. Most of his advisers were mature men, the principal exception being the Earl of Oxford. For the charge, cf. Mum, I. 88-89, and Voice, VI. 555-556.

471

[6]This paragraph refers to the events which led to the "Merciless Parliament" of 1388. With the metaphor of "poison" (l. 34) cf. II. 25-26 and see n.

[7]I. 49. A pun, as in II. 119 and 288 below, on Equs "Horse" and equus "honorable. " The allegorical designations of these three men, as of others throughout the poem, are largely derived from their heraldic badges or cognizances. Gower uses Olor or Cignus, depending upon the meter, for "Swan, " meaning Thomas Duke of Gloucester (Thomas of Woodstock). The "Horse" is Richard Earl of Arundel, the brother of Thomas Arundel. The "Bear" is Thomas Earl of Warwick. See Introduction, p. 38.

[8]I. 51. "Penna coronata. This, as the margin [here a headnote] tells us, is the Earl Marshall, that is Thomas Mowbray, earl of Nottingham, afterwards duke of Norfolk. "

[9]I. 52. "Qui gerit S: the earl of Derby [and future Henry IV], from whose badge of S, standing probably for 'Soverein, ' came the device of the well-known collar of SS. " Gower's effigy on his tomb wears such a collar, probably in token of the fact that Henry had given him one in 1393 (Works, IV, xvi-xvii). (Judges of today still wear the S-collar, a Lancastrian badge.)

[10]I. 55. "aquilonica luna, 'the northern moon, ' that is, the earl of Northumberland. The variation [in l. 56] of the text in the Harleian MS., written over erasure [and reading, 'Eclipsed by his wrongdoings, he now follows the associates of the Sun'], arises no doubt from the later disagreement between Henry IV and Northumberland. "

[11]I. 57. The sun was a badge of Richard II. He is "Phoebus" in ll. 61 and 64. (He is compared to the sun in Conf., VIII. 3006* ff.)

[12]I. 58-60. "Troy" means London. Cf. Voice, I. 880 and n., and TC, III. 174-175 and n. As the poem maintains, the London citizenry always did show hostility to Richard II.

[13]I. 65. The Boar: "The earl of Oxford, lately created duke of Ireland, whose badge was a boar's head, was chief justice of Chester in this year, and there raised forces for the king. . . . " Robert de Vere, Earl of Oxford, was the most hated of Richard's followers, partly because of his youthfulness.

[14]"The cognizance ['his banner] referred, no doubt, to the city of Chester. The same note tells us that the duke of Gloucester bore a fox-tail on his spear as an ensign. . . . "

[15]I. 79. That is, on a Friday. The date was Dec. 20, 1388.

[16]I. 80. Stat Tetis a parte. On the confusion of Thetis and Tethys cf. Voice, V. 812 and VII. 1067. Apparently Gower means that the River Thames allowed Oxford to escape. See Macaulay's n. for further details.

[17]I. 86. de fonte renatus. Sarcastic, with its overtone of "baptized. " (The line is very similar to Lucan, III. 262.)

[18]I. 95. Cf. III. 160 below.

[19]I. 103. "Noua villa Macedo, i. e. Alexander Neville: a very bad attempt on the part of our author. " For a very similar effort at translating names, cf. Chaucer's CYT, 1428, where Arnoldus de Villa Nova is rendered as "Arnold of the Newe Toun. " For the rhetorical device, see n. on Voice, I. 929.
Archibishop Neville of York had labored hard in 1386 to discomfit Richard's enemies.

[20]I. 104. "The particular form of the curse in this case was translation to the see of S. Andrew, which he could not occupy because Scotland was Clementine. "

[21]I. 107. "He is said to have especially urged the king to take strong measures against Warwick. . . . " In view of the trouble Warwick later caused, Suffolk was definitely correct.

[22]I. 109. "de puteo Michaelis, ' of Michael de la Pool. ' The same view of the meaning of the name is taken in Shakespeare, 2 Henry VI, iv. I. 70 [-71], by the murderer of William, duke of Suffolk, son of this Michael, 'Pole, Pool, sir Pool, lord! Ay, kennel, puddle, sink. '"

[23]I. 111-118. "This is Thomas Rushook, a Dominican. . . . He had incurred much suspicion and odium as the king's confessor and supposed private adviser. " See n. on Voice, IV. 723-730.

[24]I. 121-130. "All the five Appellants seem to have entered the Tower, but the three spoken of here are of course the three leaders, referred to in l. 41 and afterwards [i. e., Gloucester, Richard Earl of

Arundel, and Warwick]. Knighton says that the king invited the five to stay for the night, but only the earls of Derby and Nottingham accepted the invitation [Chronicon Henrici Knighton, ed. J. R. Lumley (Rolls Series, 1895), II, 255]. The fact that Gower here assigns no political action to his hero the earl of Derby (who was under twenty years old), but gives all the credit to the three leaders, shows clearly that the young Henry played a very subordinate part. " In the "Merciless Parliament" of 1388 the five "Lords Appellant" accused members of Richard's Court party of treason. Gower now proceeds to tell of the harsh sentences meted out.

[25]Sir Simon Burley's "chief offense seems to have been his ascendancy over the King" (Kenneth H. Vickers, England in the Later Middle Ages, [London, 1913], p. 268). He had been Richard's tutor and had helped negotiate the marriage with Anne of Bohemia. He was disliked for his irritable temper.

[26]I. 141. "senecta. Burley was then fifty-six years old. "

[27]I. 152. "Pons Aquilonis, 'Bridgenorth. ' Beauchamp was keeper of Bridgenorth Castle. . . but it does not appear from other sources that he had the title here given him by Gower of 'baron Bridgenorth. ' In 1387 he was made a peer by patent (the first instance of this) under the title of lord Beauchamp of Kidderminster. " Gower's term is one of his ways of showing scorn for Beauchamp, in that the title did not exist.

[28]I. 154. "Tribulus: i. e., Nicholas Brembel (so called by Gower). . . . He had been Mayor of London last in 1386. " (Perhaps the commonest spelling of his name is Brembre.) He is perhaps the bad Mayor of London attacked in The Voice of One Crying, V. 835 ff. Brembre was a hard-fighting politician who found favor with Richard II. Gower's punning translation of his name resembles the then common play upon "Lollard" and lollia "tares. " Cf. his Carmen, 1. 20 (Works, IV, 346), Conf., V. 1879-88, and Chaucer, MLT, 1183. See also notes to Voice, IV. 1083, and V. Chap. 15.

[29]I. 158-159. "Though he was a knight, he was not dignified with the nobler form of execution, being a citizen of London. "

[30]Chief Justice Sir Robert Tresilian had taken a leading part in punishing the rebels of 1381; but he had angered the anti-Court party in 1387 by pronouncing that the Parliament of 1386 had unwarrantedly interfered with the royal authority. See A. R. Myers, England in the Late Middle Ages (Harmondsworth, Middlesex, 1952), p. 31.

[31] I. 172. "falsa sigilla: that is, the seals set by the judges to the questions and replies submitted to them at Nottingham. . . . They all pleaded that they had set their seals to these replies under the influence of threats from the archbishop of York, the duke of Ireland, and the earl of Suffolk." The judges referred to had been asked a series of questions concerning Richard's prerogatives and whether they had been infringed upon by the commission of reform established by Parliament in 1386. "The answers were naturally all in the King's favour, since, quite apart from intimidation, the legal mind is slow to appreciate new tendencies, and the pretensions of Parliament certainly could not boast the respectability of age" (Vickers, p. 274). Gower has reversed the actual order of events. The concluding lines of this paragraph (182-187) repeat the substance of ll. 92-169, while ll. 170-181 deal with another subject.

[32] I. 183-187. Cf. Voice, I. 977-978. In l. 187, mors omnia solvit is proverbial. See Robert R. Raymo, "Mors Solvit Omnia," MLN, LXXI (1956), 249. Cf. Voice, I. 1525-26, and TC, III. 102 below; also Troilus, IV. 501, and KT, 2849.

[33] There are possible puns here on curia "court" and cura "care of souls, " and on "straw(s)" with "Jack Straw"--as in Troilus, IV. 184.

[34] I. 194. ab ordine is deliberately ambiguous: "from its path, " "from its rule or order, " etc., meaning an "irregular" clergy.

[35] I. 210. It is indeed true that Richard ruled moderately well from 1388 to 1397. He handled the French, Irish, and Lollard problems fairly competently. The realm's greatest need was peace with France, which Richard secured by annually renewing a truce, while Henry's group agitated for resumption of hostilities. In 1397, Richard became a despot. Even in his best years, however, all was not well. The well-known "Distich on the Year 1391" runs,

The axe was sharpe, the stokke was harde,
In the xiiii yere of Kyng Richarde.

[36] I. 214. There is an obvious pun on signo and Cigno.

[37] I. 215. "hirundo: a reference to the name Arundel. " Gower means Richard Earl of Arundel, not Thomas.

Notes to The Tripartite Chronicle

Part II

[1] "There is an interval of nearly ten years between the first and second part of the Chronicle. Our author proceeds to the events of 1397. He assumes that the king carried out a long-meditated plan of vengeance, cp. ll. 23 ff., but this was of course an after-thought by way of accounting for what happened."

[2] II. 4. Reading lingua with CHH3 rather than penna. Cf. ll. 233-234 below; and see n. on Voice, II. 1.

[3] II. 15-16. "A pardon was granted to all three in the Parliament of 1387-88, 'par estatut'. . ., and a special charter of pardon was granted to the earl of Arundel at Windsor, April 30, 1394 . . . ."

[4] II. 25-26. Cf. Adam of Usk, Chronicon: "eager to pour forth his pent-up venom, he thought by the help and favour of the King of France to destroy his enemies" (quoted in Vickers, p. 287). Cf. I. 34, and III. 25-26.

[5] II. 29. Cf. Voice, II. Chapters 2-4.

[6] Gower is correct concerning his accounts of Richard II's treachery, but in truth, Gloucester had already begun plotting against him and had attempted to involve Warwick and Thomas Arundel with him.

[7] II. 33. Pleshy (Pleshey) was the Duke of Gloucester's country residence in Essex. (In Richard II, I. ii. 66 it is "Plashy.")

[8] II. 60. I. e., from France back to England.

[9] II. 72. Cf. l. 293 below.

[10] II. 76. Parliament was then a sort of high court. A peer could not be tried save by his fellow peers in full Parliament. See Vickers, p. 227, and George Macaulay Trevelyan, History of England (London, 1926), p. 252.

[11] II. 77. Not to be confused with the five "Lords Appellant" of 1388. See n. on I. 121-130.

[12] II. 85-86. "From this account we should gather that the king officially announced the death of the duke of Gloucester to parliament before it had occurred; but this was not so." Macaulay's n. on ll. 85 ff. proceeds to untangle the confusion.

[13] II. 101-108. "The body seems first to have been laid in the Priory of Bermondsey: then it was buried by Richard's command in Westminster Abbey, but apart from the royal burial-place. Afterwards the body was transferred by Henry IV to the place chosen by Gloucester himself. . . ."

[14] II. 121-122. For these insults Macaulay refers to Adam of Usk, and in a long note defends the trustworthiness of that chronicler.

[15] II. 129. "The pardon pleaded by the earl of Arundel had already been revoked by parliament, therefore the plea was not accepted. From the attempts made by the king to recover Arundel's charter of pardon, even after his execution. . . we may perhaps gather that some scruples were felt about the revocation of it."

[16] II. 147. An obvious pun. With the line cf. Voice, I. 1733-34.

[17] II. 150. Centum. . . parliamentum: perhaps a sarcastic designation implying that this Parliament was as inferior a judicial body as a "Hundred Court."

[18] II. 151. ad ima: "at last" and "to the depths."

[19] II. 182. Gower wishes to place the onus upon Richard alone.

[20] II. 201-204. "By the sentence upon the earl of Warwick all his property was confiscated, . . . [and] a promise was made that he and his wife should have honourable maintenance from the forfeited revenues, [but] . . . this promise was not kept."

[21] II. 207. Gower frequently uses Aetna as a symbol of the burning flame of envy. Cf. Conf., Prol. 329-330; II. 20, 161 ff., 2837-39; and Mirour, 3805 ff. The figure is ultimately from Metam., XIII. 867-869.

[22] Lord Cobham, a son of Richard Earl of Arundel, a Lollard.

[23] II. 217-218. "It seems impossible to construe this, and I suspect that a line has dropped out." The omitted "story" may have been

a reference to Cobham's Lollardy (see n. 22 above). But Cronica can
also mean "this Chronicle," in which case Gower would seem to mean,
"This chronicle has struck at those to whom he adhered," since Gower
had attacked the Lollards in the Voice.

[24] II. 230. "His sentence of death was commuted for that of exile
to the isle of Jersey. . . . "

[25] II. 231-232. "So also below, 1. 280, our author expresses a
hope for the safe return of the archibishop of Canterbury, who came
back in company with Henry of Lancaster; cp. 330 f., where a hope is
expressed for future vengeance on the king. Yet we can hardly suppose
that this second part of the Chronicle was actually written before the
events of the third part had come to pass. All that we can say is that
the writer gives to his narrative the semblance of having been composed
as the events happened. The return of Cobham is mentioned by him
afterwards (iii. 262). " Cf. I. 9-10 and see n.

[26] II. 233-234. Cf. 1. 4 above; cf. also Voice, II. 1-2, and see
n.; cf. also Conf., VIII. 2212-13.
"Our author reserves the case of the archbishop to the last, as
a climax of the evil. He was actually sentenced on Sept. 25, [1397,] before the trial of the earl of Warwick. . . . Sir John Cobham, whose
sentence is mentioned above, was not put on his trial till Jan. 28. . . . "

[27] II. 242. "That is, the court of Rome was bribed to consent to
his translation. " References to "Simon" are frequent in Gower; cf. 1.
269 below, and see n. on Voice, III. 249.

[28] II. 246. There is no reference in the DNB to Thomas' doctorate.
At any rate, this high praise of Arundel honestly represents Gower's
own view of the man to whom he dedicated the combined Voice of One
Crying and Tripartite Chronicle. The Archbishop is perhaps most remembered in history, however, for having been a merciless persecutor
of Lollards. He became Chancellor in 1391 (see 1. 257 below) and
Archbishop of Canterbury in 1396. Upon his resumption of that office
after Henry's return, he secured passage of "that infamous act" the
Statute of Heresy, and began burning heretics. For a face-to-face re-
proval of him see The Book of Margery Kempe: A Modern Version, ed.
W. Butler-Bowdon (New York, 1944), p. 29.

[29] II. 267. "This seems to mean that other private reasons were
alleged to the Pope. "

[30] II. 293. Cf. 1. 72 above.

[31] II. 304. This could mean either that the three had permanently shut themselves off from public esteem, or that other people permannently shut their doors against them.

[32] II. 306-307. Perhaps a faint echo of Piers; see the n. on Voice, I. 1122 and cf. VII. 1473-74.

[33] II. 326-327. "An allusion to the campaign of 1380. " Gloucester led a fruitless expedition to France in that year.

[34] II. 328-329. "Referring especially to the very popular naval victory of Arundel in 1387. . . . "

[35] II. 340. "That is, in the twenty-first year of the reign (1397). "

[36] II. 345. Proverbial, after Virgil, Eclogue 3. 93; see Smith-Heseltine, s. v. "Snake, " and cf. Chaucer, SumT, 1994-95. Probably no particular "teacher" is meant in l. 344.

Notes to The Tripartite Chronicle

Part III

[1] III. 1. See n. on Voice, I. 133.

[2] III. 17. "This comparison of Richard's proceedings to the work of a mole under the ground. . . is appropriate enough as a description of the plot which he undoubtedly laid against the liberties of the kingdom, but the comparison is perhaps chiefly intended to suggest that Richard, and not Henry, was the 'talpa ore dei maledicta' of prophecy (Glendower's 'mould-warp' [in I Henry IV, III. i. 149]), cp. Archaeologia, xx. [1824], p. 258. " Cf. also Hamlet, I. v. 161.

[3] III. 21. A reference to the role of Satan as played in the cyclical drama of Gower's time. Cf. Chaucer, MillT, 3383-84.

[4] III. 25-26. Cf. II. 25-26 and see n.

[5] III. 27-30. "This refers to the appointment of a committee with full powers to deal with the petitions and other matters left unfinished in this parliament [of 1397]. "

[6]In Nov. 1397 Richard, heavily in debt, became oppressive: ". . . individuals and corporations were compelled to give blank cheques to be filled up as the Crown liked. No wealthy person escaped, and no one ever saw his money again" (Vickers, p. 296). Richard's subsequent step was to make use of the "blank charters" Gower next condemns (ll. 66-71). These were cartes blanches, signed and sealed, and hence dangerous weapons in the hand of a ruler now almost out of his mind. For details of these transactions, see Macaulay's n. on ll. 49 ff.

[7]III. 61. baratro magis auidiores: "greedy for their maw" and "intent upon hell" or "intent upon perdition. "

[8]III. 73. "pharisea: that is, hypocritically submissive to the king. " "Pharisiacal" is certainly possible here, though the Latin word can also mean "divided. "

[9]III. 85-86. "Gower attributes Henry's exile to what was probably the true cause, namely the king's jealousy of his popularity and fear that he might take the lead in opposition to the newly established arbitrary system of government. . . It is noteworthy that Gower makes no mention whatever of the duke of Norfolk here. " See Richard II, I. iii, for the scene of Henry's banishment, just before the scheduled duel with Norfolk.

[10]III. 102. Cf. TC, I. 187 and see n.

[11]III. 106. Richard's worst mistake was seizing the Lancastrian estates. This attack upon the sacred institution of property caused the entire country to rally to Henry upon his return. See l. 158 below.

[12]III. 113-114. Actually, Richard allowed him £2000 a year.

[13]"It cannot of course be supposed that Henry embarked at Calais. Probably he sailed from Boulogne. " Calais would have been in the hands of the English King. Henry's route to the coast was "carefully planned" because much of France was dangerous for him.

[14]III. 123. Proverbial. See n. on Voice, V. 879.

[15]III. 137. "nepote: that is Thomas, son of the late earl of Arundel. . . . "

[16]III. 150-152. Cf. Voice, I. 1733-34.

[17]III. 160. For leopardus ("lion passant gardant") see n. on Voice,

I. 234. The pun on lepus "hare" is obvious. For the same taunt applied to knights, cf. "Poem on the Evil Times of Edward II, " E-Text, l. 252: "And nu ben theih liouns in halle and hares in the feld. "

[18] III. 162-163. "The suggestion here that Richard foresaw the coming of Henry and went to Ireland through fear of it, is of course absurd. At the same time it is certain that he received warnings, and that in view of these his expedition to Ireland was very ill-timed. "

[19] III. 174-175. The King's three henchmen took refuge in Bristol, which betrayed them; afterwards, they were executed. The technical charge against the unpopular Brembre was that he had tried to change the name of London to "Troynovant. " Gower's dislike of him is therefore ironical, for he often calls London "Troy. " See n. on Voice, I. 880.

[20] III. 186. That is, in Ireland, where he delayed, fatally.

[21] III. 225. Gower attempts to give the impression that Richard was still alive. See n. on II. 231-232 above.

[22] III. 246. A biblical comparison (I Kings 4: 20 and elsewhere), used also in the Voice, I. 680. See n. on that line.

[23] III. 251. The harvest was also metaphorical: Henry lost no time in repossessing the Lancastrian castles of Pickering, Knaresborough, and Pontefract, in all of which he later confined Richard.

[24] III. 256. "Humfredum natum: that is Humphrey, the young son of the duke of Gloucester. Richard had taken him [as well as the future Henry V, as hostages,] to Ireland, and on hearing of the landing of Henry had ordered him to be confined, together with young Henry of Lancaster, in Trim castle. . . . "

[25] III. 268. It was Michaelmas Day, Sept. 29, 1399.

[26] III. 278-279. The expression does not seem ancient, though it is proverbial. See Smith-Heseltine, s. v. "Friendless is the dead. " These and the following two lines are inappropriate moralizing.

[27] III. 286. "dies Martis, Tuesday, Sept. 30. Richard's renunciation was made on Sept. 29.... " It has long been thought that Richard abdicated at once. But "he was tricked by Henry, who swore solemnly that Richard should remain king if the Lancastrian estates were restored and Henry made hereditary steward of England. Once in Henry's

481

hands, however, Richard was imprisoned in the Tower of London"
(Myers, p. 20).

[28]III. 291. Reading et ad with CHH3 rather than quibus with SG.

[29]III. 296. Richard's incapacity to rule was the real reason for
his deposition, despite the three-fold claims made in ll. 332-335 below.

[30]III. 300-304. "The demise of the crown made new writs necessary, but the same parliament met again six days later (Oct. 6)." See
l. 308.

[31]III. 310. "This appears to mean that the proceedings were confined to a recital of the circumstances connected with the deposition of
Richard, and that no parliamentary business was done until after the
coronation, which took place on the next Monday, Oct. 13."

[32]III. 311. This fact is explained by the next sentence. The king
was still very much the head or focus of the government, despite the
fact that a parliamentary revolution was then in progress. That Parliament could now make and unmake kings, that it was acquiring the
power of the purse, could never be ignored by Henry IV and his succes-
sors. Gower, however, could hardly have been expected to understand
the full significance of the changes he described.

[33]III. 324. "That is Oct. 13, the Translation of Edward the Confessor."

[34]III. 332-337. "The threefold right is stated here by Gower in
the same way as by Chaucer [in "The Complaint of Chaucer to his
Purse," ll. 22-25]:

'O conqueror of Brutes Albioun,
Which that by lyne and free eleccioun
Ben verray kyng, ' & c.

In the margin, however, Gower places the right by conquest last,
and tempers the idea of it by the addition 'sine sanguinis effusione. '
Henry's challenge claimed the realm by descent through 'right line of
blood' (that is, apparently setting aside descent through females...)
and by 'that right which God of his grace hath sent me...to recover it'
(that is, by conquest)...." Gower also tempers the right by conquest
in PP, 8-14, where "conquest" is represented as a divine sanction.
Vickers rightly says (p. 302), "It was the claim by election that counted."
Cf. Piers, Prol. 112-113.
On Henry's threefold right, see M. Dominica Legge, "'The

Gracious Conqueror, '" MLN, LXVIII (1953), 18-21: "Conqueror" was then an honorific, not the equivalent of "usurper." Conquest to Henry was "the acquisition by peaceful means of an inheritance vacant through the misconduct and ineptitude of his predecessors" (p. 20). See also Gaillard T. Lapsley, "The Parliamentary Title of Henry IV," EHR, XLIX (1934), 423-449.

[35]III. 352-353. That is, the future Henry V was established as heir apparent and Prince (of Wales). This action probably strengthened his father's claim of "right by descent."

[36]III. 371. Cf. 1. 418 below.

[37]III. 377. See n. 23 on 1. 251 above. Richard was frequently moved because he at once became the rallying point for disaffection.

[38]III. 383-393. "This refers to the fact that the dukes of Aumerle, Surrey, and Exeter, the marquis of Dorset, and the earl of Gloucester, were condemned to lose the titles of duke, marquis, and earl respectively." They were, then, condemned to lose the titles (and lands) which they had acquired since 1397. Bagot was confined in the Tower for one year and then released. Henry thus showed leniency to Richard's adherents, and he granted a general pardon, but his motivation was political rather than religious.

[39]III. 402-403. Gower calls them by their former, reacquired titles. Furious at their demotion, the four men at once began plotting against Henry IV. "Holland and Kent are the former dukes of Exeter and Surrey, now earls of Huntingdon and Kent. Spenser is the former earl of Gloucester."

[40]III. 410-411. It is not known who warned Henry, but he barely escaped the plot against him at Windsor on Jan. 4, 1400/01. Acting with his characteristic promptness he sent his four sons to the Tower that same night for safekeeping (see 1. 425 below).

[41]III. 418. Cf. 1. 371 above.

[42]III. 432-445. "The statement here is not that Richard deliberately starved himself to death on hearing of the failure of the rising and the death of his associates, but that he lost hope and courage and could not eat, ... and that he desired the death which came to him. This is not an incredible account, and it is fairly in accordance with the best evidence. Most of the contemporary authorities give starvation as the cause, or one of the causes, of death...." There is a difference,

however, between starvation and self-starvation. Gower cannot be blamed for accepting the account of Richard's death which was standard in those times, but "Henry's government decided that the royal prisoner in Pontefract Castle was too dangerous to be allowed to live. A fortnight later he was dead" (Myers, p. 21). Richard may well have tried to abdicate first, on condition that his followers be spared (Vickers, p. 299).

[43] III. 452-455. Richard's body was brought from Pontefract to London, with the face exposed, so that all could see he was dead. The body lay for two days at St. Paul's and was then buried at the Dominican convent at Langley.

[44] III. 462 ff. The estimate of Richard's character in this paragraph is fairly close to the mark, though modern historians (and Shakespeare) are kinder to him. Gower is much too prejudiced in favor of Henry, though honestly so. Henry IV's character is hardly any easier to fathom than Richard's, but at any rate, he was a far more efficient ruler. "The epithet 'pius, ' which Gower attaches to Henry's name in this passage, means in his mouth 'merciful, ' and in the margin [here the heading of this paragraph] the 'pietas' of the new king is contrasted with the 'cruelty' of Richard, the vice to which Gower chiefly attributes his fall. There is no doubt that the execution of Arundel and the murder of Gloucester (or the popular opinion that he had been murdered) produced a very sinister impression, and caused a general feeling of insecurity which was very favourable to Henry's enterprise. It is true also that Henry showed himself scrupulously moderate at first in his dealings with political opponents. "

[45] III. 478-487. On "lion" (l. 478) cf. l. 160 above and see n. on Voice, I. 234. These twelve lines are written over erasure in all MSS except G, which perhaps preserves the original version:
"O mirror of the world, which ought to be a reflection in advance, by which means a wise man might get a clear vision of what is foreseen for himself: This chronicle of Richard, who held sway over the realms of the lion [480*], was uttered by the people, but was not blessed by the people, as is clear. Whatsoever it had been at first, now since his destiny is borne to the depths, his honor has tarnished, his praise has become blame, his glory has died away. "
The version as given in the text (ll. 478-487) generalizes Gower's moral, using Richard as the exemplum. The concept of the world as a mirror was, of course, a medieval commonplace which had already furnished the title of Gower's major French poem. Cf. also Conf., V. 2031 ff.

[46] III. 486. "This is a perilously near approach to the Wycliffite doctrine [of Dominion]. "

Supplementary Notes

Introduction, p. 10, lines 13-14. On the reference to Edward III, see Gardiner Stillwell, "John Gower and the Last Years of Edward III, " Studies in Philology, XLV (1948), 454-471.

Introduction, note 13. Some of Gower's Balades were translated into a Northern English dialect c. 1402 by J. (?) Quixley. This translation is edited by H. N. McCracken in the Yorkshire Archeological Journal, XX (1909), 35-50.

Introduction, note 16. Professor John Fisher feels that Gower's "Robin" and "Marioun" are only conventional pastoral or rustic names, as in Adam de la Halle's Jeu de Robin et Marion, and do not indicate the English Robin Hood and Maid Marian. (See also Professor Robinson's note on Troilus, V. 1174.) The reference to "Robyn" in Mirour, 20887 ff. , however, seems quite in the same vein as that in Piers, B Passus V. 402. Both poets mention Robin only to make an unfavorable point about the clergy.

Introduction, note 22. Professor Fisher has kindly called my attention to the fact that another early reader of Vox Clamantis was Thomas Hearne. See Hearne's Historia Vitae et Regni Ricardi II. Angliae Regis . . . (Oxford, 1729), Praefatio, p. xiv. In this same Preface (pp. xiv-xvi) Hearne also purports to have read Cronica Tripertita.

Introduction, p. 24, lines 19-20. Professor David Fowler has quite rightly pointed out to me that Gower might well have been familiar with Piers' Visions of Dowel, Dobet, and Dobest from the A-Text of the poem, rather than the B-Text.

Introduction, note 70. See also John H. Mozley and Robert R. Raymo, eds., Nigel de Longchamps Speculum Stultorum (Berkeley, 1960).

Introduction, note 90. The poet's tomb, which formerly stood in St. John's Chapel, is now in the nave of the Cathedral.

I. 1055. Simon Sudbury is perhaps alluded to in Piers, B Passus XX, 555-556, as taking Thomas for his "bright mirror." I am here indebted to Professor Fowler.

II. 263-264. See also Lucienne Meyer, Les Légendes des Matières de Rome, de France, et de Bretagne dans le "Pantheon" de Godefroi de Viterbe (Paris, 1933), pp. 101-102. I am indebted to Professor Magoun for this reference.

III. 6(8*). For a somewhat different view, see J. A. W. Bennett, "The Date of the B-Text of Piers Plowman," Medium Aevum, XII (1943), 56.

III. 275. Cf. Dante, De Monarchia, III. v, where the sun denotes the Church and the moon signifies the Empire or temporal power. See Dante, On Monarchy, trans. David Michall (New York: Noonday Press, 1954), pp. 70-71.

III. 375. On the Crusade of 1383 see Alan T. Gaylord, "A85-88: Chaucer's Squire and the Glorious Campaign," Papers of the Michigan Academy of Sciences, Arts, and Letters, XLV (1960), 341-361.

IV. 12, 495-508, and 511-514. Professor Raymo notes, in "Vox Clamantis, IV. 12," MLN, LXXI (1956), 82-83, that these lines are largely plagiarized from a set of widely popular penitential verses of the thirteenth century. The verses have been edited by B. Haureau in Notices et Extraits de Quelques Manuscrits Latins de la Bibliothèque Nationale (Paris, 1890), I, 374.

VI. 937-938. Professor Fowler correctly informs me that the passage from Piers referred to here is part of a specious argument by Lady Meed, whose views can scarcely be identified with those of the poet.

This index includes the names of places, important concepts, authors, and titles mentioned in the Introduction and Notes to the translations, with minor exceptions. When book and line number(s) are given with no title, the reference is to the Notes to the Translation of The Voice of One Crying. When book and line number(s) are preceded by TC, the reference is to the Notes to the Translation of The Tripartite Chronicle. (S) refers to the Supplementary Notes.

Chronicles, II Book of, II. 321-322, 325-326, VI. 1231-34

Chrysostom, VI. 171

Cinkante Balades See Gower, John, Cinkante Balades

Clement VII, Pope (Avignon), III. 6, 955-956

Clergy, Intro. p. 19, Books III and IV, passim; - as one of the three estates, Intro. p. 4, 5, 9, 10, 12, 17, 18, 19, 23, 24, 25

Cobham, Sir John, Intro. p. 39-40, TC II. 212, 230, 231-232, 233-234

Coffman, George R., Intro. p. 13, 17, VII. 1289-1300

Confessio Amantis See Gower, John, Confessio Amantis

Constantine, Emperor, VI. 1281-82, 1285-86

Corinthians, I Epistle of Paul to the, II. 431-432, III. Prol. 45-45, III. 275-276, 403-404, 1611-12, IV. 847-848, VI. 611-612

Corinthians, II Epistle of Paul to the, III. 1211-12, VII. 831

Courtly Love, Intro. p. 22, 30 (note 76), VII. 157-168

Coxe, H. O. Intro. p. 46

Cronica Tripertita See Gower, John, Tripartite Chronicle

Crusade of 1383, III. 375(S)

Cymbeline, I. 21-24

Cyprian, Magician, VI. 1333-34

Daniel (Bible), Intro. p. 21, I. Prol. 7-8, II. 257-258, 267-268, 309, 317-318, VI. 573*-574*, VII. 5-6, 1379

Dante, Intro. p. 16, 17, 31, 43, Inferno, I. Prol. 7-8, II. 67-68, VII. 5-6; On Monarchy, III. 276(S); Paradiso, I. Prol. 7-8, VI. 835-836, 1273; Purgatorio, II. 325-326, 431-432, 623-630, III. 461, VI. 835-836, 1223, 1273, VII. 1399

Dathan, II. 287-288, VI. 1227-30

David, II. 281, 305-306, III. 363-364, VI. 863-864, 987-988

Derby, Henry, Earl of See Henry IV

Despenser, Henry, Bishop of Norwich, I. 1260, III. 375

Deuteronomy, II. Prol. 41, III. 483-484

Diogenes, VII. 1321-22

Dionysius, Bishop of Alexandria, VI. 1275-76

The Distichs of Cato, III. 541-542

Doctrine of Dominion See Wycliffe, John, and Lollardy

Dominican friars, IV. 777-778

Donation of Constantine, III. 283

Dorset, Marquis of, TC III. 383-393

Do-wel, Do-bet, Do-best, Visions of, Intro. p. 24(S), V. 921-922, VII. 1473-74

Dream vision form, Intro. p. 4, 15-17

Eacides, VI. 1293-94

Ecce Patet Tensus, Intro. p. 36, V. 175, 199-206

Ecclesiastes, II. 3, 509-512, III. 1417, IV. 207-208, VI. 473, 973

Ecclesiasticus, III. 1891-92, IV. 301-302, V. 843, VI. 269, 642

Edward III, Intro. p. 10, 10(S), VI. 1361-62

Edward, Prince of Wales, (Black Prince), Intro. p. 13, VI. Chap. 13, Heading

Edward the Confessor, Translation of, TC III. 324

Eli, II. 327-328, 329-330, III. 1145-50

Elisha, VI. 1235-36

Endor, Witch of, VI. 905-910, 1299

Eneidos Bucolis, Intro. p. 36 (note 94)

England in the 14th Century, Intro. p. 3.

Ephesians, III. 27-30, 1027, VI. 1020

Estates, Three See Society, Three Estates of

Esther (Bible and Apocrypha), II. 310, VI. 1313-14

Ex Ponto See Ovid, Ex Ponto

Exeter, Duke of, TC III. 383-393, 402-403

Exodus, I. 586, II. 251-252, 269-270, 315-316, Chap. 10, 545-550, III. 165-168, 1077-80, 1815-16

Ezekiel, I. 185-186, 767, VII. 1217-18

Fasti See Ovid, Fasti

Fisher, John H., A Calendar of Documents Relating to the Life of John Gower, Poet, Intro. p. 4, p. 4 (notes 2, 3, 4), p. 5, p. 5 (note 5), p. 10 (note 16 (S)), p. 34 (note 90), p. 37 (note 96), p. 42 (note 106)

FitzRalph, Richard, Archbishop of Armagh, IV. 723-730

Fortune (Fortuna, the goddess), Intro. p. 18, II. Chap. 1, Heading, II. 10, 623-630

Francis of Assisi, Saint, Intro. p. 20, IV. 981

Franklin's Tale, V. 613

Fraud, Intro. p. 21, V. 703

Friars, Intro. p. 20

Friar's Tale, VI. 1299

Frontispiece to MSS. CEG, Ded. Ep. 49

Fuller, Thomas, Bishop, Church History of Britain, Intro. p. 11, 15, 32, I. 783-790

Galatians, II. 333, IV. 18, 698, 1111, VI. 372, VII. 831

Gaunt, John of, Intro. p. 40, I. 929

Gehazi, VI. 1235-36

General Prologue to The Canterbury Tales. See Chaucer, General Prologue

Gower, John, - Presul, Ouile Regis, Intro. p. 36, 42; - Quicquid Homo Scribat, Intro. p. 36; - Rex Celi Deus, Intro. p. 36; VI. Chap. 18; - Traitié Pour Essampler Les Amantz Marietz, Intro. p. 35, 36, V. 53, VI. 862-864, 913, VII. 157-168, 673-676; - The Tripartite Chronicle, Intro. p. 36-42; Allegory in, 16, 37, 38; Date of, 23, 36; Henry IV, 4, 13, 32, 37, 39; historical events portrayed in, 37, 38, 39, 30; Richard II, 4, 13, 33, 37, 38, 39; style of, 3, 11, 15, 17, 29, 30, 32, 35, 36, 37, 38, 39, 40; added to Voice of One Crying, 4, 11, 12, 13, 36; - The Voice of One Crying, Intro. p. 11-32; Attitudes and ideas in, 12, 15, 16, 17, 19, 21, 22, 23, 25, 34; allegory in, 4, 15, 16, 17, 23; Peasants' revolt in, 12, 13, 14, 15, 16; revisions of, 11, 13, 21, 23; Richard II and, 13, 21, 33; source of title of, 11; sources of, 26-29, - Aurora, 26, 28, 29, Bible, 26, 29, Neckham, 26, 29, Ovid, 6, 15, 16, 26, 27, 28, 29, Pantheon, 26, 29, Piers Plowman, 24, Speculum Stultorum, 26, 29, Virgil, 6; style of, 11, 15, 17, 20, 21, 23, 30, 31, 32; theme of, 15, 17-18; three estates of society in, 4, 10, 12, 17, 18, 19, 20, 25; Tripartite Chronicle added to, 4, 11, 12, 13, 36; and other works, 10, 11, 12, 14, 15, 35, 36; source of title of, II. Prol. 83; original composition of, III. Prol.

Gower, Sir Robert, Intro. p. 4

Great Revolt of 1381 See Peasants' Revolt

Great Schism, Intro. p. 10, 13, 36, Ded. Ep. 5-6, III. 1-28, III. 6(8*), V. 1009-10, VII. 1375

Greek and Latin names, Gower's use of, Intro. p. 16, I. 929, 962-967, 985, 997, 1001, 1002, 1155

Green, Sir Henry, Intro. p. 40, TC III. 174-175

Gregory the Great, Pope, VI. 1247-48, 1273, 1283-84, VII. 639

Groundolf, Agnes, Intro. p. 6, 34, 35

Hales, Robert I. 931

Hamlet, TC III. 17

Hearne, Thomas, Intro. p. 11 (note 22 S)

Hebrews (Bible), II. 467-468

Helinand, Vers de Morte, Intro. p. 10, VII. 955-956

Henry IV, Intro. p. 4, 6, 7, 9, 13, 32, 33, 36, 37, 38, 39, 40-42, Ded. Ep. (note 1), VI. Chap. 18, VII. Prose Link, TC I. 9-10, 52, 55, 210, TC II. 101-108, 231-232, 246, TC III. 17, 85-86, 106, after 121, 162-163, 251, 286, 296, 311, 332-337, 383-393, 402-403, 410-411

1 Henry IV, TC III. 17

Henry V. TC III. 256, 352-353

2 Henry VI, TC I. 109

Heresy, Statute of, TC II. 246

Heroides See Ovid, Heroides

Historia Apollonii Tyrii, I. 2091

Holland, Thomas, TC III. 402-403

Homer, III. 1233-34

Hophni, II. 327-328, 329-330

Horace, Epistles, VI. 497

Horse, See Arundel, Richard, Earl of

Hosea, IV. 769

Humphrey, son of Duke of Gloucester, TC III. 256

Inferno See Dante, Inferno

In Praise of Peace See Gower, In Praise of Peace

Ireland, TC. III. 186

Isaiah, Book of, Intro. p. 11, I. 767, 1764, II. Prol. 83, II. 307-308, 481, Chap. 10, VI. 141-142, 151-152, VII. 809, Chap. 17, Heading, 919, 1208

Ishmael, VI. 1222

Isidore, Etymologiae, I. 765-776, IV. 587, VI. 990

Israel, Israelites, VII. 1231-32

Jacob, III. 1118-24, 1361, VII. 1231-32

Japhet, VI. 1217

Jason, Intro. p. 21, I. 263-264

Jean de Meun, Roman de la Rose, Intro. p. 12, 43

Jeremiah, Book of, III. 781-782, VI. 1222

Jersey, Isle of, TC. II. 230

Jews, Attitude toward, Intro. p. 24, II. 341-342, V. 687-688

Jezebel, VI. 1361-62

Job, Book of, II. 41, 333, III. 263, IV. 869, VI. 1135-36, VII. 922

John, Gospel of, II. Prol. 83, II. 379-390, 468, 584, III. 219-220, 303-304, 337-338, 437-438, 691, 949-950, 1005-06, 1065-66, 1219-20, 1365-66, 2142, IV. 78, 603-604, 1110, VI. 657, 1261-62

John, I Epistle of, III. 434, 1065-66, 2142, VI. 657

John of Gaunt, Intro. p. 40, I. 929

John of Northampton, V. Chap. 15, Heading

John the Baptist, Intro. p. 11, II. Prol. 83

Jonah (Bible), I. 1819-20, II. 271-272

Joseph, I. Prol. 7-8, V. 523, 527

Joshua, Book of, II. 245-246, III. 483-484

Jude, Epistle of, VI. 875-902

Judges, Book of, I. 1019-23

Julian, Emperor of Rome, VI. 1258

Justina, St., VI. 1333-34

Justinian, Emperor of Rome, VI. 1275-76

Juvenal, Satires, VI. 149

Kent, Earl of, TC III. 383-393, 402-403

494

Luke, 437-438, 574-575, 579, 599
600, 651, 800, 801-802, 861-
862, 877-878, 902, 949-950,
963-964, 1063-64, 1073-74,
1331-32, 1563, 1649-50, 1709-
14, 1721-22, 1997-98, 2071-
72, IV. 10, 41, 245-246, 579-
580, V. 175, 569, VI. 493-494,
576, 685-686, 837-838, 1056,
1259, VII. 1030, 1091-92, 1217-
18

MS. -S See All Souls MS

Macaulay, G. C. , Intro. p. 4, 5,
6 (notes 8, 9 and 11), 9 (note
14), 10 (note 18), 11, 12, 16
(note 37), 23 (note 53), 26, 27,
28, 31, 34 (note 91), 35 (note
92), 36 (note 94), 37, 39, 42
(note 105), 43 (notes 111 and
114), 46 (notes 121 and 122),
Ded. Ep. note 1 et passim

Maccabees, II Book of the, II.
289-290

Magog, I. 765-776, 767

Man as a microcosm, Intro.
p. 22, 25, II. 273-278,
VII. 645

Man of Law's Tale See Chaucer,
Man of Law's Tale

Manciple's Tale, V. 901-906

Mark, Gospel According to,
Intro. p. 11 (note 24), Ded.
Ep. 31-32, I. 377-378, II.
Prol. 57-58, 66-67, 83,
II. 55, 472, III. 437-438, 579,
599-600, 801-802, 877-878,
949-950, 1331-32, 1649-50,
1721-22, IV. 579-580, 623,
V. 893-894, VI. 383-384, 493-
494, 576, VII. 1030, 1217-18

Martin, St. , III. 79-80, VI. 1249

Mary See Blessed Virgin Mary

Matthew, Gospel According to,
Intro. p. 11 (note 24), Ded. Ep.
31-32, I. 377-378, 1869, II.
Prol. 57-58, 83, II. 55, 69-70,
247-248, 253-254, III. 137,
174-184, 207, 252, 258, 313,
319-320, 337-338, 403-404,
437-438, 574-575, 579, 593-
598, 599-600, 651, 667-668,
721, 777-778, 781-782, 800,
801-802, 805-806, 861-862,
877-878, 919, 949-950, 965-
966, 1063-64, 1073-74, 1099-
1100, 1106, 1108, 1331-32,
1400, 1563, 1569, 1649-50,
1709-14, 1721-22, 1929, 1997-
98, 2003, 2061-62, 2071-72,
2130, IV. 13-14, 324, 579-580,
623, 693, 719-720, 965-966,
1011-12, V. 175, 893-894,
VI. 443, 493-494, 576, 837-
838, 1056, 1259, VII. 1030,
1087-88, 1091-92

Mendicant friars, IV. 723-730

Merchant's Tale See Chaucer,
Merchant's Tale

Merciless Parliament, Intro.
p. 38, V. Chap. 15, Heading,
TC I. 36, 121-130

Metamorphoses See Ovid, Metamorphoses

Micaiah, VI. 1231-34

Miller's Tale See Chaucer,
Miller's Tale

Milton, John, Intro. p. 10, 19,
Paradise Lost, II. Prol. 7-8,
II. 431-432, V. 143-144, VI.
835-836

Mirour de l'Omme See Gower,
Mirour de l'Omme

Monastic and mendicant orders,
Intro. p. 20, Book IV. passim

Monk's Tale, Intro. p. 22 (note
50)

Moses, III. 1077-80, IV. 305-310

Mowbray, Thomas, Earl Marshall, Intro. p. 38, TC I. 51,
121-130, TC III. 85-86

Mum and the Sothsegger, Intro.
p. 38, TC I. 15-16

Namaan, VI. 1235-36

Nationalism, Intro. p. 18, 22,
41

Nebuchadnezzar, Intro. p. 22,
I. Prol. 7-8, VII. 5-6, 108,
136, 353, 1379

Neck(h)am, Alexander, De Vita
Monachorum, Intro. p. 26, 27,
29, 31, II. Prol. 57-58, IV. 43-
48, 395-396, 397, 401-402,
403-404, 405-430, 431-446,
461-466, 469-490, 486, 1145-
48, 1161, 1175-76, V. 335-
336, 341-342, 375, 376, 377-
378, 413-416, 417-419, 421-
428, VI. 313-326, 327-328,
329-348, 355-356, 357, 359-
372, 389, 397-398, 629-630,
1019-24, 1085-86, 1107-12,
1115-16, VII. 375-376, 379-
383, 385, 387, 389-392, 405-
410, 417-420, 437-438, 441-
442, 499-504, 685-694, 699-
708, 909-910, 911-918, 919-
924, 929-932

Neville, Alexander, Archbishop
of York, Intro. p. 38, TC I.
103, 172

Nicodemus, Gospel of, II. 555-556,
573

Nigel de Longchamps, Speculum
Stultorum See Speculum
Stultorum

Nimrod, VI. 1216

Nineveh, II. 271-272

Noah, VI. 1217

Norfolk, Duke of See Mowbray,
Thomas

Northumberland, Earl of, Intro.
p. 38, TC I. 55

Nottingham, Earl of See Mowbray,
Thomas

Numbers, Book of, II. Prol. 45, II.
261-262, 284, 287-288, III.
531-532, VI. 875-902, 1227-30

Nun's Priest's Tale See Chaucer,
Nun's Priest's Tale

O Deus Immense, Intro. p. 37

O Recolende, Intro. p. 36

Ovid, Intro. p. 6 et passim, esp.
26-28, V. 949; Amores, I. 41-
42, 849-850, 1221-22, 1775-76,
III. 41, 1595, IV. 575, V. 433-
438, VI. 659-660, 816, 825,
1345, VII. 319, 471; Ars
Amatoria, I. 903-904, 1193-
94, 1363-64, 1424, 1870, II.
Prol. 64, 77, II. 461, III. 641,
1113-14, 1213, 1215-16, 1233-
34, IV. 111, 163, 175-176, 179,
311-312, 425, 451, 617-618,
620, 951, V. 145, 185-186, 187,
217, 224, 353, 355, 359, 360,
361, 367-368, 376, 390, 399-
402, 405, 407, 953-954, 979,
981, 983-984, 985-986, VI. 765,
1178*, 1347-49, VII. 255-256,
323-324, 334, 452, 459-460,

Oxford, Earl of See Vere, Robert de

Palatine, VII. 485-486

Pamphilus, V. 613

Pantheon, Intro. p. 26, 29, I. 7-8, 17-18, 765-776, 1907-08, II. 159-161, 187, 263-264, 353-354, 357-359, 361-363, 371-374, 414, IV. 87, 97, 91, 171

Paradise Lost See Milton, John, Paradise Lost

Paradiso See Dante, Paradiso

Pardoner's Tale See Chaucer, Geoffrey, Pardoner's Tale

Parliament, TC I. 172, TC II. 76, 129, 150, TC III. 27-30, 300-304, 310, 311

Parson's Tale See Chaucer, Geoffrey, Parson's Tale

Paul, Saint, VI. 1245-46

Peasants, Intro. p. 12, 17, 19, 20, 43; - as one of three estates, Intro. p. 4, 5, 9, 10, 12, 17, 18, 19, 23, 24, 25, IV. Chap. 9, Book V., V. 4-8

Peasants' Revolt, Intro. p. 3 et passim, esp. 12-16, I. 1, 168, 321, 347-348, 767, 784, 825-826, 929, 931, 941, 1066, 1260, 1306, 2099-2100, III. Prol. 11-13, V. 599-600, VI. 545-546, TC I. 7

Peter, II Epistle of, VI. 875-902

Peter of Riga See Aurora

Perrers, Alice, VI. 1361-62

Pharisees, III. 691

Phinehas, II. 327-328, 329-330

Phirinus (or Spurina), VI. 1323

Pierce the Ploughman's Crede, IV. 1143

"Positive law, " Intro. p. 19

Piers Plowman See Langland, William, Piers Plowman

Poem on the Evil Times of Edward II, TC III. 160

Pole, Michael de la, Intro. p. 38, TC I. 109, 172

Pope, IV. 656

Presul, Ouile Regis, Intro. p. 36, 42

Priory of Bermondsey, TC II. 101-108

Priory of St. Mary Overes, Intro. p. 34, 42

Proverbs, Book of, I. 1509, IV. 1027-28, V. 299-308, 333-334, 921-922

Proverbs and proverbial phrases, Intro. p. 30, 37, 40, 44, I. Prol. 4, I. 133, 437, 1525-26, 1550, 2033-34, 2034-46, 2074, 2094, 2108, II. Prol. 41, 68, II. 41, 109, 152, 159-161, 203, 239, 461, III. Prol. 11-13, 95, III. 43, 137, 263, 403-404, 407, 409-410, 461-462, 503, 537-538, 541-542, 543, 896, 1165-66, 1211-12, 1267, 1546, 1601-04, 1631-32, 1640, 1721-22, 1891-92, 1930, 1949, 1979, 2035-40, 2073, 2074, IV. 19-20, 193-194, 277-282, 507, 659-660, 777-778, 845, 872, 874, 1010, 1121, 1125, 1127, 1171, 1177, V. 147, 175, 215-216, 671, 835-836, 843, 851-852

Proverbs and proverbial phrases, 876, 879, 949, VI. 102, 129-130, 149, 467, 497, 498, 513-514, 549, 550*, 576, 638, 640, 681, 752, 903, 911, 969, 984, 997, 999, 1125, 1135-36, 1174, 1359, VII. 109, 110, 291, 357, 369-370, 458, 461-462, 775, 922, 927, 953-954, TC Preface 7, TC I. 187, TC II. 345, TC III. 1, 102, 123, 278-279

Psalms, Book of, I. 1764, 1793-1810, II. 521-524, 531-532, III. 463, 2097-98, IV. 959-960, 969, VI. 11, Chap. 4 Heading, 987-988, 988, VII. 587-590, Chap. 17, Heading, 919, 1231-32, 1305-06

Ptolemy I, VI. 1333-34

Puns and plays on words, Intro. p. 30, 37, Ded. Ep. 6 et passim

Purgatorio, See Dante, Purgatorio

Quicquid Homo Scribat, Intro. p. 36

Rachel, V. 523, 527

Reeve's Tale, III. 1549-52, VI. 102

Reform of man, Intro. p. 17

Rehoboam, II. 325-326, VI. 1295-96

Remedia Amoris See Ovid, Remedia Amoris

Revelation of John (Bible), I. Prol. 57-58, I. 680, 749, 767, III. 337-338, 957, IV. 647-648, 657-658, 788, VI. 875-902, VII. 123, 1203-08

Rex Celi Deus, Intro. p. 36, VI. Chap. 18

Richard II., Intro. p. 3, 4, 13, 14, 15, 18, 19 (note 47), 21, 23, 25, 32, 33, 36, 37, 38, 39, 40, 41, Ded. Ep. (note 1), I. 1 1000, 1759-60, II. 86-87, IV. 723-730, VI. 545, 555, 853-856, Chap. 13, Heading, Chap. 18, VII. Prose Link, TC I. 9-10, 15-16, 57, 61, 64, 58-60, 107, 111-118, 121-130, 137, 154, 172, 210, TC II. After 29, 85-86, 101-108, 129, 182, 231-232, TC III. 17, 47, 106, 113-114, 162-163, 174-175, 186, 225, 251, 256, 286, 296, 377, 383-393, 432-445, 452-455, 462, 478-487

Richard II, TC II. 33, TC III. 85-86

Riga, Peter of, See Aurora

Robin Hood, Intro. p. 10 and note 16(S)

Roman de la Rose, Intro. p. 12, 43, III. 815, IV. 587

Romance of the Rose, I. Prol. 4

Romans, Epistle to the, I. Prol. 1-2, III. 327, IV. 873, VI. 831-832, VII. 543-544

Romeo and Juliet, I. 929, V. 53, VII. 1024

Rushook, Thomas, IV. 723-730, TC I. 111-118

Samuel, I Book of, I. 499-500, II. 305-306, 319-320, 327-328, 329-330, III. 363-364, 1145-50, 1791-92, VI. 839-940, 905-910

Swallow See Arundel, Thomas,
Archbishop of Canterbury

Swan See Gloucester, Thomas,
Duke of

Sylvester, VI. 1281-82

Tale of Melibee, V. 613

Tarquin the Proud, VI. 1277-78

Thais, VI. 1333-34

Thames River, TC I. 80

Theodosius II, Emperor of
Rome, VI. 1283-84

Thersites, VI. 1293-94

Thessalonians, I Epistle to the,
IV. 569-570

Thetis, V. 812, VII. 1067, TC
I. 80

Thomas, son of Richard, Earl
of Arundel, Intro. p. 40,
TC III. 137

Three Estates See Society,
Three Estates of

Tiberius Constantine, VI. 1285-
86

Tiburtina, I. 765-776

Timothy, I Letter of Paul to,
II. 489-492, VII. 1217-18

Titiuillis, IV. 864

Tobit, Book of, II. 233-234, 291-
292, VI. 1251

Tower of London, Intro. p. 16,
I. 997, 1759-60, TC I. 121-130,
TC III. 286

Traitié Pour Essampler Les
Amantz Marietz See Gower,
John, Traitié Pour Essampler
Les Amantz Marietz

Trajan, VI. 1273

Transubstantiation, Doctrine of,
Intro. p. 25, III. 1819-22

Tresilian, Sir Robert, Chief
Justice, TC I. (note 30)

Tripartite Chronicle See Gower,
John, The Tripartite
Chronicle

Tristia See Ovid, Tristia

Troilus and Cressida, V. 812

Troilus and Criseyde See
Chaucer, Geoffrey, Troilus
and Criseyde

Trojan Brut, I. 880

Trojan War, Intro. p. 16

Troy, Dream vision of, Intro.
p. 15-17

Troy, London as New, See
London

Tyler, Wat, Intro. p. 16, 17,
I. 321, 347-348, 652, Chap. 9,
Heading, 784, 931, 997, 1759-
60, 1861-62

Ubi sunt motif, VI. 1241, 1251-52

Usk, Thomas, Intro. p. 16
(note 36)

Usury, Intro. p. 21, V. Chap. 12,
Heading, 703

Uzzah, VI. 1223

Uzziah, II. 321-322

Valentinian III, Emperor of Rome,
VI. 1277-78

Valerius Maximus, Memorabilia,
VI. 1323

Venus, IV. 587

Vere, Robert de, Earl of Oxford, Intro. p. 38, TC I. 15-16, 65, 76, 80, 172

Vers de Morte See Helinand, Vers de Morte

Villon, Francois, Ballade, I. Prol. 7-8

Virgil, Intro. p. 6, 16-17, 43, Aeneid, Intro. p. 11, 17, I. 1793-1810, II. Prol. 51; Eclogues, VI. 999, TC II. 345

Virgin Mary See Blessed Virgin Mary

De Vita Monachorum See Neckam, Alexander, De Vita Monachorum

Viterbo, Godfrey of, Pantheon See Pantheon

Voice of One Crying See Gower, John, The Voice of One Crying

Vox Clamantis See Gower, John, The Voice of One Crying

Vox populi, vox dei, Intro. p. 17, 19, 23, 38, III. Prol. 11-13, III. 1267, VII. 1470, TC I. 9-10

Walsingham, Thomas, Chronicon Angliae, I. 855, 1173

Walworth, William, Mayor of London, I. 1861-62

Warton, Thomas, Intro. p. 11, 11 (note 23), 31 (note 85)

Warwick, Thomas, Earl of, Intro. p. 38-40, VII. Prose Link, TC I. 49, 107, 121-130, TC II. 15-16, After 29, 201-204, 233-234

Westminster Abbey, TC II. 101-108

Wickert, Maria, Gower Studien, Intro. p. 11 (note 25), 13 (note 30, 31), 17 (note 38), 19 (note 44), 27 (note 63) II. Prol. 83

Wife of Bath's Prologue and Tale See Chaucer, Geoffrey, Wife of Bath's Prologue and Tale

Witch of Endor, VI. 905-910, 1299

Wycliffe, John and Lollardy, Intro. p. 19, 24, 25, 34, 36, 42 (note 103), II. Chap. 10, III. 579, 593-598, 1025-26, 1129-30, 1141-42, 1485-86, 1671-72, 1819-22, IV. Chap. 21, Heading, 1083, 1227, VI. 1267-68, TC I. 154, 210, TC II. 212, 217-218, 246, TC III. 486

York, Archbishop of See Neville, Alexander, Archbishop of York

Zedekiah, VI. 1231-34

Zephaniah, IV. 769

Zodiac, Signs of the, I. 1630, VII. 587-590